The Tragedies of
Shakespeare

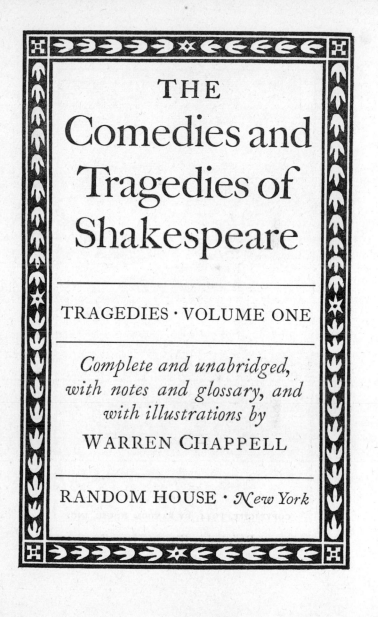

THE
Comedies and Tragedies of Shakespeare

TRAGEDIES · VOLUME ONE

---

*Complete and unabridged,
with notes and glossary, and
with illustrations by*

WARREN CHAPPELL

RANDOM HOUSE · *New York*

CONTENTS

TROILUS AND CRESSIDA

CAST OF CHARACTERS

PRIAM, *King of Troy*

HECTOR
TROILUS
PARIS } *his Sons*
DEIPHOBUS
HELENUS

MARGARELON, *a Bastard Son of Priam*

ÆNEAS } *Trojan Commanders*
ANTENOR

CALCHAS, *a Trojan Priest, taking part with the Greeks*

PANDARUS, *Uncle to Cressida*

AGAMEMNON, *the Grecian General*

MENELAUS, *his Brother*

ACHILLES
AJAX
ULYSSES
NESTOR } *Grecian Commanders*
DIOMEDES
PATROCLUS

THERSITES, *a deformed and scurrilous Grecian*

ALEXANDER, *Servant to Cressida*

Servant to Troilus

Servant to Paris

Servant to Diomedes

HELEN, *Wife to Menelaus*

ANDROMACHE, *Wife to Hector*

CASSANDRA, *Daughter to Priam; a prophetess*

CRESSIDA, *Daughter to Calchas*

Trojan and Greek Soldiers, and Attendants

SCENE

Troy, and the Grecian Camp before it

PROLOGUE

In Troy there lies the scene. From isles of Greece
The princes orgulous, their high blood chaf'd,
Have to the port of Athens sent their ships,
Fraught with the ministers and instruments
Of cruel war: sixty and nine, that wore
Their crownets regal, from the Athenian bay
Put forth toward Phrygia; and their vow is made
To ransack Troy, within whose strong immures
The ravish'd Helen, Menelaus' queen,
With wanton Paris sleeps; and that's the quarrel.
To Tenedos they come,
And the deep-drawing barks do there disgorge
Their warlike fraughtage: now on Dardan plains
The fresh and yet unbruised Greeks do pitch
Their brave pavilions: Priam's six-gated city,
Dardan, and Tymbria, Ilias, Chetas, Trojan,
And Antenorides, with massy staples
And corresponsive and fulfilling bolts,
Sperr up the sons of Troy.
Now expectation, tickling skittish spirits,
On one and other side, Trojan and Greek,
Sets all on hazard. And hither am I come
A prologue arm'd, but not in confidence
Of author's pen or actor's voice, but suited
In like conditions as our argument,
To tell you, fair beholders, that our play
Leaps o'er the vaunt and firstlings of those broils,
Beginning in the middle; starting thence away
To what may be digested in a play.
Like or find fault; do as your pleasures are:
Now good or bad, 'tis but the chance of war.

TROILUS AND CRESSIDA

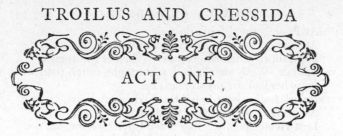

ACT ONE

SCENE ONE

Troy. Before Priam's Palace.

Enter Troilus armed, and Pandarus

TROILUS. Call here my varlet, I 'll unarm again:
Why should I war without the walls of Troy,
That find such cruel battle here within?
Each Trojan that is master of his heart,
Let him to field; Troilus, alas! has none.

PANDARUS. Will this gear ne'er be mended?

TROILUS. The Greeks are strong, and skilful to their
strength,
Fierce to their skill, and to their fierceness valiant;
But I am weaker than a woman's tear,
Tamer than sleep, fonder than ignorance,
Less valiant than the virgin in the night,
And skilless as unpractis'd infancy.

PANDARUS. Well, I have told you enough of this: for my
part, I 'll not meddle nor make no further. He that will
have a cake out of the wheat must tarry the grinding.

TROILUS. Have I not tarried?

PANDARUS. Ay, the grinding; but you must tarry the bolting.

TROILUS. Have I not tarried?

PANDARUS. Ay, the bolting; but you must tarry the leavening.

TROILUS. Still have I tarried.

PANDARUS. Ay, to the leavening; but here's yet in the word
'hereafter' the kneading, the making of the cake, the
heating of the oven, and the baking; nay, you must stay
the cooling too, or you may chance to burn your lips.

TROILUS. Patience herself, what goddess e'er she be,
Doth lesser blench at sufferance than I do.

3

At Priam's royal table do I sit;
And when fair Cressid comes into my thoughts,—
So, traitor! 'when she comes'!—When is she thence?

PANDARUS. Well, she looked yesternight fairer than ever
I saw her look, or any woman else.

TROILUS. I was about to tell thee: when my heart,
As wedged with a sigh, would rive in twain
Lest Hector or my father should perceive me,
I have—as when the sun doth light a storm—
Buried this sigh in wrinkle of a smile;
But sorrow, that is couch'd in seeming gladness,
Is like that mirth fate turns to sudden sadness.

PANDARUS. An her hair were not somewhat darker than
Helen's,—well, go to,—there were no more comparison
between the women: but, for my part, she is my kins-
woman; I would not, as they term it, praise her; but I
would somebody had heard her talk yesterday, as I did:
I will not dispraise your sister Cassandra's wit, but—

TROILUS. O Pandarus! I tell thee, Pandarus,—
When I do tell thee, there my hopes lie drown'd,
Reply not in how many fathoms deep
They lie indrench'd. I tell thee I am mad
In Cressid's love: thou answer'st, she is fair;
Pour'st in the open ulcer of my heart
Her eyes, her hair, her cheek, her gait, her voice;
Handlest in thy discourse, O! that her hand,
In whose comparison all whites are ink,
Writing their own reproach; to whose soft seizure
The cygnet's down is harsh, and spirit of sense
Hard as the palm of ploughman: this thou tell'st me,
As true thou tell'st me, when I say I love her;
But, saying thus, instead of oil and balm,
Thou lay'st in every gash that love hath given me
The knife that made it.

PANDARUS. I speak no more than truth.

TROILUS. Thou dost not speak so much.

PANDARUS. Faith, I 'll not meddle in 't. Let her be as she
is: if she be fair, 'tis the better for her; an she be not,
she has the mends in her own hands.

TROILUS. Good Pandarus, how now, Pandarus!

PANDARUS. I have had my labour for my travail; ill-thought

on of her, and ill-thought on of you: gone between, and between, but small thanks for my labour.

TROILUS. What! art thou angry, Pandarus? what! with me?

PANDARUS. Because she 's kin to me, therefore she 's not so fair as Helen: an she were not kin to me, she would be as fair on Friday as Helen is on Sunday. But what care I? I care not an she were a black-a-moor; 'tis all one to me.

TROILUS. Say I she is not fair?

PANDARUS. I do not care whether you do or no. She 's a fool to stay behind her father: let her to the Greeks; and so I 'll tell her the next time I see her. For my part, I 'll meddle nor make no more i' the matter.

TROILUS. Pandarus,—

PANDARUS. Not I.

TROILUS. Sweet Pandarus,—

PANDARUS. Pray you, speak no more to me! I will leave all as I found it, and there an end.

                                        Exit Pandarus. An alarum

TROILUS. Peace, you ungracious clamours! peace, rude sounds!
Fools on both sides! Helen must needs be fair,
When with your blood you daily paint her thus.
I cannot fight upon this argument;
It is too starv'd a subject for my sword.
But Pandarus,—O gods! how do you plague me.
I cannot come to Cressid but by Pandar;
And he 's as techy to be woo'd to woo
As she is stubborn-chaste against all suit.
Tell me, Apollo, for thy Daphne's love,
What Cressid is, what Pandar, and what we?
Her bed is India; there she lies, a pearl:
Between our Ilium and where she resides
Let it be call'd the wild and wandering flood;
Ourself the merchant, and this sailing Pandar
Our doubtful hope, our convoy and our bark.

                                        Alarum. Enter Æneas

ÆNEAS. How now, Prince Troilus! wherefore not afield?

TROILUS. Because not there: this woman's answer sorts,
For womanish it is to be from thence.
What news, Æneas, from the field to-day?

ÆNEAS. That Paris is returned home, and hurt.

TROILUS. By whom, Æneas?

ÆNEAS.   Troilus, by Menelaus.

TROILUS. Let Paris bleed: 'tis but a scar to scorn; Paris is
gor'd with Menelaus' horn.   *Alarum*

ÆNEAS. Hark, what good sport is out of town to-day!

TROILUS. Better at home, if 'would I might' were 'may.'
But to the sport abroad: are you bound thither?

ÆNEAS. In all swift haste.

TROILUS.   Come, go we then together.

                                                    Exeunt

SCENE TWO

The Same. A Street.

Enter Cressida and Alexander

CRESSIDA. Who were those went by?

ALEXANDER.   Queen Hecuba and Helen.

CRESSIDA. And whither go they?

ALEXANDER.   Up to the eastern tower,
Whose height commands as subject all the vale,
To see the battle. Hector, whose patience
Is as a virtue fix'd, to-day was mov'd:
He chid Andromache, and struck his armourer;
And, like as there were husbandry in war,
Before the sun rose he was harness'd light,
And to the field goes he; where every flower
Did, as a prophet, weep what it foresaw
In Hector's wrath.

CRESSIDA.   What was his cause of anger?

ALEXANDER. The noise goes, this: there is among the
Greeks
A lord of Trojan blood, nephew to Hector;
They call him Ajax.

CRESSIDA.   Good; and what of him?

ALEXANDER. They say he is a very man per se
And stands alone.

CRESSIDA. So do all men, unless they are drunk, sick, or
have no legs.

ALEXANDER. This man, lady, hath robbed many beasts
of their particular additions: he is as valiant as the lion,

churlish as the bear, slow as the elephant: a man into
whom nature hath so crowded humours that his valour
is crushed into folly, his folly sauced with discretion:
there is no man hath a virtue that he hath not a glimpse
of, nor any man an attaint but he carries some stain of
it. He is melancholy without cause, and merry against
the hair; he hath the joints of every thing, but every
thing so out of joint that he is a gouty Briareus, many
hands and no use; or purblind Argus, all eyes and no
sight.

CRESSIDA. But how should this man, that makes me smile,
make Hector angry?

ALEXANDER. They say he yesterday coped Hector in the
battle and struck him down; the disdain and shame
whereof hath ever since kept Hector fasting and waking.

CRESSIDA. Who comes here?

Enter Pandarus

ALEXANDER. Madam, your uncle Pandarus.

CRESSIDA. Hector 's a gallant man.

ALEXANDER. As may be in the world, lady.

PANDARUS. What 's that? what 's that?

CRESSIDA. Good-morrow, uncle Pandarus.

PANDARUS. Good-morrow, cousin Cressid. What do you
talk of? Good-morrow, Alexander. How do you, cousin?
When were you at Ilium?

CRESSIDA. This morning, uncle.

PANDARUS. What were you talking of when I came? Was
Hector armed and gone ere ye came to Ilium? Helen
was not up, was she?

CRESSIDA. Hector was gone, but Helen was not up.

PANDARUS. E'en so: Hector was stirring early.

CRESSIDA. That were we talking of, and of his anger.

PANDARUS. Was he angry?

CRESSIDA. So he says here.

PANDARUS. True, he was so; I know the cause too: he 'll lay
about him to-day, I can tell them that: and there 's
Troilus will not come far behind him; let them take heed
of Troilus, I can tell them that too.

CRESSIDA. What! is he angry too?

PANDARUS. Who, Troilus? Troilus is the better man of the
two.

CRESSIDA. O Jupiter! there 's no comparison.

PANDARUS. What! not between Troilus and Hector? Do
 you know a man if you see him?

CRESSIDA. Ay, if I ever saw him before and knew him.

PANDARUS. Well, I say Troilus is Troilus.

CRESSIDA. Then you say as I say; for I am sure he is not
 Hector.

PANDARUS. No, nor Hector is not Troilus in some degrees.

CRESSIDA. 'Tis just to each of them; he is himself.

PANDARUS. Himself! Alas, poor Troilus, I would he were.

CRESSIDA. So he is.

PANDARUS. Condition, I had gone bare-foot to India.

CRESSIDA. He is not Hector.

PANDARUS. Himself! no, he 's not himself. Would a' were
 himself: well, the gods are above; time must friend or
 end: well, Troilus, well, I would my heart were in her
 body. No, Hector is not a better man than Troilus.

CRESSIDA. Excuse me.

PANDARUS. He is elder.

CRESSIDA. Pardon me, pardon me.

PANDARUS. Th' other 's not come to 't; you shall tell me
 another tale when the other 's come to 't. Hector shall
 not have his wit this year.

CRESSIDA. He shall not need it if he have his own.

PANDARUS. Nor his qualities.

CRESSIDA. No matter.

PANDARUS. Nor his beauty.

CRESSIDA. 'Twould not become him; his own 's better.

PANDARUS. You have no judgment, niece: Helen herself
 swore th' other day, that Troilus, for a brown favour—
 for so 'tis, I must confess,—not brown neither,—

CRESSIDA. No, but brown.

PANDARUS. Faith, to say truth, brown and not brown.

CRESSIDA. To say the truth, true and not true.

PANDARUS. She prais'd his complexion above Paris.

CRESSIDA. Why, Paris hath colour enough.

PANDARUS. So he has.

CRESSIDA. Then Troilus should have too much: if she
 praised him above, his complexion is higher than his:
 he having colour enough, and the other higher, is too
 flaming a praise for a good complexion. I had as lief
 Helen's golden tongue had commended Troilus for a
 copper nose.

PANDARUS. I swear to you, I think Helen loves him better than Paris.

CRESSIDA. Then she 's a merry Greek indeed.

PANDARUS. Nay, I am sure she does. She came to him th' other day into the compassed window, and, you know, he has not past three or four hairs on his chin,—

CRESSIDA. Indeed, a tapster's arithmetic may soon bring his particulars therein to a total.

PANDARUS. Why, he is very young; and yet will he, within three pounds, lift as much as his brother Hector.

CRESSIDA. Is he so young a man, and so old a lifter?

PANDARUS. But to prove to you that Helen loves him: she came and puts me her white hand to his cloven chin,—

CRESSIDA. Juno have mercy! how came it cloven?

PANDARUS. Why, you know, 'tis dimpled. I think his smiling becomes him better than any man in all Phrygia.

CRESSIDA. O! he smiles valiantly.

PANDARUS. Does he not?

CRESSIDA. O! yes, an 'twere a cloud in autumn.

PANDARUS. Why, go to, then. But to prove to you that Helen loves Troilus,—

CRESSIDA. Troilus will stand to the proof, if you 'll prove it so.

PANDARUS. Troilus! why, he esteems her no more than I esteem an addle egg.

CRESSIDA. If you love an addle egg as well as you love an idle head, you would eat chickens i' the shell.

PANDARUS. I cannot choose but laugh, to think how she tickled his chin: indeed, she has a marvell's white hand, I must needs confess,—

CRESSIDA. Without the rack.

PANDARUS. And she takes upon her to spy a white hair on his chin.

CRESSIDA. Alas! poor chin! many a wart is richer.

PANDARUS. But there was such laughing: Queen Hecuba laughed that her eyes ran o'er.

CRESSIDA. With millstones.

PANDARUS. And Cassandra laughed.

CRESSIDA. But there was more temperate fire under the pot of her eyes: did her eyes run o'er too?

PANDARUS. And Hector laughed.

CRESSIDA. At what was all this laughing?

PANDARUS. Marry, at the white hair that Helen spied on Troilus' chin.

CRESSIDA. An't had been a green hair, I should have laughed too.

PANDARUS. They laughed not so much at the hair as at his pretty answer.

CRESSIDA. What was his answer?

PANDARUS. Quoth she, 'Here 's but two-and-fifty hairs on your chin, and one of them is white.'

CRESSIDA. This is her question.

PANDARUS. That 's true; make no question of that, 'One-and-fifty hairs,' quoth he, 'and one white: that white hair is my father, and all the rest are his sons.' 'Jupiter!' quoth she, 'which of these hairs is Paris, my husband?' 'The forked one,' quoth he; 'pluck 't out, and give it him.' But there was such laughing, and Helen so blushed, and Paris so chafed, and all the rest so laughed, that it passed.

CRESSIDA. So let it now, for it has been a great while going by.

PANDARUS. Well, cousin, I told you a thing yesterday; think on't.

CRESSIDA. So I do.

PANDARUS. I 'll be sworn 'tis true: he will weep you, an 'twere a man born in April.

CRESSIDA. And I 'll spring up in his tears, an 'twere a nettle against May.   *A retreat sounded*

PANDARUS. Hark! they are coming from the field. Shall we stand up here, and see them as they pass toward Ilium? good niece, do; sweet niece, Cressida.

CRESSIDA. At your pleasure.

PANDARUS. Here, here; here 's an excellent place: here we may see most bravely. I 'll tell you them all by their names as they pass by, but mark Troilus above the rest.

CRESSIDA. Speak not so loud.

Æneas passes

PANDARUS. That 's Æneas: is not that a brave man? he 's one of the flowers of Troy, I can tell you: but mark Troilus; you shall see anon.

Antenor passes

CRESSIDA. Who 's that?

PANDARUS. That 's Antenor: he has a shrewd wit, I can

tell you; and he 's a man good enough: he 's one o' the soundest judgments in Troy, whosoever, and a proper man of person. When comes Troilus? I 'll show you Troilus anon: if he see me, you shall see him nod at me.

CRESSIDA. Will he give you the nod?

PANDARUS. You shall see.

CRESSIDA. If he do, the rich shall have more.

Hector passes

PANDARUS. That 's Hector, that, that, look you, that; there 's a fellow! Go thy way, Hector. There 's a brave man, niece. O brave Hector! Look how he looks! there 's a countenance! Is 't not a brave man?

CRESSIDA. O! a brave man.

PANDARUS. Is a' not? It does a man's heart good. Look you what hacks are on his helmet! look you yonder, do you see? look you there? there 's no jesting; there 's laying on, take 't off who will, as they say: there be hacks!

CRESSIDA. Be those with swords?

PANDARUS. Swords? any thing, he cares not; an the devil come to him, it 's all one: by God's lid, it does one's heart good. Yonder comes Paris, yonder comes Paris.

Paris crosses

Look ye yonder, niece: is 't not a gallant man too, is 't not? Why, this is brave now. Who said he came hurt home to-day? he 's not hurt: why, this will do Helen's heart good now, ha! Would I could see Troilus now! You shall see Troilus anon.

CRESSIDA. Who 's that?

Helenus passes

PANDARUS. That 's Helenus. I marvel where Troilus is. That 's Helenus. I think he went not forth to-day. That 's Helenus.

CRESSIDA. Can Helenus fight, uncle?

PANDARUS. Helenus? no, yes, he 'll fight indifferent well. I marvel where Troilus is. Hark! do you not hear the people cry, 'Troilus'? Helenus is a priest.

CRESSIDA. What sneaking fellow comes yonder?

Troilus passes

PANDARUS. Where? yonder? that 's Deiphobus. 'Tis Troilus! there 's a man, niece! Hem! Brave Troilus! the prince of chivalry!

CRESSIDA. Peace! for shame, peace!

PANDARUS. Mark him; note him: O brave Troilus! look well upon him, niece: look you how his sword is bloodied, and his helmet more hacked than Hector's; and how he looks, and how he goes! O admirable youth! he ne'er saw three-and-twenty. Go thy way, Troilus, go thy way! Had I a sister were a grace, or a daughter a goddess, he should take his choice. O admirable man! Paris? Paris is dirt to him; and, I warrant, Helen, to change, would give an eye to boot.

CRESSIDA. Here come more.

Soldiers pass

PANDARUS. Asses, fools, dolts! chaff and bran, chaff and bran! porridge after meat! I could live and die i' the eyes of Troilus. Ne'er look, ne'er look; the eagles are gone: crows and daws, crows and daws! I had rather be such a man as Troilus than Agamemnon and all Greece.

CRESSIDA. There is among the Greeks Achilles, a better man than Troilus.

PANDARUS. Achilles! a drayman, a porter, a very camel.

CRESSIDA. Well, well.

PANDARUS. 'Well, well!' Why, have you any discretion? have you any eyes? Do you know what a man is? Is not birth, beauty, good shape, discourse, manhood, learning, gentleness, virtue, youth, liberality, and so forth, the spice and salt that season a man?

CRESSIDA. Ay, a minced man: and then to be baked with no date in the pie, for then the man's date 's out.

PANDARUS. You are such a woman! one knows not at what ward you lie.

CRESSIDA. Upon my back, to defend my belly; upon my wit, to defend my wiles; upon my secrecy, to defend mine honesty; my mask, to defend my beauty; and you, to defend all these: and at all these wards I lie, at a thousand watches.

PANDARUS. Say one of your watches.

CRESSIDA. Nay, I 'll watch you for that; and that 's one of the chiefest of them too: if I cannot ward what I would not have hit, I can watch you for telling how I took the blow; unless it swell past hiding, and then it 's past watching.

PANDARUS. You are such another!

Enter Troilus' Boy

BOY. Sir, my lord would instantly speak with you.
PANDARUS. Where?
BOY. At your own house; there he unarms him.
PANDARUS. Good boy, tell him I come.   *Exit Boy*
    I doubt he be hurt. Fare ye well, good niece.
CRESSIDA. Adieu, uncle.
PANDARUS. I'll be with you, niece, by and by.
CRESSIDA. To bring, uncle?
PANDARUS. Ay, a token from Troilus.
CRESSIDA. By the same token, you are a bawd.

                                    Exit Pandarus

    Words, vows, gifts, tears, and love's full sacrifice
    He offers in another's enterprise;
    But more in Troilus thousand-fold I see
    Than in the glass of Pandar's praise may be.
    Yet hold I off. Women are angels, wooing:
    Things won are done; joy's soul lies in the doing:
    That she belov'd knows nought that knows not this:
    Men prize the thing ungain'd more than it is:
    That she was never yet, that ever knew
    Love got so sweet as when desire did sue.
    Therefore this maxim out of love I teach:
    Achievement is command; ungain'd, beseech:
    Then though my heart's content firm love doth bear,
    Nothing of that shall from mine eyes appear.   *Exit*

SCENE THREE

The Grecian Camp. Before Agamemnon's Tent.

*Sennet. Enter Agamemnon, Nestor, Ulysses,
Menelaus, and Others*

AGAMEMNON. Princes,
    What grief hath set the jaundice on your cheeks?
    The ample proposition that hope makes
    In all designs begun on earth below
    Fails in the promis'd largeness: checks and disasters
    Grow in the veins of actions highest rear'd,
    As knots, by the conflux of meeting sap,
    Infect the sound pine and divert his grain

Tortive and errant from his course of growth.
Nor, princes, is it matter new to us
That we come short of our suppose so far
That after seven years' siege yet Troy walls stand;
Sith every action that hath gone before,
Whereof we have record, trial did draw
Bias and thwart, not answering the aim,
And that unbodied figure of the thought
That gave 't surmised shape. Why then, you princes,
Do you with cheeks abash'd behold our works,
And call them shames? which are indeed nought else
But the protractive trials of great Jove,
To find persistive constancy in men:
The fineness of which metal is not found
In Fortune's love; for then, the bold and coward,
The wise and fool, the artist and unread,
The hard and soft, seem all affin'd and kin:
But, in the wind and tempest of her frown,
Distinction, with a broad and powerful fan,
Puffing at all, winnows the light away;
And what hath mass or matter, by itself
Lies rich in virtue and unmingled.
NESTOR. With due observance of thy godlike seat,
Great Agamemnon, Nestor shall apply
Thy latest words. In the reproof of chance
Lies the true proof of men: the sea being smooth,
How many shallow bauble boats dare sail
Upon her patient breast, making their way
With those of nobler bulk!
But let the ruffian Boreas once enrage
The gentle Thetis, and anon behold
The strong-ribb'd bark through liquid mountains cut,
Bounding between the two moist elements,
Like Perseus' horse: where 's then the saucy boat
Whose weak untimber'd sides but even now
Co-rivall'd greatness? either to harbour fled,
Or made a toast for Neptune. Even so
Doth valour's show and valour's worth divide
In storms of fortune; for in her ray and brightness
The herd hath more annoyance by the breese
Than by the tiger; but when the splitting wind
Makes flexible the knees of knotted oaks,

And flies fled under shade, why then the thing of cour-
age,
As rous'd with rage, with rage doth sympathize,
And with an accent tun'd in self-same key,
Retorts to chiding fortune.

ULYSSES.   Agamemnon,
Thou great commander, nerve and bone of Greece,
Heart of our numbers, soul and only spirit,
In whom the tempers and the minds of all
Should be shut up, hear what Ulysses speaks.
Besides the applause and approbation
The which, (*To Agamemnon*) most mighty for thy
place and sway,
(*To Nestor*) And thou most reverend for thy stretch'd-
out life,
I give to both your speeches, which were such
As Agamemnon and the hand of Greece
Should hold up high in brass; and such again
As venerable Nestor, hatch'd in silver,
Should with a bond of air, strong as the axletree
On which heaven rides, knit all the Greekish ears
To his experienc'd tongue, yet let it please both,
Thou great, and wise, to hear Ulysses speak.

AGAMEMNON. Speak, Prince of Ithaca; and be 't of less
expect
That matter needless, of importless burden,
Divide thy lips, than we are confident,
When rank Thersites opes his mastick jaws,
We shall hear music, wit, and oracle.

ULYSSES. Troy, yet upon his basis, had been down,
And the great Hector's sword had lack'd a master,
But for these instances.
The specialty of rule hath been neglected:
And look, how many Grecian tents do stand
Hollow upon this plain, so many hollow factions.
When that the general is not like the hive
To whom the foragers shall all repair,
What honey is expected? Degree being vizarded,
The unworthiest shows as fairly in the mask.
The heavens themselves, the planets, and this centre
Observe degree, priority, and place,
Insisture, course, proportion, season, form,

Office, and custom, in all line of order:
And therefore is the glorious planet Sol
In noble eminence enthron'd and spher'd
Amidst the other; whose med'cinable eye
Corrects the ill aspects of planets evil,
And posts, like the commandment of a king,
Sans check, to good and bad: but when the planets
In evil mixture to disorder wander,
What plagues, and what portents, what mutiny,
What raging of the sea, shaking of earth,
Commotion in the winds, frights, changes, horrors,
Divert and crack, rend and deracinate
The unity and married calm of states
Quite from their fixure! O! when degree is shak'd,
Which is the ladder to all high designs,
The enterprise is sick. How could communities,
Degrees in schools, and brotherhoods in cities,
Peaceful commerce from dividable shores,
The primogenitive and due of birth,
Prerogative of age, crowns, sceptres, laurels,
But by degree, stand in authentic place?
Take but degree away, untune that string,
And, hark! what discord follows; each thing meets
In mere oppugnancy: the bounded waters
Should lift their bosoms higher than the shores,
And make a sop of all this solid globe:
Strength should be lord of imbecility,
And the rude son should strike his father dead:
Force should be right; or rather, right and wrong—
Between whose endless jar justice resides—
Should lose their names, and so should justice too.
Then every thing includes itself in power,
Power into will, will into appetite;
And appetite, a universal wolf,
So doubly seconded with will and power,
Must make perforce a universal prey,
And last eat up himself. Great Agamemnon,
This chaos, when degree is suffocate,
Follows the choking.
And this neglection of degree it is
That by a pace goes backward, with a purpose
It hath to climb. The general 's disdain'd

By him one step below, he by the next,
That next by him beneath; so every step,
Exampled by the first pace that is sick
Of his superior, grows to an envious fever
Of pale and bloodless emulation:
And 'tis this fever that keeps Troy on foot,
Not her own sinews. To end a tale of length,
Troy in our weakness lives, not in her strength.

NESTOR. Most wisely hath Ulysses here discover'd
The fever whereof all our power is sick.

AGAMEMNON. The nature of the sickness found, Ulysses,
What is the remedy?

ULYSSES. The great Achilles, whom opinion crowns
The sinew and the forehand of our host,
Having his ear full of his airy fame,
Grows dainty of his worth, and in his tent
Lies mocking our designs. With him Patroclus
Upon a lazy bed the livelong day
Breaks scurril jests,
And with ridiculous and awkward action—
Which, slanderer, he imitation calls—
He pageants us. Sometime, great Agamemnon,
Thy topless deputation he puts on
And, like a strutting player, whose conceit
Lies in his hamstring, and doth think it rich
To hear the wooden dialogue and sound
'Twixt his stretch'd footing and the scaffoldage,—
Such to-be-pitied and o'er-wrested seeming
He acts thy greatness in:—and when he speaks,
'Tis like a chime a-mending; with terms unsquar'd,
Which, from the tongue of roaring Typhon dropp'd,
Would seem hyperboles. At this fusty stuff
The large Achilles, on his press'd bed lolling,
From his deep chest laughs out a loud applause;
Cries, 'Excellent! 'tis Agamemnon just.
Now play me Nestor; hem, and stroke thy beard,
As he being drest to some oration.'
That 's done;—as near as the extremest ends
Of parallels, like as Vulcan and his wife:—
Yet good Achilles still cries, 'Excellent!
'Tis Nestor right. Now play him me, Patroclus,
Arming to answer in a night alarm.'

And then, forsooth, the faint defects of age
Must be the scene of mirth; to cough and spit,
And with a palsy-fumbling on his gorget,
Shake in and out the rivet: and at this sport
Sir Valour dies; cries, 'O! enough, Patroclus;
Or give me ribs of steel; I shall split all
In pleasure of my spleen.' And in this fashion,
All our abilities, gifts, natures, shapes,
Severals and generals of grace exact,
Achievements, plots, orders, preventions,
Excitements to the field, or speech for truce,
Success or loss, what is or is not, serves
As stuff for these two to make paradoxes.

NESTOR. And in the imitation of these twain—
Whom, as Ulysses says, opinion crowns
With an imperial voice—many are infect.
Ajax is grown self-will'd, and bears his head
In such a rein, in full as proud a place
As broad Achilles; keeps his tent like him;
Makes factious feasts; rails on our state of war,
Bold as an oracle, and sets Thersites—
A slave whose gall coins slanders like a mint—
To match us in comparison with dirt;
To weaken and discredit our exposure,
How rank soever rounded in with danger.

ULYSSES. They tax our policy, and call it cowardice;
Count wisdom as no member of the war;
Forestall prescience, and esteem no act
But that of hand: the still and mental parts,
That do contrive how many hands shall strike,
When fitness calls them on, and know by measure
Of their observant toil the enemies' weight,—
Why, this hath not a finger's dignity:
They call this bed-work, mappery, closet-war;
So that the ram that batters down the wall,
For the great swing and rudeness of his poise,
They place before his hand that made the engine,
Or those that with the fineness of their souls
By reason guides his execution.

NESTOR. Let this be granted, and Achilles' horse
Makes many Thetis' sons.   *A tucket.*

AGAMEMNON. What trumpet? look, Menelaus.

MENELAUS. From Troy.

Enter Æneas

AGAMEMNON. What would you 'fore our tent?

ÆNEAS. Is this great Agamemnon's tent, I pray you?

AGAMEMNON. Even this.

ÆNEAS. May one, that is a herald and a prince,
 Do a fair message to his kingly ears?

AGAMEMNON. With surety stronger than Achilles' arm
 'Fore all the Greekish heads, which with one voice
 Call Agamemnon head and general.

ÆNEAS. Fair leave and large security. How may
 A stranger to those most imperial looks
 Know them from eyes of other mortals?

AGAMEMNON.   How!

ÆNEAS. Ay;
 I ask, that I might waken reverence,
 And bid the cheek be ready with a blush
 Modest as morning when she coldly eyes
 The youthful Phœbus:
 Which is that god in office, guiding men?
 Which is the high and mighty Agamemnon?

AGAMEMNON. This Trojan scorns us; or the men of Troy
 Are ceremonious courtiers.

ÆNEAS. Courtiers as free, as debonair, unarm'd,
 As bending angels; that 's their fame in peace:
 But when they would seem soldiers, they have galls,
 Good arms, strong joints, true swords; and, Jove's ac-
     cord,
 Nothing so full of heart. But peace, Æneas!
 Peace, Trojan! lay thy finger on thy lips!
 The worthiness of praise distains his worth,
 If that the prais'd himself brings the praise forth;
 But what the repining enemy commends,
 That breath fame blows; that praise, sole pure, tran-
     scends.

AGAMEMNON. Sir, you of Troy, call you yourself Æneas?

ÆNEAS. Ay, Greek, that is my name.

AGAMEMNON. What 's your affair, I pray you?

ÆNEAS. Sir, pardon, 'tis for Agamemnon's ears.

AGAMEMNON. He hears nought privately that comes from
 Troy.

ÆNEAS. Nor I from Troy come not to whisper him:

I bring a trumpet to awake his ear,
To set his sense on the attentive bent,
And then to speak.

AGAMEMNON.   Speak frankly as the wind:
It is not Agamemnon's sleeping hour;
That thou shalt know, Trojan, he is awake,
He tells thee so himself.

ÆNEAS.   Trumpet, blow aloud,
Send thy brass voice through all these lazy tents;
And every Greek of mettle, let him know,
What Troy means fairly shall be spoke aloud.

Trumpet sounds

We have, great Agamemnon, here in Troy,
A prince called Hector,—Priam is his father,—
Who in this dull and long-continu'd truce
Is rusty grown: he bade me take a trumpet,
And to this purpose speak: kings, princes, lords!
If there be one among the fair'st of Greece
That holds his honour higher than his ease,
That seeks his praise more than he fears his peril,
That knows his valour, and knows not his fear,
That loves his mistress more than in confession,
With truant vows to her own lips he loves,
And dare avow her beauty and her worth
In other arms than hers,—to him this challenge.
Hector, in view of Trojans and of Greeks,
Shall make it good, or do his best to do it,
He hath a lady wiser, fairer, truer,
Than ever Greek did compass in his arms;
And will to-morrow with his trumpet call,
Midway between your tents and walls of Troy,
To rouse a Grecian that is true in love:
If any come, Hector shall honour him;
If none, he 'll say in Troy when he retires,
The Grecian dames are sunburnt, and not worth
The splinter of a lance. Even so much.

AGAMEMNON. This shall be told our lovers, Lord Æneas;
If none of them have soul in such a kind,
We left them all at home: but we are soldiers;
And may that soldier a mere recreant prove,
That means not, hath not, or is not in love!
If then one is, or hath, or means to be,

That one meets Hector; if none else, I am he.

NESTOR. Tell him of Nestor, one that was a man
   When Hector's grandsire suck'd: he is old now:
   But if there be not in our Grecian host
   One noble man that hath one spark of fire
   To answer for his love, tell him from me,
   I 'll hide my silver beard in a gold beaver,
   And in my vantbrace put this wither'd brawn;
   And, meeting him, will tell him that my lady
   Was fairer than his grandam, and as chaste
   As may be in the world: his youth in flood,
   I 'll prove this truth with my three drops of blood.

ÆNEAS. Now heavens forbid such scarcity of youth!

ULYSSES. Amen.

AGAMEMNON. Fair Lord Æneas, let me touch your hand;
   To our pavilion shall I lead you first.
   Achilles shall have word of this intent;
   So shall each lord of Greece, from tent to tent:
   Yourself shall feast with us before you go,
   And find the welcome of a noble foe.

                    Exeunt all but Ulysses and Nestor

ULYSSES. Nestor!

NESTOR. What says Ulysses?

ULYSSES. I have a young conception in my brain;
   Be you my time to bring it to some shape.

NESTOR. What is 't?

ULYSSES. This 'tis:
   Blunt wedges rive hard knots: the seeded pride
   That hath to this maturity blown up
   In rank Achilles, must or now be cropp'd,
   Or, shedding, breed a nursery of like evil,
   To overbulk us all.

NESTOR.   Well, and how?

ULYSSES. This challenge that the gallant Hector sends,
   However it is spread in general name,
   Relates in purpose only to Achilles.

NESTOR. The purpose is perspicuous even as substance
   Whose grossness little characters sum up:
   And, in the publication, make no strain,
   But that Achilles, were his brain as barren
   As banks of Libya,—though, Apollo knows,
   'Tis dry enough,—will with great speed of judgment,

Ay, with celerity, find Hector's purpose
Pointing on him.

ULYSSES. And wake him to the answer, think you?

NESTOR. Yes, 'tis most meet: whom may you else oppose,
That can from Hector bring those honours off,
If not Achilles? Though 't be a sportful combat,
Yet in the trial much opinion dwells;
For here the Trojans taste our dear'st repute
With their fin'st palate: and trust to me, Ulysses,
Our imputation shall be oddly pois'd
In this wild action; for the success,
Although particular, shall give a scantling
Of good or bad unto the general;
And in such indexes, although small pricks
To their subsequent volumes, there is seen
The baby figure of the giant mass
Of things to come at large. It is suppos'd
He that meets Hector issues from our choice;
And choice, being mutual act of all our souls,
Makes merit her election, and doth boil,
As 'twere from forth us all, a man distill'd
Out of our virtues; who miscarrying,
What heart receives from hence the conquering part,
To steel a strong opinion to themselves?
Which entertain'd, limbs are his instruments,
In no less working than are swords and bows
Directive by the limbs.

ULYSSES. Give pardon to my speech:
Therefore 'tis meet Achilles meet not Hector.
Let us like merchants show our foulest wares,
And think perchance they 'll sell; if not,
The lustre of the better yet to show
Shall show the better. Do not consent
That ever Hector and Achilles meet;
For both our honour and our shame in this
Are dogg'd with two strange followers.

NESTOR. I see them not with my old eyes: what are they?

ULYSSES. What glory our Achilles shares from Hector,
Were he not proud, we all should share with him:
But he already is too insolent;
And we were better parch in Afric sun
Than in the pride and salt scorn of his eyes,

Should he 'scape Hector fair: if he were foil'd,
Why then we did our main opinion crush
In taint of our best man. No; make a lottery;
And by device let blockish Ajax draw
The sort to fight with Hector: among ourselves
Give him allowance as the worthier man,
For that will physic the great Myrmidon
Who broils in loud applause; and make him fall
His crest that prouder than blue Iris bends.
If the dull brainless Ajax come safe off,
We 'll dress him up in voices: if he fail,
Yet go we under our opinion still
That we have better men. But, hit or miss,
Our project's life this shape of sense assumes:
Ajax employ'd plucks down Achilles' plumes.
NESTOR. Ulysses,
Now I begin to relish thy advice;
And I will give a taste of it forthwith
To Agamemnon: go we to him straight.
Two curs shall tame each other: pride alone
Must tarre the mastiffs on, as 'twere their bone.
                                        Exeunt

ACT TWO

SCENE ONE

A Part of the Grecian Camp.

Enter Ajax and Thersites

AJAX. Thersites!

THERSITES. Agamemnon, how if he had boils? full, all over, generally?

AJAX. Thersites!

THERSITES. And those boils did run? Say so, did not the general run then? were not that a botchy core?

AJAX. Dog!

THERSITES. Then would come some matter from him: I see none now.

AJAX. Thou bitch-wolf's son, canst thou not hear? Feel, then.   *Strikes him*

THERSITES. The plague of Greece upon thee, thou mongrel beef-witted lord!

AJAX. Speak then, thou vinewedst leaven, speak: I will beat thee into handsomeness.

THERSITES. I shall sooner rail thee into wit and holiness: but I think thy horse will sooner con an oration than thou learn a prayer without book. Thou canst strike, canst thou? a red murrain o' thy jade's tricks!

AJAX. Toadstool, learn me the proclamation.

THERSITES. Dost thou think I have no sense, thou strikest me thus?

AJAX. The proclamation!

THERSITES. Thou are proclaimed a fool, I think.

AJAX. Do not, porpentine, do not: my fingers itch.

THERSITES. I would thou didst itch from head to foot, and I had the scratching of thee; I would make thee the loathsomest scab of Greece. When thou art forth in the incursions, thou strikest as slow as another.

ninth part of a sparrow. This lord, Achilles, Ajax, who wears his wit in his belly, and his guts in his head, I 'll tell you what I say of him.

ACHILLES. What?

THERSITES. I say, this Ajax,—   *Ajax offers to strike him*

ACHILLES. Nay, good Ajax.

THERSITES. Has not so much wit—

ACHILLES. Nay, I must hold you—

THERSITES. As will stop the eye of Helen's needle, for whom he comes to fight.

ACHILLES. Peace, fool!

THERSITES. I would have peace and quietness, but the fool will not: he there; that he; look you there.

AJAX. O thou damned cur! I shall—

ACHILLES. Will you set your wit to a fool's?

THERSITES. No, I warrant you; for a fool's will shame it.

PATROCLUS. Good words, Thersites.

ACHILLES. What 's the quarrel?

AJAX. I bade the vile owl go learn me the tenour of the proclamation, and he rails upon me.

THERSITES. I serve thee not.

AJAX. Well, go to, go to.

THERSITES. I serve here voluntary.

ACHILLES. Your last service was sufferance, 'twas not voluntary; no man is beaten voluntary: Ajax was here the voluntary, and you as under an impress.

THERSITES. Even so; a great deal of your wit too lies in your sinews, or else there be liars. Hector shall have a great catch if he knock out either of your brains: a' were as good crack a fusty nut with no kernel.

ACHILLES. What, with me too, Thersites?

THERSITES. There 's Ulysses and old Nestor, whose wit was mouldy ere your grandsires had nails on their toes, yoke you like draught-oxen, and make you plough up the wars.

ACHILLES. What, what?

THERSITES. Yes, good sooth: to, Achilles! to, Ajax! to!

AJAX. I shall cut out your tongue.

THERSITES. 'Tis no matter; I shall speak as much as thou afterwards.

PATROCLUS. No more words, Thersites; peace!

AJAX. I say, the proclamation!

THERSITES. Thou grumblest and railest every hou.
Achilles, and thou art as full of envy at his greatnes
Cerberus is at Proserpina's beauty, ay, that thou bark
at him.

AJAX. Mistress Thersites!

THERSITES. Thou shouldst strike him.

AJAX. Cobloaf!

THERSITES. He would pun thee into shivers with his fist, as
a sailor breaks a biscuit.

AJAX. You whoreson cur.   *Beating him.*

THERSITES. Do, do.

AJAX. Thou stool for a witch!

THERSITES. Ay, do, do; thou sodden-witted lord! thou hast
no more brain than I have in mine elbows: an assi go
may tutor thee: thou scury-valiant ass! thou are here ut
to thrash Trojans; and thou art bought and sold a ng
those of any wit, like a barbarian slave. If thou u to
beat me, I will begin at thy heel, and tell what th art
by inches, thou thing of no bowels, thou!

AJAX. You dog!

THERSITES. You scurvy lord!

AJAX. You cur!   *Beating him*

THERSITES. Mars his idiot! do, rudeness; do, camel; do, do.

Enter Achilles and Patroclus

ACHILLES. Why, how now, Ajax! wherefore do you this?
How now, Thersites! what 's the matter, man?

THERSITES. You see him there, do you?

ACHILLES. Ay; what 's the matter?

THERSITES. Nay, look upon him.

ACHILLES. So I do: what 's the matter?

THERSITES. Nay, but regard him well.

ACHILLES. 'Well!' why, so I do.

THERSITES. But yet you look not well upon him; for, who
soever you take him to be, he is Ajax.

ACHILLES. I know that, fool.

THERSITES. Ay, but that fool knows not himself.

AJAX. Therefore I beat thee.

THERSITES. Lo, lo, lo, lo, what modicums of wit he utt
his evasions have ears thus long. I have bobbed his b
more than he has beat my bones: I will buy nine
rows for a penny, and his pia mater is not wort'

THERSITES. This lord, Achilles, Ajax, who wears his wit in his belly, and his guts in his head

THERSITES. I will hold my peace when Achilles' brach bids
   me, shall I?

ACHILLES. There's for you, Patroclus.

THERSITES. I will see you hanged, like clotpoles, ere I come
   any more to your tents: I will keep where there is wit
   stirring and leave the faction of fools.   *Exit*

PATROCLUS. A good riddance.

ACHILLES. Marry, this, sir, is proclaim'd through all our
   host:
   That Hector, by the fifth hour of the sun,
   Will, with a trumpet, 'twixt our tents and Troy
   To-morrow morning call some knight to arms
   That hath a stomach; and such a one that dare
   Maintain—I know not what: 'tis trash. Farewell.

AJAX. Farewell. Who shall answer him?

ACHILLES. I know not: it is put to lottery; otherwise,
   He knew his man.

AJAX. O, meaning you. I will go learn more of it. *Exeunt*

SCENE TWO

Troy. A Room in Priam's Palace.

Enter Priam, Hector, Troilus, Paris, and Helenus

PRIAM. After so many hours, lives, speeches spent,
   Thus once again says Nestor from the Greeks:
   'Deliver Helen, and all damage else,
   As honour, loss of time, travail, expense,
   Wounds, friends, and what else dear that is consum'd
   In hot digestion of this cormorant war,
   Shall be struck off.' Hector, what say you to 't?

HECTOR. Though no man lesser fears the Greeks than I,
   As far as toucheth my particular,
   Yet, dread Priam,
   There is no lady of more softer bowels,
   More spongy to suck in the sense of fear,
   More ready to cry out 'Who knows what follows?'
   Than Hector is. The wound of peace is surety,
   Surety secure; but modest doubt is call'd
   The beacon of the wise, the tent that searches
   To the bottom of the worst. Let Helen go:

Since the first sword was drawn about this question,
Every tithe soul, 'mongst many thousand dismes,
Hath been as dear as Helen; I mean, of ours:
If we have lost so many tenths of ours,
To guard a thing not ours nor worth to us,
Had it our name, the value of one ten,
What merit 's in that reason which denies
The yielding of her up?

TROILUS.   Fie, fie! my brother,
Weigh you the worth and honour of a king
So great as our dread father in a scale
Of common ounces? will you with counters sum
The past proportion of his infinite?
And buckle in a waist most fathomless
With spans and inches so diminutive
As fears and reasons? fie, for godly shame!

HELENUS. No marvel, though you bite so sharp at reasons,
You are so empty of them. Should not our father
Bear the great sway of his affairs with reasons,
Because your speech hath none that tells him so?

TROILUS. You are for dreams and slumbers, brother priest;
You fur your gloves with reason. Here are your reasons:
You know an enemy intends you harm;
You know a sword employ'd is perilous,
And reason flies the object of all harm:
Who marvels then, when Helenus beholds
A Grecian and his sword, if he do set
The very wings of reason to his heels,
And fly like chidden Mercury from Jove,
Or like a star disorb'd? Nay, if we talk of reason,
Let 's shut our gates and sleep: manhood and honour
Should have hare-hearts, would they but fat their
    thoughts
With this cramm'd reason: reason and respect
Make livers pale, and lustihood deject.

HECTOR. Brother, she is not worth what she doth cost
The holding.

TROILUS. What is aught but as 'tis valu'd?

HECTOR. But value dwells not in particular will;
It holds his estimate and dignity
As well wherein 'tis precious of itself
As in the prizer. 'Tis mad idolatry

To make the service greater than the god;
And the will dotes that is inclinable
To what infectiously itself affects,
Without some image of the affected merit.
TROILUS. I take to-day a wife, and my election
Is led on in the conduct of my will;
My will enkindled by mine eyes and ears,
Two traded pilots 'twixt the dangerous shores
Of will and judgment. How may I avoid,
Although my will distaste what it elected,
The wife I chose? there can be no evasion
To blench from this and to stand firm by honour.
We turn not back the silks upon the merchant
When we have soil'd them, nor the remainder viands
We do not throw in unrespective sink
Because we now are full. It was thought meet
Paris should do some vengeance on the Greeks:
Your breath of full consent bellied his sails;
The seas and winds—old wranglers—took a truce
And did him service: he touch'd the ports desir'd,
And for an old aunt whom the Greeks held captive
He brought a Grecian queen, whose youth and freshness
Wrinkles Apollo's, and makes stale the morning.
Why keep we her? the Grecians keep her aunt:
Is she worth keeping? why, she is a pearl,
Whose price hath launch'd above a thousand ships,
And turn'd crown'd kings to merchants.
If you 'll avouch 'twas wisdom Paris went,—
As you must needs, for you all cried 'Go, go,'—
If you 'll confess he brought home noble prize,—
As you must needs, for you all clapp'd your hands,
And cry'd 'Inestimable!'—why do you now
The issue of your proper wisdoms rate,
And do a deed that Fortune never did,
Beggar the estimation which you priz'd
Richer than sea and land? O! theft most base,
That we have stol'n what we do fear to keep!
But thieves unworthy of a thing so stol'n,
That in their country did them that disgrace
We fear to warrant in our native place.
CASSANDRA. (*Within*) Cry, Trojans, cry!
PRIAM.   What noise? what shriek?

TROILUS. 'Tis our mad sister, I do know her voice.
CASSANDRA. (*Within*) Cry, Trojans!
HECTOR. It is Cassandra.

Enter Cassandra, raving

CASSANDRA. Cry, Trojans, cry! lend me ten thousand eyes,
And I will fill them with prophetic tears.
HECTOR. Peace, sister, peace!
CASSANDRA. Virgins and boys, mid-age and wrinkled eld,
Soft infancy, that nothing canst but cry,
Add to my clamours! let us pay betimes
A moiety of that mass of moan to come.
Cry, Trojans, cry! practise your eyes with tears!
Troy must not be, nor goodly Ilion stand;
Our firebrand brother, Paris, burns us all.
Cry, Trojans, cry! a Helen and a woe!
Cry, cry! Troy burns, or else let Helen go.   *Exit*
HECTOR. Now, youthful Troilus, do not these high strains
Of divination in our sister work
Some touches of remorse? or is your blood
So madly hot that no discourse of reason,
Nor fear of bad success in a bad cause,
Can qualify the same?
TROILUS.   Why, brother Hector,
We may not think the justness of each act
Such and no other than event doth form it,
Nor once·deject the courage of our minds,
Because Cassandra's mad: her brain-sick raptures
Cannot distaste the goodness of a quarrel
Which hath our several honours all engag'd
To make it gracious. For my private part,
I am no more touch'd than all Priam's sons;
And Jove forbid there should be done amongst us
Such things as might offend the weakest spleen
To fight for and maintain.
PARIS. Else might the world convince of levity
As well my undertakings as your counsels;
But I attest the gods, your full consent
Gave wings to my propension and cut off
All fears attending on so dire a project:
For what, alas! can these my single arms?
What propugnation is in one man's valour,
To stand the push and enmity of those

This quarrel would excite? Yet, I protest,
Were I alone to pass the difficulties,
And had as ample power as I have will,
Paris should ne'er retract what he hath done,
Nor faint in the pursuit.

PRIAM.   Paris, you speak
Like one besotted on your sweet delights:
You have the honey still, but these the gall;
So to be valiant is no praise at all.

PARIS. Sir, I propose not merely to myself
The pleasure such a beauty brings with it;
But I would have the soil of her fair rape
Wip'd off, in honourable keeping her.
What treason were it to the ransack'd queen,
Disgrace to your great worths, and shame to me,
Now, to deliver her possession up,
On terms of base compulsion! Can it be
That so degenerate a strain as this
Should once set footing in your generous bosoms?
There 's not the meanest spirit on our party
Without a heart to dare or sword to draw
When Helen is defended, nor none so noble
Whose life were ill bestow'd or death unfam'd
Where Helen is the subject: then, I say,
Well may we fight for her, whom, we know well,
The world's large spaces cannot parallel.

HECTOR. Paris and Troilus, you have both said well;
And on the cause and question now in hand
Have gloz'd, but superficially; not much
Unlike young men, whom Aristotle thought
Unfit to hear moral philosophy.
The reasons you allege do more conduce
To the hot passion of distemper'd blood
Than to make up a free determination
'Twixt right and wrong; for pleasure and revenge
Have ears more deaf than adders to the voice
Of any true decision. Nature craves
All dues be render'd to their owners: now,
What nearer debt in all humanity
Than wife is to the husband? if this law
Of nature be corrupted through affection,
And that great minds, of partial indulgence

To their benumbed wills, resist the same;
There is a law in each well-order'd nation
To curb those raging appetites that are
Most disobedient and refractory.
If Helen then be wife to Sparta's king,
As it is known she is, these moral laws
Of nature, and of nations, speak aloud
To have her back return'd: thus to persist
In doing wrong extenuates not wrong,
But makes it much more heavy. Hector's opinion
Is this, in way of truth; yet, ne'ertheless,
My spritely brethren, I propend to you
In resolution to keep Helen still;
For 'tis a cause that hath no mean dependance
Upon our joint and several dignities.

TROILUS. Why, there you touch'd the life of our design:
Were it not glory that we more affected
Than the performance of our heaving spleens,
I would not wish a drop of Trojan blood
Spent more in her defence. But, worthy Hector,
She is a theme of honour and renown,
A spur to valiant and magnanimous deeds,
Whose present courage may beat down our foes,
And fame in time to come canonize us;
For, I presume, brave Hector would not lose
So rich advantage of a promis'd glory
As smiles upon the forehead of this action
For the wide world's revenue.

HECTOR.   I am yours,
You valiant offspring of great Priamus.
I have a roisting challenge sent amongst
The dull and factious nobles of the Greeks
Will strike amazement to their drowsy spirits.
I was advertis'd their great general slept
Whilst emulation in the army crept:
This, I presume, will wake him.   *Exeunt*

SCENE THREE

The Grecian Camp. Before Achilles' Tent.

Enter Thersites

THERSITES. How now, Thersites! what, lost in the labyrinth
of thy fury! Shall the elephant Ajax carry it thus? he
beats me, and I rail at him: O worthy satisfaction!
Would it were otherwise; that I could beat him, whilst
he railed at me. 'Sfoot, I 'll learn to conjure and raise
devils, but I 'll see some issue of my spiteful execrations.
Then there 's Achilles, a rare enginer. If Troy be not
taken till these two undermine it, the walls will stand
till they fall of themselves. O! thou great thunder-darter
of Olympus, forget that thou art Jove the king of gods,
and, Mercury, lose all the serpentine craft of thy cadu-
ceus, if ye take not that little little less than little wit
from them that they have; which short-armed ignorance
itself knows is so abundant scarce it will not in circumvention deliver a fly from a spider, without drawing
their massy irons and cutting the web. After this, the
vengeance on the whole camp! or, rather, the Neapolitan
bone-ache! for that, methinks, is the curse dependant on
those that war for a placket. I have said my prayers, and
devil Envy say Amen. What, ho! my Lord Achilles!

Enter Patroclus

PATROCLUS. Who 's there? Thersites! Good Thersites, come
in and rail.

THERSITES. If I could have remembered a gilt counterfeit,
thou wouldst not have slipped out of my contemplation:
but it is no matter; thyself upon thyself! The common
curse of mankind, folly and ignorance, be thine in great
revenue! heaven bless thee from a tutor, and discipline
come not near thee! Let thy blood be thy direction till
thy death! then, if she that lays thee out says thou art
a fair corpse, I 'll be sworn and sworn upon 't she never
shrouded any but lazars. Amen. Where 's Achilles?

PATROCLUS. What! are thou devout? wast thou in prayer?

THERSITES. Ay; the heavens hear me!

Enter Achilles

ACHILLES. Who's there?

PATROCLUS. Thersites, my lord.

ACHILLES. Where, where? Art thou come? Why, my cheese, my digestion, why hast thou not served thyself in to my table so many meals? Come, what 's Agamemnon?

THERSITES. Thy commander, Achilles. Then tell me, Patroclus, what 's Achilles?

PATROCLUS. Thy lord, Thersites. Then tell me, I pray thee, what 's thyself?

THERSITES. Thy knower, Patroclus. Then tell me, Patroclus, what are thou?

PATROCLUS. Thou mayst tell that knowest.

ACHILLES. O! tell, tell.

THERSITES. I 'll decline the whole question. Agamemnon commands Achilles; Achilles is my lord; I am Patroclus' knower; and Patroclus is a fool.

PATROCLUS. You rascal!

THERSITES. Peace, fool! I have not done.

ACHILLES. He is a privileged man. Proceed, Thersites.

THERSITES. Agamemnon is a fool; Achilles is a fool; Thersites is a fool; and, as aforesaid, Patroclus is a fool.

ACHILLES. Derive this; come.

THERSITES. Agamemnon is a fool to offer to command Achilles; Achilles is a fool to be commanded of Agamemnon; Thersites is a fool to serve such a fool; and Patroclus is a fool positive.

PATROCLUS. Why am I a fool?

THERSITES. Make that demand to the Creator. It suffices me thou art. Look you, who comes here?

ACHILLES. Patroclus, I 'll speak with nobody. Come in with me, Thersites.   *Exit*

THERSITES. Here is such patchery, such juggling, and such knavery! all the argument is a cuckold and a whore; a good quarrel to draw emulous factions and bleed to death upon. Now, the dry serpigo on the subject! and war and lechery confound all!   *Exit*

Enter Agamemnon, Ulysses, Nestor, Diomedes, and Ajax.

AGAMEMNON. Where is Achilles?

PATROCLUS. Within his tent; but ill-dispos'd, my lord.

AGAMEMNON. Let it be known to him that we are here.
He shent our messengers; and we lay by
Our appertainments, visiting of him:

Let him be told so; lest perchance he think
We dare not move the question of our place,
Or know not what we are.

PATROCLUS.   I shall say so to him.   *Exit*

ULYSSES. We saw him at the opening of his tent:
He is not sick.

AJAX. Yes, lion-sick, sick of proud heart: you may call it
melancholy if you will favour the man; but, by my head,
'tis pride: but why, why? let him show us a cause. A
word, my lord.   *Takes Agamemnon aside*

NESTOR. What moves Ajax thus to bay at him?

ULYSSES. Achilles hath inveigled his fool from him.

NESTOR. Who, Thersites?

ULYSSES. He.

NESTOR. Then will Ajax lack matter, if he have lost his
argument.

ULYSSES. No; you see, he is his argument that has his argument, Achilles.

NESTOR. All the better; their fraction is more our wish than
their faction: but it was a strong composure a fool could
disunite.

ULYSSES. The amity that wisdom knits not, folly may easily
untie. Here comes Patroclus.

Re-enter Patroclus

NESTOR. No Achilles with him.

ULYSSES. The elephant hath joints, but none for courtesy
his legs are legs for necessity, not for flexure.

PATROCLUS. Achilles bids me say, he is much sorry
If any thing more than your sport and pleasure
Did move your greatness and this noble state
To call upon him; he hopes it is no other
But, for your health and your digestion sake,
An after-dinner's breath.

AGAMEMNON.   Hear you, Patroclus:
We are too well acquainted with these answers:
But his evasion, wing'd thus swift with scorn,
Cannot outfly our apprehensions.
Much attribute he hath, and much the reason
Why we ascribe it to him; yet all his virtues,
Not virtuously on his own part beheld,
Do in our eyes begin to lose their gloss,
Yea, like fair fruit in an unwholesome dish,

Are like to rot untasted. Go and tell him,
We come to speak with him; and you shall not sin
If you do say we think him over-proud
And under-honest, in self-assumption greater
Than in the note of judgment; and worthier than himself
Here tend the savage strangeness he puts on,
Disguise the holy strength of their command,
And underwrite in an observing kind
His humorous predominance; yea, watch
His pettish lunes, his ebbs, his flows, as if
The passage and whole carriage of this action
Rode on his tide. Go tell him this, and add,
That if he overhold his price so much,
We 'll none of him; but let him, like an engine
Not portable, lie under this report:
'Bring action hither, this cannot go to war.'
A stirring dwarf we do allowance give
Before a sleeping giant: tell him so.

PATROCLUS. I shall; and bring his answer presently.   *Exit*

AGAMEMNON. In second voice we 'll not be satisfied;
We come to speak with him. Ulysses, enter you.
                                        Exit Ulysses

AJAX. What is he more than another?

AGAMEMNON. No more than what he thinks he is.

AJAX. Is he so much? Do you not think he thinks himself
a better man than I am?

AGAMEMNON. No question.

AJAX. Will you subscribe his thought, and say he is?

AGAMEMNON. No, noble Ajax; you are as strong, as valiant,
as wise, no less noble, much more gentle, and altogether
more tractable.

AJAX. Why should a man be proud? How doth pride
grow? I know not what pride is.

AGAMEMNON. Your mind is the clearer, Ajax, and your virtues the fairer. He that is proud eats up himself: pride
is his own glass, his own trumpet, his own chronicle:
and whatever praises itself but in the deed, devours the
deed in the praise.

AJAX. I do hate a proud man, as I hate the engendering
of toads.

NESTOR. (*Aside*) Yet he loves himself: is 't not strange?
                Re-enter Ulysses

ULYSSES. Achilles will not to the field to-morrow.

AGAMEMNON. What's his excuse?

ULYSSES.   He doth rely on none,
But carries on the stream of his dispose
Without observance or respect of any,
In will peculiar and in self-admission.

AGAMEMNON. Why will he not upon our fair request
Untent his person and share the air with us?

ULYSSES. Things small as nothing, for request's sake only,
He makes important: possess'd he is with greatness,
And speaks not to himself but with a pride
That quarrels at self-breath: imagin'd worth
Holds in his blood such swoln and hot discourse,
That 'twixt his mental and his active parts
Kingdom'd Achilles in commotion rages
And batters down himself: what should I say?
He is so plaguy proud, that the death-tokens of it
Cry 'No recovery.'

AGAMEMNON.   Let Ajax go to him.
Dear lord, go you and meet him in his tent:
'Tis said he holds you well, and will be led
At your request a little from himself.

ULYSSES. O Agamemnon! let it not be so.
We'll consecrate the steps that Ajax makes
When they go from Achilles: shall the proud lord
That bastes his arrogance with his own seam,
And never suffers matter of the world
Enter his thoughts, save such as do revolve
And ruminate himself, shall he be worshipp'd
Of that we hold an idol more than he?
No, this thrice-worthy and right valiant lord
Must not so stale his palm, nobly acquir'd;
Nor, by my will, assubjugate his merit,
As amply titled as Achilles is,
By going to Achilles:
That were to enlard his fat-already pride,
And add more coals to Cancer when he burns
With entertaining great Hyperion.
This lord go to him! Jupiter forbid,
And say in thunder, 'Achilles go to him.'

NESTOR. (*Aside*) O! this is well; he rubs the vein of him.

DIOMEDES. (*Aside*) And how his silence drinks up this applause!

AJAX. If I go to him, with my armed fist
I 'll pash him o'er the face.

AGAMEMNON. O, no! you shall not go.

AJAX. An a' be proud with me, I 'll pheeze his pride.
Let me go to him.

ULYSSES. Not for the worth that hangs upon our quarrel.

AJAX. A paltry, insolent fellow!

NESTOR. (*Aside*) How he describes himself!

AJAX. Can he not be sociable?

ULYSSES. (*Aside*) The raven chides blackness.

AJAX. I 'll let his humours blood.

AGAMEMNON. (*Aside*) He will be the physician that should
be the patient.

AJAX. An all men were o' my mind,—

ULYSSES. (*Aside*) Wit would be out of fashion.

AJAX. A' should not bear it so, a' should eat swords first:
shall pride carry it?

NESTOR. (*Aside*) An 't would, you 'd carry half.

ULYSSES. (*Aside*) A' would have ten shares.

AJAX. I will knead him; I will make him supple.

NESTOR. (*Aside*) He 's not yet through warm: force him
with praises: pour in, pour in; his ambition is dry.

ULYSSES. (*To Agamemnon*) My lord, you feed too much
on this dislike.

NESTOR. Our noble general, do not do so.

DIOMEDES. You must prepare to fight without Achilles.

ULYSSES. Why, 'tis this naming of him does him harm.
Here is a man—but 'tis before his face
I will be silent.

NESTOR.   Wherefore should you so?
He is not emulous, as Achilles is.

ULYSSES. Know the whole world, he is as valiant.

AJAX. A whoreson dog, that shall palter thus with us!
Would he were a Trojan!

NESTOR. What a vice were it in Ajax now,—

ULYSSES. If he were proud,—

DIOMEDES. Or covetous of praise,—

ULYSSES. Ay, or surly borne,—

DIOMEDES. Or strange, or self-affected!

ULYSSES. Thank the heavens, lord, thou art of sweet com-
    posure;
  Praise him that got thee, her that gave thee suck:
  Fam'd be thy tutor, and thy parts of nature
  Thrice-fam'd, beyond all erudition:
  But he that disciplin'd thy arms to fight,
  Let Mars divide eternity in twain,
  And give him half: and, for thy vigour,
  Bull-bearing Milo his addition yield
  To sinewy Ajax. I will not praise thy wisdom,
  Which, like a bourn, a pale, a shore, confines
  Thy spacious and dilated parts: here 's Nestor
  Instructed by the antiquary times,
  He must, he is, he cannot but be wise;
  But pardon, father Nestor, were your days
  As green as Ajax, and your brain so temper'd,
  You should not have the eminence of him,
  But be as Ajax.
AJAX.   Shall I call you father?
ULYSSES. Ay, my good son.
DIOMEDES.   Be rul'd by him, Lord Ajax.
ULYSSES. There is no tarrying here; the hart Achilles
  Keeps thicket. Please it our great general
  To call together all his state of war;
  Fresh kings are come to Troy: to-morrow,
  We must with all our main of power stand fast:
  And here 's a lord,—come knights from east to west,
  And cull their flower, Ajax shall cope the best.
AGAMEMNON. Go we to council. Let Achilles sleep:
  Light boats sail swift, though greater hulks draw deep.
                                    Exeunt

ACT THREE

SCENE ONE

Troy. Priam's Palace.

Enter Pandarus and a Servant

PANDARUS. Friend! you! pray you, a word: do not you follow the young Lord Paris?

SERVANT. Ay, sir, when he goes before me.

PANDARUS. You depend upon him, I mean?

SERVANT. Sir, I do depend upon the Lord.

PANDARUS. You depend upon a noble gentleman; I must needs praise him.

SERVANT. The Lord be praised!

PANDARUS. You know me, do you not?

SERVANT. Faith, sir, superficially.

PANDARUS. Friend, know me better, I am the Lord Pandarus.

SERVANT. I hope I shall know your honour better.

PANDARUS. I do desire it.

SERVANT. You are in the state of grace.

PANDARUS. Grace! not so, friend; honour and lordship are my titles. (*Music within*) What music is this?

SERVANT. I do but partly know, sir: it is music in parts.

PANDARUS. Know you the musicians?

SERVANT. Wholly, sir.

PANDARUS. Who play they to?

SERVANT. To the hearers, sir.

PANDARUS. At whose pleasure, friend?

SERVANT. At mine, sir, and theirs that love music.

PANDARUS. Command, I mean, friend.

SERVANT. Who shall I command, sir?

PANDARUS. Friend, we understand not one another: I am too courtly, and thou art too cunning. At whose request do these men play?

SERVANT. That 's to 't, indeed, sir. Marry, sir, at the request of Paris my lord, who is there in person; with him the mortal Venus, the heart-blood of beauty, love's invisible soul.

PANDARUS. Who, my cousin Cressida?

SERVANT. No, sir, Helen: could you not find out that by her attributes?

PANDARUS. It should seem, fellow, that thou hast not seen the Lady Cressida. I come to speak with Paris from the Prince Troilus: I will make a complimental assault upon him, for my business seethes.

SERVANT. Sodden business: there 's a stewed phrase, indeed.

Enter Paris and Helen, attended

PANDARUS. Fair be to you, my lord, and to all this fair company! fair desires, in all fair measures, fairly guide them! especially to you, fair queen! fair thoughts be your fair pillow!

HELEN. Dear lord, you are full of fair words.

PANDARUS. You speak your fair pleasure, sweet queen. Fair prince, here is good broken music.

PARIS. You have broke it, cousin; and, by my life, you shall make it whole again: you shall piece it out with a piece of your performance. Nell, he is full of harmony.

PANDARUS. Truly, lady, no.

HELEN. O, sir!

PANDARUS. Rude, in sooth; in good sooth, very rude.

PARIS. Well said, my lord! Well, you say so in fits.

PANDARUS. I have business to my lord, dear queen. My lord, will you vouchsafe me a word?

HELEN. Nay, this shall not hedge us out: we 'll hear you sing, certainly.

PANDARUS. Well, sweet queen, you are pleasant with me. But, marry, thus, my lord. My dear lord and most esteemed friend, your brother Troilus—

HELEN. My lord Pandarus; honey-sweet lord,—

PANDARUS. Go to, sweet queen, go to: commends himself most affectionately to you.

HELEN. You shall not bob us out of our melody: if you do, our melancholy upon your head!

PANDARUS. Sweet queen, sweet queen! that 's a sweet queen, i' faith.

HELEN. And to make a sweet lady sad is a sour offence.

PANDARUS. Nay, that shall not serve your turn; that shall it not, in truth, la! Nay, I care not for such words: no, no. And, my lord, he desires you, that if the king call for him at supper, you will make his excuse.

HELEN. My Lord Pandarus,—

PANDARUS. What says my sweet queen, my very sweet queen?

PARIS. What exploit 's in hand? where sups he to-night?

HELEN. Nay, but my lord,—

PANDARUS. What says my sweet queen! My cousin will fall out with you. You must know where he sups.

PARIS. I 'll lay my life, with my disposer Cressida.

PANDARUS. No, no, no such matter; you are wide. Come, your disposer is sick.

PARIS. Well, I 'll make excuse.

PANDARUS. Ay, good my lord. Why should you say Cressida? no, your poor disposer 's sick.

PARIS. I spy.

PANDARUS. You spy! what do you spy? Come, give me an instrument. Now, sweet queen.

HELEN. Why, this is kindly done.

PANDARUS. My niece is horribly in love with a thing you have, sweet queen.

HELEN. She shall have it, my lord, if it be not my Lord Paris.

PANDARUS. He! no, she 'll none of him; they two are twain.

HELEN. Falling in, after falling out, may make them three.

PANDARUS. Come, come, I 'll hear no more of this. I 'll sing you a song now.

HELEN. Ay, ay, prithee now. By my troth, sweet lord, thou hast a fine forehead.

PANDARUS. Ay, you may, you may.

HELEN. Let thy song be love: this love will undo us all. O Cupid, Cupid, Cupid!

PANDARUS. Love! ay, that it shall, i' faith.

PARIS. Ay, good now, love, love, nothing but love.

PANDARUS. In good troth, it begins so:

(*Sings*)

 Love, love, nothing but love, still more!
  For, oh! love's bow
  Shoots buck and doe:

> The shaft confounds,
>   Not that it wounds,
> But tickles still the sore.
> These lovers cry O! O! they die!
>   Yet that which seems the wound to kill,
> Doth turn O! O! to ha! ha! he!
>   So dying love lives still:
> O! O! a while, but ha! ha! ha!
> O! O! groans out for ha! ha! ha!

Heigh-ho!

HELEN. In love, i' faith, to the very tip of the nose.

PARIS. He eats nothing but doves, love; and that breeds hot blood, and hot blood begets hot thoughts, and hot thoughts beget hot deeds, and hot deeds is love.

PANDARUS. Is this the generation of love? hot blood? hot thoughts, and hot deeds? Why, they are vipers: is love a generation of vipers? Sweet lord, who 's a-field to-day?

PARIS. Hector, Deiphobus, Helenus, Antenor, and all the gallantry of Troy: I would fain have armed to-day, but my Nell would not have it so. How chance my brother Troilus went not?

HELEN. He hangs the lip at something: you know all, Lord Pandarus.

PANDARUS. Not I, honey-sweet queen. I long to hear how they sped to-day. You 'll remember your brother's excuse?

PARIS. To a hair.

PANDARUS. Farewell, sweet queen.

HELEN. Commend me to your niece.

PANDARUS. I will, sweet queen.   *Exit. A retreat sounded*

PARIS. They 're come from field: let us to Priam's hall
To greet the warriors. Sweet Helen, I must woo you
To help unarm our Hector: his stubborn buckles,
With these your white enchanting fingers touch'd,
Shall more obey than to the edge of steel
Or force of Greekish sinews; you shall do more
Than all the island kings,—disarm great Hector.

HELEN. 'Twill make us proud to be his servant, Paris;
Yea, what he shall receive of us in duty
Gives us more palm in beauty than we have,
Yea, overshines ourself.

PARIS. Sweet, above thought I love thee.   *Exeunt*

SCENE TWO

The Same. Pandarus' Orchard.

Enter Pandarus and Troilus' Boy, meeting

PANDARUS. How now! where 's thy master? at my cousin
Cressida's?

BOY. No, sir: he stays for you to conduct him thither.

Enter Troilus

PANDARUS. O! here he comes. How now, how now!

TROILUS. Sirrah, walk off.   *Exit Boy*

PANDARUS. Have you seen my cousin?

TROILUS. No, Pandarus: I stalk about her door,
Like a strange soul upon the Stygian banks
Staying for waftage. O! be thou my Charon,
And give me swift transportation to those fields
Where I may wallow in the lily-beds
Propos'd for the deserver! O gentle Pandarus!
From Cupid's shoulder pluck his painted wings,
And fly with me to Cressid.

PANDARUS. Walk here i' the orchard. I 'll bring her straight.

Exit

TROILUS. I am giddy, expectation whirls me round.
The imaginary relish is so sweet
That it enchants my sense. What will it be
When that the watery palate tastes indeed
Love's thrice-repured nectar? death, I fear me,
Swounding destruction, or some joy too fine,
Too subtle-potent, tun'd too sharp in sweetness
For the capacity of my ruder powers:
I fear it much; and I do fear besides
That I shall lose distinction in my joys;
As doth a battle, when they charge on heaps
The enemy flying.

Re-enter Pandarus

PANDARUS. She 's making her ready: she 'll come straight:
you must be witty now. She does so blush, and fetches
her wind so short, as if she were frayed with a sprite: I 'll
fetch her. It is the prettiest villain: she fetches her
breath as short as a new-ta'en sparrow.   *Exit*

TROILUS. Even such a passion doth embrace my bosom;

My heart beats thicker than a feverous pulse;
And all my powers do their bestowing lose,
Like vassalage at unawares encountering
The eye of majesty.

Re-enter Pandarus with Cressida

PANDARUS. Come, come, what need you blush? shame 's a
baby. Here she is now: swear the oaths now to her that
you have sworn to me. What! are you gone again? you
must be watched ere you be made tame, must you?
Come your ways, come your ways; an you draw backward, we 'll put you i' the fills. Why do you not speak to
her? Come, draw this curtain, and let 's see your picture.
Alas the day, how loath you are to offend day-light! an
'twere dark, you'd close sooner. So, so; rub on, and kiss
the mistress. How now! a kiss in fee-farm! build there,
carpenter; the air is sweet. Nay, you shall fight your
hearts out ere I part you. The falcon as the tercel, for all
the ducks i' the river: go to, go to.

TROILUS. You have bereft me of all words, lady.

PANDARUS. Words pay no debts, give her deeds; but she 'll
bereave you of the deeds too if she call your activity in
question. What! billing again? Here 's 'In witness whereof the parties interchangeably'—Come in, come in: I 'll
go get a fire.   *Exit*

CRESSIDA. Will you walk in, my lord?

TROILUS. O Cressida! how often have I wished me thus!

CRESSIDA. Wished, my lord! The gods grant,—O my lord!

TROILUS. What should they grant? what makes this pretty
abruption? What too curious dreg espies my sweet lady
in the fountain of our love?

CRESSIDA. More dregs than water, if my fears have eyes.

TROILUS. Fears make devils of cherubins; they never see
truly.

CRESSIDA. Blind fear, that seeing reason leads, finds safer
footing than blind reason stumbling without fear: to fear
the worst oft cures the worse.

TROILUS. O! let my lady apprehend no fear: in all Cupid's
pageant there is presented no monster.

CRESSIDA. Nor nothing monstrous neither?

TROILUS. Nothing but our undertakings; when we vow to
weep seas, live in fire, eat rocks, tame tigers; thinking it
harder for our mistress to devise imposition enough than

for us to undergo any difficulty imposed. This is the monstruosity in love, lady, that the will is infinite, and the execution confined; that the desire is boundless, and the act a slave to limit.

CRESSIDA. They say all lovers swear more performance than they are able, and yet reserve an ability that they never perform; vowing more than the perfection of ten and discharging less than the tenth part of one. They that have the voice of lions and the act of hares, are they not monsters?

TROILUS. Are there such? such are not we. Praise us as we are tasted, allow us as we prove; our head shall go bare, till merit crown it. No perfection in reversion shall have a praise in present: we will not name desert before his birth, and, being born, his addition shall be humble. Few words to fair faith: Troilus shall be such to Cressid, as what envy can say worst shall be a mock for his truth; and what truth can speak truest not truer than Troilus.

CRESSIDA. Will you walk in, my lord?

Re-enter Pandarus

PANDARUS. What! blushing still? have you not done talking yet?

CRESSIDA. Well, uncle, what folly I commit, I dedicate to you.

PANDARUS. I thank you for that: if my lord get a boy of you, you 'll give him me. Be true to my lord; if he flinch, chide me for it.

TROILUS. You know now your hostages; your uncle's word, and my firm faith.

PANDARUS. Nay, I 'll give my word for her too. Our kindred, though they be long ere they are wooed, they are constant being won: they are burrs, I can tell you; they 'll stick where they are thrown.

CRESSIDA. Boldness comes to me now, and brings me heart: Prince Troilus, I have lov'd you night and day For many weary months.

TROILUS. Why was my Cressid then so hard to win?

CRESSIDA. Hard to seem won; but I was won, my lord, With the first glance that ever—pardon me— If I confess much you will play the tyrant. I love you now; but, till now, not so much But I might master it: in faith, I lie;

My thoughts were like unbridled children, grown
Too headstrong for their mother. See, we fools!
Why have I blabb'd? who shall be true to us
When we are so unsecret to ourselves?
But, though I lov'd you well, I woo'd you not;
And yet, good faith, I wish'd myself a man,
Or that we women had men's privilege
Of speaking first. Sweet, bid me hold my tongue;
For in this rapture I shall surely speak
The thing I shall repent. See, see! your silence,
Cunning in dumbness, from my weakness draws
My very soul of counsel. Stop my mouth.

TROILUS. And shall, albeit sweet music issues thence.

PANDARUS. Pretty, i' faith.

CRESSIDA. My lord, I do beseech you, pardon me;
  'Twas not my purpose thus to beg a kiss:
  I am asham'd: O heavens! what have I done?
  For this time will I take my leave, my lord.

TROILUS. Your leave, sweet Cressid?

PANDARUS. Leave! an you take leave till to-morrow morning,—

CRESSIDA. Pray you, content you.

TROILUS.   What offends you, lady?

CRESSIDA. Sir, mine own company.

TROILUS. You cannot shun yourself.

CRESSIDA. Let me go and try:
  I have a kind of self resides with you;
  But an unkind self, that itself will leave,
  To be another's fool. I would be gone:
  Where is my wit? I speak I know not what.

TROILUS. Well know they what they speak that speak so
  wisely.

CRESSIDA. Perchance, my lord, I show more craft than love:
  And fell so roundly to a large confession,
  To angle for your thoughts: but you are wise,
  Or else you love not, for to be wise, and love,
  Exceeds man's might; that dwells with gods above.

TROILUS. O! that I thought it could be in a woman—
  As if it can I will presume in you—
  To feed for aye her lamp and flames of love;
  To keep her constancy in plight and youth.
  Outliving beauty's outward, with a mind

That doth renew swifter than blood decays:
Or that persuasion could but thus convince me,
That my integrity and truth to you
Might be affronted with the match and weight
Of such a winnow'd purity in love;
How were I then uplifted! but, alas!
I am as true as truth's simplicity,
And simpler than the infancy of truth.

CRESSIDA. In that I 'll war with you.

TROILUS.   O virtuous fight!
When right with right wars, who shall be most right?
True swains in love shall in the world to come
Approve their truths by Troilus: when their rimes,
Full of protest, of oath, and big compare,
Want similes, truth tir'd with iteration,
As true as steel, as plantage to the moon,
As sun to day, as turtle to her mate,
As iron to adamant, as earth to the centre,
Yet, after all comparisons of truth,
As truth's authentic author to be cited,
'As true as Troilus' shall crown up the verse
And sanctify the numbers.

CRESSIDA.   Prophet may you be!
If I be false, or swerve a hair from truth,
When time is old and hath forgot itself,
When waterdrops have worn the stones of Troy,
And blind oblivion swallow'd cities up,
And mighty states characterless are grated
To dusty nothing, yet let memory,
From false to false, among false maids in love
Upbraid my falsehood! when they have said 'as false
As air, as water, wind, or sandy earth,
As fox to lamb, as wolf to heifer's calf,
Pard to the hind, or stepdame to her son;'
Yea, let them say, to stick the heart of falsehood,
'As false as Cressid.'

PANDARUS. Go to, a bargain made; seal it, seal it: I 'll be the
witness. Here I hold your hand, here my cousin's. If ever
you prove false one to another, since I have taken such
pains to bring you together, let all pitiful goers-between
be called to the world's end after my name; call them all
Pandars; let all constant men be Troiluses, all false

CRESSIDA.   Yea, let them say, to stick the heart of falsehood,
  'As false as Cressid.'

women Cressids, and all brokers-between Pandars! say
Amen.

TROILUS. Amen.

CRESSIDA. Amen.

PANDARUS. Amen. Whereupon I will show you a chamber
and a bed; which bed, because it shall not speak of your
pretty encounters, press it to death: away!
And Cupid grant all tongue-tied maidens here
Bed, chamber, Pandar to provide this gear!   *Exeunt*

SCENE THREE

The Grecian Camp.

*Enter Agamemnon, Ulysses, Diomedes, Nestor, Ajax,
Menelaus, and Calchas*

CALCHAS. Now, princes, for the service I have done you,
The advantage of the time prompts me aloud
To call for recompense. Appear it to your mind
That through the sight I bear in things to love,
I have abandon'd Troy, left my possession,
Incurr'd a traitor's name; expos'd myself,
From certain and possess'd conveniences,
To doubtful fortunes; sequestering from me all
That time, acquaintance, custom, and condition
Made tame and most familiar to my nature;
And here, to do you service, have become
As new into the world, strange, unacquainted:
I do beseech you, as in way of taste,
To give me now a little benefit,
Out of those many register'd in promise,
Which, you say, live to come in my behalf.

AGAMEMNON. What wouldst thou of us, Trojan? make
demand.

CALCHAS. You have a Trojan prisoner, call'd Antenor,
Yesterday took: Troy holds him very dear.
Oft have you—often have you thanks therefore—
Desir'd my Cressid in right great exchange,
Whom Troy hath still denied; but this Antenor
I know is such a wrest in their affairs
That their negotiations all must slack,

Wanting his manage; and they will almost
Give us a prince of blood, a son of Priam,
In change of him: let him be sent, great princes,
And he shall buy my daughter; and her presence
Shall quite strike off all service I have done,
In most accepted pain.

AGAMEMNON.   Let Diomedes bear him,
And bring us Cressid hither: Calchas shall have
What he requests of us. Good Diomed,
Furnish you fairly for this interchange:
Withal bring word if Hector will to-morrow
Be answer'd in his challenge: Ajax is ready.

DIOMEDES. This shall I undertake; and 'tis a burden
Which I am proud to bear.

                    Exeunt Diomedes and Calchas
          Enter Achilles and Patroclus, before their tent

ULYSSES. Achilles stands in the entrance of his tent:
Please it our general to pass strangely by him,
As if he were forgot; and, princes all,
Lay negligent and loose regard upon him:
I will come last. 'Tis like he 'll question me
Why such unplausive eyes are bent on him:
If so, I have derision med'cinable
To use between your strangeness and his pride,
Which his own will shall have desire to drink.
It may do good: pride hath no other glass
To show itself but pride, for supple knees
Feed arrogance and are the poor man's fees.

AGAMEMNON. We 'll execute your purpose, and put on
A form of strangeness as we pass along:
So do each lord, and either greet him not,
Or else disdainfully, which shall shake him more
Than if not look'd on. I will lead the way.

ACHILLES. What! comes the general to speak with me?
You know my mind; I 'll fight no more 'gainst Troy.

AGAMEMNON. What says Achilles? would he aught with
    us?

NESTOR. Would you, my lord, aught with the general?

ACHILLES. No.

NESTOR. Nothing, my lord.

AGAMEMNON. The better.

                    Exeunt Agamemnon and Nestor

ACHILLES. Good day, good day.

MENELAUS. How do you? how do you?   *Exit*

ACHILLES. What! does the cuckold scorn me?

AJAX. How now, Patroclus?

ACHILLES. Good-morrow, Ajax.

AJAX. Ha?

ACHILLES. Good-morrow.

AJAX. Ay, and good next day too.   *Exit*

ACHILLES. What mean these fellows? Know they not Achil-
    les?

PATROCLUS. They pass by strangely: they were us'd to
    bend,
  To send their smiles before them to Achilles;
  To come as humbly as they us'd to creep
  To holy altars.

ACHILLES.   What! am I poor of late?
  'Tis certain, greatness, once fall'n out with fortune,
  Must fall out with men too; what the declin'd is
  He shall as soon read in the eyes of others
  As feel in his own fall; for men, like butterflies,
  Show not their mealy wings but to the summer,
  And not a man, for being simply man,
  Hath any honour, but honour for those honours
  That are without him, as places, riches, and favour,
  Prizes of accident as oft as merit:
  Which when they fall, as being slippery standers,
  The love that lean'd on them as slippery too,
  Do one pluck down another, and together
  Die in the fall. But 'tis not so with me:
  Fortune and I are friends: I do enjoy
  At ample point all that I did possess,
  Save these men's looks; who do, methinks, find out
  Something not worth in me such rich beholding
  As they have often given. Here is Ulysses:
  I 'll interrupt his reading.
  How now, Ulysses!

ULYSSES.   Now, great Thetis' son!

ACHILLES. What are you reading?

ULYSSES.   A strange fellow here
  Writes me,
      'That man, how dearly ever parted,
  How much in having, or without or in,

Cannot make boast to have that which he hath,
Nor feels not what he owes but by reflection;
As when his virtues shining upon others
Heat them, and they retort that heat again
To the first giver.'

ACHILLES.   This is not strange, Ulysses!
The beauty that is borne here in the face
The bearer knows not, but commends itself
To others' eyes: nor doth the eye itself—
That most pure spirit of sense—behold itself,
Not going from itself; but eye to eye oppos'd
Salutes each other with each other's form;
For speculation turns not to itself
Till it hath travell'd and is mirror'd there
Where it may see itself. This is not strange at all.

ULYSSES. I do not strain at the position,
It is familiar, but at the author's drift;
Who in his circumstance expressly proves
That no man is the lord of any thing—
Though in and of him there be much consisting—
Till he communicate his parts to others:
Nor doth he of himself know them for aught
Till he behold them form'd in the applause
Where they're extended; who, like an arch, reverberates
The voice again, or, like a gate of steel
Fronting the sun, receives and renders back
His figure and his heat. I was much rapt in this;
And apprehended here immediately
The unknown Ajax.
Heavens, what a man is there! a very horse,
That has he knows not what. Nature, what things there
    are,
Most abject in regard, and dear in use!
What things again most dear in the esteem
And poor in worth! Now shall we see to-morrow,
An act that very chance doth throw upon him,
Ajax renown'd. O heavens! what some men do;
While some men leave to do.
How some men creep in skittish Fortune's hall,
Whiles others play the idiots in her eyes!
How one man eats into another's pride,
While pride is fasting in his wantonness!

To see these Grecian lords! why, even already
They clap the lubber Ajax on the shoulder,
As if his foot were on brave Hector's breast,
And great Troy shrinking.
ACHILLES. I do believe it; for they pass'd by me
As misers do by beggars, neither gave to me
Good word or look: what! are my deeds forgot?
ULYSSES. Time hath, my lord, a wallet at his back,
Wherein he puts alms for oblivion,
A great-siz'd monster of ingratitudes:
Those scraps are good deeds past; which are devour'd
As fast as they are made, forgot as soon
As done: perseverance, dear my lord,
Keeps honour bright: to have done, is to hang
Quite out of fashion, like a rusty mail
In monumental mockery. Take the instant way;
For honour travels in a strait so narrow
Where one but goes abreast: keep, then, the path;
For emulation hath a thousand sons
That one by one pursue: if you give way,
Or hedge aside from the direct forthright,
Like to an enter'd tide they all rush by
And leave you hindmost;
Or, like a gallant horse fall'n in first rank,
Lie there for pavement to the abject rear,
O'errun and trampled on: then what they do in present
Though less than yours in past, must o'ertop yours;
For time is like a fashionable host,
That slightly shakes his parting guest by the hand,
And with his arms outstretch'd, as he would fly,
Grasps in the comer: welcome ever smiles,
And farewell goes out sighing. O! let not virtue seek
Remuneration for the thing it was;
For beauty, wit,
High birth, vigour of bone, desert in service,
Love, friendship, charity, are subjects all
To envious and calumniating time.
One touch of nature makes the whole world kin,
That all with one consent praise new-born gawds,
Though they are made and moulded of things past,
And give to dust that is a little gilt
More laud than gilt o'er-dusted.

The present eye praises the present object:
Then marvel not, thou great and complete man,
That all the Greeks begin to worship Ajax;
Since things in motion sooner catch the eye
Than what not stirs. The cry went once on thee,
And still it might, and yet it may again,
If thou wouldst not entomb thyself alive,
And case thy reputation in thy tent;
Whose glorious deeds, but in these fields of late,
Made emulous missions 'mongst the gods themselves,
And drave great Mars to faction.

ACHILLES.   Of this my privacy
I have strong reasons.

ULYSSES.   But 'gainst your privacy
The reasons are more potent and heroical.
'Tis known, Achilles, that you are in love
With one of Priam's daughters.

ACHILLES. Ha! known!

ULYSSES. Is that a wonder?
The providence that 's in a watchful state
Knows almost every grain of Plutus' gold,
Finds bottom in the uncomprehensive deeps,
Keeps place with thought, and almost, like the gods,
Does thoughts unveil in their dumb cradles.
There is a mystery—with whom relation
Durst never meddle—in the soul of state,
Which hath an operation more divine
Than breath or pen can give expressure to.
All the commerce that you have had with Troy
As perfectly is ours as yours, my lord;
And better would it fit Achilles much
To throw down Hector than Polyxena;
But it must grieve young Pyrrhus now at home,
When fame shall in our islands sound her trump,
And all the Greekish girls shall tripping sing,
'Great Hector's sister did Achilles win,
But our great Ajax bravely beat down him.'
Farewell, my lord: I as your lover speak;
The fool slides o'er the ice that you should break.   *Exit*

PATROCLUS. To this effect, Achilles, have I mov'd you.
A woman impudent and mannish grown
Is not more loath'd than an effeminate man

In time of action. I stand condemn'd for this:
They think my little stomach to the war
And your great love to me restrains you thus.
Sweet, rouse yourself; and the weak wanton Cupid
Shall from your neck unloose his amorous fold,
And, like a dew-drop from the lion's mane,
Be shook to air.

ACHILLES.   Shall Ajax fight with Hector?

PATROCLUS. Ay; and perhaps receive much honour by him.

ACHILLES. I see my reputation is at stake;
My fame is shrewdly gor'd.

PATROCLUS.   O! then, beware;
Those wounds heal ill that men do give themselves;
Omission to do what is necessary
Seals a commission to a blank of danger;
And danger, like an ague, subtly taints
Even then when we sit idly in the sun.

ACHILLES. Go call Thersites hither, sweet Patroclus:
I 'll send the fool to Ajax and desire him
T' invite the Trojan lords after the combat
To see us here unarmed. I have a woman's longing,
An appetite that I am sick withal,
To see great Hector in his weeds of peace;
To talk with him and to behold his visage,
Even to my full of view. A labour sav'd!

Enter Thersites

THERSITES. A wonder!

ACHILLES. What?

THERSITES. Ajax goes up and down the field, asking for
himself.

ACHILLES. How so?

THERSITES. He must fight singly to-morrow with Hector,
and is so prophetically proud of an heroical cudgelling
that he raves in saying nothing.

ACHILLES. How can that be?

THERSITES. Why, he stalks up and down like a peacock, a
stride and a stand; ruminates like a hostess that hath no
arithmetic but her brain to set down her reckoning; bites
his lip with a politic regard, as who should say 'There
were wit in this head, an 'twould out;' and so there is,
but it lies as coldly in him as fire in a flint, which will not
show without knocking. The man's undone for ever; for

if Hector break not his neck i' the combat, he 'll break 't himself in vain-glory. He knows not me: I said, 'Good-morrow, Ajax'; and he replies, 'Thanks, Agamemnon.' What think you of this man that takes me for the general? He's grown a very land-fish, languageless, a monster. A plague of opinion! a man may wear it on both sides, like a leather jerkin.

ACHILLES. Thou must be my ambassador to him, Thersites.

THERSITES. Who, I? why, he 'll answer nobody; he professes not answering; speaking is for beggars; he wears his tongue in his arms. I will put on his presence: let Patroclus make demands to me, you shall see the pageant of Ajax.

ACHILLES. To him, Patroclus: tell him, I humbly desire the valiant Ajax to invite the most valorous Hector to come unarmed to my tent; and to procure safe-conduct for his person of the magnanimous and most illustrious, six-or-seven-times-honoured captain-general of the Grecian army, Agamemnon, et cetera. Do this.

PATROCLUS. Jove bless great Ajax!

THERSITES. Hum!

PATROCLUS. I come from the worthy Achilles,—

THERSITES. Ha!

PATROCLUS. Who most humbly desires you to invite Hector to his tent,—

THERSITES. Hum!

PATROCLUS. And to procure safe-conduct from Agamemnon.

THERSITES. Agamemnon!

PATROCLUS. Ay, my lord.

THERSITES. Ha!

PATROCLUS. What say you to 't?

THERSITES. God be wi' you, with all my heart.

PATROCLUS. Your answer, sir.

THERSITES. If to-morrow be a fair day, by eleven o'clock it will go one way or other; howsoever, he shall pay for me ere he has me.

PATROCLUS. Your answer, sir.

THERSITES. Fare you well, with all my heart.

ACHILLES. Why, but he is not in this tune, is he?

THERSITES. No, but he 's out o' tune thus. What music will be in him when Hector has knocked out his brains, I know not; but, I am sure, none, unless the fiddler Apollo get his sinews to make catlings on.

ACHILLES. Come, thou shalt bear a letter to him straight.

THERSITES. Let me bear another to his horse, for that 's the more capable creature.

ACHILLES. My mind is troubled, like a fountain stirr'd; And I myself see not the bottom of it.

Exeunt Achilles and Patroclus

THERSITES. Would the fountain of your mind were clear again, that I might water an ass at it! I had rather be a tick in a sheep than such a valiant ignorance. *Exit*

ACT FOUR

SCENE ONE

Troy. A Street.

Enter, on one side, Æneas, and Servant, with a torch; on the other, Paris, Deiphobus, Antenor, Diomedes, and Others, with torches

PARIS. See, ho! who is that there?

DEIPHOBUS.   It is the Lord Æneas.

ÆNEAS. Is the prince there in person?
  Had I so good occasion to lie long
  As you, Prince Paris, nothing but heavenly business
  Should rob my bed-mate of my company.

DIOMEDES. That's my mind too. Good-morrow, Lord
  Æneas.

PARIS. A valiant Greek, Æneas; take his hand:
  Witness the process of your speech, wherein
  You told how Diomed, a whole week by days,
  Did haunt you in the field.

ÆNEAS.   Health to you, valiant sir,
  During all question of the gentle truce;
  But when I meet you arm'd, as black defiance
  As heart can think or courage execute.

DIOMEDES. The one and other Diomed embraces.
  Our bloods are now in calm, and, so long, health!
  But when contention and occasion meet,
  By jove, I'll play the hunter for thy life
  With all my force, pursuit, and policy.

ÆNEAS. And thou shalt hunt a lion, that will fly
  With his face backward. In humane gentleness,
  Welcome to Troy! now, by Anchises' life,
  Welcome, indeed! By Venus' hand I swear,
  No man alive can love in such a sort
  The thing he means to kill more excellently.

DIOMEDES. We sympathize. Jove, let Æneas live,
    If to my sword his fate be not the glory,
    A thousand complete courses of the sun!
    But, in mine emulous honour, let him die,
    With every joint a wound, and that to-morrow!
ÆNEAS. We know each other well.
DIOMEDES. We do; and long to know each other worse.
PARIS. This is the most despiteful gentle greeting,
    The noblest hateful love, that e'er I heard of.
    What business, lord, so early?
ÆNEAS. I was sent for to the king; but why, I know not.
PARIS. His purpose meets you: 'twas to bring this Greek
    To Calchas' house, and there to render him,
    For the enfreed Antenor, the fair Cressid.
    Let 's have your company; or, if you please,
    Haste there before us. I constantly do think—
    Or rather, call my thought a certain knowledge—
    My brother Troilus lodges there to-night:
    Rouse him and give him note of our approach,
    With the whole quality wherefore: I fear
    We shall be much unwelcome.
ÆNEAS.   That I assure you
    Troilus had rather Troy were borne to Greece
    Than Cressid borne from Troy.
PARIS.   There is no help;
    The bitter disposition of the time
    Will have it so. On, lord; we'll follow you.
ÆNEAS. Good-morrow, all.   *Exit*
PARIS. And tell me, noble Diomed; faith, tell me true,
    Even in the soul of sound good-fellowship,
    Who, in your thoughts, merits fair Helen best—
    Myself or Menelaus?
DIOMEDES.   Both alike:
    He merits well to have her that doth seek her
    Not making any scruple of her soilure—
    With such a hell of pain and world of charge,
    And you as well to keep her that defend her—
    Not palating the taste of her dishonour—
    With such a costly loss of wealth and friends:
    He, like a puling cuckold, would drink up
    The lees and dregs of a flat tamed piece;
    You, like a lecher, out of whorish loins

Are pleas'd to breed out your inheritors:
Both merits pois'd, each weighs nor less nor more;
But he as he, the heavier for a whore.

PARIS. You are too bitter to your countrywoman.

DIOMEDES. She 's bitter to her country. Hear me, Paris:
For every false drop in her bawdy veins
A Grecian's life hath sunk; for every scruple
Of her contaminated carrion weight
A Trojan hath been slain. Since she could speak,
She hath not given so many good words breath
As for her Greeks and Trojans suffer'd death.

PARIS. Fair Diomed, you do as chapmen do,
Dispraise the thing that you desire to buy;
But we in silence hold this virtue well,
We 'll not commend what we intend to sell.
Here lies our way.   *Exeunt*

SCENE TWO

The Same. A Court before Pandarus' House.

Enter Troilus and Cressida

TROILUS. Dear, trouble not yourself: the morn is cold.

CRESSIDA. Then, sweet my lord, I 'll call mine uncle down:
He shall unbolt the gates.

TROILUS.   Trouble him not;
To bed, to bed: sleep kill those pretty eyes,
And give as soft attachment to thy senses
As infants' empty of all thought!

CRESSIDA.   Good-morrow, then.

TROILUS. I prithee now, to bed.

CRESSIDA.   Are you aweary of me?

TROILUS. O Cressida! but that the busy day,
Wak'd by the lark, hath rous'd the ribald crows,
And dreaming night will hide our joys no longer,
I would not from thee.

CRESSIDA.   Night hath been too brief.

TROILUS. Beshrew the witch! with venomous wights she
    stays
As tediously as hell, but flies the grasps of love
With wings more momentary-swift than thought.

You will catch cold, and curse me.

CRESSIDA.   Prithee, tarry:

You men will never tarry.

O foolish Cressid! I might have still held off,

And then you would have tarried. Hark! there 's one up.

PANDARUS. (*Within*) What! are all the doors open here?

TROILUS. It is your uncle.

CRESSIDA. A pestilence on him! now will he be mocking: I
shall have such a life!

Enter Pandarus

PANDARUS. How now, how now! how go maiden-heads?
Here, you maid! where's my cousin Cressid?

CRESSIDA. Go hang yourself, you naughty mocking uncle!
You bring me to do—and then you flout me too.

PANDARUS. To do what? to do what? let her say what:
what have I brought you to do?

CRESSIDA. Come, come; beshrew your heart! you 'll ne'er be
good,

Nor suffer others.

PANDARUS. Ha, ha! Alas, poor wretch! a poor capocchia!
hast not slept to-night? would he not, a naughty man, let
it sleep? a bugbear take him!

CRESSIDA. Did not I tell you? 'would he were knock'd o' the
head!   *Knocking within*

Who 's that at door? good uncle, go and see.

My lord, come you again into my chamber:

You smile and mock me, as if I meant naughtily.

TROILUS. Ha, ha!

CRESSIDA. Come, you are deceiv'd, I think of no such thing.
                                    Knocking within

How earnestly they knock! Pray you, come in:

I would not for half Troy have you seen here.

                        Exeunt Troilus and Cressida

PANDARUS. (*Going to the door*) Who 's there? what 's the
matter? will you beat down the door? How now! what 's
the matter?

Enter Æneas

ÆNEAS. Good-morrow, lord, good-morrow.

PANDARUS. Who 's there? my Lord Æneas! By my troth,
I knew you not: what news with you so early?

ÆNEAS. Is not Prince Troilus here?

PANDARUS. Here! what should he do here?

ÆNEAS. Come, he is here, my lord: do not deny him: it
doth import him much to speak with me.

PANDARUS. Is he here, say you? 'tis more than I know, I 'll
be sworn: for my own part, I came in late. What should
he do here?

ÆNEAS. Who! nay, then: come, come, you 'll do him wrong
ere you 're 'ware. You 'll be so true to him, to be false to
him. Do not you know of him, but yet go fetch him
hither; go.

Re-enter Troilus

TROILUS. How now! what 's the matter?

ÆNEAS. My lord, I scarce have leisure to salute you,
My matter is so rash: there is at hand
Paris your brother, and Deiphobus,
The Grecian Diomed, and our Antenor
Deliver'd to us; and for him forthwith,
Ere the first sacrifice, within this hour,
We must give up to Diomedes' hand
The Lady Cressida.

TROILUS.   Is it so concluded?

ÆNEAS. By Priam, and the general state of Troy:
They are at hand and ready to effect it.

TROILUS. How my achievements mock me!
I will go meet them: and, my Lord Æneas,
We met by chance; you did not find me here.

ÆNEAS. Good, good, my lord; the secrets of nature
Have not more gift in taciturnity.

Exeunt Troilus and Æneas.

PANDARUS. Is 't possible? no sooner got but lost? The devil
take Antenor! the young prince will go mad: a plague
upon Antenor! I would they had broke 's neck!

Re-enter Cressida

CRESSIDA. How now! What is the matter? Who was here?

PANDARUS. Ah! ah!

CRESSIDA. Why sigh you so profoundly? where 's my lord?
gone! Tell me, sweet uncle, what 's the matter?

PANDARUS. Would I were as deep under the earth as I am
above!

CRESSIDA. O the gods! what 's the matter?

PANDARUS. Prithee, get thee in. Would thou hadst ne'er
been born! I knew thou wouldst be his death. O poor
gentleman! A plague upon Antenor!

CRESSIDA. Good uncle, I beseech you, on my knees I beseech you, what 's the matter?

PANDARUS. Thou must be gone, wench, thou must be gone;
thou art changed for Antenor. Thou must to thy father,
and be gone from Troilus: 'twill be his death; 'twill be
his bane; he cannot bear it.

CRESSIDA. O you immortal gods! I will not go.

PANDARUS. Thou must.

CRESSIDA. I will not, uncle: I have forgot my father;
I know no touch of consanguinity;
No kin, no love, no blood, no soul so near me
As the sweet Troilus. O you gods divine!
Make Cressid's name the very crown of falsehood
If ever she leave Troilus! Time, force, and death,
Do to this body what extremes you can;
But the strong base and building of my love
Is as the very centre of the earth,
Drawing all things to it. I 'll go in and weep,—

PANDARUS. Do, do.

CRESSIDA. Tear my bright hair, and scratch my praised
cheeks,
Crack my clear voice with sobs, and break my heart
With sounding Troilus. I will not go from Troy.   *Exeunt*

SCENE THREE

The Same. Before Pandarus' House.

*Enter Paris, Troilus, Æneas, Deiphobus, Antenor,
and Diomedes*

PARIS. It is great morning, and the hour prefix'd
Of her delivery to this valiant Greek
Comes fast upon. Good my brother Troilus,
Tell you the lady what she is to do,
And haste her to the purpose.

TROILUS.   Walk into her house;
I 'll bring her to the Grecian presently:
And to his hand when I deliver her,
Think it an altar, and thy brother Troilus
A priest, there offering to it his heart.   *Exit*

PARIS. I know what 'tis to love;
And would, as I shall pity, I could help!
Please you walk in, my lords.   *Exeunt*

SCENE FOUR

The Same. A Room in Pandarus' House.

Enter Pandarus and Cressida

PANDARUS. Be moderate, be moderate.
CRESSIDA. Why tell you me of moderation?
The grief is fine, full, perfect, that I taste,
And violenteth in a sense as strong
As that which causeth it: how can I moderate it?
If I could temporize with my affection,
Or brew it to a weak and colder palate,
The like allayment could I give my grief:
My love admits no qualifying dross;
No more my grief, in such a precious loss.

Enter Troilus

PANDARUS. Here, here, here he comes. Ah! sweet ducks.
CRESSIDA. (*Embracing him*) O Troilus! Troilus!
PANDARUS. What a pair of spectacles is here! Let me em-
brace too. 'O heart,' as the goodly saying is,

O heart, heavy heart,
Why sigh'st thou without breaking?

when he answers again,

Because thou canst not ease thy smart
By friendship nor by speaking.

There was never a truer rime. Let us cast away nothing,
for we may live to have need of such a verse: we see it,
we see it. How now, lambs!
TROILUS. Cressid, I love thee in so strain'd a purity,
That the bless'd gods, as angry with my fancy,
More bright in zeal than the devotion which
Cold lips blow to their deities, take thee from me.
CRESSIDA. Have the gods envy?
PANDARUS. Ay, ay, ay, ay; 'tis too plain a case.
CRESSIDA. And is it true that I must go from Troy?
TROILUS. A hateful truth.
CRESSIDA.   What! and from Troilus too?

TROILUS. From Troy and Troilus.

CRESSIDA.   Is it possible?

TROILUS. And suddenly; where injury of chance
    Puts back leave-taking, justles roughly by
    All time of pause, rudely beguiles our lips
    Of all rejoindure, forcibly prevents
    Our lock'd embrasures, strangles our dear vows
    Even in the birth of our own labouring breath.
    We two, that with so many thousand sigh
    Did buy each other, must poorly sell ourselves
    With the rude brevity and discharge of one.
    Injurious time now with a robber's haste
    Crams his rich thievery up, he knows not how:
    As many farewells as be stars in heaven,
    With distinct breath and consign'd kisses to them,
    He fumbles up into a loose adieu,
    And scants us with a single famish'd kiss,
    Distasted with the salt of broken tears.

ÆNEAS. (*Within*) My lord, is the lady ready?

TROILUS. Hark! you are call'd: some say the Genius so
    Cries 'Come!' to him that instantly must die.
    Bid them have patience; she shall come anon.

PANDARUS. Where are my tears? rain, to lay this wind, or
    my heart will be blown up by the root!   *Exit*

CRESSIDA. I must then to the Grecians?

TROILUS.   No remedy.

CRESSIDA. A woeful Cressid 'mongst the merry Greeks!
    When shall we see again?

TROILUS. Hear me, my love. Be thou but true of heart,—

CRESSIDA. I true! how now! what wicked deem is this?

TROILUS. Nay, we must use expostulation kindly,
    For it is parting from us:
    I speak not 'be thou true,' as fearing thee,
    For I will throw my glove to Death himself,
    That there 's no maculation in thy heart;
    But, 'be thou true,' say I, to fashion in
    My sequent protestation; be thou true,
    And I will see thee.

CRESSIDA. O! you shall be expos'd, my lord, to dangers
    As infinite as imminent; but I 'll be true.

TROILUS. And I 'll grow friend with danger. Wear this
    sleeve.

CRESSIDA. And you this glove. When shall I see you?

TROILUS. I will corrupt the Grecian sentinels,
To give thee nightly visitation.
But yet, be true.

CRESSIDA.   O heavens! 'be true' again!

TROILUS. Hear why I speak it, love:
The Grecian youths are full of quality;
They 're loving, well compos'd, with gifts of nature,
Flowing and swelling o'er with arts and exercise:
How novelty may move, and parts with person,
Alas! a kind of godly jealousy,—
Which, I beseech you, call a virtuous sin,—
Makes me afear'd.

CRESSIDA.   O heavens! you love me not.

TROILUS. Die I a villain, then!
In this I do not call your faith in question
So mainly as my merit: I cannot sing,
Nor heel the high lavolt, nor sweeten talk,
Nor play at subtle games; fair virtues all,
To which the Grecians are most prompt and pregnant:
But I can tell that in each grace of these
There lurks a still and dumb-discoursive devil
That tempts most cunningly. But be not tempted.

CRESSIDA. Do you think I will?

TROILUS. No.
But something may be done that we will not:
And sometimes we are devils to ourselves
When we will tempt the frailty of our powers,
Presuming on their changeful potency.

ÆNEAS. (Within) Nay, good my lord,—

TROILUS.   Come, kiss; and let us part.

PARIS. (Within) Brother Troilus!

TROILUS.   Good brother, come you hither;
And bring Æneas and the Grecian with you.

CRESSIDA. My lord, will you be true?

TROILUS. Who, I? alas, it is my vice, my fault:
While others fish with craft for great opinion,
I with great truth catch mere simplicity;
Whilst some with cunning gild their copper crowns,
With truth and plainness I do wear mine bare.
Fear not my truth; the moral of my wit
Is plain, and true; there 's all the reach of it.

Enter Æneas, Paris, Antenor, Deiphobus, and Diomedes

Welcome, Sir Diomed! Here is the lady
Which for Antenor we deliver you:
At the port, lord, I 'll give her to thy hand,
And by the way possess thee what she is.
Entreat her fair; and, by my soul, fair Greek,
If e'er thou stand at mercy of my sword,
Name Cressid, and thy life shall be as safe
As Priam is in Ilion.

DIOMEDES.   Fair Lady Cressid,
So please you, save the thanks this prince expects:
The lustre in your eye, heaven in your cheek,
Pleads your fair usage; and to Diomed
You shall be mistress, and command him wholly.

TROILUS. Grecian, thou dost not use me courteously,
To shame the zeal of my petition to thee
In praising her: I tell thee, lord of Greece,
She is as far high-soaring o'er thy praises
As thou unworthy to be call'd her servant.
I charge thee use her well, even for my charge;
For, by the dreadful Pluto, if thou dost not,
Though the great bulk Achilles be thy guard,
I 'll cut thy throat.

DIOMEDES.   O! be not mov'd, Prince Troilus:
Let me be privileg'd by my place and message
To be a speaker free; when I am hence,
I 'll answer to my lust; and know you, lord,
I 'll nothing do on charge: to her own worth
She shall be priz'd; but that you say 'be 't so,'
I 'll speak it in my spirit and honour, 'no.'

TROILUS. Come, to the port. I 'll tell thee, Diomed,
This brave shall oft make thee to hide thy head.
Lady, give me your hand, and, as we walk,
To our own selves bend we our needful talk.

                    Exeunt Troilus, Cressida,
                    and Diomedes. Trumpet sounded

PARIS. Hark! Hector's trumpet.

ÆNEAS.   How have we spent this morning!
The prince must think me tardy and remiss,
That swore to ride before him to the field.

PARIS. 'Tis Troilus' fault. Come, come, to field with him.

DEIPHOBUS. Let us make ready straight.

ÆNEAS. Yea, with a bridegroom's fresh alacrity,   1-25]
Let us address to tend on Hector's heels:
The glory of our Troy doth this day lie
On his fair worth and single chivalry.   *Exeunt*

SCENE FIVE

The Grecian Camp. Lists set out.

Enter Ajax, armed; Agamemnon, Achilles, Patroclus,
Menelaus, Ulysses, Nestor, and Others

AGAMEMNON. Here art thou in appointment fresh and fair,
Anticipating time with starting courage.
Give with thy trumpet a loud note to Troy,
Thou dreadful Ajax; that the appalled air
May pierce the head of the great combatant
And hale him hither.

AJAX.   Thou, trumpet, there 's my purse.
Now crack thy lungs, and split thy brazen pipe:
Blow, villain, till thy sphered bias cheek
Outswell the colic of puff'd Aquilon.
Come, stretch thy chest, and let thy eyes spout blood;
Thou blow'st for Hector.   *Trumpet sounds*

ULYSSES. No trumpet answers.

ACHILLES.   'Tis but early days.

AGAMEMNON. Is not yond Diomed with Calchas' daughter?

ULYSSES. 'Tis he, I ken the manner of his gait;
He rises on the toe: that spirit of his
In aspiration lifts him from the earth.
              Enter Diomedes, with Cressida

AGAMEMNON. Is this the Lady Cressid?

DIOMEDES.   Even she.

AGAMEMNON. Most dearly welcome to the Greeks, sweet
lady.

NESTOR. Our general doth salute you with a kiss.

ULYSSES. Yet is the kindness but particular;
'Twere better she were kiss'd in general.

NESTOR. And very courtly counsel: I 'll begin.
So much for Nestor.

ACHILLES. I 'll take that winter from your lips, fair lady:

Achilles bids you welcome.

MENELAUS. I had good argument for kissing once.

PATROCLUS. But that 's no argument for kissing now;
For thus popp'd Paris in his hardiment,
And parted thus you and your argument.

ULYSSES. O, deadly gall, and theme of all our scorns!
For which we lose our heads to gild his horns.

PATROCLUS. The first was Menelaus' kiss; this, mine:
Patroclus kisses you.

MENELAUS.   O! this is trim.

PATROCLUS. Paris and I, kiss evermore for him.

MENELAUS. I 'll have my kiss, sir. Lady, by your leave.

CRESSIDA. In kissing, do you render or receive?

PATROCLUS. Both take and give.

CRESSIDA.   I 'll make my match to live,
The kiss you take is better than you give;
Therefore no kiss.

MENELAUS. I 'll give you boot; I 'll give you three for one.

CRESSIDA. You 're an odd man; give even, or give none.

MENELAUS. An odd man, lady! every man is odd.

CRESSIDA. No, Paris is not; for, you know 'tis true,
That you are odd, and he is even with you.

MENELAUS. You fillip me o' the head.

CRESSIDA.   No, I 'll be sworn.

ULYSSES. It were no match, your nail against his horn. May
I, sweet lady, beg a kiss of you?

CRESSIDA. You may.

ULYSSES.   I do desire it.

CRESSIDA.   Why, beg, then.

ULYSSES. Why, then, for Venus' sake, give me a kiss,
When Helen is a maid again, and his.

CRESSIDA. I am your debtor; claim it when 'tis due.

ULYSSES. Never 's my day, and then a kiss of you.

DIOMEDES. Lady, a word: I 'll bring you to your father.

Diomedes leads out Cressida

NESTOR. A woman of quick sense.

ULYSSES.   Fie, fie upon her!
There 's language in her eye, her cheek, her lip,
Nay, her foot speaks; her wanton spirits look out
At every joint and motive of her body.
O! these encounterers, so glib of tongue,
That give a coasting welcome ere it comes,

And wide unclasp the tables of their thoughts
To every tickling reader, set them down
For sluttish spoils of opportunity
And daughters of the game.   *Trumpet within*
ALL. The Trojans' trumpet.
AGAMEMNON.   Yonder comes the troop.
             *Enter Hector, armed; Æneas, Troilus, and
                  other Trojans, with Attendants*
ÆNEAS. Hail, all you state of Greece! what shall be done
To him that victory commands? or do you purpose
A victor shall be known? will you the knights
Shall to the edge of all extremity
Pursue each other, or shall be divided
By any voice or order of the field?
Hector bade ask.
AGAMEMNON.   Which way would Hector have it?
ÆNEAS. He cares not; he 'll obey conditions.
ACHILLES. 'Tis done like Hector; but securely done,
A little proudly, and great deal misprising
The knight oppos'd.
ÆNEAS.   If not Achilles, sir,
What is your name?
ACHILLES.   If not Achilles, nothing.
ÆNEAS. Therefore Achilles; but, whate'er, know this:
In the extremity of great and little,
Valour and pride excel themselves in Hector;
The one almost as infinite as all,
The other blank as nothing. Weigh him well,
And that which looks like pride is courtesy.
This Ajax is half made of Hector's blood:
In love whereof, half Hector stays at home;
Half heart, half hand, half Hector comes to seek
This blended knight, half Trojan, and half Greek.
ACHILLES. A maiden battle, then? O! I perceive you.
                  Re-enter Diomedes
AGAMEMNON. Here is Sir Diomed. Go, gentle knight,
Stand by our Ajax: as you and Lord Æneas
Consent upon the order of their fight,
So be it; either to the uttermost,
Or else a breath: the combatants being kin
Half stints their strife before their strokes begin.
                  Ajax and Hector enter the lists

ULYSSES. They are oppos'd already.

AGAMEMNON. What Trojan is that same that looks so heavy?

ULYSSES. The youngest son of Priam, a true knight:
Not yet mature, yet matchless; firm of word,
Speaking in deeds and deedless in his tongue;
Not soon provok'd, nor being provok'd soon calm'd:
His heart and hand both open and both free;
For what he has he gives, what thinks he shows;
Yet gives he not till judgment guide his bounty,
Nor dignifies an impure thought with breath.
Manly as Hector, but more dangerous;
For Hector, in his blaze of wrath, subscribes
To tender objects; but he in heat of action
Is more vindicative than jealous love.
They call him Troilus, and on him erect
A second hope, as fairly built as Hector.
Thus says Æneas; one that knows the youth
Even to his inches, and with private soul
Did in great Ilion thus translate him to me.

Alarum. Hector and Ajax fight

AGAMEMNON. They are in action.

NESTOR. Now, Ajax, hold thine own!

TROILUS.   Hector, thou sleep'st; awake thee!

AGAMEMNON. His blows are well dispos'd: there, Ajax!

DIOMEDES. You must no more.   *Trumpets cease*

ÆNEAS.   Princes, enough, so please you.

AJAX. I am not warm yet; let us fight again.

DIOMEDES. As Hector pleases.

HECTOR.   Why, then will I no more:
Thou art, great lord, my father's sister's son,
A cousin-german to great Priam's seed;
The obligation of our blood forbids
A gory emulation 'twixt us twain.
Were thy commixtion Greek and Trojan so
That thou couldst say, 'This hand is Grecian all,
And this is Trojan; the sinews of this leg
All Greek, and this all Troy; my mother's blood
Runs on the dexter cheek, and this sinister
Bounds in my father's,' by Jove multipotent,
Thou shouldst not bear from me a Greekish member
Wherein my sword had not impressure made
Of our rank feud. But the just gods gainsay

That any drop thou borrow'dst from thy mother,
My sacred aunt, should by my mortal sword
Be drain'd! Let me embrace thee, Ajax;
By him that thunders, thou hast lusty arms;
Hector would have them fall upon him thus:
Cousin, all honour to thee!

AJAX.   I thank thee, Hector:
Thou art too gentle and too free a man:
I came to kill thee, cousin, and bear hence
A great addition earned in thy death.

HECTOR. Not Neoptolemus so mirable,
On whose bright crest Fame with her loud'st Oyes
Cries, 'This is he!' could promise to himself
A thought of added honour torn from Hector.

ÆNEAS. There is expectance here from both the sides,
What further you will do.

HECTOR.   We 'll answer it;
The issue is embracement: Ajax, farewell.

AJAX. If I might in entreaties find success,—
As seld I had the chance,—I would desire
My famous cousin to our Grecian tents.

DIOMEDES. 'Tis Agamemnon's wish, and great Achilles
Doth long to see unarm'd the valiant Hector.

HECTOR. Æneas, call my brother Troilus to me,
And signify this loving interview
To the expecters of our Trojan part;
Desire them home. Give me thy hand, my cousin;
I will go eat with thee and see your knights.

AJAX. Great Agamemnon comes to meet us here.

HECTOR. The worthiest of them tell me name by name;
But for Achilles, mine own searching eyes
Shall find him by his large and portly size.

AGAMEMNON. Worthy of arms! as welcome as to one
That would be rid of such an enemy;
But that 's no welcome; understand more clear,
What 's past and what 's to come is strew'd with husks
And formless ruin of oblivion;
But in this extant moment, faith and troth,
Strain'd purely from all hollow bias-drawing,
Bids thee, with most divine integrity,
From heart of very heart, great Hector, welcome.

HECTOR. I thank thee, most imperious Agamemnon.

ACAMEMNON. (*To Troilus*) My well-fam'd lord of Troy, no
    less to you.

MENELAUS. Let me confirm my princely brother's greeting:
    You brace of warlike brothers, welcome hither.

HECTOR. Whom must we answer?

ÆNEAS.   The noble Menelaus.

HECTOR. O! you, my lord? by Mars his gauntlet, thanks!
    Mock not that I affect the untraded oath;
    Your quondam wife swears still by Venus' glove:
    She 's well, but bade me not commend her to you.

MENELAUS. Name her not now, sir; she 's a deadly theme.

HECTOR. O! pardon; I offend.

NESTOR. I have, thou gallant Trojan, seen thee oft,
    Labouring for destiny, make cruel way
    Through ranks of Greekish youth: and I have seen thee,
    As hot as Perseus, spur thy Phrygian steed,
    Despising many forfeits and subduements,
    When thou hast hung thy advanc'd sword i' th' air,
    Not letting it decline on the declin'd;
    That I have said to some my standers-by,
    'Lo! Jupiter is yonder, dealing life!'
    And I have seen thee pause and take thy breath,
    When that a ring of Greeks have hemm'd thee in,
    Like an Olympian wrestling: this have I seen;
    But this thy countenance, still lock'd in steel,
    I never saw till now. I knew thy grandsire,
    And once fought with him: he was a soldier good;
    But, by great Mars, the captain of us all,
    Never like thee. Let an old man embrace thee;
    And, worthy warrior, welcome to our tents.

ÆNEAS. 'Tis the old Nestor.

HECTOR. Let me embrace thee, good old chronicle,
    That hast so long walk'd hand in hand with time:
    Most reverend Nestor, I am glad to clasp thee.

NESTOR. I would my arms could match thee in contention,
    As they contend with thee in courtesy.

HECTOR. I would they could.

NESTOR. Ha!
    By this white beard, I 'd fight with thee to-morrow.
    Well, welcome, welcome! I have seen the time.—

ULYSSES. I wonder now how yonder city stands,
    When we have here her base and pillar by us.

HECTOR. I know your favour, Lord Ulysses, well.
Ah! sir, there 's many a Greek and Trojan dead,
Since first I saw yourself and Diomed
In Ilion, on your Greekish embassy.

ULYSSES. Sir, I foretold you then what would ensue:
My prophecy is but half his journey yet;
For yonder walls, that pertly front your town,
Yond towers, whose wanton tops do buss the clouds,
Must kiss their own feet.

HECTOR.   I must not believe you:
There they stand yet, and modestly I think,
The fall of every Phrygian stone will cost
A drop of Grecian blood: the end crowns all,
And that old common arbitrator, Time,
Will one day end it.

ULYSSES.   So to him we leave it.
Most gentle and most valiant Hector, welcome.
After the general, I beseech you next
To feast with me and see me at my tent.

ACHILLES. I shall forestall thee, Lord Ulysses, thou!
Now, Hector, I have fed mine eyes on thee;
I have with exact view perus'd thee, Hector,
And quoted joint by joint.

HECTOR.   Is this Achilles?

ACHILLES. I am Achilles.

HECTOR. Stand fair, I pray thee: let me look on thee.

ACHILLES. Behold thy fill.

HECTOR.   Nay, I have done already.

ACHILLES. Thou art too brief: I will the second time,
As I would buy thee, view thee limb by limb.

HECTOR. O! like a book of sport thou 'lt read me o'er;
But there 's more in me than thou understand'st.
Why dost thou so oppress me with thine eye?

ACHILLES. Tell me, you heavens, in which part of his body
Shall I destroy him? whether there, or there, or there?
That I may give the local wound a name,
And make distinct the very breach whereout
Hector's great spirit flew. Answer me, heavens!

HECTOR. It would discredit the bless'd gods, proud man,
To answer such a question. Stand again:
Think'st thou to catch my life so pleasantly
As to prenominate in nice conjecture

Where thou wilt hit me dead?

ACHILLES.   I tell thee, yea.

HECTOR. Wert thou an oracle to tell me so,
I 'd not believe thee. Henceforth guard thee well,
For I 'll not kill thee there, nor there, nor there;
But, by the forge that stithied Mars his helm,
I 'll kill thee every where, yea, o'er and o'er.
You wisest Grecians, pardon me this brag;
His insolence draws folly from my lips;
But I 'll endeavour deeds to match these words,
Or may I never—

AJAX.   Do not chafe thee, cousin:
And you, Achilles, let these threats alone,
Till accident or purpose bring you to 't:
You may have every day enough of Hector,
If you have stomach. The general state, I fear,
Can scarce entreat you to be odd with him.

HECTOR. I pray you, let us see you in the field;
We have had pelting wars since you refus'd
The Grecians' cause.

ACHILLES.   Dost thou entreat me, Hector?
To-morrow do I meet thee, fell as death;
To-night all friends.

HECTOR.   Thy hand upon that match.

AGAMEMNON. First, all you peers of Greece, go to my tent;
There in the full convive we: afterwards,
As Hector's leisure and your bounties shall
Concur together, severally entreat him.
Beat loud the tabourines, let the trumpets blow,
That this great soldier may his welcome know.
                    Exeunt all except Troilus and Ulysses

TROILUS. My Lord Ulysses, tell me, I beseech you,
In what place of the field doth Calchas keep?

ULYSSES. At Menelaus' tent, most princely Troilus:
There Diomed doth feast with him to-night;
Who neither looks upon the heaven nor earth,
But gives all gaze and bent of amorous view
On the fair Cressid.

TROILUS. Shall I, sweet lord, be bound to thee so much,
After we part from Agamemnon's tent,
To bring me thither?

ULYSSES.   You shall command me, sir.

As gentle tell me, of what honour was
This Cressida in Troy? Had she no lover there
That wails her absence?
TROILUS. O, sir! to such as boasting show their scars
A mock is due. Will you walk on, my lord?
She was belov'd, she lov'd; she is, and doth:
But still sweet love is food for fortune's tooth.   *Exeunt*

ACT FIVE

SCENE ONE

The Grecian Camp. Before Achilles' Tent.

Enter Achilles and Patroclus

ACHILLES. I 'll heat his blood with Greekish wine to-night,
Which with my scimitar I 'll cool to-morrow.
Patroclus, let us feast him to the height.

PATROCLUS. Here comes Thersites.

Enter Thersites

ACHILLES.   How now, thou core of envy!
Thou crusty batch of nature, what 's the news?

THERSITES. Why, thou picture of what thou seemest, and
idol of idiot-worshippers, here 's a letter for thee.

ACHILLES. From whence, fragment?

THERSITES. Why, thou full dish of fool, from Troy.

PATROCLUS. Who keeps the tent now?

THERSITES. The surgeon's box, or the patient's wound.

PATROCLUS. Well said, adversity! and what need these
tricks?

THERSITES. Prithee, be silent, boy: I profit not by thy talk:
thou art thought to be Achilles' male varlet.

PATROCLUS. Male varlet, you rogue! what 's that?

THERSITES. Why, his masculine whore. Now, the rotten diseases of the south, the guts-griping, ruptures, catarrhs,
loads o' gravel i' the back, lethargics, cold palsies, raw
eyes, dirt-rotten livers, wheezing lungs, bladders full of
imposthume, sciaticas, lime-kilns i' the palm, incurable
bone-ache, and the rivelled fee-simple of the tetter, take
and take again such preposterous discoveries!

PATROCLUS. Why, thou damnable box of envy, thou, what
meanest thou to curse thus?

THERSITES. Do I curse thee?

PATROCLUS. Why, no, you ruinous butt, you whore-son in-
distinguishable cur, no.

THERSITES. No! why art thou then exasperate, thou idle immaterial skein of sleave silk, thou green sarcenet flap for a sore eye, thou tassel of a prodigal's purse, thou? Ah! how the poor world is pestered with such water-flies, diminutives of nature.

PATROCLUS. Out, gall!

THERSITES. Finch-egg!

ACHILLES. My sweet Patroclus, I am thwarted quite
From my great purpose in to-morrow's battle.
Here is a letter from Queen Hecuba,
A token from her daughter, my fair love,
Both taxing me and gaging me to keep
An oath that I have sworn. I will not break it:
Fall Greeks; fail fame; honour or go or stay;
My major vow lies here, this I 'll obey.
Come, come, Thersites, help to trim my tent;
This night in banqueting must all be spent.
Away, Patroclus!   *Exeunt Achilles and Patroclus*

THERSITES. With too much blood and too little brain, these two may run mad; but if with too much brain and too little blood they do, I 'll be a curer of madmen. Here 's Agamemnon, an honest fellow enough, and one that loves quails, but he has not so much brain as ear-wax: and the goodly transformation of Jupiter there, his brother, the bull, the primitive statue, and oblique memorial of cuckolds; a thrifty shoeing-horn in a chain, hanging at his brother's leg, to what form but that he is, should wit larded with malice and malice forced with wit turn him to? To an ass, were nothing: he is both ass and ox; to an ox, were nothing: he is both ox and ass. To be a dog, a mule, a cat, a fitchew, a toad, a lizard, an owl, a puttock, or a herring without a roe, I would not care; but to be Menelaus! I would conspire against destiny. Ask me not what I would be, if I were not Thersites, for I care not to be the louse of a lazar, so I were not Menelaus. Hey-day! spirits and fires!

*Enter Hector, Troilus, Ajax, Agamemnon, Ulysses,
Nestor, Menelaus, and Diomedes, with lights*

AGAMEMNON. We go wrong, we go wrong.

AJAX.   No, yonder 'tis;
There, where we see the lights.

HECTOR.   I trouble you.

AJAX. No, not a whit.

ULYSSES.   Here comes himself to guide you.

Re-enter Achilles

ACHILLES. Welcome, brave Hector; welcome, princes all.

AGAMEMNON. So now, fair prince of Troy, I bid good-night.
Ajax commands the guard to tend on you.

HECTOR. Thanks and good-night to the Greeks' general.

MENELAUS. Good-night, my lord.

HECTOR. Good-night, sweet Lord Menelaus.

THERSITES. Sweet draught: 'sweet' quoth a'! sweet sink,
sweet sewer.

ACHILLES. Good-night and welcome both at once, to those
That go or tarry.

AGAMEMNON. Good-night.

Exeunt Agamemnon and Menelaus

ACHILLES. Old Nestor tarries; and you too, Diomed,
Keep Hector company an hour or two.

DIOMEDES. I cannot, lord; I have important business,
The tide whereof is now. Good-night, great Hector.

HECTOR. Give me your hand.

ULYSSES. (*Aside to Troilus*) Follow his torch; he goes to
Calchas' tent.

I 'll keep you company.

TROILUS. Sweet sir, you honour me.

HECTOR.   .   And so, good-night.

Exit Diomedes; Ulysses and Troilus following

ACHILLES. Come, come, enter my tent.

Exeunt Achilles, Hector, Ajax, and Nestor

THERSITES. That same Diomed 's a false-hearted rogue, a
most unjust knave; I will no more trust him when he leers
than I will a serpent when he hisses. He will spend his
mouth, and promise, like Brabbler the hound; but when
he performs, astronomers foretell it: it is prodigious,
there will come some change: the sun borrows of the
moon when Diomed keeps his word. I will rather leave to
see Hector, than not to dog him: they say he keeps a
Trojan drab, and uses the traitor Calchas' tent. I 'll after.
Nothing but lechery! all incontinent varlets.   *Exit*

SCENE TWO

The Same. Before Calchas' Tent.

Enter Diomedes

DIOMEDES. What, are you up here, ho! speak.

CALCHAS. (*Within*) Who calls?

DIOMEDES. Diomed. Calchas, I think. Where 's your daughter?

CALCHAS. (*Within*) She comes to you.

Enter Troilus and Ulysses, at a distance;
after them, Thersites

ULYSSES. Stand where the torch may not discover us.

Enter Cressida

TROILUS. Cressid comes forth to him.

DIOMEDES.   How now, my charge!

CRESSIDA. Now, my sweet guardian! Hark! a word with you.   *Whispers*

TROILUS. Yea, so familiar!

ULYSSES. She will sing any man at first sight.

THERSITES. And any man may sing her, if he can take her cliff; she 's noted.

DIOMEDES. Will you remember?

CRESSIDA. Remember! yes.

DIOMEDES. Nay, but do, then;
And let your mind be coupled with your words.

TROILUS. What should she remember?

ULYSSES. List!

CRESSIDA. Sweet honey Greek, tempt me no more to folly.

THERSITES. Roguery!

DIOMEDES. Nay, then,—

CRESSIDA.   I 'll tell you what,—

DIOMEDES. Foh, foh! come, tell a pin: you are forsworn.

CRESSIDA. In faith, I cannot. What would you have me do?

THERSITES. A juggling trick,—to be secretly open.

DIOMEDES. What did you swear you would bestow on me?

CRESSIDA. I prithee, do not hold me to mine oath;
Bid me do any thing but that, sweet Greek.

DIOMEDES. Good-night.

TROILUS. Hold, patience!

ULYSSES. How now, Trojan?

CRESSIDA. Diomed,—

DIOMEDES. No, no, good-night; I 'll be your fool no more.

TROILUS. Thy better must.

CRESSIDA.   Hark! one word in your ear.

TROILUS. O plague and madness!

ULYSSES. You are mov'd, prince; let us depart, I pray you,
   Lest your displeasure should enlarge itself
   To wrathful terms. This place is dangerous;
   The time right deadly. I beseech you, go.

TROILUS. Behold, I pray you!

ULYSSES.   Nay, good my lord, go off:
   You flow to great distraction; come, my lord.

TROILUS. I pray thee, stay.

ULYSSES.   You have not patience; come.

TROILUS. I pray you, stay. By hell, and all hell's torments,
   I will not speak a word!

DIOMEDES.   And so, good-night.

CRESSIDA. Nay, but you part in anger.

TROILUS.   Doth that grieve thee?
   O wither'd truth!

ULYSSES.   Why, how now, lord!

TROILUS.   By Jove,
   I will be patient.

CRESSIDA.   Guardian!—why, Greek!

DIOMEDES. Foh, foh! adieu; you palter.

CRESSIDA. In faith, I do not: come hither once again.

ULYSSES. You shake, my lord, at something: will you go?
   You will break out.

TROILUS.   She strokes his cheek!

ULYSSES.   Come, come

TROILUS. Nay, stay; by Jove, I will not speak a word:
   There is between my will and all offences
   A guard of patience: stay a little while.

THERSITES. How the devil Luxury, with his fat rump and
   potato-finger, tickles these together! Fry, lechery, fry!

DIOMEDES. But will you, then?

CRESSIDA. In faith, I will, la; never trust me else.

DIOMEDES. Give me some token for the surety of it.

CRESSIDA. I 'll fetch you one.   *Exit*

ULYSSES. You have sworn patience.

TROILUS.   Fear me not, sweet lord;
   I will not be myself, nor have cognition

Of what I feel: I am all patience.

Re-enter Cressida

THERSITES. Now the pledge! now, now, now!

CRESSIDA. Here, Diomed, keep this sleeve.

TROILUS. O beauty! where is thy faith?

ULYSSES.   My lord,—

TROILUS. I will be patient; outwardly I will.

CRESSIDA. You look upon that sleeve; behold it well.
He lov'd me—O false wench!—Give 't to me again.

DIOMEDES. Whose was 't?

CRESSIDA.   It is no matter, now I have 't again.
I will not meet with you to-morrow night.
I prithee, Diomed, visit me no more.

THERSITES. Now she sharpens: well said, whetstone!

DIOMEDES. I shall have it.

CRESSIDA.   What, this?

DIOMEDES.   Ay, that.

CRESSIDA. O! all you gods. O pretty, pretty pledge!
Thy master now lies thinking in his bed
Of thee and me; and sighs, and takes my glove,
And gives memorial dainty kisses to it,
As I kiss thee. Nay, do not snatch it from me;
He that takes that doth take my heart withal.

DIOMEDES. I had your heart before; this follows it.

TROILUS. I did swear patience.

CRESSIDA. You shall not have it, Diomed; faith you shall
    not;
I 'll give you something else.

DIOMEDES. I will have this. Whose was it?

CRESSIDA.   'Tis no matter.

DIOMEDES. Come, tell me whose it was.

CRESSIDA. 'Twas one's that loved me better than you will.
But, now you have it, take it.

DIOMEDES.   Whose was it?

CRESSIDA. By all Diana's waiting-women yond,
And by herself, I will not tell you whose.

DIOMEDES. To-morrow will I wear it on my helm,
And grieve his spirit that dares not challenge it.

TROILUS. Wert thou the devil, and wor'st it on thy horn,
It should be challeng'd.

CRESSIDA. Well, well, 'tis done, 'tis past: and yet it is not:
I will not keep my word.

DIOMEDES.   Why then, farewell;
  Thou never shalt mock Diomed again.
CRESSIDA. You shall not go: one cannot speak a word,
  But it straight starts you.
DIOMEDES.   I do not like this fooling.
THERSITES. Nor I, by Pluto: but that that likes not me
  Pleases me best.
DIOMEDES. What, shall I come? the hour?
CRESSIDA.   Ay, come:—O Jove!—
  Do come:—I shall be plagu'd.
DIOMEDES.   Farewell till then.
CRESSIDA. Good-night: I prithee, come.—
                              Exit Diomedes
  Troilus, farewell! one eye yet looks on thee,
  But with my heart the other eye doth see.
  Ah! poor our sex; this fault in us I find,
  The error of our eye directs our mind.
  What error leads must err. O! then conclude
  Minds sway'd by eyes are full of turpitude.   *Exit*
THERSITES. A proof of strength she could not publish more,
  Unless she said, 'My mind is now turn'd whore.'
ULYSSES. All 's done, my lord.
TROILUS.   It is.
ULYSSES.   Why stay we, then?
TROILUS. To make a recordation to my soul
  Of every syllable that here was spoke.
  But if I tell how these two did co-act,
  Shall I not lie in publishing a truth?
  Sith yet there is a credence in my heart,
  An esperance so obstinately strong,
  That doth invert the attest of eyes and ears,
  As if those organs had deceptious functions,
  Created only to calumniate.
  Was Cressid here?
ULYSSES.   I cannot conjure, Trojan.
TROILUS. She was not, sure.
ULYSSES.   Most sure she was.
TROILUS. Why, my negation hath no taste of madness.
ULYSSES. Nor mine, my lord: Cressid was here but now.
TROILUS. Let it not be believ'd for womanhood!
  Think we had mothers; do not give advantage
  To stubborn critics, apt, without a theme,

For depravation, to square the general sex
By Cressid's rule: rather think this not Cressid.

ULYSSES. What hath she done, prince, that can soil our
mothers?

TROILUS. Nothing at all, unless that this were she.

THERSITES. Will he swagger himself out on 's own eyes?

TROILUS. This she? no, this is Diomed's Cressida.
If beauty have a soul, this is not she;
If souls guide vows, if vows be sanctimony,
If sanctimony be the gods' delight,
If there be rule in unity itself,
This is not she. O madness of discourse,
That cause sets up with and against itself;
Bi-fold authority! where reason can revolt
Without perdition, and loss assume all reason
Without revolt: this is, and is not, Cressid.
Within my soul there doth conduce a fight
Of this strange nature that a thing inseparate
Divides more wider than the sky and earth;
And yet the spacious breadth of this division
Admits no orifice for a point as subtle
As Ariachne's broken woof to enter.
Instance, O instance! strong as Pluto's gates;
Cressid is mine, tied with the bonds of heaven:
Instance, O instance! strong as heaven itself;
The bonds of heaven are slipp'd, dissolv'd, and loos'd;
And with another knot, five-finger-tied,
The fractions of her faith, orts of her love,
The fragments, scraps, the bits, and greasy reliques
Of her o'er-eaten faith, are bound to Diomed.

ULYSSES. May worthy Troilus be half attach'd
With that which here his passion doth express?

TROILUS. Ay, Greek; and that shall be divulged well
In characters as red as Mars his heart
Inflam'd with Venus: never did young man fancy
With so eternal and so fix'd a soul.
Hark, Greek: as much as I do Cressid love,
So much by weight hate I her Diomed:
That sleeve is mine that he 'll bear on his helm;
Were it a casque compos'd by Vulcan's skill,
My sword should bite it. Not the dreadful spout
Which shipmen do the hurricano call,

Constring'd in mass by the almighty sun,
Shall dizzy with more clamour Neptune's ear
In his descent than shall my prompted sword
Falling on Diomed.

THERSITES. He 'll tickle it for his concupy.

TROILUS. O Cressid! O false Cressid! false, false, false!
Let all untruths stand by thy stained name,
And they 'll seem glorious.

ULYSSES.   O! contain yourself;
Your passion draws ears hither.

Enter Æneas

ÆNEAS. I have been seeking you this hour, my lord.
Hector, by this, is arming him in Troy:
Ajax, your guard, stays to conduct you home.

TROILUS. Have with you, prince. My courteous lord, adieu.
Farewell, revolted fair! and Diomed,
Stand fast, and wear a castle on thy head!

ULYSSES. I 'll bring you to the gates.

TROILUS. Accept distracted thanks.

Exeunt Troilus, Æneas, and Ulysses

THERSITES. Would I could meet that rogue Diomed! I
would croak like a raven; I would bode, I would bode.
Patroclus would give me any thing for the intelligence of
this whore: the parrot will not do more for an almond
than he for a commodious drab. Lechery, lechery; still,
wars and lechery: nothing else holds fashion. A burning
devil take them!   *Exit*

SCENE THREE

Troy. Before Priam's Palace.

Enter Hector and Andromache

ANDROMACHE. When was my lord so much ungently tem-
per'd,
To stop his ears against admonishment?
Unarm, unarm, and do not fight to-day.

HECTOR. You train me to offend you; get you in:
By all the everlasting gods, I 'll go.

ANDROMACHE. My dreams will, sure, prove ominous to the
day.

HECTOR. No more, I say.

Enter Cassandra

CASSANDRA.   Where is my brother Hector?

ANDROMACHE. Here, sister; arm'd, and bloody in intent.
Consort with me in loud and dear petition;
Pursue we him on knees; for I have dream'd
Of bloody turbulence, and this whole night
Hath nothing been but shapes and forms of slaughter.

CASSANDRA. O! 'tis true.

HECTOR.   Ho! bid my trumpet sound.

CASSANDRA. No notes of sally, for the heavens, sweet
brother.

HECTOR. Be gone, I say: the gods have heard me swear.

CASSANDRA. The gods are deaf to hot and peevish vows:
They are polluted offerings, more abhorred
Than spotted livers in the sacrifice.

ANDROMACHE. O! be persuaded: do not count it holy
To hurt by being just: it is as lawful,
For we would give much, to use violent thefts,
And rob in the behalf of charity.

CASSANDRA. It is the purpose that makes strong the vow;
But vows to every purpose must not hold.
Unarm, sweet Hector.

HECTOR.   Hold you still, I say;
Mine honour keeps the weather of my fate:
Life every man holds dear; but the dear man
Holds honour far more precious-dear than life.

Enter Troilus

How now, young man! mean'st thou to fight to-day?

ANDROMACHE. Cassandra, call my father to persuade.

Exit Cassandra

HECTOR. No, faith, young Troilus; doff thy harness, youth;
I am to-day i' the vein of chivalry:
Let grow thy sinews till their knots be strong,
And tempt not yet the brushes of the war.
Unarm thee, go, and doubt thou not, brave boy,
I 'll stand to-day for thee and me and Troy.

TROILUS. Brother, you have a vice of mercy in you,
Which better fits a lion than a man.

HECTOR. What vice is that, good Troilus? chide me for it

TROILUS. When many times the captive Grecian falls,
Even in the fan and wind of your fair sword,

You bid them rise, and live.

HECTOR. O! 'tis fair play.

TROILUS.   Fool's play, by heaven, Hector.

HECTOR. How now! how now!

TROILUS.   For the love of all the gods,
Let's leave the hermit pity with our mothers,
And when we have our armours buckled on,
The venom'd vengeance ride upon our swords,
Spur them to ruthful work, rein them from ruth.

HECTOR. Fie, savage, fie!

TROILUS.   Hector, then 'tis wars.

HECTOR. Troilus, I would not have you fight to-day.

TROILUS. Who should withhold me?
Not fate, obedience, nor the hand of Mars
Beckoning with fiery truncheon my retire;
Not Priamus and Hecuba on knees,
Their eyes o'ergalled with recourse of tears;
Nor you, my brother, with your true sword drawn
Oppos'd to hinder me, should stop my way
But by my ruin.

Re-enter Cassandra, with Priam

CASSANDRA. Lay hold upon him, Priam, hold him fast:
He is thy crutch; now if thou lose thy stay,
Thou on him leaning, and all Troy on thee,
Fall all together.

PRIAM.   Come, Hector, come; go back:
Thy wife hath dreamed; thy mother hath had visions
Cassandra doth foresee; and I myself
Am like a prophet suddenly enrapt,
To tell thee that this day is ominous
Therefore, come back.

HECTOR.   Æneas is a-field;
And I do stand engaged to many Greeks,
Even in the faith of valour, to appear
This morning to them.

PRIAM.   Ay, but thou shalt not go.

HECTOR. I must not break my faith.
You know me dutiful; therefore, dear sir,
Let me not shame respect, but give me leave
To take that course by your consent and voice,
Which you do here forbid me, royal Priam.

CASSANDRA. O Priam! yield not to him.

ANDROMACHE. Do not, dear father.

HECTOR. Andromache, I am offended with you:
    Upon the love you bear me, get you in. *Exit Andromache*

TROILUS. This foolish, dreaming, superstitious girl
    Makes all these bodements.

CASSANDRA. O farewell! dear Hector.
    Look! how thou diest; look! how thy eye turns pale;
    Look! how thy wounds do bleed at many vents:
    Hark! how Troy roars: how Hecuba cries out!
    How poor Andromache shrills her dolours forth!
    Behold, distraction, frenzy, and amazement,
    Like witless anticks, one another meet,
    And all cry Hector! Hector 's dead! O Hector!

TROILUS. Away! Away!

CASSANDRA. Farewell. Yet, soft! Hector, I take my leave:
    Thou dost thyself and all our Troy deceive. *Exit*

HECTOR. You are amaz'd my liege, at her exclaim.
    Go in and cheer the town: we 'll forth and fight;
    Do deeds worth praise and tell you them at night.

PRIAM. Farewell: the gods with safety stand about thee!
            Exeunt severally Priam and Hector. Alarums

TROILUS. They are at it, hark! Proud Diomed, believe, I
    come to lose my arm, or win my sleeve.

As Troilus is going out, enter, from the other side, Pandarus

PANDARUS. Do you hear, my lord? do you hear?

TROILUS. What now?

PANDARUS. Here 's a letter come from yond poor girl.

TROILUS. Let me read.

PANDARUS. A whoreson tisick, a whoreson rascally tisick
    so troubles me, and the foolish fortune of this girl; and
    what one thing, what another, that I shall leave you one
    o' these days: and I have a rheum in mine eyes too, and
    such an ache in my bones that, unless a man were cursed,
    I cannot tell what to think on 't. What says she there?

TROILUS. Words, words, mere words, no matter from the
    heart;
    The effect doth operate another way. *Tearing the letter*
    Go, wind to wind, there turn and change together.
    My love with words and errors still she feeds,
    But edifies another with her deeds. *Exeunt severally*

SCENE FOUR

Between Troy and the Grecian Camp.

Alarums. Excursions. Enter Thersites

THERSITES. Now they are clapper-clawing one another; I 'll
go look on. That dissembling abominable varlet, Diomed,
has got that same scurvy doting foolish young knave's
sleeve of Troy there in his helm: I would fain see them
meet; that that same young Trojan ass, that loves the
whore there, might send that Greekish whoremasterly
villain, with the sleeve, back to the dissembling luxurious
drab, on a sleeveless errand. O' the other side, the policy
of those crafty swearing rascals,—that stale old mouse-
eaten dry cheese, Nestor, and that same dog-fox, Ulysses,
is not proved worth a blackberry: they set me up, in
policy, that mongrel cur, Ajax, against that dog of as bad
a kind, Achilles; and now is the cur Ajax prouder than
the cur Achilles, and will not arm to-day; whereupon the
Grecians begin to proclaim barbarism, and policy grows
into an ill opinion. Soft! here comes sleeve, and t' other.

Enter Diomedes, Troilus following

TROILUS. Fly not; for shouldst thou take the river Styx,
I would swim after.

DIOMEDES.   Thou dost miscall retire:
I do not fly; but advantageous care
Withdrew me from the odds of multitude.
Have at thee!

THERSITES. Hold thy whore, Grecian! now for thy whore,
Trojan! now the sleeve, now the sleeve!

Exeunt Troilus and Diomedes, fighting
Enter Hector

HECTOR. What art thou, Greek? art thou for Hector's match?
Art thou of blood and honour?

THERSITES. No, no, I am a rascal; a scurvy railing knave;
a very filthy rogue.

HECTOR. I do believe thee: live.   *Exit*

THERSITES. God-a-mercy, that thou wilt believe me; but
a plague break thy neck for frighting me! What 's become of the wenching rogues? I think they have swal-
lowed one another: I would laugh at that miracle; yet,
in a sort, lechery eats itself. I 'll seek them.   *Exit*

SCENE FIVE

Another Part of the Plains.

Enter Diomedes and a Servant

DIOMEDES. Go, go, my servant, take thou Troilus' horse;
  Present the fair steed to my Lady Cressid:
  Fellow, commend my service to her beauty:
  Tell her I have chastis'd the amorous Trojan,
  And am her knight by proof.

SERVANT.   I go, my lord.   *Exit*

Enter Agamemnon

AGAMEMNON. Renew, renew! The fierce Polydamas
  Hath beat down Menon; bastard Margarelon
  Hath Doreus prisoner,
  And stands colossus-wise, waving his beam,
  Upon the pashed corses of the kings
  Epistrophus and Cedius; Polixenes is slain;
  Amphimachus, and Thoas, deadly hurt;
  Patroclus ta'en, or slain; and Palamedes
  Sore hurt and bruis'd; the dreadful Sagittary
  Appals our numbers: haste we, Diomed,
  To reinforcement, or we perish all.

Enter Nestor

NESTOR. Go, bear Patroclus' body to Achilles;
  And bid the snail-pac'd Ajax arm for shame.
  There is a thousand Hectors in the field:
  Now here he fights on Galathe his horse,
  And there lacks work; anon he's there afoot,
  And there they fly or die, like scaled sculls
  Before the belching whale; then is he yonder,
  And there the strawy Greeks, ripe for his edge,
  Fall down before him, like the mower's swath:
  Here, there, and every where, he leaves and takes,
  Dexterity so obeying appetite
  That what he will he does; and does so much
  That proof is called impossibility.

Enter Ulysses

ULYSSES. O! courage, courage, princes; great Achilles

Is arming, weeping, cursing, vowing vengeance:
Patroclus' wounds have rous'd his drowsy blood,
Together with his mangled Myrmidons,
That noseless, handless, hack'd and chipp'd, come to him,
Crying on Hector. Ajax hath lost a friend,
And foams at mouth, and he is arm'd and at it,
Roaring for Troilus, who hath done to-day
Mad and fantastic execution,
Engaging and redeeming of himself
With such a careless force and forceless care
As if that luck, in very spite of cunning,
Bade him win all.

Enter Ajax

AJAX. Troilus! thou coward Troilus!   *Exit*
DIOMEDES.   Ay, there, there.
NESTOR. So, so, we draw together.

Enter Achilles

ACHILLES.   Where is this Hector?
Come, come, thou boy-queller, show thy face;
Know what it is to meet Achilles angry:
Hector! where 's Hector? I will none but Hector.

Exeunt

SCENE SIX

Another Part of the Plains.

Enter Ajax

AJAX. Troilus, thou coward Troilus, show thy head!

Enter Diomedes

DIOMEDES. Troilus, I say! where 's Troilus?
AJAX.   What wouldst thou?
DIOMEDES. I would correct him.
AJAX. Were I the general, thou shouldst have my office
Ere that correction. Troilus, I say! what, Troilus!

Enter Troilus

TROILUS. O traitor Diomed! Turn thy false face, thou
      traitor!
And pay thy life thou owest me for my horse!
DIOMEDES. Ha! art thou there?
AJAX. I 'll fight with him alone: stand, Diomed.
DIOMEDES. He is my prize; I will not look upon.

TROILUS. Come, both you cogging Greeks; have at you
both!   *Exeunt, fighting*

Enter Hector

HECTOR. Yea, Troilus? O, well fought, my youngest brother!

Enter Achilles

ACHILLES. Now I do see thee. Ha! have at thee, Hector!

HECTOR. Pause, if thou wilt.

ACHILLES. I do disdain thy courtesy, proud Trojan.
Be happy that my arms are out of use:
My rest and negligence befriend thee now,
But thou anon shalt hear of me again;
Till when, go seek thy fortune.   *Exit*

HECTOR.   Fare thee well:—
I would have been much more a fresher man,
Had I expected thee. How now, my brother!

Re-enter Troilus

TROILUS. Ajax hath ta'en Æneas: shall it be?
No, by the flame of yonder glorious heaven,
He shall not carry him: I 'll be ta'en too,
Or bring him off. Fate, hear me what I say!
I reck not though I end my life to-day.   *Exit*

Enter One in sumptuous armour

HECTOR. Stand, stand, thou Greek; thou art a goodly mark.
No? wilt thou not? I like thy armour well;
I 'll frush it, and unlock the rivets all,
But I 'll be master of it. Wilt thou not, beast, abide?
Why then, fly on, I 'll hunt thee for thy hide.   *Exeunt*

SCENE SEVEN

Another Part of the Plains.

Enter Achilles, with Myrmidons

ACHILLES. Come here about me, you my Myrmidons;
Mark what I say. Attend me where I wheel:
Strike not a stroke, but keep yourselves in breath:
And when I have the bloody Hector found,
Empale him with your weapons round about;
In fellest manner execute your aims.
Follow me, sirs, and my proceedings eye:
It is decreed, Hector the great must die.   *Exeunt*

Enter Menelaus and Paris, fighting; then Thersites

THERSITES. The cuckold and the cuckold-maker are at it.
Now, bull! now, dog! 'Loo, Paris, 'loo! now, my double-
henned sparrow! 'loo, Paris, 'loo! The bull has the game:
'ware horns, ho!   *Exeunt Paris and Menelaus*

Enter Margarelon

MARGARELON. Turn, slave, and fight.

THERSITES. What art thou?

MARGARELON. A bastard son of Priam's.

THERSITES. I am a bastard too; I love bastards: I am a bastard begot, bastard instructed, bastard in mind, bastard
in valour, in every thing illegitimate. One bear will not
bite another, and wherefore should one bastard? Take
heed, the quarrel 's most ominous to us: if the son of a
whore fight for a whore, he tempts judgment. Farewell,
bastard.   *Exit*

MARGARELON. The devil take thee, coward!   *Exit*

SCENE EIGHT

Another Part of the Plains.

Enter Hector

HECTOR. Most putrefied core, so fair without,
Thy goodly armour thus hath cost thy life.
Now is my day's work done; I 'll take good breath:
Rest, sword; thou hast thy fill of blood and death.
    Puts off his helmet, and hangs his shield behind him
    Enter Achilles and Myrmidons

ACHILLES. Look, Hector, how the sun begins to set;
How ugly night comes breathing at his heels:
Even with the vail and darking of the sun,
To close the day up, Hector's life is done.

HECTOR. I am unarm'd; forego this vantage, Greek.

ACHILLES. Strike, fellows, strike! this is the man I seek.
    Hector falls

So Ilion, fall thou next! now, Troy, sink down!
Here lies thy heart, thy sinews, and thy bone.
On! Myrmidons, and cry you all amain,
'Achilles hath the mighty Hector slain.'—
    A retreat sounded

Hark! a retreat upon our Grecian part.

MYRMIDON. The Trojan trumpets sound the like, my lord.

ACHILLES. The dragon wing of night o'erspreads the earth,
  And, stickler-like, the armies separates.
  My half-supp'd sword, that frankly would have fed,
  Pleas'd with this dainty bait, thus goes to bed.—

Sheathes his sword

  Come, tie his body to my horse's tail;
  Along the field I will the Trojan trail.   *Exeunt*

SCENE NINE

Another Part of the Plains.

*Enter Agamemnon, Ajax, Menelaus, Nestor, Diomedes,
and Others marching. Shouts within*

AGAMEMNON. Hark! hark! what shout is that?

NESTOR.   Peace, drums!

Within. Achilles!

  Achilles! Hector 's slain! Achilles:

DIOMEDES. The bruit is, Hector 's slain, and by Achilles.

AJAX. If it be so, yet bragless let it be;
  Great Hector was a man as good as he.

AGAMEMNON. March patiently along. Let one be sent
  To pray Achilles see us at our tent.
  If in his death the gods have us befriended,
  Great Troy is ours, and our sharp wars are ended.

Exeunt, marching

SCENE TEN

Another Part of the Plains.

Enter Æneas and Trojans

ÆNEAS. Stand, ho! yet are we masters of the field.
  Never go home; here starve we out the night.

Enter Troilus

TROILUS. Hector is slain.

ALL.   Hector! the gods forbid!

TROILUS. He 's dead; and at the murderer's horse's tail,
  In beastly sort, dragg'd through the shameful field.
  Frown on, you heavens, effect your rage with speed!

HECTOR.　　I am unarm'd; forego this vantage, Greek.

Sit, gods, upon your thrones, and smile at Troy!
I say, at once let your brief plagues be mercy,
And linger not our sure destructions on!

ÆNEAS. My lord, you do discomfort all the host.

TROILUS. You understand me not that tell me so.
I do not speak of flight, of fear, of death;
But dare all imminence that gods and men
Address their dangers in. Hector is gone:
Who shall tell Priam so, or Hecuba?
Let him that will a screech-owl aye be call'd
Go in to Troy, and say there Hector 's dead:
There is a word will Priam turn to stone,
Make wells and Niobes of the maids and wives,
Cold statues of the youth; and, in a word,
Scare Troy out of itself. But march away:
Hector is dead; there is no more to say.
Stay yet. You vile abominable tents,
Thus proudly pight upon our Phrygian plains,
Let Titan rise as early as he dare,
I 'll through and through you! And, thou great-siz'd
    coward,
No space of earth shall sunder our two hates:
I 'll haunt thee like a wicked conscience still,
That mouldeth goblins swift as frenzy's thoughts.
Strike a free march to Troy! with comfort go:
Hope of revenge shall hide our inward woe.

                    Exeunt Æneas and Trojan Forces

As Troilus is going out, enter, from the other side, Pandarus

PANDARUS. But hear you, hear you!

TROILUS. Hence, broker lackey! ignomy and shame
Pursue thy life, and live aye with thy name!   *Exit*

PANDARUS. A goodly medicine for my aching bones!
O world! world! world! thus is the poor agent despised.
O traitors and bawds, how earnestly are you set a-work,
and how ill requited! why should our endeavour be so
loved, and the performance so loathed? what verse for it?
what instance for it?—Let me see!—

Full merrily the humble-bee doth sing,
Till he hath lost his honey and his sting;
And being once subdu'd in armed tail,
Sweet honey and sweet notes together fail.

Good traders in the flesh, set this in your painted cloths.
As many as be here of pander's hall,
Your eyes, half out, weep out at Pandar's fall;
Or if you cannot weep, yet give some groans,
Though not for me, yet for your aching bones.
Brethren and sisters of the hold-door trade,
Some two months hence my will shall here be made:
It should be now, but that my fear is this,
Some galled goose of Winchester would hiss.
Till then I 'll sweat, and seek about for eases;
And at that time bequeath you my diseases.   *Exit*

CORIOLANUS

CAST OF CHARACTERS

CAIUS MARCIUS, *afterwards Caius Marcius Coriolanus*

TITUS LARTIUS }
COMINIUS } *Generals against the Volscians*

MENENIUS AGRIPPA, *Friend to Coriolanus*

SICINIUS VELUTUS }
JUNIUS BRUTUS } *Tribunes of the People*

YOUNG MARCIUS, *Son to Coriolanus*
A Roman Herald
TULLUS AUFIDIUS, *General of the Volscians*
Lieutenant to Aufidius
Conspirators with Aufidius
NICANOR, *a Roman*
A Citizen of Antium
ADRIAN, *a Volsce*
Two Volscian Guards

VOLUMNIA, *Mother to Coriolanus*
VIRGILIA, *Wife to Coriolanus*
VALERIA, *Friend to Virgilia*
Gentlewoman, attending on Virgilia

Roman and Volscian Senators, Patricians, Ædiles, Lictors, Soldiers, Citizens, Messengers, Servants to Aufidius, and other Attendants

SCENE

Rome and the Neighbourhood; Corioli and the Neighbourhood; Antium

CORIOLANUS

ACT ONE

SCENE ONE

Rome. A Street.

*Enter a Company of mutinous Citizens, with staves,
clubs, and other weapons*

FIRST CITIZEN. Before we proceed any further, hear me speak.

ALL. Speak, speak.

FIRST CITIZEN. You are all resolved rather to die than to
famish?

ALL. Resolved, resolved.

FIRST CITIZEN. First, you know Caius Marcius is chief
enemy to the people.

ALL. We know 't, we know 't.

FIRST CITIZEN. Let us kill him, and we 'll have corn at our
own price. Is 't a verdict?

ALL. No more talking on 't; let it be done. Away, away!

SECOND CITIZEN. One word, good citizens.

FIRST CITIZEN. We are accounted poor citizens, the patricians good. What authority surfeits on would relieve us.
If they would yield us but the superfluity, while it were
wholesome, we might guess they relieved us humanely;
but they think we are too dear: the leanness that afflicts
us, the object of our misery, is as an inventory to par-
ticularize their abundance; our sufferance is a gain to
them. Let us revenge this with our pikes, ere we become
rakes: for the gods know I speak this in hunger for
bread, not in thirst for revenge.

SECOND CITIZEN. Would you proceed especially against Caius Marcius?

FIRST CITIZEN. Against him first: he 's a very dog to the
commonalty.

SECOND CITIZEN. Consider you what services he has done
for his country?

FIRST CITIZEN. Very well; and could be content to give
him good report for 't, but that he pays himself with
being proud.

SECOND CITIZEN. Nay, but speak not maliciously.

FIRST CITIZEN. I say unto you, what he hath done fa-
mously he did it to that end: though soft-conscienced
men can be content to say it was for his country, he did
it to please his mother, and to be partly proud; which
he is, even to the altitude of his virtue.

SECOND CITIZEN. What he cannot help in his nature, you
account a vice in him. You must in no way say he is
covetous.

FIRST CITIZEN. If I must not, I need not be barren of accusations: he hath faults, with surplus, to tire in repetition. (*Shouts within*) What shouts are these? The other
side o' the city is risen: why stay we prating here? To the
Capitol!

ALL. Come, come.

FIRST CITIZEN. Soft! who comes here?

Enter Menenius Agrippa

SECOND CITIZEN. Worthy Menenius Agrippa; one that hath
always loved the people.

FIRST CITIZEN. He 's one honest enough: would all the
rest were so!

MENENIUS. What work 's, my countrymen, in hand? Where
go you
With bats and clubs? The matter? Speak, I pray you.

FIRST CITIZEN. Our business is not unknown to the senate;
they have had inkling this fortnight what we intend to
do, which now we 'll show 'em in deeds. They say poor
suitors have strong breaths: they shall know we have
strong arms too.

MENENIUS. Why, masters, my good friends, mine honest
neighbours,
Will you undo yourselves?

FIRST CITIZEN. We cannot, sir; we are undone already.

MENENIUS. I tell you, friends, most charitable care
Have the patricians of you. For your wants,
Your suffering in this dearth, you may as well
Strike at the heaven with your staves as lift them
Against the Roman state, whose course will on

The way it takes, cracking ten thousand curbs
Of more strong link asunder than can ever
Appear in your impediment. For the dearth,
The gods, not the patricians, make it, and
Your knees to them, not arms, must help. Alack!
You are transported by calamity
Thither where more attends you; and you slander
The helms o' the state, who care for you like fathers,
When you curse them as enemies.

FIRST CITIZEN. Care for us! True, indeed! They ne'er cared
for us yet: suffer us to famish, and their storehouses
crammed with grain; make edicts for usury, to support
usurers; repeal daily any wholesome act established
against the rich, and provide more piercing statutes
daily to chain up and restrain the poor. If the wars eat
us not up, they will; and there 's all the love they bear
us.

MENENIUS. Either you must
Confess yourselves wondrous malicious,
Or be accus'd of folly. I shall tell you
A pretty tale: it may be you have heard it;
But, since it serves my purpose, I will venture
To scale 't a little more.

FIRST CITIZEN. Well, I 'll hear it, sir; yet you must not think
to fob off our disgrace with a tale; but, an 't please you,
deliver.

MENENIUS. There was a time when all the body's members
Rebell'd against the belly; thus accus'd it:
That only like a gulf it did remain
I' the midst o' the body, idle and unactive,
Still cupboarding the viand, never bearing
Like labour with the rest, where the other instruments
Did see and hear, devise, instruct, walk, feel,
And, mutually participate, did minister
Unto the appetite and affection common
Of the whole body. The belly answer'd,—

FIRST CITIZEN. Well, sir, what answer made the belly?

MENENIUS. Sir, I shall tell you.—With a kind of smile,
Which ne'er came from the lungs, but even thus—
For, look you, I may make the belly smile
As well as speak—it tauntingly replied

To the discontented members, the mutinous parts
That envied his receipt; even so most fitly
As you malign our senators for that
They are not such as you.

FIRST CITIZEN.   Your belly's answer? What!
The kingly crowned head, the vigilant eye,
The counsellor heart, the arm our soldier,
Our steed the leg, the tongue our trumpeter,
With other muniments and petty helps
In this our fabric, if that they—

MENENIUS.   What then?—
'Fore me, this fellow speaks! what then? what then?

FIRST CITIZEN. Should by the cormorant belly be restrain'd,
Who is the sink o' the body,—

MENENIUS.   Well, what then?

FIRST CITIZEN. The former agents, if they did complain,
What could the belly answer?

MENENIUS.   I will tell you;
If you 'll bestow a small, of what you have little,
Patience a while, you 'll hear the belly's answer.

FIRST CITIZEN. You 're long about it.

MENENIUS.   Note me this, good friend;
Your most grave belly was deliberate,
Not rash like his accusers, and thus answer'd:
'True is it, my incorporate friends,' quoth he,
'That I receive the general food at first,
Which you do live upon; and fit it is;
Because I am the store-house and the shop
Of the whole body: but, if you do remember,
I send it through the rivers of your blood,
Even to the court, the heart, to the seat o' the brain;
And, through the cranks and offices of man,
The strongest nerves and small inferior veins
From me receive that natural competency
Whereby they live. And though that all at once,
You, my good friends,'—this says the belly, mark me,—

FIRST CITIZEN. Ay, sir; well, well.

MENENIUS.   'Though all at once cannot
See what I do deliver out to each,
Yet I can make my audit up, that all
From me do back receive the flour of all,

And leave me but the bran.' What say you to 't?

FIRST CITIZEN. It was an answer: how apply you this?

MENENIUS. The senators of Rome are this good belly,
And you the mutinous members; for, examine
Their counsels and their cares, digest things rightly
Touching the weal o' the common, you shall find
No public benefit which you receive
But it proceeds or comes from them to you,
And no way from yourselves. What do you think,
You, the great toe of this assembly?

FIRST CITIZEN. I the great toe? Why the great toe?

MENENIUS. For that, being one o' the lowest, basest, poorest,
Of this most wise rebellion, thou go'st foremost:
Thou rascal, that are worst in blood to run,
Lead'st first to win some vantage.
But make you ready your stiff bats and clubs:
Rome and her rats are at the point of battle;
The one side must have bale.
                    Enter Caius Marcius
                              Hail, noble Marcius!

MARCIUS. Thanks.—What 's the matter, you dissentious rogues,
That, rubbing the poor itch of your opinion,
Make yourselves scabs?

FIRST CITIZEN.   We have ever your good word.

MARCIUS. He that will give good words to thee will flatter
Beneath abhorring. What would you have, you curs,
That like nor peace nor war? the one affrights you,
The other makes you proud. He that trusts to you,
Where he should find you lions, finds you hares;
Where foxes, geese: you are no surer, no,
Than is the coal of fire upon the ice,
Or hailstone in the sun. Your virtue is,
To make him worthy whose offence subdues him,
And curses that justice did it. Who deserves greatness
Deserves your hate; and your affections are
A sick man's appetite, who desires most that
Which would increase his evil. He that depends
Upon your favours swims with fins of lead
And hews down oaks with rushes. Hang ye! Trust ye?

With every minute you do change a mind,
And call him noble that was now your hate,
Him vile that was your garland. What 's the matter,
That in these several places of the city
You cry against the noble senate, who,
Under the gods, keep you in awe, which else
Would feed on one another? What 's their seeking?

MENENIUS. For corn at their own rates; whereof they say
The city is well stor'd.

MARCIUS.   Hang 'em! They say!
They 'll sit by the fire, and presume to know
What 's done i' the Capitol; who 's like to rise,
Who thrives, and who declines; side factions, and give
    out
Conjectural marriages; making parties strong,
And feebling such as stand not in their liking,
Below their cobbled shoes. They say there 's grain
    enough!
Would the nobility lay aside their ruth,
And let me use my sword, I 'd make a quarry
With thousands of these quarter'd slaves, as high
As I could pick my lance.

MENENIUS. Nay, these are almost thoroughly persuaded;
For though abundantly they lack discretion,
Yet are they passing cowardly. But, I beseech you,
What says the other troop?

MARCIUS.   They are dissolv'd: hang 'em!
They said they were an-hungry; sigh'd forth proverbs:
That hunger broke stone walls; that dogs must eat;
That meat was made for mouths; that the gods sent not
Corn for the rich men only. With these shreds
They vented their complainings; which being answer'd,
And a petition granted them, a strange one,—
To break the heart of generosity,
And make bold power look pale,—they threw their caps
As they would hang them on the horns o' the moon,
Shouting their emulation.

MENENIUS.   What is granted them?

MARCIUS. Five tribunes to defend their vulgar wisdoms,
Of their own choice: one 's Junius Brutus,
Sicinius Velutus, and I know not—'Sdeath!
The rabble should have first unroof'd the city,

Ere so prevail'd with me; it will in time
Win upon power, and throw forth greater themes
For insurrection's arguing.

MENENIUS.   This is strange.

MARCIUS. Go; get you home, you fragments!

Enter a Messenger, hastily

MESSENGER. Where 's Caius Marcius?

MARCIUS.   Here: what 's the matter?

MESSENGER. The news is, sir, the Volsces are in arms.

MARCIUS. I am glad on 't; then we shall ha' means to vent
Our musty superfluity. See, our best elders.

Enter Cominius, Titus Lartius, and other Senators;
Junius Brutus and Sicinius Velutus

FIRST SENATOR. Marcius, 'tis true that you have lately told
us;
The Volsces are in arms.

MARCIUS.   They have a leader,
Tullus Aufidius, that will put you to 't.
I sin in envying his nobility,
And were I anything but what I am,
I would wish me only he.

COMINIUS.   You have fought together.

MARCIUS. Were half to half the world by the ears, and he
Upon my party, I 'd revolt, to make
Only my wars with him: he is a lion
That I am proud to hunt.

FIRST SENATOR.   Then, worthy Marcius,
Attend upon Cominius to these wars.

COMINIUS. It is your former promise.

MARCIUS.   Sir, it is;
And I am constant. Titus Lartius, thou
Shalt see me once more strike at Tullus' face.
What! art thou stiff? stand'st out?

TITUS.   No, Caius Marcius;
I 'll lean upon one crutch and fight with t'other,
Ere stay behind this business.

MENENIUS.   O! true-bred.

FIRST SENATOR. Your company to the Capitol; where I
know
Our greatest friends attend us.

TITUS. (*To Cominius*)   Lead you on:

(*To Marcius*) Follow Cominius; we must follow you;
Right worthy you priority.

COMINIUS.   Noble Marcius!

FIRST SENATOR. (*To the Citizens*) Hence! to your homes!
  be gone.

MARCIUS.   Nay, let them follow:
The Volsces have much corn; take these rats thither
To gnaw their garners. Worshipful mutineers,
Your valour puts well forth; pray, follow.

> *Exeunt Senators, Cominius, Marcius,*
> *Titus, and Menenius. Citizens steal away*

SICINIUS. Was ever man so proud as is this Marcius?

BRUTUS. He has no equal.

SICINIUS. When we were chosen tribunes for the people,—

BRUTUS. Mark'd you his lip and eyes?

SICINIUS.   Nay, but his taunts.

BRUTUS. Being mov'd, he will not spare to gird the gods.

SICINIUS. Bemock the modest moon.

BRUTUS. The present wars devour him; he is grown
  Too proud to be so valiant.

SICINIUS.   Such a nature,
Tickled with good success, disdains the shadow
Which he treads on at noon. But I do wonder
His insolence can brook to be commanded
Under Cominius.

BRUTUS.   • Fame, at the which he aims,
In whom already he is well grac'd, cannot
Better be held nor more attain'd than by
A place below the first; for what miscarries
Shall be the general's fault, though he perform
To the utmost of a man; and giddy censure
Will then cry out of Marcius 'O! if he
Had borne the business.'

SICINIUS.   Besides, if things go well,
Opinion, that so sticks on Marcius, shall
Of his demerits rob Cominius.

BRUTUS.   Come:
Half all Cominius' honours are to Marcius,
Though Marcius earn'd them not; and all his faults
To Marcius shall be honours, though indeed
In aught he merit not.

SICINIUS.   Let 's hence and hear

How the dispatch is made; and in what fashion,
More than his singularity, he goes
Upon this present action.

BRUTUS.   Let 's along.   *Exeunt*

SCENE TWO

Corioli. The Senate-house.

Enter Tullus Aufidius and Senators

FIRST SENATOR. So, your opinion is, Aufidius,
That they of Rome are enter'd in our counsels,
And know how we proceed.

AUFIDIUS.   Is it not yours?
What ever have been thought on in this state,
That could be brought to bodily act ere Rome
Had circumvention? 'Tis not four days gone
Since I heard thence; these are the words: I think
I have the letter here; yes, here it is.
'They have press'd a power, but it is not known
Whether for east, or west: the dearth is great;
The people mutinous; and it is rumour'd,
Cominius, Marcius, your old enemy,—
Who is of Rome worse hated than of you,—
And Titus Lartius, a most valiant Roman,
These three lead on this preparation
Whither 'tis bent: most likely 'tis for you:
Consider of it.'

FIRST SENATOR. Our army 's in the field:
We never yet made doubt but Rome was ready
To answer us.

AUFIDIUS.   Nor did you think it folly
To keep your great pretences veil'd till when
They needs must show themselves; which in the hatch-
   ing,
It seem'd, appear'd to Rome. By the discovery
We shall be shorten'd in our aim, which was
To take in many towns ere almost Rome
Should know we were afoot.

SECOND SENATOR.   Noble Aufidius,
Take your commission; hie you to your bands;

Let us alone to guard Corioli:
If they set down before 's, for the remove
Bring up your army; but, I think you 'll find
They 've not prepared for us.

AUFIDIUS.   O! doubt not that;
I speak from certainties. Nay, more;
Some parcels of their power are forth already,
And only hitherward. I leave your honours.
If we and Caius Marcius chance to meet,
'Tis sworn between us we shall ever strike
Till one can do no more.

ALL.   The gods assist you!
AUFIDIUS. And keep your honours safe!
FIRST SENATOR.   Farewell.
SECOND SENATOR.   Farewell.
ALL. Farewell.   *Exeunt*

SCENE THREE

Rome. A Room in Marcius' House.

*Enter Volumnia and Virgilia: they set them down
on two low stools and sew*

VOLUMNIA. I pray you, daughter, sing; or express yourself
in a more comfortable sort. If my son were my husband,
I would freelier rejoice in that absence wherein he won
honour than in the embracements of his bed where he
would show most love. When yet he was but tender-
bodied and the only son of my womb, when youth with
comeliness plucked all gaze his way, when for a day of
kings' entreaties a mother should not sell him an hour
from her beholding, I, considering how honour would
become such a person, that it was no better than pic-
ture-like to hang by the wall, if renown made it not
stir, was pleased to let him seek danger where he was
like to find fame. To a cruel war I sent him; from
whence he returned, his brows bound with oak. I tell
thee, daughter, I sprang not more in joy at first hearing
he was a man-child than now in first seeing he had
proved himself a man.

VIRGILIA. But had he died in the business, madam; how
then?

VOLUMNIA. Then, his good report should have been my
son; I therein would have found issue. Hear me profess
sincerely: had I a dozen sons, each in my love alike,
and none less dear than thine and my good Marcius, I
had rather had eleven die nobly for their country than
one voluptuously surfeit out of action.

Enter a Gentlewoman

GENTLEWOMAN. Madam, the Lady Valeria is come to visit
you.

VIRGILIA. Beseech you, give me leave to retire myself.

VOLUMNIA. Indeed, you shall not.
Methinks I hear hither your husband's drum,
See him pluck Aufidius down by the hair,
As children from a bear, the Volsces shunning him:
Methinks I see him stamp thus, and call thus:
'Come on, you cowards! you were got in fear,
Though you were born in Rome.' His bloody brow
With his mail'd hand then wiping, forth he goes,
Like to a harvestman that 's task'd to mow
Or all or lose his hire.

VIRGILIA. His bloody brow! O Jupiter! no blood.

VOLUMNIA. Away, you fool! it more becomes a man
Than gilt his trophy: the breasts of Hecuba,
When she did suckle Hector, look'd not lovelier
Than Hector's forehead when it spit forth blood
At Grecian swords, contemning. Tell Valeria
We are fit to bid her welcome.   *Exit Gentlewoman*

VIRGILIA. Heavens bless my lord from fell Aufidius!

VOLUMNIA. He 'll beat Aufidius' head below his knee,
And tread upon his neck.

Re-enter Gentlewoman, with Valeria and an Usher

VALERIA. My ladies both, good day to you.

VOLUMNIA. Sweet madam.

VIRGILIA. I am glad to see your ladyship.

VALERIA. How do you both? you are manifest housekeep-
ers. What are you sewing here? A fine spot, in good
faith. How does your little son?

VIRGILIA. I thank your ladyship; well, good madam.

VOLUMNIA. He had rather see the swords and hear a drum,
than look upon his schoolmaster.

VALERIA. O' my word, the father's son; I 'll swear 'tis a very pretty boy. O' my troth, I looked upon him o' Wednesday half an hour together: he has such a confirmed countenance. I saw him run after a gilded butterfly; and when he caught it, he let it go again; and after it again; and over and over he comes, and up again; catched it again: or whether his fall enraged him, or how 'twas, he did so set his teeth and tear it; O! I warrant, how he mammocked it!

VOLUMNIA. One on 's father's moods.

VALERIA. Indeed, la, 'tis a noble child.

VIRGILIA. A crack, madam.

VALERIA. Come, lay aside your stitchery; I must have you play the idle huswife with me this afternoon.

VIRGILIA. No, good madam; I will not out of doors.

VALERIA. Not out of doors!

VOLUMNIA. She shall, she shall.

VIRGILIA. Indeed, no, by your patience; I 'll not over the threshold till my lord return from the wars.

VOLUMNIA. Fie! you confine yourself most unreasonably. Come; you must go visit the good lady that lies in.

VIRGILIA. I will wish her speedy strength, and visit her with my prayers; but I cannot go thither.

VOLUMNIA. Why, I pray you?

VIRGILIA. 'Tis not to save labour, nor that I want love.

VALERIA. You would be another Penelope; yet, they say, all the yarn she spun in Ulysses' absence did but fill Ithaca full of moths. Come; I would your cambric were sensible as your finger, that you might leave pricking it for pity. Come, you shall go with us.

VIRGILIA. No, good madam, pardon me; indeed, I will not forth.

VALERIA. In truth, la, go with me; and I 'll tell you excellent news of your husband.

VIRGILIA. O, good madam, there can be none yet.

VALERIA. Verily, I do not jest with you; there came news from him last night.

VIRGILIA. Indeed, madam?

VALERIA. In earnest, it 's true; I heard a senator speak it. Thus it is: The Volsces have an army forth; against whom Cominius the general is gone, with one part of our Roman power: your lord and Titus Lartius are set down

before their city Corioli; they nothing doubt prevailing
and to make it brief wars. This is true, on mine honour;
and so, I pray, go with us.

VIRGILIA. Give me excuse, good madam; I will obey you
in every thing hereafter.

VOLUMNIA. Let her alone, lady: as she is now she will but
disease our better mirth.

VALERIA. In troth, I think she would. Fare you well then.
Come, good sweet lady. Prithee, Virgilia, turn thy sol-
emness out o' door, and go along with us.

VIRGILIA. No, at a word, madam; indeed I must not. I wish
you much mirth.

VALERIA. Well then, farewell.   *Exeunt*

SCENE FOUR

Before Corioli.

Enter, with drum and colours, Marcius, Titus Lartius,
Officers, and Soldiers. To them a Messenger

MARCIUS. Yonder comes news: a wager they have met.

LARTIUS. My horse to yours, no.

MARCIUS.   'Tis done.

LARTIUS.   Agreed.

MARCIUS. Say, has our general met the enemy?

MESSENGER. They lie in view, but have not spoke as yet.

LARTIUS. So the good horse is mine.

MARCIUS.   I 'll buy him of you.

LARTIUS. No, I 'll nor sell nor give him; lend you him I will
For half a hundred years. Summon the town.

MARCIUS. How far off lie these armies?

MESSENGER.   Within this mile and half.

MARCIUS. Then shall we hear their 'larum, and they ours.
Now, Mars, I prithee, make us quick in work,
That we with smoking swords may march from hence,
To help our fielded friends! Come, blow thy blast.

        A Parley sounded. Enter, on the Walls, two
                Senators, and Others

Tullus Aufidius, is he within your walls?

FIRST SENATOR. No, nor a man that fears you less than he,
That 's lesser than a little. Hark, our drums
                              Drums afar off
Are bringing forth our youth: we 'll break our walls,
Rather than they shall pound us up: our gates,
Which yet seem shut, we have but pinn'd with rushes:
They 'll open of themselves. Hark you, far off!
                              Alarum afar off
There is Aufidius: list, what work he makes
Amongst your cloven army.
MARCIUS.   O! they are at it!
LARTIUS. Their noise be our instruction. Ladders ho!
    The Volsces enter, and pass over the stage
MARCIUS. They fear us not, but issue forth their city.
Now put your shields before your hearts, and fight
With hearts more proof than shields. Advance, brave
    Titus:
They do disdain us much beyond our thoughts,
Which makes me sweat with wrath. Come on, my fel-
    lows:
He that retires, I 'll take him for a Volsce,
And he shall feel mine edge.
Alarum. The Romans are beaten back to their trenches.
                Re-enter Marcius
MARCIUS. All the contagion of the south light on you,
You shames of Rome! you herd of—Boils and plagues
Plaster you o'er, that you may be abhorr'd
Farther than seen, and one infect another
Against the wind a mile! You souls of geese,
That bear the shapes of men, how have you run
From slaves that apes would beat! Pluto and hell!
All hurt behind; backs red, and faces pale
With flight and agu'd fear! Mend and charge home,
Or, by the fires of heaven, I 'll leave the foe
And make my wars on you; look to 't: come on;
If you 'll stand fast, we 'll beat them to their wives,
As they us to our trenches. Follow me!
    Another alarum. The Volsces and Romans re-enter,
and the fight is renewed. The Volsces retire into Corioli.
    Marcius follows them to the gates, and is shut in
So, now the gates are ope: now prove good seconds:
'Tis for the followers Fortune widens them.

Not for the fliers: mark me, and do the like.

He enters the gates

FIRST SOLDIER. Foolhardiness! not I.

SECOND SOLDIER.   Nor I;

THIRD SOLDIER. See, they have shut him in.

Alarum continues

ALL.   To the pot, I warrant him.

Re-enter Titus Lartius

LARTIUS. What is become of Marcius?

ALL.   Slain, sir, doubtless.

FIRST SOLDIER. Following the fliers at the very heels
With them he enters; who, upon the sudden,
Clapp'd to their gates; he is himself alone,
To answer all the city.

LARTIUS.   O noble fellow!
Who, sensibly, outdares his senseless sword,
And, when it bows, stands up. Thou art left, Marcius:
A carbuncle, entire, as big as thou art,
Were not so rich a jewel. Thou wast a soldier
Even to Cato's wish, not fierce and terrible
Only in strokes; but, with thy grim looks and
The thunder-like percussion of thy sounds,
Thou mad'st thine enemies shake, as if the world
Were feverous and did tremble.

Re-enter Marcius, bleeding, assaulted by the enemy

FIRST SOLDIER.   Look, sir!

LARTIUS.   O! tis Marcius

Let's fetch him off, or make remain alike.

They fight, and all enter the city

SCENE FIVE

Corioli. A Street.

Enter certain Romans, with spoils

FIRST ROMAN. This will I carry to Rome.

SECOND ROMAN. And I this.

THIRD ROMAN. A murrain on 't! I took this for silver.

Alarum continues still afar off

Enter Marcius and Titus Lartius, with a trumpet

MARCIUS. See here these movers that do prize their hours

At a crack'd drachme! Cushions, leaden spoons,
Irons of a doit, doublets that hangmen would
Bury with those that wore them, these base slaves,
Ere yet the fight be done, pack up. Down with them!
And hark, what noise the general makes! To him!
There is the man of my soul's hate, Aufidius,
Piercing our Romans: then, valiant Titus, take
Convenient numbers to make good the city,
Whilst I, with those that have the spirit, will haste
To help Cominius.
LARTIUS.   Worthy sir, thou bleed'st;
Thy exercise hath been too violent
For a second course of fight.
MARCIUS.   Sir, praise me not;
My work hath yet not warm'd me: fare you well:
The blood I drop is rather physical
Than dangerous to me: to Aufidius thus
I will appear, and fight.
LARTIUS.   Now the fair goddess, Fortune,
Fall deep in love with thee; and her great charms
Misguide thy opposers' swords! Bold gentleman,
Prosperity be thy page!
MARCIUS.   Thy friend no less
Than those she places highest: So, farewell.
LARTIUS. Thou worthiest Marcius!—   *Exit Marcius*
Go, sound thy trumpet in the market-place;
Call thither all the officers of the town,
Where they shall know our mind. Away!   *Exeunt*

SCENE SIX

Near the Camp of Cominius.

Enter Cominius and Forces, retreating

COMINIUS. Breathe you, my friends: well fought; we are
    come off
Like Romans, neither foolish in our stands,
Nor cowardly in retire: believe me, sirs,
We shall be charg'd again. Whiles we have struck,
By interims and conveying gusts we have heard
The charges of our friends. Ye Roman gods!

Lead their successes as we wish our own,
That both our powers, with smiling fronts encountering,
May give you thankful sacrifice

Enter a Messenger

Thy news?

MESSENGER. The citizens of Corioli have issu'd,
And given to Lartius and to Marcius battle:
I saw our party to their trenches driven,
And then I came away.

COMINIUS.   Though thou speak'st truth,
Methinks thou speak'st not well. How long is 't since?

MESSENGER. Above an hour, my lord.

COMINIUS. 'Tis not a mile; briefly we heard their drums:
How couldst thou in a mile confound an hour,
And bring thy news so late?

MESSENGER.   Spies of the Volsces
Held me in chase, that I was forc'd to wheel
Three or four miles about; else had I, sir,
Half an hour since brought my report.

COMINIUS.   Who 's yonder,
That does appear as he were flay'd? O gods!
He has the stamp of Marcius; and I have
Before-time seen him thus.

MARCIUS. (*Within*)   Come I too late?

COMINIUS. The shepherd knows not thunder from a tabor,
More than I know the sound of Marcius' tongue
From every meaner man.

Enter Marcius

MARCIUS.   Come I too late?

COMINIUS. Ay, if you come not in the blood of others,
But mantled in your own.

MARCIUS.   O! let me clip ye
In arms as sound as when I woo'd, in heart
As merry as when our nuptial day was done,
And tapers burn'd to bedward.

COMINIUS.   Flower of warriors
How is 't with Titus Lartius?

MARCIUS. As with a man busied about decrees:
Condemning some to death, and some to exile;
Ransoming him, or pitying, threatening the other;
Holding Corioli in the name of Rome,
Even like a fawning greyhound in the leash,

To let him slip at will.

COMINIUS.   Where is that slave
Which told me they had beat you to your trenches?
Where is he? Call him hither.

MARCIUS.   Let him alone:
He did inform the truth; but for our gentlemen,
The common file—a plague! tribunes for them!—
The mouse ne'er shunn'd the cat as they did budge
From rascals worse than they.

COMINIUS.   But how prevail'd you?

MARCIUS. Will the time serve to tell? I do not think.
Where is the enemy? Are you lords o' the field?
If not, why cease you till you are so?

COMINIUS. Marcius, we have at disadvantage fought,
And did retire to win our purpose.

MARCIUS. How lies their battle? Know you on which side
They have plac'd their men of trust?

COMINIUS.   As I guess, Marcius,
Their bands i' the vaward are the Antiates,
Of their best trust; o'er them Aufidius,
Their very heart of hope.

MARCIUS.   I do beseech you,
By all the battles wherein we have fought,
By the blood we have shed together, by the vows
We have made to endure friends, that you directly
Set me against Aufidius and his Antiates;
And that you not delay the present, but,
Filling the air with swords advanc'd and darts,
We prove this very hour.

COMINIUS.   Though I could wish
You were conducted to a gentle bath,
And balms applied to you, yet dare I never
Deny your asking: take your choice of those
That best can aid your action.

MARCIUS.   Those are they
That most are willing. If any such be here—
As it were sin to doubt—that love this painting
Wherein you see me smear'd; if any fear
Lesser his person than an ill report;
If any think brave death outweighs bad life,
And that his country's dearer than himself;
Let him, alone, or so many so minded,

Wave thus, to express his disposition,
And follow Marcius.

> *They all shout, and wave their swords; take him*
> *up in their arms, and cast up their caps*

O! me alone? Make you a sword of me?
If these shows be not outward, which of you
But is four Volsces? None of you but is
Able to bear against the great Aufidius
A shield as hard as his. A certain number,
Though thanks to all, must I select from all: the rest
Shall bear the business in some other fight,
As cause will be obey'd. Please you to march;
And four shall quickly draw out my command,
Which men are best inclin'd.

COMINIUS.   March on, my fellows:
Make good this ostentation, and you shall
Divide in all with us.   *Exeunt*

SCENE SEVEN

The Gates of Corioli.

Titus Lartius, having set a guard upon Corioli, going with
drum and trumpet towards Cominius and Caius Marcius,
enters with a Lieutenant, a party of
Soldiers, and a Scout

LARTIUS. So; let the ports be guarded: keep your duties,
As I have set them down. If I do send, dispatch
Those centuries to our aid; the rest will serve
For a short holding: if we lose the field,
We cannot keep the town.

LIEUTENANT.   Fear not our care, sir.

LARTIUS. Hence, and shut your gates upon us.
Our guider, come; to the Roman camp conduct us.
                                        Exeunt

SCENE EIGHT

*A Field of Battle between the Roman and
the Volscian Camps*

Alarum. Enter from opposite sides Marcius and Aufidius

MARCIUS. I 'll fight with none but thee; for I do hate thee
Worse than a promise-breaker.
AUFIDIUS.   We hate alike:
Not Afric owns a serpent I abhor
More than thy fame and envy. Fix thy foot.
MARCIUS. Let the first budger die the other's slave,
And the gods doom him after!
AUFIDIUS.   If I fly, Marcius,
Halloo me like a hare.
MARCIUS. Within these three hours, Tullus,
Alone I fought in your Corioli walls,
And made what work I pleas'd; 'tis not my blood
Wherein thou seest me mask'd; for thy revenge
Wrench up thy power to the highest.
AUFIDIUS.   Wert thou the Hector
That was the whip of your bragg'd progeny,
Thou shouldst not 'scape me here.—

> *They fight, and certain Volsces come
> to the aid of Aufidius*

Officious, and not valiant, you have sham'd me
In your condemned seconds.

> *Exeunt fighting, all driven in by Marcius*

SCENE NINE

The Roman Camp.

*Alarum. A retreat sounded. Flourish. Enter from one side,
Cominius and Romans; from the other side, Marcius,
with his arm in a scarf, and other Romans*

COMINIUS. If I should tell thee o'er this thy day's work,
Thou 'lt not believe thy deeds: but I 'll report it
Where senators shall mingle tears with smiles,
Where great patricians shall attend and shrug,

MARCIUS.   Let the first budger die the other's slave,
   And the gods doom him after!

I' the end, admire; where ladies shall be frighted,
And, gladly quak'd, hear more; where the dull tribunes,
That, with the fusty plebeians, hate thine honours,
Shall say, against their hearts,
'We thank the gods our Rome hath such a soldier!'
Yet cam'st thou to a morsel of this feast,
Having fully din'd before.

Enter Titus Lartius, with his power, from the pursuit

LARTIUS.   O general.
Here is the steed, we the caparison:
Had'st thou beheld—

MARCIUS.   Pray now, no more: my mother,
Who has a charter to extol her blood,
When she does praise me grieves me. I have done
As you have done; that 's what I can; induc'd
As you have been; that 's for my country:
He that has but effected his good will
Hath overta'en mine act.

COMINIUS.   You shall not be
The grave of your deserving; Rome must know
The value of her own: 'twere a concealment
Worse than a theft, no less than a traducement,
To hide your doings; and to silence that,
Which, to the spire and top of praises vouch'd,
Would seem but modest. Therefore, I beseech you,—
In sign of what you are, not to reward
What you have done,—before our army hear me.

MARCIUS. I have some wounds upon me, and they smart
To hear themselves remember'd.

COMINIUS.   Should they not,
Well might they fester 'gainst ingratitude,
And tent themselves with death. Of all the horses,
Whereof we have' ta'en good, and good store, of all
The treasure, in this field achiev'd and city,
We render you the tenth; to be ta'en forth,
Before the common distribution,
At your only choice.

MARCIUS.   I thank you, general;
But cannot make my heart consent to take
A bribe to pay my sword: I do refuse it;
And stand upon my common part with those
That have beheld the doing.

A long flourish. They all cry
'Marcius! Marcius!' cast up their caps
and lances; Cominius and Lartius stand bare

MARCIUS. May these same instruments, which you profane,
  Never sound more! When drums and trumpets shall
  I' the field prove flatterers, let courts and cities be
  Made all of false-fac'd soothing!
  When steel grows soft as is the parasite's silk,
  Let him be made a coverture for the wars!
  No more, I say! For that I have not wash'd
  My nose that bled, or foil'd some debile wretch,
  Which, without note, here 's many else have done,
  You shout me forth
  In acclamations hyperbolical;
  As if I lov'd my little should be dieted
  In praises sauc'd with lies.
COMINIUS.   Too modest are you;
  More cruel to your good report than grateful
  To us that give you truly. By your patience,
  If 'gainst yourself you be incens'd, we 'll put you,
  Like one that means his proper harm, in manacles,
  Then reason safely with you. Therefore, be it known,
  As to us, to all the world, that Caius Marcius
  Wears this war's garland; in token of the which,
  My noble steed, known to the camp, I give him,
  With all his trim belonging; and from this time,
  For what he did before Corioli, call him,
  With all the applause and clamour of the host,
  CAIUS MARCIUS CORIOLANUS! Bear
  The addition nobly ever!
ALL. Caius Marcius Coriolanus!
                Flourish. Trumpets sound, and drums
CORIOLANUS. I will go wash;
  And when my face is fair, you shall perceive
  Whether I blush, or no: howbeit, I thank you.
  I mean to stride your steed, and at all times
  To undercrest your good addition
  To the fairness of my power.
COMINIUS.   So, to our tent;
  Where, ere we do repose us, we will write
  To Rome of our success. You, Titus Lartius,
  Must to Corioli back: send us to Rome

    The best, with whom we may articulate,
    For their own good and ours.
LARTIUS.   I shall, my lord.
CORIOLANUS. The gods begin to mock me. I, that now
    Refus'd most princely gifts, am bound to beg
    Of my lord general.
COMINIUS.   Take it; 'tis yours. What is 't?
CORIOLANUS. I sometime lay here in Corioli
    At a poor man's house; he us'd me kindly:
    He cried to me; I saw him prisoner;
    But then Aufidius was within my view,
    And wrath o'erwhelm'd my pity: I request you
    To give my poor host freedom.
COMINIUS   O! well begg'd!
    Were he the butcher of my son, he should
    Be free as is the wind. Deliver him, Titus.
LARTIUS. Marcius, his name?
CORIOLANUS.   By Jupiter! forgot.
    I am weary; yea, my memory is tir'd.
    Have we no wine here?
COMINIUS.   Go we to our tent:
    The blood upon your visage dries; 'tis time
    It should be look'd to: come.   *Exeunt*

SCENE TEN

The Camp of the Volsces.

*A Flourish. Cornets. Enter Tullus Aufidius, bloody,
with two or three Soldiers*

AUFIDIUS. The town is ta'en!
FIRST SOLDIER. 'Twill be deliver'd back on good condition.
AUFIDIUS. Condition!
    I would I were a Roman; for I cannot,
    Being a Volsce, be that I am. Condition!
    What good condition can a treaty find
    I' the part that is at mercy? Five times, Marcius,
    I have fought with thee; so often hast thou beat me,
    And wouldst do so, I think, should we encounter
    As often as we eat. By the elements,
    If e'er again I meet him beard to beard,

He is mine, or I am his: mine emulation
Hath not that honour in 't it had; for where
I thought to crush him in an equal force—
True sword to sword—I 'll potch at him some way
Or wrath or craft may get him.

FIRST SOLDIER.   He 's the devil.

AUFIDIUS. Bolder, though not so subtle. My valour's
    poison'd
With only suffering stain by him; for him
Shall fly out of itself. Nor sleep nor sanctuary,
Being naked, sick, nor fane nor Capitol,
The prayers of priests, nor times of sacrifice,
Embarquements all of fury, shall lift up
Their rotten privilege and custom 'gainst
My hate to Marcius. Where I find him, were it
At home, upon my brother's guard, even there,
Against the hospitable canon, would I
Wash my fierce hand in 's heart. Go you to the city;
Learn how 'tis held, and what they are that must
Be hostages for Rome.

FIRST SOLDIER.   Will not you go?

AUFIDIUS. I am attended at the cypress grove: I pray you—
'Tis south the city mills—bring me word thither
How the world goes, that to the pace of it
I may spur on my journey.

FIRST SOLDIER.   I shall, sir.   *Exeunt*

ACT TWO

SCENE ONE

Rome. A Public Place.

Enter Menenius, Sicinius, and Brutus

MENENIUS. The augurer tells me we shall have news to-night.

BRUTUS. Good or bad?

MENENIUS. Not according to the prayer of the people, for they love not Marcius.

SICINIUS. Nature teaches beasts to know their friends.

MENENIUS. Pray you, who does the wolf love?

SICINIUS. The lamb.

MENENIUS. Ay, to devour him; as the hungry plebeians would the noble Marcius.

BRUTUS. He 's a lamb indeed, that baes like a bear.

MENENIUS. He 's a bear indeed, that lives like a lamb. You two are old men; tell me one thing that I shall ask you.

SICINIUS. } Well, sir.
BRUTUS. }

MENENIUS. In what enormity is Marcius poor in, that you two have not in abundance?

BRUTUS. He 's poor in no one fault, but stored with all.

SICINIUS. Especially in pride.

BRUTUS. And topping all others in boasting.

MENENIUS. This is strange now: do you two know how you are censured here in the city, I mean of us o' the right-hand file? Do you?

BOTH. Why, how are we censured?

MENENIUS. Because you talk of pride now,—Will you not be angry?

BOTH. Well, well, sir; well.

MENENIUS. Why, 'tis no great matter; for a very little thief of occasion will rob you of a great deal of patience: give your dispositions the reins, and be angry at your pleasures; at the least, if you take it as a pleasure to you in being so. You blame Marcius for being proud?

BRUTUS. We do it not alone, sir.

MENENIUS. I know you can do very little alone; for your helps are many, or else your actions would grow wondrous single: your abilities are too infant-like, for doing much alone. You talk of pride: O! that you could turn your eyes towards the napes of your necks, and make but an interior survey of your good selves. O! that you could.

BRUTUS. What then, sir?

MENENIUS. Why, then you should discover a brace of unmeriting, proud, violent, testy magistrates—alias fools—as any in Rome.

SICINIUS. Menenius, you are known well enough too.

MENENIUS. I am known to be a humorous patrician, and one that loves a cup of hot wine with not a drop of allaying Tiber in 't; said to be something imperfect in favouring the first complaint; hasty and tinder-like upon too trivial motion; one that converses more with the buttock of the night than with the forehead of the morning. What I think I utter, and spend my malice in my breath. Meeting two such wealsmen as you are,—I cannot call you Lycurguses,—if the drink you give me touch my palate adversely, I make a crooked face at it. I cannot say your worships have delivered the matter well when I find the ass in compound with the major part of your syllables; and though I must be content to bear with those that say you are reverend grave men, yet they lie deadly that tell you you have good faces. If you see this in the map of my microcosm, follows it that I am known well enough to? What harm can your bisson conspectuities glean out of this character, if I be known well enough too?

BRUTUS. Come, sir, come, we know you well enough.

MENENIUS. You know neither me, yourselves, nor anything. You are ambitious for poor knaves' caps and legs; you wear out a good wholesome forenoon in hearing a cause between an orange-wife and a fosset-seller, and then rejourn the controversy of three-pence to a second

day of audience. When you are hearing a matter between party and party, if you chance to be pinched
with the colic, you make faces like mummers, set up the
bloody flag against all patience, and, in roaring for a
chamber-pot, dismiss the controversy bleeding, the more
entangled by your hearing: all the peace you make in
their cause is, calling both the parties knaves. You are a
pair of strange ones.

BRUTUS. Come, come, you are well understood to be a per-
fecter giber for the table than a necessary bencher in the
Capitol.

MENENIUS. Our very priests must become mockers if they
shall encounter such ridiculous subjects as you are.
When you speak best unto the purpose it is not worth
the wagging of your beards; and your beards deserve
not so honourable a grave as to stuff a botcher's cushion,
or to be entombed in an ass's pack-saddle. Yet you must
be saying Marcius is proud; who, in a cheap estimation,
is worth all your predecessors since Deucalion, though
peradventure some of the best of 'em were hereditary
hangmen. Good den to your worships: more of your con-
versation would infect my brain, being the herdsmen of
the beastly plebeians: I will be bold to take my leave of
you.   *Brutus and Sicinius go aside*
        Enter Volumnia, Virgilia, and Valeria
How now, my as fair as noble ladies,—and the moon,
were she earthly, no nobler,—whither do you follow your
eyes so fast?

VOLUMNIA. Honourable Menenius, my boy Marcius approaches; for the love of Juno, let 's go.

MENENIUS. Ha! Marcius coming home?

VOLUMNIA. Ay, worthy Menenius; and with most prosperous approbation.

MENENIUS. Take my cap, Jupiter, and I thank thee. Hoo!
Marcius coming home!

VOLUMNIA. }
VIRGILIA. } Nay, 'tis true.

VOLUMNIA. Look, here 's a letter from him: the state hath
another, his wife another; and, I think, there 's one at
home for you.

MENENIUS. I will make my very house reel to-night. A letter for me!

VIRGILIA. Yes, certain, there 's a letter for you; I saw it.

MENENIUS. A letter for me! It gives me an estate of seven years' health; in which time I will make a lip at the physician: the most sovereign prescription in Galen is but empiricutic, and, to this preservative, of no better report than a horse-drench. Is he not wounded? he was wont to come home wounded.

VIRGILIA. O! no, no, no.

VOLUMNIA. O! he is wounded, I thank the gods for 't.

MENENIUS. So do I too, if it be not too much. Brings a' victory in his pocket? The wounds become him.

VOLUMNIA. On 's brows, Menenius; he comes the third time home with the oaken garland.

MENENIUS. Has he disciplined Aufidius soundly?

VOLUMNIA. Titus Lartius writes they fought together, but Aufidius got off.

MENENIUS. And 'twas time for him too, I 'll warrant him that: an he had stayed by him I would not have been so fidiused for all the chests in Corioli, and the gold that 's in them. Is the senate possessed of this?

VOLUMNIA. Good ladies, let 's go. Yes, yes, yes; the senate has letters from the general, wherein he gives my son the whole name of the war. He hath in this action outdone his former deeds doubly.

VALERIA. In troth there 's wondrous things spoke of him.

MENENIUS. Wondrous! ay, I warrant you, and not without his true purchasing.

VIRGILIA. The gods grant them true!

VOLUMNIA. True! pow, wow.

MENENIUS. True! I 'll be sworn they are true. Where is he wounded? (*To the Tribunes*) God save your good worships! Marcius is coming home: he has more cause to be proud. (*To Volumnia*) Where is he wounded?

VOLUMNIA. I' the shoulder, and i' the left arm: there will be large cicatrices to show the people when he shall stand for his place. He received in the repulse of Tarquin seven hurts i' the body.

MENENIUS. One i' the neck, and two i' the thigh, there 's nine that I know.

VOLUMNIA. He had, before this last expedition, twenty-five wounds upon him.

MENENIUS. Now, it 's twenty-seven: every gash was an

enemy's grave. (*A shout and flourish*) Hark! the trumpets.

VOLUMNIA. These are the ushers of Marcius: before him
he carries noise, and behind him he leaves tears:
Death, that dark spirit, in 's nervy arm doth lie;
Which, being advanc'd, declines, and then men die.

A Sennet. Trumpets sound. Enter Cominius and
Titus Lartius; between them, Coriolanus, crowned with an
oaken garland; with Captains, Soldiers, and a Herald

HERALD. Know, Rome, that all alone Marcius did fight
Within Corioli gates: where he hath won,
With fame, a name to Caius Marcius; these
In honour follows Coriolanus.
Welcome to Rome, renowned Coriolanus!   *Flourish*

ALL. Welcome to Rome, renowned Coriolanus!

CORIOLANUS. No more of this; it does offend my heart:
Pray now, no more.

COMINIUS.   Look, sir, your mother!

CORIOLANUS.   O!
You have, I know, petition'd all the gods
For my prosperity.   *Kneels*

VOLUMNIA.   Nay, my good soldier, up;
My gentle Marcius, worthy Caius, and
By deed-achieving honour newly nam'd,—
What is it?—Coriolanus must I call thee?
But O! thy wife!—

CORIOLANUS.   . My gracious silence, hail!
Wouldst thou have laugh'd had I come coffin'd home,
That weep'st to see me triumph? Ah! my dear,
Such eyes the widows in Corioli wear,
And mothers that lack sons.

MENENIUS.   Now, the gods crown thee!

CORIOLANUS. And live you yet? (*To Valeria*) O my sweet
lady, pardon.

VOLUMNIA. I know not where to turn: O! welcome home;
And welcome, general; and ye're welcome all.

MENENIUS. A hundred thousand welcomes: I could weep,
And I could laugh; I am light, and heavy. Welcome.
A curse begnaw at very root on 's heart
That is not glad to see thee! You are three
That Rome should dote on; yet, by the faith of men,
We have some old crab-trees here at home that will not

Be grafted to your relish. Yet, welcome, warriors:
We call a nettle but a nettle, and
The faults of fools but folly.

COMINIUS.   Ever right.

CORIOLANUS. Menenius, ever, ever.

HERALD. Give way there, and go on!

CORIOLANUS. (*To Volumnia and Virgilia*) Your hand, and
yours:
Ere in our own house I do shade my head,
The good patricians must be visited;
From whom I have receiv'd not only greetings,
But with them change of honours.

VOLUMNIA.   I have liv'd
To see inherited my very wishes,
And the buildings of my fancy: only
There 's one thing wanting, which I doubt not but
Our Rome will cast upon thee.

CORIOLANUS.   Know, good mother,
I had rather be their servant in my way
Than sway with them in theirs.

COMINIUS. On, to the Capitol!

> *Flourish. Cornets. Exeunt*
> *in state, as before. The Tribunes remain*

BRUTUS. All tongues speak of him, and the bleared sights
Are spectacled to see him: your prattling nurse
Into a rapture lets her baby cry
While she chats him; the kitchen malkin pins
Her richest lockram 'bout her reechy neck,
Clambering the walls to eye him: stalls, bulks, windows,
Are smother'd up, leads fill'd, and ridges hors'd
With variable complexions, all agreeing
In earnestness to see him: seld-shown flamens
Do press among the popular throngs, and puff
To win a vulgar station: our veil'd dames
Commit the war of white and damask in
Their nicely-gawded cheeks to the wanton spoil
Of Phœbus' burning kisses: such a pother
As if that whatsoever god who leads him
Were slily crept into his human powers,
And gave him graceful posture.

SICINIUS.   On the sudden
I warrant him consul.

BRUTUS.   Then our office may,
  During his power, go sleep.
SICINIUS. He cannot temperately transport his honours
  From where he should begin and end, but will
  Lose those he hath won.
BRUTUS.   In that there 's comfort.
SICINIUS. Doubt not, the commoners, for whom we stand,
  But they upon their ancient malice will
  Forget with the least cause these his new honours,
  Which that he'll give them, make I as little question
  As he is proud to do 't.
BRUTUS.   I heard him swear,
  Were he to stand for consul, never would he
  Appear i' the market-place, nor on him put
  The napless vesture of humility;
  Nor, showing, as the manner is, his wounds
  To the people, beg their stinking breaths.
SICINIUS.   'Tis right.
BRUTUS. It was his word. O! he would miss it rather
  Than carry it but by the suit o' the gentry to him
  And the desire of the nobles.
SICINIUS.   I wish no better
  Than have him hold that purpose and to put it
  In execution.
BRUTUS.   'Tis most like he will.
SICINIUS. It shall be to him then, as our good wills,
  A sure destruction.
BRUTUS.   So it must fall out
  To him or our authorities. For an end,
  We must suggest the people in what hatred
  He still hath held them; that to his power he would
  Have made them mules, silenc'd their pleaders, and
  Dispropertied their freedoms; holding them,
  In human action and capacity,
  Of no more soul nor fitness for the world
  Than camels in the war; who have their provand
  Only for bearing burdens, and sore blows
  For sinking under them.
SICINIUS.   This, as you say, suggested
  At some time when his soaring insolence
  Shall teach the people—which time shall not want,
  If he be put upon 't; and that 's as easy

As to set dogs on sheep—will be his fire
To kindle their dry stubble; and their blaze
Shall darken him for ever.

Enter a Messenger

BRUTUS.   What 's the matter?

MESSENGER. You are sent for to the Capitol. 'Tis thought
That Marcius shall be consul.
I have seen the dumb men throng to see him, and
The blind to hear him speak: matrons flung gloves,
Ladies and maids their scarfs and handkerchers
Upon him as he pass'd; the nobles bended
As to Jove's statue, and the commons made
A shower and thunder with their caps and shouts:
I never saw the like.

BRUTUS.   Let 's to the Capitol;
And carry with us ears and eyes for the time,
But hearts for the event.

SICINIUS.   Have with you.   *Exeunt*

SCENE TWO

The Same. The Capitol.

Enter two Officers to lay cushions

FIRST OFFICER. Come, come, they are almost here. How
many stand for consulships?

SECOND OFFICER. Three, they say; but 'tis thought of every
one Coriolanus will carry it.

FIRST OFFICER. That 's a brave fellow; but he 's vengeance
proud, and loves not the common people.

SECOND OFFICER. Faith, there have been many great men
that have flattered the people, who ne'er loved them;
and there be many that they have lov'd, they know not
wherefore: so that if they love they know not why, they
hate upon no better a ground. Therefore, for Coriolanus
neither to care whether they love or hate him manifests
the true knowledge he has in their disposition; and out
of his noble carelessness lets them plainly see 't.

FIRST OFFICER. If he did not care whether he had their
love or no, he waved indifferently 'twixt doing them
neither good nor harm; but he seeks their hate with

greater devotion than they can render it him; and leaves
nothing undone that may fully discover him their opposite. Now, to seem to affect the malice and displeasure
of the people is as bad as that which he dislikes, to flatter them for their love.

SECOND OFFICER. He hath deserved worthily of his country; and his ascent is not by such easy degrees as those
who, having been supple and courteous to the people,
bonneted, without any further deed to have them at all
into their estimation and report; but he hath so planted
his honours in their eyes, and his actions in their hearts,
that for their tongues to be silent, and not confess so
much, were a kind of ingrateful injury; to report otherwise, were a malice, that, giving itself the lie, would
pluck reproof and rebuke from every ear that heard it.

FIRST OFFICER. No more of him; he is a worthy man: make
way, they are coming.

A Sennet. Enter, with Lictors before them, Cominius
the Consul, Menenius, Coriolanus, many other Senators,
Sicinius and Brutus. The Senators take their places; the
Tribunes take theirs also by themselves

MENENIUS. Having determin'd of the Volsces, and
To send for Titus Lartius, it remains
As the main point of this our after-meeting,
To gratify his noble service that
Hath thus stood for his country: therefore, please you,
Most reverend and grave elders, to desire
The present consul, and last general
In our well-found successes, to report
A little of that worthy work perform'd
By Caius Marcius Coriolanus, whom
We meet here both to thank and to remember
With honours like himself.

FIRST SENATOR.   Speak, good Cominius:
Leave nothing out for length, and make us think
Rather our state 's defective for requital,
Than we to stretch it out. (*To the Tribunes*) Masters o'
the people,
We do request your kindest ears, and, after,
Your loving motion toward the common body,
To yield what passes here.

SICINIUS.   We are convented

Upon a pleasing treaty, and have hearts
Inclinable to honour and advance
The theme of our assembly.

BRUTUS.   Which the rather
We shall be bless'd to do, if he remember
A kinder value of the people than
He hath hereto priz'd them at.

MENENIUS.   That 's off, that 's off;
I would you rather had been silent. Please you
To hear Cominius speak?

BRUTUS.   Most willingly;
But yet my caution was more pertinent
Than the rebuke you give it.

MENENIUS.   He loves your people;
But tie him not to be their bedfellow.
Worthy Cominius, speak.
                    Coriolanus rises, and offers to go away
                    Nay, keep your place.

FIRST SENATOR. Sit, Coriolanus; never shame to hear
What you have nobly done.

CORIOLANUS.   Your honours' pardon:
I had rather have my wounds to heal again
Than hear say how I got them.

BRUTUS.   Sir, I hope
My words disbench'd you not.

CORIOLANUS.   No, sir; yet oft,
When blows have made me stay, I fled from words.
You sooth'd not, therefore hurt not. But your people,
I love them as they weigh.

MENENIUS.   Pray now, sit down.

CORIOLANUS. I had rather have one scratch my head
     i' the sun
When the alarum were struck than idly sit
To hear my nothings monster'd.   *Exit*

MENENIUS.   Masters of the people,
Your multiplying spawn how can he flatter,—
That 's thousand to one good one,—when you now see
He had rather venture all his limbs for honour
Than one on 's ear to hear it. Proceed, Cominius.

COMINIUS. I shall lack voice: the deeds of Coriolanus
Should not be utter'd feebly. It is held
That valour is the chiefest virtue, and

Most dignifies the haver: if it be,
The man I speak of cannot in the world
Be singly counterpois'd. At sixteen years,
When Tarquin made a head for Rome, he fought
Beyond the mark of others; our then dictator,
Whom with all praise I point at, saw him fight,
When with his Amazonian chin he drove
The bristled lips before him. He bestrid
An o'er-press'd Roman, and i' the consul's view
Slew three opposers: Tarquin's self he met,
And struck him on his knee: in that day's feats,
When he might act the woman in the scene,
He prov'd best man i' the field, and for his meed
Was brow-bound with the oak. His pupil age
Man-enter'd thus, he waxed like a sea,
And in the brunt of seventeen battles since
He lurch'd all swords of the garland. For this last,
Before and in Corioli, let me say,
I cannot speak him home: he stopp'd the fliers,
And by his rare example made the coward
Turn terror into sport: as weeds before
A vessel under sail, so men obey'd,
And fell below his stem: his sword, death's stamp,
Where it did mark, it took; from face to foot
He was a thing of blood, whose every motion
Was tim'd with dying cries: alone he enter'd
The mortal gate of the city, which he painted
With shunless destiny; aidless came off,
And with a sudden re-enforcement struck
Corioli like a planet. Now all 's his:
When by and by the din of war 'gan pierce
His ready sense; then straight his doubled spirit
Re-quicken'd what in flesh was fatigate,
And to the battle came he; where he did
Run reeking o'er the lives of men, as if
'Twere a perpetual spoil; and till we call'd
Both field and city ours, he never stood
To ease his breast with panting.

MENENIUS.   Worthy man!

FIRST SENATOR. He cannot but with measure fit the hon-
    ours
    Which we devise him.

COMINIUS.   Our spoils he kick'd at,
And look'd upon things precious as they were
The common muck o' the world: he covets less
Than misery itself would give; rewards
His deeds with doing them, and is content
To spend the time to end it.
MENENIUS.   He 's right noble:
Let him be call'd for.
FIRST SENATOR.   Call Coriolanus.
OFFICER. He doth appear.

Re-enter Coriolanus

MENENIUS. The senate, Coriolanus, are well pleas'd
To make thee consul.
CORIOLANUS.   I do owe them still
My life and services.
MENENIUS.   It then remains
That you do speak to the people.
CORIOLANUS.   I do beseech you,
Let me o'erleap that custom, for I cannot
Put on the gown, stand naked, and entreat them,
For my wounds' sake, to give their suffrage: please you,
That I may pass this doing.
SICINIUS.   Sir, the people
Must have their voices; neither will they bate
One jot of ceremony.
MENENIUS.   Put them not to 't:
Pray you, go fit you to the custom, and
Take to you, as your predecessors have,
Your honour with your form.
CORIOLANUS.   It is a part
That I shall blush in acting, and might well
Be taken from the people.
BRUTUS. (*Aside to Sicinius*) Mark you that?
CORIOLANUS. To brag unto them, thus I did, and thus;
Show them the unaching scars which I should hide,
As if I had receiv'd them for the hire
Of their breath only!
MENENIUS.   Do not stand upon 't.
We recommend to you, tribunes of the people,
Our purpose to them; and to our noble consul
Wish we all joy and honour.

SENATORS. To Coriolanus come all joy and honour!
>*Flourish. Exeunt all but Sicinius and Brutus*

BRUTUS. You see how he intends to use the people.

SICINIUS. May they perceive 's intent! He will require
  them,
  As if he did contemn what he requested
  Should be in them to give.

BRUTUS.   Come; we 'll inform them
  Of our proceedings here: on the market-place
  I know they do attend us.   *Exeunt*

SCENE THREE

The Same. The Forum.

Enter several Citizens

FIRST CITIZEN. Once, if he do require our voices, we ought
  not to deny him.

SECOND CITIZEN. We may, sir, if we will.

THIRD CITIZEN. We have power in ourselves to do it, but it
  is a power that we have no power to do; for if he show
  us his wounds, and tell us his deeds, we are to put our
  tongues into those wounds and speak for them; so, if he
  tell us his noble deeds, we must also tell him our noble
  acceptance of them. Ingratitude is monstrous, and for
  the multitude to be ingrateful were to make a monster
  of the multitude; of the which, we being members,
  should bring ourselves to be monstrous members.

FIRST CITIZEN. And to make us no better thought of, a
  little help will serve; for once we stood up about the
  corn, he himself stuck not to call us the many-headed
  multitude.

THIRD CITIZEN. We have been called so of many; not that
  our heads are some brown, some black, some abram,
  some bald, but that our wits are so diversely coloured:
  and truly I think, if all our wits were to issue out of one
  skull, they would fly east, west, north, south; and their
  consent of one direct way should be at once to all the
  points o' the compass.

SECOND CITIZEN. Think you so? Which way do you judge
  my wit would fly?

THIRD CITIZEN. Nay, your wit will not so soon out as another man's will; 'tis strongly wedged up in a block-
head; but if it were at liberty, 'twould, sure, southward.

SECOND CITIZEN. Why that way?

THIRD CITIZEN. To lose itself in a fog; where being three
parts melted away with rotten dews, the fourth would
return for conscience' sake, to help to get thee a wife.

SECOND CITIZEN. You are never without your tricks: you
may, you may.

THIRD CITIZEN. Are you all resolved to give your voices?
But that 's no matter, the greater part carries it. I say, if
he would incline to the people, there was never a
worthier man.

Re-enter Coriolanus, in a gown of humility, and Menenius
Here he comes, and in a gown of humility: mark his behaviour. We are not to stay all together, but to come by
him where he stands, by ones, by twos, and by threes.
He 's to make his requests by particulars; wherein every
one of us has a single honour, in giving him our own
voices with our own tongues: therefore follow me, and
I 'll direct you how you shall go by him.

ALL. Content, content.   *Exeunt Citizens*

MENENIUS. O, sir, you are not right: have you not known
The worthiest men have done 't?

CORIOLANUS.   What must I say?
'I pray, sir,'—Plague upon 't! I cannot bring
My tongue to such a pace. 'Look, sir, my wounds:
I got them in my country's service, when
Some certain of your brethren roar'd and ran
From the noise of our own drums.'

MENENIUS.   O me! the gods!
You must not speak of that: you must desire them
To think upon you.

CORIOLANUS.   Think upon me! Hang 'em!
I would they would forget me, like the virtues
Which our divines lose by 'em.

MENENIUS.   You 'll mar all:
I 'll leave you. Pray you, speak to 'em, I pray you,
In wholesome manner.

CORIOLANUS.   Bid them wash their faces,
And keep their teeth clean.   *Exit Menenius*
          So here comes a brace.

Re-enter two Citizens

You know the cause, sir, of my standing here?

FIRST CITIZEN. We do, sir; tell us what hath brought you to 't.

CORIOLANUS. Mine own desert.

SECOND CITIZEN. Your own desert!

CORIOLANUS. Ay, not mine own desire.

FIRST CITIZEN. How! not your own desire?

CORIOLANUS. No, sir, 'twas never my desire yet to trouble the poor with begging.

FIRST CITIZEN. You must think, if we give you any thing, we hope to gain by you.

CORIOLANUS. Well, then, I pray, your price o' the consulship?

FIRST CITIZEN. The price is, to ask it kindly.

CORIOLANUS. Kindly! sir, I pray, let me ha 't: I have wounds to show you, which shall be yours in private. Your good voice, sir; what say you?

SECOND CITIZEN. You shall ha 't, worthy sir.

CORIOLANUS. A match, sir. There is in all two worthy voices begged. I have your alms: adieu.

FIRST CITIZEN. But this is something odd.

SECOND CITIZEN. An 'twere to give again,—but 'tis no matter.   *Exeunt the two Citizens*

Re-enter two other Citizens

CORIOLANUS. Pray you now, if it may stand with the tune of your voices that I may be consul, I have here the customary gown.

THIRD CITIZEN. You have deserved nobly of your country, and you have not deserved nobly.

CORIOLANUS. Your enigma?

THIRD CITIZEN. You have been a scourge to her enemies, you have been a rod to her friends; you have not indeed loved the common people.

CORIOLANUS. You should account me the more virtuous that I have not been common in my love. I will, sir, flatter my sworn brother the people, to earn a dearer estimation of them; 'tis a condition they account gentle: and since the wisdom of their choice is rather to have my hat than my heart, I will practise the insinuating nod, and be off to them most counterfeitly; that is, sir, I will counterfeit the bewitchment of some popular man, and

give it bountifully to the desirers. Therefore, beseech
you, I may be consul.

FOURTH CITIZEN. We hope to find you our friend, and
therefore give you our voices heartily.

THIRD CITIZEN. You have received many wounds for your
country.

CORIOLANUS. I will not seal your knowledge with showing
them. I will make much of your voices, and so trouble
you no further.

BOTH CITIZENS. The gods give you joy, sir, heartily!

Exeunt

CORIOLANUS. Most sweet voices!
Better it is to die, better to starve,
Than crave the hire which first we do deserve.
Why in this woolvish toge should I stand here,
To beg of Hob and Dick, that do appear,
Their needless vouches? Custom calls me to 't:
What custom wills, in all things should we do 't,
The dust on antique time would lie unswept,
And mountainous error be too highly heap'd
For truth to o'er-peer. Rather than fool it so,
Let the high office and the honour go
To one that would do thus. I am half through;
The one part suffer'd, the other will I do.
Here come more voices.

Re-enter three other Citizens

Your voices: for your voices I have fought;
Watch'd for your voices; for your voices bear
Of wounds two dozen odd; battles thrice six
I have seen and heard of; for your voices have
Done many things, some less, some more; your voices:
Indeed, I would be consul.

FIFTH CITIZEN. He has done nobly and cannot go without
any honest man's voice.

SIXTH CITIZEN. Therefore let him be consul. The gods give
him joy, and make him good friend to the people!

ALL. Amen, amen.
God save thee, noble consul!   *Exeunt Citizens*

CORIOLANUS.   Worthy voices!

Re-enter Menenius, with Brutus and Sicinius

MENENIUS. You have stood your limitation; and the tribunes

Endue you with the people's voice: remains
That, in the official marks invested, you
Anon do meet the senate.
CORIOLANUS.   Is this done?
SICINIUS. The custom of request you have discharg'd:
The people do admit you, and are summon'd
To meet anon, upon your approbation.
CORIOLANUS. Where? at the senate-house?
SICINIUS.   There, Coriolanus.
CORIOLANUS. May I change these garments?
SICINIUS. You may, sir.
CORIOLANUS. That I'll straight do; and, knowing myself
again,
Repair to the senate-house.
MENENIUS. I'll keep you company. Will you along?
BRUTUS. We stay here for the people.
SICINIUS.   Fare you well.
Exeunt Coriolanus and Menenius
He has it now; and by his looks, methinks,
'Tis warm at's heart.
BRUTUS.   With a proud heart he wore
His humble weeds. Will you dismiss the people?
Re-enter Citizens
SICINIUS. How now, my masters! have you chose this man?
FIRST CITIZEN. He has our voices, sir.
BRUTUS. We pray the gods he may deserve your love.
SECOND CITIZEN. Amen, sir. To my poor unworthy notice,
He mock'd us when he begg'd our voices.
THIRD CITIZEN.   Certainly,
He flouted us downright.
FIRST CITIZEN. No, 'tis his kind of speech; he did not mock
us.
SECOND CITIZEN. Not one amongst us, save yourself but
says
He used us scornfully: he should have show'd us
His marks of merit, wounds receiv'd for's country.
SICINIUS. Why, so he did, I am sure.
ALL.   No, no; no man saw 'em.
THIRD CITIZEN. He said he had wounds, which he could
show in private;
And with his hat, thus waving it in scorn,
'I would be consul,' says he: 'aged custom,

But by your voices, will not so permit me;
Your voices therefore:' when we granted that,
Here was, 'I thank you for your voices, thank you,
Your most sweet voices: now you have left your voices
I have no further with you.' Was not this mockery?

SICINIUS. Why, either were you ignorant to see 't,
Or, seeing it, of such childish friendliness
To yield your voices?

BRUTUS.   Could you not have told him
As you were lesson'd, when he had no power,
But was a petty servant to the state,
He was your enemy, ever spake against
Your liberties and the charters that you bear
I' the body of the weal; and now, arriving
A place of potency and sway o' the state,
If he should still malignantly remain
Fast foe to the plebeii, your voices might
Be curses to yourselves? You should have said
That as his worthy deeds did claim no less
Than what he stood for, so his gracious nature
Would think upon you for your voices and
Translate his malice towards you into love,
Standing your friendly lord.

SICINIUS.   Thus to have said,
As you were fore-advis'd, had touch'd his spirit
And tried his inclination; from him pluck'd
Either his gracious promise, which you might,
As cause had call'd you up, have held him to;
Or else it would have gall'd his surly nature,
Which easily endures not article
Tying him to aught; so, putting him to rage,
You should have ta'en the advantage of his choler,
And pass'd him unelected.

BRUTUS.   Did you perceive
He did solicit you in free contempt
When he did need your loves, and do you think
That his contempt shall not be bruising to you
When he hath power to crush? Why, had your bodies
No heart among you? or had you tongues to cry
Against the rectorship of judgment?

SICINIUS.   Have you
Ere now denied the asker? and now again

Of him that did not ask, but mock, bestow
Your su'd-for tongues?
THIRD CITIZEN. He 's not confirm'd; we may deny him yet.
SECOND CITIZEN. And will deny him:
I 'll have five hundred voices of that sound.
FIRST CITIZEN. Ay, twice five hundred and their friends to
     piece 'em.
BRUTUS. Get you hence instantly, and tell those friends,
They have chose a consul that will from them take
Their liberties; make them of no more voice
Than dogs that are as often beat for barking
As therefore kept to do so.
SICINIUS.   Let them assemble;
And, on a safer judgment, all revoke
Your ignorant election. Enforce his pride,
And his old hate unto you: besides, forget not
With what contempt he wore the humble weed;
How in his suit he scorn'd you; but your loves,
Thinking upon his services, took from you
The apprehension of his present portance,
Which most gibingly, ungravely, he did fashion
After the inveterate hate he bears you.
BRUTUS.   Lay
A fault on us, your tribunes; that we labour'd,—
No impediment between,—but that you must
Cast your election on him.
SICINIUS.   Say, you chose him
More after our commandment than as guided
By your own true affections; and that your minds,
Pre-occupied with what you rather must do
Than what you should, made you against the grain
To voice him consul: lay the fault on us.
BRUTUS. Ay, spare us not. Say we read lectures to you,
How youngly he began to serve his country,
How long continu'd, and what stock he springs of,
The noble house o' the Marcians, from whence came
That Ancus Marcius, Numa's daughter's son,
Who, after great Hostilius, here was king;
Of the same house Publius and Quintus were,
That our best water brought by conduits hither;
And Censorinus, that was so surnam'd,—
And nobly nam'd so, twice being censor,—

Was his great ancestor.

SICINIUS.   One thus descended,
That hath, beside, well in his person wrought
To be set high in place, we did commend
To your remembrances: but you have found,
Scaling his present bearing with his past,
That he 's your fixed enemy, and revoke
Your sudden approbation.

BRUTUS.   Say you ne'er had done 't—
Harp on that still—but by our putting on;
And presently, when you have drawn your number,
Repair to the Capitol.

ALL.   We will so; almost all
Repent in their election.   *Exeunt Citizens*

BRUTUS.   Let them go on;
This mutiny were better put in hazard
Than stay, past doubt, for greater.
If, as his nature is, he fall in rage
With their refusal, both observe and answer
The vantage of his anger.

SICINIUS.   To the Capitol, come:
We will be there before the stream o' the people;
And this shall seem, as partly 'tis, their own,
Which we have goaded onward.   *Exeunt*

ACT THREE

SCENE ONE

Rome. A Street.

Cornets. Enter Coriolanus, Menenius, Cominius, Titus Lartius, Senators, and Patricians

CORIOLANUS. Tullus Aufidius then had made new head?

LARTIUS. He had, my lord; and that it was which caus'd
Our swifter composition.

CORIOLANUS. So then the Volsces stand but as at first,
Ready, when time shall prompt them, to make road
Upon 's again.

COMINIUS.   They are worn, lord consul, so,
That we shall hardly in our ages see
Their banners wave again.

CORIOLANUS.   Saw you Aufidius?

LARTIUS. On safe-guard he came to me; and did curse
Against the Volsces, for they had so vilely
Yielded the town: he is retir'd to Antium.

CORIOLANUS. Spoke he of me?

LARTIUS.   He did my lord.

CORIOLANUS.   How? what?

LARTIUS. How often he had met you, sword to sword;
That of all things upon the earth he hated
Your person most, that he would pawn his fortunes
To hopeless restitution, so he might
Be call'd your vanquisher.

CORIOLANUS.   At Antium lives he?

LARTIUS. At Antium.

CORIOLANUS. I wish I had a cause to seek him there.
To oppose his hatred fully. Welcome home.

Enter Sicinius and Brutus

Behold! these are the tribunes of the people,
The tongues o' the common mouth: I do despise them

For they do prank them in authority
Against all noble sufferance.

SICINIUS.   Pass no further.

CORIOLANUS. Ha! what is that?

BRUTUS. It will be dangerous to go on: no further.

CORIOLANUS. What makes this change?

MENENIUS.   The matter?

COMINIUS. Hath he not pass'd the noble and the common?

BRUTUS. Cominius, no.

CORIOLANUS.   Have I had children's voices?

FIRST SENATOR. Tribunes, give way; he shall to the market-
place.

BRUTUS. The people are incens'd against him.

SICINIUS.   Stop,
Or all will fall in broil.

CORIOLANUS.   Are these your herd?
Must these have voices, that can yield them now,
And straight disclaim their tongues? What are your of-
fices?
You being their mouths, why rule you not their teeth?
Have you not set them on?

MENENIUS.   Be calm, be calm.

CORIOLANUS. It is a purpos'd thing, and grows by plot,
To curb the will of the nobility:
Suffer 't, and live with such as cannot rule
Nor ever will be rul'd.

BRUTUS.   Call 't not a plot:
The people cry you mock'd them, and of late,
When corn was given them gratis, you repin'd;
Scandall'd the suppliants for the people, call'd them
Time-pleasers, flatterers, foes to nobleness.

CORIOLANUS. Why, this was known before.

BRUTUS.   Not to them all.

CORIOLANUS. Have you inform'd them sithence?

BRUTUS.   How! I inform them!

CORIOLANUS. You are like to do such business.

BRUTUS.   Not unlike,
Each way, to better yours.

CORIOLANUS. Why then should I be consul? By yond
clouds,
Let me deserve so ill as you, and make me
Your fellow tribune.

SICINIUS.   You show too much of that
For which the people stir; if you will pass
To where you are bound, you must inquire your way,
Which you are out of, with a gentler spirit;
Or never be so noble as a consul
Nor yoke with him for tribune.
MENENIUS.   Let 's be calm.
COMINIUS. The people are abus'd; set on. This paltering
Becomes not Rome, nor has Coriolanus
Deserv'd this so dishonour'd rub, laid falsely
I' the plain way of his merit.
CORIOLANUS.   Tell me of corn!
This was my speech, and I will speak 't again,—
MENENIUS. Not now, not now.
FIRST SENATOR.   Not in this heat, sir, now.
CORIOLANUS. Now, as I live, I will. My nobler friends,
I crave their pardons:
For the mutable, rank-scented many, let them
Regard me as I do not flatter, and
Therein behold themselves: I say again,
In soothing them we nourish 'gainst our senate
The cockle of rebellion, insolence, sedition,
Which we ourselves have plough'd for, sow'd and scat-
ter'd,
By mingling them with us, the honour'd number;
Who lack'd not virtue, no, nor power, but that
Which they have given to beggars.
MENENIUS.   Well, no more.
FIRST SENATOR. No more words, we beseech you.
CORIOLANUS.   How! no more!
As for my country I have shed my blood,
Not fearing outward force, so shall my lungs
Coin words till they decay against those measles,
Which we disdain should tetter us, yet sought
The very way to catch them.
BRUTUS.   You speak o' the people,
As if you were a god to punish, not
A man of their infirmity.
SICINIUS.   'Twere well
We let the people know 't.
MENENIUS.   What, what? his choler?
CORIOLANUS. Choler!

Were I as patient as the midnight sleep,
By Jove, 'twould be my mind!

SICINIUS.   It is a mind
That shall remain a poison where it is
Not poison any further.

CORIOLANUS.   Shall remain!
Hear you this Triton of the minnows? mark you
His absolute 'shall'?

COMINIUS.   'Twas from the canon.

CORIOLANUS.   'Shall!'
O good but most unwise patricians! why,
You grave but reckless senators, have you thus
Given Hydra here to choose an officer,
That with his peremptory 'shall,' being but
The horn and noise o' the monster's, wants not spirit
To say he 'll turn your current in a ditch,
And make your channel his? If he have power,
Then vail your ignorance; if none, awake
Your dangerous lenity. If you are learned,
Be not as common fools; if you are not,
Let them have cushions by you. You are plebeians
If they be senators; and they are no less,
When, both your voices blended, the great'st taste
Most palates theirs. They choose their magistrate,
And such a one as he, who puts his 'shall,'
His popular 'shall,' against a graver bench
Than ever frown'd in Greece. By Jove himself!
It makes the consuls base; and my soul aches
To know, when two authorities are up,
Neither supreme, how soon confusion
May enter 'twixt the gap of both and take
The one by the other.

COMINIUS.   Well, on to the market-place.

CORIOLANUS. Whoever gave that counsel, to give forth
The corn o' the store-house gratis, as 'twas us'd
Sometime in Greece,—

MENENIUS.   Well, well; no more of that.

CORIOLANUS. Though there the people had more absolute
    power,
I say, they nourish'd disobedience, fed
The ruin of the state.

BRUTUS.   Why, shall the people give

One that speaks thus their voice?

CORIOLANUS.   I 'll give my reasons,
More worthier than their voices. They know the corn
Was not our recompense, resting well assur'd
They ne'er did service for 't. Being press'd to the war,
Even when the navel of the state was touch'd,
They would not thread the gates: this kind of service
Did not deserve corn gratis. Being i' the war,
Their mutinies and revolts, wherein they show'd
Most valour, spoke not for them. The accusation
Which they have often made against the senate,
All cause unborn, could never be the motive
Of our so frank donation. Well, what then?
How shall this bisson multitude digest
The senate's courtesy? Let deeds express
What 's like to be their words: 'We did request it;
We are the greater poll, and in true fear
They gave us our demands.' Thus we debase
The nature of our seats, and make the rabble
Call our cares, fears; which will in time break ope
The locks o' the senate, and bring in the crows
To peck the eagles.

MENENIUS.   Come, enough.

BRUTUS. Enough, with over-measure.

CORIOLANUS.   No, take more:
What may be sworn by, both divine and human,
Seal what I end withal! This double worship,
Where one part does disdain with cause, the other
Insult without all reason; where gentry, title, wisdom,
Cannot conclude, but by the yea and no
Of general ignorance,—it must omit
Real necessities, and give way the while
To unstable slightness: purpose so barr'd, it follows
Nothing is done to purpose. Therefore, beseech you,—
You that will be less fearful than discreet,
That love the fundamental part of state
More than you doubt the change on 't, that prefer
A noble life before a long, and wish
To jump a body with a dangerous physic
That 's sure of death without it, at once pluck out
The multitudinous tongue; let them not lick
The sweet which is their poison. Your dishonour

Mangles true judgment, and bereaves the state
Of that integrity which should become it,
Not having the power to do the good it would,
For the ill which doth control 't.

BRUTUS.   He has said enough.

SICINIUS. He has spoken like a traitor, and shall answer
As traitors do.

CORIOLANUS. Thou wretch! despite o'erwhelm thee!
What should the people do with these bald tribunes?
On whom depending, their obedience fails
To the greater bench. In a rebellion,
When what 's not meet, but what must be, was law,
Then were they chosen: in a better hour,
Let what is meet be said it must be meet,
And throw their power i' the dust.

BRUTUS. Manifest treason!

SICINIUS.   This a consul? no.

BRUTUS. The ædiles, ho! Let him be apprehended.

Enter an Ædile

SICINIUS. Go, call the people; (*Exit Ædile*) in whose name,
myself
Attach thee as a traitorous innovator,
A foe to the public weal: obey, I charge thee,
And follow to thine answer.

CORIOLANUS.   Hence, old goat!

SENATORS. We 'll surety him.

COMINIUS.   Aged sir, hands off.

CORIOLANUS. Hence, rotten thing! or I shall shake thy
bones
Out of thy garments.

SICINIUS.   Help, ye citizens!

Re-enter Ædiles, with Others, and a rabble of Citizens

MENENIUS. On both sides more respect.

SICINIUS. Here 's he that would take from you all your
power.

BRUTUS. Seize him, ædiles!

CITIZENS. Down with him!—down with him!—

SENATORS. Weapons!—weapons!—weapons!—
                    They all bustle about Coriolanus, crying
Tribunes!—patricians!—citizens!—What ho!—
Sicinius!—Brutus!—Coriolanus!—Citizens!
Peace!—Peace!—Peace!—Stay!—Hold!—Peace!

MENENIUS. What is about to be?—I am out of breath;
  Confusion 's near; I cannot speak. You, tribunes
  To the people! Coriolanus, patience!
  Speak, good Sicinius.
SICINIUS.   Hear me, people; peace!
CITIZENS. Let 's hear our tribune:—Peace!—Speak, speak,
    speak.
SICINIUS. You are at point to lose your liberties:
  Marcius would have all from you; Marcius,
  Whom late you have nam'd for consul.
MENENIUS.   Fie, fie, fie!
  This is the way to kindle, not to quench.
FIRST SENATOR. To unbuild the city and to lay all flat.
SICINIUS. What is the city but the people?
CITIZENS.   True,
  The people are the city.
BRUTUS. By the consent of all, we were establish'd
  The people's magistrates.
CITIZENS.   You so remain.
MENENIUS. And so are like to do.
COMINIUS. That is the way to lay the city flat;
  To bring the roof to the foundation,
  And bury all, which yet distinctly ranges,
  In heaps and piles of ruin.
SICINIUS.   This deserves death.
BRUTUS. Or let us stand to our authority,
  Or let us lose it. We do here pronounce,
  Upon the part o' the people, in whose power
  We were elected theirs, Marcius is worthy
  Of present death.
SICINIUS.   Therefore lay hold of him;
  Bear him to the rock Tarpeian, and from thence
  Into destruction cast him.
BRUTUS.   Ædiles, seize him!
CITIZENS. Yield, Marcius, yield!
MENENIUS.   Hear me one word;
  Beseech you, tribunes, hear me but a word.
ÆDILES. Peace, peace!
MENENIUS. (*To Brutus*) Be that you seem, truly your
    country's friends,
  And temperately proceed to what you would
  Thus violently redress.

BRUTUS.   Sir, those cold ways,
That seem like prudent helps, are very poisonous
Where the disease is violent. Lay hands upon him,
And bear him to the rock.
CORIOLANUS.   No, I 'll die here.

                              Drawing his sword
There 's some among you have beheld me fighting:
Come, try upon yourselves what you have seen me.
MENENIUS. Down with that sword! Tribunes, withdraw
    awhile.
BRUTUS. Lay hands upon him.
MENENIUS.   Help, Marcius, help,
You that be noble; help him, young and old!
CITIZENS. Down with him!—down with him!

                    In this mutiny the Tribunes,
          the Ædiles, and the People are beat in
MENENIUS. Go, get you to your house; be gone, away!
All will be naught else.
SECOND SENATOR.   Get you gone.
CORIOLANUS.   Stand fast;
We have as many friends as enemies.
MENENIUS. Shall it be put to that?
FIRST SENATOR.   The gods forbid!
I prithee, noble friend, home to thy house;
Leave us to cure this cause.
MENENIUS.   For 'tis a sore upon us,
You cannot tent yourself: be gone, beseech you.
COMINIUS. Come, sir, along with us.
CORIOLANUS. I would they were barbarians,—as they are,
Though in Rome litter'd,—not Romans,—as they are not,
Though calv'd i' the porch o' the Capitol,—
MENENIUS.   Be gone;
Put not your worthy rage into your tongue;
One time will owe another.
CORIOLANUS.   On fair ground
I could beat forty of them.
MENENIUS.   I could myself
Take up a brace o' the best of them; yea, the two trib-
    unes.
COMINIUS. But now 'tis odds beyond arithmetic;
And manhood is call'd foolery when it stands
Against a falling fabric. Will you hence,

Before the tag return? whose rage doth rend
Like interrupted waters and o'erbear
What they are us'd to bear.
MENENIUS.　　　　　　　　　Pray you, be gone.
I 'll try whether my old wit be in request
With those that have but little: this must be patch'd
With cloth of any colour.
COMINIUS.　　　　　　　　　Nay, come away.
　　　　Exeunt Coriolanus, Cominius, and Others
FIRST PATRICIAN. This man has marr'd his fortune.
MENENIUS. His nature is too noble for the world:
He would not flatter Neptune for his trident,
Or Jove for 's power to thunder. His heart 's his mouth:
What his breast forges, that his tongue must vent;
And, being angry, does forget that ever
He heard the name of death.　　　　*A noise within*
Here 's goodly work!
SECOND PATRICIAN. I would they were a-bed!
MENENIUS. I would they were in Tiber! What the venge-
　　ance!
Could he not speak 'em fair?
　　　　Re-enter Brutus and Sicinius, with the rabble
SICINIUS.　　　　　　　　　Where is this viper
That would depopulate the city and
Be every man himself?
MENENIUS　　　　　　　　　You worthy tribunes,—
SICINIUS. He shall be thrown down the Tarpeian rock
With rigorous hands; he hath resisted law,
And therefore law shall scorn him further trial
Than the severity of the public power,
Which he so sets at nought.
FIRST CITIZEN.　　　　　　　He shall well know
The noble tribunes are the people's mouths,
And we their hands.
CITIZENS.　　　　　　　He shall, sure on 't.
MENENIUS.　　　　　　　　　　　　Sir, sir,—
SICINIUS. Peace!
MENENIUS. Do not cry havoc, where you should but hunt
With modest warrant.
SICINIUS.　　　　　　　Sir, how comes 't that you
Have holp to make this rescue?
MENENIUS.　　　　　　　　Hear me speak:

As I do know the consul's worthiness,
So can I name his faults.

SICINIUS.   Consul! what consul?

MENENIUS. The consul Coriolanus.

BRUTUS.   He consul!

CITIZENS. No, no, no, no, no.

MENENIUS. If, by the tribunes' leave, and yours, good
    people,
I may be heard, I would crave a word or two,
The which shall turn you to no further harm
Than so much loss of time.

SICINIUS.   Speak briefly then;
For we are peremptory to dispatch
This viperous traitor. To eject him hence
Were but one danger, and to keep him here
Our certain death; therefore it is decreed
He dies to-night.

MENENIUS.   Now the good gods forbid
That our renowned Rome, whose gratitude
Towards her deserved children is enroll'd
In Jove's own book, like an unnatural dam
Should now eat up her own!

SICINIUS. He 's a disease that must be cut away.

MENENIUS. O! he 's a limb that has but a disease;
Mortal to cut it off; to cure it easy.
What has he done to Rome that 's worthy death?
Killing our enemies, the blood he hath lost,—
Which, I dare vouch, is more than that he hath
By many an ounce,—he dropp'd it for his country;
And what is left, to lose it by his country,
Were to us all, that do 't and suffer it,
A brand to the end o' the world.

SICINIUS.   This is clean kam.

BRUTUS. Merely awry: when he did love his country
It honour'd him.

MENENIUS.   The service of the foot
Being once gangren'd, is not then respected
For what before it was.

BRUTUS.   We 'll hear no more.
Pursue him to his house, and pluck him thence,
Lest his infection, being of catching nature,
Spread further.

MENENIUS.   One word more, one word.
This tiger-footed rage, when it shall find
The harm of unscann'd swiftness, will, too late,
Tie leaden pounds to 's heels. Proceed by process;
Lest parties—as he is belov'd—break out,
And sack great Rome with Romans.

BRUTUS.   If 'twere so,—
SICINIUS. What do ye talk?
Have we not had a taste of his obedience?
Our ædiles smote? ourselves resisted? Come!

MENENIUS. Consider this: he has been bred i' the wars
Since he could draw a sword, and is ill school'd
In bolted language; meal and bran together
He throws without distinction. Give me leave,
I 'll go to him, and undertake to bring him
Where he shall answer by a lawful form,—
In peace,—to his utmost peril.

FIRST SENATOR.   Noble tribunes,
It is the humane way: the other course
Will prove too bloody, and the end of it
Unknown to the beginning.

SICINIUS.   Noble Menenius,
Be you then as the people's officer.
Masters, lay down your weapons.

BRUTUS.   Go not home.
SICINIUS. Meet on the market-place. We 'll attend you
    there:
Where, if you bring not Marcius, we 'll proceed
In our first way.

MENENIUS.   I 'll bring him to you.
    (To the Senators) Let me desire your company. He must
    come,
Or what is worst will follow.

FIRST SENATOR.   Pray you, let 's to him.
                                        Exeunt

SCENE TWO

The Same. A Room in Coriolanus' House.

Enter Coriolanus and Patricians

CORIOLANUS. Let them pull all about mine ears; present me
  Death on the wheel, or at wild horses' heels;
  Or pile ten hills on the Tarpeian rock,
  That the precipitation might down stretch
  Below the beam of sight; yet will I still
  Be thus to them.

FIRST PATRICIAN. You do the nobler.

CORIOLANUS.   I muse my mother
  Does not approve me further, who was wont
  To call them woollen vassals, things created
  To buy and sell with groats, to show bare heads
  In congregations, to yawn, be still, and wonder,
  When one but of my ordinance stood up
  To speak of peace or war.
                Enter Volumnia
                      I talk of you:
  Why did you wish me milder? Would you have me
  False to my nature? Rather say I play
  The man I am.

VOLUMNIA.   O! sir, sir, sir,
  I would have had you put your power well on
  Before you had worn it out.

CORIOLANUS.   Let go.

VOLUMNIA. You might have been enough the man you are
  With striving less to be so: lesser had been
  The thwarting of your dispositions if
  You had not show'd them how you were dispos'd,
  Ere they lack'd power to cross you.

CORIOLANUS.   Let them hang.

VOLUMNIA. Ay, and burn too.
            Enter Menenius and Senators

MENENIUS. Come, come; you have been too rough, some-
      thing too rough;
  You must return and mend it.

FIRST SENATOR.   There 's no remedy;
  Unless, by not so doing, our good city

Cleave in the midst, and perish.

VOLUMNIA.   Pray be counsell'd.
  I have a heart of mettle, apt as yours.
  But yet a brain that leads my use of anger
  To better vantage.

MENENIUS.   Well said, noble woman!
  Before he should thus stoop to the herd, but that
  The violent fit o' the time craves it as physic
  For the whole state, I would put mine armour on,
  Which I can scarcely bear.

CORIOLANUS.   What must I do?

MENENIUS. Return to the tribunes.

CORIOLANUS.   Well, what then? what then?

MENENIUS. Repent what you have spoke.

CORIOLANUS. For them! I cannot do it to the gods;
  Must I then do 't to them?

VOLUMNIA.   You are too absolute;
  Though therein you can never be too noble,
  But when extremities speak. I have heard you say,
  Honour and policy, like unsever'd friends,
  I' the war do grow together: grant that, and tell me,
  In peace what each of them by the other lose,
  That they combine not there.

CORIOLANUS.   Tush, tush!

MENENIUS.   A good demand.

VOLUMNIA. If it be honour in your wars to seem
  The same you are not,—which, for your best ends,
  You adopt your policy,—how is it less or worse,
  That it shall hold companionship in peace
  With honour, as in war, since that to both
  It stands in like request?

CORIOLANUS.   Why force you this?

VOLUMNIA. Because that now it lies you on to speak
  To the people; not by your own instruction,
  Nor by the matter which your heart prompts you,
  But with such words that are but rooted in
  Your tongue, though but bastards and syllables
  Of no allowance to your bosom's truth.
  Now, this no more dishonours you at all
  Than to take in a town with gentle words,
  Which else would put you to your fortune and
  The hazard of much blood.

I would dissemble with my nature where
My fortunes and my friends at stake requir'd
I should do so in honour: I am in this,
Your wife, your son, these senators, the nobles;
And you will rather show our general louts
How you can frown than spend a fawn upon 'em,
For the inheritance of their loves and safeguard
Of what that want might ruin.

MENENIUS.   Noble lady!
Come, go with us; speak fair; you may salve so,
Not what is dangerous present, but the loss
Of what is past.

VOLUMNIA.   I prithee now, my son,
Go to them, with this bonnet in thy hand;
And thus far having stretch'd it,—here be with them,
Thy knee bussing the stones,—for in such business
Action is eloquence, and the eyes of the ignorant
More learned than the ears,—waving thy head,
Which often, thus, correcting thy stout heart,
Now humble as the ripest mulberry
That will not hold the handling: or say to them,
Thou art their soldier, and being bred in broils
Hast not the soft way which, thou dost confess,
Were fit for thee to use as they to claim,
In asking their good loves; but thou wilt frame
Thyself, forsooth, hereafter theirs, so far
As thou hast power and person.

MENENIUS.   This but done,
Even as she speaks, why, their hearts were yours;
For they have pardons, being ask'd, as free
As words to little purpose.

VOLUMNIA.   Prithee now,
Go, and be rul'd; although I know thou'hadst rather
Follow thine enemy in a fiery gulf
Than flatter him in a bower. Here is Cominius.

Enter Cominius

COMINIUS. I have been i' the market-place; and, sir, 'tis fit
You make strong party, or defend yourself:
By calmness or by absence: all 's in anger.

MENENIUS. Only fair speech.

COMINIUS.   I think 'twill serve if he
Can thereto frame his spirit.

VOLUMNIA.   He must, and will.
  Prithee now, say you will, and go about it.
CORIOLANUS. Must I go show them my unbarbed sconce?
  Must I with my base tongue give to my noble heart
  A lie that it must bear? Well, I will do 't:
  Yet, were there but this single plot to lose,
  This mould of Marcius, they to dust should grind it,
  And throw 't against the wind. To the market-place!
  You have put me now to such a part which never
  I shall discharge to the life.
COMINIUS.   Come, come, we 'll prompt you.
VOLUMNIA. I prithee now, sweet son, as thou hast said
  My praises made thee first a soldier, so,
  To have my praise for this, perform a part
  Thou hast not done before.
CORIOLANUS.   Well, I must do 't:
  Away, my disposition, and possess me
  Some harlot's spirit! My throat of war be turn'd,
  Which quired with my drum, into a pipe
  Small as a eunuch, or the virgin voice
  That babies lulls asleep! The smiles of knaves
  Tent in my cheeks, and schoolboys' tears take up
  The glasses of my sight! A beggar's tongue
  Make motion through my lips, and my arm'd knees,
  Who bow'd but in my stirrup, bend like his
  That hath receiv'd an alms! I will not do 't,
  Lest I surcease to honour mine own truth,
  And by my body's action teach my mind
  A most inherent baseness.
VOLUMNIA.   At thy choice then:
  To beg of thee it is my more dishonour
  Than thou of them. Come all to ruin; let
  Thy mother rather feel thy pride than fear
  Thy dangerous stoutness, for I mock at death
  With as big heart as thou. Do as thou list,
  Thy valiantness was mine, thou suck'dst it from me
  But owe thy pride thyself.
CORIOLANUS.   Pray, be content:
  Mother, I am going to the market-place;
  Chide me no more. I 'll mountebank their loves,
  Cog their hearts from them, and come home belov'd
  Of all the trades in Rome. Look, I am going:

Commend me to my wife. I 'll return consul,
Or never trust to what my tongue can do
I' the way of flattery further.
VOLUMNIA.   Do your will.   *Exit*
COMINIUS. Away! the tribunes do attend you: arm yourself
To answer mildly; for they are prepar'd
With accusations, as I hear, more strong
Than are upon you yet.
MENENIUS. The word is 'mildly.'
CORIOLANUS.   Pray you, let us go:
Let them accuse me by invention, I
Will answer in mine honour.
MENENIUS.   Ay, but mildly.
CORIOLANUS. Well, mildly be it then. Mildly!   *Exeunt*

SCENE THREE

The Same. The Forum.

Enter Sicinius and Brutus

BRUTUS. In this point charge him home, that he affects
Tyrannical power: if he evade us there,
Enforce him with his envy to the people,
And that the spoil got on the Antiates
Was ne'er distributed.—
                    Enter an Ædile
What, will he come?
ÆDILE.   He 's coming.
BRUTUS.   How accompanied?
ÆDILE. With old Menenius, and those senators
That always favour'd him.
SICINIUS.   Have you a catalogue
Of all the voices that we have procur'd,
Set down by the poll?
ÆDILE.   I have; 'tis ready.
SICINIUS. Have you collected them by tribes?
ÆDILE.   I have.
SICINIUS. Assemble presently the people hither;
And when they hear me say, 'It shall be so,
I' the right and strength o' the commons,' be it either
For death, for fine, or banishment, then let them,

If I say, fine, cry 'fine,'—if death, cry 'death,'
Insisting on the old prerogative
And power i' the truth o' the cause.

ÆDILE.   I shall inform them.

BRUTUS. And when such time they have begun to cry,
Let them not cease, but with a din confus'd
Enforce the present execution
Of what we chance to sentence.

ÆDILE.   Very well.

SICINIUS. Make them be strong and ready for this hint.
When we shall hap to give 't them.

BRUTUS.   Go about it.

Exit Ædile

Put him to choler straight. He hath been us'd
Ever to conquer, and to have his worth
Of contradiction: being once chaf'd, he cannot
Be rein'd again to temperance; then he speaks
What 's in his heart; and that is there which looks
With us to break his neck.

SICINIUS.   Well, here he comes.

Enter Coriolanus, Menenius, Cominius, Senators,
and Patricians

MENENIUS. Calmly, I do beseech you.

CORIOLANUS. Ay, as an ostler, that for the poorest piece
Will bear the knave by the volume. The honour'd gods
Keep Rome in safety, and the chairs of justice
Supplied with worthy men! plant love among us!
Throng our large temples with the shows of peace,
And not our streets with war!

FIRST SENATOR.   Amen, amen.

MENENIUS. A noble wish.

Re-enter Ædile, with Citizens

SICINIUS.   Draw near, ye people.

ÆDILE. List to your tribunes; audience; peace! I say.

CORIOLANUS. First, hear me speak.

BOTH TRIBUNES.   Well, say, Peace, ho!

CORIOLANUS. Shall I be charg'd no further than this present?
Must all determine here?

SICINIUS.   I do demand,
If you submit you to the people's voices,
Allow their officers, and are content

To suffer lawful censure for such faults
As shall be prov'd upon you?

CORIOLANUS.   I am content.

MENENIUS. Lo! citizens, he says he is content:
The warlike service he has done, consider; think
Upon the wounds his body bears, which show
Like graves i' the holy churchyard.

CORIOLANUS.   Scratches with briers,
Scars to move laughter only.

MENENIUS.   Consider further,
That when he speaks not like a citizen,
You find him like a soldier: do not take
His rougher accents for malicious sounds,
But, as I say, such as become a soldier,
Rather than envy you.

COMINIUS. (*To Coriolanus*) Well, well; no more.

CORIOLANUS. What is the matter,
That being pass'd for consul with full voice
I am so dishonour'd that the very hour
You take it off again?

SICINIUS.   Answer to us.

CORIOLANUS. Say, then: 'tis true, I ought so.

SICINIUS. We charge you, that you have contriv'd to take
From Rome all season'd office, and to wind
Yourself into a power tyrannical;
For which you are a traitor to the people.

CORIOLANUS. How! Traitor!

MENENIUS.   Nay, temperately; your promise.

CORIOLANUS. The fires i' the lowest hell fold-in the people!
Call me their traitor! Thou injurious tribune!
Within thine eyes sat twenty thousand deaths,
In thy hands clutch'd as many millions, in
Thy lying tongue both numbers, I would say
'Thou liest' unto thee with a voice as free
As I do pray the gods.

SICINIUS.   Mark you this, people?

CITIZENS. To the rock.—to the rock with him!

SICINIUS.   Peace!
We need not put new matter to his charge:
What you have seen him do, and heard him speak,
Beating your officers, cursing yourselves,
Opposing laws with strokes, and here defying

Those whose great power must try him; even this,
So criminal and in such capital kind,
Deserves the extremest death.

BRUTUS.   But since he hath
Serv'd well for Rome,—

CORIOLANUS.   What do you prate of service?

BRUTUS. I talk of that, that know it.

CORIOLANUS.   You!

MENENIUS. Is this the promise that you made your mother?

COMINIUS. Know, I pray you,—

CORIOLANUS.   I 'll know no further:
Let them pronounce the steep Tarpeian death,
Vagabond exile, flaying, pent to linger
But with a grain a day, I would not buy
Their mercy at the price of one fair word,
Nor check my courage for what they can give,
To have 't with saying 'Good-morrow.'

SICINIUS.   For that he has,—
As much as in him lies,—from time to time
Envied against the people, seeking means
To pluck away their power, as now at last
Given hostile strokes, and that not in the presence
Of dreaded justice, but on the ministers
That do distribute it; in the name o' the people,
And in the power of us the tribunes, we,
Even from this instant, banish him our city,
In peril of precipitation
From off the rock Tarpeian, never more
To enter our Rome gates: i' the people's name,
I say, it shall be so.

CITIZENS. It shall be so,—It shall be so,—Let him away.—
He 's banish'd, and it shall be so.

COMINIUS. Hear me, my masters, and my common
     friends,—

SICINIUS. He 's sentenc'd; no more hearing.

COMINIUS.   Let me speak:
I have been consul, and can show for Rome
Her enemies' marks upon me. I do love
My country's good with a respect more tender,
More holy, and profound, than mine own life,
My dear wife's estimate, her womb's increase,
And treasure of my loins; then if I would

    Speak that—

SICINIUS.   We know your drift: speak what?

BRUTUS. There 's no more to be said, but he is banish'd,
    As enemy to the people and his country:
    It shall be so.

CITIZENS.   It shall be so,—it shall be so.

CORIOLANUS. You common cry of curs! whose breath I hate
    As reek o' the rotten fens, whose loves I prize
    As the dead carcases of unburied men
    That do corrupt my air, I banish you;
    And here remain with your uncertainty!
    Let every feeble rumour shake your hearts!
    Your enemies, with nodding of their plumes,
    Fan you into despair! Have the power still
    To banish your defenders; till at length
    Your ignorance,—which finds not, till it feels,—
    Making but reservation of yourselves,—
    Still your own foes,—deliver you as most
    Abated captives to some nation
    That won you without blows! Despising,
    For you, the city, thus I turn my back:
    There is a world elsewhere.

                        Exeunt Coriolanus,
        Cominius, Menenius, Senators, and Patricians

ÆDILE. The people's enemy is gone, is gone!

CITIZENS.   Our enemy is banish'd!—he is gone!—
  Hoo! hoo!   *They all shout and throw up their caps*

SICINIUS. Go, see him out at gates, and follow him,
    As he hath follow'd you, with all despite;
    Give him deserv'd vexation. Let a guard
    Attend us through the city.

CITIZENS. Come, come,—let us see him out at gates! come!
    The gods preserve our noble tribunes! Come!   *Exeunt*

CORIOLANUS.   I would not buy
Their mercy at the price of one fair word

ACT FOUR

SCENE ONE

Rome. Before a Gate of the City.

Enter Coriolanus, Volumnia, Virgilia, Menenius, Cominius, and several young Patricians

CORIOLANUS. Come, leave your tears: a brief farewell: the beast
With many heads butts me away. Nay, mother,
Where is your ancient courage? You were us'd,
To say extremity was the trier of spirits;
That common chances common men could bear;
That when the sea was calm all boats alike
Show'd mastership in floating; fortune's blows,
When most struck home, being gentle wounded, craves
A noble cunning: you were us'd to load me
With precepts that would make invincible
The heart that conn'd them.
VIRGILIA. O heavens! O heavens!
CORIOLANUS.   Nay, I prithee, woman,—
VOLUMNIA. Now the red pestilence strike all trades in Rome,
And occupations perish!
CORIOLANUS.   What, what, what!
I shall be lov'd when I am lack'd. Nay, mother,
Resume that spirit, when you were wont to say,
If you had been the wife of Hercules,
Six of his labours you'd have done, and sav'd
Your husband so much sweat. Cominius,
Droop not; adieu. Farewell, my wife! my mother!
I 'll do well yet. Thou old and true Menenius,
Thy tears are salter than a younger man's,
And venomous to thine eyes. My sometime general,
I have seen thee stern, and thou hast oft beheld

Heart-hardening spectacles; tell these sad women
'Tis fond to wail inevitable strokes
As 'tis to laugh at them. My mother, you wot well
My hazards still have been your solace; and
Believe 't not lightly,—though I go alone
Like to a lonely dragon, that his fen
Makes fear'd and talk'd of more than seen,—your son
Will or exceed the common or be caught
With cautelous baits and practice.

VOLUMNIA.   My first son,
Whither wilt thou go? Take good Cominius
With thee awhile: determine on some course,
More than a wild expouture to each chance
That starts i' the way before thee.

CORIOLANUS.   O the gods!

COMINIUS. I 'll follow thee a month, devise with thee
Where thou shalt rest, that thou mayst hear of us,
And we of thee: so, if the time thrust forth
A cause for thy repeal, we shall not send
O'er the vast world to seek a single man,
And lose advantage, which doth ever cool,
I' the absence of the needer.

CORIOLANUS.   Fare ye well:
Thou hast years upon thee; and thou art too full
Of the wars' surfeits, to go rove with one
That 's yet unbruis'd: bring me but out at gate.
Come, my sweet wife, my dearest mother, and
My friends of noble touch, when I am forth,
Bid me farewell, and smile. I pray you, come.
While I remain above the ground you shall
Hear from me still; and never of me aught
But what is like me formerly.

MENENIUS.   That 's worthily
As any ear can hear. Come, let 's not weep.
If I could shake off but one seven years
From these old arms and legs, by the good gods,
I'd with thee every foot.

CORIOLANUS.   Give me thy hand:
Come.   *Exeunt*

SCENE TWO

The Same. A Street near the Gate.

Enter Sicinius, Brutus, and an Ædile

SICINIUS. Bid them all home; he 's gone, and we 'll no fur-
 ther.
 The nobility are vex'd, whom we see have sided
 In his behalf.
BRUTUS.   Now we have shown our power,
 Let us seem humbler after it is done
 Than when it was a-doing.
SICINIUS.   Bid them home;
 Say their great enemy is gone, and they
 Stand in their ancient strength.
BRUTUS.   Dismiss them home.
                Exit Ædile

Enter Volumnia, Virgilia, and Menenius
 Here comes his mother.
SICINIUS.   Let 's not meet her.
BRUTUS.   Why?
SICINIUS. They say she 's mad.
BRUTUS. They have ta'en note of us: keep on your way.
VOLUMNIA. O! you 're well met. The hoarded plague o' the
 gods
 Requite your love!
MENENIUS.   Peace, peace! be not so loud.
VOLUMNIA. If that I could for weeping, you should hear,—
 Nay, and you shall hear some. (*To Brutus*) Will you be
 gone?
VIRGILIA. (*To Sicinius*) You shall stay too: I would I had
 the power
 To say so to my husband.
SICINIUS.   Are you mankind?
VOLUMNIA. Ay, fool; is that a shame? Note but this fool.
 Was not a man my father? Hadst thou foxship
 To banish him that struck more blows for Rome
 Than thou hast spoken words?
SICINIUS.   O blessed heavens!
VOLUMNIA. More noble blows than ever thou wise words;
 And for Rome's good. I 'll tell thee what; yet go:

Nay, but thou shalt stay too: I would my son
Were in Arabia, and thy tribe before him,
His good sword in his hand.

SICINIUS.   What then?

VIRGILIA.   What then!
He 'd make an end of thy posterity.

VOLUMNIA. Bastards and all.
Good man, the wounds that he does bear for Rome!

MENENIUS. Come, come: peace!

SICINIUS. I would he had continu'd to his country
As he began, and not unknit himself
The noble knot he made.

BRUTUS.   I would he had.

VOLUMNIA. 'I would he had'! 'Twas you incens'd the
rabble:
Cats, that can judge as fitly of his worth
As I can of those mysteries which heaven
Will not have earth to know.

BRUTUS.   Pray, let us go.

VOLUMNIA. Now, pray, sir, get you gone:
You have done a brave deed. Ere you go, hear this:
As far as doth the Capitol exceed
The meanest house in Rome, so far my son,—
This lady's husband here, this, do you see,—
Whom you have banish'd, does exceed you all.

BRUTUS. Well, well, we 'll leave you.

SICINIUS.   Why stay we to be baited
With one that wants her wits?

VOLUMNIA.   Take my prayers with you.
                                Exeunt Tribunes
I would the gods had nothing else to do
But to confirm my curses! Could I meet 'em
But once a day, it would unclog my heart
Of what lies heavy to 't.

MENENIUS.   You have told them home,
And, by my troth, you have cause. You'll sup with me?

VOLUMNIA. Anger's my meat; I sup upon myself,
And so shall starve with feeding. Come, let 's go.
Leave this faint puling and lament as I do,
In anger, Juno-like. Come, come, come.

MENENIUS. Fie, fie, fie!
                                        Exeunt

SCENE THREE

A Highway between Rome and Antium.

Enter a Roman and a Volsce, meeting

ROMAN. I know you well, sir, and you know me: your name I think is Adrian.

VOLSCE. It is so, sir: truly, I have forgot you.

ROMAN. I am a Roman; and my services are, as you are, against 'em: know you me yet?

VOLSCE. Nicanor? No.

ROMAN. The same, sir.

VOLSCE. You had more beard, when I last saw you; but your favour is well approved by your tongue. What 's the news in Rome? I have a note from the Volscian state to find you out there: you have well saved me a day's journey.

ROMAN. There hath been in Rome strange insurrections: the people against the senators, patricians, and nobles.

VOLSCE. Hath been! Is it ended then? Our state thinks not so; they are in a most warlike preparation, and hope to come upon them in the heat of their division.

ROMAN. The main blaze of it is past, but a small thing would make it flame again. For the nobles receive so to heart the banishment of that worthy Coriolanus, that they are in a ripe aptness to take all power from the people and to pluck from them their tribunes for ever. This lies glowing, I can tell you, and is almost mature for the violent breaking out.

VOLSCE. Coriolanus banished!

ROMAN. Banished, sir.

VOLSCE. You will be welcome with this intelligence, Nicanor.

ROMAN. The day serves well for them now. I have heard it said, the fittest time to corrupt a man's wife is when she 's fallen out with her husband. Your noble Tullus Aufidius will appear well in these wars, his great opposer, Coriolanus, being now in no request of his country.

VOLSCE. He cannot choose. I am most fortunate, thus accidentally to encounter you: you have ended my business, and I will merrily accompany you home.

ROMAN. I shall, between this and supper, tell you most strange things from Rome; all tending to the good of their adversaries. Have you an army ready, say you?

VOLSCE. A most royal one: the centurions and their charges distinctly billeted, already in the entertainment, and to be on foot at an hour's warning.

ROMAN. I am joyful to hear of their readiness, and am the man, I think, that shall set them in present action. So, sir, heartily well met, and most glad of your company.

VOLSCE. You take my part from me, sir; I have the most cause to be glad of yours.

ROMAN. Well, let us go together. *Exeunt*

SCENE FOUR

Antium. Before Aufidius' House.

Enter Coriolanus, in mean apparel, disguised and muffled

CORIOLANUS. A goodly city is this Antium. City,
'Tis I that made thy widows: many an heir
Of these fair edifices 'fore my wars
Have I heard groan and drop: then, know me not,
Lest that thy wives with spits and boys with stones
In puny battle slay me.

Enter a Citizen

Save you, sir.

CITIZEN. And you.

CORIOLANUS. Direct me, if it be your will,
Where great Aufidius lies. Is he in Antium?

CITIZEN. He is, and feasts the nobles of the state
At his house this night.

CORIOLANUS. Which is his house, beseech you?

CITIZEN. This, here before you.

CORIOLANUS. Thank you, sir. Farewell.

Exit Citizen

O world! thy slippery turns. Friends now fast sworn,
Whose double bosoms seem to wear one heart,
Whose hours, whose bed, whose meal, and exercise,
Are still together, who twin, as 'twere, in love

Unseparable, shall within this hour,
On a dissension of a doit, break out
To bitterest enmity: so, fellest foes,
Whose passions and whose plots have broke their sleep
To take the one the other, by some chance,
Some trick not worth an egg, shall grow dear friends
And interjoin their issues. So with me:
My birth-place hate I, and my love 's upon
This enemy town. I 'll enter: if he slay me,
He does fair justice; if he give me way,
I 'll do his country service.   *Exit*

SCENE FIVE

The Same. A Hall in Aufidius' House.

Music within. Enter a Servingman

FIRST SERVINGMAN. Wine, wine, wine! What service is
   here! I think our fellows are asleep.   *Exit*
             Enter a Second Servingman
SECOND SERVINGMAN. Where 's Cotus? my master calls for
   him. Cotus!   *Exit*
             Enter Coriolanus
CORIOLANUS. A goodly house: the feast smells well; but I
   Appear not like a guest.
             Re-enter the First Servingman
FIRST SERVINGMAN. What would you have, friend?
   Whence are you? Here 's no place for you: pray, go to
   the door.   *Exit*
CORIOLANUS. I have deserv'd no better entertainment,
   In being Coriolanus.
             Re-enter Second Servingman
SECOND SERVINGMAN. Whence are you, sir? Has the porter
   his eyes in his head, that he gives entrance to such com-
   panions? Pray, get you out.
CORIOLANUS. Away!
SECOND SERVINGMAN. 'Away'! Get you away.
CORIOLANUS. Now, thou art troublesome.
SECOND SERVINGMAN. Are you so brave? I 'll have you
   talked with anon.
       Enter a Third Servingman. Re-enter the First

THIRD SERVINGMAN. What fellow 's this?

FIRST SERVINGMAN. A strange one as ever I looked on: I cannot get him out o' the house: prithee, call my master to him.

THIRD SERVINGMAN. What have you to do here, fellow? Pray you, avoid the house.

CORIOLANUS. Let me but stand; I will not hurt your hearth.

THIRD SERVINGMAN. What are you?

CORIOLANUS. A gentleman.

THIRD SERVINGMAN. A marvellous poor one.

CORIOLANUS. True, so I am.

THIRD SERVINGMAN. Pray you, poor gentleman, take up some other station; here's no place for you; pray you, avoid: come.

CORIOLANUS. Follow your function; go, and batten on cold bits.   *Pushes him away*

THIRD SERVINGMAN. What, you will not? Prithee tell my master what a strange guest he has here.

SECOND SERVINGMAN. And I shall.   *Exit*

THIRD SERVINGMAN. Where dwell'st thou?

CORIOLANUS. Under the canopy.

THIRD SERVINGMAN. 'Under the canopy'!

CORIOLANUS. Ay.

THIRD SERVINGMAN. Where 's that?

CORIOLANUS. I' the city of kites and crows.

THIRD SERVINGMAN. 'I' the city of kites and crows'! What an ass it is! Then thou dwell'st with daws too?

CORIOLANUS. No; I serve not thy master.

THIRD SERVINGMAN. How sir! Do you meddle with my master?

CORIOLANUS. Ay; 'tis an honester service than to meddle with thy mistress.

Thou prat'st, and prat'st: serve with thy trencher. Hence.
                                           Beats him away

Enter Aufidius and First Servingman

AUFIDIUS. Where is this fellow?

SECOND SERVINGMAN. Here, sir: I 'd have beaten him like a dog, but for disturbing the lords within.

AUFIDIUS. Whence com'st thou? what wouldst thou? Thy name?

Why speak'st not? Speak, man: what 's thy name?

CORIOLANUS. (*Unmuffling*) If, Tullus,

Not yet thou know'st me, and, seeing me, dost not
Think me for the man I am, necessity
Commands me name myself.
AUFIDIUS.   What is thy name?
                                        Servants retire
CORIOLANUS. A name unmusical to the Volscians' ears,
And harsh in sound to thine.
AUFIDIUS.   Say, what's thy name?
Thou hast a grim appearance, and thy face
Bears a command in 't; though thy tackle's torn,
Thou show'st a noble vessel. What 's thy name?
CORIOLANUS. Prepare thy brow to frown. Know'st thou me
    yet?
AUFIDIUS. I know thee not. Thy name?
CORIOLANUS. My name is Caius Marcius, who hath done
To thee particularly, and to all the Volsces,
Great hurt and mischief; thereto witness may
My surname, Coriolanus: the painful service,
The extreme dangers, and the drops of blood
Shed for my thankless country, are requited
But with that surname; a good memory,
And witness of the malice and displeasure
Which thou shouldst bear me: only that name remains;
The cruelty and envy of the people,
Permitted by our dastard nobles, who
Have all forsook me, hath devour'd the rest;
And suffer'd me by the voice of slaves to be
Whoop'd out of Rome. Now this extremity
Hath brought me to thy hearth; not out of hope,
Mistake me not, to save my life, for if
I had fear'd death, of all the men i' the world
I would have 'voided thee; but in mere spite,
To be full quit of those my banishers,
Stand I before thee here. Then if thou hast
A heart of wreak in thee, that will revenge
Thine own particular wrongs and stop those maims
Of shame seen through thy country, speed thee straight,
And make my misery serve thy turn: so use it,
That my revengeful services may prove
As benefits to thee, for I will fight
Against my canker'd country with the spleen
Of all the under fiends. But if so be

Thou dar'st not this, and that to prove more fortunes
Thou art tir'd, then, in a word, I also am
Longer to live most weary, and present
My throat to thee and to thy ancient malice;
Which not to cut would show thee but a fool,
Since I have ever follow'd thee with hate,
Drawn tuns of blood out of thy country's breast,
And cannot live but to thy shame, unless
It be to do thee service.

AUFIDIUS.   O Marcius, Marcius!
Each word thou hast spoke hath weeded from my heart
A root of ancient envy. If Jupiter
Should from yond cloud speak divine things,
And say, ' 'Tis true,' I'd not believe them more
Than thee, all noble Marcius. Let me twine
Mine arms about that body, where against
My grained ash a hundred times hath broke,
And scarr'd the moon with splinters: here I clip
The anvil of my sword, and do contest
As hotly and as nobly with thy love
As ever in ambitious strength I did
Contend against thy valour. Know thou first,
I lov'd the maid I married; never man
Sigh'd truer breath; but that I see thee here,
Thou noble thing! more dances my rapt heart
Than when I first my wedded mistress saw
Bestride my threshold. Why, thou Mars! I tell thee,
We have a power on foot; and I had purpose
Once more to hew thy target from thy brawn,
Or lose mine arm for 't. Thou hast beat me out
Twelve several times, and I have nightly since
Dreamt of encounters 'twixt thyself and me;
We have been down together in my sleep,
Unbuckling helms, fisting each other's throat,
And wak'd half dead with nothing. Worthy Marcius,
Had we no quarrel else to Rome, but that
Thou art thence banish'd, we would muster all
From twelve to seventy, and, pouring war
Into the bowels of ungrateful Rome,
Like a bold flood o'er-bear. O! come; go in,
And take our friendly senators by the hands,
Who now are here, taking their leaves of me,

Who am prepar'd against your territories,
Though not for Rome itself.

CORIOLANUS.   You bless me, gods!

AUFIDIUS. Therefore, most absolute sir, if thou wilt have
The leading of thine own revenges, take
The one half of my commission, and set down,
As best thou art experienc'd, since thou know'st
Thy country's strength and weakness, thine own ways;
Whether to knock against the gates of Rome,
Or rudely visit them in parts remote,
To fright them, ere destroy. But come in:
Let me command thee first to those that shall
Say yea to thy desires. A thousand welcomes!
And more a friend than e'er an enemy;
Yet, Marcius, that was much. Your hand: most welcome!
                    Exeunt Coriolanus and Aufidius

FIRST SERVINGMAN. (*Advancing*) Here's a strange alteration!

SECOND SERVINGMAN. By my hand, I had thought to have
strucken him with a cudgel; and yet my mind gave me
his clothes made a false report of him.

FIRST SERVINGMAN. What an arm he has! He turned me
about with his finger and his thumb, as one would set
up a top.

SECOND SERVINGMAN. Nay, I knew by his face that there
was something in him: he had, sir, a kind of face, methought,—I cannot tell how to term it.

FIRST SERVINGMAN. He had so; looking as it were,—would
I were hanged but I thought there was more in him than
I could think.

SECOND SERVINGMAN. So did I, I'll be sworn: he is simply
the rarest man i' the world.

FIRST SERVINGMAN. I think he is; but a greater soldier than
he you wot on.

SECOND SERVINGMAN. Who? my master?

FIRST SERVINGMAN. Nay, it's no matter for that.

SECOND SERVINGMAN. Worth six on him.

FIRST SERVINGMAN. Nay, not so neither; but I take him to
be the greater soldier.

SECOND SERVINGMAN. Faith, look you, one cannot tell how
to say that: for the defence of a town our general is excellent.

FIRST SERVINGMAN. Ay, and for an assault too.

Re-enter Third Servingman

THIRD SERVINGMAN. O slaves! I can tell you news; news, you rascals.

FIRST SERVINGMAN. } What, what, what? let 's partake.
SECOND SERVINGMAN. }

THIRD SERVINGMAN. I would not be a Roman, of all nations; I had as lief be a condemned man.

FIRST SERVINGMAN. } Wherefore? wherefore?
SECOND SERVINGMAN. }

THIRD SERVINGMAN. Why, here 's he that was wont to thwack our general, Caius Marcius.

FIRST SERVINGMAN. Why do you say 'thwack our general'?

THIRD SERVINGMAN. I do not say, 'thwack our general'; but he was always good enough for him.

SECOND SERVINGMAN. Come, we are fellows and friends: he was ever too hard for him; I have heard him say so himself.

FIRST SERVINGMAN. He was too hard for him,—directly to say the truth on 't: before Corioli he scotched him and notched him like a carbonado.

SECOND SERVINGMAN. An he had been cannibally given, he might have broiled and eaten him too.

FIRST SERVINGMAN. But, more of thy news.

THIRD SERVINGMAN. Why, he is so made on here within, as if he were son and heir to Mars; set at upper end o' the table; no question asked him by any of the senators, but they stand bald before him. Our general himself makes a mistress of him; sanctifies himself with 's hand, and turns up the white o' the eye to his discourse. But the bottom of the news is, our general is cut i' the middle, and but one half of what he was yesterday, for the other has half, by the entreaty and grant of the whole table. He 'll go, he says, and sowle the porter of Rome gates by the ears: he will mow down all before him, and leave his passage polled.

SECOND SERVINGMAN. And he 's as like to do 't as any man I can imagine.

THIRD SERVINGMAN. Do 't! he will do 't; for—look you, sir—he has as many friends as enemies; which friends, sir—as it were—durst not—look you, sir—show themselves—as we term it—his friends, whilst he 's in directitude.

FIRST SERVINGMAN. Directitude! what 's that?

SECOND SERVINGMAN. But when they shall see, sir, his crest up again, and the man in blood, they will out of their burrows, like conies after rain, and revel all with him.

FIRST SERVINGMAN. But when goes this forward?

THIRD SERVINGMAN. To-morrow; to-day; presently. You shall have the drum struck up this afternoon; 'tis, as it were, a parcel of their feast, and to be executed ere they wipe their lips.

SECOND SERVINGMAN. Why, then we shall have a stirring world again. This peace is nothing but to rust iron, increase tailors, and breed ballad-makers.

FIRST SERVINGMAN. Let me have war, say I; it exceeds peace as far as day does night; it 's spritely, waking, audible, and full of vent. Peace is a very apoplexy, lethargy; mulled, deaf, sleepy, insensible; a getter of more bastard children than war 's a destroyer of men.

SECOND SERVINGMAN. 'Tis so: and as war, in some sort, may be said to be a ravisher, so it cannot be denied but peace is a great maker of cuckolds.

FIRST SERVINGMAN. Ay, and it makes men hate one another.

THIRD SERVINGMAN. Reason: because they then less need one another. The wars for my money. I hope to see Romans as cheap as Volscians. They are rising, they are rising.

ALL. In, in, in, in!   *Exeunt*

SCENE SIX

Rome. A Public Place.

Enter Sicinius and Brutus

SICINIUS. We hear not of him, neither need we fear him;
His remedies are tame i' the present peace
And quietness o' the people, which before
Were in wild hurry. Here do we make his friends
Blush that the world goes well, who rather had,
Though they themselves did suffer by 't, behold
Dissentious numbers pestering streets, than see

Our tradesmen singing in their shops and going
About their functions friendly.

Enter Menenius

BRUTUS. We stood to 't in good time. Is this Menenius?

SICINIUS. 'Tis he, 'tis he. O! he is grown most kind
Of late. Hail, sir!

MENENIUS.   Hail to you both!

SICINIUS. Your Coriolanus is not much miss'd
But with his friends: the commonwealth doth stand,
And so would do, were he more angry at it.

MENENIUS. All 's well; and might have been much better, if
He could have temporiz'd.

SICINIUS.   Where is he, hear you?

MENENIUS. Nay, I hear nothing: his mother and his wife
Hear nothing from him.

Enter three or four Citizens

CITIZENS. The gods preserve you both!

SICINIUS.   Good den, our neighbours.

BRUTUS. Good den to you all, good den to you all.

FIRST CITIZEN. Ourselves, our wives, and children, on our knees,
Are bound to pray for you both.

SICINIUS.   Live, and thrive!

BRUTUS. Farewell, kind neighbours: we wish'd Coriolanus
had lov'd you as we did.

CITIZENS.   Now the gods keep you!

SICINIUS. }
BRUTUS. } Farewell, farewell.   *Exeunt Citizens*

SICINIUS. This is a happier and more comely time
Than when these fellows ran about the streets
Crying confusion.

BRUTUS.   Caius Marcius was
A worthy officer i' the war; but insolent,
O'ercome with pride, ambitious past all thinking,
Self-loving,—

SICINIUS.   And affecting one sole throne,
Without assistance.

MENENIUS.   I think not so.

SICINIUS. We should by this, to all our lamentation,
If he had gone forth consul, found it so.

BRUTUS. The gods have well prevented it, and Rome

Sits safe and still without him.

Enter an Ædile

ÆDILE.   Worthy tribunes,
There is a slave, whom we have put in prison,
Reports, the Volsces with two several powers
Are enter'd in the Roman territories,
And with the deepest malice of the war
Destroy what lies before them.

MENENIUS.   'Tis Aufidius,
Who, hearing of our Marcius' banishment,
Thrusts forth his horns again into the world;
Which were inshell'd when Marcius stood for Rome
And durst not once peep out.

SICINIUS. Come, what talk you of Marcius?

BRUTUS. Go see this rumourer whipp'd. It cannot be
The Volsces dare break with us.

MENENIUS.   Cannot be!
We have record that very well it can,
And three examples of the like have been
Within my age. But reason with the fellow,
Before you punish him, where he heard this,
Lest you shall chance to whip your information,
And beat the messenger who bids beware
Of what is to be dreaded.

SICINIUS.   Tell not me:
I know this cannot be.

BRUTUS.   Not possible.

Enter a Messenger

MESSENGER. The nobles in great earnestness are going
All to the senate-house: some news is come,
That turns their countenances.

SICINIUS.   'Tis this slave.—
Go whip him 'fore the people's eyes: his raising,
Nothing but his report.

MESSENGER.   Yes, worthy sir,
The slave's report is seconded; and more,
More fearful, is deliver'd.

SICINIUS.   What more fearful?

MESSENGER. It is spoke freely out of many mouths—
How probable I do not know—that Marcius,
Join'd with Aufidius, leads a power 'gainst Rome,
And vows revenge as spacious as between

The young'st and oldest thing.

SICINIUS. This is most likely.

BRUTUS. Rais'd only, that the weaker sort may wish
Good Marcius home again.

SICINIUS. The very trick on 't.

MENENIUS. This is unlikely:
He and Aufidius can no more atone,
Than violentest contrariety.

Enter another Messenger

SECOND MESSENGER. You are sent for to the senate:
A fearful army, led by Caius Marcius,
Associated with Aufidius, rages
Upon our territories; and have already
O'erborne their way, consum'd with fire, and took
What lay before them.

Enter Cominius

COMINIUS. O! you have made good work!

MENENIUS. What news? what news?

COMINIUS. You have holp to ravish your own daughters,
and
To melt the city leads upon your pates,
To see your wives dishonour'd to your noses,—

MENENIUS. What 's the news? what 's the news?

COMINIUS. Your temples burned in their cement and
Your franchises, whereon you stood, confin'd
Into an auger's bore.

MENENIUS. Pray now, your news?—
You have made fair work, I fear me. Pray, your news?
If Marcius should be join'd with Volscians,—

COMINIUS. If!
He is their god: he leads them like a thing
Made by some other deity than Nature,
That shapes man better; and they follow him,
Against us brats, with no less confidence
Than boys pursuing summer butterflies,
Or butchers killing flies.

MENENIUS. You have made good work,
You, and your apron-men; you that stood so much
Upon the voice of occupation and
The breath of garlic-eaters!

COMINIUS. He will shake
Your Rome about your ears.

MENENIUS.   As Hercules
Did shake down mellow fruit. You have made fair work!
BRUTUS. But is this true, sir?
COMINIUS.   Ay; and you 'll look pale
Before you find it other. All the regions
Do smilingly revolt; and who resist
Are mock'd for valiant ignorance,
And perish constant fools. Who is 't can blame him?
Your enemies, and his, find something in him.
MENENIUS. We are all undone unless
The noble man have mercy.
COMINIUS.   Who shall ask it?
The tribunes cannot do 't for shame; the people
Deserve such pity of him as the wolf
Does of the shepherds: for his best friends, if they
Should say 'Be good to Rome,' they charg'd him even
As those should do that had deserv'd his hate,
And therein show'd like enemies.
MENENIUS.   'Tis true:
If he were putting to my house the brand
That should consume it, I have not the face
To say 'Beseech you, cease.'—You have made fair hands,
You and your crafts! you have crafted fair!
COMINIUS.   You have brought
A trembling upon Rome, such as was never
So incapable of help.
SICINIUS. ⎱
BRUTUS. ⎰   Say not we brought it.
MENENIUS. How! Was it we? We lov'd him; but, like
    beasts
And cowardly nobles, gave way unto your clusters,
Who did hoot him out o' the city.
COMINIUS.   But I fear
They 'll roar him in again. Tullus Aufidius,
The second name of men, obeys his points
As if he were his officer: desperation
Is all the policy, strength, and defence,
That Rome can make against them.
              Enter a troop of Citizens
MENENIUS.   Here come the clusters.
And is Aufidius with him? You are they
That made the air unwholesome, when you cast

Your stinking greasy caps in hooting at
Coriolanus' exile. Now he 's coming;
And not a hair upon a soldier's head
Which will not prove a whip: as many coxcombs
As you threw caps up will he tumble down,
And pay you for your voices. 'Tis no matter;
If he could burn us all into one coal,
We have deserv'd it.

CITIZENS. Faith, we hear fearful news.

FIRST CITIZEN.   For mine own part,
When I said banish him, I said 'twas pity.

SECOND CITIZEN. And so did I.

THIRD CITIZEN. And so did I; and, to say the truth, so did
very many of us. That we did we did for the best; and
though we willingly consented to his banishment, yet it
was against our will.

COMINIUS. You 're goodly things, you voices!

MENENIUS.   You have made
Good work, you and your cry! Shall 's to the Capitol?

COMINIUS. O! ay; what else?

Exeunt Cominius and Menenius

SICINIUS. Go, masters, get you home; be not dismay'd;
These are a side that would be glad to have
This true which they so seem to fear. Go home,
And show no sign of fear.

FIRST CITIZEN. The gods be good to us. Come, masters,
let 's home. I ever said we were i' the wrong when we
banished him.

SECOND CITIZEN. So did we all. But come, let 's home.

Exeunt Citizens

BRUTUS. I do not like this news.

SICINIUS. Nor I.

BRUTUS. Let 's to the Capitol. Would half my wealth
Would buy this for a lie!

SICINIUS.   Pray let us go.   *Exeunt*

SCENE SEVEN

A Camp at a small distance from Rome.

Enter Aufidius and his Lieutenant

AUFIDIUS. Do they still fly to the Roman?

LIEUTENANT. I do not know what witchcraft 's in him, but
  Your soldiers use him as the grace 'fore meat,
  Their talk at table, and their thanks at end;
  And you are darken'd in this action, sir,
  Even by your own.

AUFIDIUS.   I cannot help it now,
  Unless, by using means, I lame the foot
  Of our design. He bears himself more proudlier,
  Even to my person, than I thought he would
  When first I did embrace him; yet his nature
  In that 's no changeling, and I must excuse
  What cannot be amended.

LIEUTENANT.   Yet, I wish, sir,—
  I mean for your particular,—you had not
  Join'd in commission with him; but either
  Had borne the action of yourself, or else
  To him had left it solely.

AUFIDIUS. I understand thee well; and be thou sure,
  When he shall come to his account, he knows not
  What I can urge against him. Although it seems,
  And so he thinks, and is no less apparent
  To the vulgar eye, that he bears all things fairly,
  And shows good husbandry for the Volscian state,
  Fights dragon-like, and does achieve as soon
  As draw his sword; yet he hath left undone
  That which shall break his neck or hazard mine,
  Whene'er we come to our account.

LIEUTENANT. Sir, I beseech you, think you he 'll carry
  Rome?

AUFIDIUS. All places yield to him ere he sits down;
  And the nobility of Rome are his:
  The senators and patricians love him too;
  The tribunes are no soldiers; and their people
  Will be as rash in the repeal as hasty
  To expel him thence. I think he 'll be to Rome

As is the osprey to the fish, who takes it
By sovereignty of nature. First he was
A noble servant to them, but he could not
Carry his honours even; whether 'twas pride,
Which out of daily fortune ever taints
The happy man; whether defect of judgment,
To fail in the disposing of those chances
Which he was lord of; or whether nature
Not to be other than one thing, not moving
From the casque to the cushion, but commanding peace
Even with the same austerity and garb
As he controll'd the war; but one of these,
As he hath spices of them all, not all,
For I dare so far free him, made him fear'd,
So hated, and so banish'd: but he has a merit
To choke it in the utterance. So our virtues
Lie in the interpretation of the time;
And power, unto itself most commendable,
Hath not a tomb so evident as a chair
To extol what it hath done.
One fire drives out one fire; one nail, one nail;
Rights by rights falter, strengths by strengths do fail.
Come, let 's away. When, Caius, Rome is thine,
Thou art poor'st of all; then shortly art thou mine.

Exeunt

ACT FIVE

SCENE ONE

Rome. A Public Place.

Enter Menenius, Cominius, Sicinius, Brutus, and Others

MENENIUS. No, I 'll not go: you hear what he hath said
   Which was sometime his general; who lov'd him
   In a most dear particular. He call'd me father:
   But what o' that? Go, you that banish'd him;
   A mile before his tent fall down, and knee
   The way into his mercy. Nay, if he coy'd
   To hear Cominius speak, I 'll keep at home.

COMINIUS. He would not seem to know me.

MENENIUS.   Do you hear?

COMINIUS. Yet one time he did call me by my name.
   I urg'd our old acquaintance, and the drops
   That we have bled together. Coriolanus
   He would not answer to; forbad all names;
   He was a kind of nothing, titleless,
   Till he had forg'd himself a name o' the fire
   Of burning Rome.

MENENIUS.   Why, so: you have made good work!
   A pair of tribunes that have rack'd for Rome,
   To make coals cheap: a noble memory!

COMINIUS. I minded him how royal 'twas to pardon
   When it was less expected: he replied,
   It was a bare petition of a state
   To one whom they had punish'd.

MENENIUS.   Very well.
   Could he say less?

COMINIUS. I offer'd to awaken his regard
   For 's private friends: his answer to me was,
   He could not stay to pick them in a pile
   Of noisome musty chaff: he said 'twas folly.

For one poor grain or two, to leave unburnt,
And still to nose the offence.

MENENIUS.   For one poor grain or two!
I am one of those; his mother, wife, his child,
And this brave fellow too, we are the grains:
You are the musty chaff, and you are smelt
Above the moon. We must be burnt for you.

SICINIUS. Nay, pray, be patient: if you refuse your aid
In this so-never-needed help, yet do not
Upbraid 's with our distress. But, sure, if you
Would be your country's pleader, your good tongue,
More than the instant army we can make,
Might stop our countryman.

MENENIUS.   No; I 'll not meddle.

SICINIUS. Pray you, go to him.

MENENIUS. What should I do?

BRUTUS. Only make trial what your love can do
For Rome, towards Marcius.

MENENIUS.   Well; and say that Marcius
Return me, as Cominius is return'd,
Unheard; what then?
But as a discontented friend, grief-shot
With his unkindness? say 't be so?

SICINIUS.   Yet your good will
Must have that thanks from Rome, after the measure
As you intended well.

MENENIUS.   I 'll undertake it:
I think he 'll hear me. Yet, to bite his lip
And hum at good Cominius, much unhearts me.
He was not taken well; he had not din'd:
The veins unfill'd, our blood is cold, and then
We pout upon the morning, are unapt
To give or to forgive; but when we have stuff'd
These pipes and these conveyances of our blood
With wine and feeding, we have suppler souls
Than in our priest-like fasts: therefore, I 'll watch him
Till he be dieted to my request,
And then I 'll set upon him.

BRUTUS. You know the very road into his kindness,
And cannot lose your way.

MENENIUS.   Good faith, I 'll prove him,
Speed how it will. I shall ere long have knowledge

Of my success.

COMINIUS.   He 'll never hear him.

SICINIUS.   Not?

COMINIUS. I tell you he does sit in gold, his eye
Red as 'twould burn Rome, and his injury
The gaoler to his pity. I kneel'd before him;
'Twas very faintly he said 'Rise'; dismiss'd me
Thus, with his speechless hand: what he would do
He sent in writing after me; what he would not,
Bound with an oath to yield to his conditions:
So that all hope is vain
Unless his noble mother and his wife,
Who, as I hear, mean to solicit him
For mercy to his country. Therefore let 's hence,
And with our fair entreaties haste them on.   *Exeunt*

SCENE TWO

*The Volscian Camp before Rome. The Guards
at their stations.*

Enter to them, Menenius

FIRST GUARD. Stay! whence are you?

SECOND GUARD.   Stand! and go back.

MENENIUS. You guard like men; 'tis well; but, by your
leave,
I am an officer of state, and come
To speak with Coriolanus.

FIRST GUARD.   From whence?

MENENIUS.   From Rome.

FIRST GUARD. You may not pass; you must return: our
general
Will no more hear from thence.

SECOND GUARD. You 'll see your Rome embrac'd with fire
before
You 'll speak with Coriolanus.

MENENIUS.   Good my friends,
If you have heard your general talk of Rome,
And of his friends there, it is lots to blanks
My name hath touch'd your ears: it is Menenius.

FIRST GUARD. Be it so; go back: the virtue of your name
Is not here passable.

MENENIUS.   I tell thee, fellow,
Thy general is my lover: I have been
The book of his good acts, whence men have read
His fame unparallel'd, haply amplified;
For I have ever glorified my friends—
Of whom he 's chief—with all the size that verity
Would without lapsing suffer: nay, sometimes,
Like to a bowl upon a subtle ground,
I have tumbled past the throw, and in his praise
Have almost stamp'd the leasing. Therefore, fellow,
I must have leave to pass.

FIRST GUARD. Faith, sir, if you had told as many lies in his
behalf as you have uttered words in your own, you
should not pass here; no, though it were as virtuous to
lie as to live chastely. Therefore go back.

MENENIUS. Prithee, fellow, remember my name is Menenius, always factionary on the party of your general.

SECOND GUARD. Howsoever you have been his liar—as you
say you have—I am one that, telling true under him,
must say you cannot pass. Therefore go back.

MENENIUS. Has he dined, canst thou tell? for I would not
speak with him till after dinner.

FIRST GUARD. You are a Roman, are you?

MENENIUS. I am as thy general is.

FIRST GUARD. Then you should hate Rome, as he does.
Can you, when you have pushed out your gates the very
defender of them, and, in a violent popular ignorance,
given your enemy your shield, think to front his revenges with the easy groans of old women, the virginal
palms of your daughters, or with the palsied intercession
of such a decayed dotant as you seem to be? Can you
think to blow out the intended fire your city is ready to
flame in, with such weak breath as this? No, you are
deceived; therefore, back to Rome, and prepare for your
execution: you are condemned, our general has sworn
you out of reprieve and pardon.

MENENIUS. Sirrah, if thy captain knew I were here, he
would use me with estimation.

SECOND GUARD. Come, my captain knows you not.

MENENIUS. I mean, thy general.

FIRST GUARD. My general cares not for you. Back, I say:
go, lest I let forth your half-pint of blood; back, that 's
the utmost of your having: back.

MENENIUS. Nay, but, fellow, fellow,—
    Enter Coriolanus and Aufidius

CORIOLANUS. What 's the matter?

MENENIUS. Now, you companion, I 'll say an errand for
you: you shall know now that I am in estimation; you
shall perceive that a Jack guardant cannot office me from
my son Coriolanus: guess, but by my entertainment
with him, if thou standest not i' the state of hanging, or
of some death more long in spectatorship, and crueller
in suffering; behold now presently, and swound for
what 's to come upon thee. (*To Coriolanus*) The glorious gods sit in hourly synod about thy particular prosperity, and love thee no worse than thy old father Menenius does! O my son! my son! thou art preparing fire
for us; look thee, here 's water to quench it. I was hardly
moved to come to thee; but being assured none but myself could move thee, I have been blown out of your
gates with sighs; and conjure thee to pardon Rome, and
thy petitionary countrymen. The good gods assuage thy
wrath, and turn the dregs of it upon this varlet here;
this, who, like a block, hath denied my access to thee.

CORIOLANUS. Away!

MENENIUS. How! away!

CORIOLANUS. Wife, mother, child, I know not. My affairs
Are servanted to others: though I owe
My revenge properly, my remission lies
In Volscian breasts. That we have been familiar,
Ingrate forgetfulness shall poison, rather
Than pity note how much. Therefore, be gone:
Mine ears against your suits are stronger than
Your gates against my force. Yet, for I lov'd thee,
Take this along; I writ it for thy sake,   *Gives a paper*
And would have sent it. Another word, Menenius,
I will not hear thee speak. This man, Aufidius,
Was my belov'd in Rome: yet thou behold'st!

AUFIDIUS. You keep a constant temper.
            Exeunt Coriolanus and Aufidius

FIRST GUARD. Now, sir, is your name Menenius?

SECOND GUARD. 'Tis a spell, you see, of much power. You
know the way home again.

FIRST GUARD. Do you hear how we are shent for keeping
your greatness back?

SECOND GUARD. What cause, do you think, I have to
swound?

MENENIUS. I neither care for the world nor your general:
for such things as you, I can scarce think there 's any,
ye 're so slight. He that hath a will to die by himself
fears it not from another. Let your general do his worst.
For you, be that you are, long; and your misery increase
with your age! I say to you, as I was said to, Away!

Exit

FIRST GUARD. A noble fellow, I warrant him.

SECOND GUARD. The worthy fellow is our general: he is the
rock, the oak not to be wind-shaken.   *Exeunt*

SCENE THREE

The Tent of Coriolanus.

Enter Coriolanus, Aufidius, and Others

CORIOLANUS. We will before the walls of Rome to-morrow
Set down our host. My partner in this action,
You must report to the Volscian lords, how plainly
I have borne this business.

AUFIDIUS.   Only their ends
You have respected; stopp'd your ears against
The general suit of Rome; never admitted
A private whisper; no, not with such friends
That thought them sure of you.

CORIOLANUS.   This last old man,
Whom with a crack'd heart I have sent to Rome,
Lov'd me above the measure of a father;
Nay, godded me indeed. Their latest refuge
Was to send him; for whose old love I have,
Though I show'd sourly to him, once more offer'd
The first conditions, which they did refuse,
And cannot now accept, to grace him only
That thought he could do more. A very little
I have yielded to; fresh embassies and suits,

Nor from the state, nor private friends, hereafter
Will I lend ear to. (*Shout within*) Ha! what shout is
  this?
Shall I be tempted to infringe my vow
In the same time 'tis made? I will not.
  Enter, in mourning habits, Virgilia, Volumnia, leading
      young Marcius, Valeria, and Attendants
My wife comes foremost; then the honour'd mould
Wherein this trunk was fram'd, and in her hand
The grandchild to her blood. But out, affection!
All bond and privilege of nature, break!
Let it be virtuous to be obstinate.
What is that curtsy worth? or those doves' eyes,
Which can make gods forsworn? I melt, and am not
Of stronger earth than others. My mother bows,
As if Olympus to a molehill should
In supplication nod; and my young boy
Hath an aspect of intercession, which
Great nature cries 'Deny not.' Let the Volsces
Plough Rome, and harrow Italy; I 'll never
Be such a gosling to obey instinct, but stand
As if a man were author of himself
And knew no other kin.
VIRGILIA.   My lord and husband!
CORIOLANUS. These eyes are not the same I wore in Rome.
VIRGILIA. The sorrow that delivers us thus chang'd
  Makes you think so.
CORIOLANUS.   Like a dull actor now,
  I have forgot my part, and I am out,
  Even to a full disgrace. Best of my flesh,
  Forgive my tyranny; but do not say
  For that, 'Forgive our Romans.' O! a kiss
  Long as my exile, sweet as my revenge!
  Now, by the jealous queen of heaven, that kiss
  I carried from thee, dear, and my true lip
  Hath virgin'd it e'er since. You gods! I prate,
  And the most noble mother of the world
  Leave unsaluted. Sink, my knee, i' the earth;   *Kneels*
  Of thy deep duty more impression show
  Than that of common sons.
VOLUMNIA.   O! stand up bless'd;
  Whilst, with no softer cushion than the flint,

I kneel before thee, and unproperly
Show duty, as mistaken all this while
Between the child and parent.   *Kneels*

CORIOLANUS.   What is this?
Your knees to me! to your corrected son!
Then let the pebbles on the hungry beach
Fillip the stars; then let the mutinous winds
Strike the proud cedars 'gainst the fiery sun,
Murdering impossibility, to make
What cannot be, slight work.

VOLUMNIA.   Thou art my warrior;
I holp to frame thee. Do you know this lady?

CORIOLANUS. The noble sister of Publicola,
The moon of Rome; chaste as the icicle
That 's curdied by the frost from purest snow,
And hangs on Dian's temple: dear Valeria!

VOLUMNIA. This is a poor epitome of yours,
                    Pointing to the Child
Which by the interpretation of full time
May show like all yourself.

CORIOLANUS.   The god of soldiers,
With the consent of supreme Jove, inform
Thy thoughts with nobleness; that thou mayst prove
To shame unvulnerable, and stick i' the wars
Like a great sea-mark, standing every flaw,
And saving those that eye thee!

VOLUMNIA.   Your knee, sirrah.

CORIOLANUS. That 's my brave boy!

VOLUMNIA. Even he, your wife, this lady, and myself,
Are suitors to you.

CORIOLANUS.   I beseech you, peace:
Or, if you 'd ask, remember this before:
The things I have forsworn to grant may never
Be held by you denials. Do not bid me
Dismiss my soldiers, or capitulate
Again with Rome's mechanics: tell me not
Wherein I seem unnatural: desire not
To allay my rages and revenges with
Your colder reasons.

VOLUMNIA.   O! no more, no more;
You have said you will not grant us any thing;
For we have nothing else to ask but that

CORIOLANUS.   What is this?
Your knees to me! to your corrected son!

　　Which you deny already: yet we will ask;
　　That, if you fail in our request, the blame
　　May hang upon your hardness. Therefore, hear us.
CORIOLANUS. Aufidius, and you Volsces, mark; for we 'll
　　Hear nought from Rome in private. Your request?
VOLUMNIA. Should we be silent and not speak, our raiment
　　And state of bodies would bewray what life
　　We have led since thy exile. Think with thyself
　　How more unfortunate than all living women
　　Are we come hither: since that thy sight, which should
　　Make our eyes flow with joy, hearts dance with comforts,
　　Constrains them weep, and shake with fear and sorrow;
　　Making the mother, wife, and child to see
　　The son, the husband, and the father tearing
　　His country's bowels out. And to poor we
　　Thine enmity 's most capital: thou barr'st us
　　Our prayers to the gods, which is a comfort
　　That all but we enjoy; for how can we,
　　Alas! how can we for our country pray,
　　Whereto we are bound, together with thy victory,
　　Whereto we are bound? Alack! or we must lose
　　The country, our dear nurse, or else thy person,
　　Our comfort in the country. We must find
　　An evident calamity, though we had
　　Our wish, which side should win; for either thou
　　Must, as a foreign recreant, be led
　　With manacles through out streets, or else
　　Triumphantly tread on thy country's ruin,
　　And bear the palm for having bravely shed
　　Thy wife and children's blood. For myself, son,
　　I purpose not to wait on Fortune till
　　These wars determine: if I cannot persuade thee
　　Rather to show a noble grace to both parts
　　Than seek the end of one, thou shalt no sooner
　　March to assault thy country than to tread—
　　Trust to 't, thou shalt not—on thy mother's womb,
　　That brought thee to this world.
VIRGILIA.　　　　　　　　　　　Ay, and mine,
　　That brought you forth this boy, to keep your name
　　Living to time.
BOY.　　　　　A' shall not tread on me:
　　I 'll run away till I am bigger, but then I 'll fight.

CORIOLANUS. Not of a woman's tenderness to be,
Requires nor child nor woman's face to see.
I have sat too long.   *Rising*
VOLUMNIA.   Nay, go not from us thus.
If it were so, that our request did tend
To save the Romans, thereby to destroy
The Volsces whom you serve, you might condemn us,
As poisonous of your honour: no; our suit
Is, that you reconcile them: while the Volsces
May say 'This mercy we have show'd'; the Romans,
'This we receiv'd'; and each in either side
Give the all-hail to thee, and cry 'Be bless'd
For making up this peace!' Thou know'st, great son,
The end of war 's uncertain; but this certain,
That, if thou conquer Rome, the benefit
Which thou shalt thereby reap is such a name
Whose repetition will be dogg'd with curses;
Whose chronicle thus writ: 'The man was noble,
But with his last attempt he wip'd it out,
Destroy'd his country, and his name remains
To the ensuing age abhorr'd.' Speak to me, son!
Thou hast affected the fine strains of honour,
To imitate the graces of the gods;
To tear with thunder the wide cheeks o' the air,
And yet to charge thy sulphur with a bolt
That should but rive an oak. Why dost not speak?
Think'st thou it honourable for a noble man
Still to remember wrongs? Daughter, speak you:
He cares not for your weeping. Speak thou, boy:
Perhaps thy childishness will move him more
Than can our reasons. There is no man in the world
More bound to 's mother; yet here he lets me prate
Like one i' the stocks. Thou hast never in thy life
Show'd thy dear mother any courtesy;
When she—poor hen! fond of no second brood—
Has cluck'd thee to the wars, and safely home,
Loaden with honour. Say my request 's unjust,
And spurn me back; but if it be not so,
Thou art not honest, and the gods will plague thee,
That thou restrain'st from me the duty which
To a mother's part belongs. He turns away:
Down, ladies; let us shame him with our knees.

To his surname Coriolanus 'longs more pride
Than pity to our prayers. Down: an end;
This is the last: so we will home to Rome,
And die among our neighbours. Nay, behold us.
This boy, that cannot tell what he would have,
But kneels and holds up hands for fellowship,
Does reason our petition with more strength
Than thou hast to deny 't. Come, let us go:
This fellow had a Volscian to his mother;
His wife is in Corioli, and his child
Like him by chance. Yet give us our dispatch:
I am hush'd until our city be a-fire,
And then I 'll speak a little.

CORIOLANUS. (*Holding Volumnia by the hand, silent*)
                    O, mother, mother!
What have you done? Behold! the heavens do ope,
The gods look down, and this unnatural scene
They laugh at. O my mother! mother! O!
You have won a happy victory to Rome;
But, for your son, believe it, O! believe it,
Most dangerously you have with him prevail'd,
If not most mortal to him. But let it come.
Aufidius, though I cannot make true wars,
I 'll frame convenient peace. Now, good Aufidius,
Were you in my stead, would you have heard
A mother less, or granted less, Aufidius?

AUFIDIUS. I was mov'd withal.

CORIOLANUS.   I dare be sworn you were:
And, sir, it is no little thing to make
Mine eyes to sweat compassion. But, good sir,
What peace you'll make, advise me: for my part,
I 'll not to Rome, I 'll back with you; and pray you,
Stand to me in this cause. O mother! wife!

AUFIDIUS. (*Aside*) I am glad thou hast set thy mercy and
    thy honour
At difference in thee: out of that I 'll work
Myself a former fortune.

CORIOLANUS.   Ay, by and by;
But we will drink together; and you shall bear
A better witness back than words, which we,
On like conditions, would have counter-seal'd.
Come, enter with us. Ladies, you deserve

To have a temple built you: all the swords
In Italy, and her confederate arms,
Could not have made this peace.   *Exeunt*

SCENE FOUR

Rome. A Public Place.

Enter Menenius and Sicinius

MENENIUS. See you yond coign o' the Capitol, yond corner-stone?

SICINIUS. Why, what of that?

MENENIUS. If it be possible for you to displace it with your little finger, there is some hope the ladies of Rome, especially his mother, may prevail with him. But I say, there is no hope in 't. Our throats are sentenced and stay upon execution.

SICINIUS. Is 't possible that so short a time can alter the condition of a man?

MENENIUS. There is differency between a grub and a butterfly; yet your butterfly was a grub. This Marcius is grown from man to dragon: he has wings; he 's more than a creeping thing.

SICINIUS. He loved his mother dearly.

MENENIUS. So did he me; and he no more remembers his mother now than an eight-year-old horse. The tartness of his face sours ripe grapes: when he walks, he moves like an engine, and the ground shrinks before his treading: he is able to pierce a corslet with his eye; talks like a knell, and his hum is a battery. He sits in his state, as a thing made for Alexander. What he bids be done is finished with his bidding. He wants nothing of a god but eternity and a heaven to throne in.

SICINIUS. Yes, mercy, if you report him truly.

MENENIUS. I paint him in the character. Mark what mercy his mother shall bring from him: there is no more mercy in him than there is milk in a male tiger; that shall our poor city find: and all this is 'long of you.

SICINIUS. The gods be good unto us!

MENENIUS. No, in such a case the gods will not be good unto us. When we banished him, we respected not

them; and, he returning to break our necks, they respect
not us.

Enter a Messenger

MESSENGER. Sir, if you 'd save your life, fly to your house:
The plebeians have got your fellow-tribune,
And hale him up and down; all swearing, if
The Roman ladies bring not comfort home,
They 'll give him death by inches.

Enter a second Messenger

SICINIUS.   What 's the news?
SECOND MESSENGER. Good news, good news! the ladies
    have prevail'd,
The Volscians are dislodg'd, and Marcius gone.
A merrier day did never yet greet Rome,
No, not the expulsion of the Tarquins.
SICINIUS.   Friend,
Art thou certain this is true? is it most certain?
SECOND MESSENGER. As certain as I know the sun is fire:
Where have you lurk'd that you make doubt of it?
Ne'er through an arch so hurried the blown tide,
As the recomforted through the gates. Why, hark you!

Trumpets and hautboys sounded,
and drums beaten, all together. Shouting also within

The trumpets, sackbuts, psalteries, and fifes,
Tabors, and cymbals, and the shouting Romans,
Make the sun dance. Hark you!   *A shout within*
MENENIUS.   This is good news:
I will go meet the ladies. This Volumnia
Is worth of consuls, senators, patricians,
A city full; of tribunes, such as you,
A sea and land full. You have pray'd well to-day:
This morning for ten thousand of your throats
I 'd not have given a doit. Hark, how they joy!

Music still and shouts

SICINIUS. First, the gods bless you for your tidings; next,
Accept my thankfulness.
SECOND MESSENGER.   Sir, we have all
Great cause to give great thanks.
SICINIUS.   They are near the city?
SECOND MESSENGER. Almost at point to enter.
SICINIUS.   We will meet them,
And help the joy.   *Going*

SCENE FIVE

Rome. A Street Near the Gate.

*Enter the Ladies, accompanied by Senators, Patricians,
and People. They pass over the stage*

FIRST SENATOR. Behold our patroness, the life of Rome!
Call all your tribes together, praise the gods,
And make triumphant fires; strew flowers before them:
Unshout the noise that banish'd Marcius;
Repeal him with the welcome of his mother;
Cry, 'Welcome, ladies, welcome!'

ALL.   Welcome ladies,
Welcome!   *A flourish with drums and trumpets. Exeunt*

SCENE SIX

Corioli. A Public Place.

Enter Aufidius, with Attendants

AUFIDIUS. Go tell the lords o' the city I am here:
Deliver them this paper: having read it,
Bid them repair to the market-place; where I,
Even in theirs and in the commons' ears,
Will vouch the truth of it. Him I accuse
The city ports by this hath enter'd, and
Intends to appear before the people, hoping
To purge himself with words: dispatch.

                              Exeunt Attendants
     Enter three or four Conspirators of Aufidius' faction
Most welcome!

FIRST CONSPIRATOR. How is it with our general?
AUFIDIUS.   Even so
As with a man by his own alms empoison'd,
And with his charity slain.

SECOND CONSPIRATOR.   Most noble sir,
If you do hold the same intent wherein
You wish'd us parties, we 'll deliver you
Of your great danger.

AUFIDIUS.   Sir, I cannot tell:
  We must proceed as we do find the people.
THIRD CONSPIRATOR. The people will remain uncertain
      whilst
  'Twixt you there 's difference; but the fall of either
  Makes the survivor heir of all.
AUFIDIUS.   I know it;
  And my pretext to strike at him admits
  A good construction. I rais'd him, and I pawn'd
  Mine honour for his truth: who being so heighten'd,
  He water'd his new plants with dews of flattery,
  Seducing so my friends; and, to this end,
  He bow'd his nature, never known before
  But to be rough, unswayable, and free.
THIRD CONSPIRATOR. Sir, his stoutness
  When he did stand for consul, which he lost
  By lack of stooping,—
AUFIDIUS.   That I would have spoke of:
  Being banish'd for 't, he came unto my hearth;
  Presented to my knife his throat: I took him;
  Made him joint-servant with me; gave him way
  In all his own desires; nay, let him choose
  Out of my files, his projects to accomplish,
  My best and freshest men; serv'd his designments
  In mine own person; holp to reap the fame
  Which he did end all his; and took some pride
  To do myself this wrong: till, at the last,
  I seem'd his follower, not partner; and
  He wag'd me with his countenance, as if
  I had been mercenary.
FIRST CONSPIRATOR. So he did, my lord:
  The army marvell'd at it; and, in the last,
  When we had carried Rome, and that we look'd
  For no less spoil than glory,—
AUFIDIUS.   There was it;
  For which my sinews shall be stretch'd upon him.
  At a few drops of women's rheum, which are
  As cheap as lies, he sold the blood and labour
  Of our great action: therefore shall he die,
  And I 'll renew me in his fall. But, hark!

                    Drums and trumpets
                sound, with great shouts of the People

FIRST CONSPIRATOR. Your native town you enter'd like a
          post,
    And had no welcomes home; but he returns,
    Splitting the air with noise.

SECOND CONSPIRATOR.   And patient fools,
    Whose children he hath slain, their base throats tear
    With giving him glory.

THIRD CONSPIRATOR.   Therefore, at your vantage,
    Ere he express himself, or move the people
    With what he would say, let him feel your sword,
    Which we will second. When he lies along,
    After your way his tale pronounc'd shall bury
    His reasons with his body.

AUFIDIUS.   Say no more:
    Here come the lords.

          Enter the Lords of the city

LORDS. You are most welcome home.

AUFIDIUS.   I have not deserv'd it.
    But, worthy lords, have you with heed perus'd
    What I have written to you?

LORDS.   We have.

FIRST LORD.   And grieve to hear 't
    What faults he made before the last, I think
    Might have found easy fines; but there to end
    Where he was to begin, and give away
    The benefit of our levies, answering us
    With our own charge, making a treaty where
    There was a yielding, this admits no excuse.

AUFIDIUS. He approaches: you shall hear him.

          Enter Coriolanus, with drums and colours;
          a crowd of Citizens with him

CORIOLANUS. Hail, lords! I am return'd your soldier;
    No more infected with my country's love
    Than when I parted hence, but still subsisting
    Under your great command. You are to know,
    That prosperously I have attempted and
    With bloody passage led your wars even to
    The gates of Rome. Our spoils we have brought home
    Do more than counterpoise a full third part
    The charges of the action. We have made peace
    With no less honour to the Antiates
    Than shame to the Romans; and we here deliver,

Subscrib'd by the consuls and patricians,
Together with the seal o' the senate, what
We have compounded on.

AUFIDIUS.   Read it not, noble lords;
But tell the traitor in the highest degree
He hath abus'd your powers.

CORIOLANUS. Traitor! How now?

AUFIDIUS.   Ay, traitor, Marcius.

CORIOLANUS.   Marcius!

AUFIDIUS. Ay, Marcius, Caius Marcius. Dost thou think
I 'll grace thee with that robbery, thy stol'n name
Coriolanus in Corioli?
You lords and heads of the state, perfidiously
He has betray'd your business, and given up,
For certain drops of salt, your city Rome,
I say 'your city,' to his wife and mother;
Breaking his oath and resolution like
A twist of rotten silk, never admitting
Counsel o' the war, but at his nurse's tears
He whin'd and roar'd away your victory,
That pages blush'd at him, and men of heart
Look'd wondering each at other.

CORIOLANUS.   Hear'st thou, Mars?

AUFIDIUS. Name not the god, thou boy of tears.

CORIOLANUS.   Ha!

AUFIDIUS. No more.

CORIOLANUS. Measureless liar, thou hast made my heart
Too great for what contains it. Boy! O slave!
Pardon me, lords, 'tis the first time that ever
I was forc'd to scold. Your judgments, my grave lords,
Must give this cur the lie: and his own notion—
Who wears my stripes impress'd upon him, that
Must bear my beating to his grave—shall join
To thrust the lie unto him.

FIRST LORD. Peace, both, and hear my speak.

CORIOLANUS. Cut me to pieces, Volsces; men and lads,
Stain all your edges on me. Boy! False hound!
If you have writ your annals true, 'tis there,
That, like an eagle in a dove-cote, I
Flutter'd your Volscians in Corioli:
Alone I did it. Boy!

AUFIDIUS.   Why, noble lords,

Will you be put in mind of his blind fortune,
Which was your shame, by this unholy braggart,
'Fore your own eyes and ears?

CONSPIRATORS.   Let him die for 't.

ALL THE PEOPLE. Tear him to pieces.—Do it presently.—
He killed my son.—My daughter.—He killed my cousin
Marcus.—He killed my father.

SECOND LORD. Peace, ho! no outrage! peace!
The man is noble and his fame folds in
This orb o' the earth. His last offences to us
Shall have judicious hearing. Stand, Aufidius,
And trouble not the peace.

CORIOLANUS.   O! that I had him,
With six Aufidiuses, or more, his tribe,
To use my lawful sword!

AUFIDIUS.   Insolent villain!

CONSPIRATORS. Kill, kill, kill, kill, kill him!

                    The Conspirators draw, and kill
          Coriolanus, who falls: Aufidius stands on his body

LORDS.   Hold, hold, hold, hold!

AUFIDIUS. My noble masters, hear me speak.

FIRST LORD.   O Tullus!

SECOND LORD. Thou hast done a deed whereat valour will
    weep.

THIRD LORD. Tread not upon him. Masters all, be quiet.
Put up your swords.

AUFIDIUS. My lords, when you shall know,—as in this rage,
Provok'd by him, you cannot,—the great danger
Which this man's life did owe you, you 'll rejoice
That he is thus cut off. Please it your honours
To call me to your senate, I 'll deliver.
Myself your loyal servant, or endure
Your heaviest censure.

FIRST LORD.   Bear from hence his body;
And mourn you for him! Let him be regarded
As the most noble corse that ever herald
Did follow to his urn.

SECOND LORD.   His own impatience
Takes from Aufidius a great part of blame.
Let 's make the best of it.

AUFIDIUS.   My rage is gone,
And I am struck with sorrow. Take him up:

Help, three o' the chiefest soldiers; I 'll be one.
Beat thou the drum, that it speak mournfully;
Trail your steel pikes. Though in this city he
Hath widow'd and unchilded many a one,
Which to this hour bewail the injury,
Yet he shall have a noble memory.
Assist.   *Exeunt, bearing the body
                    of Coriolanus. A dead march sounded*

TITUS ANDRONICUS

CAST OF CHARACTERS

SATURNINUS, *Son to the late Emperor of Rome, and afterwards declared Emperor*

BASSIANUS, *Brother to Saturninus, in love with Lavinia*

TITUS ANDRONICUS, *a Roman, General against the Goths*

MARCUS ANDRONICUS, *Tribune of the People, and brother to Titus*

LUCIUS
QUINTUS } *Sons to Titus Andronicus*
MARTIUS
MUTIUS

YOUNG LUCIUS, *a Boy, Son to Lucius*
PUBLIUS, *Son to Marcus Andronicus*

SEMPRONIUS
CAIUS } *Kinsmen to Titus*
VALENTINE

ÆMILIUS, *a noble Roman*

ALARBUS
DEMETRIUS } *Sons to Tamora*
CHIRON

AARON, *a Moor, beloved by Tamora*
A Captain, Tribune, Messenger, and Clown; Romans
Goths and Romans

TAMORA, *Queen of the Goths*
LAVINIA, *Daughter to Titus Andronicus*
A Nurse, and a black Child

Senators, Tribunes, Officers, Soldiers, and Attendants

SCENE

Rome, and the Country near it

TITUS ANDRONICUS

ACT ONE

SCENE ONE

Rome.

*The Tomb of the Andronici appearing. The Tribunes and
Senators aloft; and then enter Saturninus and his Followers
at one door, and Bassianus and his Followers
at the other, with drum and colours*

SATURNINUS. Noble patricians, patrons of my right,
Defend the justice of my cause with arms;
And, countrymen, my loving followers,
Plead my successive title with your swords:
I am his first-born son that was the last
That wore the imperial diadem of Rome;
Then let my father's honours live in me,
Nor wrong mine age with this indignity.

BASSIANUS. Romans, friends, followers, favourers of my
right,
If ever Bassianus, Cæsar's son,
Were gracious in the eyes of royal Rome,
Keep then this passage to the Capitol,
And suffer not dishonour to approach
The imperial seat, to virtue consecrate,
To justice, continence, and nobility;
But let desert in pure election shine,
And, Romans, fight for freedom in your choice.
Enter Marcus Andronicus, aloft, with the crown

MARCUS. Princes, that strive by factions and by friends
Ambitiously for rule and empery,
Know that the people of Rome, for whom we stand
A special party, have, by common voice,
In election for the Roman empery,
Chosen Andronicus, surnamed Pius,
For many good and great deserts to Rome:

A nobler man, a braver warrior,
Lives not this day within the city walls:
He by the senate is accited home
From weary wars against the barbarous Goths;
That, with his sons, a terror to our foes,
Hath yok'd a nation strong, train'd up in arms.
Ten years are spent since first he undertook
This cause of Rome, and chastised with arms
Our enemies' pride: five times he hath return'd
Bleeding to Rome, bearing his valiant sons
In coffins from the field;
And now at last, laden with honour's spoils,
Returns the good Andronicus to Rome,
Renowned Titus, flourishing in arms.
Let us entreat, by honour of his name,
Whom worthily you would have now succeed,
And in the Capitol and senate's right,
Whom you pretend to honour and adore
That you withdraw you and abate your strength;
Dismiss your followers, and, as suitors should,
Plead your deserts in peace and humbleness.

SATURNINUS. How fair the tribune speaks to calm my
    thoughts!

BASSIANUS. Marcus Andronicus, so I do affy
In thy uprightness and integrity,
And so I love and honour thee and thine,
Thy noble brother Titus and his sons,
And her to whom my thoughts are humbled all,
Gracious Lavinia, Rome's rich ornament,
That I will here dismiss my loving friends,
And to my fortunes and the people's favour
Commit my cause in balance to be weigh'd.

           Exeunt the Followers of Bassianus

SATURNINUS. Friends, that have been thus forward in my
    right,
I thank you all and here dismiss you all;
And to the love and favour of my country
Commit myself, my person, and the cause.

          Exeunt the Followers of Saturninus

Rome, be as just and gracious unto me
As I am confident and kind to thee.

Open the gates, and let me in.
BASSIANUS. Tribunes, and me, a poor competitor.

Flourish. They go up into the Senate-house
Enter a Captain

CAPTAIN. Romans, make way! the good Andronicus,
Patron of virtue, Rome's best champion,
Successful in the battles that he fights,
With honour and with fortune is return'd
From where he circumscribed with his sword,
And brought to yoke, the enemies of Rome.

Drums and trumpets sounded, and then enter
Martius and Mutius; after them two men bearing a coffin
covered with black; then Lucius and Quintus. After them
Titus Andronicus; and then Tamora, with Alarbus, Chiron,
Demetrius, Aaron, and other Goths, prisoners; Soldiers and
People following. The bearers set down the coffin,
and Titus speaks

TITUS. Hail, Rome, victorious in thy mourning weeds!
Lo! as the bark, that hath discharg'd her fraught,
Returns with precious lading to the bay
From whence at first she weigh'd her anchorage,
Cometh Andronicus, bound with laurel boughs,
To re-salute his country with his tears,
Tears of true joy for his return to Rome.
Thou great defender of this Capitol,
Stand gracious to the rites that we intend!
Romans, of five-and-twenty valiant sons,
Half of the number that King Priam had,
Behold the poor remains, alive, and dead!
These that survive let Rome reward with love;
These that I bring unto their latest home,
With burial among their ancestors:
Here Goths have given me leave to sheathe my sword.
Titus, unkind and careless of thine own,
Why suffer'st thou thy sons, unburied yet
To hover on the dreadful shore of Styx?
Make way to lay them by their brethren.

The tomb is opened

There greet in silence, as the dead are wont,
And sleep in peace, slain in your country's wars!
O sacred receptacle of my joys,

    Sweet cell of virtue and nobility,
    How many sons of mine hast thou in store,
    That thou wilt never render to me more!
LUCIUS. Give us the proudest prisoner of the Goths,
    That we may hew his limbs, and on a pile
    'Ad manes fratrum' sacrifice his flesh,
    Before this earthly prison of their bones;
    That so the shadows be not unappeas'd,
    Nor we disturb'd with prodigies on earth.
TITUS. I give him you, the noblest that survives
    The eldest son of this distressed queen.
TAMORA. Stay, Roman brethren! Gracious conqueror,
    Victorious Titus, rue the tears I shed,
    A mother's tears in passion for her son:
    And if thy sons were ever dear to thee,
    O! think my son to be as dear to me.
    Sufficeth not that we are brought to Rome,
    To beautify thy triumphs and return,
    Captive to thee and to thy Roman yoke;
    But must my sons be slaughter'd in the streets
    For valiant doings in their country's cause?
    O! if to fight for king and commonweal
    Were piety in thine, it is in these.
    Andronicus, stain not thy tomb with blood:
    Wilt thou draw near the nature of the gods?
    Draw near them then in being merciful;
    Sweet mercy is nobility's true badge:
    Thrice-noble Titus, spare my first-born son.
TITUS. Patient yourself, madam, and pardon me.
    These are their brethren, whom your Goths beheld
    Alive and dead, and for their brethren slain
    Religiously they ask a sacrifice:
    To this your son is mark'd, and die he must,
    To appease their groaning shadows that are gone.
LUCIUS. Away with him! and make a fire straight;
    And with our swords, upon a pile of wood,
    Let 's hew his limbs till they be clean consum'd.

                            Exeunt Lucius,
        Quintus, Martius, and Mutius, with Alarbus
TAMORA. O cruel, irreligious piety!
CHIRON. Was every Scythia half so barbarous?

DEMETRIUS. Oppose not Scythia to ambitious Rome.
  Alarbus goes to rest, and we survive
  To tremble under Titus' threatening look.
  Then, madam, stand resolv'd; but hope withal
  The self-same gods, that arm'd the Queen of Troy
  With opportunity of sharp revenge
  Upon the Thracian tyrant in his tent,
  May favour Tamora, the Queen of Goths—
  When Goths were Goths, and Tamora was queen—
  To quit the bloody wrongs upon her foes.
        Re-enter Lucius, Quintus, Martius, and Mutius,
                with their swords bloody
LUCIUS. See, lord and father, how we have perform'd
  Our Roman rites. Alarbus' limbs are lopp'd,
  And entrails feed the sacrificing fire,
  Whose smoke, like incense, doth perfume the sky.
  Remaineth nought but to inter our brethren,
  And with loud 'larums welcome them to Rome.
TITUS. Let it be so; and let Andronicus
  Make this his latest farewell to their souls.
        Trumpets sounded, and the coffin laid in the tomb
  In peace and honour rest you here, my sons;
  Rome's readiest champions, repose you here in rest,
  Secure from worldly chances and mishaps!
  Here lurks no treason, here no envy swells,
  Here grow no damned drugs, here are no storms,
  No noise, but silence and eternal sleep:
  In peace and honour rest you here, my sons!
        Enter Lavinia
LAVINIA. In peace and honour live Lord Titus long;
  My noble lord and father, live in fame!
  Lo! at this tomb my tributary tears
  I render for my brethren's obsequies;
  And at thy feet I kneel, with tears of joy
  Shed on the earth for thy return to Rome.
  O! bless me here with thy victorious hand,
  Whose fortunes Rome's best citizens applaud.
TITUS. Kind Rome, that hast thus lovingly reserv'd
  The cordial of mine age to glad my heart!
  Lavinia, live; outlive thy father's days,
  And fame's eternal date, for virtue's praise!

Enter Marcus Andronicus and Tribunes; re-enter
Saturninus, Bassianus, and Others

MARCUS. Long live Lord Titus, my beloved brother,
  Gracious triumpher in the eyes of Rome!
TITUS. Thanks, gentle tribune, noble brother Marcus.
MARCUS. And welcome, nephews, from successful wars,
  You that survive, and you that sleep in fame!
  Fair lords, your fortunes are alike in all,
  That in your country's service drew your swords;
  But safer triumph is this funeral pomp,
  That hath aspir'd to Solon's happiness,
  And triumphs over chance in honour's bed.
  Titus Andronicus, the people of Rome,
  Whose friend in justice thou hast ever been,
  Send thee by me, their tribune and their trust,
  This palliament of white and spotless hue;
  And name thee in election for the empire,
  With these our late-deceased emperor's sons:
  Be candidatus then, and put it on,
  And help to set a head on headless Rome.
TITUS. A better head her glorious body fits
  Than his that shakes for age and feebleness.
  What should I don this robe, and trouble you?
  Be chosen with proclamations to-day,
  To-morrow yield up rule, resign my life,
  And set abroad new business for you all?
  Rome, I have been thy soldier forty years,
  And led my country's strength successfully,
  And buried one-and-twenty valiant sons,
  Knighted in field, slain manfully in arms,
  In right and service of their noble country.
  Give me a staff of honour for mine age,
  But not a sceptre to control the world:
  Upright he held it, lords, that held it last.
MARCUS. Titus, thou shalt obtain and ask the empery.
SATURNINUS. Proud and ambitious tribune, canst thou tell?
TITUS. Patience, Prince Saturninus.
SATURNINUS.   Romans, do me right:
  Patricians, draw your swords, and sheathe them not
  Till Saturninus be Rome's emperor.
  Andronicus, would thou wert shipp'd to hell,
  Rather than rob me of the people's hearts!

LUCIUS. Proud Saturnine, interrupter of the good
   That noble-minded Titus means to thee!
TITUS. Content thee, prince; I will restore to thee
   The people's hearts, and wean them from themselves.
BASSIANUS. Andronicus, I do not flatter thee,
   But honour thee, and will do till I die:
   My faction if thou strengthen with thy friends,
   I will most thankful be; and thanks to men
   Of noble minds is honourable meed.
TITUS. People of Rome, and people's tribunes here,
   I ask your voices and your suffrages:
   Will you bestow them friendly on Andronicus?
TRIBUNES. To gratify the good Andronicus,
   And gratulate his safe return to Rome,
   The people will accept whom he admits.
TITUS. Tribunes, I thank you; and this suit I make,
   That you create your emperor's eldest son,
   Lord Saturnine, whose virtues will, I hope,
   Reflect on Rome as Titan's rays on earth,
   And ripen justice in this commonweal:
   Then, if you will elect by my advice,
   Crown him, and say, 'Long live our emperor!'
MARCUS. With voices and applause of every sort,
   Patricians and plebeians, we create
   Lord Saturninus Rome's great emperor,
   And say, 'Long live our Emperor Saturnine!'

                               A long flourish

SATURNINUS. Titus Andronicus, for thy favours done
   To us in our election this day,
   I give thee thanks in part of thy deserts,
   And will with deeds requite thy gentleness:
   And, for an onset, Titus, to advance
   Thy name and honourable family
   Lavinia will I make my empress,
   Rome's royal mistress, mistress of my heart,
   And in the sacred Pantheon her espouse.
   Tell me, Andronicus, doth this motion please thee?
TITUS. It doth, my worthy lord; and in this match
   I hold me highly honour'd of your Grace:
   And here in sight of Rome to Saturnine,
   King and commander of our commonweal,
   The wide world's emperor, do I consecrate

My sword, my chariot, and my prisoners;
Presents well worthy Rome's imperious lord:
Receive them then, the tribute that I owe,
Mine honour's ensigns humbled at thy feet.

SATURNINUS. Thanks, noble Titus, father of my life!
How proud I am of thee and of thy gifts
Rome shall record, and, when I do forget
The least of these unspeakable deserts,
Romans, forget your fealty to me.

TITUS. (*To Tamora*) Now, madam, are you prisoner to an
    emperor;
To him that, for your honour and your state,
Will use you nobly and your followers.

SATURNINUS. A goodly lady, trust me; of the hue
That I would choose, were I to choose anew.
Clear up, fair queen, that cloudy countenance:
Though chance of war hath wrought this change of
    cheer,
Thou com'st not to be made a scorn in Rome:
Princely shall be thy usage every way.
Rest on my word, and let not discontent
Daunt all your hopes: madam, he comforts you
Can make you greater than the Queen of Goths.
Lavinia, you are not displeas'd with this?

LAVINIA. Not I, my lord; sith true nobility
Warrants these words in princely courtesy.

SATURNINUS. Thanks, sweet Lavinia, Romans, let us go;
Ransomless here we set our prisoners free:
Proclaim our honours, lords, with trump and drum.
        Flourish. Saturninus courts Tamora in dumb show

BASSIANUS. Lord Titus, by your leave, this maid is mine.
                                    Seizing Lavinia

TITUS. How, sir! Are you in earnest then, my lord?

BASSIANUS. Ay, noble Titus; and resolv'd withal
To do myself this reason and this right.

MARCUS. 'Suum cuique' is our Roman justice:
This prince in justice seizeth but his own.

LUCIUS. And that he will, and shall, if Lucius live.

TITUS. Traitors, avaunt! Where is the emperor's guard?
Treason, my lord! Lavinia is surpris'd.

SATURNINUS. Surpris'd! By whom?

BASSIANUS.   By him that justly may

Bear his betroth'd from all the world away.

Exeunt Marcus and Bassianus with Lavinia

MUTIUS. Brothers, help to convey her hence away,
And with my sword I 'll keep this door safe.

Exeunt Lucius, Quintus, and Martius

TITUS. Follow, my lord, and I 'll soon bring her back.

MUTIUS. My lord, you pass not here.

TITUS.   What! villain boy;
Barr'st me my way in Rome?   *Stabs Mutius*

MUTIUS.   Help, Lucius, help!   *Dies*

Re-enter Lucius

LUCIUS. My lord, you are unjust; and, more than so,
In wrongful quarrel you have slain your son.

TITUS. Nor thou, nor he, are any sons of mine;
My sons would never so dishonour me.
Traitor, restore Lavinia to the emperor.

LUCIUS. Dead, if you will; but not to be his wife
That is another's lawful promis'd love.   *Exit*

SATURNINUS. No, Titus, no; the emperor needs her not,
Nor her, nor thee, nor any of thy stock:
I 'll trust, by leisure, him that mocks me once;
Thee never, nor thy traitorous haughty sons,
Confederates all thus to dishonour me.
Was none in Rome to make a stale
But Saturnine? Full well, Andronicus,
Agreed these deeds with that proud brag of thine,
That saidst I begg'd the empire at thy hands.

TITUS. O monstrous! what reproachful words are these!

SATURNINUS. But go thy ways; go, give that changing piece
To him that flourish'd for her with his sword.
A valiant son-in-law thou shalt enjoy;
One fit to bandy with thy lawless sons,
To ruffle in the commonwealth of Rome.

TITUS. These words are razors to my wounded heart.

SATURNINUS. And therefore, lovely Tamora, Queen of
   Goths,
That like the stately Phœbe 'mongst her nymphs,
Dost overshine the gallant'st dames of Rome,
If thou be pleas'd with this my sudden choice,
Behold, I choose thee, Tamora, for my bride,
And will create thee Empress of Rome.
Speak, Queen of Goths, dost thou applaud my choice?

And here I swear by all the Roman gods,
Sith priest and holy water are so near,
And tapers burn so bright, and every thing
In readiness for Hymenæus stand,
I will not re-salute the streets of Rome,
Or climb my palace, till from forth this place
I lead espous'd my bride along with me.

TAMORA. And here in sight of heaven, to Rome I swear,
If Saturnine advance the Queen of Goths,
She will a handmaid be to his desires,
A loving nurse, a mother to his youth.

SATURNINUS. Ascend, fair queen, Pantheon. Lords, accompany
Your noble emperor, and his lovely bride,
Sent by the heavens for Prince Saturnine,
Whose wisdom hath her fortune conquered:
There shall we consummate our spousal rights.

Exeunt all but Titus

TITUS. I am not bid to wait upon this bride.
Titus, when wert thou wont to walk alone,
Dishonour'd thus, and challenged of wrongs?

Re-enter Marcus, Lucius, Quintus, and Martius

MARCUS. O! Titus, see, O! see what thou hast done;
In a bad quarrel slain a virtuous son.

TITUS. No, foolish tribune, no; no son of mine,
Nor thou, nor these, confederates in the deed
That hath dishonour'd all our family:
Unworthy brother, and unworthy sons!

LUCIUS. But let us give him burial, as becomes;
Give Mutius burial with our brethren.

TITUS. Traitors, away! he rests not in this tomb.
This monument five hundred years hath stood,
Which I have sumptuously re-edified:
Here none but soldiers and Rome's servitors
Repose in fame; none basely slain in brawls.
Bury him where you can; he comes not here.

MARCUS. My lord, this is impiety in you.
My nephew Mutius' deeds do plead for him;
He must be buried with his brethren.

QUINTUS.
MARTIUS. } And shall, or him we will accompany.

TITUS. And shall! What villain was it spake that word?

QUINTUS. He that would vouch it in any place but here.
TITUS. What! would you bury him in my despite?
MARCUS. No, noble Titus; but entreat of thee
　　To pardon Mutius, and to bury him.
TITUS. Marcus, even thou hast struck upon my crest,
　　And, with these boys, mine honour thou hast wounded:
　　My foes I do repute you every one;
　　So, trouble me no more, but get you gone.
MARTIUS. He is not with himself; let us withdraw.
QUINTUS. Not I, till Mutius' bones be buried.

　　　　　　　　Marcus and the sons of Titus kneel

MARCUS. Brother, for in that name doth nature plead,—
QUINTUS. Father, and in that name doth nature speak,—
TITUS. Speak thou no more, if all the rest will speed.
MARCUS. Renowned Titus, more than half my soul,—
LUCIUS. Dear father, soul and substance of us all,—
MARCUS. Suffer thy brother Marcus to inter
　　His noble nephew here in virtue's nest,
　　That died in honour and Lavinia's cause.
　　Thou art a Roman; be not barbarous:
　　The Greeks upon advice did bury Ajax
　　That slew himself; and wise Laertes' son
　　Did graciously plead for his funerals.
　　Let not young Mutius then, that was thy joy,
　　Be barr'd his entrance here.
TITUS.　　　　　　　Rise, Marcus, rise.

　　　　　　　　　　　　　　They rise

　　The dismall'st day is this that e'er I saw,
　　To be dishonour'd by my sons in Rome!
　　Well, bury him, and bury me the next.

　　　　　　　　Mutius is put into the tomb

LUCIUS. There lie thy bones, sweet Mutius, with thy
　　　friends,
　　Till we with trophies do adorn thy tomb.
ALL. (*Kneeling*) No man shed tears for noble Mutius;
　　He lives in fame that died in virtue's cause.
MARCUS. My lord,—to step out of these dreary dumps,—
　　How comes it that the subtle Queen of Goths
　　Is of a sudden thus advanc'd in Rome?
TITUS. I know not, Marcus; but I know it is,
　　Whether by device or no, the heavens can tell.
　　Is she not, then, beholding to the man

That brought her for this high good turn so far?

MARCUS. Yes, and will nobly him remunerate.

Flourish. Re-enter, on one side, Saturninus, attended;
Tamora, Demetrius, Chiron, and Aaron: on the other side,
Bassianus, Lavinia and Others

SATURNINUS. So, Bassianus, you have play'd your prize:
God give you joy, sir, of your gallant bride.

BASSIANUS. And you of yours, my lord! I say no more,
Nor wish no less; and so I take my leave.

SATURNINUS. Traitor, if Rome have law or we have power,
Thou and thy faction shall repent this rape.

BASSIANUS. Rape call you it, my lord, to seize my own,
My true-betrothed love and now my wife?
But let the laws of Rome determine all;
Meanwhile, I am possess'd of that is mine.

SATURNINUS. 'Tis good, sir: you are very short with us;
But, if we live, we 'll be as sharp with you.

BASSIANUS. My lord, what I have done, as best I may,
Answer I must and shall do with my life.
Only thus much I give your Grace to know:
By all the duties that I owe to Rome,
This noble gentleman, Lord Titus here,
Is in opinion and in honour wrong'd;
That, in the rescue of Lavinia,
With his own hand did slay his youngest son,
In zeal to you and highly mov'd to wrath
To be controll'd in that he frankly gave:
Receive him then to favour, Saturnine,
That hath express'd himself in all his deeds
A father and a friend to thee and Rome.

TITUS. Prince Bassianus, leave to plead my deeds:
'Tis thou and those that have dishonour'd me.
Rome and the righteous heavens be my judge,
How I have lov'd and honour'd Saturnine!

TAMORA. My worthy lord, if ever Tamora
Were gracious in those princely eyes of thine,
Then hear me speak indifferently for all;
And at my suit, sweet, pardon what is past.

SATURNINUS. What, madam! be dishonour'd openly,
And basely put it up without revenge?

TAMORA. Not so, my lord; the gods of Rome forfend
I should be author to dishonour you!

But on mine honour dare I undertake
For good Lord Titus' innocence in all,
Whose fury not dissembled speaks his griefs.
Then, at my suit, look graciously on him;
Lose not so noble a friend on vain suppose,
Nor with sour looks afflict his gentle heart.
(*Aside to Saturninus*) My lord, be rul'd by me, be
      won at last;
Dissemble all your griefs and discontents:
You are but newly planted in your throne;
Lest then, the people, and patricians too,
Upon a just survey, take Titus' part,
And so supplant you for ingratitude,
Which Rome reputes to be a heinous sin,
Yield at entreats, and then let me alone.
I 'll find a day to massacre them all,
And raze their faction and their family,
The cruel father, and his traitorous sons,
To whom I sued for my dear son's life;
And make them know what 'tis to let a queen
Kneel in the streets and beg for grace in vain.
(*Aloud*) Come, come, sweet emperor; come, Andron-
      icus;
Take up this good old man, and cheer the heart
That dies in tempest of thy angry frown.
SATURNINUS. Rise, Titus, rise; my empress hath prevail'd.
TITUS. I thank your majesty, and her, my lord.
These words, these looks, infuse new life in me.
TAMORA. Titus, I am incorporate in Rome,
A Roman now adopted happily,
And must advise the emperor for his good.
This day all quarrels die, Andronicus;
And let it be mine honour, good my lord,
That I have reconcil'd your friends and you.
For you, Prince Bassianus, I have pass'd
My word and promise to the emperor,
That you will be more mild and tractable.
And fear not, lords, and you, Lavinia,
By my advice, all humbled on your knees,
You shall ask pardon of his majesty.
LUCIUS. We do; and vow to heaven and to his highness,
That what we did was mildly, as we might,

Tendering our sister's honour and our own.

MARCUS. That on mine honour here I do protest.

SATURNINUS. Away, and talk not; trouble us no more.

TAMORA. Nay, nay, sweet emperor, we must all be friends:
The tribune and his nephews kneel for grace;
I will not be denied: sweet heart, look back.

SATURNINUS. Marcus, for thy sake, and thy brother's here,
And at my lovely Tamora's entreats,
I do remit these young men's heinous faults:
Stand up.
Lavinia, though you left me like a churl,
I found a friend, and sure as death I swore
I would not part a bachelor from the priest.
Come; if the emperor's court can feast two brides,
You are my guest, Lavinia, and your friends.
This day shall be a love-day, Tamora.

TITUS. To-morrow, an it please your majesty
To hunt the panther and the hart with me,
With horn and hound we 'll give your Grace bon jour.

SATURNINUS. Be it so, Titus, and gramercy too.

Trumpets. Exeunt

ACT TWO

SCENE ONE

Rome. Before the Palace.

Enter Aaron

AARON. Now climbeth Tamora Olympus' top,
Safe out of Fortune's shot; and sits aloft,
Secure of thunder's crack or lightning flash,
Advanc'd above pale envy's threatening reach.
As when the golden sun salutes the morn,
And, having gilt the ocean with his beams,
Gallops the zodiac in his glistering coach,
And overlooks the highest-peering hills;
So Tamora.
Upon her wit doth earthly honour wait
And virtue stoops and trembles at her frown.
Then, Aaron, arm thy heart, and fit thy thoughts
To mount aloft with thy imperial mistress,
And mount her pitch, whom thou in triumph long
Hast prisoner held, fetter'd in amorous chains,
And faster bound to Aaron's charming eyes
Than is Prometheus tied to Caucasus.
Away with slavish weeds and servile thoughts!
I will be bright, and shine in pearl and gold,
To wait upon this new-made empress.
To wait, said I? to wanton with this queen,
This goddess, this Semiramis, this nymph,
This siren, that will charm Rome's Saturnine,
And see his shipwrack and his commonweal's
Holla! what storm is this?
         Enter Demetrius and Chiron, braving
DEMETRIUS. Chiron, thy years want wit, thy wit wants edge
And manners, to intrude where I am grac'd,
And may, for aught thou know'st, affected be.

CHIRON. Demetrius, thou dost over-ween in all
    And so in this, to bear me down with braves.
    'Tis not the difference of a year or two
    Makes me less gracious or thee more fortunate:
    I am as able and as fit as thou
    To serve, and to deserve my mistress' grace;
    And that my sword upon thee shall approve,
    And plead my passions for Lavinia's love.
AARON. (*Aside*) Clubs, clubs! these lovers will not keep
        the peace.
DEMETRIUS. Why, boy, although our mother, unadvis'd,
    Gave you a dancing-rapier by your side,
    Are you so desperate grown, to threat your friends?
    Go to; have your lath glued within your sheath
    Till you know better how to handle it.
CHIRON. Meanwhile, sir, with the little skill I have,
    Full well shalt thou perceive how much I dare.
DEMETRIUS. Ay, boy, grow ye so brave?   *They draw*
AARON.   Why, how now, lords!
    So near the emperor's palace dare you draw,
    And maintain such a quarrel openly?
    Full well I wot the ground of all this grudge:
    I would not for a million of gold
    The cause were known to them it most concerns;
    Nor would your noble mother for much more
    Be so dishonour'd in the court of Rome.
    For shame, put up.
DEMETRIUS.   Not I, till I have sheath'd
    My rapier in his bosom, and withal
    Thrust those reproachful speeches down his throat
    That he hath breath'd in my dishonour here.
CHIRON. For that I am prepar'd and full resolv'd,
    Foul-spoken coward, that thunder'st with thy tongue,
    And with thy weapon nothing dar'st perform!
AARON. Away, I say!
    Now, by the gods that warlike Goths adore,
    This petty brabble will undo us all.
    Why, lords, and think you not how dangerous
    It is to jet upon a prince's right?
    What! is Lavinia then become so loose,
    Or Bassianus so degenerate,
    That for her love such quarrels may be broach'd

 Without controlment, justice, or revenge?
 Young lords, beware! an should the empress know
 This discord's ground, the music would not please.

CHIRON. I care not, I, knew she and all the world:
 I love Lavinia more than all the world.

DEMETRIUS. Youngling, learn thou to make some meaner
  choice:
 Lavinia is thine elder brother's hope.

AARON. Why, are ye mad? or know ye not in Rome
 How furious and impatient they be,
 And cannot brook competitors in love?
 I tell you, lords, you do but plot your deaths
 By this device.

CHIRON.   Aaron, a thousand deaths
 Would I propose, to achieve her whom I love.

AARON. To achieve her! how?

DEMETRIUS.   Why mak'st thou it so strange?
 She is a woman, therefore may be woo'd;
 She is a woman, therefore may be won;
 She is Lavinia, therefore must be lov'd.
 What, man! more water glideth by the mill
 That wots the miller of; and easy it is
 Of a cut loaf to steal a shive, we know:
 Though Bassianus be the emperor's brother,
 Better than he have worn Vulcan's badge.

AARON. (Aside) Ay, and as good as Saturninus may.

DEMETRIUS. Then why should he despair that knows to
  court it
 With words, fair looks, and liberality?
 What! hast thou not full often struck a doe,
 And borne her cleanly by the keeper's nose?

AARON. Why, then, it seems, some certain snatch or so
 Would serve your turns.

CHIRON.   Ay, so the turn were serv'd.

DEMETRIUS. Aaron, thou hast hit it.

AARON.   Would you had hit it too!
 Then should not we be tir'd with this ado.
 Why, hark ye, hark ye! and are you such fools
 To square for this? Would it offend you then
 That both should speed?

CHIRON.   Faith, not me.

DEMETRIUS. Nor me, so I were one.

AARON. For shame, be friends, and join for that you jar:
'Tis policy and stratagem must do
That you affect; and so must you resolve,
That what you cannot as you would achieve,
You must perforce accomplish as you may,
Take this of me: Lucrece was not more chaste
Than this Lavinia, Bassianus' love.
A speedier course than lingering languishment
Must we pursue, and I have found the path.
My lords, a solemn hunting is in hand;
There will the lovely Roman ladies troop:
The forest walks are wide and spacious,
And many unfrequented plots there are
Fitted by kind for rape and villany:
Single you thither then this dainty doe,
And strike her home by force, if not by words:
This way, or not at all, stand you in hope.
Come, come, our empress, with her sacred wit
To villany and vengeance consecrate,
Will we acquaint with all that we intend;
And she shall file our engines with advice,
That will not suffer you to square yourselves,
But to your wishes' height advance you both.
The emperor's court is like the house of Fame,
The palace full of tongues, of eyes, and ears:
The woods are ruthless, dreadful, deaf, and dull;
There speak, and strike, brave boys, and take your turns;
There serve your lusts, shadow'd from heaven's eye,
And revel in Lavinia's treasury.
CHIRON. Thy counsel, lad, smells of no cowardice.
DEMETRIUS. Sit fas aut nefas, till I find the stream
To cool this heat, a charm to calm these fits,
Per Styga, per manes vehor.   *Exeunt*

SCENE TWO

A Forest.

*Horns and cry of hounds heard. Enter Titus Andronicus,
with Hunters, &c.; Marcus, Lucius, Quintus,
and Martius*

TITUS. The hunt is up, the morn is bright and grey,
 The fields are fragrant and the woods are green.
 Uncouple here and let us make a bay,
 And wake the emperor and his lovely bride,
 And rouse the prince and ring a hunter's peal,
 That all the court may echo with the noise.
 Sons, let it be your charge, as it is ours,
 To attend the emperor's person carefully:
 I have been troubled in my sleep this night,
 But dawning day new comfort hath inspir'd.
   *A cry of hounds, and horns winded in a peal
   Enter Saturninus, Tamora, Bassianus, Lavinia,
   Demetrius, Chiron, and Attendants*
 Many good-morrows to your Majesty;
 Madam, to you as many and as good;
 I promised your Grace a hunter's peal.
SATURNINUS. And you have rung it lustily, my lord;
 Somewhat too early for new-married ladies.
BASSIANUS. Lavinia, how say you?
LAVINIA.   I say, no;
 I have been broad awake two hours and more.
SATURNINUS. Come on, then; horse and chariots let us have,
 And to our sport.—(*To Tamora*) Madam, now shall ye
   300
 Our Roman hunting.
MARCUS.   I have dogs, my lord,
 Will rouse the proudest panther in the chase,
 And climb the highest promontory top.
TITUS. And I have horse will follow where the game
 Makes way, and run like swallows o'er the plain.
DEMETRIUS. (*Aside*) Chiron, we hunt not, we, with horse
   nor hound,
 But hope to pluck a dainty doe to ground.   *Exeunt*

SCENE THREE

A lonely Part of the Forest.

Enter Aaron, with a bag of gold

AARON. He that had wit would think that I had none,
    To bury so much gold under a tree,
    And never after to inherit it.
    Let him that thinks of me so abjectly
    Know that this gold must coin a stratagem,
    Which, cunningly effected, will beget
    A very excellent piece of villany:
    And so repose, sweet gold, for their unrest
    That have their alms out of the empress' chest.

                                        Hides the gold

Enter Tamora

TAMORA. My lovely Aaron, wherefore look'st thou sad,
    When every thing doth make a gleeful boast?
    The birds chant melody on every bush,
    The snake lies rolled in the cheerful sun,
    The green leaves quiver with the cooling wind,
    And make a chequer'd shadow on the ground.
    Under their sweet shade, Aaron, let us sit,
    And, whilst the babbling echo mocks the hounds,
    Replying shrilly to the well-tun'd horns,
    As if a double hunt were heard at once,
    Let us sit down and mark their yelping noise;
    And after conflict, such as was suppos'd
    The wandering prince and Dido once enjoy'd,
    When with a happy storm they were surpris'd,
    And curtain'd with a counsel-keeping cave,
    We may, each wreathed in the other's arms,
    Our pastimes done, possess a golden slumber;
    Whiles hounds and horns and sweet melodious birds
    Be unto us as is a nurse's song
    Of lullaby to bring her babe asleep.
AARON. Madam, though Venus govern your desires,
    Saturn is dominator over mine:
    What signifies my deadly-standing eye,
    My silence and my cloudy melancholy,
    My fleece of woolly hair that now uncurls

Even as an adder when she doth unroll
To do some fatal execution?
No, madam, these are no venereal signs:
Vengeance is in my heart, death in my hand,
Blood and revenge are hammering in my head.
Hark, Tamora, the empress of my soul,
Which never hopes more heaven than rests in thee,
This is the day of doom for Bassianus;
His Philomel must lose her tongue to-day,
Thy sons make pillage of her chastity,
And wash their hands in Bassianus' blood.
Seest thou this letter? take it up, I pray thee,
And give the king this fatal-plotted scroll.
Now question me no more; we are espied;
Here comes a parcel of our hopeful booty,
Which dreads not yet their lives' destruction.

TAMORA. Ah! my sweet Moor, sweeter to me than life.

AARON. No more, great empress; Bassianus comes:
Be cross with him; and I 'll go fetch thy sons
To back thy quarrels, whatsoe'er they be.   *Exit*
          Enter Bassianus and Lavinia

BASSIANUS. Who have we here? Rome's royal empress,
Unfurnish'd of her well-beseeming troop?
Or is it Dian, habited like her,
Who hath abandoned her holy groves,
To see the general hunting in this forest?

TAMORA. Saucy controller of our private steps!
Had I the power that some say Dian had,
Thy temples should be planted presently
With horns, as was Actæon's; and the hounds
Should drive upon thy new-transformed limbs,
Unmannerly intruder as thou art!

LAVINIA. Under your patience, gentle empress,
'Tis thought you have a goodly gift in horning;
And to be doubted that your Moor and you
Are singled forth to try experiments.
Jove shield your husband from his hounds to-day!
'Tis pity they should take him for a stag.

BASSIANUS. Believe me, queen, your swarth Cimmerian
Doth make your honour of his body's hue,
Spotted, detested, and abominable.
Why are you sequester'd from all your train,

Dismounted from your snow-white goodly steed,
And wander'd hither to an obscure plot,
Accompanied but with a barbarous Moor,
If foul desire had not conducted you?

LAVINIA. And, being intercepted in your sport,
Great reason that my noble lord be rated
For sauciness. I pray you, let us hence,
And let her joy her raven-colour'd love;
This valley fits the purpose passing well.

BASSIANUS. The king my brother shall have note of this.

LAVINIA. Ay, for these slips have made him noted long:
Good king to be so mightily abus'd!

TAMORA. Why have I patience to endure all this?

Enter Demetrius and Chiron

DEMETRIUS. How now, dear sovereign, and our gracious
mother!
Why doth your Highness look so pale and wan?

TAMORA. Have I not reason, think you, to look pale?
These two have 'tic'd me hither to this place:
A barren detested vale, you see, it is;
The trees, though summer, yet forlorn and lean,
O'ercome with moss and baleful mistletoe:
Here never shines the sun; here nothing breeds,
Unless the nightly owl or fatal raven:
And when they show'd me this abhorred pit,
They told me, here, at dead time of the night,
A thousand fiends, a thousand hissing snakes,
Ten thousand swelling toads, as many urchins,
Would make such fearful and confused cries,
As any mortal body hearing it
Should straight fall mad, or else die suddenly.
No sooner had they told this hellish tale,
But straight they told me they would bind me here
Unto the body of a dismal yew,
And leave me to this miserable death:
And then they called me foul adulteress,
Lascivious Goth, and all the bitterest terms
That ever ear did hear to such effect;
And, had you not by wondrous fortune come,
This vengeance on me had they executed.
Revenge it, as you love your mother's life,
Or be ye not henceforth call'd my children.

AARON. Vengeance is in my heart, death in my hand,
   Blood and revenge are hammering in my head.

DEMETRIUS. This is a witness that I am thy son.
                              Stabs Bassianus

CHIRON. And this for me, struck home to show my
  strength.   *Also stabs Bassianus, who dies*

LAVINIA. Ay, come, Semiramis, nay, barbarous Tamora;
 For no name fits thy nature but thy own.

TAMORA. Give me thy poniard; you shall know, my boys,
 Your mother's hand shall right your mother's wrong.

DEMETRIUS. Stay, madam; here is more belongs to her:
 First thrash the corn, then after burn the straw.
 This minion stood upon her chastity,
 Upon her nuptial vow, her loyalty,
 And with that painted hope she braves your mightiness:
 And shall she carry this unto her grave?

CHIRON. And if she do, I would I were an eunuch.
 Drag hence her husband to some secret hole,
 And make his dead trunk pillow to our lust.

TAMORA. But when ye have the honey ye desire,
 Let not this wasp outlive, us both to sting.

CHIRON. I warrant you, madam, we will make that sure.
 Come, mistress, now perforce we will enjoy
 That nice-preserved honesty of yours.

LAVINIA. O Tamora! thou bear'st a woman's face,—

TAMORA. I will not hear her speak; away with her!

LAVINIA. Sweet lords, entreat her hear me but a word.

DEMETRIUS. Listen, fair madam: let it be your glory
 To see her tears; but be your heart to them
 As unrelenting flint to drops of rain.

LAVINIA. When did the tiger's young ones teach the dam?
 O! do not learn her wrath; she taught it thee;
 The milk thou suck'dst from her did turn to marble;
 Even at thy teat thou hadst thy tyranny.
 Yet every mother breeds not sons alike:
 (*To Chiron*) Do thou entreat her show a woman's pity.

CHIRON. What! wouldst thou have me prove myself a
  bastard?

LAVINIA. 'Tis true! the raven doth not hatch a lark:
 Yet have I heard, O! could I find it now,
 The lion moved with pity did endure
 To have his princely paws par'd all away.
 Some say that ravens foster forlorn children,
 The whilst their own birds famish in their nests:

O! be to me, though thy hard heart say no,
Nothing so kind, but something pitiful.

TAMORA. I know not what it means; away with her!

LAVINIA. O, let me teach thee! for my father's sake,
That gave thee life when well he might have slain thee,
Be not obdurate, open thy deaf ears.

TAMORA. Hadst thou in person ne'er offended me,
Even for his sake am I pitiless.
Remember, boys, I pour'd forth tears in vain
To save your brother from the sacrifice;
But fierce Andronicus would not relent:
Therefore, away with her, and use her as you will:
The worse to her, the better lov'd of me.

LAVINIA. O Tamora! be call'd a gentle queen,
And with thine own hands kill me in this place;
For 'tis not life that I have begg'd so long;
Poor I was slain when Bassianus died.

TAMORA. What begg'st thou then? fond woman, let me go.

LAVINIA. 'Tis present death I beg; and one thing more
That womanhood denies my tongue to tell,
O! keep me from their worse than killing lust,
And tumble me into some loathsome pit,
Where never man's eye may behold my body:
Do this, and be a charitable murderer.

TAMORA. So should I rob my sweet sons of their fee:
No, let them satisfy their lust on thee.

DEMETRIUS. Away! for thou hast stay'd us here too long.

LAVINIA. No grace! no womanhood! Ah, beastly creature,
The blot and enemy to our general name.
Confusion fall—

CHIRON. Nay, then I'll stop your mouth. Bring thou her
husband:
This is the hole where Aaron bid us hide him.

*Demetrius throws the body of Bassianus into the pit;
then exeunt Demetrius and Chiron, dragging off Lavinia*

TAMORA. Farewell, my sons: see that you make her sure.
Ne'er let my heart know merry cheer indeed
Till all the Andronici be made away.
Now will I hence to seek my lovely Moor,
And let my spleenful sons this trull deflower.   *Exit*

Enter Aaron, with Quintus and Martius

AARON. Come on, my lords, the better foot before:

Straight will I bring you to the loathsome pit
Where I espied the panther fast asleep.

QUINTUS. My sight is very dull, whate'er it bodes.

MARTIUS. And mine, I promise you: were 't not for shame,
Well could I leave our sport to sleep awhile.

Falls into the pit

QUINTUS. What! art thou fall'n? What subtle hole is this,
Whose mouth is cover'd with rude-growing briers,
Upon whose leaves are drops of new-shed blood
As fresh as morning's dew distill'd on flowers?
A very fatal place it seems to me.
Speak, brother, hast thou hurt thee with the fall?

MARTIUS. O brother! with the dismall'st object hurt
That ever eye with sight made heart lament.

AARON. (*Aside*) Now will I fetch the king to find them
here,
That he thereby may give a likely guess
How these were they that made away his brother. *Exit*

MARTIUS. Why dost not comfort me, and help me out
From this unhallow'd and blood-stained hole?

QUINTUS. I am surprised with an uncouth fear:
A chilling sweat o'erruns my trembling joints:
My heart suspects more than mine eye can see.

MARTIUS. To prove thou hast a true-divining heart,
Aaron and thou look down into this den,
And see a fearful sight of blood and death.

QUINTUS. Aaron is gone; and my compassionate heart
Will not permit mine eyes once to behold
The thing whereat it trembles by surmise.
O! tell me how it is; for ne'er till now
Was I a child, to fear I know not what.

MARTIUS. Lord Bassianus lies embrewed here,
All on a heap, like to a slaughter'd lamb,
In this detested, dark, blood-drinking pit.

QUINTUS. If it be dark, how dost thou know 'tis he?

MARTIUS. Upon his bloody finger he doth wear
A precious ring, that lightens all the hole,
Which, like a taper in some monument,
Doth shine upon the dead man's earthy cheeks,
And shows the ragged entrails of the pit:
So pale did shine the moon on Pyramus
When he by night lay bath'd in maiden blood.

O brother! help me with thy fainting hand,
If fear hath made thee faint, as me it hath,
Out of this fell devouring receptacle,
As hateful as Cocytus' misty mouth.

QUINTUS. Reach me thy hand, that I may help thee out;
Or, wanting strength to do thee so much good
I may be pluck'd into the swallowing womb
Of this deep pit, poor Bassianus' grave.
I have no strength to pluck thee to the brink.

MARTIUS. Nor I no strength to climb without thy help.

QUINTUS. Thy hand once more; I will not loose again,
Till thou art here aloft, or I below.
Thou canst not come to me: I come to thee. *Both fall in*
                    Re-enter Aaron with Saturninus

SATURNINUS. Along with me: I 'll see what hole is here,
And what he is that now is leap'd into it.
Say, who art thou that lately didst descend
Into this gaping hollow of the earth?

MARTIUS. The unhappy son of old Andronicus;
Brought hither in a most unlucky hour,
To find thy brother Bassianus dead.

SATURNINUS. My brother dead! I know thou dost but jest:
He and his lady both are at the lodge,
Upon the north side of this pleasant chase;
'Tis not an hour since I left him there.

MARTIUS. We know not where you left him all alive;
But, out alas! here have we found him dead.
          Re-enter Tamora, with Attendants; Titus Andronicus,
                    and Lucius

TAMORA. Where is my lord, the king?

SATURNINUS. Here, Tamora; though griev'd with killing
    grief.

TAMORA. Where is thy brother Bassianus?

SATURNINUS. Now to the bottom dost thou search my
    wound:
Poor Bassianus here lies murdered.

TAMORA. Then all too late I bring this fatal writ,
                              Giving a letter
The complot of this timeless tragedy;
And wonder greatly that man's face can fold
In pleasing smiles such murderous tyranny.

SATURNINUS. (*Reading*) 'And if we miss to meet him hand-
    somely,
  Sweet huntsman, Bassianus 'tis we mean,
  Do thou so much as dig the grave for him:
  Thou know'st our meaning. Look for thy reward
  Among the nettles at the elder-tree
  Which overshades the mouth of that same pit
  Where we decreed to bury Bassianus:
  Do this, and purchase us thy lasting friends.'
  O Tamora! was ever heard the like?
  This is the pit, and this the elder-tree.
  Look, sirs, if you can find the huntsman out
  That should have murder'd Bassianus here.
AARON. My gracious lord, here is the bag of gold.
SATURNINUS. (*To Titus*) Two of thy whelps, fell curs of
    bloody kind,
  Have here bereft my brother of his life.
  Sirs, drag them from the pit unto the prison:
  There let them bide until we have devis'd
  Some never-heard-of torturing pain for them.
TAMORA. What! are they in this pit? O wondrous thing!
  How easily murder is discovered!
TITUS. High emperor, upon my feeble knee
  I beg this boon with tears not lightly shed;
  That this fell fault of my accursed sons,
  Accursed, if the fault be prov'd in them,—
SATURNINUS. If it be prov'd! you see it is apparent.
  Who found this letter? Tamora, was it you?
TAMORA. Andronicus himself did take it up.
TITUS. I did, my lord: yet let me be their bail;
  For, by my father's reverend tomb, I vow
  They shall be ready at your Highness' will
  To answer their suspicion with their lives.
SATURNINUS. Thou shalt not bail them: see thou follow me.
  Some bring the murder'd body, some the murderers:
  Let them not speak a word; the guilt is plain;
  For, by my soul, were there worse end than death,
  That end upon them should be executed.
TAMORA. Andronicus, I will entreat the king:
  Fear not thy sons, they shall do well enough.
TITUS. Come, Lucius, come; stay not to talk with them.
                        Exeunt severally

SCENE FOUR

Another Part of the Forest.

Enter Demetrius and Chiron, with Lavinia, ravished; her hands cut off, and her tongue cut out

DEMETRIUS. So, now go tell, an if thy tongue can speak,
  Who 'twas that cut thy tongue and ravish'd thee.
CHIRON. Write down thy mind, bewray thy meaning so;
  An if thy stumps will let thee play the scribe.
DEMETRIUS. See, how with signs and tokens she can
    scrowl.
CHIRON. Go home, call for sweet water, wash thy hands.
DEMETRIUS. She hath no tongue to call, nor hands to wash;
  And so let 's leave her to her silent walks.
CHIRON. An 'twere my case, I should go hang myself.
DEMETRIUS. If thou hadst hands to help thee knit the cord.
                    Exeunt Demetrius and Chiron
                    Enter Marcus
MARCUS. Who 's this? my niece, that flies away so fast?
  Cousin, a word; where is your husband?
  If I do dream, would all my wealth would wake me!
  If I do wake, some planet strike me down,
  That I may slumber in eternal sleep!
  Speak, gentle niece, what stern ungentle hands
  Have lopp'd and hew'd and made thy body bare
  Of her two branches, those sweet ornaments,
  Whose circling shadows kings have sought to sleep in,
  And might not gain so great a happiness
  As have thy love? Why dost not speak to me?
  Alas! a crimson river of warm blood,
  Like to a bubbling fountain stirr'd with wind,
  Doth rise and fall between thy rosed lips,
  Coming and going with thy honey breath.
  But, sure, some Tereus hath deflower'd thee,
  And, lest thou shouldst detect him, cut thy tongue.
  Ah! now thou turn'st away thy face for shame
  And, notwithstanding all this loss of blood,
  As from a conduit with three issuing spouts,
  Yet do thy cheeks look red as Titan's face
  Blushing to be encounter'd with a cloud.

Shall I speak for thee? shall I say 'tis so?
O! that I knew thy heart; and knew the beast,
That I might rail at him to ease my mind.
Sorrow concealed, like to an oven stopp'd,
Doth burn the heart to cinders where it is.
Fair Philomela, she but lost her tongue,
And in a tedious sampler sew'd her mind:
But, lovely niece, that mean is cut from thee;
A craftier Tereus hast thou met withal,
And he hath cut those pretty fingers off,
That could have better sew'd than Philomel.
O! had the monster seen those lily hands
Tremble, like aspen-leaves, upon a lute,
And make the silken strings delight to kiss them,
He would not, then, have touch'd them for his life;
Or had he heard the heavenly harmony
Which that sweet tongue hath made,
He would have dropp'd his knife, and fell asleep,
As Cerberus at the Thracian poet's feet.
Come, let us go, and make thy father blind;
For such a sight will blind a father's eye:
One hour's storm will drown the fragrant meads;
What will whole months of tears thy father's eyes?
Do not draw back, for we will mourn with thee:
O! could our mourning ease thy misery.   *Exeunt*

ACT THREE

SCENE ONE

Rome. A Street.

*Enter Senators, Tribunes, and Officers of Justice, with
Martius and Quintus, bound, passing on to the place
of execution; Titus going before, pleading*

TITUS. Hear me, grave fathers! noble tribunes, stay!
For pity of mine age, whose youth was spent
In dangerous wars, whilst you securely slept;
For all my blood in Rome's great quarrel shed;
For all the frosty nights that I have watched;
And for these bitter tears, which now you see
Filling the aged wrinkles in my cheeks;
Be pitiful to my condemned sons,
Whose souls are not corrupted as 'tis thought.
For two and twenty sons I never wept,
Because they died in honour's lofty bed.
For these, these, tribunes, in the dust I write
              He throws himself on the ground
My heart's deep languor and my soul's sad tears.
Let my tears stanch the earth's dry appetite;
My sons' sweet blood will make it shame and blush.
      Exeunt Senators, Tribunes, &c., with the Prisoners
O earth! I will befriend thee more with rain,
That shall distil from these two ancient urns,
Than youthful April shall with all his showers:
In summer's drought I 'll drop upon thee still;
In winter with warm tears I 'll melt the snow,
And keep eternal spring-time on thy face,
So thou refuse to drink my dear sons' blood.
        Enter Lucius, with his sword drawn
O reverend tribunes! O gentle, aged men!
Unbind my sons, reverse the doom of death:

And let me say, that never wept before,
My tears are now prevailing orators.

LUCIUS. O noble father, you lament in vain:
The tribunes hear you not, no man is by;
And you recount your sorrows to a stone.

TITUS. Ah! Lucius, for thy brothers let me plead.
Grave tribunes, once more I entreat of you,—

LUCIUS. My gracious lord, no tribune hears you speak.

TITUS. Why, 'tis no matter, man: if they did hear,
They would not mark me, or if they did mark,
They would not pity me, yet plead I must,
All bootless unto them.
Therefore I tell my sorrows to the stones,
Who, though they cannot answer my distress,
Yet in some sort they are better than the tribunes,
For that they will not intercept my tale.
When I do weep, they humbly at my feet
Receive my tears, and seem to weep with me
And, were they but attired in grave weeds,
Rome could afford no tribune like to these.
A stone is soft as wax, tribunes more hard than stones.
A stone is silent, and offendeth not,
And tribunes with their tongues doom men to death.

Rises

But wherefore stand'st thou with thy weapon drawn?

LUCIUS. To rescue my two brothers from their death;
For which attempt the judges have pronounc'd
My everlasting doom of banishment.

TITUS. O happy man! they have befriended thee.
Why, foolish Lucius, dost thou not perceive
That Rome is but a wilderness of tigers?
Tigers must prey; and Rome affords no prey
But me and mine: how happy art thou then,
From these devourers to be banished!
But who comes with our brother Marcus here?

Enter Marcus and Lavinia

MARCUS. Titus, prepare thy aged eyes to weep;
Or, if not so, thy noble heart to break:
I bring consuming sorrow to thine age.

TITUS. Will it consume me? let me see it then.

MARCUS. This was thy daughter.

TITUS. Why, Marcus, so she is.

LUCIUS. Ay me! this object kills me.

TITUS. Faint-hearted boy, arise, and look upon her.
Speak, Lavinia, what accursed hand
Hath made thee handless in thy father's sight?
What fool hath added water to the sea,
Or brought a faggot to bright-burning Troy?
My grief was at the height before thou cam'st;
And now, like Nilus, it disdaineth bounds.
Give me a sword, I 'll chop off my hands too;
For they have fought for Rome, and all in vain;
And they have nurs'd this woe, in feeding life;
In bootless prayer have they been held up,
And they have serv'd me to effectless use:
Now all the service I require of them
Is that the one will help to cut the other.
'Tis well, Lavinia, that thou hast no hands,
For hands, to do Rome service, are but vain.

LUCIUS. Speak, gentle sister, who hath martyr'd thee?

MARCUS. O! that delightful engine of her thoughts,
That blabb'd them with such pleasing eloquence,
Is torn from forth that pretty hollow cage,
Where, like a sweet melodious bird, it sung
Sweet varied notes, enchanting every ear.

LUCIUS. O! say thou for her, who hath done this deed?

MARCUS. O! thus I found her straying in the park,
Seeking to hide herself, as doth the deer,
That hath receiv'd some unrecuring wound.

TITUS. It was my dear; and he that wounded her
Hath hurt me more than had he kill'd me dead:
For now I stand as one upon a rock
Environ'd with a wilderness of sea,
Who marks the waxing tide grow wave by wave,
Expecting ever when some envious surge
Will in his brinish bowels swallow him.
This way to death my wretched sons are gone;
Here stands my other son, a banished man,
And here my brother, weeping at my woes:
But that which gives my soul the greatest spurn,
Is dear Lavinia, dearer than my soul.
Had I but seen thy picture in this plight
It would have madded me: what shall I do
Now I behold thy lively body so?

Thou hast no hands to wipe away thy tears,
Nor tongue to tell me who hath martyr'd thee:
Thy husband he is dead, and for his death
Thy brothers are condemn'd, and dead by this.
Look! Marcus; ah! son Lucius, look on her:
When I did name her brothers, then fresh tears
Stood on her cheeks, as doth the honey-dew
Upon a gather'd lily almost wither'd.

MARCUS. Perchance she weeps because they kill'd her husband;
Perchance because she knows them innocent.

TITUS. If they did kill thy husband, then be joyful,
Because the law hath ta'en revenge on them.
No, no, they would not do so foul a deed;
Witness the sorrow that their sister makes.
Gentle Lavinia, let me kiss thy lips;
Or make some sign how I may do thee ease.
Shall thy good uncle, and thy brother Lucius,
And thou, and I, sit round about some fountain,
Looking all downwards, to behold our cheeks
How they are stain'd, like meadows yet not dry,
With miry slime left on them by a flood?
And in the fountain shall we gaze so long
Till the fresh taste be taken from that clearness,
And made a brine-pit with our bitter tears?
Or shall we cut away our hands, like thine?
Or shall we bite our tongues, and in dumb shows
Pass the remainder of our hateful days?
What shall we do? let us, that have our tongues,
Plot some device of further misery,
To make us wonder'd at in time to come.

LUCIUS. Sweet father, cease your tears; for at your grief
See how my wretched sister sobs and weeps.

MARCUS. Patience, dear niece. Good Titus, dry thine eyes.

TITUS. Ah! Marcus, Marcus, brother; well I wot
Thy napkin cannot drink a tear of mine,
For thou, poor man, hast drown'd it with thine own.

LUCIUS. Ah! my Lavinia, I will wipe thy cheeks.

TITUS. Mark, Marcus, mark! I understand her signs:
Had she a tongue to speak, now would she say
That to her brother which I said to thee:
His napkin, with his true tears all bewet,

Can do no service on her sorrowful cheeks.
O! what a sympathy of woe is this;
As far from help as limbo is from bliss.

Enter Aaron

AARON. Titus Andronicus, my lord the emperor
Sends thee this word: that, if thou love thy sons,
Let Marcus, Lucius, or thyself, old Titus,
Or any one of you, chop off your hand,
And send it to the king: he for the same
Will send thee hither both thy sons alive;
And that shall be the ransom for their fault.

TITUS. O gracious emperor! O gentle Aaron!
Did ever raven sing so like a lark,
That gives sweet tidings of the sun's uprise?
With all my heart, I 'll send the emperor my hand:
Good Aaron, wilt thou help to chop it off?

LUCIUS. Stay, father! for that noble hand of thine,
That hath thrown down so many enemies,
Shall not be sent; my hand will serve the turn:
My youth can better spare my blood than you;
And therefore mine shall save my brothers' lives.

MARCUS. Which of your hands hath not defended Rome,
And rear'd aloft the bloody battle-axe,
Writing destruction on the enemy's castle?
O! none of both but are of high desert:
My hand hath been but idle; let it serve
To ransom my two nephews from their death;
Then have I kept it to a worthy end.

AARON. Nay, come, agree whose hand shall go along,
For fear they die before their pardon come.

MARCUS. My hand shall go.

LUCIUS.   By heaven, it shall not go!

TITUS. Sirs, strive no more: such wither'd herbs as these
Are meet for plucking up, and therefore mine.

LUCIUS. Sweet father, if I shall be thought thy son,
Let me redeem my brothers both from death.

MARCUS. And for our father's sake, and mother's care,
Now let me show a brother's love to thee.

TITUS. Agree between you; I will spare my hand.

LUCIUS. Then I 'll go fetch an axe.

MARCUS.   But I will use the axe.

Exeunt Lucius and Marcus

TITUS. Come hither, Aaron; I 'll deceive them both:
    Lend me thy hand, and I will give thee mine.
AARON. (*Aside*) If that be call'd deceit, I will be honest,
    And never, whilst I live, deceive men so:
    But I 'll deceive you in another sort,
    And that you 'll say, ere half an hour pass.

                                Cuts off Titus' hand
            Re-enter Lucius and Marcus

TITUS. Now stay your strife: what shall be is dispatch'd.
    Good Aaron, give his majesty my hand:
    Tell him it was a hand that warded him
    From thousand dangers; bid him bury it;
    More hath it merited; that let it have.
    As for my sons, say I account of them
    As jewels purchas'd at an easy price;
    And yet dear too, because I bought mine own.
AARON. I go, Andronicus; and for thy hand,
    Look by and by to have thy sons with thee.
    (*Aside*) Their heads, I mean. O! how this villany
    Doth fat me with the very thoughts of it.
    Let fools do good, and fair men call for grace,
    Aaron will have his soul black like his face.   *Exit*
TITUS. O! here I lift this one hand up to heaven,
    And bow this feeble ruin to the earth:
    If any power pities wretched tears,
    To that I call! (*To Lavinia*) What! wilt thou kneel with
        me?
    Do, then, dear heart; for heaven shall hear our prayers,
    Or with our sighs we'll breathe the welkin dim,
    And stain the sun with fog, as sometime clouds
    When they do hug him in their melting bosoms.
MARCUS. O! brother, speak with possibilities,
    And do not break into these deep extremes.
TITUS. Is not my sorrow deep, having no bottom?
    Then be my passions bottomless with them.
MARCUS. But yet let reason govern thy lament.
TITUS. If there were reason for these miseries,
    Then into limits could I bind my woes.
    When heaven doth weep, doth not the earth o'erflow?
    If the winds rage, doth not the sea wax mad,
    Threatening the welkin with his big-swoln face?
    And wilt thou have a reason for this coil?

I am the sea; hark! how her sighs do blow
She is the weeping welkin, I the earth:
Then must my sea be moved with her sighs;
Then must my earth with her continual tears
Become a deluge, overflow'd and drown'd;
For why my bowels cannot hide her woes,
But like a drunkard must I vomit them.
Then give me leave, for losers will have leave
To ease their stomachs with their bitter tongues.

Enter a Messenger, with two heads and a hand

MESSENGER. Worthy Andronicus, ill art thou repaid
For that good hand thou sent'st the emperor.
Here are the heads of thy two noble sons,
And here 's thy hand, in scorn to thee sent back:
Thy griefs their sports, thy resolution mock'd;
That woe is me to think upon thy woes,
More than remembrance of my father's death.   *Exit*

MARCUS. Now let hot Ætna cool in Sicily,
And be my heart an ever burning hell!
These miseries are more than may be borne.
To weep with them that weep doth ease some deal,
But sorrow flouted at is double death.

LUCIUS. Ah! that this sight should make so deep a wound,
And yet detested life not shrink thereat,
That ever death should let life bear his name,
Where life hath no more interest but to breathe.

Lavinia kisses Titus

MARCUS. Alas! poor heart; that kiss is comfortless
As frozen water to a starved snake.

TITUS. When will this fearful slumber have an end?

MARCUS. Now, farewell, flattery: die, Andronicus;
Thou dost not slumber: see, thy two sons' heads,
Thy warlike hand, thy mangled daughter here;
Thy other banish'd son, with this dear sight
Struck pale and bloodless; and thy brother, I,
Even like a stony image, cold and numb.
Ah! now no more will I control thy griefs.
Rent off thy silver hair, thy other hand
Gnawing with thy teeth; and be this dismal sight
The closing up of our most wretched eyes!
Now is a time to storm; why art thou still?

TITUS. Ha, ha, ha!

MARCUS. Why dost thou laugh? it fits not with this hour.
TITUS. Why, I have not another tear to shed:
  Besides, this sorrow is an enemy,
  And would usurp upon my watery eyes,
  And make them blind with tributary tears:
  Then which way shall I find Revenge's cave?
  For these two heads do seem to speak to me,
  And threat me I shall never come to bliss
  Till all these mischiefs be return'd again
  Even in their throats that have committed them.
  Come, let me see what task I have to do.
  You heavy people, circle me about,
  That I may turn me to each one of you,
  And swear unto my soul to right your wrongs.
  The vow is made. Come, brother, take a head;
  And in this hand the other will I bear.
  Lavinia, thou shalt be employ'd in these things:
  Bear thou my hand, sweet wench, between thy teeth.
  As for thee, boy, go get thee from my sight;
  Thou art an exile, and thou must not stay:
  Hie to the Goths, and raise an army there:
  And if you love me, as I think you do,
  Let 's kiss and part, for we have much to do.
              Exeunt Titus, Marcus, and Lavinia
LUCIUS. Farewell, Andronicus, my noble father;
  The woefull'st man that ever liv'd in Rome:
  Farewell, proud Rome; till Lucius come again,
  He leaves his pledges dearer than his life.
  Farewell, Lavinia, my noble sister;
  O! would thou wert as thou tofore hast been;
  But now nor Lucius nor Lavinia lives
  But in oblivion and hateful griefs.
  If Lucius live, he will requite your wrongs,
  And make proud Saturnine and his empress
  Beg at the gates like Tarquin and his queen.
  Now will I to the Goths, and raise a power,
  To be reveng'd on Rome and Saturnine.   *Exit*

SCENE TWO

The Same. A Room in Titus' House. A Banquet set out.

Enter Titus, Marcus, Lavinia, and young Lucius, a Boy

TITUS. So, so; now sit; and look you eat no more
    Than will preserve just so much strength in us
    As will revenge these bitter woes of ours.
    Marcus, unknit that sorrow-wreathen knot:
    Thy niece and I, poor creatures, want our hands,
    And cannot passionate our tenfold grief
    With folded arms. This poor right hand of mine
    Is left to tyrannize upon my breast;
    And when my heart, all mad with misery,
    Beats in this hollow prison of my flesh,
    Then thus I thump it down.
    (*To Lavinia*) Thou map of woe, that thus dost talk in
      signs!
    When thy poor heart beats with outrageous beating
    Thou canst not strike it thus to make it still.
    Wound it with sighing, girl, kill it with groans;
    Or get some little knife between thy teeth,
    And just against thy heart make thou a hole;
    That all the tears that thy poor eyes let fall
    May run into that sink, and, soaking in,
    Drown the lamenting fool in sea-salt tears.
MARCUS. Fie, brother, fie! teach her not thus to lay
    Such violent hands upon her tender life.
TITUS. How now! has sorrow made thee dote already?
    Why, Marcus, no man should be mad but I.
    What violent hands can she lay on her life?
    Ah! wherefore dost thou urge the name of hands;
    To bid Æneas tell the tale twice o'er,
    How Troy was burnt and he made miserable?
    O! handle not the theme, to talk of hands,
    Lest we remember still that we have none.
    Fie, fie! how franticly I square my talk,
    As if we should forget we had no hands,
    If Marcus did not name the word of hands.
    Come, let 's fall to; and, gentle girl, eat this:
    Here is no drink. Hark, Marcus, what she says;

I can interpret all her martyr'd signs:
She says she drinks no other drink but tears,
Brew'd with her sorrow, mash'd upon her cheeks.
Speechless complainer, I will learn thy thought;
In thy dumb action will I be as perfect
As begging hermits in their holy prayers:
Thou shalt not sigh, nor hold thy stumps to heaven,
Nor wink, nor nod, nor kneel, nor make a sign,
But I of these will wrest an alphabet,
And by still practice learn to know thy meaning.

BOY. Good grandsire, leave these bitter deep laments:
Make my aunt merry with some pleasing tale.

MARCUS. Alas! the tender boy, in passion mov'd,
Doth weep to see his grandsire's heaviness.

TITUS. Peace, tender sapling; thou art made of tears,
And tears will quickly melt thy life away.

Marcus strikes the dish with a knife

What dost thou strike at, Marcus, with thy knife?

MARCUS. At that that I have kill'd, my lord; a fly.

TITUS. Out on thee, murderer! thou kill'st my heart;
Mine eyes are cloy'd with view of tyranny:
A deed of death, done on the innocent,
Becomes not Titus' brother. Get thee gone;
I see, thou art not for my company.

MARCUS. Alas! my lord, I have but kill'd a fly.

TITUS. But how if that fly had a father and a mother?
How would he hang his slender gilded wings
And buzz lamenting doings in the air!
Poor harmless fly,
That, with his pretty buzzing melody,
Came here to make us merry! and thou hast kill'd him.

MARCUS. Pardon me, sir; it was a black ill-favour'd fly,
Like to the empress' Moor; therefore I kill'd him.

TITUS. O, O, O!
Then pardon me for reprehending thee,
For thou hast done a charitable deed.
Give me thy knife, I will insult on him;
Flattering myself, as if it were the Moor
Come hither purposely to poison me.
There 's for thyself, and that 's for Tamora.
Ah! sirrah.
Yet I think we are not brought so low,

But that between us we can kill a fly
That comes in likeness of a coal-black Moor.
MARCUS. Alas! poor man; grief has so wrought on him,
He takes false shadows for true substances.
TITUS. Come, take away. Lavinia, go with me:
I 'll to thy closet; and go read with thee
Sad stories chanced in the times of old.
Come, boy, and go with me: thy sight is young,
And thou shalt read when mine begins to dazzle.

Exeunt

ACT FOUR

SCENE ONE

Rome. Titus' Garden.

*Enter Titus and Marcus. Then enter young Lucius, with
his books under his arm, Lavinia
running after him*

BOY. Help, grandsire, help! my aunt Lavinia
Follows me every where, I know not why:
Good uncle Marcus, see how swift she comes!
Alas! sweet aunt, I know not what you mean.
MARCUS. Stand by me, Lucius; do not fear thine aunt.
TITUS. She loves thee, boy, too well to do thee harm.
BOY. Ay, when my father was in Rome, she did.
MARCUS. What means my niece Lavinia by these signs?
TITUS. Fear her not, Lucius: somewhat doth she mean.
See, Lucius, see how much she makes of thee;
Somewhither would she have thee go with her.
Ah! boy; Cornelia never with more care
Read to her sons, than she hath read to thee
Sweet poetry and Tully's Orator.
MARCUS. Canst thou not guess wherefore she plies thee
    thus?
BOY. My Lord, I know not, I, nor can I guess,
Unless some fit or frenzy do possess her;
For I have heard my grandsire say full oft,
Extremity of griefs would make men mad;
And I have read that Hecuba of Troy
Ran mad through sorrow; that made me to fear,
Although, my lord, I know my noble aunt
Loves me as dear as e'er my mother did,
And would not, but in fury, fright my youth;
Which made me down to throw my books and fly,
Causeless, perhaps. But pardon me, sweet aunt;

And, madam, if my uncle Marcus go,
I will most willingly attend your ladyship.
MARCUS. Lucius, I will.   *Lavinia turns over*
                              the books which Lucius had let fall
TITUS. How now, Lavinia! Marcus, what means this?
Some book there is that she desires to see.
Which is it, girl, of these? Open them, boy.
But thou art deeper read, and better skill'd;
Come, and take choice of all my library,
And so beguile thy sorrow, till the heavens
Reveal the damn'd contriver of this deed.
Why lifts she up her arms in sequence thus?
MARCUS. I think she means that there was more than one
Confederate in the fact: ay, more there was;
Or else to heaven she heaves them for revenge.
TITUS. Lucius, what book is that she tosseth so?
BOY. Grandsire, 'tis Ovid's Metamorphoses;
My mother gave it me.
MARCUS.   For love of her that 's gone,
Perhaps, she cull'd it from among the rest.
TITUS. Soft! see how busily she turns the leaves!
                              Helping her
What would she find? Lavinia, shall I read?
This is the tragic tale of Philomel,
And treats of Tereus' treason and his rape;
And rape, I fear, was root of thine annoy.
MARCUS. See, brother, see! note how she quotes the leaves.
TITUS. Lavinia, wert thou thus surpris'd, sweet girl,
Ravish'd and wrong'd, as Philomela was,
Forc'd in the ruthless, vast, and gloomy woods?
See, see!
Ay, such a place there is, where we did hunt,
O! had we never, never hunted there,—
Pattern'd by that the poet here describes,
By nature made for murders and for rapes.
MARCUS. O! why should nature build so foul a den,
Unless the gods delight in tragedies?
TITUS. Give signs, sweet girl, for here are none but friends,
What Roman lord it was durst do the deed:
Or slunk not Saturnine, as Tarquin erst,
That left the camp to sin in Lucrece' bed?
MARCUS. Sit down, sweet niece: brother, sit down by me.

MARCUS.   Write thou, good niece, and here display at last
    What God will have discover'd for revenge.

Apollo, Pallas, Jove, or Mercury,
Inspire me, that I may this treason find!
My lord, look here; look here, Lavinia:
This sandy plot is plain; guide, if thou canst,
This after me.   *He writes his name with
                his staff, and guides it with his feet and mouth*
              I have writ my name
Without the help of any hand at all.
Curs'd be that heart that forc'd us to this shift!
Write thou, good niece, and here display at last
What God will have discover'd for revenge.
Heaven guide thy pen to print thy sorrows plain,
That we may know the traitors and the truth!
                          *She takes the staff in her
              mouth, and guides it with her stumps, and writes*
TITUS. O! do you read, my lord, what she hath writ?
  'Stuprum—Chiron—Demetrius.'
MARCUS. What, what! the lustful sons of Tamora
  Performers of this heinous bloody deed?
TITUS. Magni dominator poli,
  Tam lentus audis scelera? tam lentus vides?
MARCUS. O! calm thee, gentle lord; although I know
  There is enough written upon this earth
  To stir a mutiny in the mildest thoughts
  And arm the minds of infants to exclaims.
  My lord, kneel down with me; Lavinia, kneel;
  And kneel, sweet boy, the Roman Hector's hope;
  And swear with me, as, with the woeful fere
  And father of that chaste dishonour'd dame,
  Lord Junius Brutus sware for Lucrece' rape,
  That we will prosecute by good advice
  Mortal revenge upon these traitorous Goths,
  And see their blood, or die with this reproach.
TITUS. 'Tis sure enough, an you knew how;
  But if you hunt these bear-whelps, then beware:
  The dam will wake, an if she wind you once:
  She's with the lion deeply still in league,
  And lulls him whilst she playeth on her back,
  And when he sleeps will she do what she list.
  You're a young huntsman, Marcus; let it alone;
  And, come, I will go get a leaf of brass,
  And with a gad of steel will write these words,

And lay it by: the angry northern wind
Will blow these sands like Sibyl's leaves abroad,
And where 's your lesson then? Boy, what say you?

BOY. I say, my lord, that if I were a man,
Their mother's bed-chamber should not be safe
For these bad bondmen to the yoke of Rome.

MARCUS. Ay, that 's my boy; thy father hath full oft
For his ungrateful country done the like.

BOY. And, uncle, so will I, and if I live.

TITUS. Come, go with me into mine armoury:
Lucius, I 'll fit thee; and withal my boy
Shall carry from me to the empress' sons
Presents that I intend to send them both:
Come, come; thou 'lt do thy message, wilt thou not?

BOY. Ay, with my dagger in their bosoms, grandsire.

TITUS. No, boy, not so; I 'll teach thee another course.
Lavinia, come. Marcus, look to my house;
Lucius and I 'll go brave it at the court:
Ay, marry, will we, sir; and we 'll be waited on.
                              Exeunt Titus, Lavinia, and Boy

MARCUS. O heavens! can you hear a good man groan,
And not relent or not compassion him?
Marcus, attend him in his ecstasy,
That hath more scars of sorrow in his heart
Than foemen's marks upon his batter'd shield;
But yet so just that he will not revenge.
Revenge, ye heavens, for old Andronicus!   *Exit*

SCENE TWO

The Same. A Room in the Palace.

*Enter, from one side, Aaron, Demetrius, and Chiron; from
the other young Lucius, and an Attendant, with a
bundle of weapons, and verses writ upon them*

CHIRON. Demetrius, here 's the son of Lucius;
He hath some message to deliver us.

AARON. Ay, some mad message from his mad grandfather.

BOY. My lords, with all the humbleness I may,
I greet your honours from Andronicus;
(*Aside*) And pray the Roman gods, confound you both!

DEMETRIUS. Gramercy, lovely Lucius: what 's the news?

BOY. (*Aside*) That you are both decipher'd, that 's the news,
For villains mark'd with rape. (*Aloud*) May it please you,
My grandsire, well advis'd, hath sent by me
The goodliest weapons of his armoury,
To gratify your honourable youth,
The hope of Rome, for so he bade me say;
And so I do, and with his gifts present
Your lordships, that whenever you have need,
You may be armed and appointed well.
And so I leave you both: (*Aside*) like bloody villains.
                              Exeunt Boy and Attendant

DEMETRIUS. What 's here? A scroll; and written round
     about?
Let 's see:—
     (*Reads*) 'Integer vitae, scelerisque purus,
               Non eget Mauri jaculis, nec arcu.'

CHIRON. O! 'tis a verse in Horace, I know it well.
I read it in the grammar long ago.

AARON. Ay just, a verse in Horace; right, you have it.
(*Aside*) Now, what a thing it is to be an ass!
Here 's no sound jest! the old man hath found their guilt.
And sends them weapons wrapp'd about with lines,
That wound, beyond their feeling, to the quick;
But were our witty empress well afoot,
She would applaud Andronicus' conceit:
But let her rest in her unrest awhile;
(*To them*) And now, young lords, was 't not a happy star
Led us to Rome, strangers, and more than so,
Captives, to be advanced to this height?
It did me good before the palace gate
To brave the tribune in his brother's hearing.

DEMETRIUS. But me more good, to see so great a lord
Basely insinuate and send us gifts.

AARON. Had he not reason, Lord Demetrius?
Did you not use his daughter very friendly?

DEMETRIUS. I would we had a thousand Roman dames
At such a bay, by turn to serve our lust.

CHIRON. A charitable wish and full of love.

AARON. Here lacks but your mother for to say amen.

CHIRON. And that would she for twenty thousand more.

DEMETRIUS. Come, let us go and pray to all the gods

For our beloved mother in her pains.

AARON. (*Aside*) Pray to the devils; the gods have given us
   over.   *Trumpets sound*

DEMETRIUS. Why do the emperor's trumpets flourish thus?

CHIRON. Belike, for joy the emperor hath a son.

DEMETRIUS. Soft! who comes here?

   Enter a Nurse, with a blackamoor Child

NURSE. Good-morrow, lords. O! tell me, did you see Aaron
   the Moor?

AARON. Well, more or less, or ne'er a whit at all,
   Here Aaron is; and what with Aaron now?

NURSE. O gentle Aaron! we are all undone.
   Now help, or woe betide thee evermore!

AARON. Why, what a caterwauling dost thou keep!
   What dost thou wrap and fumble in thine arms?

NURSE. O! that which I would hide from heaven's eye,
   Our empress' shame, and stately Rome's disgrace!
   She is deliver'd, lords, she is deliver'd.

AARON. To whom?

NURSE.   I mean, she 's brought a-bed.

AARON. Well, God give her good rest! What hath he sent
   her?

NURSE. A devil.

AARON. Why, then she 's the devil's dam: a joyful issue.

NURSE. A joyless, dismal, black, and sorrowful issue.
   Here is the babe, as loathsome as a toad
   Amongst the fairest breeders of our clime.
   The empress sends it thee, thy stamp, thy seal,
   And bids thee christen it with thy dagger's point.

AARON. 'Zounds, ye whore! is black so base a hue?
   Sweet blowse, you are a beauteous blossom, sure.

DEMETRIUS. Villain, what hast thou done?

AARON. That which thou canst not undo.

CHIRON. Thou hast undone our mother.

AARON. Villain, I have done thy mother.

DEMETRIUS. And therein, hellish dog, thou hast undone.
   Woe to her chance, and damn'd her loathed choice!
   Accurs'd the offspring of so foul a fiend!

CHIRON. It shall not live.

AARON. It shall not die.

NURSE. Aaron, it must; the mother wills it so.

AARON. What! must it, nurse? then let no man but I

Do execution on my flesh and blood.

DEMETRIUS. I 'll broach the tadpole on my rapier's point:
Nurse, give it me; my sword shall soon dispatch it.

AARON. Sooner this sword shall plough thy bowels up.
            Takes the Child from the Nurse, and draws
Stay, murderous villains! will you kill your brother?
Now, by the burning tapers of the sky,
That shone so brightly when this boy was got,
He dies upon my scimitar's sharp point
That touches this my first-born son and heir.
I tell you, younglings, not Enceladus,
With all his threatening band of Typhon's brood,
Nor great Alcides, nor the god of war,
Shall seize this prey out of his father's hands.
What, what, ye sanguine, shallow-hearted boys!
Ye white-lim'd walls! ye alehouse painted signs!
Coal-black is better than another hue,
In that it scorns to bear another hue;
For all the water in the ocean
Can never turn the swan's black legs to white,
Although she lave them hourly in the flood.
Tell the empress from me, I am of age
To keep mine own, excuse it how she can.

DEMETRIUS. Wilt thou betray thy noble mistress thus?

AARON. My mistress is my mistress; this myself;
The vigour, and the picture of my youth:
This before all the world do I prefer;
This maugre all the world will I keep safe,
Or some of you shall smoke for it in Rome.

DEMETRIUS. By this our mother is for ever sham'd.

CHIRON. Rome will despise her for this foul escape.

NURSE. The emperor in his rage will doom her death.

CHIRON. I blush to think upon this ignomy.

AARON. Why, there 's the privilege your beauty bears.
Fie, treacherous hue! that will betray with blushing
The close enacts and counsels of the heart:
Here 's a young lad fram'd of another leer:
Look how the black slave smiles upon the father,
As who should say, 'Old lad, I am thine own.'
He is your brother, lords, sensibly fed
Of that self blood that first gave life to you;
And from that womb where you imprisoned were

He is enfranchised and come to light:
Nay, he is your brother by the surer side,
Although my seal be stamped in his face.

NURSE. Aaron, what shall I say unto the empress?

DEMETRIUS. Advise thee, Aaron, what is to be done,
And we will all subscribe to thy advice:
Save thou the child, so we may all be safe.

AARON. Then sit we down, and let us all consult,
My son and I will have the wind of you:
Keep there; now talk at pleasure of your safety.

They sit

DEMETRIUS. How many women saw this child of his?

AARON. Why, so, brave lords! when we join in league,
I am a lamb; but if you brave the Moor,
The chafed boar, the mountain lioness,
The ocean swells not so as Aaron storms.
But say, again, how many saw the child?

NURSE. Cornelia the midwife, and myself,
And no one else but the deliver'd empress.

AARON. The empress, the midwife, and yourself:
Two may keep counsel when the third 's away.
Go to the empress; tell her this I said: *Stabbing her*
'Weke, weke!'
So cries a pig prepared to the spit.

DEMETRIUS. What mean'st thou, Aaron? Wherefore didst
thou this?

AARON. O lord, sir, 'tis a deed of policy:
Shall she live to betray this guilt of ours,
A long-tongu'd babbling gossip? no, lords, no.
And now be it known to you my full intent.
Not far, one Muli lives, my countryman;
His wife but yesternight was brought to bed.
His child is like to her, fair as you are:
Go pack with him, and give the mother gold,
And tell them both the circumstance of all,
And how by this their child shall be advanc'd,
And be received for the emperor's heir,
And substituted in the place of mine,
To calm this tempest whirling in the court;
And let the emperor dandle him for his own.
Hark ye, lords; you see, I have given her physic,

Pointing to the Nurse

And you must needs bestow her funeral;
'The fields are near, and you are gallant grooms.
This done, see that you take no longer days,
But send the midwife presently to me.
The midwife and the nurse well made away,
Then let the ladies tattle what they please.

CHIRON. Aaron, I see thou wilt not trust the air
With secrets.

DEMETRIUS. For this care of Tamora,
Herself and hers are highly bound to thee.

Exeunt Demetrius and
Chiron, bearing off the Nurse's body

AARON. Now to the Goths, as swift as swallow flies;
There to dispose this treasure in mine arms,
And secretly to greet the empress' friends.
Come on, you thick-lipp'd slave, I 'll bear you hence;
For it is you that puts us to our shifts:
I 'll make you feed on berries and on roots,
And feed on curds and whey, and suck the goat,
And cabin in a cave, and bring you up
To be a warrior, and command a camp.

Exit with the Child

SCENE THREE

The Same. A Public Place.

Enter Titus, bearing arrows, with letters on the ends of them;
with him Marcus, young Lucius, Publius, Sempronius,
Caius, and other Gentlemen, with bows

TITUS. Come, Marcus, come; kinsmen, this is the way.
Sir boy, now let me see your archery:
Look ye draw home enough, and 'tis there straight.
Terras Astræa reliquit:
Be you remember'd, Marcus, she 's gone, she 's fled.
Sirs, take you to your tools. You, cousins, shall
Go sound the ocean, and cast your nets;
Happily you may find her in the sea;
Yet there 's as little justice as at land.
No; Publius and Sempronius, you must do it;
'Tis you must dig with mattock and with spade,

And pierce the inmost centre of the earth:
Then, when you come to Pluto's region,
I pray you, deliver him this petition;
Tell him, it is for justice and for aid,
And that it comes from old Andronicus,
Shaken with sorrows in ungrateful Rome.
Ah! Rome. Well, well; I made thee miserable
What time I threw the people's suffrages
On him that thus doth tyrannize o'er me.
Go, get you gone; and pray be careful all,
And leave you not a man-of-war unsearch'd:
This wicked emperor may have shipp'd her hence;
And, kinsmen, then we may go pipe for justice.

MARCUS. O Publius! is not this a heavy case,
To see thy noble uncle thus distract?

PUBLIUS. Therefore, my lord, it highly us concerns
By day and night to attend him carefully,
And feed his humour kindly as we may,
Till time beget some careful remedy.

MARCUS. Kinsmen, his sorrows are past remedy.
Join with the Goths, and with revengeful war
Take wreak on Rome for his ingratitude,
And vengeance on the traitor Saturnine.

TITUS. Publius, how now! how now, my masters!
What! have you met with her?

PUBLIUS. No, my good lord; but Pluto sends you word,
If you will have Revenge from hell, you shall:
Marry, for Justice, she is so employ'd,
He thinks, with Jove in heaven, or somewhere else,
So that perforce you must needs stay a time.

TITUS. He doth me wrong to feed me with delays.
I 'll dive into the burning lake below,
And pull her out of Acheron by the heels.
Marcus, we are but shrubs, no cedars we;
No big-bon'd men fram'd of the Cyclops' size;
But metal, Marcus, steel to the very back,
Yet wrung with wrongs more than our backs can bear:
And sith there 's no justice in earth nor hell,
We will solicit heaven and move the gods
To send down Justice for to wreak our wrongs.
Come, to this gear. You are a good archer, Marcus.

He gives them the arrows

'Ad Jovem,' that 's for you: here 'ad Apollinem':
'Ad Martem,' that 's for myself:
Here boy, to Pallas: here, to Mercury:
To Saturn, Caius, not to Saturnine;
You were as good to shoot against the wind.
To it, boy! Marcus, loose when I bid.
Of my word, I have written to effect;
There 's not a god left unsolicited.

MARCUS. Kinsmen, shoot all your shafts into the court:
We will afflict the emperor in his pride.

TITUS. Now, masters, draw. (*They shoot*) O! well said,
Lucius!
Good boy, in Virgo's lap: give it Pallas.

MARCUS. My lord, I aim a mile beyond the moon:
Your letter is with Jupiter by this.

TITUS. Ha! Publius, Publius, what hast thou done?
See, see! thou hast shot off one of Taurus' horns.

MARCUS. This was the sport, my lord: when Publius shot,
The Bull, being gall'd, gave Aries such a knock
That down fell both the Ram's horns in the court;
And who should find them but the empress' villain?
She laugh'd, and told the Moor, he should not choose
But give them to his master for a present.

TITUS. Why, there it goes: God give his lordship joy!
Enter a Clown, with a basket, and two pigeons in it
News! news from heaven! Marcus, the post is come.
Sirrah, what tidings? have you any letters?
Shall I have justice? what says Jupiter?

CLOWN. O! the gibbet-maker? He says that he hath taken
them down again, for the man must not be hanged till
the next week.

TITUS. But what says Jupiter, I ask thee?

CLOWN. Alas! sir, I know not Jupiter; I never drank with
him in all my life.

TITUS. Why, villain, art not thou the carrier?

CLOWN. Ay, of my pigeons, sir; nothing else.

TITUS. Why, didst thou not come from heaven?

CLOWN. From heaven! alas! sir, I never came there. God
forbid I should be so bold to press to heaven in my
young days. Why I am going with my pigeons to the
tribunal plebs, to take up a matter of brawl betwixt my
uncle and one of the emperial's men.

MARCUS. Why, sir, that is as fit as can be to serve for your
  oration; and let him deliver the pigeons to the emperor
  from you.

TITUS. Tell me, can you deliver an oration to the emperor
  with a grace?

CLOWN. Nay, truly, sir, I could never say grace in all my
  life.

TITUS. Sirrah, come hither: make no more ado,
  But give your pigeons to the emperor:
  By me thou shalt have justice at his hands.
  Hold, hold; meanwhile, here 's money for thy charges.
  Give me pen and ink.
  Sirrah, can you with a grace deliver a supplication?

CLOWN. Ay, sir.

TITUS. Then here is a supplication for you. And when you
  come to him, at the first approach you must kneel; then
  kiss his foot; then deliver up your pigeons; and then
  look for your reward. I 'll be at hand, sir; see you do it
  bravely.

CLOWN. I warrant you, sir; let me alone.

TITUS. Sirrah, hast thou a knife? Come, let me see it.
  Here, Marcus, fold it in the oration;
  For thou hast made it like a humble suppliant:
  And when thou hast given it to the emperor,
  Knock at my door, and tell me what he says.

CLOWN. God be with you, sir; I will.

TITUS. Come, Marcus, let us go. Publius, follow me.

                                              Exeunt

SCENE FOUR

The Same. Before the Palace.

*Enter Saturninus, Tamora, Demetrius, Chiron, Lords, and
  Others: Saturninus with the arrows in his hand
  that Titus shot at him*

SATURNINUS. Why, lords, what wrongs are these! Was ever
    seen
  An emperor of Rome thus overborne,
  Troubled, confronted thus; and, for the extent
  Of egal justice, us'd in such contempt?
  My lords, you know, as do the mightful gods,—

However these disturbers of our peace
Buzz in the people's ears,—there nought hath pass'd,
But even with law, against the wilful sons
Of old Andronicus. And what an if
His sorrows have so overwhelm'd his wits,
Shall we be thus afflicted in his wreaks,
His fits, his frenzy, and his bitterness?
And now he writes to heaven for his redress:
See, here 's to Jove, and this to Mercury;
This to Apollo; this to the god of war;
Sweet scrolls to fly about the streets of Rome!
What 's this but libelling against the senate,
And blazoning our injustice every where?
A goodly humour, is it not, my lords?
As who would say, in Rome no justice were.
But if I live, his feigned ecstasies
Shall be no shelter to these outrages;
But he and his shall know that justice lives
In Saturninus' health; whom, if she sleep,
He 'll so awake, as she in fury shall
Cut off the proud'st conspirator that lives.
TAMORA. My gracious lord, my lovely Saturnine,
Lord of my life, commander of my thoughts,
Calm thee, and bear the faults of Titus' age,
The effects of sorrow for his valiant sons,
Whose loss hath pierc'd him deep and scarr'd his heart;
And rather comfort his distressed plight
Than prosecute the meanest or the best
For these contempts.—(*Aside*) Why, thus it shall
　　become
High-witted Tamora to gloze with all:
But, Titus, I have touch'd thee to the quick,
Thy life-blood out: if Aaron now be wise,
Then is all safe, the anchor's in the port.

Enter Clown

How now, good fellow! wouldst thou speak with us?
CLOWN. Yea, forsooth, an your mistership be emperial.
TAMORA. Empress I am, but yonder sits the emperor.
CLOWN. 'Tis he. God and Saint Stephen give you good den.
I have brought you a letter and a couple of pigeons here.
　　　　　　　　　　Saturninus reads the letter
SATURNINUS. Go, take him away, and hang him presently.

CLOWN. How much money must I have?

TAMORA. Come, sirrah, you must be hanged.

CLOWN. Hanged! By 'r lady, then I have brought up a
neck to a fair end.   *Exit, guarded*

SATURNINUS. Despiteful and intolerable wrongs!
Shall I endure this monstrous villany?
I know from whence this same device proceeds.
May this be borne? As if his traitorous sons,
That died by law for murder of our brother,
Have by my means been butcher'd wrongfully!
Go, drag the villain hither by the hair;
Nor age·nor honour shall shape privilege.
For this proud mock I 'll be thy slaughterman;
Sly frantic wretch, that holp'st to make me great,
In hope thyself should govern Rome and me.

Enter Æmilius

What news with thee, Æmilius?

ÆMILIUS. Arm, arm, my lord! Rome never had more cause.
The Goths have gather'd head, and with a power
Of high-resolved men, bent to the spoil,
They hither march amain, under conduct
Of Lucius, son to old Andronicus;
Who threats, in course of this revenge, to do
As much as ever Coriolanus did.

SATURNINUS. Is warlike Lucius general of the Goths?
These tidings nip me, and I hang the head
As flowers with frost or grass beat down with storms.
Ay, now begin our sorrows to approach:
'Tis he the common people love so much;
Myself hath often heard them say,
When I have walked like a private man,
That Lucius' banishment was wrongfully,
And they have wish'd that Lucius were their emperor.

TAMORA. Why should you fear? is not your city strong?

SATURNINUS. Ay, but the citizens favour Lucius,
And will revolt from me to succour him.

TAMORA. King, be thy thoughts imperious like thy name.
Is the sun dimm'd, that gnats do fly in it?
The eagle suffers little birds to sing,
And is not careful what they mean thereby,
Knowing that with the shadow of his wings
He can at pleasure stint their melody;

Even so mayst thou the giddy men of Rome.
Then cheer thy spirit; for know, thou emperor,
I will enchant the old Andronicus
With words more sweet, and yet more dangerous,
Than baits to fish, or honey-stalks to sheep,
Whenas the one is wounded with the bait,
The other rotted with delicious feed.

SATURNINUS. But he will not entreat his son for us.

TAMORA. If Tamora entreat him, then he will:
For I can smooth and fill his aged ear
With golden promises, that, were his heart
Almost impregnable, his old ears deaf,
Yet should both ear and heart obey my tongue.
(*To Æmilius*) Go thou before, be our ambassador:
Say that the emperor requests a parley
Of warlike Lucius, and appoint the meeting,
Even at his father's house, the old Andronicus.

SATURNINUS. Æmilius, do this message honourably.
And if he stand on hostage for his safety,
Bid him demand what pledge will please him best.

ÆMILIUS. Your bidding shall I do effectually.   *Exit*

TAMORA. Now will I to that old Andronicus,
And temper him with all the art I have,
To pluck proud Lucius from the warlike Goths.
And now, sweet emperor, be blithe again,
And bury all thy fear in my devices.

SATURNINUS. Then go successantly, and plead to him.
                                        Exeunt

ACT FIVE

SCENE ONE

Plains near Rome.

*Flourish. Enter Lucius, and an army of Goths,
with drums and colours*

LUCIUS. Approved warriors, and my faithful friends,
I have received letters from great Rome,
Which signify what hate they bear their emperor,
And how desirous of our sight they are.
Therefore, great lords, be, as your titles witness,
Imperious and impatient of your wrongs;
And wherein Rome hath done you any scath,
Let him make treble satisfaction.

FIRST GOTH. Brave slip, sprung from the great Andronicus,
Whose name was once our terror, now our comfort;
Whose high exploits and honourable deeds
Ingrateful Rome requites with foul contempt,
Be bold in us: we 'll follow where thou lead'st,
Like stinging bees in hottest summer's day
Led by their master to the flower'd fields,
And be aveng'd on cursed Tamora.

GOTHS. And, as he saith, so say we all with him.

LUCIUS. I humbly thank him, and I thank you all.
But who comes here, led by a lusty Goth?
Enter a Goth, leading Aaron, with his Child in his arms

SECOND GOTH. Renowned Lucius, from our troops I stray'd,
To gaze upon a ruinous monastery;
And as I earnestly did fix mine eye
Upon the wasted building, suddenly
I heard a child cry underneath a wall.
I made unto the noise; when soon I heard
The crying babe controll'd with this discourse:
'Peace, tawny slave, half me and half thy dam!

Did not thy hue bewray whose brat thou art,
Had nature lent thee but thy mother's look,
Villain, thou mightst have been an emperor:
But where the bull and cow are both milk-white,
They never do beget a coal-black calf.
Peace, villain, peace!—even thus he rates the babe,—
'For I must bear thee to a trusty Goth;
Who, when he knows thou art the empress' babe,
Will hold thee dearly for thy mother's sake.'
With this, my weapon drawn, I rush'd upon him,
Surpris'd him suddenly, and brought him hither,
To use as you think needful of the man.

LUCIUS. O worthy Goth, this is the incarnate devil
That robb'd Andronicus of his good hand:
This is the pearl that pleas'd your empress' eye,
And here 's the base fruit of his burning lust.
Say, wall-eye'd slave, whither wouldst thou convey
This growing image of thy fiend-like face?
Why dost not speak? What! deaf? not a word?
A halter, soldiers! hang him on this tree,
And by his side his fruit of bastardy.

AARON. Touch not the boy; he is of royal blood.

LUCIUS. Too like the sire for ever being good.
First hang the child, that he may see it sprawl;
A sight to vex the father's soul withal.
Get me a ladder.   *A ladder brought,*
                              which Aaron is made to ascend

AARON.   Lucius, save the child;
And bear it from me to the empress.
If thou do this, I 'll show thee wondrous things,
That highly may advantage thee to hear:
If thou wilt not, befall what may befall,
I 'll speak no more but 'Vengeance rot you all!'

LUCIUS. Say on; and if it please me which thou speak'st,
Thy child shall live, and I will see it nourish'd.

AARON. An if it please thee! why, assure thee, Lucius,
'Twill vex thy soul to hear what I shall speak;
For I must talk of murders, rapes, and massacres,
Acts of black night, abominable deeds,
Complots of mischief, treason, villanies
Ruthful to hear, yet piteously perform'd:
And this shall all be buried by my death,

Unless thou swear to me my child shall live.

LUCIUS. Tell on thy mind: I say, thy child shall live.

AARON. Swear that he shall, and then I will begin.

LUCIUS. Who should I swear by? thou believ'st no god:
That granted, how canst thou believe an oath?

AARON. What if I do not? as, indeed, I do not;
Yet, for I know thou art religious,
And hast a thing within thee called conscience,
With twenty popish tricks and ceremonies,
Which I have seen thee careful to observe,
Therefore I urge thy oath; for that I know
An idiot holds his bauble for a god,
And keeps the oath which by that god he swears,
To that I 'll urge him: therefore thou shalt vow
By that same god, what god soe'er it be,
That thou ador'st and hast in reverence,
To save my boy, to nourish and bring him up:
Or else I will discover nought to thee.

LUCIUS. Even by my god I swear to thee I will.

AARON. First, know thou, I begot him on the empress.

LUCIUS. O most insatiate and luxurious woman!

AARON. Tut! Lucius, this was but a deed of charity
To that which thou shalt hear of me anon.
'Twas her two sons that murder'd Bassianus;
They cut thy sister's tongue and ravish'd her,
And cut her hands and trimm'd her as thou saw'st.

LUCIUS. O detestable villain! call'st thou that trimming?

AARON. Why, she was wash'd, and cut, and trimm'd, and
'twas
Trim sport for them that had the doing of it.

LUCIUS. O barbarous, beastly villains, like thyself!

AARON. Indeed, I was their tutor to instruct them.
That codding spirit had they from their mother,
As sure a card as ever won the set;
That bloody mind, I think, they learn'd of me
As true a dog as ever fought at head.
Well, let my deeds be witness of my worth.
I train'd thy brethren to that guileful hole
Where the dead corpse of Bassianus lay;
I wrote the letter that thy father found,
And hid the gold within the letter mention'd,
Confederate with the queen and her two sons:

And what not done, that thou hast cause to rue,
Wherein I had no stroke of mischief in it?
I play'd the cheater for thy father's hand,
And, when I had it, drew myself apart,
And almost broke my heart with extreme laughter.
I pry'd me through the crevice of a wall
When, for his hand, he had his two sons' heads;
Beheld his tears, and laugh'd so heartily,
That both mine eyes were rainy like to his:
And when I told the empress of this sport,
She swounded almost at my pleasing tale,
And for my tidings gave me twenty kisses.

FIRST GOTH. What! canst thou say all this, and never
blush?

AARON. Ay, like a black dog, as the saying is.

LUCIUS. Art thou not sorry for these heinous deeds?

AARON. Ay, that I had not done a thousand more.
Even now I curse the day, and yet, I think,
Few come within the compass of my curse,
Wherein I did not some notorious ill:
As kill a man, or else devise his death;
Ravish a maid, or plot the way to do it;
Accuse some innocent, and forswear myself;
Set deadly enmity between two friends;
Make poor men's cattle break their necks;
Set fire on barns and hay-stacks in the night,
And bid the owners quench them with their tears,
Oft have I digg'd up dead men from their graves,
And set them upright at their dear friends' doors,
Even when their sorrows almost were forgot;
And on their skins, as on the bark of trees,
Have with my knife carved in Roman letters,
'Let not your sorrow die, though I am dead.'
Tut! I have done a thousand dreadful things
As willingly as one would kill a fly,
And nothing grieves me heartily indeed
But that I cannot do ten thousand more.

LUCIUS. Bring down the devil, for he must not die
So sweet a death as hanging presently.

Aaron is brought down from the ladder

AARON. If there be devils, would I were a devil,
To live and burn in everlasting fire,

So I might have your company in hell,
But to torment you with my bitter tongue!
LUCIUS. Sirs, stop his mouth, and let him speak no more.

Enter a Goth

GOTH. My lord, there is a messenger from Rome
Desires to be admitted to your presence.
LUCIUS. Let him come near.

Enter Æmilius

Welcome, Æmilius! what 's the news from Rome?
ÆMILIUS. Lord Lucius, and you princes of the Goths,
The Roman emperor greets you all by me;
And, for he understands you are in arms,
He craves a parley at your father's house,
Willing you to demand your hostages,
And they shall be immediately deliver'd.
FIRST GOTH. What says our general?
LUCIUS. Æmilius, let the emperor give his pledges
Unto my father and my uncle Marcus,
And we will come. March away.   *Exeunt*

SCENE TWO

Rome. Before Titus' House.

Enter Tamora, Demetrius, and Chiron, disguised

TAMORA. Thus, in this strange and sad habiliment,
I will encounter with Andronicus,
And say I am Revenge, sent from below
To join with him and right his heinous wrongs.
Knock at his study, where, they say, he keeps,
To ruminate strange plots of dire revenge;
Tell him, Revenge is come to join with him,
And work confusion on his enemies.   *They knock*

Enter Titus, above

TITUS. Who doth molest my contemplation?
Is it your trick to make me ope the door,
That so my sad decrees may fly away,
And all my study be to no effect?
You are deceiv'd; for what I mean to do,
See here, in bloody lines I have set down;
And what is written shall be executed.

TAMORA. Titus, I am come to talk with thee.

TITUS. No, not a word; how can I grace my talk,
  Wanting a hand to give it action?
  Thou hast the odds of me; therefore no more.

TAMORA. If thou didst know me, thou wouldst talk with
    me.

TITUS. I am not mad; I know thee well enough:
  Witness this wretched stump, witness these crimson lines;
  Witness these trenches made by grief and care;
  Witness the tiring day and heavy night;
  Witness all sorrow, that I know thee well
  For our proud empress, mighty Tamora.
  Is not thy coming for my other hand?

TAMORA. Know, thou sad man, I am not Tamora;
  She is thy enemy, and I thy friend:
  I am Revenge, sent from the infernal kingdom,
  To ease the gnawing vulture of thy mind,
  By working wreakful vengeance on thy foes.
  Come down, and welcome me to this world's light;
  Confer with me of murder and of death.
  There's not a hollow cave or lurking-place,
  No vast obscurity or misty vale,
  Where bloody murder or detested rape
  Can couch for fear, but I will find them out;
  And in their ears tell them my dreadful name,
  Revenge, which makes the foul offender quake.

TITUS. Art thou Revenge? and art thou sent to me,
  To be a torment to mine enemies?

TAMORA. I am; therefore come down, and welcome me.

TITUS. Do me some service ere I come to thee.
  Lo, by thy side where Rape and Murder stands;
  Now give some surance that thou art Revenge·
  Stab them, or tear them on thy chariot-wheels,
  And then I'll come and be thy waggoner,
  And whirl along with thee about the globe.
  Provide two proper palfreys, black as jet,
  To hale thy vengeful waggon swift away,
  And find out murderers in their guilty caves:
  And when thy car is loaden with their heads,
  I will discount, and by the waggon-wheel
  Trot like a servile footman all day long,
  Even from Hyperion's rising in the east

Until his very downfall in the sea:
And day by day I 'll do this heavy task,
So thou destroy Rapine and Murder there.
TAMORA. These are my ministers, and come with me.
TITUS. Are these thy ministers? what are they call'd?
TAMORA. Rapine and Murder; therefore called so,
'Cause they take vengeance of such kind of men.
TITUS. Good Lord, how like the empress' sons they are,
And you the empress! but we worldly men
Have miserable, mad, mistaking eyes.
O sweet Revenge! now do I come to thee;
And, if one arm's embracement will content thee,
I will embrace thee in it by and by.   *Exit above*
TAMORA. This closing with him fits his lunacy.
Whate'er I forge to feed his brain-sick fits,
Do you uphold and maintain in your speeches,
For now he firmly takes me for Revenge;
And, being credulous in this mad thought,
I 'll make him send for Lucius his son;
And, whilst I at a banquet hold him sure,
I 'll find some cunning practice out of hand
To scatter and disperse the giddy Goths,
Or, at the least, make them his enemies.
See, here he comes, and I must ply my theme.
Enter Titus
TITUS. Long have I been forlorn, and all for thee:
Welcome, dread Fury, to my woeful house:
Rapine and Murder, you are welcome too.
How like the empress and her sons you are!
Well are you fitted had you but a Moor:
Could not all hell afford you such a devil?
For well I wot the empress never wags
But in her company there is a Moor;
And would you represent our queen aright,
It were convenient you had such a devil.
But welcome as you are. What shall we do?
TAMORA. What wouldst thou have us do, Andronicus?
DEMETRIUS. Show me a murderer, I 'll deal with him.
CHIRON. Show me a villain that hath done a rape,
And I am sent to be reveng'd on him.
TAMORA. Show me a thousand that have done thee wrong,
And I will be revenged on them all.

TITUS. Look round about the wicked streets of Rome,
    And when thou find'st a man that 's like thyself,
    Good Murder, stab him; he 's a murderer.
    Go thou with him; and when it is thy hap
    To find another that is like to thee,
    Good Rapine, stab him; he 's a ravisher.
    Go thou with them; and in the emperor's court
    There is a queen attended by a Moor;
    Well mayst thou know her by thy own proportion,
    For up and down she doth resemble thee:
    I pray thee, do on them some violent death;
    They have been violent to me and mine.
TAMORA. Well hast thou lesson'd us; this shall we do.
    But would it please thee, good Andronicus,
    To send for Lucius, thy thrice-valiant son,
    Who leads towards Rome a band of warlike Goths,
    And bid him come and banquet at thy house:
    When he is here, even at thy solemn feast,
    I will bring in the empress and her sons,
    The emperor himself, and all thy foes,
    And at thy mercy shall they stoop and kneel,
    And on them shalt thou ease thy angry heart.
    What says Andronicus to this device?
TITUS. Marcus, my brother! 'tis sad Titus calls.

Enter Marcus

    Go, gentle Marcus, to thy nephew Lucius;
    Thou shalt inquire him out among the Goths:
    Bid him repair to me, and bring with him
    Some of the chiefest princes of the Goths;
    Bid him encamp his soldiers where they are:
    Tell him, the emperor and the empress too
    Feast at my house, and he shall feast with them.
    This do thou for my love; and so let him,
    As he regards his aged father's life.
MARCUS. This will I do, and soon return again.   *Exit*
TAMORA. Now will I hence about thy business,
    And take my ministers along with me.
TITUS. Nay, nay, let Rape and Murder stay with me;
    Or else I 'll call my brother back again,
    And cleave to no revenge but Lucius.
TAMORA. (*Aside to her sons*) What say you, boys? will
    you abide with him,

Whiles I go tell my lord the emperor
How I have govern'd our determin'd jest?
Yield to his humour, smooth and speak him fair,
And tarry with him till I turn again.

TITUS. (*Aside*) I know them all, though they suppose me
    mad;
And will o'er-reach them in their own devices;
A pair of cursed hell-hounds and their dam.

DEMETRIUS. (*Aside to Tamora*) Madam, depart at pleasure;
    leave us here.

TAMORA. Farewell, Andronicus: Revenge now goes
    To lay a complot to betray thy foes.   *Exit Tamora*

TITUS. I know thou dost; and, sweet Revenge, farewell.

CHIRON. Tell us, old man, how shall we be employ'd?

TITUS. Tut! I have work enough for you to do.
    Publius, come hither, Caius, and Valentine!
                Enter Publius and Others

PUBLIUS. What is your will?

TITUS. Know you these two?

PUBLIUS. The empress' sons,
    I take them, Chiron and Demetrius.

TITUS. Fie, Publius, fie! thou art too much deceiv'd;
The one is Murder, Rape is the other's name;
And therefore bind them, gentle Publius;
Caius and Valentine, lay hands on them;
Oft have you heard me wish for such an hour,
And now I find it: therefore bind them sure,
And stop their mouths, if they begin to cry.
       Exit. Publius, &c., seize Chiron and Demetrius

CHIRON. Villains, forbear! we are the empress' sons.

PUBLIUS. And therefore do we what we are commanded.
Stop close their mouths, let them not speak a word.
Is he sure bound? look that you bind them fast.
    Re-enter Titus, with Lavinia; she bearing a basin,
             and he a knife

TITUS. Come, come, Lavinia; look, thy foes are bound.
Sirs, stop their mouths, let them not speak to me,
But let them hear what fearful words I utter.
O villains, Chiron and Demetrius!
Here stands the spring whom you have stain'd with mud,
This goodly summer with your winter mix'd.
You kill'd her husband, and for that vile fault

Two of her brothers were condemn'd to death,
My hand cut off and made a merry jest:
Both her sweet hands, her tongue, and that more dear
Than hands or tongue, her spotless chastity,
Inhuman traitors, you constrain'd and forc'd.
What would you say if I should let you speak?
Villains! for shame you could not beg for grace.
Hark, wretches! how I mean to martyr you.
This one hand yet is left to cut your throats,
Whilst that Lavinia 'tween her stumps doth hold
The basin that receives your guilty blood.
You know your mother means to feast with me,
And calls herself Revenge, and thinks me mad.
Hark! villains, I will grind your bones to dust,
And with your blood and it I 'll make a paste;
And of the paste a coffin I will rear,
And make two pasties of your shameful heads·
And bid that strumpet, your unhallow'd dam,
Like to the earth swallow her own increase.
This is the feast that I have bid her to,
And this the banquet she shall surfeit on;
For worse than Philomel you us'd my daughter,
And worse than Procne I will be reveng'd.
And now prepare your throats. Lavinia, come.

He cuts their throats

Receive the blood: and when that they are dead,
Let me go grind their bones to powder small,
And with this hateful liquor temper it;
And in that paste let their vile heads be bak'd.
Come, come, be every one officious
To make this banquet, which I wish may prove
More stern and bloody than the Centaurs' feast.
So, now bring them in, for I will play the cook,
And see them ready 'gainst their mother comes.

Exeunt, bearing the dead bodies

SCENE THREE

The Same. Court of Titus' House. A banquet set out.

Enter Lucius, Marcus, and Goths, with Aaron prisoner

LUCIUS. Uncle Marcus, since it is my father's mind
    That I repair to Rome, I am content.
FIRST GOTH. And ours with thine, befall what fortune will.
LUCIUS. Good uncle, take you in this barbarous Moor,
    This ravenous tiger, this accursed devil;
    Let him receive no sustenance, fetter him,
    Till he be brought unto the empress' face,
    For testimony of her foul proceedings:
    And see the ambush of our friends be strong;
    I fear the emperor means no good to us.
AARON. Some devil whisper curses in mine ear,
    And prompt me, that my tongue may utter forth
    The venomous malice of my swelling heart!
LUCIUS. Away, inhuman dog! unhallow'd slave!
    Sirs, help our uncle to convey him in.
          Exeunt Goths, with Aaron. Trumpets sound
    The trumpets show the emperor is at hand.
      Enter Saturninus and Tamora, with Æmilius,
        Senators, Tribunes, and Others
SATURNINUS. What! hath the firmament more suns than
    one?
LUCIUS. What boots it thee, to call thyself a sun?
MARCUS. Rome's emperor, and nephew, break the parle;
    These quarrels must be quietly debated.
    The feast is ready which the careful Titus
    Hath ordain'd   an honourable end,
    For peace, for love, for league, and good to Rome:
    Please you, therefore, draw nigh, and take your places.
SATURNINUS. Marcus, we will.
          A table is brought in. Hautboys sound
*Enter Titus, dressed like a cook, Lavinia, veiled, young
Lucius, and Others. Titus places the dishes on the table*
TITUS. Welcome, my gracious lord; welcome, dread queen;
    Welcome, ye warlike Goths; welcome, Lucius;
    And welcome all. Although the cheer be poor,
    'Twill fill your stomachs; please you eat of it.

SATURNINUS. Why art thou thus attir'd, Andronicus?
TITUS. Because I would be sure to have all well
    To entertain your highness, and your empress.
TAMORA. We are beholding to you, good Andronicus.
TITUS. An if your highness knew my heart, you were.
    My lord the emperor, resolve me this:
    Was it well done of rash Virginius
    To slay his daughter with his own right hand,
    Because she was enforced, stain'd, and deflower'd?
SATURNINUS. It was, Andronicus.
TITUS. Your reason, mighty lord?
SATURNINUS. Because the girl should not survive her
        shame,
    And by her presence still renew his sorrows.
TITUS. A reason mighty, strong, and effectual;
    A pattern, precedent, and lively warrant,
    For me most wretched, to perform the like.
    Die, die, Lavinia, and thy shame with thee;
    And with thy shame thy father's sorrow die!

                                    Kills Lavinia

SATURNINUS. What hast thou done, unnatural and unkind?
TITUS. Kill'd her, for whom my tears have made me blind.
    I am as woeful as Virginius was,
    And have a thousand times more cause than he
    To do this outrage: and it is now done.
SATURNINUS. What! was she ravish'd? tell who did the deed.
TITUS. Will 't please you eat? will 't please your highness
        feed?
TAMORA. Why hast thou slain thine only daughter thus?
TITUS. Not I; 'twas Chiron and Demetrius:
    They ravish'd her, and cut away her tongue:
    And they, 'twas they, that did her all this wrong.
SATURNINUS. Go fetch them hither to us presently.
TITUS. Why, there they are both, baked in that pie;
    Whereof their mother daintily hath fed,
    Eating the flesh that she herself hath bred.
    'Tis true, 'tis true; witness my knife's sharp point.

                                    Kills Tamora

SATURNINUS. Die, frantic wretch, for this accursed deed!

                                    Kills Titus

LUCIUS. Can the son's eye behold his father bleed?
    There 's meed for meed, death for a deadly deed!

Kills Saturninus. A great
tumult. The people in confusion disperse.
Marcus, Lucius, and their partisans, go up into the balcony

MARCUS. You sad-fac'd men, people and sons of Rome,
By uproar sever'd, like a flight of fowl
Scatter'd by winds and high tempestuous gusts,
O! let me teach you how to knit again
This scatter'd corn into one mutual sheaf,
These broken limbs again into one body;
Lest Rome herself be bane unto herself,
And she whom mighty kingdoms curtsy to,
Like a forlorn and desperate castaway,
Do shameful execution on herself.
But if my frosty signs and chaps of age,
Grave witnesses of true experience,
Cannot induce you to attend my words,
(To Lucius) Speak, Rome's dear friend, as erst our
    ancestor,
When with his solemn tongue he did discourse
To love-sick Dido's sad attending ear
The story of that baleful burning night
When subtle Greeks surpris'd King Priam's Troy;
Tell us what Sinon hath bewitch'd our ears,
Or who hath brought the fatal engine in
That gives our Troy, our Rome, the civil wound.
My heart is not compact of flint nor steel,
Nor can I utter all our bitter grief,
But floods of tears will drown my oratory,
And break my very utterance, even in the time
When it should move you to attend me most,
Lending your kind commiseration.
Here is a captain, let him tell the tale;
Your hearts will throb and weep to hear him speak.
LUCIUS. Then, noble auditory, be it known to you,
That cursed Chiron and Demetrius
Were they that murdered our emperor's brother;
And they it was that ravished our sister.
For their fell faults our brothers were beheaded,
Our father's tears despis'd, and basely cozen'd
Of that true hand that fought Rome's quarrel out,
And sent her enemies unto the grave:
Lastly, myself unkindly banished,

   The gates shut on me, and turn'd weeping out,
To beg relief among Rome's enemies;
Who drown'd their enmity in my true tears,
And op'd their arms to embrace me as a friend:
And I am the turn'd forth, be it known to you,
That have preserv'd her welfare in my blood,
And from her bosom took the enemy's point,
Sheathing the steel in my adventurous body.
Alas! you know I am no vaunter, I;
My scars can witness, dumb although they are,
That my report is just and full of truth.
But, soft! methinks I do digress too much,
Citing my worthless praise: O! pardon me;
For when no friends are by, men praise themselves.
MARCUS. Now is my turn to speak. Behold this child;
                    Indicates Child in the arms of an Attendant
Of this was Tamora delivered,
The issue of an irreligious Moor,
Chief architect and plotter of these woes.
The villain is alive in Titus' house,
Damn'd as he is, to witness this is true.
Now judge what cause had Titus to revenge
These wrongs, unspeakable, past patience,
Or more than any living man could bear.
Now you have heard the truth, what say you, Romans?
Have we done aught amiss, show us wherein,
And, from the place where you behold us now,
The poor remainder of Andronici
Will, hand in hand, all headlong cast us down,
And on the ragged stones beat forth our brains,
And make a mutual closure of our house.
Speak, Romans, speak! and if you say we shall,
Lo! hand in hand, Lucius and I will fall.
ÆMILIUS. Come, come, thou reverend man of Rome,
And bring our emperor, gently in thy hand,
Lucius, our emperor; for well I know
The common voice do cry it shall be so.
ROMANS. Lucius, all hail! Rome's royal emperor!
MARCUS. (*To Attendants*) Go, go into old Titus' sorrowful
      house,
And hither hale that misbelieving Moor,
To be adjudg'd some direful slaughtering death,

As punishment for his most wicked life.

Exeunt Attendants

Lucius, Marcus, and the Others descend

ROMANS. Lucius, all hail! Rome's gracious governor!

LUCIUS. Thanks, gentle Romans: may I govern so,
To heal Rome's harms, and wipe away her woe!
But, gentle people, give me aim awhile,
For nature puts me to a heavy task.
Stand all aloof; but, uncle, draw you near,
To shed obsequious tears upon this trunk.
O! take this warm kiss on thy pale cold lips,

Kisses Titus

These sorrowful drops upon thy blood-stain'd face,
The last true duties of thy noble son!

MARCUS. Tear for tear, and loving kiss for kiss,
Thy brother Marcus tenders on thy lips:
O! were the sum of these that I should pay
Countless and infinite, yet would I pay them.

LUCIUS. Come hither, boy; come, come, and learn of us
To melt in showers: thy grandsire lov'd thee well:
Many a time he danc'd thee on his knee,
Sung thee asleep, his loving breast thy pillow;
Many a matter hath he told to thee,
Meet and agreeing with thine infancy;
In that respect, then, like a loving child,
Shed yet some small drops from thy tender spring,
Because kind nature doth require it so:
Friends should associate friends in grief and woe.
Bid him farewell; commit him to the grave;
Do him that kindness, and take leave of him.

BOY. O grandsire, grandsire! even with all my heart
Would I were dead, so you did live again.
O Lord! I cannot speak to him for weeping;
My tears will choke me if I ope my mouth.

Re-enter Attendants, with Aaron

FIRST ROMAN. You sad Andronici, have done with woes:
Give sentence on this execrable wretch,
That hath been breeder of these dire events.

LUCIUS. Set him breast-deep in earth, and famish him;
There let him stand, and rave, and cry for food:
If any one relieves or pities him,
For the offence he dies. This is our doom:

TITUS.   'Tis true, 'tis true; witness my knife's sharp point.

Some stay to see him fasten'd in the earth.
AARON. O! why should wrath be mute, and fury dumb?
I am no baby, I, that with base prayers
I should repent the evils I have done.
Ten thousand worse than ever yet I did
Would I perform, if I might have my will:
If one good deed in all my life I did,
I do repent it from my very soul.
LUCIUS. Some loving friends convey the emperor hence,
And give him burial in his father's grave.
My father and Lavinia shall forthwith
Be closed in our household's monument.
As for that heinous tiger, Tamora,
No funeral rite, nor man in mournful weeds,
No mournful bell shall ring her burial;
But throw her forth to beasts and birds of prey.
Her life was beast-like, and devoid of pity;
And, being so, shall have like want of pity.
See justice done on Aaron, that damn'd Moor,
By whom our heavy haps had their beginning:
Then, afterwards, to order well the state,
That like events may ne'er it ruinate.   *Exeunt*

ROMEO AND JULIET

CAST OF CHARACTERS

ESCALUS, *Prince of Verona*
PARIS, *a young Nobleman, Kinsman to the Prince*

MONTAGUE ⎱ *Heads of two Houses at variance*
CAPULET ⎰ *with each other*

Uncle to Capulet
ROMEO, *son to Montague*

MERCUTIO, *Kinsman to the Prince* ⎱ *Friends*
BENVOLIO, *Nephew to Montague* ⎰ *to Romeo*

TYBALT, *Nephew to Lady Capulet*
FRIAR LAURENCE, *a Franciscan*
FRIAR JOHN, *of the same Order*
BALTHASAR, *Servant to Romeo*

SAMPSON ⎱ *Servants to Capulet*
GREGORY ⎰

PETER, *Servant to Juliet's Nurse*
ABRAHAM, *Servant to Montague*
An Apothecary
Three Musicians
Page to Mercutio; Page to Paris, another Page; an
Officer

LADY MONTAGUE, *Wife to Montague*
LADY CAPULET, *Wife to Capulet*
JULIET, *Daughter to Capulet*
Nurse to Juliet

Chorus

Citizens of Verona; male and female Kinsfolk to
both Houses; Maskers, Guards, Watchmen, and
Attendants

SCENE

Verona; at Mantua

PROLOGUE

Enter Chorus

CHORUS. Two households, both alike in dignity,
 In fair Verona, where we lay our scene,
From ancient grudge break to new mutiny,
 Where civil blood makes civil hands unclean.
From forth the fatal loins of these two foes
 A pair of star-cross'd lovers take their life;
Whose misadventur'd piteous overthrows
 Do with their death bury their parents' strife.
The fearful passage of their death-mark'd love,
 And the continuance of their parents' rage,
Which, but their children's end, nought could remove,
 Is now the two hours' traffick of our stage;
The which if you with patient ears attend,
What here shall miss, our toil shall strive to mend. *Exit*

ROMEO AND JULIET

ACT ONE

SCENE ONE

Verona. A Public Place.

*Enter Sampson and Gregory, armed with
swords and bucklers*

SAMPSON. Gregory, o' my word, we 'll not carry coals.

GREGORY. No, for then we should be colliers.

SAMPSON. I mean, an we be in choler, we 'll draw.

GREGORY. Ay, while you live, draw your neck out o' the
collar.

SAMPSON. I strike quickly, being moved.

GREGORY. But thou art not quickly moved to strike.

SAMPSON. A dog of the house of Montague moves me.

GREGORY. To move is to stir, and to be valiant is to stand;
therefore, if thou art moved, thou runnest away.

SAMPSON. A dog of that house shall move me to stand: I
will take the wall of any man or maid of Montague's.

GREGORY. That shows thee a weak slave; for the weakest
goes to the wall.

SAMPSON. 'Tis true; and therefore women, being the
weaker vessels, are ever thrust to the wall: therefore I
will push Montague's men from the wall, and thrust his
maids to the wall.

GREGORY. The quarrel is between our masters and us their
men.

SAMPSON. 'Tis all one, I will show myself a tyrant: when
I have fought with the men, I will be cruel with the
maids; I will cut off their heads.

GREGORY. The heads of the maids?

SAMPSON. Ay, the heads of the maids, or their maiden-
heads; take it in what sense thou wilt.

GREGORY. They must take it in sense that feel it.

SAMPSON. Me they shall feel while I am able to stand; and 'tis known I am a pretty piece of flesh.

GREGORY. 'Tis well thou art not fish; if thou hadst, thou hadst been poor John. Draw thy tool; here comes two of the house of the Montagues.

Enter Abraham and Balthasar

SAMPSON. My naked weapon is out; quarrel, I will back thee.

GREGORY. How! turn thy back and run?

SAMPSON. Fear me not.

GREGORY. No, marry; I fear thee!

SAMPSON. Let us take the law of our sides; let them begin.

GREGORY. I will frown as I pass by, and let them take it as they list.

SAMPSON. Nay, as they dare. I will bite my thumb at them; which is a disgrace to them, if they bear it.

ABRAHAM. Do you bite your thumb at us, sir?

SAMPSON. I do bite my thumb, sir.

ABRAHAM. Do you bite your thumb at us, sir?

SAMPSON. (*Aside to Gregory*) Is the law of our side if I say ay?

GREGORY. (*Aside to Sampson*) No.

SAMPSON. No, sir, I do not bite my thumb at you, sir; but I bite my thumb, sir.

GREGORY. Do you quarrel, sir?

ABRAHAM. Quarrel, sir! no, sir.

SAMPSON. If you do, sir, I am for you: I serve as good a man as you.

ABRAHAM. No better.

SAMPSON. Well, sir.

GREGORY. (*Aside to Sampson*) Say 'better'; here comes one of my master's kinsmen.

SAMPSON. Yes, better, sir.

ABRAHAM. You lie.

SAMPSON. Draw, if you be men. Gregory, remember thy swashing blow.   *They fight*

Enter Benvolio

BENVOLIO. Part, fools!
Put up your swords; you know not what you do.

Beats down their swords
Enter Tybalt

TYBALT. What! art thou drawn among these heartless hinds?
  Turn thee, Benvolio, look upon thy death.
BENVOLIO. I do but keep the peace: put up thy sword,
  Or manage it to part these men with me.
TYBALT. What! drawn, and talk of peace? I hate the word,
  As I hate hell, all Montagues, and thee.
  Have at thee, coward!   *They fight*
Enter several persons of both houses, who join the fray;
    then enter Citizens, with clubs and partisans
CITIZENS. Clubs, bills, and partisans! strike! beat them
    down!
  Down with the Capulets! down with Montagues!
      Enter Capulet in his gown, and Lady Capulet
CAPULET. What noise is this? Give me my long sword, ho!
LADY CAPULET. A crutch, a crutch! Why call you for a
    sword?
CAPULET. My sword, I say! Old Montague is come,
  And flourishes his blade in spite of me.
        Enter Montague and Lady Montague
MONTAGUE. Thou villain Capulet! Hold me not; let me go.
LADY MONTAGUE. Thou shalt not stir one foot to seek a foe.
        Enter Prince with his Train
PRINCE. Rebellious subjects, enemies to peace,
  Profaners of this neighbour-stained steel,—
  Will they not hear? What ho! you men, you beasts,
  That quench the fire of your pernicious rage
  With purple fountains issuing from your veins,
  On pain of torture, from those bloody hands
  Throw your mis-temper'd weapons to the ground,
  And hear the sentence of your moved prince.
  Three civil brawls, bred of an airy word,
  By thee, old Capulet, and Montague,
  Have thrice disturb'd the quiet of our streets,
  And made Verona's ancient citizens
  Cast by their grave beseeming ornaments,
  To wield old partisans, in hands as old,
  Canker'd with peace, to part your canker'd hate.
  If ever you disturb our streets again
  Your lives shall pay the forfeit of the peace.
  For this time, all the rest depart away:
  You, Capulet, shall go along with me;

And, Montague, come you this afternoon
To know our further pleasure in this case,
To old Free-town, our common judgment-place.
Once more, on pain of death, all men depart.

Exeunt all but Montague,
Lady Montague, and Benvolio

MONTAGUE. Who set this ancient quarrel new abroach?
Speak, nephew, were you by when it began?
BENVOLIO. Here were the servants of your adversary
And yours close fighting ere I did approach:
I drew to part them; in the instant came
The fiery Tybalt, with his sword prepar'd,
Which, as he breath'd defiance to my ears,
He swung about his head, and cut the winds,
Who, nothing hurt withal, hiss'd him in scorn.
While we were interchanging thrusts and blows,
Came more and more, and fought on part and part,
Till the prince came, who parted either part.
LADY MONTAGUE. O! where is Romeo? saw you him to-day?
Right glad I am he was not at this fray.
BENVOLIO. Madam, an hour before the worshipp'd sun
Peer'd forth the golden window of the east,
A troubled mind drave me to walk abroad;
Where, underneath the grove of sycamore
That westward rooteth from the city's side,
So early walking did I see your son:
Towards him I made; but he was ware of me,
And stole into the covert of the wood:
I, measuring his affections by my own,
That most are busied when they 're most alone,
Pursu'd my humour not pursuing his,
And gladly shunn'd who gladly fled from me.
MONTAGUE. Many a morning hath he there been seen,
With tears augmenting the fresh morning's dew,
Adding to clouds more clouds with his deep sighs:
But all so soon as the all-cheering sun
Should in the furthest east begin to draw
The shady curtains from Aurora's bed,
Away from light steals home my heavy son,
And private in his chamber pens himself,
Shuts up his windows, locks fair daylight out,
And makes himself an artificial night.

    Black and portentous must this humour prove
    Unless good counsel may the cause remove.

BENVOLIO. My noble uncle, do you know the cause?

MONTAGUE. I neither know it nor can learn of him.

BENVOLIO. Have you importun'd him by any means?

MONTAGUE. Both by myself and many other friends:
    But he, his own affections' counsellor,
    Is to himself, I will not say how true,
    But to himself so secret and so close,
    So far from sounding and discovery,
    As is the bud bit with an envious worm,
    Ere he can spread his sweet leaves to the air,
    Or dedicate his beauty to the sun.
    Could we but learn from whence his sorrows grow,
    We would as willingly give cure as know.

BENVOLIO. See where he comes: so please you, step aside;
    I 'll know his grievance, or be much denied.

MONTAGUE. I would thou wert so happy by thy stay,
    To hear true shrift. Come, madam, let 's away.

                Exeunt Montague and Lady
                Enter Romeo

BENVOLIO. Good-morrow, cousin.

ROMEO.   Is the day so young?

BENVOLIO. But new struck nine.

ROMEO.   Ay me! sad hours seem long.
    Was that my father that went hence so fast?

BENVOLIO. It was. What sadness lengthens Romeo's hours?

ROMEO. Not having that, which having, makes them short.

BENVOLIO. In love?

ROMEO. Out—

BENVOLIO. Of love?

ROMEO. Out of her favour, where I am in love.

BENVOLIO. Alas! that love, so gentle in his view,
    Should be so tyrannous and rough in proof.

ROMEO. Alas! that love, whose view is muffled still,
    Should, without eyes, see pathways to his will.
    Where shall we dine? O me! What fray was here?
    Yet tell me not, for I have heard it all.
    Here 's much to do with hate, but more with love.
    Why then, O brawling love! O loving hate!
    O any thing! of nothing first create.
    O heavy lightness! serious vanity!

Mis-shapen chaos of well-seeming forms!
Feather of lead, bright smoke, cold fire, sick health!
Still-waking sleep, that is not what it is!
This love feel I, that feel no love in this.
Dost thou not laugh?

BENVOLIO.   No, coz, I rather weep.

ROMEO. Good heart, at what?

BENVOLIO. At thy good heart's oppression.

ROMEO. Why, such is love's transgression.
Griefs of mine own lie heavy in my breast,
Which thou wilt propagate to have it press'd
With more of thine: this love that thou hast shown
Doth add more grief to too much of mine own.
Love is a smoke rais'd with the fume of sighs;
Being purg'd, a fire sparkling in lovers' eyes;
Being vex'd, a sea nourish'd with lovers' tears:
What is it else? a madness most discreet,
A choking gall, and a preserving sweet.
Farewell, my coz.   *Going*

BENVOLIO.   Soft, I will go along;
An if you leave me so, you do me wrong.

ROMEO. Tut! I have lost myself; I am not here;
This is not Romeo, he 's some other where.

BENVOLIO. Tell me in sadness, who is that you love.

ROMEO. What! shall I groan and tell thee?

BENVOLIO.   Groan! why, no;
But sadly tell me who.

ROMEO. Bid a sick man in sadness make his will;
Ah! word ill urg'd to one that is so ill.
In sadness, cousin, I do love a woman.

BENVOLIO. I aim'd so near when I suppos'd you lov'd.

ROMEO. A right good mark-man! And she 's fair I love.

BENVOLIO. A right fair mark, fair coz, is soonest hit.

ROMEO. Well, in that hit you miss: she 'll not be hit
With Cupid's arrow; she hath Dian's wit;
And, in strong proof of chastity well arm'd,
From love's weak childish bow she lives unharm'd.
She will not stay the siege of loving terms,
Nor bide the encounter of assailing eyes,
Nor ope her lap to saint-seducing gold:
O! she is rich in beauty; only poor
That, when she dies, with beauty dies her store.

BENVOLIO. Then she hath sworn that she will still live
    chaste?

ROMEO. She hath, and in that sparing makes huge waste;
  For beauty, starv'd with her severity,
  Cuts beauty off from all posterity.
  She is too fair, too wise, wisely too fair,
  To merit bliss by making me despair:
  She hath forsworn to love, and in that vow
  Do I live dead that live to tell it now.

BENVOLIO. Be rul'd by me; forget to think of her.

ROMEO. O! teach me how I should forget to think.

BENVOLIO. By giving liberty unto thine eyes:
  Examine other beauties.

ROMEO.   'Tis the way
  To call hers exquisite, in question more.
  These happy masks that kiss fair ladies' brows
  Being black put us in mind they hide the fair:
  He, that is strucken blind cannot forget
  The precious treasure of his eyesight lost:
  Show me a mistress that is passing fair,
  What doth her beauty serve but as a note
  Where I may read who pass'd that passing fair?
  Farewell: thou canst not teach me to forget.

BENVOLIO. I'll pay that doctrine, or else die in debt.

                                 Exeunt

SCENE TWO

A Street.

Enter Capulet, Paris, and Servant

CAPULET. But Montague is bound as well as I,
  In penalty alike; and 'tis not hard, I think,
  For men so old as we to keep the peace.

PARIS. Of honourable reckoning are you both;
  And pity 'tis you liv'd at odds so long.
  But now, my lord, what say you to my suit?

CAPULET. But saying o'er what I have said before:
  My child is yet a stranger in the world,
  She hath not seen the change of fourteen years;
  Let two more summers wither in their pride

Ere we may think her ripe to be a bride.

PARIS. Younger than she are happy mothers made.

CAPULET. And too soon marr'd are those so early made.
Earth hath swallow'd all my hopes but she,
She is the hopeful lady of my earth:
But woo her, gentle Paris, get her heart,
My will to her consent is but a part;
An she agree, within her scope of choice
Lies my consent and fair according voice.
This night I hold an old accustom'd feast,
Whereto I have invited many a guest
Such as I love; and you, among the store,
Once more, most welcome, makes my number more.
At my poor house look to behold this night
Earth-treading stars that make dark heaven light:
Such comfort as do lusty young men feel
When well-apparell'd April on the heel
Of limping winter treads, even such delight
Among fresh female buds shall you this night
Inherit at my house; hear all, all see,
And like her most whose merit most shall be:
Which on more view, of many mine being one
May stand in number, though in reckoning none.
Come, go with me. (*To Servant, giving him a paper*) Go,
sirrah, trudge about
Through fair Verona; find those persons out
Whose names are written there, and to them say,
My house and welcome on their pleasure stay.

Exeunt Capulet and Paris

SERVANT. Find them out whose names are written here!
It is written that the shoemaker should meddle with his
yard, and the tailor with his last, the fisher with his pen-
cil, and the painter with his nets; but I am sent to find
those persons, whose names are here writ, and can never
find what names the writing person hath here writ. I
must to the learned. In good time.

Enter Benvolio and Romeo

BENVOLIO. Tut! man, one fire burns out another's burning.
One pain is lessen'd by another's anguish;
Turn giddy, and be holp by backward turning;
One desperate grief cures with another's languish:
Take thou some new infection to thy eye,

And the rank poison of the old will die.

ROMEO. Your plantain leaf is excellent for that.

BENVOLIO. For what, I pray thee?

ROMEO.   For your broken shin.

BENVOLIO. Why, Romeo, art thou mad?

ROMEO. Not mad, but bound more than a madman is;
  Shut up in prison, kept without my food,
  Whipp'd and tormented, and—Good den, good fellow.

SERVANT. God gi' good den. I pray, sir, can you read?

ROMEO. Ay, mine own fortune in my misery.

SERVANT. Perhaps you have learn'd it without book: but, I
  pray, can you read any thing you see?

ROMEO. Ay, if I know the letters and the language.

SERVANT. Ye say honestly; rest you merry!   *Offering to go*

ROMEO. Stay, fellow; I can read. (*He reads*) 'Signior Mar-
  tino and his wife and daughters; County Anselme and
  his beauteous sisters; the lady widow of Vitruvio; Signior Placentio, and his lovely nieces; Mercutio and his
  brother Valentine; mine uncle Capulet, his wife and
  daughters; my fair niece Rosaline; Livia; Signior Valentio
  and his cousin Tybalt; Lucio and the lively Helena.'
  A fair assembly: whither should they come?

SERVANT. Up.

ROMEO. Whither?

SERVANT. To supper; to our house.

ROMEO. Whose house?

SERVANT. My master's.

ROMEO. Indeed, I should have asked you that before.

SERVANT. Now I 'll tell you without asking. My master is
  the great rich Capulet; and if you be not of the house of
  Montagues, I pray, come and crush a cup of wine. Rest
  you merry!   *Exit*

BENVOLIO. At this same ancient feast of Capulet's,
  Sups the fair Rosaline, whom thou so lov'st,
  With all the admired beauties of Verona:
  Go thither; and, with unattainted eye,
  Compare her face with some that I shall show,
  And I will make thee think thy swan a crow.

ROMEO. When the devout religion of mine eye
    Maintains such falsehood, then turn tears to fires!
  And these, who often drown'd could never die,
    Transparent heretics, be burnt for liars!

One fairer than my love! the all-seeing sun
Ne'er saw her match since first the world begun.
BENVOLIO. Tut! you saw her fair, none else being by,
Herself pois'd with herself in either eye;
But in that crystal scales let there be weigh'd
Your lady's love against some other maid
That I will show you shining at this feast,
And she shall scant show well that now shows best.
ROMEO. I 'll go along, no such sight to be shown,
But to rejoice in splendour of mine own.   *Exeunt*

SCENE THREE

A Room in Capulet's House.

Enter Lady Capulet and Nurse

LADY CAPULET. Nurse, where 's my daughter? Call her forth
to me.
NURSE. Now, by my maidenhead, at twelve year old,
I bade her come. What, lamb! what, lady-bird!
God forbid! where 's this girl? what, Juliet!
Enter Juliet
JULIET. How now! who calls?
NURSE.   Your mother.
JULIET.   Madam, I am here.
What is your will?
LADY CAPULET. This is the matter. Nurse, give leave awhile.
We must talk in secret: nurse, come back again;
I have remember'd me, thou 's hear our counsel.
Thou know'st my daughter 's of a pretty age.
NURSE. Faith, I can tell her age unto an hour.
LADY CAPULET. She 's not fourteen.
NURSE.   I 'll lay fourteen of my teeth—
And yet to my teen be it spoken I have but four—
She is not fourteen. How long is it now
To Lammas-tide?
LADY CAPULET. A fortnight and odd days.
NURSE. Even or odd, of all days in the year,
Come Lammas-eve at night shall she be fourteen.
Susan and she—God rest all Christian souls!—
Were of an age. Well, Susan is with God;

She was too good for me. But, as I said,
On Lammas-eve at night shall she be fourteen;
That shall she, marry; I remember it well.
'Tis since the earthquake now eleven years;
And she was wean'd, I never shall forget it,
Of all the days of the year, upon that day;
For I had then laid wormwood to my dug,
Sitting in the sun under the dove-house wall;
My lord and you were then at Mantua.
Nay, I do bear a brain:—but, as I said,
When it did taste the wormwood on the nipple
Of my dug and felt it bitter, pretty fool!
To see it tetchy and fall out with the dug.
'Shake,' quoth the dove-house: 'twas no need, I trow,
To bid me trudge:
And since that time it is eleven years;
For then she could stand high lone; nay, by the rood,
She could have run and waddled all about;
For even the day before she broke her brow:
And then my husband—God be with his soul!
A' was a merry man—took up the child:
'Yea,' quoth he, 'dost thou fall upon thy face?
Thou wilt fall backward when thou hast more wit;
Wilt thou not, Jule?' and, by my halidom,
The pretty wretch left crying, and said 'Ay.'
To see now how a jest shall come about!
I warrant, an I should live a thousand years,
I never should forget it: 'Wilt thou not, Jule?' quoth he;
And, pretty fool, it stinted and said 'Ay.'
LADY CAPULET. Enough of this; I pray thee, hold thy
    peace.
NURSE. Yes, madam. Yet I cannot choose but laugh,
    To think it should leave crying, and say 'Ay.'
    And yet, I warrant, it had upon its brow
    A bump as big as a young cockerel's stone;
    A parlous knock; and it cried bitterly:
    'Yea,' quoth my husband, 'fall'st upon thy face?
    Thou wilt fall backward when thou com'st to age;
    Wilt thou not, Jule?' it stinted and said 'Ay.'
JULIET. And stint thou too, I pray thee, nurse, say I.
NURSE. Peace, I have done. God mark thee to his grace!
    Thou wast the prettiest babe that e'er I nursed:

An I might live to see thee married once,
I have my wish.

LADY CAPULET. Marry, that 'marry' is the very theme
I came to talk of. Tell me, daughter Juliet,
How stands your disposition to be married?

JULIET. It is an honour that I dream not of.

NURSE. An honour! were not I thine only nurse,
I would say thou hadst suck'd wisdom from thy teat.

LADY CAPULET. Well, think of marriage now; younger than
you,
Here in Verona, ladies of esteem,
Are made already mothers: by my count,
I was your mother much upon these years
That you are now a maid. Thus then in brief,
The valiant Paris seeks you for his love.

NURSE. A man, young lady! lady, such a man
As all the world—why, he 's a man of wax.

LADY CAPULET. Verona's summer hath not such a flower.

NURSE. Nay, he 's a flower; in faith, a very flower.

LADY CAPULET. What say you? can you love the gentle-
man?
This night you shall behold him at our feast;
Read o'er the volume of young Paris' face
And find delight writ there with beauty's pen;
Examine every married lineament,
And see how one another lends content;
And what obscur'd in this fair volume lies
Find written in the margent of his eyes.
This precious book of love, this unbound lover,
To beautify him, only lacks a cover:
The fish lives in the sea, and 'tis much pride
For fair without the fair within to hide:
That book in many eyes doth share the glory,
That in gold clasps locks in the golden story:
So shall you share all that he doth possess,
By having him making yourself no less.

NURSE. No less! nay, bigger; women grow by men.

LADY CAPULET. Speak briefly, can you like of Paris' love?

JULIET. I 'll look to like, if looking liking move;
But no more deep will I endart mine eye
Than your consent gives strength to make it fly.

Enter a Servant

SERVANT. Madam, the guests are come, supper served up,
 you called, my young lady asked for, the nurse cursed
 in the pantry, and everything in extremity. I must hence
 to wait; I beseech you, follow straight.
LADY CAPULET. We follow thee. Juliet, the county stays.
NURSE. Go, girl, seek happy nights to happy days.

Exeunt

SCENE FOUR

A Street.

*Enter Romeo, Mercutio, Benvolio, with five or six
Maskers, Torchbearers, and Others*

ROMEO. What! shall this speech be spoke for our excuse,
 Or shall we on without apology?
BENVOLIO. The date is out of such prolixity.
 We 'll have no Cupid hood-wink'd with a scarf,
 Bearing a Tartar's painted bow of lath,
 Scaring the ladies like a crow-keeper;
 Nor no without-book prologue, faintly spoke
 After the prompter, for our entrance:
 But, let them measure us by what they will,
 We 'll measure them a measure, and be gone.
ROMEO. Give me a torch: I am not for this ambling;
 Being but heavy, I will bear the light.
MERCUTIO. Nay, gentle Romeo, we must have you dance.
ROMEO. Not I, believe me; you have dancing shoes
 With nimble soles; I have a soul of lead
 So stakes me to the ground I cannot move.
MERCUTIO. You are a lover; borrow Cupid's wings,
 And soar with them above a common bound.
ROMEO. I am too sore enpierced with his shaft
 To soar with his light feathers; and so bound
 I cannot bound a pitch above dull woe:
 Under love's heavy burden do I sink.
MERCUTIO. And, to sink in it, should you burden love;
 Too great oppression for a tender thing.
ROMEO. Is love a tender thing? it is too rough,
 Too rude, too boisterous; and it pricks like thorn.
MERCUTIO. If love be rough with you, be rough with love;

Prick love for pricking, and you beat love down.
Give me a case to put my visage in: *Putting on a mask*
A visor for a visor! what care I,
What curious eye doth quote deformities?
Here are the beetle brows shall blush for me.

BENVOLIO. Come, knock and enter; and no sooner in,
But every man betake him to his legs.

ROMEO. A torch for me; let wantons, light of heart,
Tickle the senseless rushes with their heels,
For I am proverb'd with a grandsire phrase;
I 'll be a candle-holder, and look on.
The game was ne'er so fair, and I am done.

MERCUTIO. Tut! dun 's the mouse, the constable's own
word:
If thou art Dun, we 'll draw thee from the mire,
Of—save your reverence—love, wherein thou stick'st
Up to the ears. Come, we burn daylight, ho!

ROMEO. Nay, that 's not so.

MERCUTIO.   I mean, sir, in delay
We waste our lights in vain, like lamps by day.
Take our good meaning, for our judgment sits
Five times in that ere once in our five wits.

ROMEO. And we mean well in going to this mask;
But 'tis no wit to go.

MERCUTIO.   Why, may one ask?

ROMEO. I dream'd a dream to-night.

MERCUTIO.   And so did I.

ROMEO. Well, what was yours?

MERCUTIO.   That dreamers often lie.

ROMEO. In bed asleep, while they do dream things true.

MERCUTIO. O! then, I see, Queen Mab hath been with you.

BENVOLIO. Queen Mab! What 's she?

MERCUTIO. She is the fairies' midwife, and she comes
In shape no bigger than an agate-stone
On the fore-finger of an alderman,
Drawn with a team of little atomies
Athwart men's noses as they lie asleep:
Her waggon-spokes made of long spinners' legs;
The cover, of the wings of grasshoppers;
The traces, of the smallest spider's web;
The collars, of the moonshine's watery beams;
Her whip, of cricket's bone; the lash, of film;

MERCUTIO.   Give me a case to put my visage in:
  A visor for a visor! what care I,
  What curious eye doth quote deformities?
  Here are the beetle brows shall blush for me.

Her waggoner, a small grey-coated gnat,
Not half so big as a round little worm
Prick'd from the lazy finger of a maid;
Her chariot is an empty hazel-nut,
Made by the joiner squirrel or old grub,
Time out o' mind the fairies' coach-makers.
And in this state she gallops night by night
Through lovers' brains, and then they dream of love;
O'er courtiers' knees, that dream on curtsies straight;
O'er lawyers' fingers, who straight dream on fees;
O'er ladies' lips, who straight on kisses dream;
Which oft the angry Mab with blisters plagues,
Because their breaths with sweetmeats tainted are.
Sometimes she gallops o'er a courtier's nose,
And then dreams he of smelling out a suit;
And sometimes comes she with a tithe-pig's tail,
Tickling a parson's nose as a' lies asleep,
Then dreams he of another benefice;
Sometime she driveth o'er a soldier's neck,
And then dreams he of cutting foreign throats,
Of breaches, ambuscadoes, Spanish blades,
Of healths five fathom deep; and then anon
Drums in his ear, at which he starts and wakes;
And, being thus frighted, swears a prayer or two,
And sleeps again. This is that very Mab
That plats the manes of horses in the night;
And bakes the elf-locks in foul sluttish hairs,
Which once untangled much misfortune bodes;
This is the hag, when maids lie on their backs,
That presses them and learns them first to bear,
Making them women of good carriage:
This is she—

ROMEO.   Peace, peace! Mercutio, peace!
Thou talk'st of nothing.

MERCUTIO.   True, I talk of dreams,
Which are the children of an idle brain,
Begot of nothing but vain fantasy;
Which is as thin of substance as the air,
And more inconstant than the wind, who woos
Even now the frozen bosom of the north,
And, being anger'd, puffs away from thence,
Turning his face to the dew-dropping south.

BENVOLIO. This wind you talk of blows us from ourselves;
  Supper is done, and we shall come too late.

ROMEO. I fear too early; for my mind misgives
  Some consequence yet hanging in the stars
  Shall bitterly begin his fearful date
  With this night's revels, and expire the term
  Of a despised life clos'd in my breast
  By some vile forfeit of untimely death.
  But he, that hath the steerage of my course,
  Direct my sail! On, lusty gentlemen.

BENVOLIO. Strike, drum.   *Exeunt*

SCENE FIVE

A Hall in Capulet's House.

Musicians waiting. Enter Servingmen

FIRST SERVINGMAN. Where 's Potpan, that he helps not to
  take away? he shift a trencher! he scrape a trencher!

SECOND SERVINGMAN. When good manners shall lie all in
  one or two men's hands, and they unwashed too, 'tis a
  foul thing.

FIRST SERVINGMAN. Away with the joint-stools, remove the
  court-cupboard, look to the plate. Good thou, save me a
  piece of marchpane; and, as thou lovest me, let the
  porter let in Susan Grindstone and Nell. Antony! and
  Potpan!

SECOND SERVINGMAN. Ay, boy; ready.

FIRST SERVINGMAN. You are looked for and called for,
  asked for and sought for in the great chamber.

THIRD SERVINGMAN. We cannot be here and there too.

SECOND SERVINGMAN. Cheerly, boys; be brisk awhile, and
  the longer liver take all.   *They retire behind*
    Enter Capulet and Juliet and Others of his house,
          meeting the Guests and Maskers

CAPULET. Welcome, gentlemen! ladies that have their toes
  Unplagu'd with corns will walk a bout with you.
  Ah ha! my mistresses, which of you all
  Will now deny to dance? she that makes dainty, she,
  I 'll swear, hath corns; am I come near ye now?

Welcome, gentlemen! I have seen the day
That I have worn a visor, and could tell
A whispering tale in a fair lady's ear
Such as would please; 'tis gone, 'tis gone, 'tis gone.
You are welcome, gentlemen! Come, musicians, play.
A hall! a hall! give room, and foot it, girls.

Music plays, and they dance

More light, ye knaves! and turn the tables up,
And quench the fire, the room has grown too hot.
Ah! sirrah, this unlook'd-for sport comes well.
Nay, sit, nay, sit, good cousin Capulet,
For you and I are past our dancing days;
How long is 't now since last yourself and I
Were in a mask?

SECOND CAPULET. By 'r Lady, thirty years.

CAPULET. What, man! 'tis not so much, 'tis not so much:
'Tis since the nuptial of Lucentio,
Come Pentecost as quickly as it will,
Some five and twenty years; and then we mask'd.

SECOND CAPULET. 'Tis more, 'tis more; his son is elder, sir.
His son is thirty.

CAPULET. Will you tell me that?
His son was but a ward two years ago.

ROMEO. What lady is that which doth enrich the hand
Of yonder knight?

SERVINGMAN. I know not, sir.

ROMEO. O! she doth teach the torches to burn bright.
It seems she hangs upon the cheek of night
Like a rich jewel in an Ethiop's ear;
Beauty too rich for use, for earth too dear!
So shows a snowy dove trooping with crows,
As yonder lady o'er her fellows shows.
The measure done, I 'll watch her place of stand,
And, touching hers, make blessed my rude hand.
Did my heart love till now? forswear it, sight!
For I ne'er saw true beauty till this night.

TYBALT. This, by his voice, should be a Montague.
Fetch me my rapier, boy. What! dares the slave
Come hither, cover'd with an antick face,
To fleer and scorn at our solemnity?
Now, by the stock and honour of my kin,
To strike him dead I hold it not a sin.

CAPULET. Why, how now, kinsman! wherefore storm you
     so?

TYBALT. Uncle, this is a Montague, our foe;
     A villain that is hither come in spite,
     To scorn at our solemnity this night.

CAPULET. Young Romeo, is it?

TYBALT.   'Tis he, that villain Romeo.

CAPULET. Content thee, gentle coz, let him alone:
     He bears him like a portly gentleman;
     And, to say truth, Verona brags of him
     To be a virtuous and well-govern'd youth.
     I would not for the wealth of all this town
     Here in my house do him disparagement;
     Therefore be patient, take no note of him:
     It is my will; the which if thou respect,
     Show a fair presence and put off these frowns,
     An ill-beseeming semblance for a feast.

TYBALT. It fits, when such a villain is a guest:
     I 'll not endure him.

CAPULET.   He shall be endur'd:
     What! goodman boy; I say, he shall, go to;
     Am I the master here, or you? go to.
     You 'll not endure him! God shall mend my soul!
     You 'll make a mutiny among my guests!
     You will set cock-a-hoop! you'll be the man!

TYBALT. Why, uncle, 'tis a shame.

CAPULET.   Go to, go to;
     You are a saucy boy—is 't so indeed?—
     This trick may chance to scathe you.—I know what:
     You must contrary me! marry, 'tis time.
     Well said, my hearts! You are a princox; go:
     Be quiet, or—More light, more light!—For shame!
     I 'll make you quiet. What! cheerly, my hearts!

TYBALT. Patience perforce with wilful choler meeting
     Makes my flesh tremble in their different greeting.
     I will withdraw; but this intrusion shall
     Now seeming sweet convert to bitter gall.   *Exit*

ROMEO. (*To Juliet*) If I profane with my unworthiest hand
     This holy shrine, the gentle sin is this;
     My lips, two blushing pilgrims, ready stand
     To smooth that rough touch with a tender kiss.

JULIET. Good pilgrim, you do wrong your hand too much,

Which mannerly devotion shows in this;
For saints have hands that pilgrims' hands do touch,
    And palm to palm is holy palmer's kiss.
ROMEO. Have not saints lips, and holy palmers too?
JULIET. Ay, pilgrim, lips that they must use in prayer.
ROMEO. O! then, dear saint, let lips do what hands do;
    They pray, grant thou, lest faith turn to despair.
JULIET. Saints do not move, though grant for prayer's sake.
ROMEO. Then move not, while my prayers' effect I take.
    Thus from my lips, by thine, my sin is purg'd.

> *Kissing her*

JULIET. Then have my lips the sin that they have took.
ROMEO. Sin from my lips? O trespass sweetly urg'd!
    Give me my sin again.
JULIET.   You kiss by the book.
NURSE. Madam, your mother craves a word with you.
ROMEO. What is her mother?
NURSE.   Marry, bachelor,
    Her mother is the lady of the house,
    And a good lady, and a wise, and virtuous:
    I nurs'd her daughter, that you talk'd withal;
    I tell you he that can lay hold of her
    Shall have the chinks.
ROMEO.   Is she a Capulet?
    O dear account! my life is my foe's debt.
BENVOLIO. Away, be gone; the sport is at the best.
ROMEO. Ay, so I fear; the more is my unrest.
CAPULET. Nay, gentlemen, prepare not to be gone;
    We have a trifling foolish banquet towards.
    Is it e'en so? Why then, I thank you all;
    I thank you, honest gentlemen; good-night.
    More torches here! Come on then, let 's to bed.
    Ah! sirrah, by my fay, it waxes late;
    I 'll to my rest.   *Exeunt all except Juliet and Nurse*
JULIET. Come hither, nurse. What is yond gentleman?
NURSE. The son and heir of old Tiberio.
JULIET. What 's he that now is going out of door?
NURSE. Marry, that, I think, be young Petruchio.
JULIET. What 's he, that follows there that would not
    dance?
NURSE. I know not.
JULIET. Go, ask his name.—If he be married,

My grave is like to be my wedding-bed.

NURSE. His name is Romeo, and a Montague;
The only son of your great enemy.

JULIET. My only love sprung from my only hate!
Too early seen unknown, and known too late!
Prodigious birth of love it is to me,
That I must love a loathed enemy.

NURSE. What 's this, what 's this?

JULIET.   A rime I learn'd even now
Of one I danc'd withal.   *One calls within, 'Juliet!'*

NURSE.   Anon, anon!—
Come, let 's away; the strangers are all gone.   *Exeunt*

ACT TWO

PROLOGUE

Enter Chorus

CHORUS. Now old desire doth in his death-bed lie,
　　And young affection gapes to be his heir;
That fair for which love groan'd for and would die,
　　With tender Juliet match'd, is now not fair.
Now Romeo is belov'd and loves again,
　　Alike bewitched by the charm of looks,
But to his foe suppos'd he must complain,
　　And she steal love's sweet bait from fearful hooks:
Being held a foe, he may not have access
　　To breathe such vows as lovers us'd to swear;
And she as much in love, her means much less
　　To meet her new-beloved any where:
But passion lends them power, time means, to meet,
Tempering extremity with extreme sweet.　　　*Exit*

SCENE ONE

Verona. A Lane by the Wall of Capulet's Orchard

Enter Romeo

ROMEO. Can I go forward when my heart is here?
Turn back, dull earth, and find thy centre out.
　　　　　He climbs the wall, and leaps down within it
　　　　　Enter Benvolio and Mercutio
BENVOLIO. Romeo! my cousin Romeo!
MERCUTIO.　　　　　　　　　　　He is wise;
And, on my life, hath stol'n him home to bed.
BENVOLIO. He ran this way, and leap'd this orchard wall:
　　Call, good Mercutio.

MERCUTIO.   Nay, I 'll conjure too.
  Romeo! humours! madman! passion! lover!
  Appear thou in the likeness of a sigh:
  Speak but one rime and I am satisfied;
  Cry but 'Ay me!' couple but 'love' and 'dove';
  Speak to my gossip Venus one fair word,
  One nickname for her purblind son and heir,
  Young Adam Cupid, he that shot so trim
  When King Cophetua lov'd the beggar-maid.
  He heareth not, he stirreth not, he moveth not;
  The ape is dead, and I must conjure him.
  I conjure thee by Rosaline's bright eyes,
  By her high forehead, and her scarlet lip,
  By her fine foot, straight leg, and quivering thigh,
  And the demesnes that there adjacent lie,
  That in thy likeness thou appear to us.
BENVOLIO. An if he hear thee, thou wilt anger him.
MERCUTIO. This cannot anger him: 'twould anger him
  To raise a spirit in his mistress' circle
  Of some strange nature, letting it there stand
  Till she had laid it, and conjur'd it down;
  That were some spite: my invocation
  Is fair and honest, and in his mistress' name
  I conjure only but to raise up him.
BENVOLIO. Come, he hath hid himself among these trees,
  To be consorted with the humorous night:
  Blind is his love and best befits the dark.
MERCUTIO. If love be blind, love cannot hit the mark.
  Now will he sit under a medlar tree,
  And wish his mistress were that kind of fruit
  As maids call medlars, when they laugh alone.
  O Romeo! that she were, O! that she were
  An open 'et cætera,' thou a poperin pear.
  Romeo, good-night: I 'll to my truckle-bed;
  This field-bed is too cold for me to sleep:
  Come, shall we go?
BENVOLIO.   Go, then; for 'tis in vain
  To seek him here that means not to be found.

                                        Exeunt

SCENE TWO

Capulet's Orchard.

Enter Romeo

ROMEO. He jests at scars, that never felt a wound.
                    Juliet appears above at a window
But, soft! what light through yonder window breaks?
It is the east, and Juliet is the sun!
Arise, fair sun, and kill the envious moon,
Who is already sick and pale with grief,
That thou her maid art far more fair than she:
Be not her maid, since she is envious;
Her vestal livery is but sick and green,
And none but fools do wear it; cast it off.
It is my lady; O! it is my love:
O! that she knew she were.
She speaks, yet she says nothing: what of that?
Her eye discourses; I will answer it.
I am too bold, 'tis not to me she speaks:
Two of the fairest stars in all the heaven,
Having some business, do entreat her eyes
To twinkle in their spheres till they return.
What if her eyes were there, they in her head?
The brightness of her cheek would shame those stars
As daylight doth a lamp; her eyes in heaven
Would through the airy region stream so bright
That birds would sing and think it were not night.
See! how she leans her cheek upon her hand:
O! that I were a glove upon that hand,
That I might touch that cheek.
JULIET.   Ay me!
ROMEO.   She speaks:
O! speak again, bright angel; for thou art
As glorious to this night, being o'er my head,
As is a winged messenger of heaven
Unto the white-upturned wondering eyes
Of mortals, that fall back to gaze on him
When he bestrides the lazy-pacing clouds,
And sails upon the bosom of the air.
JULIET. O Romeo, Romeo! wherefore art thou Romeo?

  Deny thy father, and refuse thy name;
  Or, if thou wilt not, be but sworn my love,
  And I 'll no longer be a Capulet.

ROMEO. (*Aside*) Shall I hear more, or shall I speak at this?

JULIET. 'Tis but thy name that is my enemy;
  Thou art thyself though, not a Montague.
  What 's Montague? it is nor hand, nor foot,
  Nor arm, nor face, nor any other part
  Belonging to a man. O! be some other name:
  What 's in a name? That which we call a rose
  By any other name would smell as sweet;
  So Romeo would, were he not Romeo call'd,
  Retain that dear perfection which he owes
  Without that title. Romeo, doff thy name;
  And for that name, which is no part of thee,
  Take all myself.

ROMEO.   I take thee at thy word.
  Call me but love, and I 'll be new baptiz'd;
  Henceforth I never will be Romeo.

JULIET. What man art thou, that, thus bescreen'd in night,
  So stumblest on my counsel?

ROMEO.   By a name
  I know not how to tell thee who I am:
  My name, dear saint, is hateful to myself,
  Because it is an enemy to thee:
  Had I it written, I would tear the word.

JULIET. My ears have not yet drunk a hundred words
  Of that tongue's uttering, yet I know the sound:
  Art thou not Romeo, and a Montague?

ROMEO. Neither, fair maid, if either thee dislike.

JULIET. How cam'st thou hither, tell me, and wherefore?
  The orchard walls are high and hard to climb,
  And the place death, considering who thou art,
  If any of my kinsmen find thee here.

ROMEO. With love's light wings did I o'erperch these walls;
  For stony limits cannot hold love out,
  And what love can do that dares love attempt;
  Therefore thy kinsmen are no stop to me.

JULIET. If they do see thee they will murder thee.

ROMEO. Alack! there lies more peril in thine eye
  Than twenty of their swords: look thou but sweet,
  And I am proof against their enmity.

JULIET. I would not for the world they saw thee here.

ROMEO. I have night's cloak to hide me from their eyes;
And but thou love me, let them find me here;
My life were better ended by their hate,
Than death prorogued, wanting of thy love.

JULIET. By whose direction found'st thou out this place?

ROMEO. By Love, that first did prompt me to inquire;
He lent me counsel, and I lent him eyes.
I am no pilot; yet wert thou as far
As that vast shore wash'd with the furthest sea,
I would adventure for such merchandise.

JULIET. Thou know'st the mask of night is on my face,
Else would a maiden blush bepaint my cheek
For that which thou hast heard me speak to-night.
Fain would I dwell on form, fain, fain deny
What I have spoke: but farewell compliment!
Dost thou love me? I know thou wilt say 'Ay';
And I will take thy word; yet, if thou swear'st,
Thou mayst prove false; at lovers' perjuries,
They say, Jove laughs. O gentle Romeo!
If thou dost love, pronounce it faithfully:
Or if thou think'st I am too quickly won,
I 'll frown and be perverse and say thee nay,
So thou wilt woo; but else, not for the world.
In truth, fair Montague, I am too fond,
And therefore thou mayst think my haviour light:
But trust me, gentleman, I 'll prove more true
Than those that have more cunning to be strange.
I should have been more strange, I must confess,
But that thou over-heard'st, ere I was ware,
My true love's passion: therefore pardon me,
And not impute this yielding to light love,
Which the dark night hath so discovered.

ROMEO. Lady, by yonder blessed moon I swear
That tips with silver all these fruit-tree tops,—

JULIET. O! swear not by the moon, the inconstant moon,
That monthly changes in her circled orb,
Lest that thy love prove likewise variable.

ROMEO. What shall I swear by?

JULIET.   Do not swear at all;
Or, if thou wilt, swear by thy gracious self,
Which is the god of my idolatry,

And I 'll believe thee.

ROMEO.   If my heart's dear love—

JULIET. Well, do not swear. Although I joy in thee,
  I have no joy of this contract to-night:
  It is too rash, too unadvis'd, too sudden;
  Too like the lightning, which doth cease to be
  Ere one can say it lightens. Sweet, good-night!
  This bud of love, by summer's ripening breath,
  May prove a beauteous flower when next we meet.
  Good-night, good-night! as sweet repose and rest
  Come to thy heart as that within my breast!

ROMEO. O! wilt thou leave me so unsatisfied?

JULIET. What satisfaction canst thou have to-night?

ROMEO. The exchange of thy love's faithful vow for mine.

JULIET. I gave thee mine before thou didst request it;
  And yet I would it were to give again.

ROMEO. Wouldst thou withdraw it? for what purpose, love?

JULIET. But to be frank, and give it thee again.
  And yet I wish but for the thing I have:
  My bounty is as boundless as the sea,
  My love as deep; the more I give to thee,
  The more I have, for both are infinite.

                       Nurse calls within

  I hear some noise within; dear love, adieu!
  Anon, good nurse! Sweet Montague, be true.
  Stay but a little, I will come again.   *Exit above*

ROMEO. O blessed, blessed night! I am afeard,
  Being in night, all this is but a dream,
  Too flattering-sweet to be substantial.

               Re-enter Juliet, above

JULIET. Three words, dear Romeo, and good-night indeed.
  If that thy bent of love be honourable,
  Thy purpose marriage, send me word to-morrow,
  By one that I 'll procure to come to thee,
  Where, and what time, thou wilt perform the rite;
  And all my fortunes at thy foot I 'll lay,
  And follow thee my lord throughout the world.

NURSE. (*Within*) Madam!

JULIET. I come, anon.—But if thou mean'st not well, I do
    beseech thee,—

NURSE. (*Within*) Madam!

JULIET.   By and by; I come;—

> To cease thy suit, and leave me to my grief:
> To-morrow will I send.

ROMEO.   So thrive my soul,—

JULIET. A thousand times good-night!   *Exit above*

ROMEO. A thousand times the worse, to want thy light.
> Love goes toward love, as schoolboys from their books;
> But love from love, toward school with heavy looks.

Retiring

Re-enter Juliet, above

JULIET. Hist! Romeo, hist! O! for a falconer's voice,
> To lure this tassel-gentle back again.
> Bondage is hoarse, and may not speak aloud,
> Else would I tear the cave where Echo lies,
> And make her airy tongue more hoarse than mine,
> With repetition of my Romeo's name.

ROMEO. It is my soul that calls upon my name:
> How silver-sweet sound lovers' tongues by night,
> Like softest music to attending ears!

JULIET. Romeo!

ROMEO.   My dear!

JULIET.   At what o'clock to-morrow
> Shall I send to thee?

ROMEO.   At the hour of nine.

JULIET. I will not fail; 'tis twenty years till then.
> I have forgot why I did call thee back.

ROMEO. Let me stand here till thou remember it.

JULIET. I shall forget, to have thee still stand there,
> Remembering how I love thy company.

ROMEO. And I 'll still stay, to have thee still forget,
> Forgetting any other home but this.

JULIET. 'Tis almost morning; I would have thee gone;
> And yet no further than a wanton's bird,
> Who lets it hop a little from her hand,
> Like a poor prisoner in his twisted gyves,
> And with a silk thread plucks it back again,
> So loving-jealous of his liberty.

ROMEO. I would I were thy bird.

JULIET.   Sweet, so would I:
> Yet I should kill thee with much cherishing.
> Good-night, good-night! parting is such sweet sorrow
> That I shall say good-night till it be morrow.   *Exit*

ROMEO. Sleep dwell upon thine eyes, peace in thy breast!

Would I were sleep and peace, so sweet to rest!
Hence will I to my ghostly father's cell,
His help to crave, and my dear hap to tell.   *Exit*

SCENE THREE

Friar Laurence's Cell.

Enter Friar Laurence, with a basket

FRIAR LAURENCE. The grey-ey'd morn smiles on the frown-
  ing night,
Chequering the eastern clouds with streaks of light,
And flecked darkness like a drunkard reels
From forth day's path and Titan's fiery wheels:
Now, ere the sun advance his burning eye
The day to cheer and night's dank dew to dry,
I must up-fill this osier cage of ours
With baleful weeds and precious-juiced flowers.
The earth that 's nature's mother is her tomb;
What is her burying grave that is her womb,
And from her womb children of divers kind
We sucking on her natural bosom find,
Many for many virtues excellent,
None but for some, and yet all different.
O! mickle is the powerful grace that lies
In herbs, plants, stones, and their true qualities:
For nought so vile that on the earth doth live
But to the earth some special good doth give,
Nor aught so good but strain'd from that fair use
Revolts from true birth, stumbling on abuse:
Virtue itself turns vice, being misapplied,
And vice sometime 's by action dignified.
Within the infant rind of this weak flower
Poison hath residence and medicine power:
For this, being smelt, with that part cheers each part;
Being tasted, slays all senses with the heart.
Two such opposed foes encamp them still
In man as well as herbs, grace and rude will;
And where the worser is predominant,
Full soon the canker death eats up that plant.
                    Enter Romeo

ROMEO. Good-morrow, father!

FRIAR LAURENCE.   Benedicite!
  What early tongue so sweet saluteth me?
  Young son, it argues a distemper'd head
  So soon to bid good-morrow to thy bed:
  Care keeps his watch in every old man's eye,
  And where care lodges, sleep will never lie;
  But where unbruised youth with unstuff'd brain
  Doth couch his limbs, there golden sleep doth reign:
  Therefore thy earliness doth me assure
  Thou art up-rous'd by some distemperature;
  Or if not so, then here I hit it right,
  Our Romeo hath not been in bed to-night.

ROMEO. That last is true; the sweeter rest was mine.

FRIAR LAURENCE. God pardon sin! wast thou with Rosa-
    line?

ROMEO. With Rosaline, my ghostly father? no;
  I have forgot that name, and that name 's woe.

FRIAR LAURENCE. That 's my good son: but where hast
    thou been, then?

ROMEO. I 'll tell thee, ere thou ask it me again.
  I have been feasting with mine enemy,
  Where on a sudden one hath wounded me,
  That 's by me wounded: both our remedies
  Within thy help and holy physics lies:
  I bear no hatred, blessed man; for, lo!
  My intercession likewise steads my foe.

FRIAR LAURENCE. Be plain, good son, and homely in thy
    drift;
  Riddling confession finds but riddling shrift.

ROMEO. Then plainly know my heart's dear love is set
  On the fair daughter of rich Capulet:
  As mine on hers, so hers is set on mine;
  And all combin'd, save what thou must combine
  By holy marriage: when and where and how
  We met, we woo'd and made exchange of vow,
  I 'll tell thee as we pass; but this I pray,
  That thou consent to marry us to-day.

FRIAR LAURENCE. Holy Saint Francis! what a change is
    here;
  Is Rosaline, whom thou didst love so dear,
  So soon forsaken? young men's love then lies

Not truly in their hearts, but in their eyes.
Jesu Maria! what a deal of brine
Hath wash'd thy sallow cheeks for Rosaline;
How much salt water thrown away in waste,
To season love, that of it doth not taste!
The sun not yet thy sighs from heaven clears,
Thy old groans ring yet in my ancient ears;
Lo! here upon thy cheek the stain doth sit
Of an old tear that is not wash'd off yet.
If e'er thou wast thyself and these woes thine,
Thou and these woes were all for Rosaline:
And art thou chang'd? pronounce this sentence then:
Women may fall, when there 's no strength in men.

ROMEO. Thou chidd'st me oft for loving Rosaline.

FRIAR LAURENCE. For doting, not for loving, pupil mine.

ROMEO. And bad'st me bury love.

FRIAR LAURENCE.   Not in a grave,
To lay one in, another out to have.

ROMEO. I pray thee, chide not; she, whom I love now
Doth grace for grace and love for love allow;
The other did not so.

FRIAR LAURENCE.   O! she knew well
Thy love did read by rote and could not spell.
But come, young waverer, come, go with me,
In one respect I 'll thy assistant be;
For this alliance may so happy prove,
To turn your households' rancour to pure love.

ROMEO. O! let us hence; I stand on sudden haste.

FRIAR LAURENCE. Wisely and slow; they stumble that run
    fast.   *Exeunt*

SCENE FOUR

A Street.

Enter Benvolio and Mercutio

MERCUTIO. Where the devil should this Romeo be?
    Came he not home to-night?

BENVOLIO. Not to his father's; I spoke with his man.

MERCUTIO. Why, that same pale hard-hearted wench, that
    Rosaline,

Torments him so, that he will sure run mad.

BENVOLIO. Tybalt, the kinsman of old Capulet,
Hath sent a letter to his father's house.

MERCUTIO. A challenge, on my life.

BENVOLIO. Romeo will answer it.

MERCUTIO. Any man that can write may answer a letter.

BENVOLIO. Nay, he will answer the letter's master, how he
dares, being dared.

MERCUTIO. Alas! poor Romeo, he is already dead; stabbed
with a white wench's black eye; shot through the ear
with a love-song; the very pin of his heart cleft with
the blind bow-boy's butt-shaft; and is he a man to encounter Tybalt?

BENVOLIO. Why, what is Tybalt?

MERCUTIO. More than prince of cats, I can tell you. O! he
is the courageous captain of compliments. He fights as
you sing prick-song, keeps time, distance, and proportion; rests me his minim rest, one, two, and the third in
your bosom; the very butcher of a silk button, a duellist,
a duellist; a gentleman of the very first house, of the
first and second cause. Ah! the immortal passado! the
punto reverso! the hay!

BENVOLIO. The what?

MERCUTIO. The pox of such antick, lisping, affecting fan-
tasticoes, these new tuners of accents!—'By Jesu, a very
good blade! a very tall man! a very good whore.'—Why,
is not this a lamentable thing, grandsire, that we should
be thus afflicted with these strange flies, these fashion-
mongers, these pardonnez-mois, who stand so much on
the new form that they cannot sit at ease on the old
bench? O, their bons, their bons!

Enter Romeo

BENVOLIO. Here comes Romeo, here comes Romeo.

MERCUTIO. Without his roe, like a dried herring. O flesh,
flesh, how art thou fishified! Now is he for the numbers
that Petrarch flowed in: Laura to his lady was but a
kitchen-wench; marry, she had a better love to be-rime
her; Dido a dowdy; Cleopatra a gipsy; Helen and Hero
hildings and harlots; Thisbe, a grey eye or so, but not
to the purpose. Signior Romeo, bon jour! there's a
French salutation to your French slop. You gave us the
counterfeit fairly last night.

ROMEO. Good-morrow to you both. What counterfeit did I give you?

MERCUTIO. The slip, sir, the slip; can you not conceive?

ROMEO. Pardon, good Mercutio, my business was great; and in such a case as mine a man may strain courtesy.

MERCUTIO. That 's as much as to say, such a case as yours constrains a man to bow in the hams.

ROMEO. Meaning—to curtsy.

MERCUTIO. Thou hast most kindly hit it.

ROMEO. A most courteous exposition.

MERCUTIO. Nay, I am the very pink of courtesy.

ROMEO. Pink for flower.

MERCUTIO. Right.

ROMEO. Why, then, is my pump well flowered.

MERCUTIO. Well said; follow me this jest now till thou hast worn out the pump, that, when the single sole of it is worn, the jest may remain after the wearing sole singular.

ROMEO. O single-soled jest! solely singular for the singleness.

MERCUTIO. Come between us, good Benvolio; my wit faints.

ROMEO. Switch and spurs, switch and spurs; or I 'll cry a match.

MERCUTIO. Nay, if thy wits run the wild-goose chase, I have done, for thou hast more of the wild-goose in one of thy wits than, I am sure, I have in my whole five. Was I with you there for the goose?

ROMEO. Thou wast never with me for anything when thou wast not here for the goose.

MERCUTIO. I will bite thee by the ear for that jest.

ROMEO. Nay, good goose, bite not.

MERCUTIO. Thy wit is a very bitter sweeting; it is a most sharp sauce.

ROMEO. And is it not then well served in to a sweet goose?

MERCUTIO. O! here 's a wit of cheveril, that stretches from an inch narrow to an ell broad.

ROMEO. I stretch it out for that word 'broad'; which added to the goose, proves thee far and wide a broad goose.

MERCUTIO. Why, is not this better now than groaning for love? now art thou sociable, now art thou Romeo; now art thou what thou art, by art as well as by nature: for this drivelling love is like a great natural, that runs lolling up and down to hide his bauble in a hole.

BENVOLIO. Stop there, stop there.

MERCUTIO. Thou desirest me to stop in my tale against the hair.

BENVOLIO. Thou wouldst else have made thy tale large.

MERCUTIO. O! thou art deceived; I would have made it short; for I was come to the whole depth of my tale, and meant indeed to occupy the argument no longer.

ROMEO. Here 's goodly gear!

Enter Nurse and Peter

MERCUTIO. A sail, a sail!

BENVOLIO. Two, two; a shirt and a smock.

NURSE. Peter!

PETER. Anon!

NURSE. My fan, Peter.

MERCUTIO. Good Peter, to hide her face; for her fan 's the fairer face.

NURSE. God ye good morrow, gentlemen.

MERCUTIO. God ye good den, fair gentlewoman.

NURSE. Is it good den?

MERCUTIO. 'Tis no less, I tell you; for the bawdy hand of the dial is now upon the prick of noon.

NURSE. Out upon you! what a man are you!

ROMEO. One, gentlewoman, that God hath made for himself to mar.

NURSE. By my troth, it is well said; 'for himself to mar,' quoth a'?—Gentlemen, can any of you tell me where I may find the young Romeo?

ROMEO. I can tell you; but young Romeo will be older when you have found him than he was when you sought him: I am the youngest of that name, for fault of a worse.

NURSE. You say well.

MERCUTIO. Yea! is the worst well? very well took, i' faith; wisely, wisely.

NURSE. If you be he, sir, I desire some confidence with you.

BENVOLIO. She will indite him to some supper.

MERCUTIO. A bawd, a bawd, a bawd! So ho!

ROMEO. What hast thou found?

MERCUTIO. No hare, sir; unless a hare, sir, in a lenten pie, that is something stale and hoar ere it be spent.   *Sings*

> An old hare hoar, and an old hare hoar,
>> Is very good meat in Lent:
> But a hare that is hoar, is too much for a score,
>> When it hoars ere it be spent.

Romeo, will you come to your father's? we 'll to dinner thither.

ROMEO. I will follow you.

MERCUTIO. Farewell, ancient lady; farewell.

> (*Sings*) Lady, lady, lady.

Exeunt Mercutio and Benvolio

NURSE. Marry, farewell! I pray you, sir, what saucy merchant was this, that was so full of his ropery?

ROMEO. A gentleman, nurse, that loves to hear himself talk, and will speak more in a minute than he will stand to in a month.

NURSE. An a' speak anything against me, I 'll take him down, an a' were lustier than he is, and twenty such Jacks; and if I cannot, I 'll find those that shall. Scurvy knave! I am none of his flirt-gills; I am none of his skeins-mates. (*To Peter*) And thou must stand by too, and suffer every knave to use me at his pleasure!

PETER. I saw no man use you at his pleasure; if I had, my weapon should quickly have been out, I warrant you. I dare draw as soon as another man, if I see occasion in a good quarrel, and the law on my side.

NURSE. Now, afore God, I am so vexed, that every part about me quivers. Scurvy knave! Pray you, sir, a word; and as I told you, my young lady bade me inquire you out; what she bid me say I will keep to myself; but first let me tell ye, if ye should lead her into a fool's paradise, as they say, it were a very gross kind of behaviour, as they say: for the gentlewoman is young; and, therefore, if you should deal double with her, truly it were an ill thing to be offered to any gentlewoman, and very weak dealing.

ROMEO. Nurse, commend me to thy lady and mistress. I protest unto thee,—

NURSE. Good heart! and, i' faith, I will tell her as much. Lord, Lord! she will be a joyful woman.

ROMEO. What wilt thou tell her, nurse? thou dost not mark me.

NURSE. I will tell her, sir, that you do protest; which, as I take it, is a gentlemanlike offer.

ROMEO. Bid her devise
Some means to come to shrift this afternoon;
And there she shall at Friar Laurence' cell
Be shriv'd and married. Here is for thy pains.

NURSE. No, truly, sir; not a penny.

ROMEO. Go to; I say, you shall.

NURSE. This afternoon, sir? well, she shall be there.

ROMEO. And stay, good nurse; behind the abbey wall:
Within this hour my man shall be with thee,
And bring thee cords made like a tackled stair;
Which to the high top-gallant of my joy
Must be my convoy in the secret night.
Farewell! Be trusty, and I 'll quit thy pains.
Farewell! Commend me to thy mistress.

NURSE. Now God in heaven bless thee! Hark you, sir.

ROMEO. What sayst thou, my dear nurse?

NURSE. Is your man secret? Did you ne'er hear say,
Two may keep counsel, putting one away?

ROMEO. I warrant thee my man 's as true as steel.

NURSE. Well, sir; my mistress is the sweetest lady—Lord, Lord!—when 'twas a little prating thing,—O! there 's a nobleman in town, one Paris, that would fain lay knife aboard; but she, good soul, had as lief see a toad, a very toad, as see him. I anger her sometimes and tell her that Paris is the properer man; but, I 'll warrant you, when I say so, she looks as pale as any clout in the versal world. Doth not rosemary and Romeo begin both with a letter?

ROMEO. Ay, nurse: what of that? both with an R.

NURSE. Ah! mocker; that 's the dog's name. R is for the—No; I know it begins with some other letter: and she had the prettiest sententious of it, of you and rosemary, that it would do you good to hear it.

ROMEO. Commend me to thy lady.

NURSE. Ay, a thousand times. (*Exit Romeo*) Peter!

PETER. Anon!

NURSE. Before, and apace.   *Exeunt*

SCENE FIVE

Capulet's Garden.

Enter Juliet

JULIET. The clock struck nine when I did send
 the nurse;
 In half an hour she promis'd to return.
 Perchance she cannot meet him: that 's not so.
 O! she is lame: love's heralds should be thoughts,
 Which ten times faster glide than the sun's beams,
 Driving back shadows over lowering hills:
 Therefore do nimble-pinion'd doves draw Love,
 And therefore hath the wind-swift Cupid wings.
 Now is the sun upon the highmost hill
 Of this day's journey, and from nine till twelve
 Is three long hours, yet she is not come.
 Had she affections, and warm youthful blood,
 She 'd be as swift in motion as a ball;
 My words would bandy her to my sweet love,
 And his to me:
 But old folks, many feign as they were dead;
 Unwieldy, slow, heavy and pale as lead.
    Enter Nurse and Peter
 O God! she comes. O honey nurse! what news?
 Hast thou met with him? Send thy man away.
NURSE. Peter, stay at the gate.   *Exit Peter*
JULIET. Now, good sweet nurse; O Lord! why look'st thou
 sad?
 Though news be sad, yet tell them merrily;
 If good, thou sham'st the music of sweet news
 By playing it to me with so sour a face.
NURSE. I am aweary, give me leave awhile:
 Fie, how my bones ache! What a jaunce have I had!
JULIET. I would thou hadst my bones, and I thy news.
 Nay, come, I pray thee, speak; good, good nurse, speak.
NURSE. Jesu! what haste? can you not stay awhile?
 Do you not see that I am out of breath?
JULIET. How art thou out of breath when thou hast breath
 To say to me that thou art out of breath?
 The excuse that thou dost make in this delay

Is longer than the tale thou dost excuse.
Is thy news good, or bad? answer to that;
Say either, and I 'll stay the circumstance:
Let me be satisfied, is 't good or bad?

NURSE. Well, you have made a simple choice; you know
not how to choose a man: Romeo! no, not he; though
his face be better than any man's, yet his leg excels all
men's; and for a hand, and a foot, and a body, though
they be not to be talked on, yet they are past compare.
He is not the flower of courtesy, but, I 'll warrant him,
as gentle as a lamb. Go thy ways, wench; serve God.
What! have you dined at home?

JULIET. No, no: but all this did I know before.
What says he of our marriage? what of that?

NURSE. Lord! how my head aches; what a head have I!
It beats as it would fall in twenty pieces.
My back o' t'other side; O! my back, my back!
Beshrew your heart for sending me about,
To catch my death with jauncing up and down.

JULIET. I' faith, I am sorry that thou art not well.
Sweet, sweet, sweet nurse, tell me, what says my love?

NURSE. Your love says, like an honest gentleman, and a
courteous, and a kind, and a handsome, and, I warrant,
a virtuous,—Where is your mother?

JULIET. Where is my mother! why, she is within;
Where should she be? How oddly thou repliest:
'Your love says, like an honest gentleman,
Where is your mother?'

NURSE.   O! God's lady dear,
Are you so hot? Marry, come up, I trow;
Is this the poultice for my aching bones?
Henceforward do your messages yourself.

JULIET. Here 's such a coil! come, what says Romeo?

NURSE. Have you got leave to go to shrift to-day?

JULIET. I have.

NURSE. Then hie you hence to Friar Laurence' cell,
There stays a husband to make you a wife:
Now comes the wanton blood up in your cheeks,
They 'll be in scarlet straight at any news.
Hie you to church; I must another way,
To fetch a ladder, by the which your love
Must climb a bird's nest soon when it is dark;

I am the drudge and toil in your delight,
But you shall bear the burden soon at night.
Go; I 'll to dinner; hie you to the cell.

JULIET. Hie to high fortune! Honest nurse, farewell.

Exeunt

SCENE SIX

Friar Laurence's Cell.

Enter Friar Laurence and Romeo

FRIAR LAURENCE. So smile the heaven upon this holy act,
That after hours with sorrow chide us not!

ROMEO. Amen, amen! but come what sorrow can,
It cannot countervail the exchange of joy
That one short minute gives me in her sight:
Do thou but close our hands with holy words,
Then love-devouring death do what he dare;
It is enough I may but call her mine.

FRIAR LAURENCE. These violent delights have violent ends,
And in their triumph die, like fire and powder
Which, as they kiss, consume: the sweetest honey
Is loathsome in his own deliciousness
And in the taste confounds the appetite:
Therefore love moderately; long love doth so;
Too swift arrives as tardy as too slow.

Enter Juliet

Here comes the lady: O! so light a foot
Will ne'er wear out the everlasting flint:
A lover may bestride the gossamer
That idles in the wanton summer air,
And yet not fall; so light is vanity.

JULIET. Good-even to my ghostly confessor.

FRIAR LAURENCE. Romeo shall thank thee, daughter, for
us both.

JULIET. As much to him, else are his thanks too much.

ROMEO. Ah! Juliet, if the measure of thy joy
Be heap'd like mine, and that thy skill be more
To blazon it, then sweeten with thy breath
This neighbour air, and let rich music's tongue
Unfold the imagin'd happiness that both

Receive in either by this dear encounter.

JULIET. Conceit, more rich in matter than in words.
Brags of his substance, not of ornament:
They are but beggars that can count their worth;
But my true love is grown to such excess
I cannot sum up half my sum of wealth.

FRIAR LAURENCE. Come, come with me, and we will make
short work;
For, by your leaves, you shall not stay alone
Till holy church incorporate two in one.   *Exeunt*

ACT THREE

SCENE ONE

Verona. A Public Place.

Enter Mercutio, Benvolio, Page, and Servants

BENVOLIO. I pray thee, good Mercutio, let 's retire:
  The day is hot, the Capulets abroad,
  And, if we meet, we shall not 'scape a brawl;
  For now, these hot days, is the mad blood stirring.

MERCUTIO. Thou art like one of those fellows that when
  he enters the confines of a tavern claps me his sword
  upon the table, and says 'God send me no need of thee!'
  and by the operation of the second cup draws him on
  the drawer, when, indeed, there is no need.

BENVOLIO. Am I like such a fellow?

MERCUTIO. Come, come, thou art as hot a Jack in thy
  mood as any in Italy; and as soon moved to be moody,
  and as soon moody to be moved.

BENVOLIO. And what to?

MERCUTIO. Nay, an there were two such, we should have
  none shortly, for one would kill the other. Thou! why,
  thou wilt quarrel with a man that hath a hair more or a
  hair less in his beard than thou hast. Thou wilt quarrel
  with a man for cracking nuts, having no other reason but
  because thou hast hazel eyes. What eye, but such an
  eye, would spy out such a quarrel? Thy head is as full
  of quarrels as an egg is full of meat, and yet thy head
  hath been beaten as addle as an egg for quarrelling.
  Thou has quarrelled with a man for coughing in the
  street, because he hath wakened thy dog that hath lain
  asleep in the sun. Didst thou not fall out with a tailor for
  wearing his new doublet before Easter? with another,
  for tying his new shoes with old riband? and yet thou
  wilt tutor me from quarrelling!

BENVOLIO. An I were so apt to quarrel as thou art, any
man should buy the fee-simple of my life for an hour
and a quarter.

MERCUTIO. The fee-simple! O simple!

BENVOLIO. By my head, here come the Capulets.

MERCUTIO. By my heel, I care not.

Enter Tybalt, and Others

TYBALT. Follow me close, for I will speak to them. Gentlemen, good den! a word with one of you.

MERCUTIO. And but one word with one of us? Couple it
with something; make it a word and a blow.

TYBALT. You shall find me apt enough to that, sir, an you
will give me occasion.

MERCUTIO. Could you not take some occasion without
giving?

TYBALT. Mercutio, thou consort'st with Romeo,—

MERCUTIO. Consort! What! dost thou make us minstrels?
an thou make minstrels of us, look to hear nothing but
discords: here 's my fiddlestick; here 's that shall make
you dance. 'Zounds! consort!

BENVOLIO. We talk here in the public haunt of men:
Either withdraw unto some private place,
Or reason coldly of your grievances,
Or else depart; here all eyes gaze on us.

MERCUTIO. Men's eyes were made to look, and let them
gaze;
I will not budge for no man's pleasure, I.

Enter Romeo

TYBALT. Well, peace be with you, sir. Here comes my
man.

MERCUTIO. But I 'll be hang'd, sir, if he wear your livery:
Marry, go before to field, he 'll be your follower;
Your worship in that sense may call him 'man.'

TYBALT. Romeo, the hate I bear thee can afford
No better term than this,—thou art a villain.

ROMEO. Tybalt, the reason that I have to love thee
Doth much excuse the appertaining rage
To such a greeting; villain am I none,
Therefore farewell; I see thou know'st me not.

TYBALT. Boy, this shall not excuse the injuries
That thou hast done me; therefore turn and draw.

ROMEO. I do protest I never injur'd thee,

But love thee better than thou canst devise,
Till thou shalt know the reason of my love:
And so, good Capulet, which name I tender
As dearly as my own, be satisfied.

MERCUTIO. O calm, dishonourable, vile submission!
Alla stoccata carries it away.   *Draws*
Tybalt, you rat-catcher, will you walk?

TYBALT. What wouldst thou have with me?

MERCUTIO. Good king of cats, nothing but one of your nine
lives, that I mean to make bold withal, and, as you shall
use me hereafter, dry-beat the rest of the eight. Will you
pluck your sword out of his pilcher by the ears? make
haste, lest mine be about your ears ere it be out.

TYBALT. (*Drawing*) I am for you.

ROMEO. Gentle Mercutio, put thy rapier up.

MERCUTIO. Come, sir, your passado.   *They fight*

ROMEO. Draw, Benvolio; beat down their weapons.
Gentlemen, for shame, forbear this outrage!
Tybalt, Mercutio, the prince expressly hath
Forbidden bandying in Verona streets.
Hold, Tybalt! good Mercutio!

Exeunt Tybalt and his Partisans

MERCUTIO.   I am hurt.
A plague o' both your houses! I am sped.
Is he gone, and hath nothing?

BENVOLIO.   What! art thou hurt?

MERCUTIO. Ay, ay, a scratch, a scratch; marry, 'tis enough.
Where is my page? Go, villain, fetch a surgeon.

Exit Page

ROMEO. Courage, man; the hurt cannot be much.

MERCUTIO. No, 'tis not so deep as a well, nor so wide as a
church door; but 'tis enough, 'twill serve: ask for me
to-morrow, and you shall find me a grave man. I am
peppered, I warrant, for this world. A plague o' both
your houses! Zounds, a dog, a rat, a mouse, a cat, to
scratch a man to death! a braggart, a rogue, a villain,
that fights by the book of arithmetic! Why the devil
came you between us? I was hurt under your arm.

ROMEO. I thought all for the best.

MERCUTIO. Help me into some house, Benvolio,
Or I shall faint. A plague o' both your houses!
They have made worms' meat of me: I have it

And soundly too:—your houses!

Exeunt Mercutio and Benvolio

ROMEO. This gentleman, the prince's near ally,
My very friend, hath got his mortal hurt
In my behalf; my reputation stain'd
With Tybalt's slander, Tybalt, that an hour
Hath been my kinsman. O sweet Juliet!
Thy beauty hath made me effeminate,
And in my temper soften'd valour's steel!

Re-enter Benvolio

BENVOLIO. O Romeo, Romeo! brave Mercutio's dead;
That gallant spirit hath aspir'd the clouds,
Which too untimely here did scorn the earth.

ROMEO. This day's black fate on more days doth depend;
This but begins the woe others must end.

Re-enter Tybalt

BENVOLIO. Here comes the furious Tybalt back again.

ROMEO. Alive! in triumph! and Mercutio slain!
Away to heaven, respective lenity,
And fire-ey'd fury be my conduct now!
Now, Tybalt, take the villain back again
That late thou gav'st me; for Mercutio's soul
Is but a little way above our heads,
Staying for thine to keep him company:
Either thou, or I, or both, must go with him.

TYBALT. Thou wretched boy, that didst consort him here,
Shalt with him hence.

ROMEO.   This shall determine that.

They fight: Tybalt falls

BENVOLIO. Romeo, away! be gone!
The citizens are up, and Tybalt slain.
Stand not amaz'd: the prince will doom thee death
If thou art taken: hence! be gone! away!

ROMEO. O! I am Fortune's fool.

BENVOLIO.   Why dost thou stay?

Exit Romeo

Enter Citizens, &c.

FIRST CITIZEN. Which way ran he that kill'd Mercutio?
Tybalt, that murderer, which way ran he?

BENVOLIO. There lies that Tybalt.

FIRST CITIZEN.   Up, sir, go with me.
I charge thee in the prince's name, obey.

Enter Prince, attended; Montague, Capulet,
their Wives, and Others

PRINCE. Where are the vile beginners of this fray?

BENVOLIO. O noble prince! I can discover all
The unlucky manage of this fatal brawl:
There lies the man, slain by young Romeo,
That slew thy kinsman, brave Mercutio.

LADY CAPULET. Tybalt, my cousin! O my brother's child!
O prince! O cousin! husband! O! the blood is spill'd
Of my dear kinsman. Prince, as thou art true,
For blood of ours shed blood of Montague.
O cousin, cousin!

PRINCE. Benvolio, who began this bloody fray?

BENVOLIO. Tybalt, here slain, whom Romeo's hand did
slay:
Romeo, that spoke him fair, bade him bethink
How nice the quarrel was, and urg'd withal
Your high displeasure: all this, uttered
With gentle breath, calm look, knees humbly bow'd,
Could not take truce with the unruly spleen
Of Tybalt deaf to peace, but that he tilts
With piercing steel at bold Mercutio's breast,
Who, all as hot, turns deadly point to point,
And, with a martial scorn, with one hand beats
Cold death aside, and with the other sends
It back to Tybalt, whose dexterity
Retorts it: Romeo he cries aloud,
'Hold, friends! friends, part!' and, swifter than his
tongue,
His agile arm beats down their fatal points,
And 'twixt them rushes; underneath whose arm
An envious thrust from Tybalt hit the life
Of stout Mercutio, and then Tybalt fled;
But by and by comes back to Romeo,
Who had but newly entertain'd revenge,
And to 't they go like lightning, for, ere I
Could draw to part them, was stout Tybalt slain,
And, as he fell, did Romeo turn and fly.
This is the truth, or let Benvolio die.

LADY CAPULET. He is a kinsman to the Montague;
Affection makes him false, he speaks not true:
Some twenty of them fought in this black strife

And all those twenty could but kill one life.
I beg for justice, which thou, prince must give;
Romeo slew Tybalt, Romeo must not live.

PRINCE. Romeo slew him, he slew Mercutio;
Who now the price of his dear blood doth owe?

MONTAGUE. Not Romeo, prince, he was Mercutio's friend,
His fault concludes but what the law should end,
The life of Tybalt.

PRINCE.   And for that offence
Immediately we do exile him hence:
I have an interest in your hate's proceeding,
My blood for your rude brawls doth lie a-bleeding;
But I 'll amerce you with so strong a fine
That you shall all repent the loss of mine.
I will be deaf to pleading and excuses;
Nor tears nor prayers shall purchase out abuses;
Therefore use none; let Romeo hence in haste,
Else, when he 's found, that hour is his last.
Bear hence this body and attend our will:
Mercy but murders, pardoning those that kill.   *Exeunt*

SCENE TWO

Capulet's Orchard.

Enter Juliet

JULIET. Gallop apace, you fiery-footed steeds,
Towards Phoebus' lodging; such a waggoner
As Phaethon would whip you to the west,
And bring in cloudy night immediately.
Spread thy close curtain, love-performing night!
That runaway's eyes may wink, and Romeo
Leap to these arms, untalk'd of and unseen!
Lovers can see to do their amorous rites
By their own beauties; or, if love be blind,
It best agrees with night. Come, civil night,
Thou sober-suited matron, all in black,
And learn me how to lose a winning match,
Play'd for a pair of stainless maidenhoods:
Hood my unmann'd blood, bating in my cheeks,
With thy black mantle; till strange love, grown bold,

Think true love acted simple modesty.
Come, night! come, Romeo! come, thou day in night!
For thou wilt lie upon the wings of night,
Whiter than new snow on a raven's back.
Come, gentle night; come, loving, black-brow'd night,
Give me my Romeo: and, when he shall die,
Take him and cut him out in little stars,
And he will make the face of heaven so fine
That all the world will be in love with night,
And pay no worship to the garish sun.
O! I have bought the mansion of a love,
But not possess'd it, and, though I am sold,
Not yet enjoy'd. So tedious is this day
As is the night before some festival
To an impatient child that hath new robes
And may not wear them. O! here comes my nurse,

     Enter Nurse with cords

And she brings news; and every tongue that speaks
But Romeo's name speaks heavenly eloquence.
Now, nurse, what news? What hast thou there? the cords
That Romeo bade thee fetch?

NURSE.   Ay, ay, the cords.

            Throws them down

JULIET. Ah me! what news? why dost thou wring thy
 hands?

NURSE. Ah well-a-day! he's dead, he's dead, he's dead!
 We are undone, lady, we are undone!
 Alack the day! he's gone, he's kill'd, he's dead!

JULIET. Can heaven be so envious?

NURSE.   Romeo can,
 Though heaven cannot. O! Romeo, Romeo;
 Who ever would have thought it? Romeo!

JULIET. What devil art thou that dost torment me thus?
 This torture should be roar'd in dismal hell.
 Hath Romeo slain himself? say thou but 'I,'
 And that bare vowel, 'I,' shall poison more
 Than the death-darting eye of cockatrice:
 I am not I, if there be such an 'I';
 Or those eyes shut that make thee answer 'I.'
 If he be slain, say 'I'; or if not, 'no':
 Brief sounds determine of my weal or woe.

NURSE. I saw the wound, I saw it with mine eyes,
  God save the mark! here on his manly breast:
  A piteous corse, a bloody piteous corse;
  Pale, pale as ashes, all bedaub'd in blood,
  All in gore blood; I swounded at the sight.
JULIET. O break, my heart!—poor bankrupt, break at once!
  To prison, eyes, ne'er look on liberty!
  Vile earth, to earth resign; end motion here;
  And thou and Romeo press one heavy bier!
NURSE. O Tybalt, Tybalt! the best friend I had:
  O courteous Tybalt! honest gentleman!
  That ever I should live to see thee dead!
JULIET. What storm is this that blows so contrary?
  Is Romeo slaughter'd, and is Tybalt dead?
  My dearest cousin, and my dearer lord?
  Then, dreadful trumpet, sound the general doom!
  For who is living if those two are gone?
NURSE. Tybalt is gone, and Romeo banished;
  Romeo, that kill'd him, he is banished.
JULIET. O God! did Romeo's hand shed Tybalt's blood?
NURSE. It did, it did; alas the day! it did.
JULIET. O serpent heart, hid with a flowering face!
  Did ever dragon keep so fair a cave?
  Beautiful tyrant! fiend angelical!
  Dove-feather'd raven! wolvish-ravening lamb!
  Despised substance of divinest show!
  Just opposite to what thou justly seem'st;
  A damned saint, an honourable villain!
  O, nature! what hadst thou to do in hell
  When thou didst bower the spirit of a fiend
  In mortal paradise of such sweet flesh?
  Was ever book containing such vile matter
  So fairly bound? O! that deceit should dwell
  In such a gorgeous palace.
NURSE.   There 's no trust,
  No faith, no honesty in men; all naught,
  All perjur'd, all dissemblers, all forsworn.
  Ah! where 's my man? give me some aqua vitæ:
  These griefs, these woes, these sorrows make me old.
  Shame come to Romeo!
JULIET.   Blister'd be thy tongue
  For such a wish! he was not born to shame:

Upon his brow shame is asham'd to sit;
For 'tis a throne where honour may be crown'd
Sole monarch of the universal earth.
O! what a beast was I to chide at him.
NURSE. Will you speak well of him that kill'd your cousin?
JULIET. Shall I speak ill of him that is my husband?
Ah! poor my lord, what tongue shall smooth thy name,
When I, thy three-hours wife, have mangled it?
But, wherefore, villain, didst thou kill my cousin?
That villain cousin would have kill'd my husband:
Back, foolish tears, back to your native spring;
Your tributary drops belong to woe,
Which you, mistaking, offer up to joy.
My husband lives, that Tybalt would have slain;
And Tybalt 's dead, that would have slain my husband:
All this is comfort; wherefore weep I then?
Some word there was, worser than Tybalt's death,
That murder'd me: I would forget it fain;
But O! it presses to my memory,
Like damned guilty deeds to sinners' minds.
'Tybalt is dead, and Romeo banished!'
That 'banished,' that one word 'banished,'
Hath slain ten thousand Tybalts. Tybalt's death
Was woe enough, if it had ended there:
Or, if sour woe delights in fellowship,
And needly will be rank'd with other griefs,
Why follow'd not, when she said 'Tybalt 's dead,'
Thy father, or thy mother, nay, or both,
Which modern lamentation might have mov'd?
But with a rearward following Tybalt's death,
'Romeo is banished!' to speak that word
Is father, mother, Tybalt, Romeo, Juliet,
All slain, all dead: 'Romeo is banished!'
There is no end, no limit, measure, bound
In that word's death; no words can that woe sound.—
Where is my father and my mother, nurse?
NURSE. Weeping and wailing over Tybalt's corse:
Will you go to them? I will bring you thither.
JULIET. Wash they his wounds with tears: mine shall be
spent,
When theirs are dry, for Romeo's banishment.
Take up those cords. Poor ropes, you are beguil'd,

Both you and I, for Romeo is exil'd:
He made you for a highway to my bed,
But I, a maid, die maiden-widowed.
Come, cords; come, nurse; I'll to my wedding-bed;
And death, not Romeo, take my maidenhead!

NURSE. Hie to your chamber; I'll find Romeo
To comfort you: I wot well where he is.
Hark ye, your Romeo will be here to-night:
I'll to him; he is hid at Laurence' cell.

JULIET. O! find him; give this ring to my true knight,
And bid him come to take his last farewell.   *Exeunt*

SCENE THREE

Friar Laurence's Cell.

Enter Friar Laurence

FRIAR LAURENCE. Romeo, come forth; come forth, thou
    fearful man:
Affliction is enamour'd of thy parts,
And thou art wedded to calamity.

Enter Romeo

ROMEO. Father, what news? what is the prince's doom?
What sorrow craves acquaintance at my hand,
That I yet know not?

FRIAR LAURENCE. Too familiar
Is my dear son with such sour company:
I bring thee tidings of the prince's doom.

ROMEO. What less than doomsday is the prince's doom?

FRIAR LAURENCE. A gentler judgment vanish'd from his
    lips,
Not body's death, but body's banishment.

ROMEO. Ha! banishment! be merciful, say 'death';
For exile hath more terror in his look,
Much more than death: do not say 'banishment.'

FRIAR LAURENCE. Hence from Verona art thou banished.
Be patient, for the world is broad and wide.

ROMEO. There is no world without Verona walls,
But purgatory, torture, hell itself.
Hence banished is banish'd from the world,
And world's exile is death; then 'banished,'

Is death mis-term'd. Calling death 'banished,'
Thou cutt'st my head off with a golden axe,
And smil'st upon the stroke that murders me.

FRIAR LAURENCE. O deadly sin! O rude unthankfulness!
Thy fault our law calls death; but the kind prince,
Taking thy part, hath rush'd aside the law,
And turn'd that black word death to banishment:
This is dear mercy, and thou seest it not.

ROMEO. 'Tis torture, and not mercy: heaven is here,
Where Juliet lives; and every cat and dog
And little mouse, every unworthy thing,
Live here in heaven and may look on her;
But Romeo may not: more validity,
More honourable state, more courtship lives
In carrion flies than Romeo: they may seize
On the white wonder of dear Juliet's hand,
And steal immortal blessing from her lips,
Who, even in pure and vestal modesty,
Still blush, as thinking their own kisses sin;
Flies may do this, but I from this must fly:
They are free men, but I am banished.
And sayst thou yet that exile is not death?
Hadst thou no poison mix'd, no sharp-ground knife,
No sudden mean of death, though ne'er so mean,
But 'banished' to kill me? 'Banished!'
O friar! the damned use that word in hell;
Howlings attend it: how hast thou the heart,
Being a divine, a ghostly confessor,
A sin-absolver, and my friend profess'd,
To mangle me with that word 'banished'?

FRIAR LAURENCE. Thou fond mad man, hear me but speak
    a word.

ROMEO. O! thou wilt speak again of banishment.

FRIAR LAURENCE. I 'll give thee armour to keep off that
    word;
Adversity's sweet milk, philosophy,
To comfort thee, though thou art banished.

ROMEO. Yet 'banished!' Hang up philosophy.
Unless philosophy can make a Juliet,
Displant a town, reverse a prince's doom,
It helps not, it prevails not: talk no more.

FRIAR LAURENCE. O! then I see that madmen have no ears

ROMEO. How should they, when that wise men have no eyes?
FRIAR LAURENCE. Let me dispute with thee of thy estate.
ROMEO. Thou canst not speak of that thou dost not feel:
    Wert thou as young as I, Juliet thy love,
    An hour but married, Tybalt murdered,
    Doting like me, and like me banished,
    Then mightst thou speak, then mightst thou tear thy hair,
    And fall upon the ground, as I do now,
    Taking the measure of an unmade grave.
                       Knocking within

FRIAR LAURENCE. Arise; one knocks: good Romeo, hide
    thyself.
ROMEO. Not I; unless the breath of heart-sick groans,
    Mist-like, infold me from the search of eyes.   *Knocking*
FRIAR LAURENCE. Hark! how they knock. Who 's there?
    Romeo, arise;
    Thou wilt be taken. Stay awhile! Stand up;   *Knocking*
    Run to my study. By and by! God's will!
    What wilfulness is this! I come, I come!   *Knocking*
    Who knocks so hard? whence come you? what 's your
    will?
NURSE. (*Within*) Let me come in, and you shall know my
    errand:
    I come from Lady Juliet.
FRIAR LAURENCE.   Welcome, then.
                  Enter Nurse
NURSE. O holy friar! O! tell me, holy friar,
    Where is my lady's lord? where 's Romeo?
FRIAR LAURENCE. There on the ground, with his own tears
    made drunk.
NURSE. O! he is even in my mistress' case,
    Just in her case!
FRIAR LAURENCE. O woeful sympathy!
    Piteous predicament! Even so lies she,
    Blubbering and weeping, weeping and blubbering.
    Stand up, stand up; stand, an you be a man:
    For Juliet's sake, for her sake, rise and stand;
    Why should you fall into so deep an O?
ROMEO. Nurse!
NURSE. Ah, sir! ah, sir! Well, death 's the end of all.
ROMEO. Spak'st thou of Juliet? how is it with her?
    Doth she not think me an old murderer,

Now I have stain'd the childhood of our joy
With blood remov'd but little from her own?
Where is she? and how doth she? and what says
My conceal'd lady to our cancell'd love?

NURSE. O! she says nothing, sir, but weeps and weeps;
And now falls on her bed; and then starts up,
And Tybalt calls, and then on Romeo cries,
And then down falls again.

ROMEO.   As if that name,
Shot from the deadly level of a gun,
Did murder her; as that name's cursed hand
Murder'd her kinsman. O! tell me, friar, tell me,
In what vile part of this anatomy
Doth my name lodge? tell me, that I may sack
The hateful mansion.   *Drawing his sword*

FRIAR LAURENCE.   Hold thy desperate hand:
Art thou a man? thy form cries out thou art:
Thy tears are womanish; thy wild acts denote
The unreasonable fury of a beast:
Unseemly woman in a seeming man;
Or ill-beseeming beast in seeming both!
Thou hast amaz'd me: by my holy order,
I thought thy disposition better temper'd.
Hast thou slain Tybalt? wilt thou slay thyself?
And slay thy lady that in thy life lives,
By doing damned hate upon thyself?
Why rail'st thou on thy birth, the heaven, and earth?
Since birth, and heaven, and earth, all three do meet
In thee at once, which thou at once wouldst lose.
Fie, fie! thou sham'st thy shape, thy love, thy wit,
Which, like a usurer, abound'st in all,
And usest none in that true use indeed
Which should bedeck thy shape, thy love, thy wit.
Thy noble shape is but a form of wax,
Digressing from the valour of a man;
Thy dear love, sworn, but hollow perjury,
Killing that love which thou hast vow'd to cherish;
Thy wit, that ornament to shape and love,
Misshapen in the conduct of them both,
Like powder in a skilless soldier's flask,
To set a-fire by thine own ignorance,
And thou dismember'd with thine own defence.

What! rouse thee, man; thy Juliet is alive,
For whose dear sake thou wast but lately dead;
There art thou happy: Tybalt would kill thee,
But thou slew'st Tybalt; there art thou happy too:
The law that threaten'd death becomes thy friend,
And turns it to exile; there art thou happy:
A pack of blessings light upon thy back;
Happiness courts thee in her best array;
But, like a misbehav'd and sullen wench,
Thou pout'st upon thy fortune and thy love.
Take heed, take heed, for such die miserable.
Go, get thee to thy love, as was decreed,
Ascend her chamber, hence and comfort her;
But look thou stay not till the watch be set,
For then thou canst not pass to Mantua;
Where thou shalt live, till we can find a time
To blaze your marriage, reconcile your friends,
Beg pardon of the prince, and call thee back
With twenty hundred thousand times more joy
Than thou went'st forth in lamentation.
Go before, nurse: commend me to thy lady;
And bid her hasten all the house to bed,
Which heavy sorrow makes them apt unto:
Romeo is coming.

NURSE. O Lord! I could have stay'd here all the night
To hear good counsel: O! what learning is.
My lord, I 'll tell my lady you will come.

ROMEO. Do so, and bid my sweet prepare to chide.

NURSE. Here, sir, a ring she bid me give you, sir.
Hie you, make haste, for it grows very late.   *Exit*

ROMEO. How well my comfort is reviv'd by this!

FRIAR LAURENCE. Go hence; good-night; and here stands
    all your state:
Either be gone before the watch be set,
Or by the break of day disguis'd from hence:
Sojourn in Mantua; I 'll find out your man,
And he shall signify from time to time
Every good hap to you that chances here.
Give me thy hand; 'tis late: farewell; good-night.

ROMEO. But that a joy past joy calls out on me,
It were a grief so brief to part with thee:
Farewell.   *Exeunt*

SCENE FOUR

A Room in Capulet's House.

Enter Capulet, Lady Capulet, and Paris

CAPULET. Things have fall'n out, sir, so unluckily,
　That we have had no time to move our daughter:
　Look you, she lov'd her kinsman Tybalt dearly,
　And so did I: well, we were born to die.
　'Tis very late, she 'll not come down to-night:
　I promise you, but for your company,
　I would have been a-bed an hour ago.
PARIS. These times of woe afford no time to woo.
　Madam, good-night: commend me to your daughter.
LADY CAPULET. I will, and know her mind, early to-morrow;
　To-night she 's mew'd up to her heaviness.
CAPULET. Sir Paris, I will make a desperate tender
　Of my child's love: I think she will be rul'd
　In all respects by me; nay, more, I doubt it not.
　Wife, go you to her ere you go to bed;
　Acquaint her here of my son Paris' love;
　And bid her, mark you me, on Wednesday next—
　But, soft! what day is this?
PARIS. 　　　　　　　　　　Monday, my lord.
CAPULET. Monday! ha, ha! Well, Wednesday is too soon;
　O' Thursday let it be: o' Thursday, tell her,
　She shall be married to this noble earl.
　Will you be ready? do you like this haste?
　We 'll keep no great ado; a friend or two;
　For, hark you, Tybalt being slain so late,
　It may be thought we held him carelessly,
　Being our kinsman, if we revel much.
　Therefore we 'll have some half a dozen friends,
　And there an end. But what say you to Thursday?
PARIS. My lord, I would that Thursday were to-morrow.
CAPULET. Well, get you gone: o' Thursday be it then.
　Go you to Juliet ere you go to bed,
　Prepare her, wife, against this wedding-day.
　Farewell, my lord. Light to my chamber, ho!
　Afore me! it is so very very late,
　That we may call it early by and by.
　Good-night. 　　　　　　　　　　　*Exeunt*

SCENE FIVE

Capulet's Orchard.

Enter Romeo and Juliet, above, at the window

JULIET. Wilt thou be gone? it is not yet near day.
It was the nightingale, and not the lark,
That pierc'd the fearful hollow of thine ear;
Nightly she sings on yon pomegranate-tree:
Believe me, love, it was the nightingale.

ROMEO. It was the lark, the herald of the morn,
No nightingale: look, love, what envious streaks
Do lace the severing clouds in yonder east:
Night's candles are burnt out, and jocund day
Stands tiptoe on the misty mountain tops:
I must be gone and live, or stay and die.

JULIET. Yon light is not daylight, I know it, I:
It is some meteor that the sun exhales,
To be to thee this night a torch-bearer,
And light thee on thy way to Mantua:
Therefore stay yet; thou need'st not to be gone.

ROMEO. Let me be ta'en, let me be put to death;
I am content, so thou wilt have it so.
I 'll say yon grey is not the morning's eye,
'Tis but the pale reflex of Cynthia's brow;
Nor that is not the lark, whose notes do beat
The vaulty heaven so high above our heads:
I have more care to stay than will to go:
Come, death, and welcome! Juliet wills it so.
How is 't, my soul? let 's talk; it is not day.

JULIET. It is, it is; hie hence, be gone, away!
It is the lark that sings so out of tune,
Straining harsh discords and unpleasing sharps.
Some say the lark makes sweet division;
This doth not so, for she divideth us:
Some say the lark and loathed toad change eyes;
O! now I would they had chang'd voices too,
Since arm from arm that voice doth us affray,
Hunting thee hence with hunts-up to the day.
O! now be gone; more light and light it grows.

ROMEO. More light and light; more dark and dark our woes.

Enter Nurse

NURSE. Madam!

JULIET. Nurse!

NURSE. Your lady mother is coming to your chamber:
　The day is broke; be wary, look about.   *Exit*

JULIET. Then, window, let day in, and let life out.

ROMEO. Farewell, farewell! one kiss, and I 'll descend.

　　　　　　　　　　　　　　　　　　　　Descends

JULIET. Art thou gone so? my lord, my love, my friend!
　I must hear from thee every day in the hour,
　For in a minute there are many days:
　O! by this count I shall be much in years
　Ere I again behold my Romeo.

ROMEO. Farewell!
　I will omit no opportunity
　That may convey my greetings, love, to thee.

JULIET. O! think'st thou we shall ever meet again?

ROMEO. I doubt it not; and all these woes shall serve
　For sweet discourses in our time to come.

JULIET. O God! I have an ill-divining soul:
　Methinks I see thee, now thou art so low,
　As one dead in the bottom of a tomb:
　Either my eyesight fails, or thou look'st pale.

ROMEO. And trust me, love, in my eye so do you:
　Dry sorrow drinks our blood. Adieu! adieu!   *Exit*

JULIET. O fortune, fortune! all men call thee fickle:
　If thou art fickle, what dost thou with him
　That is renown'd for faith? Be fickle, fortune;
　For then, I hope, thou wilt not keep him long,
　But send him back.

LADY CAPULET. (*Within*) Ho, daughter! are you up?

JULIET. Who is 't that calls? is it my lady mother?
　Is she not down so late, or up so early?
　What unaccustom'd cause procures her hither?

Enter Lady Capulet

LADY CAPULET. Why, how now, Juliet!

JULIET.　　　　　　　　　　Madam, I am not well.

LADY CAPULET. Evermore weeping for your cousin's death?
　What! wilt thou wash him from his grave with tears?
　And if thou couldst, thou couldst not make him live;
　Therefore, have done: some grief shows much of love;
　But much of grief shows still some want of wit.

ROMEO. Night's candles are burnt out, and jocund day
Stands tiptoe on the misty mountain tops:
I must be gone and live, or stay and die.

JULIET. Yet let me weep for such a feeling loss.

LADY CAPULET. So shall you feel the loss, but not the friend
Which you weep for.

JULIET.   Feeling so the loss,
I cannot choose but ever weep the friend.

LADY CAPULET. Well, girl, thou weep'st not so much for his death,
As that the villain lives which slaughter'd him.

JULIET. What villain, madam?

LADY CAPULET.   That same villain, Romeo.

JULIET. (*Aside*) Villain and he be many miles asunder.
God pardon him! I do, with all my heart;
And yet no man like he doth grieve my heart.

LADY CAPULET. That is because the traitor murderer lives.

JULIET. Ay, madam, from the reach of these my hands.
Would none but I might venge my cousin's death!

LADY CAPULET. We will have vengeance for it, fear thou not:
Then weep no more. I 'll send to one in Mantua,
Where that same banish'd runagate doth live,
Shall give him such an unaccustom'd dram
That he shall soon keep Tybalt company:
And then, I hope, thou wilt be satisfied.

JULIET. Indeed, I never shall be satisfied
With Romeo, till I behold him—dead—
Is my poor heart so for a kinsman vex'd:
Madam, if you could find out but a man
To bear a poison, I would temper it,
That Romeo should, upon receipt thereof,
Soon sleep in quiet. O! how my heart abhors
To hear him nam'd, and cannot come to him,
To wreak the love I bore my cousin Tybalt
Upon his body that hath slaughter'd him.

LADY CAPULET. Find thou the means, and I 'll find such a man.
But now I 'll tell thee joyful tidings, girl.

JULIET. And joy comes well in such a needy time:
What are they, I beseech your ladyship?

LADY CAPULET. Well, well, thou hast a careful father, child;
One who, to put thee from thy heaviness,
Hath sorted out a sudden day of joy

That thou expect'st not, nor I look'd not for.

JULIET. Madam, in happy time, what day is that?

LADY CAPULET. Marry, my child, early next Thursday morn
The gallant, young, and noble gentleman,
The County Paris, at Saint Peter's church,
Shall happily make thee there a joyful bride.

JULIET. Now, by Saint Peter's church, and Peter too,
He shall not make me there a joyful bride.
I wonder at this haste; that I must wed
Ere he that should be husband comes to woo.
I pray you, tell my lord and father, madam,
I will not marry yet; and, when I do, I swear,
It shall be Romeo, whom you know I hate,
Rather than Paris. These are news indeed!

LADY CAPULET. Here comes your father; tell him so yourself,
And see how he will take it at your hands.

Enter Capulet and Nurse

CAPULET. When the sun sets, the air doth drizzle dew;
But for the sunset of my brother's son
It rains downright.
How now! a conduit, girl? what! still in tears?
Evermore showering? In one little body
Thou counterfeit'st a bark, a sea, a wind;
For still thy eyes, which I may call the sea,
Do ebb and flow with tears; the bark thy body is,
Sailing in this salt flood; the winds, thy sighs;
Who, raging with thy tears, and they with them,
Without a sudden calm, will overset
Thy tempest-tossed body. How now, wife!
Have you deliver'd to her our decree?

LADY CAPULET. Ay, sir; but she will none, she gives you
thanks.
I would the fool were married to her grave!

CAPULET. Soft! take me with you, take me with you, wife.
How! will she none? doth she not give us thanks?
Is she not proud? doth she not count her bless'd,
Unworthy as she is, that we have wrought
So worthy a gentleman to be her bridegroom?

JULIET. Not proud, you have; but thankful, that you have:
Proud can I never be of what I hate;
But thankful even for hate, that is meant love.

CAPULET. How now! how now, chop-logic! What is this?
  'Proud,' and 'I thank you,' and 'I thank you not';
  And yet 'not proud'; mistress minion, you,
  Thank me no thankings, nor proud me no prouds,
  But fettle your fine joints 'gainst Thursday next,
  To go with Paris to Saint Peter's church,
  Or I will drag thee on a hurdle thither.
  Out, you green-sickness carrion! out, you baggage!
  You tallow face!
LADY CAPULET. Fie, fie! what, are you mad?
JULIET. Good father, I beseech you on my knees,
  Hear me with patience but to speak a word.
CAPULET. Hang thee, young baggage! disobedient wretch!
  I tell thee what, get thee to church o' Thursday,
  Or never after look me in the face,
  Speak not, reply not, do not answer me;
  My fingers itch.—Wife, we scarce thought us bless'd
  That God had lent us but this only child;
  But now I see this one is one too much,
  And that we have a curse in having her.
  Out on her, hilding!
NURSE.   God in heaven bless her!
  You are to blame, my lord, to rate her so.
CAPULET. And why, my lady wisdom? hold your tongue,
  Good prudence; smatter with your gossips, go.
NURSE. I speak no treason.
CAPULET.   O! God ye good den.
NURSE. May not one speak?
CAPULET.   Peace, you mumbling fool;
  Utter your gravity o'er a gossip's bowl;
  For here we need it not.
LADY CAPULET.   You are too hot.
CAPULET. God's bread! it makes me mad.
  Day, night, hour, tide, time, work, play,
  Alone, in company, still my care hath been
  To have her match'd; and having now provided
  A gentleman of noble parentage,
  Of fair demesnes, youthful, and nobly train'd,
  Stuff'd, as they say, with honourable parts,
  Proportion'd as one's thought would wish a man!
  And then to have a wretched puling fool,
  A whining mammet, in her fortune's tender,

To answer 'I 'll not wed,' 'I cannot love,'
'I am too young,' 'I pray you, pardon me';
But, an you will not wed, I 'll pardon you:
Graze where you will, you shall not house with me:
Look to 't, think on 't, I do not use to jest.
Thursday is near; lay hand on heart, advise.
An you be mine, I 'll give you to my friend;
An you be not, hang, beg, starve, die in the streets,
For, by my soul, I 'll ne'er acknowledge thee,
Nor what is mine shall never do thee good.
Trust to 't, bethink you; I 'll not be forsworn. *Exit*

JULIET. Is there no pity sitting in the clouds,
That sees into the bottom of my grief?
O! sweet my mother, cast me not away:
Delay this marriage for a month, a week;
Or, if you do not, make the bridal bed
In that dim monument where Tybalt lies.

LADY CAPULET. Talk not to me, for I 'll not speak a word.
Do as thou wilt, for I have done with thee. *Exit*

JULIET. O God!—O nurse! how shall this be prevented?
My husband is on earth, my faith in heaven;
How shall that faith return again to earth,
Unless that husband send it me from heaven
By leaving earth? comfort me, counsel me.
Alack, alack! that heaven should practise stratagems
Upon so soft a subject as myself!
What sayst thou? hast thou not a word of joy?
Some comfort, nurse?

NURSE. Faith, here it is. Romeo
Is banished; and all the world to nothing
That he dares ne'er come back to challenge you;
Or, if he do, it needs must be by stealth.
Then, since the case so stands as now it doth,
I think it best you married with the county.
O! he 's a lovely gentleman;
Romeo 's a dishclout to him: an eagle, madam,
Hath not so green, so quick, so fair an eye
As Paris hath. Beshrew my very heart,
I think you are happy in this second match,
For it excels your first: or if it did not,
Your first is dead; or 'twere as good he were,
As living here and you no use of him.

JULIET. Speakest thou from thy heart?

NURSE.   And from my soul too;
  Or else beshrew them both.

JULIET.   Amen!

NURSE.   What!

JULIET. Well, thou hast comforted me marvellous much.
  Go in; and tell my lady I am gone,
  Having displeas'd my father, to Laurence' cell,
  To make confession and to be absolv'd.

NURSE. Marry, I will; and this is wisely done.   *Exit*

JULIET. Ancient damnation! O most wicked fiend!
  Is it more sin to wish me thus forsworn,
  Or to dispraise my lord with that same tongue
  Which she hath prais'd him with above compare
  So many thousand times? Go, counsellor;
  Thou and my bosom henceforth shall be twain.
  I 'll to the friar, to know his remedy:
  If all else fail, myself have power to die.   *Exit*

ACT FOUR

SCENE ONE

Verona. Friar Laurence's Cell.

Enter Friar Laurence and Paris

FRIAR LAURENCE. On Thursday, sir? the time is very short.
PARIS. My father Capulet will have it so;
　And I am nothing slow to slack his haste.
FRIAR LAURENCE. You say you do not know the lady's
　　mind:
　Uneven is the course, I like it not.
PARIS. Immoderately she weeps for Tybalt's death,
　And therefore have I little talk'd of love;
　For Venus smiles not in a house of tears.
　Now, sir, her father counts it dangerous
　That she doth give her sorrow so much sway,
　And in his wisdom hastes our marriage
　To stop the inundation of her tears;
　Which, too much minded by herself alone,
　May be put from her by society.
　Now do you know the reason of this haste.
FRIAR LAURENCE. (*Aside*) I would I knew not why it should
　　be slow'd.
　Look, sir, here comes the lady towards my cell.
　　　　　　　Enter Juliet
PARIS. Happily met, my lady and my wife!
JULIET. That may be, sir, when I may be a wife.
PARIS. That may be must be, love, on Thursday next.
JULIET. What must be shall be.
FRIAR LAURENCE. 　　　　　　　　That 's a certain text.
PARIS. Come you to make confession to this father?
JULIET. To answer that, I should confess to you.
PARIS. Do not deny to him that you love me.
JULIET. I will confess to you that I love him.

PARIS. So will ye, I am sure, that you love me.

JULIET. If I do so, it will be of more price,
Being spoke behind your back, than to your face.

PARIS. Poor soul, thy face is much abus'd with tears.

JULIET. The tears have got small victory by that;
For it was bad enough before their spite.

PARIS. Thou wrong'st it, more than tears, with that report.

JULIET. That is no slander, sir, which is a truth;
And what I spake, I spake it to my face.

PARIS. Thy face is mine, and thou hast slander'd it.

JULIET. It may be so, for it is not mine own.
Are you at leisure, holy father, now;
Or shall I come to you at evening mass?

FRIAR LAURENCE. My leisure serves me, pensive daughter,
now:
My lord, we must entreat the time alone.

PARIS. God shield I should disturb devotion!
Juliet, on Thursday early will I rouse you:
Till then, adieu: and keep this holy kiss.   *Exit*

JULIET. O! shut the door! and when thou hast done so,
Come weep with me; past hope, past cure, past help!

FRIAR LAURENCE. Ah! Juliet, I already know thy grief;
It strains me past the compass of my wits:
I hear thou must, and nothing may prorogue it,
On Thursday next be married to this county.

JULIET. Tell me not, friar, that thou hear'st of this,
Unless thou tell me how I may prevent it:
If, in thy wisdom, thou canst give no help,
Do thou but call my resolution wise,
And with this knife, I 'll help it presently.
God join'd my heart and Romeo's, thou our hands;
And ere this hand, by thee to Romeo seal'd,
Shall be the label to another deed,
Or my true heart with treacherous revolt
Turn to another, this shall slay them both.
Therefore, out of thy long-experienc'd time,
Give me some present counsel; or behold,
'Twixt my extremes and me this bloody knife
Shall play the umpire, arbitrating that
Which the commission of thy years and art
Could to no issue of true honour bring.
Be not so long to speak; I long to die,

If what thou speak'st speak not of remedy.

FRIAR LAURENCE. Hold, daughter; I do spy a kind of hope,
Which craves as desperate an execution
As that is desperate which we would prevent.
If, rather than to marry County Paris,
Thou hast the strength of will to slay thyself,
Then is it likely thou wilt undertake
A thing like death to chide away this shame,
That cop'st with death himself to 'scape from it;
And, if thou dar'st, I 'll give thee remedy.

JULIET. O! bid me leap, rather than marry Paris,
From off the battlements of yonder tower;
Or walk in thievish ways; or bid me lurk
Where serpents are; chain me with roaring bears;
Or shut me nightly in a charnel-house,
O'er-cover'd quite with dead men's rattling bones,
With reeky shanks, and yellow chapless skulls;
Or bid me go into a new-made grave
And hide me with a dead man in his shroud;
Things that, to hear them told, have made me tremble;
And I will do it without fear or doubt,
To live an unstain'd wife to my sweet love.

FRIAR LAURENCE. Hold, then; go home, be merry, give
        consent
To marry Paris: Wednesday is to-morrow:
To-morrow night look that thou lie alone,
Let not thy nurse lie with thee in thy chamber:
Take thou this vial, being then in bed,
And this distilled liquor drink thou off;
When presently through all thy veins shall run
A cold and drowsy humour, for no pulse
Shall keep his native progress, but surcease;
No warmth, no breath, shall testify, thou liv'st;
The roses in thy lips and cheeks shall fade
To paly ashes; thy eyes' windows fall,
Like death, when he shuts up the day of life;
Each part, depriv'd of supple government,
Shall, stiff and stark and cold, appear like death;
And in this borrow'd likeness of shrunk death
Thou shalt continue two-and-forty hours,
And then awake as from a pleasant sleep.
Now, when the bridegroom in the morning comes

To rouse thee from thy bed, there art thou dead:
Then—as the manner of our country is—
In thy best robes uncover'd on the bier,
Thou shalt be borne to that same ancient vault
Where all the kindred of the Capulets lie.
In the mean time, against thou shalt awake,
Shall Romeo by my letters know our drift,
And hither shall he come; and he and I
Will watch thy waking, and that very night
Shall Romeo bear thee hence to Mantua.
And this shall free thee from this present shame;
If no unconstant toy, nor womanish fear,
Abate thy valour in the acting it.

JULIET. Give me, give me! O! tell me not of fear!
FRIAR LAURENCE. Hold; get you gone, be strong and pros-
     perous
In this resolve. I 'll send a friar with speed
To Mantua, with my letters to thy lord.
JULIET. Love, give me strength! and strength shall help
     afford.
Farewell, dear father!   *Exeunt*

SCENE TWO

Hall in Capulet's House.

Enter Capulet, Lady Capulet, Nurse, and Servingmen

CAPULET. So many guests invite as here are writ.
                                        Exit Servant
Sirrah, go hire me twenty cunning cooks.
SECOND SERVANT. You shall have none ill, sir; for I 'll try if
     they can lick their fingers.
CAPULET. How canst thou try them so?
SECOND SERVANT. Marry, sir, 'tis an ill cook that cannot lick
     his own fingers: therefore he that cannot lick his fingers
     goes not with me.
CAPULET. Go, be gone.   *Exit Second Servant*
We shall be much unfurnish'd for this time.
What! is my daughter gone to Friar Laurence?
NURSE. Ay, forsooth.

CAPULET. Well, he may chance to do some good on her:
A peevish self-will'd harlotry it is.

NURSE. See where she comes from shrift with merry look.

Enter Juliet

CAPULET. How now, my headstrong! where have you been
gadding?

JULIET. Where I have learn'd me to repent the sin
Of disobedient opposition
To you and your behests; and am enjoin'd
By holy Laurence to fall prostrate here,
And beg your pardon. Pardon, I beseech you!
Henceforward I am ever rul'd by you.

CAPULET. Send for the county; go tell him of this:
I 'll have this knot knit up to-morrow morning.

JULIET. I met the youthful lord at Laurence' cell;
And gave him what becomed love I might,
Not stepping o'er the bounds of modesty.

CAPULET. Why, I'm glad on 't; this is well: stand up:
This is as 't should be. Let me see the county;
Ay, marry, go, I say, and fetch him hither.
Now, afore God! this reverend holy friar,
All our whole city is much bound to him.

JULIET. Nurse, will you go with me into my closet,
To help me sort such needful ornaments
As you think fit to furnish me to-morrow?

LADY CAPULET. No, not till Thursday; there is time enough.

CAPULET. Go, nurse, go with her. We 'll to church to-
morrow.   *Exeunt Juliet and Nurse*

LADY CAPULET. We shall be short in our provision:
'Tis now near night.

CAPULET.   Tush! I will stir about,
And all things shall be well, I warrant thee, wife:
Go thou to Juliet, help to deck up her;
I 'll not to bed to-night; let me alone;
I 'll play the housewife for this once. What, ho!
They are all forth: well, I will walk myself
To County Paris, to prepare him up
Against to-morrow. My heart is wondrous light,
Since this same wayward girl is so reclaim'd.   *Exeunt*

SCENE THREE

Juliet's Chamber.

Enter Juliet and Nurse

JULIET. Ay, those attires are best; but, gentle nurse,
  I pray thee, leave me to myself to-night;
  For I have need of many orisons
  To move the heavens to smile upon my state,
  Which, well thou know'st, is cross and full of sin.
              Enter Lady Capulet
LADY CAPULET. What! are you busy, ho? need you my
  help?
JULIET. No, madam; we have cull'd such necessaries
  As are behoveful for our state to-morrow:
  So please you, let me now be left alone,
  And let the nurse this night sit up with you;
  For, I am sure, you have your hands full all
  In this so sudden business.
LADY CAPULET.   Good-night:
  Get thee to bed, and rest; for thou hast need.
       Exeunt Lady Capulet and Nurse
JULIET. Farewell! God knows when we shall meet again.
  I have a faint cold fear thrills through my veins,
  That almost freezes up the heat of life:
  I 'll call them back again to comfort me:
  Nurse! What should she do here?
  My dismal scene I needs must act alone.
  Come, vial.
  What if this mixture do not work at all?
  Shall I be married then to-morrow morning?
  No, no; this shall forbid it: lie thou there.
         Laying down a dagger
  What if it be a poison, which the friar
  Subtly hath minister'd to have me dead,
  Lest in this marriage he should be dishonour'd
  Because he married me before to Romeo?
  I fear it is: and yet, methinks, it should not,
  For he hath still been tried a holy man.
  I will not entertain so bad a thought.
  How if, when I am laid into the tomb,

I wake before the time that Romeo
Come to redeem me? there 's a fearful point!
Shall I not then be stifled in the vault,
To whose foul mouth no healthsome air breathes in,
And there die strangled ere my Romeo comes?
Or, if I live, is it not very like,
The horrible conceit of death and night,
Together with the terror of the place,
As in a vault, an ancient receptacle,
Where, for these many hundred years, the bones
Of all my buried ancestors are pack'd;
Where bloody Tybalt, yet but green in earth,
Lies festering in his shroud; where, as they say,
At some hours in the night spirits resort:
Alack, alack! is it not like that I,
So early waking, what with loathsome smells,
And shrieks like mandrakes' torn out of the earth,
That living mortals, hearing them, run mad:
O! if I wake, shall I not be distraught,
Environed with all these hideous fears,
And madly play with my forefathers' joints,
And pluck the mangled Tybalt from his shroud?
And, in this rage, with some great kinsman's bone,
As with a club, dash out my desperate brains?
O, look! methinks I see my cousin's ghost
Seeking out Romeo, that did spit his body
Upon a rapier's point. Stay, Tybalt, stay!
Romeo, I come! this do I drink to thee.

She falls upon her bed within the curtains

SCENE FOUR

Hall in Capulet's House.

Enter Lady Capulet and Nurse

LADY CAPULET. Hold, take these keys, and fetch more
    spices, nurse.
NURSE. They call for dates and quinces in the pastry.
Enter Capulet
CAPULET. Come, stir, stir, stir! the second cock hath crow'd,
    The curfew bell hath rung, 'tis three o'clock:

Look to the bak'd meats, good Angelica:
Spare not for cost.

NURSE.   Go, go, you cot-quean, go;
Get you to bed; faith, you 'll be sick to-morrow
For this night's watching.

CAPULET. No, not a whit; what! I have watch'd ere now
All night for lesser cause, and ne'er been sick.

LADY CAPULET. Ay, you have been a mouse-hunt in your
    time;
But I will watch you from such watching now.
                    Exeunt Lady Capulet and Nurse

CAPULET. A jealous-hood, a jealous-hood!

            Enter three or four Servingmen, with spits,
                    logs, and baskets

                                Now, fellow,
What 's there?

FIRST SERVINGMAN. Things for the cook, sir; but I know
    not what.

CAPULET. Make haste, make haste.
                    Exit first Servingman
Sirrah, fetch drier logs:
Call Peter, he will show thee where they are.

SECOND SERVINGMAN. I have a head, sir, that will find out
    logs,
And never trouble Peter for the matter.   *Exit*

CAPULET. Mass, and well said; a merry whoreson, ha!
Thou shalt be logger-head. Good faith! 'tis day:
The county will be here with music straight,
For so he said he would. (*Music within*) I hear him near.
Nurse! Wife! what, ho! What, nurse, I say!

                    Re-enter Nurse

Go waken Juliet, go and trim her up;
I 'll go and chat with Paris. Hie, make haste,
Make haste; the bridegroom he is come already:
Make haste, I say.   *Exeunt*

SCENE FIVE

Juliet's Chamber.

Enter Nurse

NURSE. Mistress! what, mistress! Juliet! fast, I warrant her,
    she:
  Why, lamb! why, lady! fie, you slug-a-bed!
  Why, love, I say! madam! sweet-heart! why, bride!
  What! not a word? you take your pennyworths now:
  Sleep for a week; for the next night, I warrant,
  The County Paris hath set up his rest,
  That you shall rest but little. God forgive me,
  Marry, and amen, how sound is she asleep!
  I needs must wake her. Madam, madam, madam!
  Ay, let the county take you in your bed;
  He 'll fright you up, i' faith. Will it not be?
  What, dress'd! and in your clothes! and down again!
  I must needs wake you. Lady! lady! lady!
  Alas! alas! Help! help! my lady 's dead!
  O! well-a-day, that ever I was born.
  Some aqua-vitæ, ho! My lord! my lady!

Enter Lady Capulet

LADY CAPULET. What noise is here?

NURSE.   O lamentable day!

LADY CAPULET. What is the matter?

NURSE.   Look, look! O heavy day!

LADY CAPULET. O me, O me! my child, my only life,
  Revive, look up, or I will die with thee!
  Help, help! Call help.

Enter Capulet

CAPULET. For shame! bring Juliet forth; her lord is come.

NURSE. She 's dead, deceas'd, she 's dead; alack the day!

LADY CAPULET. Alack the day! she 's dead! she 's dead!
  she 's dead!

CAPULET. Ha! let me see her. Out, alas! she 's cold;
  Her blood is settled, and her joints are stiff;
  Life and these lips have long been separated:
  Death lies on her like an untimely frost
  Upon the sweetest flower of all the field.

NURSE. O lamentable day!

LADY CAPULET.   O woeful time!

CAPULET. Death, that hath ta'en her hence to make me wail,
  Ties up my tongue, and will not let me speak.

Enter Friar Laurence, and Paris, with Musicians

FRIAR LAURENCE. Come, is the bride ready to go to church?

CAPULET. Ready to go, but never to return.
  O son! the night before thy wedding-day
  Hath Death lain with thy wife. There she lies,
  Flower as she was, deflowered by him.
  Death is my son-in-law, Death is my heir;
  My daughter he hath wedded: I will die,
  And leave him all; life, living, all is Death's!

PARIS. Have I thought long to see this morning's face,
  And doth it give me such a sight as this?

LADY CAPULET. Accurs'd, unhappy, wretched, hateful day!
  Most miserable hour that e'er time saw
  In lasting labour of his pilgrimage!
  But one, poor one, one poor and loving child,
  But one thing to rejoice and solace in,
  And cruel death hath catch'd it from my sight!

NURSE. O woe! O woeful, woeful, woeful day!
  Most lamentable day, most woeful day,
  That ever, ever, I did yet behold!
  O day! O day! O day! O hateful day!
  Never was seen so black a day as this:
  O woeful day, O woeful day!

PARIS. Beguil'd, divorced, wronged, spited, slain!
  Most detestable death, by thee beguil'd,
  By cruel cruel thee quite overthrown!
  O love! O life! not life, but love in death!

CAPULET. Despis'd, distressed, hated, martyr'd, kill'd!
  Uncomfortable time, why cam'st thou now
  To murder, murder our solemnity?
  O child! O child! my soul, and not my child!
  Dead art thou! dead! alack, my child is dead;
  And with my child my joys are buried!

FRIAR LAURENCE. Peace, ho! for shame! confusion's cure lives not
  In these confusions. Heaven and yourself
  Had part in this fair maid; now heaven hath all,
  And all the better is it for the maid:

Your part in her you could not keep from death,
But heaven keeps his part in eternal life.
The most you sought was her promotion,
For 'twas your heaven she should be advanc'd;
And weep ye now, seeing she is advanc'd
Above the clouds, as high as heaven itself?
O! in this love, you love your child so ill,
That you run mad, seeing that she is well:
She 's not well married that lives married long;
But she 's best married that dies married young.
Dry up your tears, and stick your rosemary
On this fair corse; and, as the custom is,
In all her best array bear her to church;
For though fond nature bids us all lament,
Yet nature's tears are reason's merriment.

CAPULET. All things that we ordained festival,
Turn from their office to black funeral;
Our instruments to melancholy bells,
Our wedding cheer to a sad burial feast,
Our solemn hymns to sullen dirges change,
Our bridal flowers serve for a buried corse,
And all things change them to the contrary.

FRIAR LAURENCE. Sir, go you in; and, madam, go with
     him;
And go, Sir Paris; every one prepare
To follow this fair corse unto her grave.
The heavens do lower upon you for some ill;
Move them no more by crossing their high will.

               Exeunt Capulet, Lady Capulet, Paris, and Friar

FIRST MUSICIAN. Faith, we may put up our pipes, and be
gone.

NURSE. Honest good fellows, ah! put up, put up, for, well
you know, this is a pitiful case.   *Exit*

FIRST MUSICIAN. Ay, by my troth, the case may be
amended.

                    Enter Peter

PETER. Musicians! O! musicians, 'Heart's ease, Heart's
ease': O! an ye will have me live, play 'Heart's ease.'

FIRST MUSICIAN. Why 'Heart's ease'?

PETER. O! musicians, because my heart itself plays 'My
heart is full of woe'; O! play me some merry dump, to
comfort me.

SECOND MUSICIAN. Not a dump we; 'tis no time to play now.

PETER. You will not then?

MUSICIANS. No.

PETER. I will then give it you soundly.

FIRST MUSICIAN. What will you give us?

PETER. No money, on my faith! but the gleek; I will give you the minstrel.

FIRST MUSICIAN. Then will I give you the serving-creature.

PETER. Then will I lay the serving-creature's dagger on your pate, I will carry no crotchets: I 'll re you, I 'll fa you. Do you note me?

FIRST MUSICIAN. An you re us, and fa us, you note us.

SECOND MUSICIAN. Pray you, put up your dagger, and put out your wit.

PETER. Then have at you with my wit! I will dry-beat you with an iron wit, and put up my iron dagger. Answer me like men:

> When gripping grief the heart doth wound,
>   And doleful dumps the mind oppress,
>   Then music with her silver sound—

Why 'silver sound'? why 'music with her silver sound'? What say you, Simon Catling?

FIRST MUSICIAN. Marry, sir, because silver hath a sweet sound.

PETER. Pretty! What say you, Hugh Rebeck?

SECOND MUSICIAN. I say 'silver sound,' because musicians sound for silver.

PETER. Pretty too! What say you, James Soundpost?

THIRD MUSICIAN. Faith, I know not what to say.

PETER. O! I cry you mercy; you are the singer; I will say for you. It is, 'music with her silver sound,' because musicians have no gold for sounding:

> Then music with her silver sound
>   With speedy help doth lend redress.   *Exit*

FIRST MUSICIAN. What a pestilent knave is this same!

SECOND MUSICIAN. Hang him, Jack! Come, we 'll in here; tarry for the mourners, and stay dinner.   *Exeunt*

ACT FIVE

SCENE ONE

Mantua. A Street.

Enter Romeo

ROMEO. If I may trust the flattering truth of sleep,
My dreams presage some joyful news at hand:
My bosom's lord sits lightly in his throne;
And all this day an unaccustom'd spirit
Lifts me above the ground with cheerful thoughts.
I dreamt my lady came and found me dead;—
Strange dream, that gives a dead man leave to think,—
And breath'd such life with kisses in my lips,
That I reviv'd, and was an emperor.
Ah me! how sweet is love itself possess'd,
When but love's shadows are so rich in joy!

Enter Balthasar, booted

News from Verona! How now, Balthasar?
Dost thou not bring me letters from the friar?
How doth my lady? Is my father well?
How fares my Juliet? That I ask again;
For nothing can be ill if she be well.

BALTHASAR. Then she is well, and nothing can be ill;
Her body sleeps in Capel's monument,
And her immortal part with angels lives.
I saw her laid low in her kindred's vault,
And presently took post to tell it you.
O! pardon me for bringing these ill news,
Since you did leave it for my office, sir.

ROMEO. Is it even so? then I defy you, stars!
Thou know'st my lodging: get me ink and paper,
And hire post-horses; I will hence to-night.

BALTHASAR. I do beseech you, sir, have patience:

Your looks are pale and wild, and do import
Some misadventure.

ROMEO.   Tush, thou art deceiv'd;
Leave me, and do the thing I bid thee do.
Hast thou no letters to me from the friar?

BALTHASAR. No, my good lord.

ROMEO.   No matter; get thee gone,
And hire those horses: I'll be with thee straight.

Exit Balthasar

Well, Juliet, I will lie with thee to-night.
Let's see for means: O mischief! thou art swift
To enter in the thoughts of desperate men.
I do remember an apothecary,
And hereabouts he dwells, which late I noted
In tatter'd weeds, with overwhelming brows,
Culling of simples; meagre were his looks,
Sharp misery had worn him to the bones;
And in his needy shop a tortoise hung,
An alligator stuff'd, and other skins
Of ill-shap'd fishes; and about his shelves
A beggarly account of empty boxes,
Green earthen pots, bladders, and musty seeds,
Remnants of packthread, and old cakes of roses,
Were thinly scatter'd, to make up a show.
Noting this penury, to myself I said
An if a man did need a poison now,
Whose sale is present death in Mantua,
Here lives a caitiff wretch would sell it him.
O! this same thought did but fore-run my need,
And this same needy man must sell it me.
As I remember, this should be the house:
Being holiday, the beggar's shop is shut.
What, ho! apothecary!

Enter Apothecary

APOTHECARY.   Who calls so loud?

ROMEO. Come hither, man. I see that thou art poor;
Hold, there is forty ducats; let me have
A dram of poison, such soon-speeding gear
As will disperse itself through all the veins
That the life-weary taker may fall dead,
And that the trunk may be discharg'd of breath
As violently as hasty powder fir'd

Doth hurry from the fatal cannon's womb.

APOTHECARY. Such mortal drugs I have; but Mantua's law
Is death to any he that utters them.

ROMEO. Art thou so bare, and full of wretchedness,
And fear'st to die? famine is in thy cheeks,
Need and oppression starveth in thine eyes,
Contempt and beggary hang upon thy back;
The world is not thy friend nor the world's law:
The world affords no law to make thee rich;
Then be not poor, but break it, and take this.

APOTHECARY. My poverty, but not my will, consents.

ROMEO. I pay thy poverty, and not thy will.

APOTHECARY. Put this in any liquid thing you will,
And drink it off; and, if you had the strength
Of twenty men, it would dispatch you straight.

ROMEO. There is thy gold, worse poison to men's souls,
Doing more murders in this loathsome world
Than these poor compounds that thou mayst not sell:
I sell thee poison, thou hast sold me none.
Farewell; buy food, and get thyself in flesh.
Come, cordial and not poison, go with me
To Juliet's grave, for there must I use thee.   *Exeunt*

SCENE TWO

Verona. Friar Laurence's Cell.

Enter Friar John

FRIAR JOHN. Holy Franciscan friar; brother, ho!
                    Enter Friar Laurence

FRIAR LAURENCE. This same should be the voice of Friar
John.
Welcome from Mantua: what says Romeo?
Or, if his mind be writ, give me his letter.

FRIAR JOHN. Going to find a bare-foot brother out,
One of our order, to associate me,
Here in this city visiting the sick,
And finding him, the searchers of the town,
Suspecting that we both were in a house,
Where the infectious pestilence did reign,
Seal'd up the doors, and would not let us forth;

So that my speed to Mantua there was stay'd.

FRIAR LAURENCE. Who bare my letter then to Romeo?

FRIAR JOHN. I could not send it, here it is again,
Nor get a messenger to bring it thee,
So fearful were they of infection.

FRIAR LAURENCE. Unhappy fortune! by my brotherhood,
The letter was not nice, but full of charge
Of dear import; and the neglecting it
May do much danger. Friar John, go hence;
Get me an iron crow, and bring it straight
Unto my cell.

FRIAR JOHN. Brother, I 'll go and bring it thee.   *Exit*

FRIAR LAURENCE. Now must I to the monument alone;
Within these three hours will fair Juliet wake:
She will beshrew me much that Romeo
Hath had no notice of these accidents;
But I will write again to Mantua,
And keep her at my cell till Romeo come:
Poor living corse, clos'd in a dead man's tomb!   *Exit*

SCENE THREE

*Verona. A Churchyard; in it a Monument
belonging to the Capulets.*

Enter Paris, and his Page, bearing flowers and a torch

PARIS. Give me thy torch, boy: hence, and stand aloof;
Yet put it out, for I would not be seen.
Under yond yew-trees lay thee all along,
Holding thine ear close to the hollow ground:
So shall no foot upon the churchyard tread,
Being loose, unfirm with digging up of graves,
But thou shalt hear it: whistle then to me,
As signal that thou hear'st something approach.
Give me those flowers. Do as I bid thee; go.

PAGE. (*Aside*) I am almost afraid to stand alone
Here in the churchyard; yet I will adventure.   *Retires*

PARIS. Sweet flower, with flowers thy bridal bed I strew,—
O woe! thy canopy is dust and stones;—
Which with sweet water nightly I will dew,

Or, wanting that, with tears distill'd by moans:
The obsequies that I for thee will keep
Nightly shall be to strew thy grave and weep.

The Page whistles

The boy gives warning something doth approach.
What cursed foot wanders this way to-night,
To cross my obsequies and true love's rite?
What! with a torch?—muffle me, night, awhile.

Retires

Enter Romeo and Balthasar, with a torch, mattock, &c.

ROMEO. Give me that mattock, and the wrenching iron.
Hold, take this letter; early in the morning
See thou deliver it to my lord and father.
Give me the light: upon thy life I charge thee,
Whate'er thou hear'st or seest, stand all aloof,
And do not interrupt me in my course.
Why I descend into this bed of death,
Is partly to behold my lady's face;
But chiefly to take thence from her dead finger
A precious ring, a ring that I must use
In dear employment: therefore hence, be gone:
But, if thou, jealous, dost return to pry
In what I further shall intend to do,
By heaven, I will tear thee joint by joint,
And strew this hungry churchyard with thy limbs.
The time and my intents are savage-wild,
More fierce and more inexorable far
Than empty tigers or the roaring sea.

BALTHASAR. I will be gone, sir, and not trouble you.

ROMEO. So shalt thou show me friendship. Take thou that:
Live, and be prosperous; and farewell, good fellow.

BALTHASAR. (*Aside*) For all this same, I 'll hide me here
about:
His looks I fear, and his intents I doubt.   *Retires*

ROMEO. Thou detestable maw, thou womb of death,
Gorg'd with the dearest morsel of the earth,
Thus I enforce thy rotten jaws to open,   *Opens the tomb*
And, in despite, I 'll cram thee with more food!

PARIS. This is that banish'd haughty Montague,
That murder'd my love's cousin, with which grief
It is supposed the fair creature died;
And here is come to do some villanous shame

To the dead bodies: I will apprehend him.—
Comes forward

Stop thy unhallow'd toil, vile Montague,
Can vengeance be pursu'd further than death?
Condemned villain, I do apprehend thee:
Obey, and go with me; for thou must die.

ROMEO. I must, indeed; and therefore came I hither.
Good gentle youth, tempt not a desperate man;
Fly hence and leave me: think upon these gone;
Let them affright thee. I beseech thee, youth,
Put not another sin upon my head
By urging me to fury: O! be gone:
By heaven, I love thee better than myself,
For I come hither arm'd against myself:
Stay not, be gone; live, and hereafter say
A madman's mercy bade thee run away.

PARIS. I do defy thy conjurations,
And apprehend thee for a felon here.

ROMEO. Wilt thou provoke me? then have at thee, boy!
They fight

PAGE. O Lord! they fight: I will go call the watch.   *Exit*

PARIS. (*Falls*) O, I am slain!—If thou be merciful,
Open the tomb, lay me with Juliet.   *Dies*

ROMEO. In faith, I will. Let me peruse this face:
Mercutio's kinsman, noble County Paris!
What said my man when my betossed soul
Did not attend him as we rode? I think
He told me Paris should have married Juliet:
Said he not so? or did I dream it so?
Or am I mad, hearing him talk of Juliet,
To think it was so? O! give me thy hand,
One writ with me in sour misfortune's book:
I 'll bury thee in a triumphant grave;
A grave? O, no! a lanthorn, slaughter'd youth,
For here lies Juliet, and her beauty makes
This vault a feasting presence full of light.
Death, lie thou there, by a dead man interr'd.
Laying Paris in the tomb

How oft when men are at the point of death
Have they been merry! which their keepers call
A lightning before death: O! how may I
Call this a lightning? O my love! my wife!

Death, that hath suck'd the honey of thy breath,
Hath had no power yet upon thy beauty:
Thou art not conquer'd; beauty's ensign yet
Is crimson in thy lips and in thy cheeks,
And death's pale flag is not advanced there.
Tybalt, liest thou there in thy bloody sheet?
O! what more favour can I do to thee,
Than with that hand that cut thy youth in twain
To sunder his that was thine enemy?
Forgive me, cousin! Ah! dear Juliet,
Why art thou yet so fair? Shall I believe
That unsubstantial Death is amorous,
And that the lean abhorred monster keeps
Thee here in dark to be his paramour?
For fear of that I still will stay with thee,
And never from this palace of dim night
Depart again: here, here will I remain
With worms that are thy chambermaids; O! here
Will I set up my everlasting rest,
And shake the yoke of inauspicious stars
From this world-wearied flesh. Eyes, look your last!
Arms, take your last embrace! and, lips, O you
The doors of breath, seal with a righteous kiss
A dateless bargain to engrossing death!
Come, bitter conduct, come, unsavory guide!
Thou desperate pilot, now at once run on
The dashing rocks thy sea-sick weary bark!
Here's to my love! (*Drinks*) O true apothecary!
Thy drugs are quick. Thus with a kiss I die.   *Dies*

Enter, at the other end of the Churchyard, Friar
Laurence, with a lanthorn, crow, and spade

FRIAR LAURENCE. Saint Francis be my speed! how oft to-
night
Have my old feet stumbled at graves! Who's there?

BALTHASAR. Here's one, a friend, and one that knows you
well.

FRIAR LAURENCE. Bliss be upon you! Tell me, good my
friend,
What torch is yond, that vainly lends his light
To grubs and eyeless skulls? as I discern,
It burneth in the Capel's monument.

BALTHASAR. It doth so, holy sir; and there's my master,
  One that you love.
FRIAR LAURENCE. Who is it?
BALTHASAR.   Romeo.
FRIAR LAURENCE. How long hath he been there?
BALTHASAR.   Full half an hour.
FRIAR LAURENCE. Go with me to the vault.
BALTHASAR.   I dare not, sir
  My master knows not but I am gone hence;
  And fearfully did menace me with death
  If I did stay to look on his intents.
FRIAR LAURENCE. Stay then, I 'll go alone. Fear comes upon
    me;
  O! much I fear some ill unlucky thing.
BALTHASAR. As I did sleep under this yew-tree here,
  I dreamt my master and another fought,
  And that my master slew him.
FRIAR LAURENCE. (*Advances*) Romeo!
  Alack, alack! what blood is this which stains
  The stony entrance of this sepulchre?
  What mean these masterless and gory swords
  To lie discolour'd by this place of peace?
                                   Enters the tomb
  Romeo! O pale! Who else? what! Paris too?
  And steep'd in blood? Ah! what an unkind hour
  Is guilty of this lamentable chance.
  The lady stirs.   *Juliet wakes*
JULIET. O, comfortable friar! where is my lord?
  I do remember well where I should be,
  And there I am. Where is my Romeo?   *Noise within*
FRIAR LAURENCE. I hear some noise. Lady, come from that
    nest
  Of death, contagion, and unnatural sleep:
  A greater power than we can contradict
  Hath thwarted our intents: come, come away.
  Thy husband in thy bosom there lies died:
  And Paris too: come, I 'll dispose of thee
  Among a sisterhood of holy nuns.
  Stay not to question, for the watch is coming;
  Come, go, good Juliet.—(*Noise again*) I dare no longer
    stay.

JULIET. Go, get thee hence, for I will not away.

Exit Friar Laurence

What 's here? a cup, clos'd in my true love's hand?
Poison, I see, hath been his timeless end.
O churl! drunk all, and left no friendly drop
To help me after! I will kiss thy lips;
Haply, some poison yet doth hang on them,
To make me die with a restorative.   *Kisses him*
Thy lips are warm!

FIRST WATCH. (*Within*) Lead, boy: which way?

JULIET. Yea, noise? then I 'll be brief. O happy dagger!

Snatching Romeo's dagger

This is thy sheath; (*Stabs herself.*) there rest, and let me
    die.   *Falls on Romeo's body and dies*

Enter Watch, with the Page of Paris

PAGE. This is the place; there where the torch doth burn.

FIRST WATCH. The ground is bloody; search about the
    churchyard.

Go, some of you; who'er you find, attach.

Exeunt some of the Watch

Pitiful sight! here lies the county slain,
And Juliet bleeding, warm, and newly dead,
Who here hath lain these two days buried.
Go, tell the prince, run to the Capulets,
Raise up the Montagues, some others search:

Exeunt others of the Watch

We see the ground whereon these woes do lie;
But the true ground of all these piteous woes
We cannot without circumstance descry.

Re-enter some of the Watch, with Balthasar

SECOND WATCH. Here 's Romeo's man; we found him in the
    churchyard.

FIRST WATCH. Hold him in safety, till the prince come
    hither.

Re-enter other of the Watch, with Friar Laurence

THIRD WATCH. Here is a friar, that trembles, sighs, and
    weeps;

We took this mattock and this spade from him,
As he was coming from this churchyard side.

FIRST WATCH. A great suspicion: stay the friar too.

Enter the Prince and Attendants

PRINCE. What misadventure is so early up,

That calls our person from our morning's rest?
Enter Capulet, Lady Capulet, and Others

CAPULET. What should it be, that they so shriek abroad?

LADY CAPULET. The people in the street cry Romeo,
Some Juliet, and some Paris; and all run
With open outcry toward our monument.

PRINCE. What fear is this which startles in our ears?

FIRST WATCH. Sovereign, here lies the County Paris slain;
And Romeo dead; and Juliet, dead before,
Warm and new kill'd.

PRINCE. Search, seek, and know how this foul murder
comes.

FIRST WATCH. Here is a friar, and slaughter'd Romeo's
man;
With instruments upon them, fit to open
These dead men's tombs.

CAPULET. O, heaven!—O wife! look how our daughter
bleeds!
This dagger hath mista'en!—for, lo, his house
Is empty on the back of Montague—
And is mis-sheathed in my daughter's bosom.

LADY CAPULET. O me! this sight of death is as a bell,
That warns my old age to a sepulchre.
Enter Montague and Others

PRINCE. Come, Montague: for thou art early up,
To see thy son and heir more early down.

MONTAGUE. Alas! my liege, my wife is dead to-night;
Grief of my son's exile hath stopp'd her breath.
What further woe conspires against mine age?

PRINCE. Look, and thou shalt see.

MONTAGUE. O thou untaught! what manners is in this,
To press before thy father to a grave?

PRINCE. Seal up the mouth of outrage for a while,
Till we can clear these ambiguities,
And know their spring, their head, their true descent;
And then will I be general of your woes,
And lead you even to death: meantime forbear,
And let mischance be slave to patience.
Bring forth the parties of suspicion.

FRIAR LAURENCE. I am the greatest, able to do least,
Yet most suspected, as the time and place
Doth make against me, of this direful murder;

And here I stand, both to impeach and purge
Myself condemned and myself excus'd.

PRINCE. Then say at once what thou dost know in this.

FRIAR LAURENCE. I will be brief, for my short date of
  breath
Is not so long as is a tedious tale.
Romeo, there dead, was husband to that Juliet;
And she, there dead, that Romeo's faithful wife:
I married them; and their stolen marriage-day
Was Tybalt's doomsday, whose untimely death
Banish'd the new-made bridegroom from this city;
For whom, and not for Tybalt, Juliet pin'd.
You, to remove that siege of grief from her,
Betroth'd, and would have married her perforce,
To County Paris: then comes she to me,
And, with wild looks bid me devise some mean
To rid her from this second marriage,
Or in my cell there would she kill herself.
Then gave I her,—so tutor'd by my art,—
A sleeping potion; which so took effect
As I intended, for it wrought on her
The form of death: meantime I writ to Romeo
That he should hither come as this dire night,
To help to take her from her borrow'd grave,
Being the time the potion's force should cease.
But he which bore my letter, Friar John,
Was stay'd by accident, and yesternight
Return'd my letter back. Then, all alone,
At the prefixed hour of her waking,
Came I to take her from her kindred's vault,
Meaning to keep her closely at my cell,
Till I conveniently could send to Romeo:
But, when I came,—some minute ere the time
Of her awakening,—here untimely lay
The noble Paris and true Romeo dead.
She wakes; and I entreated her come forth,
And bear this work of heaven with patience;
But then a noise did scare me from the tomb,
And she, too desperate, would not go with me,
But, as it seems, did violence on herself.
All this I know; and to the marriage

JULIET. Yea, noise? then I 'll be brief. O happy dagger!
This is thy sheath; there rest, and let me die.

Her nurse is privy: and, if aught in this
Miscarried by my fault, let my old life
Be sacrific'd, some hour before his time,
Unto the rigour of severest law.

PRINCE. We still have known thee for a holy man.
Where 's Romeo's man? what can he say in this?

BALTHASAR. I brought my master news of Juliet's death;
And then in post he came from Mantua
To this same place, to this same monument.
This letter he early bid me give his father,
And threaten'd me with death, going in the vault,
If I departed not and left him there.

PRINCE. Give me the letter; I will look on it.
Where is the county's page that rais'd the watch?
Sirrah, what made your master in this place?

PAGE. He came with flowers to strew his lady's grave,
And bid me stand aloof, and so I did;
Anon, comes one with light to ope the tomb;
And by and by my master drew on him;
And then I ran away to call the watch.

PRINCE. This letter doth make good the friar's words,
Their course of love, the tidings of her death;
And here he writes that he did buy a poison
Of a poor 'pothecary, and therewithal
Came to this vault to die, and lie with Juliet.
Where be these enemies?—Capulet! Montague!
See what a scourge is laid upon your hate,
That heaven finds means to kill your joys with love;
And I, for winking at your discords too,
Have lost a brace of kinsmen: all are punish'd.

CAPULET. O brother Montague! give me thy hand:
This is my daughter's jointure, for no more
Can I demand.

MONTAGUE. But I can give thee more;
For I will raise her statue in pure gold;
That while Verona by that name is known,
There shall no figure at such rate be set
As that of true and faithful Juliet.

CAPULET. As rich shall Romeo by his lady lie;
Poor sacrifices of our enmity!

PRINCE. A glooming peace this morning with it brings;

The sun, for sorrow, will not show his head:
Go hence, to have more talk of these sad things;
Some shall be pardon'd, and some punished:
For never was a story of more woe
Than this of Juliet and her Romeo.   *Exeunt*

TIMON OF ATHENS

CAST OF CHARACTERS

TIMON, *a noble Athenian*

LUCIUS
LUCULLUS } *flattering Lords*
SEMPRONIUS

VENTIDIUS, *one of Timon's false Friends*
APEMANTUS, *a churlish Philosopher*
ALCIBIADES, *an Athenian Captain*
FLAVIUS, *Steward to Timon*

FLAMINIUS
LUCILIUS } *Servants to Timon*
SERVILIUS

CAPHIS
PHILOTUS
TITUS } *Servants to Timon's Creditors*
LUCIUS
HORTENSIUS

Servants of Ventidius, and of Varro and Isidore
  (two of Timon's Creditors)
Three Strangers
An Old Athenian
A Page
A Fool
Poet, Painter, Jeweller, and Merchant

PHRYNIA } *Mistresses to Alcibiades*
TIMANDRA

CUPID *and Amazons in the Mask*

Lords, Senators, Officers, Soldiers, Thieves, and
Attendants

SCENE

Athens, and the neighbouring Woods

TIMON OF ATHENS

ACT ONE

SCENE ONE

Athens. A Hall in Timon's House.

Enter Poet, Painter, Jeweller, Merchant, and Others, at several doors

POET. Good day, sir.

PAINTER.   I am glad you 're well.

POET. I have not seen you long. How goes the world?

PAINTER. It wears, sir, as it grows.

POET.   Ay, that 's well known;
But what particular rarity? what strange,
Which manifold record not matches? See,
Magic of bounty! all these spirits thy power
Hath conjur'd to attend. I know the merchant.

PAINTER. I know them both: th' other 's a jeweller.

MERCHANT. O! 'tis a worthy lord.

JEWELLER.   Nay, that 's most fix'd.

MERCHANT. A most incomparable man, breath'd, as it
     were,
To an untirable and continuate goodness:
He passes.

JEWELLER. I have a jewel here—

MERCHANT. O! pray, let 's see 't: for the Lord Timon, sir?

JEWELLER. If he will touch the estimate: but, for that—

POET. 'When we for recompense have prais'd the vile,
It stains the glory in that happy verse
Which aptly sings the good.'

MERCHANT. (*Looking at the jewel*) 'Tis a good form.

JEWELLER. And rich: here is a water, look ye.

PAINTER. You are rapt, sir, in some work, some dedication
To the great lord.

POET.   A thing slipp'd idly from me.
Our poesy is as a gum, which oozes

From whence 'tis nourish'd: the fire i' the flint
Shows not till it be struck; our gentle flame
Provokes itself, and, like the current, flies
Each bound it chafes. What have you there?

PAINTER. A picture, sir. When comes your book forth?

POET. Upon the heels of my presentment, sir.
Let 's see your piece.

PAINTER. 'Tis a good piece.

POET. So 'tis: this comes off well and excellent.

PAINTER. Indifferent.

POET.   Admirable! How this grace
Speaks his own standing! what a mental power
This eye shoots forth! how big imagination
Moves in this lip! to the dumbness of the gesture
One might interpret.

PAINTER. It is a pretty mocking of the life.
Here is a touch; is 't good?

POET.   I 'll say of it,
It tutors nature: artificial strife
Lives in these touches, livelier than life.

        Enter certain Senators, who pass over the stage

PAINTER. How this lord is follow'd!

POET. The senators of Athens: happy man!

PAINTER. Look, more!

POET. You see this confluence, this great flood of visitors.
I have, in this rough work, shap'd out a man,
Whom this beneath world doth embrace and hug
With amplest entertainment: my free drift
Halts not particularly, but moves itself
In a wide sea of wax: no levell'd malice
Infects one comma in the course I hold;
But flies an eagle flight, bold and forth on,
Leaving no tract behind.

PAINTER. How shall I understand you?

POET.   I will unbolt to you.
You see how all conditions, how all minds—
As well of glib and slippery creatures as
Of grave and austere quality—tender down
Their services to Lord Timon: his large fortune,
Upon his good and gracious nature hanging,
Subdues and properties to his love and tendance

All sorts of hearts; yea, from the glass-fac'd flatterer
To Apemantus, that few things loves better
Than to abhor himself: even he drops down
The knee before him and returns in peace
Most rich in Timon's nod.

PAINTER.   I saw them speak together.

POET. Sir, I have upon a high and pleasant hill
Feign'd Fortune to be thron'd: the base o' the mount
Is rank'd with all deserts, all kinds of natures,
That labour on the bosom of this sphere
To propagate their states: amongst them all,
Whose eyes are on this sovereign lady fix'd,
One do I personate of Lord Timon's frame,
Whom Fortune with her ivory hand wafts to her;
Whose present grace to present slaves and servants
Translates his rivals.

PAINTER.   'Tis conceiv'd to scope.
This throne, this Fortune, and this hill, methinks,
With one man beckon'd from the rest below,
Bowing his head against the steepy mount
To climb his happiness, would be well express'd
In our condition.

POET.   Nay, sir, but hear me on.
All those which were his fellows but of late,
Some better than his value, on the moment
Follow his strides, his lobbies fill with tendance,
Rain sacrificial whisperings in his ear,
Make sacred even his stirrup, and through him
Drink the free air.

PAINTER.   Ay, marry, what of these?

POET. When Fortune in her shift and change of mood
Spurns down her late belov'd, all his dependants
Which labour'd after him to the mountain's top
Even on their knees and hands, let him slip down,
Not one accompanying his declining foot.

PAINTER. 'Tis common:
A thousand moral paintings I can show
That shall demonstrate these quick blows of Fortune's
More pregnantly than words. Yet you do well
To show Lord Timon that mean eyes have seen
The foot above the head.

Trumpets sound. Enter Lord Timon,
addressing himself courteously to every suitor; a Messenger
from Ventidius talking with him; Lucilius and other
servants following.

TIMON.   Imprison'd is he, say you?

MESSENGER. Ay, my good lord: five talents is his debt,
His means most short, his creditors most strait:
Your honourable letter he desires
To those have shut him up; which failing,
Periods his comfort.

TIMON.   Noble Ventidius! Well;
I am not of that feather to shake off
My friend when he must need me. I do know him
A gentleman that well deserves a help,
Which he shall have: I 'll pay the debt and free him.

MESSENGER. Your lordship ever binds him.

TIMON. Commend me to him. I will send his ransom;
And being enfranchis'd, bid him come to me.
'Tis not enough to help the feeble up,
But to support him after. Fare you well.

MESSENGER. All happiness to your honour.   *Exit*

Enter an old Athenian

OLD ATHENIAN. Lord Timon, hear me speak.

TIMON.   Freely, good father.

OLD ATHENIAN. Thou hast a servant nam'd Lucilius.

TIMON. I have so: what of him?

OLD ATHENIAN. Most noble Timon, call the man before
thee.

TIMON. Attends he here or no? Lucilius!

LUCILIUS. Here, at your lordship's service.

OLD ATHENIAN. This fellow here, Lord Timon, this thy
creature,
By night frequents my house. I am a man
That from my first have been inclin'd to thrift,
And my estate deserves an heir more rais'd
Than one which holds a trencher.

TIMON.   Well; what further?

OLD ATHENIAN. One only daughter have I, no kin else,
On whom I may confer what I have got:
The maid is fair, o' the youngest for a bride,
And I have bred her at my dearest cost
In qualities of the best. This man of thine

Attempts her love: I prithee, noble lord,
Join with me to forbid him her resort;
Myself have spoke in vain.

TIMON.   The man is honest.

OLD ATHENIAN. Therefore he will be, Timon:
His honesty rewards him in itself;
It must not bear my daughter.

TIMON.   Does she love him?

OLD ATHENIAN. She is young and apt:
Our own precedent passions do instruct us
What levity 's in youth.

TIMON. (*To Lucilius*) Love you the maid?

LUCILIUS. Ay, my good lord, and she accepts of it.

OLD ATHENIAN. If in her marriage my consent be missing,
I call the gods to witness, I will choose
Mine heir from forth the beggars of the world,
And dispossess her all.

TIMON.   How shall she be endow'd,
If she be mated with an equal husband?

OLD ATHENIAN. Three talents on the present; in future, all.

TIMON. This gentleman of mine hath serv'd me long:
To build his fortune, I will strain a little,
For 'tis a bond in men. Give him thy daughter;
What you bestow, in him I 'll counterpoise,
And make him weigh with her.

OLD ATHENIAN.   Most noble lord,
Pawn me to this your honour, she is his.

TIMON. My hand to thee; mine honour on my promise.

LUCILIUS. Humbly I thank your lordship: never may
That state or fortune fall into my keeping
Which is not ow'd to you!

              Exeunt Lucilius and Old Athenian

POET. Vouchsafe my labour, and long live your lordship!

TIMON. I thank you; you shall hear from me anon:
Go not away. What have you there, my friend?

PAINTER. A piece of painting, which I do beseech
Your lordship to accept.

TIMON.   Painting is welcome.
The painting is almost the natural man;
For since dishonour traffics with man's nature,
He is but outside: these pencill'd figures are
Even such as they give out. I like your work;

And you shall find I like it: wait attendance
Till you hear further from me.

PAINTER.   The gods preserve you!

TIMON. Well fare you, gentleman: give me your hand;
We must needs dine together. Sir, your jewel
Hath suffer'd under praise.

JEWELLER.   What, my lord! dispraise?

TIMON. A mere satiety of commendations.
If I should pay you for 't as 'tis extoll'd,
It would unclew me quite.

JEWELLER.   My lord, 'tis rated
As those which sell would give: but you well know,
Things of live value, differing in the owners,
Are prized by their masters. Believe 't, dear lord,
You mend the jewel by the wearing it.

TIMON. Well mock'd.

MERCHANT. No, my good lord; he speaks the common
      tongue,
Which all men speak with him.

TIMON. Look, who comes here. Will you be chid?

Enter Apemantus

JEWELLER. We 'll bear, with your lordship.

MERCHANT.   He 'll spare none.

TIMON. Good-morrow to thee, gentle Apemantus!

APEMANTUS. Till I be gentle, stay thou for thy good-mor-
      row;
When thou art Timon's dog, and these knaves honest.

TIMON. Why dost thou call them knaves? thou know'st them
      not.

APEMANTUS. Are they not Athenians?

TIMON. Yes.

APEMANTUS. Then I repent not.

JEWELLER. You know me, Apemantus?

APEMANTUS. Thou know'st I do; I call'd thee by thy name.

TIMON. Thou art proud, Apemantus.

APEMANTUS. Of nothing so much as that I am not like
      Timon.

TIMON. Whither art going?

APEMANTUS. To knock out an honest Athenian's brains.

TIMON. That 's a deed thou 'lt die for.

APEMANTUS. Right, if doing nothing be death by the law.

TIMON. How likest thou this picture, Apemantus?

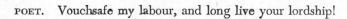

POET.   Vouchsafe my labour, and long live your lordship!

APEMANTUS. The best, for the innocence.

TIMON. Wrought he not well that painted it?

APEMANTUS. He wrought better that made the painter; and yet he 's but a filthy piece of work.

PAINTER. You 're a dog.

APEMANTUS. Thy mother 's of my generation: what 's she, if I be a dog?

TIMON. Wilt dine with me, Apemantus?

APEMANTUS. No; I eat not lords.

TIMON. An thou shouldst, thou 'dst anger ladies.

APEMANTUS. O! they eat lords; so they come by great bellies.

TIMON. That 's a lascivious apprehension.

APEMANTUS. So thou apprehendest it, take it for thy labour.

TIMON. How dost thou like this jewel, Apemantus?

APEMANTUS. Not so well as plain-dealing, which will not cost a man a doit.

TIMON. What dost thou think 'tis worth?

APEMANTUS. Not worth my thinking. How now, poet!

POET. How now, philosopher!

APEMANTUS. Thou liest.

POET. Art not one?

APEMANTUS. Yes.

POET. Then I lie not.

APEMANTUS. Art not a poet?

POET. Yes.

APEMANTUS. Then thou liest: look in thy last work, where thou hast feigned him a worthy fellow.

POET. That 's not feigned; he is so.

APEMANTUS. Yes, he is worthy of thee, and to pay thee for thy labour: he that loves to be flattered is worthy o' the flatterer. Heavens, that I were a lord!

TIMON. What wouldst do then, Apemantus?

APEMANTUS. Even as Apemantus does now; hate a lord with my heart.

TIMON. What, thyself?

APEMANTUS. Ay.

TIMON. Wherefore?

APEMANTUS. That I had no angry wit to be a lord. Art not thou a merchant?

MERCHANT. Ay, Apemantus.

APEMANTUS. Traffic confound thee, if the gods will not!

MERCHANT. If traffic do it, the gods do it.

APEMANTUS. Traffic 's thy god, and thy god confound thee!

Trumpet sounds. Enter a Servant

TIMON. What trumpet 's that?

SERVANT. 'Tis Alcibiades, and some twenty horse,
All of companionship.

TIMON. Pray, entertain them: give them guide to us.

Exeunt some Attendants

You must needs dine with me. Go not you hence
Till I have thanked you; when dinner 's done,
Show me this piece. I am joyful of your sights.

Enter Alcibiades, with his Company

Most welcome, sir!

APEMANTUS.   So, so, there!
Aches contract and starve your supple joints!
That there should be small love 'mongst these sweet
knaves,
And all this courtesy! The strain of man 's bred out
Into baboon and monkey.

ALCIBIADES. Sir, you have sav'd my longing, and I feed
Most hungerly on your sight.

TIMON.   Right welcome, sir!
Ere we depart, we 'll share a bounteous time
In different pleasures. Pray you, let us in.

Exeunt all except Apemantus

Enter two Lords

FIRST LORD. What time o' day is 't, Apemantus?

APEMANTUS. Time to be honest.

FIRST LORD. That time serves still.

APEMANTUS. The more accursed thou, that still omitt'st it.

SECOND LORD. Thou art going to Lord Timon's feast?

APEMANTUS. Ay; to see meat fill knaves and wine heat
fools.

SECOND LORD. Fare thee well, fare thee well.

APEMANTUS. Thou art a fool to bid me farewell twice.

SECOND LORD. Why, Apemantus?

APEMANTUS. Shouldst have kept one to thyself, for I mean
to give thee none.

FIRST LORD. Hang thyself!

APEMANTUS. No, I will do nothing at thy bidding: make
thy requests to thy friend.

SECOND LORD. Away, unpeaceable dog! or I 'll spurn thee
   hence.

APEMANTUS. I will fly, like a dog, the heels of an ass.

Exit

FIRST LORD. He 's opposite to humanity. Come, shall we in,
   And taste Lord Timon's bounty? he outgoes
   The very heart of kindness.

SECOND LORD. He pours it out; Plutus, the god of gold,
   Is but his steward: no meed but he repays
   Sevenfold above itself; no gift to him
   But breeds the giver a return exceeding
   All use of quittance.

FIRST LORD.   The noblest mind he carries
   That ever govern'd man.

SECOND LORD. Long may he live in fortunes! Shall we in?

FIRST LORD. I 'll keep you company.   *Exeunt*

SCENE TWO

A Room of State in Timon's House.

*Hautboys playing loud music. A great
banquet served in; Flavius and Others attending: then enter
Lord Timon, Alcibiades, Lords, and Senators, Ventidius and
Attendants. Then comes, dropping after all, Apemantus,
discontentedly, like himself*

VENTIDIUS. Most honour'd Timon,
   It hath pleas'd the gods to remember my father's age,
   And call him to long peace.
   He is gone happy, and has left me rich:
   Then, as in grateful virtue I am bound
   To your free heart, I do return those talents,
   Doubled with thanks and service, from whose help
   I deriv'd liberty.

TIMON.   O! by no means,
   Honest Ventidius; you mistake my love;
   I gave it freely ever; and there 's none
   Can truly say he gives, if he receives:
   If our betters play at that game, we must not dare
   To imitate them; faults that are rich are fair.

VENTIDIUS. A noble spirit.

They all stand ceremoniously looking on Timon

TIMON. Nay, my lords, ceremony was but devis'd at first
To set a gloss on faint deeds, hollow welcomes,
Recanting goodness, sorry ere 'tis shown;
But where there is true friendship, there needs none.
Pray, sit; more welcome are ye to my fortunes
Than my fortunes to me.   *They sit*

FIRST LORD. My lord, we always have confess'd it.

APEMANTUS. Ho, ho! confess'd it; hang'd it, have you not?

TIMON. O! Apemantus, you are welcome.

APEMANTUS.   No,
You shall not make me welcome:
I come to have thee thrust me out of doors.

TIMON. Fie! thou 'rt a churl; ye 've got a humour there
Does not become a man; 'tis much to blame.
They say, my lords, 'Ira furor brevis est';
But yond man is ever angry.
Go, let him have a table by himself,
For he does neither affect company,
Nor is he fit for it, indeed.

APEMANTUS. Let me stay at thine apperil, Timon: I come
to observe; I give thee warning on 't.

TIMON. I take no heed of thee; thou 'rt an Athenian, therefore, welcome. I myself would have no power; prithee,
let my meat make thee silent.

APEMANTUS. I scorn thy meat; 'twould choke me, for I
should
Ne'er flatter thee. O you gods! what a number
Of men eat Timon, and he sees them not.
It grieves me to see so many dip their meat
In one man's blood; and all the madness is,
He cheers them up too.
I wonder men dare trust themselves with men:
Methinks thy should invite them without knives;
Good for their meat, and safer for their lives.
There 's much example for 't; the fellow that
Sits next him now, parts bread with him, and pledges
The breath of him in a divided draught,
Is the readiest man to kill him: 't has been prov'd.
If I were a huge man, I should fear to drink at meals;
Lest they should spy my windpipe's dangerous notes:

Great men should drink with harness on their throats.

TIMON. My lord, in heart; and let the health go round.

SECOND LORD. Let it flow this way, my good lord.

APEMANTUS. Flow this way! A brave fellow! he keeps his
tides well. Those healths will make thee and thy state
look ill, Timon.
Here 's that which is too weak to be a sinner,
Honest water, which ne'er left man i' the mire:
This and my food are equals, there 's no odds:
Feasts are too proud to give thanks to the gods.

> Immortal gods, I crave no pelf;
> I pray for no man but myself:
> Grant I may never prove so fond,
> To trust man on his oath or bond;
> Or a harlot for her weeping;
> Or a dog that seems a-sleeping;
> Or a keeper with my freedom;
> Or my friends, if I should need 'em.
> Amen. So fall to 't:
> Rich men sin, and I eat root.   *Eats and drinks*

Much good dich thy good heart, Apemantus!

TIMON. Captain Alcibiades, your heart 's in the field now.

ALCIBIADES. My heart is ever at your service, my lord.

TIMON. You had rather be at a breakfast of enemies than a
dinner of friends.

ALCIBIADES. So they were bleeding-new, my lord, there 's
no meat like 'em: I could wish my best friend at such a
feast.

APEMANTUS. 'Would all those flatterers were thine enemies
then, that then thou mightst kill 'em and bid me to 'em.

FIRST LORD. Might we but have that happiness, my lord,
that you would once use our hearts, whereby we might
express some part of our zeals, we should think ourselves
for ever perfect.

TIMON. O! no doubt, my good friends, but the gods themselves have provided that I shall have much help from
you: how had you been my friends else? why have you
that charitable title from thousands, did not you chiefly
belong to my heart? I have told more of you to myself
than you can with modesty speak in your own behalf;
and thus far I confirm you. O you gods! think I, what
need we have any friends, if we should ne'er have need

of 'em? they were the most needless creatures living,
should we ne'er have use for 'em, and would most re-
semble sweet instruments hung up in cases, that keep
their sounds to themselves. Why, I have often wished
myself poorer that I might come nearer to you. We are
born to do benefits; and what better or properer can we
call our own than the riches of our friends? O! what a
precious comfort 'tis, to have so many, like brothers,
commanding one another's fortunes. O joy! e'en made
away ere it can be born. Mine eyes cannot hold out
water, methinks: to forget their faults, I drink to you.

APEMANTUS. Thou weepest to make them drink, Timon.

SECOND LORD. Joy had the like conception in our eyes,
And, at that instant, like a babe, sprung up.

APEMANTUS. Ho, ho! I laugh to think that babe a bastard.

THIRD LORD. I promise you, my lord, you mov'd me much.

APEMANTUS. Much!   *Tucket sounded*

TIMON. What means that trump?

Enter a Servant

                    How now!

SERVANT. Please you, my lord, there are certain ladies most
desirous of admittance.

TIMON. Ladies! What are their wills?

SERVANT. There comes with them a forerunner, my lord,
which bears that office, to signify their pleasures.

TIMON. I pray, let them be admitted.   *Exit Servant*

Enter Cupid

CUPID. Hail to thee, worthy Timon; and to all
That of his bounties taste! The five best senses
Acknowledge thee their patron; and come freely
To gratulate thy plenteous bosom. Th' ear,
Taste, touch, smell, pleas'd from thy table rise;
They only now come but to feast thine eyes.

TIMON. They are welcome all; let 'em have kind admittance:

Music, make their welcome!   *Exit Cupid*

FIRST LORD. You see, my lord, how ample you 're belov'd.

*Music. Re-enter Cupid, with a mask of Ladies as Amazons,
with lutes in their hands, dancing and playing.*

APEMANTUS. Hoy-day! what a sweep of vanity comes this
way:
They dance! they are mad women.

Like madness is the glory of this life,
As this pomp shows to a little oil and root.
We make ourselves fools to disport ourselves;
And spend our flatteries to drink those men
Upon whose age we void it up again,
With poisonous spite and envy,
Who lives that 's not depraved or depraves?
Who dies that bears not one spurn to their graves
Of their friend's gift?
I should fear those that dance before me now
Would one day stamp upon me: it has been done;
Men shut their doors against a setting sun.

The Lords rise from table,
with much adoring of Timon; and to show
their loves each singles out an Amazon, and all dance, men
with women, a lofty strain or two to the hautboys, and cease

TIMON. You have done our pleasures much grace, fair
    ladies,
Set a fair fashion on our entertainment,
Which was not half so beautiful and kind;
You have added worth unto 't and lustre,
And entertain'd me with mine own device:
I am to thank you for 't.

FIRST LADY. My lord, you take us even at the best.

APEMANTUS. Faith, for the worst is filthy; and would not
    hold taking, I doubt me.

TIMON. Ladies, there is an idle banquet
Attends you: please you to dispose yourselves.

ALL LADIES. Most thankfully, my lord.

                    Exeunt Cupid and Ladies

TIMON. Flavius!

FLAVIUS. My lord?

TIMON.   The little casket bring me hither.

FLAVIUS. Yes, my lord. (*Aside*) More jewels yet!
There is no crossing him in 's humour;
Else I should tell him well, i' faith, I should,
When all 's spent, he 'd be cross'd then, an he could.
'Tis pity bounty had not eyes behind,
That man might ne'er be wretched for his mind.   *Exit*

FIRST LORD. Where be our men?

SERVANT. Here, my lord, in readiness.

SECOND LORD. Our horses!

Re-enter Flavius, with the Casket

TIMON. O, my friends! I have one word to say to you;
   Look you, my good lord,
   I must entreat you, honour me so much
   As to advance this jewel; accept it and wear it,
   Kind my lord.
FIRST LORD. I am so far already in your gifts—
ALL. So are we all.

Enter a Servant

SERVANT. My lord, there are certain nobles of the senate
   Newly alighted, and come to visit you.
TIMON. They are fairly welcome.   *Exit Servant*
FLAVIUS.   I beseech your honour,
   Vouchsafe me a word; it does concern you near.
TIMON. Near! why then another time I 'll hear thee.
   I prithee let 's be provided to show them entertainment.
FLAVIUS. (*Aside*) I scarce know how.

Enter another Servant

SECOND SERVANT. May it please your honour, Lord Lucius,
   Out of his free love, hath presented to you
   Four milk-white horses, trapp'd in silver.
TIMON. I shall accept them fairly; let the presents
   Be worthily entertain'd.   *Exit Servant*

Enter a third Servant

          How now! what news?

THIRD SERVANT. Please you, my lord, that honourable
   gentleman, Lord Lucullus, entreats your company to-
   morrow to hunt with him, and has sent your honour two
   brace of greyhounds.
TIMON. I 'll hunt with him; and let them be receiv'd,
   Not without fair reward.   *Exit Servant*
FLAVIUS.   (*Aside*) What will this come to?
   He commands us to provide, and give great gifts,
   And all out of an empty coffer:
   Nor will he know his purse, or yield me this,
   To show him what a beggar his heart is,
   Being of no power to make his wishes good.
   His promises fly so beyond his state
   That what he speaks is all in debt; he owes
   For every word: he is so kind that he now
   Pays interest for 't; his land 's put to their books.
   Well, would I were gently put out of office

Before I were forc'd out!
Happier he that has no friend to feed
Than such as do e'en enemies exceed.
I bleed inwardly for my lord.   *Exit*

TIMON.   You do yourselves
Much wrong, you bate too much of your own merits:
Here, my lord, a trifle of our love.

SECOND LORD. With more than common thanks I will
    receive it.

THIRD LORD. O! he 's the very soul of bounty.

TIMON. And now I remember, my lord, you gave
Good words the other day of a bay courser
I rode on: it is yours, because you lik'd it.

THIRD LORD. O! I beseech you, pardon me, my lord, in that.

TIMON. You may take my word, my lord: I know no man
Can justly praise but what he does affect:
I weigh my friend's affection with mine own;
I 'll tell you true. I 'll call to you.

ALL LORDS.   O! none so welcome.

TIMON. I take all and your several visitations
So kind to heart, 'tis not enough to give;
Methinks, I could deal kingdoms to my friends,
And ne'er be weary. Alcibiades.
Thou art a soldier, therefore seldom rich;
It comes in charity to thee; for all thy living
Is 'mongst the dead, and all the lands thou hast
Lie in a pitch'd field.

ALCIBIADES.   Ay, defil'd land, my lord.

FIRST LORD. We are so virtuously bound,—

TIMON.   And so
Am I to you.

SECOND LORD. So infinitely endear'd,—

TIMON. All to you. Lights, more lights!

FIRST LORD.   The best of happiness,
Honour, and fortunes, keep with you, Lord Timon!

TIMON. Ready for his friends.

                    Exeunt Alcibiades, Lords, &c.

APEMANTUS.   What a coil 's here!
Serving of becks and jutting out of bums!
I doubt whether their legs be worth the sums
That are given for 'em. Friendship 's full of dregs:
Methinks, false hearts should never have sound legs.

Thus honest fools lay out their wealth on curtsies.

TIMON. Now, Apemantus, if thou wert not sullen,
I would be good to thee.

APEMANTUS. No, I 'll nothing; for if I should be bribed too,
there would be none left to rail upon thee, and then thou
wouldst sin the faster. Thou givest so long, Timon, I fear
me thou wilt give away thyself in paper shortly: what
need these feasts, pomps, and vain-glories?

TIMON. Nay, an you begin to rail on society once, I am
sworn not to give regard to you. Farewell; and come
with better music.   *Exit*

APEMANTUS. So:
Thou wilt not hear me now; thou shalt not then;
I 'll lock thy heaven from thee.
O! that men's ears should be
To counsel deaf, but not to flattery.   *Exit*

ACT TWO

SCENE ONE

Athens. A Room in a Senator's House.

Enter a Senator, with papers in his hand

SENATOR. And late, five thousand: to Varro and to Isidore
He owes nine thousand; besides my former sum,
Which makes it five-and-twenty. Still in motion
Of raging waste! It cannot hold; it will not.
If I want gold, steal but a beggar's dog
And give it Timon, why, the dog coins gold;
If I would sell my horse, and buy twenty more
Better than he, why, give my horse to Timon,
Ask nothing, give it him, it foals me, straight,
And able horses. Nor porter at his gate,
But rather one that smiles and still invites
All that pass by. It cannot hold; no reason
Can found his state in safety. Caphis, ho!
Caphis, I say!

Enter Caphis

CAPHIS.   Here, sir; what is your pleasure?
SENATOR. Get on your cloak, and haste you to Lord Timon;
Importune him for my moneys; be not ceas'd
With slight denial, nor then silenc'd when—
'Commend me to your master'—and the cap
Plays in the right hand, thus;—but tell him,
My uses cry to me; I must serve my turn
Out of mine own; his days and times are past,
And my reliances on his fracted dates
Have smit my credit: I love and honour him,
But must not break my back to heal his finger;
Immediate are my needs, and my relief
Must not be toss'd and turn'd to me in words,
But find supply immediate. Get you gone:

Put on a most importunate aspect,
A visage of demand; for, I do fear,
When every feather sticks in his own wing,
/ Lord Timon will be left a naked gull,
Which flashes now a phœnix. Get you gone.

CAPHIS. I go, sir.

SENATOR. 'I go, sir!' Take the bonds along with you,
And have the dates in compt.

CAPHIS.   I will, sir.

SENATOR.   Go.   *Exeunt*

SCENE TWO

A Hall in Timon's House.

Enter Flavius, with many bills in his hand

FLAVIUS. No care, no stop! so senseless of expense,
That he will neither know how to maintain it,
Nor cease his flow of riot: takes no account
How things go from him, nor resumes no care
Of what is to continue: never mind
Was to be so unwise, to be so kind.
What shall be done? He will not hear, till feel:
I must be round with him, now he comes from hunting.
Fie, fie, fie, fie!

Enter Caphis, and the Servants of Isidore and Varro

CAPHIS.   Good even, Varro. What!
You come for money?

VARRO'S SERVANT. Is 't not your business too?

CAPHIS. It is: and yours too, Isidore?

ISIDORE'S SERVANT.   It is so.

CAPHIS. Would we were all discharg'd!

VARRO'S SERVANT.   I fear it.

CAPHIS. Here comes the lord!

Enter Timon, Alcibiades, and Lords, &c.

TIMON. So soon as dinner 's done, we 'll forth again,
My Alcibiades. With me? what is your will?

CAPHIS. My lord, here is a note of certain dues.

TIMON. Dues! Whence are you?

CAPHIS.   Of Athens here, my lord.

TIMON. Go to my steward.

CAPHIS. Please it your lordship, he hath put me off
  To the succession of new days this month:
  My master is awak'd by great occasion
  To call upon his own; and humbly prays you
  That with your other noble parts you 'll suit
  In giving him his right.
TIMON.   Mine honest friend,
  I prithee, but repair to me next morning.
CAPHIS. Nay, good my lord,—
TIMON.   Contain thyself, good friend.
VARRO'S SERVANT. One Varro's servant, my good lord,—
ISIDORE'S SERVANT.   From Isidore;
  He humbly prays your speedy payment.
CAPHIS. If you did know, my lord, my master's wants,—
VARRO'S SERVANT. 'Twas due on forfeiture, my lord, six
    weeks
  And past.
ISIDORE'S SERVANT. Your steward puts me off, my lord;
  And I am sent expressly to your lordship.
TIMON. Give me breath.
  I do beseech you, good my lords, keep on;
  I 'll wait upon you instantly.
                    Exeunt Alcibiades and Lords
          (*To Flavius*) Come hither: pray you,
  How goes the world, that I am thus encounter'd
  With clamorous demands of date-broke bonds,
  And the detention of long-since-due debts,
  Against my honour?
FLAVIUS.   Please you, gentlemen,
  The time is unagreeable to this business:
  Your importunacy cease till after dinner,
  That I may make his lordship understand
  Wherefore you are not paid.
TIMON.   Do so, my friends.
  See them well entertained.   *Exit*
FLAVIUS.   Pray, draw near.   *Exit*
          Enter Apemantus and Fool
CAPHIS. Stay, stay; here comes the fool with Apemantus:
  let 's ha' some sport with 'em.
VARRO'S SERVANT. Hang him, he 'll abuse us.
ISIDORE'S SERVANT. A plague upon him, dog!
VARRO'S SERVANT. How dost, fool?

APEMANTUS. Dost dialogue with thy shadow?

VARRO'S SERVANT. I speak not to thee.

APEMANTUS. No; 'tis to thyself. (*To the Fool*) Come away.

ISIDORE'S SERVANT. (*To Varro's Servant*) There 's the fool hangs on your back already.

APEMANTUS. No, thou stand'st single; thou 'rt not on him yet.

CAPHIS. Where 's the fool now?

APEMANTUS. He last asked the question. Poor rogues, and usurers' men! bawds between gold and want!

ALL SERVANTS. What are we, Apemantus?

APEMANTUS. Asses.

ALL SERVANTS. Why?

APEMANTUS. That you ask me what you are, and do not know yourselves. Speak to 'em, fool.

FOOL. How do you, gentlemen?

ALL SERVANTS. Gramercies, good fool. How does your mistress?

FOOL. She 's e'en setting on water to scald such chickens as you are. Would we could see you at Corinth!

APEMANTUS. Good! gramercy.

Enter Page

FOOL. Look you, here comes my mistress' page.

PAGE. (*To the Fool*) Why, how now, captain! what do you in this wise company? How dost thou, Apemantus?

APEMANTUS. Would I had a rod in my mouth, that I might answer thee profitably.

PAGE. Prithee, Apemantus, read me the superscription of these letters: I know not which is which.

APEMANTUS. Canst not read?

PAGE. No.

APEMANTUS. There will little learning die then, that day thou art hanged. This is to Lord Timon; this to Alcibiades. Go; thou wast born a bastard, and thou 'lt die a bawd.

PAGE. Thou wast whelped a dog, and thou shalt famish a dog's death. Answer not; I am gone.   *Exit Page*

APEMANTUS. E'en so thou outrunn'st grace.—Fool, I will go with you to Lord Timon's.

FOOL. Will you leave me there?

APEMANTUS. If Timon stay at home. You three serve three usurers?

ALL SERVANTS. Ay; would they served us!

APEMANTUS. So would I, as good a trick as ever hangman
served thief.

FOOL. Are you three usurers' men?

ALL SERVANTS. Ay, fool.

FOOL. I think no usurer but has a fool to his servant: my
mistress is one, and I am her fool. When men come to
borrow of your masters, they approach sadly, and go
away merry; but they enter my mistress' house merrily,
and go away sadly: the reason of this?

VARRO'S SERVANT. I could render one.

APEMANTUS. Do it, then, that we may account thee a
whoremaster and a knave; which, notwithstanding, thou
shalt be no less esteemed.

VARRO'S SERVANT. What is a whoremaster, fool?

FOOL. A fool in good clothes, and something like thee. 'Tis
a spirit: sometime 't appears like a lord, sometime like a
lawyer; sometime like a philosopher, with two stones
more than 's artificial one. He is very often like a knight;
and generally in all shapes that man goes up and down
in from fourscore to thirteen, this spirit walks in.

VARRO'S SERVANT. Thou art not altogether a fool.

FOOL. Nor thou altogether a wise man: as much foolery as
I have, so much wit thou lackest.

APEMANTUS. That answer might have become Apemantus.

ALL SERVANTS. Aside, aside; here comes Lord Timon.

Re-enter Timon and Flavius

APEMANTUS. Come with me, fool, come.

FOOL. I do not always follow lover, elder brother and
woman; sometime the philosopher.

Exeunt Apemantus and Fool

FLAVIUS. Pray you, walk near: I 'll speak with you anon.

Exeunt Servants

TIMON. You make me marvel: wherefore, ere this time,
Had you not fully laid my state before me,
That I might so have rated my expense
As I had leave of means?

FLAVIUS.   You would not hear me,
At many leisures I propos'd.

TIMON.   Go to:
Perchance some single vantages you took,
When my indisposition put you back;

And that unaptness made your minister,
Thus to excuse yourself.

FLAVIUS.   O my good lord
At many times I brought in my accounts,
Laid them before you; you would throw them off,
And say you found them in mine honesty.
When for some trifling present you have bid me
Return so much, I have shook my head, and wept;
Yea, 'gainst the authority of manners, pray'd you
To hold your hand more close: I did endure
Not seldom, nor no slight checks, when I have
Prompted you in the ebb of your estate
And your great flow of debts. My loved lord,
Though you hear now, too late, yet now 's a time,
The greatest of your having lacks a half
To pay your present debts.

TIMON.   Let all my land be sold.

FLAVIUS. 'Tis all engag'd, some forfeited and gone;
And what remains will hardly stop the mouth
Of present dues; the future comes apace:
What shall defend the interim? and at length
How goes our reckoning?

TIMON. To Lacedæmon did my land extend.

FLAVIUS. O my good lord! the world is but a word;
Were it all yours to give it in a breath,
How quickly were it gone!

TIMON.   You tell me true.

FLAVIUS. If you suspect my husbandry or falsehood,
Call me before the exactest auditors,
And set me on the proof. So the gods bless me,
When all our offices have been oppress'd
With riotous feeders, when our vaults have wept
With drunken spilth of wine, when every room
Hath blaz'd with lights and bray'd with minstrelsy,
I have retir'd me to a wasteful cock,
And set mine eyes at flow.

TIMON.   Prithee, no more.

FLAVIUS. Heavens! have I said, the bounty of this lord!
How many prodigal bits have slaves and peasants
This night englutted! Who is not Timon's?
What heart, head, sword, force, means, but is Lord
    Timon's?

Great Timon, noble, worthy, royal Timon!
Ah! when the means are gone that buy this praise,
The breath is gone whereof this praise is made:
Feast-won, fast-lost; one cloud of winter showers,
These flies are couch'd.

TIMON.   Come, sermon me no further;
No villanous bounty yet hath pass'd my heart;
Unwisely, not ignobly, have I given.
Why dost thou weep? Canst thou the conscience lack,
To think I shall lack friends? Secure thy heart;
If I would broach the vessels of my love,
And try the argument of hearts by borrowing,
Men and men's fortunes could I frankly use
As I can bid thee speak.

FLAVIUS.   Assurance bless your thoughts!

TIMON. And, in some sort, these wants of mine are
    crown'd,
That I account them blessings; for by these
Shall I try friends. You shall perceive how you
Mistake my fortunes; I am wealthy in my friends.
Within there! Flaminius! Servilius!

    Enter Flaminius, Servilius, and other Servants

SERVANTS. My lord! my lord!

TIMON. I will dispatch you severally: you, to Lord Lucius;
to Lord Lucullus you: I hunted with his honour to-day;
you, to Sempronius. Commend me to their loves; and I
am proud, say, that my occasions have found time to use
them toward a supply of money: let the request be fifty
talents.

FLAMINIUS. As you have said, my lord.

FLAVIUS. (*Aside*) Lord Lucius, and Lucullus? hum!

TIMON. (*To another Servant*) Go you, sir, to the senators,—
Of whom, even to the state's best health, I have
Deserv'd this hearing,—bid 'em send o' the instant
A thousand talents to me.   *Exeunt Servants*

FLAVIUS.   I have been bold,—
For that I knew it the most general way,—
To them to use your signet and your name;
But they do shake their heads, and I am here
No richer in return.

TIMON.   Is 't true? can 't be?

FLAVIUS. They answer, in a joint and corporate voice,

That now they are at fall, want treasure, cannot
Do what they would; are sorry; you are honourable;
But yet they could have wish'd; they know not;
Something hath been amiss; a noble nature
May catch a wrench; would all were well; 'tis pity;
And so, intending other serious matters,
After distasteful looks and these hard fractions,
With certain half-caps and cold-moving nods
They froze me into silence.

TIMON.   You gods, reward them!
Prithee, man, look cheerly. These old fellows
Have their ingratitude in them hereditary;
Their blood is cak'd, 'tis cold, it seldom flows;
'Tis lack of kindly warmth they are not kind;
And nature, as it grows again toward earth,
Is fashion'd for the journey, dull and heavy.
(*To a Servant*) Go to Ventidius.—(*To Flavius*) Prithee,
    be not sad,
Thou art true and honest; ingenuously I speak,
No blame belongs to thee.—(*To Servant*) Ventidius lately
Buried his father; by whose death he 's stepp'd
Into a great estate; when he was poor,
Imprison'd and in scarcity of friends,
I clear'd him with five talents; greet him from me;
Bid him suppose some good necessity
Touches his friend, which craves to be remember'd
With those five talents. (*Exit Servant*) (*To Flavius*)
    That had, give 't these fellows
To whom 'tis instant due. Ne'er speak, or think
That Timon's fortunes 'mong his friends can sink.

FLAVIUS. I would I could not think it: that thought is
    bounty's foe;
Being free itself, it thinks all others so.   *Exeunt*

ACT THREE

SCENE ONE

Athens. A Room in Lucullus' House.

Flaminius waiting. Enter a Servant to him

SERVANT. I have told my lord of you; he is coming down to you.

FLAMINIUS. I thank you, sir.

Enter Lucullus

SERVANT. Here 's my lord.

LUCULLUS. (*Aside*) One of Lord Timon's men! a gift, I warrant. Why, this hits right; I dreamt of a silver basin and ewer to-night. Flaminius, honest Flaminius, you are very respectively welcome, sir. Fill me some wine. (*Exit Servant*) And how does that honourable, complete, free-hearted gentleman of Athens, thy very bountiful good lord and master?

FLAMINIUS. His health is well, sir.

LUCULLUS. I am right glad that his health is well, sir. And what hast thou there under thy cloak, pretty Flaminius?

FLAMINIUS. Faith, nothing but an empty box, sir; which, in my lord's behalf, I come to entreat your honour to supply; who, having great and instant occasion to use fifty talents, hath sent to your lordship to furnish him, nothing doubting your present assistance therein.

LUCULLUS. La, la, la, la! 'nothing doubting,' says he? Alas! good lord; a noble gentleman 'tis, if he would not keep so good a house. Many a time and often I ha' dined with him, and told him on 't; and come again to supper to him, of purpose to have him spend less; and yet he would embrace no counsel, take no warning by my coming. Every man has his fault, and honesty is his; I ha' told him on 't, but I could ne'er get him from it.

Re-enter Servant, with wine

SERVANT. Please your lordship, here is the wine.

LUCULLUS. Flaminius, I have noted thee always wise.
Here 's to thee.

FLAMINIUS. Your lordship speaks your pleasure.

LUCULLUS. I have observed thee always for a towardly
prompt spirit, give thee thy due, and one that knows
what belongs to reason; and canst use the time well, if
the time use thee well: good parts in thee. (*To the
Servant*)—Get you gone, sirrah.—(*Exit Servant*) Draw
nearer, honest Flaminius. Thy lord 's a bountiful gentleman; but thou art wise, and thou knowest well enough,
although thou comest to me, that this is no time to lend
money, especially upon bare friendship, without security. Here 's three solidares for thee: good boy, wink
at me, and say thou sawest me not. Fare thee well.

FLAMINIUS. Is 't possible the world should so much differ,
And we alive that liv'd? Fly, damned baseness,
To him that worships thee.   *Throwing the money away*

LUCULLUS. Ha! now I see thou art a fool, and fit for thy
master.   *Exit*

FLAMINIUS. May these add to the number that may scald
thee!
Let molten coin be thy damnation,
Thou disease of a friend, and not himself!
Has friendship such a faint and milky heart
It turns in less than two nights? O you gods!
I feel my master's passion. This slave unto his honour
Has my lord's meat in him:
Why should it thrive and turn to nutriment
When he is turn'd to poison?
O! may diseases only work upon 't.
And, when he 's sick to death, let not that part of nature
Which my lord paid for, be of any power
To expel sickness, but prolong his hour.   *Exit*

SCENE TWO

A Public Place.

Enter Lucius, with three Strangers

LUCIUS. Who, the Lord Timon? he is my very good friend,
and an honourable gentleman.

FIRST STRANGER. We know him for no less, though we are but strangers to him. But I can tell you one thing, my lord, and which I hear from common rumours: now Lord Timon's happy hours are done and past, and his estate shrinks from him.

LUCIUS. Fie, no, do not believe it; he cannot want for money.

SECOND STRANGER. But believe you this, my lord, that, not long ago, one of his men was with the Lord Lucullus, to borrow so many talents, nay, urged extremely for 't, and showed what necessity belonged to 't, and yet was denied.

LUCIUS. How!

SECOND STRANGER. I tell you, denied, my lord.

LUCIUS. What a strange case was that! now, before the gods, I am ashamed on 't. Denied that honourable man! there was very little honour showed in 't. For my own part, I must needs confess, I have received some small kindnesses from him, as money, plate, jewels, and such like trifles, nothing comparing to his; yet, had he mistook him, and sent to me, I should ne'er have denied his occasion so many talents.

Enter Servilius

SERVILIUS. See, by good hap, yonder 's my lord; I have sweat to see his honour. (*To Lucius*) My honoured lord!

LUCIUS. Servilius! you are kindly met, sir. Fare thee well: commend me to thy honourable virtuous lord, my very exquisite friend.

SERVILIUS. May it please your honour, my lord hath sent—

LUCIUS. Ha! what has he sent? I am so much endeared to that lord; he 's ever sending: how shall I thank him, thinkest thou? And what has he sent now?

SERVILIUS. He has only sent his present occasion now, my lord; requesting your lordship to supply his instant use with so many talents.

LUCIUS. I know his lordship is but merry with me;
He cannot want fifty-five hundred talents.

SERVILIUS. But in the mean time he wants less, my lord.
If his occasion were not virtuous,
I should not urge it half so faithfully.

LUCIUS. Dost thou speak seriously, Servilius?

SERVILIUS. Upon my soul, 'tis true, sir.

LUCIUS. What a wicked beast was I to disfurnish myself
against such a good time, when I might ha' shown myself honourable! how unluckily it happened, that I
should purchase the day before for a little part, and undo
a great deal of honour! Servilius, now, before the gods, I
am not able to do; the more beast, I say; I was sending
to use Lord Timon myself, these gentlemen can witness;
but I would not, for the wealth of Athens, I had done it
now. Commend me bountifully to his good lordship; and
I hope his honour will conceive the fairest of me, because I have no power to be kind: and tell him this from
me, I count it one of my greatest afflictions, say, that I
cannot pleasure such an honourable gentleman. Good
Servilius, will you befriend me so far as to use mine own
words to him?

SERVILIUS. Yes, sir, I shall.

LUCIUS. I 'll look you out a good turn, Servilius.

                                        Exit Servilius

True, as you said, Timon is shrunk indeed;
And he that 's once denied will hardly speed.   *Exit*

FIRST STRANGER. Do you observe this, Hostilius?

SECOND STRANGER.   Ay, too well.

FIRST STRANGER. Why, this is the world's soul; and just of
    the same piece
Is every flatterer's spirit. Who can call him
His friend that dips in the same dish? for, in
My knowing, Timon has been this lord's father,
And kept his credit with his purse,
Supported his estate; nay, Timon's money
Has paid his men their wages: he ne'er drinks
But Timon's silver treads upon his lip;
And yet, O! see the monstrousness of man,
When he looks out in an ungrateful shape,
He does deny him, in respect of his,
What charitable men afford to beggars.

THIRD STRANGER. Religion groans at it.

FIRST STRANGER.   For mine own part,
I never tasted Timon in my life,
Nor came any of his bounties over me,
To mark me for his friend; yet, I protest,
For his right noble mind, illustrious virtue,
And honourable carriage,

Had his necessity made use of me,
I would have put my wealth into donation,
And the best half should have return'd to him,
So much I love his heart. But, I perceive,
Men must learn now with pity to dispense;
For policy sits above conscience.   *Exeunt*

SCENE THREE

A Room in Sempronius' House.

Enter Sempronius and a Servant of Timon's

SEMPRONIUS. Must he needs trouble me in 't. Hum! 'bove
  all others?
He might have tried Lord Lucius, or Lucullus;
And now Vontidius is wealthy too,
Whom he redeem'd from prison: all these
Owe their estates unto him.
SERVANT.   My lord,
They have all been touch'd and found base metal, for
They have all denied him.
SEMPRONIUS.   How! have they denied him?
Have Ventidius and Lucullus denied him?
And does he send to me? Three? hum
It shows but little love or judgment in him:
Must I be his last refuge? His friends, like physicians,
Thrice give him over; must I take the cure upon me?
He has much disgrac'd me in 't; I 'm angry at him,
That might have known my place. I see no sense for 't,
But his occasions might have woo'd me first;
For, in my conscience, I was the first man
That e'er received gift from him:
And does he think so backwardly of me now,
That I 'll requite it last? No:
So it may prove an argument of laughter
To the rest, and I 'mongst lords be thought a fool.
I had rather than the worth of thrice the sum,
He had sent to me first, but for my mind's sake;
I 'd such a courage to do him good. But now return,
And with their faint reply this answer join;
Who bates mine honour shall not know my coin.   *Exit*

SERVANT. Excellent! Your lordship 's a goodly villain. The
    devil knew not what he did when he made man politic;
    he crossed himself by 't: and I cannot think but in the
    end the villanies of man will set him clear. How fairly
    this lord strives to appear foul! takes virtuous copies to
    be wicked, like those that under hot ardent zeal would
    set whole realms on fire:
    Of such a nature is his politic love.
    This was my lord's best hope; now all are fled
    Save only the gods. Now his friends are dead,
    Doors, that were ne'er acquainted with their wards
    Many a bounteous year, must be employ'd
    Now to guard sure their master:
    And this is all a liberal course allows;
    Who cannot keep his wealth must keep his house.   *Exit*

SCENE FOUR

A Hall in Timon's House.

*Enter two Servants of Varro, and the Servant of Lucius,
meeting Titus, Hortensius, and other Servants to
Timon's Creditors, waiting his coming out*

VARRO'S SERVANT I. Well met; good-morrow, Titus and Hor-
    tensius.
TITUS. The like to you, kind Varro.
HORTENSIUS.   Lucius!
    What! do we meet together!
LUCIUS'S SERVANT.   Ay, and I think
    One business does command us all; for mine
    Is money.
TITUS. So is theirs and ours.
                        Enter Philotus
LUCIUS'S SERVANT.   And Sir Philotus too!
PHILOTUS. Good day at once.
LUCIUS'S SERVANT.   Welcome, good brother.
    What do you think the hour?
PHILOTUS.   Labouring for nine.
LUCIUS'S SERVANT. So much?
PHILOTUS.   Is not my lord seen yet?
LUCIUS'S SERVANT.   Not yet.

PHILOTUS. I wonder on 't; he was wont to shine at seven.

LUCIUS'S SERVANT. Ay, but the days are waxed shorter with
 him:
 You must consider that a prodigal course
 Is like the sun's; but not, like his, recoverable.
 I fear
 'Tis deepest winter in Lord Timon's purse;
 That is, one may reach deep enough, and yet
• Find little.

PHILOTUS. I am of your fear for that.

TITUS. I 'll show you how to observe a strange event.
 Your lord sends now for money.

HORTENSIUS.   Most true, he does.

TITUS. And he wears jewels now of Timon's gift,
 For which I wait for money.

HORTENSIUS. It is against my heart.

LUCIUS'S SERVANT.   Mark, how strange it shows,
 Timon in this should pay more than he owes:
 And e'en as if your lord should wear rich jewels,
 And send for money for 'em.

HORTENSIUS. I 'm weary of this charge, the gods can wit-
 ness:
 I know my lord hath spent of Timon's wealth,
 And now ingratitude makes it worse than stealth.

VARRO'S SERVANT I. Yes, mine 's three thousand crowns;
 what 's yours?

LUCIUS'S SERVANT. Five thousand mine.

VARRO'S SERVANT I. 'Tis much deep: and it should seem by
 the sum,
 Your master's confidence was above mine;
 Else, surely, his had equall'd.

     Enter Flaminius

TITUS. One of Lord Timon's men.

LUCIUS'S SERVANT. Flaminius! Sir, a word. Pray, is my lord
 ready to come forth?

FLAMINIUS. No, indeed, he is not.

TITUS. We attend his lordship; pray, signify so much.

FLAMINIUS. I need not tell him that; he knows you are too
 diligent.   *Exit Flaminius*

   Enter Flavius in a cloak, muffled

LUCIUS'S SERVANT. Ha! is not that his steward muffled so?
 He goes away in a cloud: call him, call him.

TITUS. Do you hear, sir?

VARRO'S SERVANT II. By your leave, sir.

FLAVIUS. What do you ask of me, my friend?

TITUS. We wait for certain money here, sir.

FLAVIUS.   Ay,
If money were as certain as your waiting,
'Twere sure enough.
Why then preferr'd you not your sums and bills,
When your false masters eat of my lord's meat?
Then they could smile and fawn upon his debts,
And take down the interest into their gluttonous maws.
You do yourselves but wrong to stir me up;
Let me pass quietly:
Believe 't, my lord and I have made an end;
I have no more to reckon, he to spend.

LUCIUS'S SERVANT. Ay, but this answer will not serve.

FLAVIUS. If 'twill not serve, 'tis not so base as you;
For you serve knaves.   *Exit*

VARRO'S SERVANT I. How! what does his cashiered worship
mutter?

VARRO'S SERVANT II. No matter what; he 's poor, and that 's
revenge enough. Who can speak broader than he that
has no house to put his head in? such may rail against
great buildings.

Enter Servilius

TITUS. O! here 's Servilius; now we shall know some answer.

SERVILIUS. If I might beseech you, gentlemen, to repair
some other hour, I should derive much from 't; for, take
't of my soul, my lord leans wondrously to discontent.
His comfortable temper has forsook him; he 's much out
of health, and keeps his chamber.

LUCIUS'S SERVANT. Many do keep their chambers are not
sick:
And, if it be so far beyond his health,
Methinks he should the sooner pay his debts,
And make a clear way to the gods.

SERVILIUS.   Good gods!

TITUS. We cannot take this for answer, sir.

FLAMINIUS. (*Within*) Servilius, help! my lord! my lord!

Enter Timon, in a rage; Flaminius following

TIMON. What! are my doors oppos'd against my passage?

Have I been ever free, and must my house
Be my retentive enemy, my gaol?
The place which I have feasted, does it now,
Like all mankind, show me an iron heart?

LUCIUS'S SERVANT. Put it now, Titus.

TITUS. My lord, here is my bill.

LUCIUS'S SERVANT. Here 's mine.

HORTENSIUS. And mine, my lord.

BOTH VARRO'S SERVANTS. And ours, my lord.

PHILOTUS. All our bills.

TIMON. Knock me down with 'em: cleave me to the girdle.

LUCIUS'S SERVANT. Alas! my lord,—

TIMON. Cut my heart in sums.

TITUS. Mine, fifty talents.

TIMON. Tell out my blood.

LUCIUS'S SERVANT. Five thousand crowns, my lord.

TIMON. Five thousand drops pays that. What yours? and
yours?

VARRO'S SERVANT I. My lord,—

VARRO'S SERVANT II. My lord,—

TIMON. Tear me, take me; and the gods fall upon you!   *Exit*

HORTENSIUS. Faith, I perceive our masters may throw their
caps at their money: these debts may well be called desperate ones, for a madman owes 'em.   *Exeunt*

Re-enter Timon and Flavius

TIMON. They have e'en put my breath from me, the slaves.
Creditors? devils!

FLAVIUS. My dear lord,—

TIMON. What if it should be so?

FLAVIUS. My lord,—

TIMON. I 'll have it so. My steward!

FLAVIUS. Here, my lord.

TIMON. So fitly! Go, bid all my friends again,
Lucius, Lucullus, and Sempronius; all:
I 'll once more feast the rascals.

FLAVIUS.   O my lord!
You only speak from your distracted soul;
There is not so much left to furnish out
A moderate table.

TIMON.   Be 't not in thy care: go.
I charge thee, invite them all: let in the tide
Of knaves once more; my cook and I 'll provide.   *Exeunt*

SCENE FIVE

The Senate-House.

The Senate sitting

FIRST SENATOR. My lord, you have my voice to it; the
    fault 's
  Bloody; 'tis necessary he should die;
  Nothing emboldens sin so much as mercy.
SECOND SENATOR. Most true; the law shall bruise him.
                  Enter Alcibiades, attended
ALCIBIADES. Honour, health, and compassion to the senate!
FIRST SENATOR. Now, captain.
ALCIBIADES. I am a humble suitor to your virtues;
  For pity is the virtue of the law,
  And none but tyrants use it cruelly.
  It pleases time and fortune to lie heavy
  Upon a friend of mine, who, in hot blood,
  Hath stepp'd into the law, which is past depth
  To those that without heed do plunge into 't.
  He is a man, setting his fate aside,
  Of comely virtues;
  Nor did he soil the fact with cowardice,—
  An honour in him which buys out his fault,—
  But, with a noble fury and fair spirit,
  Seeing his reputation touch'd to death,
  He did oppose his foe;
  And with such sober and unnoted passion
  He did behave his anger, ere 'twas spent,
  As if he had but prov'd an argument.
FIRST SENATOR. You undergo too strict a paradox,
  Striving to make an ugly deed look fair:
  Your words have took such pains as if they labour'd
  To bring manslaughter into form, and set quarrelling
  Upon the head of valour; which indeed
  Is valour misbegot, and came into the world
  When sects and factions were newly born.
  He 's truly valiant that can wisely suffer
  The worst that man can breathe, and make his wrongs
  His outsides, to wear them like his raiment, carelessly,
  And ne'er prefer his injuries to his heart,

   To bring it into danger.
   If wrongs be evils and enforce us kill,
   What folly 'tis to hazard life for ill!
ALCIBIADES. My lord,—
FIRST SENATOR. You cannot make gross sins look clear;
   To revenge is no valour, but to bear.
ALCIBIADES. My lords, then, under favour, pardon me,
   If I speak like a captain.
   Why do fond men expose themselves to battle,
   And not endure all threats? sleep upon 't,
   And let the foes quietly cut their throats
   Without repugnancy? If there be
   Such valour in the bearing, what make we
   Abroad? why then, women are more valiant
   That stay at home, if bearing carry it,
   And the ass more captain than the lion, the felon
   Loaden with irons wiser than the judge,
   If wisdom be in suffering. O my lords!
   As you are great, be pitifully good:
   Who cannot condemn rashness in cold blood?
   To kill, I grant, is sin's extremest gust;
   But, in defence, by mercy, 'tis most just.
   To be in anger is impiety;
   But who is man that is not angry?
   Weigh but the crime with this.
SECOND SENATOR. You breathe in vain.
ALCIBIADES.   In vain! his service done
   At Lacedæmon and Byzantium
   Were a sufficient briber for his life.
FIRST SENATOR. What 's that?
ALCIBIADES. I say, my lords, he has done fair service,
   And slain in fight many of your enemies.
   How full of valour did he bear himself
   In the last conflict, and made plenteous wounds!
SECOND SENATOR. He has made too much plenty with 'em;
   He 's a sworn rioter; he has a sin that often
   Drowns him and takes his valour prisoner;
   If there were no foes, that were enough
   To overcome him; in that beastly fury
   He has been known to commit outrages
   And cherish factions; 'tis inferr'd to us,
   His days are foul and his drink dangerous.

FIRST SENATOR. He dies.

ALCIBIADES. Hard fate! he might have died in war.
My lords, if not for any parts in him,—
Though his right arm might purchase his own time,
And be in debt to none,—yet, more to move you,
Take my deserts to his, and join 'em both;
And, for I know your reverend ages love
Security, I 'll pawn my victories, all
My honour to you, upon his good returns.
If by this crime he owes the law his life,
Why, let the war receive 't in valiant gore;
For law is strict, and war is nothing more.

FIRST SENATOR. We are for law; he dies: urge it no more,
On height of our displeasure. Friend, or brother
He forfeits his own blood that spills another.

ALCIBIADES. Must it be so? it must not be. My lords,
I do beseech you, know me.

SECOND SENATOR. How!

ALCIBIADES. Call me to your remembrances.

THIRD SENATOR.   What!

ALCIBIADES. I cannot think but your age has forgot me;
It could not else be I should prove so base,
To sue, and be denied such common grace.
My wounds ache at you.

FIRST SENATOR.   Do you dare our anger?
'Tis in few words, but spacious in effect;
We banish thee for ever.

ALCIBIADES.   Banish me!
Banish your dotage; banish usury,
That makes the senate ugly.

FIRST SENATOR. If, after two days' shine, Athens contain
    thee,
Attend our weightier judgment. And, not to swell our
    spirit,
He shall be executed presently.   *Exeunt Senators*

ALCIBIADES. Now the gods keep you old enough; that you
    may live
Only in bone, that none may look on you!
I am worse than mad: I have kept back their foes,
While they have told their money and let out
Their coin upon large interest; I myself

Rich only in large hurts: all those for this?
Is this the balsam that the usuring senate
Pours into captains' wounds? Banishment!
It comes not ill; I hate not to be banish'd;
It is a cause worthy my spleen and fury,
That I may strike at Athens. I 'll cheer up
My discontented troops, and lay for hearts.
'Tis honour with most lands to be at odds;
Soldiers should brook as little wrongs as gods.   *Exit*

SCENE SIX

A Room of State in Timon's House.

*Music. Tables set out: Servants attending. Enter divers
Lords, Senators, and Others, at several doors.*

FIRST LORD. The good time of day to you, sir.

SECOND LORD. I also wish it you. I think this honourable
lord did but try us this other day.

FIRST LORD. Upon that were my thoughts tiring when we
encountered: I hope it is not so low with him as he made
it seem in the trial of his several friends.

SECOND LORD. It should not be, by the persuasion of his
new feasting.

FIRST LORD. I should think so: he hath sent me an earnest
inviting, which many my near occasions did urge me to
put off; but he hath conjured me beyond them, and I
must needs appear.

SECOND LORD. In like manner was I in debt to my importunate business, but he would not hear my excuse. I am
sorry, when he sent to borrow of me, that my provision
was out.

FIRST LORD. I am sick of that grief too, as I understand how
all things go.

SECOND LORD. Every man here 's so. What would he have
borrowed you?

FIRST LORD. A thousand pieces.

SECOND LORD. A thousand pieces!

FIRST LORD. What of you?

THIRD LORD. He sent to me, sir,—Here he comes.

Enter Timon and Attendants

TIMON. With all my heart, gentlemen both; and how fare you?

FIRST LORD. Ever at the best, hearing well of your lordship.

SECOND LORD. The swallow follows not summer more willing than we your lordship.

TIMON. (*Aside*) Nor more willingly leaves winter; such summer-birds are men. Gentlemen, our dinner will not recompense this long stay: feast your ears with the music awhile, if they will fare so harshly o' the trumpet's sound; we shall to 't presently.

FIRST LORD. I hope it remains not unkindly with your lordship that I returned you an empty messenger.

TIMON. O! sir, let it not trouble you.

SECOND LORD. My noble lord,—

TIMON. Ah! my good friend, what cheer?

SECOND LORD. My most honourable lord, I am e'en sick of shame, that when your lordship this other day sent to me I was so unfortunate a beggar.

TIMON. Think not on 't, sir.

SECOND LORD. If you had sent but two hours before,—

TIMON. Let it not cumber your better remembrance. (*The banquet brought in*) Come, bring in all together.

SECOND LORD. All covered dishes!

FIRST LORD. Royal cheer, I warrant you.

THIRD LORD. Doubt not that, if money and the season can yield it.

FIRST LORD. How do you? What 's the news?

THIRD LORD. Alcibiades is banished; hear you of it?

FIRST LORD. }
SECOND LORD. } Alcibiades banished!

THIRD LORD. 'Tis so, be sure of it.

FIRST LORD. How? how?

SECOND LORD. I pray you, upon what?

TIMON. My worthy friends, will you draw near?

THIRD LORD. I 'll tell you more anon. Here 's a noble feast toward.

SECOND LORD. This is the old man still.

THIRD LORD. Will 't hold? will 't hold?

SECOND LORD. It does; but time will—and so—

THIRD LORD. I do conceive.

TIMON. Each man to his stool, with that spur as he would
  to the lip of his mistress; your diet shall be in all places
  alike. Make not a city feast of it, to let the meat cool ere
  we can agree upon the first place: sit, sit. The gods require our thanks.—
You great benefactors, sprinkle our society with thankfulness. For your own gifts, make yourselves praised:
  but reserve still to give, lest your deities be despised.
  Lend to each man enough, that one need not lend to another; for, were your godheads to borrow of men, men
  would forsake the gods. Make the meat be beloved more
  than the man that gives it. Let no assembly of twenty be
  without a score of villains: if there sit twelve women at
  the table, let a dozen of them be as they are. The rest of
  your fees, O gods! the senators of Athens, together with
  the common lag of people, what is amiss in them, you
  gods, make suitable for destruction. For these my present
  friends, as they are to me nothing, so in nothing bless
  them, and to nothing are they welcome.
Uncover, dogs, and lap.
          The dishes uncovered are full of warm water.
SOME SPEAK. What does his lordship mean?
SOME OTHER. I know not.
TIMON. May you a better feast never behold,
  You knot of mouth-friends! smoke and lukewarm water
  Is your perfection. This is Timon's last;
  Who, stuck and spangled with your flatteries,
  Washes it off, and sprinkles in your faces
              Throwing the water in their faces
  Your reeking villany. Live loath'd, and long,
  Most smiling, smooth, detested parasites,
  Courteous destroyers, affable wolves, meek bears,
  You fools of fortune, trencher-friends, time's flies,
  Cap and knee slaves, vapours, and minute-jacks!
  Of man and beast the infinite malady
  Crust you quite o'er! What! dost thou go?
  Soft! take thy physic first,—thou too,—and thou;—
  Stay, I will lend thee money, borrow none.
              Throws the dishes at them
  What! all in motion? Henceforth be no feast,
  Whereat a villain 's not a welcome guest.
  Burn, house! sink, Athens! henceforth hated be

Of Timon man and all humanity!   *Exit*
Re-enter the Lords, Senators, &c.

FIRST LORD. How now, my lords!

SECOND LORD. Know you the quality of Lord Timon's fury?

THIRD LORD. Push! did you see my cap?

FOURTH LORD. I have lost my gown.

FIRST LORD. He 's but a mad lord, and nought but humour
  sways him. He gave me a jewel th' other day, and now
  he has beat it out of my hat: did you see my jewel?

THIRD LORD. Did you see my cap?

SECOND LORD. Here 'tis.

FOURTH LORD. Here lies my gown.

FIRST LORD. Let 's make no stay.

SECOND LORD. Lord Timon 's mad.

THIRD LORD.   I feel 't upon my bones.

FOURTH LORD. One day he gives us diamonds, next day
  stones.   *Exeunt*

ACT FOUR

SCENE ONE

Without the Walls of Athens.

Enter Timon

TIMON. Let me look back upon thee. O thou wall,
That girdlest in those wolves, dive in the earth,
And fence not Athens! Matrons, turn incontinent!
Obedience fail in children! slaves and fools,
Pluck the grave wrinkled senate from the bench,
And minister in their steads! To general filths
Convert, o' the instant, green virginity!
Do 't in your parents' eyes! Bankrupts, hold fast;
Rather than render back, out with your knives,
And cut your trusters' throats! Bound servants, steal!—
Large-handed robbers your grave masters are,
And pill by law. Maid, to thy master's bed;
Thy mistress is o' the brothel! Son of sixteen,
Pluck the lin'd crutch from thy old limping sire,
With it beat out his brains! Piety, and fear,
Religion to the gods, peace, justice, truth,
Domestic awe, night-rest and neighbourhood,
Instruction, manners, mysteries and trades,
Degrees, observances, customs and laws,
Decline to your confounding contraries,
And let confusion live! Plagues incident to men,
Your potent and infectious fevers heap
On Athens, ripe for stroke! Thou cold sciatica,
Cripple our senators, that their limbs may halt
As lamely as their manners! Lust and liberty
Creep in the minds and marrows of our youth,
That 'gainst the stream of virtue they may strive,
And drown themselves in riot! Itches, blains,
Sow all the Athenian bosoms, and their crop

Be general leprosy! Breath infect breath,
That their society, as their friendship, may
Be merely poison! Nothing I 'll bear from thee
But nakedness, thou detestable town!
Take thou that too, with multiplying bans!
Timon will to the woods; where he shall find
The unkindest beast more kinder than mankind.
The gods confound—hear me, you good gods all—
The Athenians both within and out that wall!
And grant, as Timon grows, his hate may grow
To the whole race of mankind, high and low!

                       Amen.   *Exit*

SCENE TWO

Athens. A Room in Timon's House.

Enter Flavius, with two or three Servants

FIRST SERVANT. Hear you, Master steward! where 's our
    master?
Are we undone? cast off? nothing remaining?
FLAVIUS. Alack! my fellows, what should I say to you?
Let me be recorded by the righteous gods,
I am as poor as you.
FIRST SERVANT.   Such a house broke!
So noble a master fall'n! All gone! and not
One friend to take his fortune by the arm,
And go along with him!
SECOND SERVANT.   As we do turn our backs
From our companion thrown into his grave,
So his familiars to his buried fortunes
Slink all away, leave their false vows with him,
Like empty purses pick'd; and his poor self,
A dedicated beggar to the air,
With his disease of all-shunn'd poverty,
Walks, like contempt, alone. More of our fellows.
              Enter other Servants
FLAVIUS. All broken implements of a ruin'd house.
THIRD SERVANT. Yet do our hearts wear Timon's livery,
That see I by our faces; we are fellows still,
Serving alike in sorrow. Leak'd is our bark,

TIMON.   Henceforth be no feast,
  Whereat a villain 's not a welcome guest.

And we, poor mates, stand on the dying deck,
Hearing the surges threat: we must all part
Into the sea of air.

FLAVIUS.   Good fellows all,
The latest of my wealth I 'll share amongst you.
Wherever we shall meet, for Timon's sake
Let 's yet be fellows; let 's shake our heads, and say,
As 'twere a knell unto our master's fortunes,
'We have seen better days.' Let each take some;

                          Giving them money

Nay, put out all your hands. Not one word more:
Thus part we rich in sorrow, parting poor.

                  They embrace, and part several ways

O! the fierce wretchedness that glory brings us.
Who would not wish to be from wealth exempt,
Since riches point to misery and contempt?
Who would be so mock'd with glory? or so live,
But in a dream of friendship?
To have his pomp and all what state compounds
But only painted, like his varnish'd friends?
Poor honest lord! brought low by his own heart,
Undone by goodness. Strange, unusual blood,
When man's worst sin is, he does too much good!
Who then dares to be half so kind agen?
For bounty, that makes gods, does still mar men.
My dearest lord, bless'd, to be most accurs'd,
Rich, only to be wretched, thy great fortunes
Are made thy chief afflictions. Alas! kind lord,
He 's flung in rage from this ingrateful seat
Of monstrous friends;
Nor has he with him to supply his life,
Or that which can command it.
I 'll follow and inquire him out:
I 'll ever serve his mind with my best will;
Whilst I have gold I'll be his steward still.   *Exit*

SCENE THREE

Woods and Cave near the Sea-shore.

Enter Timon from the Cave

TIMON. O blessed breeding sun! draw from the earth
  Rotten humidity; below thy sister's orb
  Infect the air! Twinn'd brothers of one womb,
  Whose procreation, residence and birth,
  Scarce is dividant, touch them with several fortunes;
  The greater scorns the lesser: not nature,
  To whom all sores lay siege, can bear great fortune,
  But by contempt of nature.
  Raise me this beggar, and deny 't that lord;
  The senator shall bear contempt hereditary,
  The beggar native honour.
  It is the pasture lards the rother's sides,
  The want that makes him lean. Who dares, who dares,
  In purity of manhood stand upright,
  And say, 'This man 's a flatterer'? if one be,
  So are they all; for every grize of fortune
  Is smooth'd by that below: the learned pate
  Ducks to the golden fool: all is oblique;
  There 's nothing level in our cursed natures
  But direct villany. Therefore, be abhorr'd
  All feasts, societies, and throngs of men!
  His semblable, yea, himself, Timon disdains:
  Destruction fang mankind! Earth, yield me roots!
                                            Digging

  Who seeks for better of thee, sauce his palate
  With thy most operant poison! What is here?
  Gold! yellow, glittering, precious gold! No, gods,
  I am no idle votarist. Roots, you clear heavens!
  Thus much of this will make black white, foul fair,
  Wrong right, base noble, old young, coward valiant.
  Ha! you gods, why this? What this, you gods? Why, this
  Will lug your priests and servants from your sides,
  Pluck stout men's pillows from below their head:
  This yellow slave
  Will knit and break religions; bless the accurs'd;
  Make the hoar leprosy ador'd; place thieves,

And give them title, knee, and approbation,
With senators on the bench; this is it
That makes the wappen'd widow wed again;
She, whom the spital-house and ulcerous sores
Would cast the gorge at, this embalms and spices
To the April day again. Come, damned earth,
Thou common whore of mankind, that putt'st odds
Among the rout of nations, I will make thee
Do thy right nature.—(*March afar off*) Ha! a drum?
   thou'rt quick,
But yet I 'll bury thee: thou 'lt go, strong thief,
When gouty keepers of thee cannot stand:
Nay, stay thou out for earnest.   *Keeping some gold*
   Enter Alcibiades, with drum and fife, in warlike
      manner; Phrynia and Timandra

ALCIBIADES. What art thou there? speak.
TIMON. A beast, as thou art. The canker gnaw thy heart,
For showing me again the eyes of man!
ALCIBIADES. What is thy name? Is man so hateful to thee,
That art thyself a man?
TIMON. I am Misanthropos, and hate mankind.
For thy part, I do wish thou wert a dog,
That I might love thee something.
ALCIBIADES.   I know thee well,
But in thy fortunes am unlearn'd and strange.
TIMON. I know thee too; and more than that I know thee
I not desire to know. Follow thy drum;
With man's blood paint the ground, gules, gules;
Religious canons, civil laws are cruel;
Then what should war be? This fell whore of thine
Hath in her more destruction than thy sword,
For all her cherubin look.
PHRYNIA.   Thy lips rot off!
TIMON. I will not kiss thee; then the rot returns
To thine own lips again.
ALCIBIADES. How came the noble Timon to this change?
TIMON. As the moon does, by wanting light to give:
But then renew I could not like the moon;
There were no suns to borrow of.
ALCIBIADES. Noble Timon, what friendship may I do thee?
TIMON. None, but to maintain my opinion.
ALCIBIADES. What is it, Timon?

TIMON. Promise me friendship, but perform none: if thou
wilt not promise, the gods plague thee, for thou art a
man! if thou dost perform, confound thee, for thou art a
man!

ALCIBIADES. I have heard in some sort of thy miseries.

TIMON. Thou saw'st them, when I had prosperity.

ALCIBIADES. I see them now! then was a blessed time.

TIMON. As thine is now, held with a brace of harlots.

TIMANDRA. Is this the Athenian minion, whom the world
Voic'd so regardfully?

TIMON.   Art thou Timandra?

TIMANDRA.   Yes.

TIMON. Be a whore still; they love thee not that use thee;
Give them diseases, leaving with thee their lust.
Make use of thy salt hours; season the slaves
For tubs and baths; bring down rose-cheeked youth
To the tub-fast and the diet.

TIMANDRA.   Hang thee, monster!

ALCIBIADES. Pardon him, sweet Timandra, for his wits
Are drown'd and lost in his calamities.
I have but little gold of late, brave Timon,
The want whereof doth daily make revolt
In my penurious band: I have heard and griev'd
How cursed Athens, mindless of thy worth,
Forgetting thy great deeds, when neighbour states,
But for thy sword and fortune, trod upon them,—

TIMON. I prithee, beat thy drum, and get thee gone.

ALCIBIADES. I am thy friend, and pity thee, dear Timon.

TIMON. How dost thou pity him whom thou dost trouble?
I had rather be alone.

ALCIBIADES.   Why, fare thee well:
Here is some gold for thee.

TIMON.   Keep it, I cannot eat it.

ALCIBIADES. When I have laid proud Athens on a heap,—

TIMON. Warr'st thou 'gainst Athens?

ALCIBIADES. Ay, Timon, and have cause.

TIMON. The gods confound them all in thy conquest; and
Thee after, when thou hast conquer'd!

ALCIBIADES.   Why me, Timon?

TIMON. That, by killing of villains, thou wast born to conquer
My country.

Put up thy gold: go on,—here's gold,—go on;
Be as a planetary plague, when Jove
Will o'er some high-vic'd city hang his poison
In the sick air: let not thy sword skip one.
Pity not honour'd age for his white beard;
He is a usurer. Strike me the counterfeit matron;
It is her habit only that is honest,
Herself's a bawd. Let not the virgin's cheek
Make soft thy trenchant sword; for those milk-paps,
That through the window-bars bore at men's eyes,
Are not within the leaf of pity writ,
But set them down horrible traitors. Spare not the babe,
Whose dimpled smiles from fools exhaust their mercy;
Think it a bastard, whom the oracle
Hath doubtfully pronounc'd thy throat shall cut,
And mince it sans remorse. Swear against objects;
Put armour on thine ears and on thine eyes,
Whose proof nor yells of mothers, maids, nor babes,
Nor sight of priests in holy vestments bleeding,
Shall pierce a jot. There's gold to pay thy soldiers:
Make large confusion; and, thy fury spent,
Confounded be thyself! Speak not, be gone.

ALCIBIADES. Hast thou gold yet? I'll take the gold thou
     giv'st me,
   Not all thy counsel.

TIMON. Dost thou, or dost thou not, heaven's curse upon
     thee!

PHRYNIA.) Give us some gold, good Timon: hast thou
TIMANDRA.)   more?

TIMON. Enough to make a whore forswear her trade,
   And to make whores a bawd. Hold up, you sluts,
   Your aprons mountant: you are not oathable,
   Although, I know, you'll swear, terribly swear
   Into strong shudders and to heavenly agues
   The immortal gods that hear you, spare your oaths,
   I'll trust to your conditions: be whores still;
   And he whose pious breath seeks to convert you,
   Be strong in whore, allure him, burn him up;
   Let your close fire predominate his smoke,
   And be no turncoats: yet may your pains, six months,
   Be quite contrary: and thatch your poor thin roofs
   With burdens of the dead; some that were hang'd,

No matter; wear them, betray with them: whore still;
Paint till a horse may mire upon your face:
A pox of wrinkles!

PHRYNIA. \
TIMANDRA. / Well, more gold. What then?

Believe 't, that we 'll do anything for gold.

TIMON. Consumptions sow
In hollow bones of man; strike their sharp shins,
And mar men's spurring. Crack the lawyer's voice,
That he may never more false title plead,
Nor sound his quillets shrilly: hoar the flamen,
That scolds against the quality of flesh,
And not believes himself: down with the nose,
Down with it flat; take the bridge quite away
Of him that, his particular to foresee,
Smells from the general weal: make curl'd-pate ruffians
    bald,
And let the unscarr'd braggarts of the war
Derive some pain from you: plague all,
That your activity may defeat and quell
The source of all erection. There 's more gold;
Do you damn others, and let this damn you,
And ditches grave you all!

PHRYNIA. \ More counsel with more money, bounteous
TIMANDRA. /   Timon.

TIMON. More whore, more mischief first; I have given you
    earnest.

ALCIBIADES. Strike up the drum towards Athens! Farewell,
    Timon:
If I thrive well, I 'll visit thee again.

TIMON. If I hope well, I 'll never see thee more.

ALCIBIADES. I never did thee harm.

TIMON. Yes, thou spok'st well of me.

ALCIBIADES.   Call'st thou that harm?

TIMON. Men daily find it. Get thee away, and take
    Thy beagles with thee.

ALCIBIADES.   We but offend him. Strike!
    Drum beats. Exeunt Alcibiades, Phrynia, and Timandra

TIMON. That nature, being sick of man's unkindness,
    Should yet be hungry! Common mother, thou,   *Digging*
Whose womb unmeasurable, and infinite breast,
Teems, and feeds all; whose self-same mettle,

Whereof thy proud child, arrogant man, is puff'd,
Engenders the black toad and adder blue,
The gilded newt and eyeless venom'd worm,
With all the abhorred births below crisp heaven
Whereon Hyperion's quickening fire doth shine;
Yield him, who all thy human sons doth hate,
From forth thy plenteous bosom, one poor root!
Ensear thy fertile and conceptious womb,
Let it no more bring out ingrateful man!
Go great with tigers, dragons, wolves, and bears;
Teem with new monsters, whom thy upward face
Hath to the marbled mansion all above
Never presented! O! a root; dear thanks:
Dry up thy marrows, vines and plough-torn leas;
Whereof ungrateful man, with liquorish draughts
And morsels unctuous, greases his pure mind,
That from it all consideration slips!

Enter Apemantus

More man! Plague! plague!

APEMANTUS. I was directed hither: men report
Thou dost affect my manners, and dost use them.

TIMON. 'Tis, then, because thou dost not keep a dog
Whom I would imitate: consumption catch thee!

APEMANTUS. This is in thee a nature but infected;
A poor unmanly melancholy sprung
From change of fortune. Why this spade? this place?
This slave-like habit? and these looks of care?
Thy flatterers yet wear silk, drink wine, lie soft,
Hug their diseas'd perfumes, and have forgot
That ever Timon was. Shame not these woods
By putting on the cunning of a carper.
Be thou a flatterer now, and seek to thrive
By that which has undone thee: hinge thy knee,
And let his very breath, whom thou 'lt observe,
Blow off thy cap; praise his most vicious strain,
And call it excellent. Thou wast told thus;
Thou gav'st thine ears, like tapsters that bid welcome,
To knaves and all approachers: 'tis most just
That thou turn rascal; hadst thou wealth again,
Rascals should have 't. Do not assume my likeness.

TIMON. Were I like thee I 'd throw away myself.

APEMANTUS. Thou hast cast away thyself, being like thyself:

A madman so long, now a fool. What! think'st
That the bleak air, thy boisterous chamberlain,
Will put thy shirt on warm? will these moss'd trees,
That have outliv'd the eagle, page thy heels
And skip when thou point'st out? will the cold brook,
Candied with ice, caudle thy morning taste
To cure the o'er-night surfeit? Call the creatures
Whose naked natures live in all the spite
Of wreakful heaven, whose bare unhoused trunks
To the conflicting elements expos'd,
Answer mere nature; bid them flatter thee;
O! thou shalt find—

TIMON.   A fool of thee. Depart.

APEMANTUS. I love thee better now than e'er I did.

TIMON. I hate thee worse.

APEMANTUS.   Why?

TIMON.   Thou flatter'st misery.

APEMANTUS. I flatter not, but say thou art a caitiff.

TIMON. Why dost thou seek me out?

APEMANTUS.   To vex thee.

TIMON. Always a villain's office, or a fool's.
    Dost please thyself in 't?

APEMANTUS.   Ay.

TIMON.   What! a knave too?

APEMANTUS. If thou didst put this sour-cold habit on
    To castigate thy pride, 'twere well; but thou
    Dost it enforcedly: thou 'dst courtier be again
    Wert thou not beggar. Willing misery
    Outlives incertain pomp, is crown'd before;
    The one is filling still, never complete;
    The other, at high wish: best state, contentless,
    Hath a distracted and most wretched being,
    Worse than the worst, content.
    Thou shouldst desire to die, being miserable.

TIMON. Not by his breath that is more miserable.
    Thou art a slave, whom Fortune's tender arm
    With favour never clasp'd, but bred a dog.
    Hadst thou, like us from our first swath, proceeded
    The sweet degrees that this brief world affords
    To such as may the passive drudges of it
    Freely command, thou wouldst have plung'd thyself
    In general riot; melted down thy youth

In different beds of lust; and never learn'd
The icy precepts of respect, but follow'd
The sugar'd game before thee. But myself,
Who had the world as my confectionary,
The mouths, the tongues, the eyes, and hearts of men
At duty, more than I could frame employment,
That numberless upon me stuck as leaves
Do on the oak, have with one winter's brush
Fell from their boughs and left me open, bare
For every storm that blows; I, to bear this,
That never knew but better, is some burden:
Thy nature did commence in sufferance, time
Hath made thee hard in 't. Why shouldst thou hate men?
They never flatter'd thee: what hast thou given?
If thou wilt curse, thy father, that poor rag,
Must be thy subject, who in spite put stuff
To some she beggar and compounded thee
Poor rogue hereditary. Hence! be gone!
If thou hadst not been born the worst of men,
Thou hadst been a knave and flatterer.

APEMANTUS.   Art thou proud yet?

TIMON. Ay, that I am not thee.

APEMANTUS.   I, that I was
No prodigal.

TIMON.   I, that I am one now:
Were all the wealth I have shut up in thee,
I 'd give thee leave to hang it. Get thee gone.
That the whole life of Athens were in this!
Thus would I eat it.   *Eating a root*

APEMANTUS.   Here; I will mend thy feast.

TIMON. First mend my company, take away thyself.

APEMANTUS. So I shall mend mine own, by the lack of
thine.

TIMON. 'Tis not well mended so, it is but botch'd;
If not, I would it were.

APEMANTUS. What wouldst thou have to Athens?

TIMON. Thee thither in a whirlwind. If thou wilt,
Tell them there I have gold; look, so I have.

APEMANTUS. Here is no use for gold.

TIMON.   The best and truest;
For here it sleeps, and does no tired harm.

APEMANTUS. Where liest o' nights, Timon?

TIMON.   Under that 's above me.
  Where feed'st thou o' days, Apemantus?

APEMANTUS. Where my stomach finds meat; or, rather,
  where I eat it.

TIMON. Would poison were obedient and knew my mind!

APEMANTUS. Where wouldst thou send it?

TIMON. To sauce thy dishes.

APEMANTUS. The middle of humanity thou never knewest,
  but the extremity of both ends. When thou wast in thy
  gilt and thy perfume, they mocked thee for too much
  curiosity; in thy rags thou knowest none, but art despised
  for the contrary. There 's a medlar for thee; eat it.

TIMON. On what I hate I feed not.

APEMANTUS. Dost hate a medlar?

TIMON. Ay, though it look like thee.

APEMANTUS. An thou hadst hated meddlers sooner, thou
  shouldst have loved thyself better now. What man didst
  thou ever know unthrift that was beloved after his means?

TIMON. Who, without those means thou talkest of, didst
  thou ever know beloved?

APEMANTUS. Myself.

TIMON. I understand thee; thou hadst some means to keep
  a dog.

APEMANTUS. What things in the world canst thou nearest
  compare to thy flatterers?

TIMON. Women nearest; but men, men are the things
  themselves. What wouldst thou do with the world, Apemantus, if it lay in thy power?

APEMANTUS. Give it the beasts, to be rid of the men.

TIMON. Wouldst thou have thyself fall in the confusion of
  men, and remain a beast with the beasts?

APEMANTUS. Ay, Timon.

TIMON. A beastly ambition, which the gods grant thee to
  attain to. If thou wert the lion, the fox would beguile
  thee; if thou wert the lamb, the fox would eat thee; if
  thou wert the fox, the lion would suspect thee, when peradventure thou wert accused by the ass; if thou wert the
  ass, thy dulness would torment thee, and still thou livedst
  but as a breakfast to the wolf; if thou wert the wolf, thy
  greediness would afflict thee, and oft thou shouldst hazard thy life for thy dinner; wert thou the unicorn, pride
  and wrath would confound thee and make thine own self

the conquest of thy fury; wert thou a bear, thou wouldst
be killed by the horse; wert thou a horse, thou wouldst
be seized by the leopard; wert thou a leopard, thou wert
german to the lion, and the spots of thy kindred were
jurors on thy life; all thy safety were remotion, and thy
defence absence. What beast couldst thou be, that were
not subject to a beast? and what a beast art thou already,
that seest not thy loss in transformation!

APEMANTUS. If thou couldst please me with speaking to
me, thou mightst have hit it upon it here; the commonwealth of Athens is become a forest of beasts.

TIMON. How has the ass broke the wall, that thou art out
of the city?

APEMANTUS. Yonder comes a poet and a painter: the
plague of company light upon thee! I will fear to catch
it, and give way. When I know not what else to do, I 'll
see thee again.

TIMON. When there is nothing living but thee, thou shalt
be welcome. I had rather be a beggar's dog than Apemantus.

APEMANTUS. Thou art the cap of all the fools alive.

TIMON. Would thou wert clean enough to spit upon!

APEMANTUS. A plague on thee! thou art too bad to curse!

TIMON. All villains that do stand by thee are pure.

APEMANTUS. There is no leprosy but what thou speak'st.

TIMON. If I name thee,
I 'll beat thee, but I should infect my hands.

APEMANTUS. I would my tongue could rot them off!

TIMON. Away, thou issue of a mangy dog!
Choler does kill me that thou art alive;
I swound to see thee.

APEMANTUS.　　　　　Would thou wouldst burst!

TIMON.　　　　　　　　　　　　　　　Away,
Thou tedious rogue! I am sorry I shall lose
A stone by thee.　　　　　*Throws a stone at him*

APEMANTUS. Beast!

TIMON.　　　　Slave!

APEMANTUS.　　　　　Toad!

TIMON.　　　　　　　　　Rogue, rogue, rogue!
I am sick of this false world, and will love nought
But even the mere necessities upon 't.
Then, Timon, presently prepare thy grave;

Lie where the light foam of the sea may beat
Thy grave-stone daily: make thine epitaph,
That death in me at others' lives may laugh.

Looking on the gold

O thou sweet king-killer, and dear divorce
'Twixt natural son and sire! thou bright defiler
Of Hymen's purest bed! thou valiant Mars!
Thou ever young, fresh, lov'd, and delicate wooer,
Whose blush doth thaw the consecrated snow
That lies on Dian's lap! thou visible god,
That solder'st close impossibilities,
And mak'st them kiss! that speak'st with every tongue,
To every purpose! O thou touch of hearts!
Think, thy slave man rebels, and by thy virtue
Set them into confounding odds, that beasts
May have the world in empire.

APEMANTUS.   Would 'twere so:
But not till I am dead; I 'll say thou 'st gold:
Thou wilt be throng'd to shortly.

TIMON.   Throng'd to?

APEMANTUS.   Ay.

TIMON. Thy back, I prithee.

APEMANTUS.   Live, and love thy misery!

TIMON. Long live so, and so die!   *Exit Apemantus*
                    I am quit.
More things like men! Eat, Timon, and abhor them.

Enter Thieves

FIRST THIEF. Where should he have this gold? It is some
    poor fragment, some slender ort of his remainder. The
    mere want of gold, and the falling-from of his friends,
    drove him into this melancholy.

SECOND THIEF. It is noised he hath a mass of treasure.

THIRD THIEF. Let us make the assay upon him: if he care
    not for 't, he will supply us easily; if he covetously re-
    serve it, how shall 's get it?

SECOND THIEF. True; for he bears it not about him, 'tis hid.

FIRST THIEF. Is not this he?

THIEVES. Where?

SECOND THIEF. 'Tis his description.

THIRD THIEF. He; I know him.

ALL. Save thee, Timon.

TIMON. Now, thieves?

ALL. Soldiers, not thieves.

TIMON. Both too; and women's sons.

THIEVES. We are not thieves, but men that much do want.

TIMON. Your greatest want is, you want much of meat.
　　Why should you want? Behold, the earth hath roots;
　　Within this mile break forth a hundred springs;
　　The oaks bear mast, the briers scarlet hips;
　　The bounteous housewife, nature, on each bush
　　Lays her full mess before you. Want! why want?

FIRST THIEF. We cannot live on grass, on berries, water,
　　As beasts, and birds, and fishes.

TIMON. Nor on the beasts themselves, the birds, and fishes;
　　You must eat men. Yet thanks I must you con
　　That you are thieves profess'd, that you work not
　　In holier shapes; for there is boundless theft
　　In limited professions. Rascal thieves,
　　Here 's gold. Go, suck the subtle blood o' the grape,
　　Till the high fever seethe your blood to froth,
　　And so 'scape hanging; trust not the physician;
　　His antidotes are poison, and he slays
　　More than you rob: take wealth and lives together;
　　Do villany, do, since you protest to do 't,
　　Like workmen. I 'll example you with thievery:
　　The sun 's a thief, and with his great attraction
　　Robs the vast sea; the moon 's an arrant thief,
　　And her pale fire she snatches from the sun;
　　The sea 's a thief, whose liquid surge resolves
　　The moon into salt tears; the earth 's a thief,
　　That feeds and breeds by a composture stolen
　　From general excrement; each thing 's a thief;
　　The laws, your curb and whip, in their rough power
　　Have unchcck'd theft. Love not yourselves; away!
　　Rob one another. There 's more gold: cut throats;
　　All that you meet are thieves. To Athens go,
　　Break open shops; nothing can you steal
　　But thieves do lose it: steal no less for this
　　I give you; and gold confound you howsoe'er!
　　Amen.

THIRD THIEF. He has almost charmed me from my profes-
　　sion, by persuading me to it.

FIRST THIEF. 'Tis in the malice of mankind that he thus ad-
　　vises us; not to have us thrive in our mystery.

SECOND THIEF. I 'll believe him as an enemy, and give over
  my trade.

FIRST THIEF. Let us first see peace in Athens; there is no
  time so miserable but a man may be true.

                                            Exeunt Thieves
                    Enter Flavius

FLAVIUS. O you gods!
  Is yond despised and ruinous man my lord?
  Full of decay and failing? O monument
  And wonder of good deeds evilly bestow'd!
  What an alteration of honour
  Has desperate want made!
  What viler thing upon the earth than friends
  Who can bring noblest minds to basest ends!
  How rarely does it meet with this time's guise,
  When man was wish'd to love his enemies!
  Grant I may ever love, and rather woo
  Those that would mischief me than those that do!
  He hath caught me in his eye: I will present
  My honest grief unto him; and, as my lord,
  Still serve him with my life. My dearest master!
                    Timon comes forward

TIMON. Away! what are thou?
FLAVIUS.   Have you forgot me, sir?
TIMON. Why dost ask that? I have forgot all men;
  Then, if thou grant'st thou'rt a man, I have forgot thee.
FLAVIUS. An honest poor servant of yours.
TIMON.   Then I know thee not:
  I never had an honest man about me; ay, all
  I kept were knaves, to serve in meat to villains.
FLAVIUS. The gods are witness,
  Ne'er did poor steward wear a truer grief
  For his undone lord than mine eyes for you.
TIMON. What! dost thou weep? Come nearer. Then I love
    thee,
  Because thou art a woman, and disclaim'st
  Flinty mankind; whose eyes do never give,
  But thorough lust and laughter. Pity 's sleeping:
  Strange times, that weep with laughing, not with weep-
    ing!
FLAVIUS. I beg of you to know me, good my lord,
  To accept my grief and whilst this poor wealth lasts

    To entertain me as your steward still.

TIMON. Had I a steward
    So true, so just, and now so comfortable?
    It almost turns my dangerous nature mild.
    Let me behold thy face. Surely, this man
    Was born of woman.
    Forgive my general and exceptless rashness,
    You perpetual-sober gods! I do proclaim
    One honest man, mistake me not, but one;
    No more, I pray, and he 's a steward.
    How fain would I have hated all mankind!
    And thou redeem'st thyself: but all, save thee,
    I fell with curses.
    Methinks thou art more honest now than wise;
    For, by oppressing and betraying me,
    Thou mightst have sooner got another service:
    For many so arrive at second masters
    Upon their first lord's neck. But tell me true,—
    For I must ever doubt, though ne'er so sure,—
    Is not thy kindness subtle, covetous,
    If not a usuring kindness and as rich men deal gifts,
    Expecting in return twenty for one?

FLAVIUS. No, my most worthy master; in whose breast
    Doubt and suspect, alas! are plac'd too late.
    You should have fear'd false times when you did feast;
    Suspect still comes when an estate is least
    That which I show, heaven knows, is merely love,
    Duty and zeal to your unmatched mind,
    Care of your food and living; and, believe it
    My most honour'd lord,
    For any benefit that points to me,
    Either in hope, or present, I 'd exchange
    For this one wish, that you had power and wealth
    To requite me by making rich yourself.

TIMON. Look thee, 'tis so. Thou singly honest man,
    Here, take: the gods out of my misery,
    Have sent thee treasure. Go, live rich and happy;
    But thus condition'd: thou shalt build from men;
    Hate all, curse all, show charity to none,
    But let the famish'd flesh slide from the bone,
    Ere thou relieve the beggar; give to dogs
    What thou deny'st to men; let prisons swallow 'em,

Debts wither 'em to nothing; be men like blasted woods,
And may diseases lick up their false bloods!
And so, farewell and thrive.

FLAVIUS.   O! let me stay
And comfort you, my master.

TIMON.   If thou hatest
Curses, stay not; fly, whilst thou 'rt bless'd and free:
Ne'er see thou man, and let me ne'er see thee.

Exeunt, severally

ACT FIVE

SCENE ONE

The Woods. Before Timon's Cave.

Enter Poet and Painter.

PAINTER. As I took note of the place, it cannot be far where he abides.

POET. What 's to be thought of him? Does the rumour hold for true that he is so full of gold?

PAINTER. Certain: Alcibiades reports it; Phrynia and Timandra had gold of him: he likewise enriched poor straggling soldiers with great quantity. 'Tis said he gave unto his steward a mighty sum.

POET. Then this breaking of his has been but a try for his friends.

PAINTER. Nothing else; you shall see him a palm in Athens again, and flourish with the highest. Therefore 'tis not amiss we tender our loves to him, in this supposed distress of his: it will show honestly in us, and is very likely to load our purposes with what they travel for, if it be a just and true report that goes of his having.

POET. What have you now to present unto him?

PAINTER. Nothing at this time but my visitation; only, I will promise him an excellent piece.

POET. I must serve him so too; tell him of an intent that 's coming towards him.

PAINTER. Good as the best. Promising is the very air o' the time; it opens the eyes of expectation; performance is ever the duller for his act; and, but in the plainer and simpler kind of people, the deed of saying is quite out of use. To promise is most courtly and fashionable; performance is a kind of will or testament which argues a great sickness in his judgment that makes it.

Enter Timon from his cave

TIMON. (*Aside*) Excellent workman! Thou canst not paint
a man so bad as is thyself.

POET. I am thinking what I shall say I have provided for
him: it must be a personating of himself; a satire against
the softness of prosperity, with a discovery of the infinite
flatteries that follow youth and opulency.

TIMON. (*Aside*) Must thou needs stand for a villain in
thine own work? Wilt thou whip thine own faults in
other men? Do so, I have gold for thee.

POET. Nay, let's seek him:
Then do we sin against our own estate,
When we may profit meet, and come too late.

PAINTER. True;
When the day serves, before black-corner'd night,
Find what thou want'st by free and offer'd light.
Come.

TIMON. (*Aside*) I'll meet you at the turn. What a god's gold,
That he is worshipp'd in a baser temple
Than where swine feed!
'Tis thou that rigg'st the bark and plough'd the foam,
Settlest admired reverence in a slave:
To thee be worship; and thy saints for aye
Be crown'd with plagues that thee alone obey.
Fit I meet them.   *Advancing*

POET. Hail, worthy Timon!

PAINTER.   Our late noble master!

TIMON. Have I once liv'd to see two honest men?

POET. Sir,
Having often of your open bounty tasted,
Hearing you were retir'd, your friends fall'n off,
Whose thankless natures—O abhorred spirits!
Not all the whips of heaven are large enough—
What! to you,
Whose star-like nobleness gave life and influence
To their whole being! I am rapt, and cannot cover
The monstrous bulk of this ingratitude
With any size of words.

TIMON. Let it go naked, men may see 't the better:
You, that are honest, by being what you are,
Make them best seen and known.

PAINTER.   He and myself
Have travell'd in the great shower of your gifts,

And sweetly felt it.

TIMON.   Ay, you are honest men.

PAINTER. We are hither come to offer you our service.

TIMON. Most honest men! Why, how shall I requite you?
Can you eat roots and drink cold water? no.

BOTH. What we can do, we 'll do, to do you service.

TIMON. Ye 're honest men. Ye 've heard that I have gold;
I am sure you have: speak truth; ye 're honest men.

PAINTER. So it is said, my noble lord; but therefore
Came not my friend nor I.

TIMON. Good honest men! Thou draw'st a counterfeit
Best in all Athens: thou 'rt, indeed, the best;
Thou counterfeit'st most lively.

PAINTER.   So, so, my lord.

TIMON. E'en so, sir, as I say. And, for thy fiction,
Why, thy verse swells with stuff so fine and smooth
That thou art even natural in thine art.
But for all this, my honest-natur'd friends,
I must needs say you have a little fault:
Marry, 'tis not monstrous in you, neither wish I
You take much pains to mend.

BOTH.   Beseech your honour
To make it known to us.

TIMON.   You 'll take it ill.

BOTH. Most thankfully, my lord.

TIMON.   Will you indeed?

BOTH. Doubt it not, worthy lord.

TIMON. There 's never a one of you but trusts a knave,
That mightily deceives you.

BOTH.   Do we, my lord?

TIMON. Ay, and you hear him cog, see him dissemble,
Know his gross patchery, love him, feed him,
Keep in your bosom; yet remain assur'd
That he 's a made-up villain.

PAINTER. I know none such, my lord.

POET.   Nor I.

TIMON. Look you, I love you well; I 'll give you gold,
Rid me these villains from your companies:
Hang them or stab them, drown them in a draught,
Confound them by some course, and come to me,
I 'll give you gold enough.

BOTH. Name them, my lord; let 's know them.

TIMON. You that way and you this, but two in company;
    Each man apart, all single and alone,
    Yet an arch-villain keeps him company.
    If, where thou art two villains shall not be,
    Come not near him. (*To the Poet*) If thou would not
        reside
    But where one villain is, then him abandon.
    Hence! pack! there 's gold; ye came for gold, ye slaves:
    You have done work for me, there 's payment: hence!
    You are an alchemist, make gold of that.
    Out, rascal dogs!   *Beats them out*
                                 and then returns to his cave
            Enter Flavius and two Senators
FLAVIUS. It is in vain that you would speak with Timon;
    For he is set so only to himself
    That nothing but himself, which looks like man,
    Is friendly with him.
FIRST SENATOR. Bring us to his cave:
    It is our part and promise to the Athenians
    To speak with Timon.
SECOND SENATOR.   At all times alike
    Men are not still the same: 'twas time and griefs
    That fram'd him thus: time, with his fairer hand,
    Offering the fortunes of his former days,
    The former man may make him. Bring us to him,
    And chance it as it may.
FLAVIUS.   Here is his cave.
    Peace and content be here! Lord Timon! Timon!
    Look out, and speak to friends. The Athenians,
    By two of their most reverend senate, greet thee:
    Speak to them, noble Timon.
            Enter Timon, from his cave
TIMON. Thou sun, that comfort'st, burn! Speak, and be
        hang'd:
    For each true word, a blister! and each false
    Be as a cauterizing to the root o' the tongue,
    Consuming it with speaking!
FIRST SENATOR.   Worthy Timon,—
TIMON. Of none but such as you, and you of Timon.
SECOND SENATOR. The senators of Athens greet thee, Timon.
TIMON. I thank them; and would send them back the
        plague,

TIMON. Most honest men! Why, how shall I requite you? Can you eat roots and drink cold water? no.

Could I but catch it for them.

FIRST SENATOR.   O! forget
What we are sorry for ourselves in thee.
The senators with one consent of love
Entreat thee back to Athens: who have thought
On special dignities, which vacant lie
For thy best use and wearing.

SECOND SENATOR.   They confess
Toward thee forgetfulness too general, gross;
Which now the public body, which doth seldom
Play the recanter, feeling in itself
A lack of Timon's aid, hath sense withal
Of its own fail, restraining aid to Timon;
And send forth us, to make their sorrow'd render,
Together with a recompense more fruitful
Than their offence can weigh down by the dram;
Ay, even such heaps and sums of love and wealth
As shall to thee block out what wrongs were theirs,
And write in thee the figures of their love,
Ever to read them thine.

TIMON.   You witch me in it;
Surprise me to the very brink of tears:
Lend me a fool's heart and a woman's eyes,
And I 'll beweep these comforts, worthy senators.

FIRST SENATOR. Therefore so please thee to return with us,
And of our Athens—thine and ours—to take
The captainship, thou shalt be met with thanks,
Allow'd with absolute power, and thy good name
Live with authority: so soon we shall drive back
Of Alcibiades the approaches wild;
Who, like a boar too savage, doth root up
His country's peace.

SECOND SENATOR. And shakes his threatening sword
Against the walls of Athens.

FIRST SENATOR.   Therefore, Timon,—

TIMON. Well, sir, I will; therefore, I will, sir; thus:—
If Alcibiades kill my countrymen,
Let Alcibiades know this of Timon,
That Timon cares not. But if he sack fair Athens,
And take our goodly aged men by the beards,
Giving our holy virgins to the stain
Of contumelious, beastly, mad-brain'd war;

Then let him know, and tell him Timon speaks it,
In pity of our aged and our youth
I cannot choose but tell him, that I care not,
And let him take 't at worst; for their knives care not
While you have throats to answer: for myself,
There 's not a whittle in the unruly camp
But I do prize it at my love before
The reverend'st throat in Athens. So I leave you
To the protection of the prosperous gods,
As thieves to keepers.

FLAVIUS.   Stay not; all 's in vain.

TIMON. Why, I was writing of my epitaph;
It will be seen to-morrow. My long sickness
Of health and living now begins to mend,
And nothing brings me all things. Go; live still:
Be Alcibiades your plague, you his,
And last so long enough!

FIRST SENATOR. We speak in vain.

TIMON. But yet I love my country, and am not
One that rejoices in the common wrack,
As common bruit doth put it.

FIRST SENATOR.   That 's well spoke.

TIMON. Commend me to my loving countrymen,—

FIRST SENATOR. These words become your lips as they pass
through them.

SECOND SENATOR. And enter in our ears like great tri-
umphers
In their applauding gates.

TIMON.   Commend me to them;
And tell them, that, to ease them of their griefs,
Their fears of hostile strokes, their aches, losses,
Their pangs of love, with other incident throes
That nature's fragile vessel doth sustain
In life's uncertain voyage, I will some kindness do them:
I 'll teach them to prevent wild Alcibiades' wrath.

SECOND SENATOR. I like this well; he will return again.

TIMON. I have a tree which grows here in my close,
That mine own use invites me to cut down,
And shortly must I fell it: tell my friends,
Tell Athens, in the sequence of degree,
From high to low throughout, that whoso please
To stop affliction, let him take his haste,

Come hither, ere my tree hath felt the axe,
And hang himself. I pray you, do my greeting.
FLAVIUS. Trouble him no further; thus you still shall find
   him.
TIMON. Come not to me again; but say to Athens,
Timon hath made his everlasting mansion
Upon the beached verge of the salt flood;
Who once a day with his embossed froth
The turbulent surge shall cover: thither come,
And let my grave-stone be your oracle.   ·
Lips, let sour words go by and language end:
What is amiss plague and infection mend!
Graves only be men's works and death their gain!
Sun, hide thy beams! Timon hath done his reign.   *Exit*
FIRST SENATOR. His discontents are unremovably
Coupled to nature.
SECOND SENATOR. Our hope in him is dead· let us return,
And strain what other means is left unto us
In our dear peril.
FIRST SENATOR. It requires swift foot.   *Exeunt*

SCENE TWO

Before the Walls of Athens.

Enter two Senators and a Messenger

FIRST SENATOR. Thou hast painfully discover'd: are his files
   As full as thy report?
MESSENGER.   I have spoke the least;
Besides, his expedition promises
Present approach.
SECOND SENATOR. We stand much hazard if they bring not
   Timon.
MESSENGER. I met a courier, one mine ancient friend,
Whom, though in general part we were oppos'd,
Yet our old love made a particular force,
And made us speak like friends: this man was riding
From Alcibiades to Timon's cave,
With letters of entreaty, which imported
His fellowship i' the cause against your city,
In part for his sake mov'd.

FIRST SENATOR.   Here come our brothers.
            Enter Senators from Timon
THIRD SENATOR. No talk of Timon, nothing of him expect.
    The enemies' drum is heard, and fearful scouring
    Doth choke the air with dust. In, and prepare:
    Ours is the fall, I fear; our foes the snare.   *Exeunt*

SCENE THREE

The Woods. Timon's Cave, and a rude Tomb seen.

Enter a Soldier, seeking Timon

SOLDIER. By all description this should be the place.
    Who 's here? speak, ho! No answer! What is this?
    Timon is dead, who hath outstretch'd his span:
    Some beast rear'd this; here does not live a man.
    Dead, sure; and this his grave. What 's on this tomb
    I cannot read; the character I 'll take with wax:
    Our captain hath in every figure skill;
    An ag'd interpreter, though young in days.
    Before proud Athens he 's set down by this,
    Whose fall the mark of his ambition is.   *Exit*

SCENE FOUR

Before the Walls of Athens.

Trumpets sound. Enter Alcibiades with his Powers

ALCIBIADES. Sound to this coward and lascivious town
    Our terrible approach.   *A parley sounded*
            Enter Senators, on the Walls
    Till now you have gone on, and fill'd the time
    With all licentious measure, making your wills
    The scope of justice: till now myself and such
    As slept within the shadow of your power
    Have wander'd with our travers'd arms, and breath'd
    Our sufferance vainly. Now the time is flush,
    When crouching marrow, in the bearer strong,
    Cries of itself, 'No more': now breathless wrong

Shall sit and pant in your great chairs of ease,
And pursy insolence shall break his wind
With fear and horrid flight.
FIRST SENATOR. Noble and young,
When thy first griefs were but a mere conceit,
Ere thou hadst power or we had cause of fear,
We sent to thee, to give thy rages balm,
To wipe out our ingratitude with loves
Above their quantity.
SECOND SENATOR. So did we woo
Transformed Timon to our city's love
By humble message and by promis'd means:
We were not all unkind, nor all deserve
The common stroke of war.
FIRST SENATOR. These walls of ours
Were not erected by their hands from whom
You have receiv'd your grief; nor are they such
That these great towers, trophies, and schools should fall
For private faults in them.
SECOND SENATOR.   Nor are they living
Who were the motives that you first went out;
Shame that they wanted cunning in excess
Hath broke their hearts. March, noble lord,
Into our city with thy banners spread:
By decimation, and a tithed death,—
If thy revenges hunger for that food
Which nature loathes,—take thou the destin'd tenth,
And by the hazard of the spotted die
Let die the spotted.
FIRST SENATOR. All have not offended;
For those that were, it is not square to take
On those that are, revenges: crimes, like lands,
Are not inherited. Then, dear countryman,
Bring in thy ranks, but leave without thy rage:
Spare thy Athenian cradle, and those kin
Which in the bluster of thy wrath must fall
With those that have offended: like a shepherd,
Approach the fold and cull th' infected forth,
But kill not all together.
SECOND SENATOR.   What thou wilt,
Thou rather shalt enforce it with thy smile
Than hew to 't with thy sword.

FIRST SENATOR. Set but thy foot
  Against our rampir'd gates, and they shall ope,
  So thou wilt send thy gentle heart before,
  To say thou 'lt enter friendly.
SECOND SENATOR. Throw thy glove,
  Or any token of thine honour else,
  That thou wilt use the wars as thy redress
  And not as our confusion, all thy powers
  Shall make their harbour in our town, till we
  Have seal'd thy full desire.
ALCIBIADES. Then there 's my glove;
  Descend, and open your uncharged ports:
  Those enemies of Timon's and mine own
  Whom you yourselves shall set out for reproof,
  Fall, and no more; and, to atone your fears
  With my more noble meaning, not a man
  Shall pass his quarter, or offend the stream
  Of regular justice in your city's bounds,
  But shall be render'd to your public laws
  At heaviest answer.
BOTH. 'Tis most nobly spoken.
ALCIBIADES. Descend, and keep your words.
              The Senators descend, and open the gates
                        Enter a Soldier
SOLDIER. My noble general, Timon is dead;
  Entomb'd upon the very hem o' the sea:
  And on his grave-stone this insculpture, which
  With wax I brought away, whose soft impression
  Interprets for my poor ignorance.
ALCIBIADES. 'Here lies a wretched corse, of wretched soul
    bereft:
  Seek not my name: a plague consume you wicked cai-
    tiffs left!
  Here lie I, Timon; who, alive, all living men did hate:
  Pass by, and curse thy fill; but pass and stay not here thy
    gait.'
  These well express in thee thy latter spirits:
  Though thou abhorr'dst in us our human griefs,
  Scorn'dst our brain's flow and those our droplets which
  From niggard nature fall, yet rich conceit
  Taught thee to make vast Neptune weep for aye
  On thy low grave, on faults forgiven. Dead

Is noble Timon; of whose memory
Hereafter more. Bring me into your city,
And I will use the olive with my sword;
Make war breed peace; make peace stint war; make each
Prescribe to other as each other's leech.
Let our drums strike.   *Exeunt*

JULIUS CÆSAR

CAST OF CHARACTERS

JULIUS CÆSAR

OCTAVIUS CÆSAR
MARCUS ANTONIUS } *Triumvirs after the Death*
M. ÆMILIUS LEPIDUS } *of Julius Cæsar*

CICERO
PUBLIUS } *Senators*
POPILIUS LENA }

MARCUS BRUTUS
CASSIUS
CASCA
TREBONIUS *Conspirators against Julius*
LIGARIUS *Cæsar*
DECIUS BRUTUS
METELLUS CIMBER
CINNA

FLAVIUS AND MARULLUS, *Tribunes*
ARTEMIDORUS, *a Sophist of Cnidos*
A Soothsayer
CINNA, *a Poet*
Another Poet
LUCILIUS, TITINIUS, MESSALA, Young CATO, and
   VOLUMNIUS, *Friends to Brutus and Cassius*
VARRO, CLITUS, CLAUDIUS, STRATO, LUCIUS,
   DARDANIUS, *Servants to Brutus*
PINDARUS, *Servant to Cassius*

CALPHURNIA, *Wife to Cæsar*
PORTIA, *Wife to Brutus*

Senators, Citizens, Guards, Attendants, &c.

SCENE
Rome; afterwards, Sardis and near Philippi

JULIUS CÆSAR

ACT ONE

SCENE ONE

Rome. A Street.

Enter Flavius, Marullus, and certain Commoners

FLAVIUS. Hence! home, you idle creatures, get you home:
Is this a holiday? What! know you not,
Being mechanical, you ought not walk
Upon a labouring day without the sign
Of your profession? Speak, what trade art thou?

FIRST COMMONER. Why, sir, a carpenter.

MARULLUS. Where is thy leather apron, and thy rule?
What dost thou with thy best apparel on?
You, sir, what trade are you?

SECOND COMMONER. Truly, sir, in respect of a fine workman, I am but, as you would say, a cobbler.

MARULLUS. But what trade art thou? Answer me directly.

SECOND COMMONER. A trade, sir, that, I hope, I may use
with a safe conscience; which is, indeed, sir, a mender of
bad soles.

MARULLUS. What trade, thou knave? thou naughty knave,
what trade?

SECOND COMMONER. Nay, I beseech you, sir, be not out
with me: yet, if you be out, sir, I can mend you.

MARULLUS. What meanest thou by that? Mend me, thou
saucy fellow!

SECOND COMMONER. Why, sir, cobble you.

FLAVIUS. Thou art a cobbler, art thou?

SECOND COMMONER. Truly, sir, all that I live by is with the
awl: I meddle with no tradesman's matters, nor women's
matters, but with awl. I am, indeed, sir, a surgeon to
old shoes; when they are in great danger, I recover them.

As proper men as ever trod upon neat's leather have gone
upon my handiwork.

FLAVIUS. But wherefore art not in thy shop to-day?
Why dost thou lead these men about the streets?

SECOND COMMONER. Truly, sir, to wear out their shoes, to
get myself into more work. But, indeed, sir, we make
holiday to see Cæsar and to rejoice in his triumph.

MARULLUS. Wherefore rejoice? What conquest brings he
home?
What tributaries follow him to Rome
To grace in captive bonds his chariot wheels?
You blocks, you stones, you worse than senseless things!
O you hard hearts, you cruel men of Rome,
Knew you not Pompey? Many a time and oft
Have you climb'd up to walls and battlements,
To towers and windows, yea, to chimney-tops,
Your infants in your arms, and there have sat
The livelong day, with patient expectation,
To see great Pompey pass the streets of Rome:
And when you saw his chariot but appear,
Have you not made a universal shout,
That Tiber trembled underneath her banks,
To hear the replication of your sounds
Made in her concave shores?
And do you now put on your best attire?
And do you now cull out a holiday?
And do you now strew flowers in his way,
That comes in triumph over Pompey's blood?
Be gone!
Run to your houses, fall upon your knees,
Pray to the gods to intermit the plague
That needs must light on this ingratitude.

FLAVIUS. Go, go, good countrymen, and, for this fault
Assemble all the poor men of your sort;
Draw them to Tiber banks, and weep your tears
Into the channel, till the lowest stream
Do kiss the most exalted shores of all.

Exeunt all the Commoners

See whe'r their basest metal be not mov'd;
They vanish tongue-tied in their guiltiness.
Go you down that way towards the Capitol;
This way will I: Disrobe the images

If you do find them deck'd with ceremonies.
MARULLUS. May we do so?
    You know it is the feast of Lupercal.
FLAVIUS. It is no matter; let no images
    Be hung with Cæsar's trophies. I'll about,
    And drive away the vulgar from the streets:
    So do you too where you perceive them thick.
    These growing feathers pluck'd from Cæsar's wing
    Will make him fly an ordinary pitch,
    Who else would soar above the view of men
    And keep us all in servile fearfulness.   *Exeunt*

SCENE TWO

A Public Place.

*Enter, in procession, with music, Cæsar; Antony, for the
course; Calphurnia, Portia, Decius, Cicero, Brutus, Cassius,
and Casca; a great crowd following, among them a
Soothsayer*

CÆSAR. Calphurnia!
CASCA. Peace, ho! Cæsar speaks.   *Music ceases*
CÆSAR.   Calphurnia!
CALPHURNIA. Here, my lord.
CÆSAR. Stand you directly in Antonius' way
    When he doth run his course. Antonius!
ANTONY. Cæsar, my lord.
CÆSAR. Forget not, in your speed, Antonius,
    To touch Calphurnia; for our elders say,
    The barren, touched in this holy chase,
    Shake off their sterile curse.
ANTONY.   I shall remember:
    When Cæsar says 'Do this,' it is perform'd.
CÆSAR. Set on; and leave no ceremony out.   *Music*
SOOTHSAYER. Cæsar!
CÆSAR. Ha! Who calls?
CASCA. Bid every noise be still: peace yet again!
                                        Music ceases
CÆSAR. Who is it in the press that calls on me?
    I hear a tongue, shriller than all the music,

Cry 'Cæsar.' Speak; Cæsar is turn'd to hear.

SOOTHSAYER. Beware the ides of March.

CÆSAR.   What man is that?

BRUTUS. A soothsayer bids you beware the ides of March.

CÆSAR. Set him before me; let me see his face.

CASSIUS. Fellow, come from the throng; look upon Cæsar.

CÆSAR. What sayst thou to me now? Speak once again.

SOOTHSAYER. Beware the ides of March.

CÆSAR. He is a dreamer; let us leave him: pass.

                    Sennet. Exeunt all but Brutus and Cassius

CASSIUS. Will you go see the order of the course?

BRUTUS. Not I.

CASSIUS. I pray you, do.

BRUTUS. I am not gamesome: I do lack some part
    Of that quick spirit that is in Anthony.
    Let me not hinder, Cassius, your desires;
    I 'll leave you.

CASSIUS. Brutus, I do observe you now of late:
    I have not from your eyes that gentleness
    And show of love as I was wont to have:
    You bear too stubborn and too strange a hand
    Over your friend that loves you.

BRUTUS.   Cassius,
    Be not deceiv'd: if I have veil'd my look,
    I turn the trouble of my countenance
    Merely upon myself. Vexed I am
    Of late with passions of some difference,
    Conceptions only proper to myself,
    Which give some soil perhaps to my behaviours;
    But let not therefore my good friends be griev'd,—
    Among which number, Cassius, be you one,—
    Nor construe any further my neglect,
    Than that poor Brutus, with himself at war,
    Forgets the shows of love to other men.

CASSIUS. Then, Brutus, I have much mistook your passion;
    By means whereof this breast of mine hath buried
    Thoughts of great value, worthy cogitations.
    Tell me, good Brutus, can you see your face?

BRUTUS. No, Cassius; for the eye sees not itself,
    But by reflection, by some other things.

CASSIUS. 'Tis just:
    And it is very much lamented, Brutus,

That you have no such mirrors as will turn
Your hidden worthiness into your eye,
That you might see your shadow. I have heard,
Where many of the best respect in Rome,—
Except immortal Cæsar,—speaking of Brutus,
And groaning underneath this age's yoke,
Have wish'd that noble Brutus had his eyes.

BRUTUS. Into what dangers would you lead me, Cassius,
That you would have me seek into myself
For that which is not in me?

CASSIUS. Therefore, good Brutus, be prepar'd to hear;
And, since you know you cannot see yourself
So well as by reflection, I, your glass,
Will modestly discover to yourself
That of yourself which you yet know not of.
And be not jealous on me, gentle Brutus:
Were I a common laugher, or did use
To stale with ordinary oaths my love
To every new protester; if you know
That I do fawn on men and hug them hard,
And after scandal them; or if you know
That I profess myself in banqueting
To all the rout, then hold me dangerous.

Flourish and shout

BRUTUS. What means this shouting? I do fear, the people
Choose Cæsar for their king.

CASSIUS.   Ay, do you fear it?
Then must I think you would not have it so.

BRUTUS. I would not, Cassius; yet I love him well.
But wherefore do you hold me here so long?
What is it that you would impart to me?
If it be aught toward the general good,
Set honour in one eye and death i' the other,
And I will look on both indifferently;
For let the gods so speed me as I love
The name of honour more than I fear death.

CASSIUS. I know that virtue to be in you, Brutus,
As well as I do know your outward favour.
Well, honour is the subject of my story.
I cannot tell what you and other men
Think of this life; but, for my single self,
I had as lief not be as live to be

In awe of such a thing as I myself.
I was born free as Cæsar; so were you:
We both have fed as well, and we can both
Endure the winter's cold as well as he:
For once, upon a raw and gusty day,
The troubled Tiber chafing with her shores,
Cæsar said to me, 'dar'st thou, Cassius, now
Leap in with me into this angry flood,
And swim to yonder point?' Upon the word,
Accoutred as I was, I plunged in
And bade him follow; so indeed he did.
The torrent roar'd, and we did buffet it
With lusty sinews, throwing it aside
And stemming it with hearts of controversy;
But ere we could arrive the point propos'd,
Cæsar cried, 'Help me, Cassius, or I sink!'
I, as Æneas, our great ancestor,
Did from the flames of Troy upon his shoulder
The old Anchises bear, so from the waves of Tiber
Did I the tired Cæsar. And this man
Is now become a god, and Cassius is
A wretched creature and must bend his body
If Cæsar carelessly but nod on him.
He had a fever when he was in Spain,
And when the fit was on him, I did mark
How he did shake; 'tis true, this god did shake;
His coward lips did from their colour fly,
And that same eye whose bend doth awe the world
Did lose his lustre; I did hear him groan;
Ay, and that tongue of his that bade the Romans
Mark him and write his speeches in their books,
Alas! it cried, 'Give me some drink, Titinius,'
As a sick girl. Ye gods, it doth amaze me,
A man of such a feeble temper should
So get the start of the majestic world,
And bear the palm alone.   *Flourish. Shout*
BRUTUS.   Another general shout!
I do believe that these applauses are
For some new honours that are heaped on Cæsar.
CASSIUS. Why, man, he doth bestride the narrow world
Like a Colossus; and we petty men
Walk under his huge legs, and peep about

To find ourselves dishonourable graves.
Men at some time are masters of their fates:
The fault, dear Brutus, is not in our stars,
But in ourselves, that we are underlings.
Brutus and Cæsar: what should be in that 'Cæsar'?
Why should that name be sounded more than yours?
Write them together, yours is as fair a name;
Sound them, it doth become the mouth as well;
Weigh them, it is as heavy; conjure with 'em,
'Brutus' will start a spirit as soon as 'Cæsar.'
Now, in the names of all the gods at once,
Upon what meat doth this our Cæsar feed,
That he is grown so great? Age, thou art sham'd!
Rome, thou hast lost the breed of noble bloods!
When went there by an age, since the great flood,
But it was fam'd with more than with one man?
When could they say, till now, that talk'd of Rome,
That her wide walls encompass'd but one man?
Now is it Rome indeed and room enough,
When there is in it but one only man.
O! you and I have heard our fathers say,
There was a Brutus once that would have brook'd
The eternal devil to keep his state in Rome
As easily as a king.
BRUTUS. That you do love me, I am nothing jealous;
What you would work me to, I have some aim:
How I have thought of this and of these times,
I shall recount hereafter; for this present,
I would not, so with love I might entreat you,
Be any further mov'd. What you have said
I will consider; what you have to say
I will with patience hear, and find a time
Both meet to hear and answer such high things.
Till then, my noble friend, chew upon this:
Brutus had rather be a villager
Than to repute himself a son of Rome
Under these hard conditions as this time
Is like to lay upon us.
CASSIUS.   I am glad
That my weak words have struck but thus much show
Of fire from Brutus.
BRUTUS. The games are done and Cæsar is returning.

CASSIUS. As they pass by, pluck Casca by the sleeve,
  And he will, after his sour fashion, tell you
  What hath proceeded worthy note to-day.
            Re-enter Cæsar and his Train
BRUTUS. I will do so. But, look you, Cassius,
  The angry spot doth glow on Cæsar's brow,
  And all the rest look like a chidden train:
  Calphurnia's cheek is pale, and Cicero
  Looks with such ferret and such fiery eyes
  As we have seen him in the Capitol,
  Being cross'd in conference by some senators.
CASSIUS. Casca will tell us what the matter is.
CÆSAR. Antonius!
ANTONY. Cæsar?
CÆSAR. Let me have men about me that are fat;
  Sleek-headed men and such as sleep o' nights.
  Yond Cassius has a lean and hungry look;
  He thinks too much: such men are dangerous.
ANTONY. Fear him not, Cæsar, he 's not dangerous;
  He is a noble Roman, and well given.
CÆSAR. Would he were fatter! but I fear him not:
  Yet if my name were liable to fear,
  I do not know the man I should avoid
  So soon as that spare Cassius. He reads much;
  He is a great observer, and he looks
  Quite through the deeds of men; he loves no plays,
  As thou dost, Antony; he hears no music;
  Seldom he smiles, and smiles in such a sort
  As if he mock'd himself, and scorn'd his spirit
  That could be mov'd to smile at any thing.
  Such men as he be never at heart's ease
  Whiles they behold a greater than themselves,
  And therefore are they very dangerous.
  I rather tell thee what is to be fear'd
  Than what I fear, for always I am Cæsar.
  Come on my right hand, for this ear is deaf,
  And tell me truly what thou think'st of him.
              Sennet. Exeunt Cæsar
            and his Train. Casca stays behind
CASCA. You pull'd me by the cloak; would you speak with
    me?
BRUTUS. Ay, Casca; tell us what hath chanc'd to-day,

That Cæsar looks so sad.

CASCA. Why, you were with him, were you not?

BRUTUS. I should not then ask Casca what had chanc'd.

CASCA. Why, there was a crown offered him; and, being offered him, he put it by with the back of his hand, thus; and then the people fell a-shouting.

BRUTUS. What was the second noise for?

CASCA. Why, for that too.

CASSIUS. They shouted thrice: what was the last cry for?

CASCA. Why, for that too.

BRUTUS. Was the crown offered him thrice?

CASCA. Ay, marry, was 't, and he put it by thrice, every time gentler than other; and at every putting-by mine honest neighbours shouted.

CASSIUS. Who offered him the crown?

CASCA. Why, Antony.

BRUTUS. Tell us the manner of it, gentle Casca.

CASCA. I can as well be hanged as tell the manner of it: it was mere foolery; I did not mark it. I saw Mark Antony offer him a crown; yet 'twas not a crown neither, 'twas one of these coronets; and, as I told you, he put it by once; but, for all that, to my thinking, he would fain have had it. Then he offered it to him again; then he put it by again; but, to my thinking, he was very loath to lay his fingers off it. And then he offered it the third time; he put it the third time by; and still as he refused it the rabblement shouted and clapped their chopped hands, and threw up their sweaty night-caps, and uttered such a deal of stinking breath because Cæsar refused the crown, that it had almost choked Cæsar; for he swounded and fell down at it: and for mine own part, I durst not laugh, for fear of opening my lips and receiving the bad air.

CASSIUS. But soft, I pray you: what! did Cæsar swound?

CASCA. He fell down in the market-place, and foamed at mouth, and was speechless.

BRUTUS. 'Tis very like: he hath the falling-sickness.

CASSIUS. No, Cæsar hath it not; but you, and I,
And honest Casca, we have the falling-sickness.

CASCA. I know not what you mean by that; but I am sure Cæsar fell down. If the tag-rag people did not clap him and hiss him, according as he pleased and displeased

them, as they use to do the players in the theatre, I am
no true man.

BRUTUS. What said he, when he came unto himself?

CASCA. Marry, before he fell down, when he perceiv'd the
common herd was glad he refused the crown, he plucked
me ope his doublet and offered them his throat to cut.
An I had been a man of any occupation, if I would not
have taken him at a word, I would I might go to hell
among the rogues. And so he fell. When he came to himself again, he said, if he had done or said any thing
amiss, he desired their worships to think it was his infirmity. Three or four wenches, where I stood, cried,
'Alas! good soul,' and forgave him with all their hearts:
but there 's no heed to be taken of them; if Cæsar had
stabbed their mothers, they would have done no less.

BRUTUS. And after that, he came, thus sad, away?

CASCA. Ay.

CASSIUS. Did Cicero say any thing?

CASCA. Ay, he spoke Greek.

CASSIUS. To what effect?

CASCA. Nay, an I tell you that, I 'll ne'er look you i' the face
again; but those that understood him smiled at one another and shook their heads; but, for mine own part, it
was Greek to me. I could tell you more news too; Marullus and Flavius, for pulling scarfs off Cæsar's images, are
put to silence. Fare you well. There was more foolery
yet, if I could remember it.

CASSIUS. Will you sup with me to-night, Casca?

CASCA. No, I am promised forth.

CASSIUS. Will you dine with me to-morrow?

CASCA. Ay, if I be alive, and your mind hold, and your
dinner worth the eating.

CASSIUS. Good; I will expect you.

CASCA. Do so. Farewell, both.   *Exit*

BRUTUS. What a blunt fellow is this grown to be!
He was quick mettle when he went to school.

CASSIUS. So is he now in execution
Of any bold or noble enterprise,
However he puts on this tardy form.
This rudeness is a sauce to his good wit,
Which gives men stomach to digest his words
With better appetite.

CASSIUS.   Men at some time are masters of their fates:
    The fault, dear Brutus, is not in our stars,
    But in ourselves, that we are underlings.

BRUTUS. And so it is. For this time I will leave you:
  To-morrow, if you please to speak with me,
  I will come home to you; or, if you will,
  Come home to me, and I will wait for you.
CASSIUS. I will do so: till then, think of the world.

                                Exit Brutus

  Well, Brutus, thou art noble; yet, I see,
  Thy honourable metal may be wrought
  From that it is dispos'd: therefore 'tis meet
  That noble minds keep ever with their likes;
  For who so firm that cannot be seduc'd?
  Cæsar doth bear me hard; but he loves Brutus:
  If I were Brutus now and he were Cassius
  He should not humour me. I will this night,
  In several hands, in at his windows throw,
  As if they came from several citizens,
  Writings all tending to the great opinion
  That Rome holds of his name; wherein obscurely
  Cæsar's ambition shall be glanced at:
  And after this let Cæsar seat him sure;
  For we will shake him, or worse days endure.   *Exit*

SCENE THREE

A Street.

Thunder and lightning. Enter, from opposite sides,
Casca, with his sword drawn, and Cicero

CICERO. Good even, Casca: brought you Cæsar home?
  Why are you breathless? and why stare you so?
CASCA. Are not you mov'd, when all the sway of earth
  Shakes like a thing unfirm? O Cicero!
  I have seen tempests, when the scolding winds
  Have riv'd the knotty oaks; and I have seen
  The ambitious ocean swell and rage and foam,
  To be exalted with the threatening clouds:
  But never till to-night, never till now,
  Did I go through a tempest dropping fire.
  Either there is a civil strife in heaven,
  Or else the world, too saucy with the gods,
  Incenses them to send destruction.

CICERO. Why, saw you any thing more wonderful?

CASCA. A common slave—you know him well by sight—
Held up his left hand, which did flame and burn
Like twenty torches join'd; and yet his hand,
Not sensible of fire, remain'd unscorch'd.
Besides,—I have not since put up my sword,—
Against the Capitol I met a lion,
Who glar'd upon me, and went surly by,
Without annoying me; and there were drawn
Upon a heap a hundred ghastly women,
Transformed with their fear, who swore they saw
Men all in fire walk up and down the streets.
And yesterday the bird of night did sit,
Even at noon-day, upon the market-place,
Hooting and shrieking. When these prodigies
Do so conjointly meet, let not men say
'These are their reasons, they are natural';
For, I believe, they are portentous things
Unto the climate that they point upon.

CICERO. Indeed, it is a strange-disposed time:
But men may construe things after their fashion,
Clean from the purpose of the things themselves.
Comes Cæsar to the Capitol to-morrow?

CASCA. He doth; for he did bid Antonius
Send word to you he would be there to-morrow.

CICERO. Good-night then, Casca: this disturbed sky
Is not to walk in.

CASCA.   Farewell, Cicero.   *Exit Cicero*

Enter Cassius

CASSIUS. Who's there?

CASCA.   A Roman.

CASSIUS.   Casca, by your voice.

CASCA. Your ear is good. Cassius, what night is this!

CASSIUS. A very pleasing night to honest men.

CASCA. Who ever knew the heavens menace so?

CASSIUS. Those that have known the earth so full of faults.
For my part, I have walk'd about the streets,
Submitting me unto the perilous night,
And, thus unbraced, Casca, as you see,
Have bar'd my bosom to the thunder-stone;
And, when the cross blue lightning seem'd to open
The breast of heaven, I did present myself

Even in the aim and very flash of it.

CASCA. But wherefore did you so much tempt the heavens?
It is the part of men to fear and tremble
When the most mighty gods by tokens send
Such dreadful heralds to astonish us.

CASSIUS. You are dull, Casca, and those sparks of life
That should be in a Roman you do want,
Or else you use not. You look pale, and gaze,
And put on fear, and cast yourself in wonder,
To see the strange impatience of the heavens;
But if you would consider the true cause
Why all these fires, why all these gliding ghosts,
Why birds and beasts, from quality and kind;
Why old men, fools, and children calculate;
Why all these things change from their ordinance,
Their natures, and pre-formed faculties,
To monstrous quality, why, you shall find
That heaven hath infus'd them with these spirits
To make them instruments of fear and warning
Unto some monstrous state.
Now could I, Casca, name to thee a man
Most like this dreadful night,
That thunders, lightens, opens graves, and roars
As doth the lion in the Capitol,
A man no mightier than thyself or me
In personal action, yet prodigious grown
And fearful as these strange eruptions are.

CASCA. 'Tis Cæsar that you mean; is it not, Cassius?

CASSIUS. Let it be who it is; for Romans now
Have thews and limbs like to their ancestors;
But, woe the while! our fathers' minds are dead,
And we are govern'd with our mothers' spirits;
Our yoke and sufferance show us womanish.

CASCA. Indeed, they say the senators to-morrow
Mean to establish Cæsar as a king;
And he shall wear his crown by sea and land,
In every place, save here in Italy.

CASSIUS. I know where I will wear this dagger then;
Cassius from bondage will deliver Cassius:
Therein, ye gods, you make the weak most strong;
Therein, ye gods, you tyrants do defeat:
Nor stony tower, nor walls of beaten brass,

Nor airless dungeon, nor strong links of iron,
Can be retentive to the strength of spirit;
But life, being weary of those worldly bars,
Never lacks power to dismiss itself.
If I know this, know all the world besides,
That part of tyranny that I do bear
I can shake off at pleasure.   *Thunder still*

CASCA.   So can I:
So every bondman in his own hand bears
The power to cancel his captivity.

CASSIUS. And why should Cæsar be a tyrant then?
Poor man! I know he would not be a wolf
But that he sees the Romans are but sheep;
He were no lion were not Romans hinds.
Those that with haste will make a mighty fire
Begin it with weak straws; what trash is Rome,
What rubbish, and what offal, when it serves
For the base matter to illuminate
So vile a thing as Cæsar! But, O grief!
Where hast thou led me? I, perhaps, speak this
Before a willing bondman; then I know,
My answer must be made: but I am arm'd,
And dangers are to me indifferent.

CASCA. You speak to Casca, and to such a man
That is no fleering tell-tale. Hold, my hand:
Be factious for redress of all these griefs,
And I will set this foot of mine as far
As who goes farthest.

CASSIUS.   There 's a bargain made.
Now know you, Casca, I have mov'd already
Some certain of the noblest-minded Romans
To undergo with me an enterprise
Of honourable-dangerous consequence;
And I do know by this they stay for me
In Pompey's porch: for now, this fearful night,
There is no stir, or walking in the streets;
And the complexion of the element
In favour 's like the work we have in hand,
Most bloody, fiery, and most terrible.

CASCA. Stand close awhile, for here comes one in haste.

CASSIUS. 'Tis Cinna; I do know him by his gait:
He is a friend

Enter Cinna

Cinna, where haste you so?

CINNA. To find out you. Who 's that? Metellus Cimber?

CASSIUS. No, it is Casca; one incorporate
To our attempts. Am I not stay'd for, Cinna?

CINNA. I am glad on 't. What a fearful night is this!
There 's two or three of us have seen strange sights.

CASSIUS. Am I not stay'd for? Tell mè.

CINNA.   Yes, you are.
O Cassius! if you could
But win the noble Brutus to our party—

CASSIUS. Be you content. Good Cinna, take this paper,
And look you lay it in the prætor's chair,
Where Brutus may but find it; and throw this
In at his window; set this up with wax
Upon old Brutus' statue: all this done,
Repair to Pompey's porch, where you shall find us.
Is Decius Brutus and Trebonius there?

CINNA. All but Metellus Cimber; and he 's gone
To seek you at your house. Well, I will hie,
And so bestow these papers as you bade me.

CASSIUS. That done, repair to Pompey's theatre.

                                        Exit Cinna

Come, Casca, you and I will yet ere day
See Brutus at his house: three parts of him
Is ours already, and the man entire
Upon the next encounter yields him ours.

CASCA. O! he sits high in all the people's hearts:
And that which would appear offence in us,
His countenance, like richest alchemy,
Will change to virtue and to worthiness.

CASSIUS. Him and his worth and our great need of him
You have right well conceited. Let us go,
For it is after midnight; and ere day
We will awake him and be sure of him.   *Exeunt*

ACT TWO

SCENE ONE

Rome. Brutus' Orchard.

Enter Brutus

BRUTUS. What, Lucius! ho!
I cannot, by the progress of the stars,
Give guess how near to day. Lucius, I say!
I would it were my fault to sleep so soundly.
When, Lucius, when! Awake, I say! what, Lucius!
Enter Lucius
LUCIUS. Call'd you, my lord?
BRUTUS. Get me a taper in my study, Lucius:
When it is lighted, come and call me here.
LUCIUS. I will, my lord. *Exit*
BRUTUS. It must be by his death: and, for my part,
I know no personal cause to spurn at him,
But for the general. He would be crown'd:
How that might change his nature, there 's the question:
It is the bright day that brings forth the adder;
And that craves wary walking. Crown him—that!
And then, I grant, we put a sting in him.
That at his will he may do danger with.
The abuse of greatness is when it disjoins
Remorse from power; and, to speak truth of Cæsar,
I have not known when his affections sway'd
More than his reason. But 'tis a common proof,
That lowliness is young ambition's ladder,
Whereto the climber-upward turns his face;
But when he once attains the upmost round,
He then unto the ladder turns his back,
Looks in the clouds, scorning the base degrees
By which he did ascend. So Cæsar may:
Then, lest he may, prevent. And, since the quarrel

Will bear no colour for the thing he is,
Fashion it thus; that what he is, augmented,
Would run to these and these extremities;
And therefore think him as a serpent's egg
Which, hatch'd, would, as his kind, grow mischievous,
And kill him in the shell.

Re-enter Lucius

LUCIUS. The taper burneth in your closet, sir.
Searching the window for a flint, I found
This paper, thus seal'd up: and I am sure
It did not lie there when I went to bed.
BRUTUS. Get you to bed again; it is not day.
Is not to-morrow, boy, the ides of March?
LUCIUS. I know not, sir.
BRUTUS. Look in the calendar, and bring me word.
LUCIUS. I will, sir.   *Exit*
BRUTUS. The exhalations whizzing in the air
Give so much light that I may read by them.

Opens the letter

'Brutus, thou sleep'st: awake and see thyself.
Shall Rome, &c. Speak, strike, redress!
Brutus, thou sleep'st: awake!'
Such instigations have been often dropp'd
Where I have took them up.
'Shall Rome, &c.' Thus must I piece it out:
Shall Rome stand under one man's awe? What, Rome?
My ancestors did from the streets of Rome
The Tarquin drive, when he was call'd a king.
'Speak, strike, redress!' Am I entreated
To speak, and strike? O Rome! I make thee promise;
If the redress will follow, thou receiv'st
Thy full petition at the hand of Brutus!

Re-enter Lucius

LUCIUS. Sir, March is wasted fourteen days.

Knocking within

BRUTUS. 'Tis good. Go to the gate: somebody knocks.

Exit Lucius

Since Cassius first did whet me against Cæsar,
I have not slept.
Between the acting of a dreadful thing
And the first motion, all the interim is
Like a phantasma, or a hideous dream:

The genius and the mortal instruments
Are then in council; and the state of man,
Like to a little kingdom, suffers then
The nature of an insurrection.

Re-enter Lucius

LUCIUS. Sir, 'tis your brother Cassius at the door,
Who doth desire to see you.

BRUTUS. Is he alone?

LUCIUS. No, sir, there are more with him.

BRUTUS. Do you know them?

LUCIUS. No, sir; their hats are pluck'd about their ears,
And half their faces buried in their cloaks,
That by no means I may discover them
By any mark of favour.

BRUTUS. Let 'em enter. *Exit Lucius*
They are the faction. O conspiracy!
Sham'st thou to show thy dangerous brow by night,
When evils are most free? O! then by day
Where wilt thou find a cavern dark enough
To mask thy monstrous visage? Seek none, conspiracy;
Hide it in smiles and affability:
For if thou path, thy native semblance on,
Not Erebus itself were dim enough
To hide thee from prevention.

*Enter the Conspirators, Cassius, Casca, Decius, Cinna,
Metellus Cimber, and Trebonius*

CASSIUS. I think we are too bold upon your rest:
Good-morrow, Brutus; do we trouble you?

BRUTUS. I have been up this hour, awake all night.
Know I these men that come along with you?

CASSIUS. Yes, every man of them; and no man here
But honours you; and every one doth wish
You had but that opinion of yourself
Which every noble Roman bears of you.
This is Trebonius.

BRUTUS. He is welcome hither.

CASSIUS. This, Decius Brutus.

BRUTUS. He is welcome too.

CASSIUS. This, Casca; this, Cinna;
And this, Metellus Cimber.

BRUTUS. They are all welcome.
What watchful cares do interpose themselves

Betwixt your eyes and night?

CASSIUS. Shall I entreat a word?

Brutus and Cassius whisper

DECIUS. Here lies the east: doth not the day break here?

CASCA. No.

CINNA. O! pardon, sir, it doth; and yon grey lines
That fret the clouds are messengers of day.

CASCA. You shall confess that you are both deceiv'd.
Here, as I point my sword, the sun arises;
Which is a great way growing on the south,
Weighing the youthful season of the year.
Some two months hence up higher toward the north
He first presents his fire; and the high east
Stands, as the Capitol, directly here.

BRUTUS. Give me your hands all over, one by one.

CASSIUS. And let us swear our resolution.

BRUTUS. No, not an oath: if not the face of men,
The sufferance of our souls, the time's abuse,—
If these be motives weak, break off betimes,
And every man hence to his idle bed;
So let high-sighted tyranny range on,
Till each man drop by lottery. But if these,
As I am sure they do, bear fire enough
To kindle cowards and to steel with valour
The melting spirits of women, then, countrymen,
What need we any spur but our own cause
To prick us to redress? what other bond
Than secret Romans, that have spoke the word
And will not palter? and what other oath
Than honesty to honesty engag'd,
That this shall be, or we will fall for it?
Swear priests and cowards and men cautelous,
Old feeble carrions and such suffering souls
That welcome wrongs; unto bad causes swear
Such creatures as men doubt; but do not stain
The even virtue of our enterprise,
Nor the insuppressive mettle of our spirits,
To think that or our cause or our performance
Did need an oath; when every drop of blood
That every Roman bears, and nobly bears,
Is guilty of a several bastardy,
If he do break the smallest particle

Of any promise that hath pass'd from him.

CASSIUS. But what of Cicero? Shall we sound him?
I think he will stand very strong with us.

CASCA. Let us not leave him out.

CINNA.   No, by no means.

METELLUS. O! let us have him; for his silver hairs
Will purchase us a good opinion
And buy men's voices to commend our deeds:
It shall be said his judgment rul'd our hands;
Our youths and wildness shall no whit appear,
But all be buried in his gravity.

BRUTUS. O! name him not: let us not break with him;
For he will never follow any thing
That other men begin.

CASSIUS.   Then leave him out.

CASCA. Indeed he is not fit.

DECIUS. Shall no man else be touch'd but only Cæsar?

CASSIUS. Decius, well urg'd. I think it is not meet,
Mark Antony, so well belov'd of Cæsar,
Should outlive Cæsar: we shall find of him
A shrewd contriver; and, you know, his means,
If he improve them, may well stretch so far
As to annoy us all; which to prevent,
Let Antony and Cæsar fall together.

BRUTUS. Our course will seem too bloody, Caius Cassius,
To cut the head off and then hack the limbs,
Like wrath in death and envy afterwards;
For Antony is but a limb of Cæsar;
Let us be sacrificers, but not butchers, Caius.
We all stand up against the spirit of Cæsar;
And in the spirit of men there is no blood:
O! that we then could come by Cæsar's spirit,
And not dismember Cæsar. But, alas!
Cæsar must bleed for it. And, gentle friends,
Let 's kill him boldly, but not wrathfully;
Let 's carve him as a dish fit for the gods,
Not hew him as a carcass fit for hounds:
And let our hearts, as subtle masters do,
Stir up their servants to an act of rage,
And after seem to chide 'em. This shall make
Our purpose necessary and not envious;
Which so appearing to the common eyes,

We shall be call'd purgers, not murderers.
And, for Mark Antony, think not of him;
For he can do no more than Cæsar's arm
When Cæsar's head is off.

CASSIUS.   Yet I fear him;
For in the engrafted love he bears to Cæsar—

BRUTUS. Alas! good Cassius, do not think of him:
If he love Cæsar, all that he can do
Is to himself, take thought and die for Cæsar:
And that were much he should; for he is given
To sports, to wildness, and much company.

TREBONIUS. There is no fear in him; let him not die:
For he will live, and laugh at this hereafter.

BRUTUS. Peace! count the clock.   *Clock strikes*

CASSIUS.   The clock hath stricken three.

TREBONIUS. 'Tis time to part.

CASSIUS.   But it is doubtful yet
Whether Cæsar will come forth to-day or no;
For he is superstitious grown of late,
Quite from the main opinion he held once
Of fantasy, of dreams, and ceremonies.
It may be, these apparent prodigies,
The unaccustom'd terror of this night,
And the persuasion of his augurers,
May hold him from the Capitol to-day.

DECIUS. Never fear that: if he be so resolv'd,
I can o'ersway him; for he loves to hear
That unicorns may be betray'd with trees,
And bears with glasses, elephants with holes,
Lions with toils, and men with flatterers;
But when I tell him he hates flatterers,
He says he does, being then most flattered.
Let me work;
For I can give his humour the true bent,
And I will bring him to the Capitol.

CASSIUS. Nay, we will all of us be there to fetch him.

BRUTUS. By the eighth hour: is that the uttermost?

CINNA. Be that the uttermost, and fail not then.

METELLUS. Caius Ligarius doth bear Cæsar hard,
Who rated him for speaking well of Pompey:
I wonder none of you have thought of him.

BRUTUS. Now, good Metellus, go along by him:

He loves me well, and I have given him reasons;
Send him but hither, and I 'll fashion him.

CASSIUS. The morning comes upon 's: we 'll leave you,
    Brutus.
And, friends, disperse yourselves; but all remember
What you have said, and show yourselves true Romans.

BRUTUS. Good gentlemen, look fresh and merrily;
    Let not our looks put on our purposes,
    But bear it as our Roman actors do,
    With untir'd spirits and formal constancy:
    And so good-morrow to you every one.

                              Exeunt all except Brutus

Boy! Lucius! Fast asleep? It is no matter;
Enjoy the honey-heavy dew of slumber:
Thou hast no figures nor no fantasies,
Which busy care draws in the brains of men;
Therefore thou sleep'st so sound.

                    Enter Portia

PORTIA.   Brutus, my lord!

BRUTUS. Portia, what mean you? Wherefore rise you now?
    It is not for your health thus to commit
    Your weak condition to the raw cold morning.

PORTIA. Nor for yours neither. You 've ungently, Brutus,
    Stole from my bed; and yesternight at supper
    You suddenly arose, and walk'd about,
    Musing and sighing, with your arms across,
    And when I ask'd you what the matter was,
    You star'd upon me with ungentle looks.
    I urg'd you further; then you scratch'd your head,
    And too impatiently stamp'd with your foot;
    Yet I insisted, yet you answer'd not,
    But, with an angry wafture of your hand,
    Gave sign for me to leave you. So I did,
    Fearing to strengthen that impatience
    Which seem'd too much enkindled, and withal
    Hoping it was but an effect of humour,
    Which sometime hath his hour with every man.
    It will not let you eat, nor talk, nor sleep,
    And could it work so much upon your shape
    As it hath much prevail'd on your condition,
    I should not know you, Brutus. Dear my lord,
    Make me acquainted with your cause of grief.

BRUTUS. I am not well in health, and that is all.
PORTIA. Brutus is wise, and were he not in health,
  He would embrace the means to come by it.
BRUTUS. Why, so I do. Good Portia, go to bed.
PORTIA. Is Brutus sick, and is it physical
  To walk unbraced and suck up the humours
  Of the dank morning? What! is Brutus sick,
  And will he steal out of his wholesome bed
  To dare the vile contagion of the night,
  And tempt the rheumy and unpurged air
  To add unto his sickness? No, my Brutus;
  You have some sick offence within your mind,
  Which, by the right and virtue of my place,
  I ought to know of; and, upon my knees,
  I charm you, by my once-commended beauty,
  By all your vows of love, and that great vow
  Which did incorporate and make us one,
  That you unfold to me, your self, your half,
  Why are you heavy, and what men to-night
  Have had resort to you; for here have been
  Some six or seven, who did hide their faces
  Even from darkness.
BRUTUS.   Kneel not, gentle Portia.
PORTIA. I should not need, if you were gentle Brutus.
  Within the bond of marriage, tell me, Brutus,
  Is it excepted, I should know no secrets
  That appertain to you? Am I yourself
  But, as it were, in sort or limitation,
  To keep with you at meals, comfort your bed,
  And talk to you sometimes? Dwell I but in the suburbs
  Of your good pleasure? If it be no more,
  Portia is Brutus' harlot, not his wife.
BRUTUS. You are my true and honourable wife,
  As dear to me as are the ruddy drops
  That visit my sad heart.
PORTIA. If this were true, then should I know this secret.
  I grant I am a woman, but, withal,
  A woman that Lord Brutus took to wife;
  I grant I am a woman, but, withal,
  A woman well-reputed, Cato's daughter.
  Think you I am no stronger than my sex,
  Being so father'd and so husbanded?

Tell me your counsels, I will not disclose 'em.
I have made strong proof of my constancy,
Giving myself a voluntary wound
Here, in the thigh: can I bear that with patience
And not my husband's secrets?

BRUTUS.　　　　　　　　　　　O ye gods!
Render me worthy of this noble wife.　*Knocking within*
Hark, hark! one knocks. Portia, go in awhile;
And by and by thy bosom shall partake
The secrets of my heart.
All my engagements I will construe to thee,
All the charactery of my sad brows.
Leave me with haste.　　　　　　　*Exit Portia*
　　　　　　Lucius, who 's that knocks?
　　　　Re-enter Lucius with Ligarius

LUCIUS. Here is a sick man that would speak with you.

BRUTUS. Caius Ligarius, that Metellus spoke of.
Boy, stand aside. Caius Ligarius! how?

LIGARIUS. Vouchsafe good-morrow from a feeble tongue.

BRUTUS. O! what a time have you chose out, brave Caius,
To wear a kerchief. Would you were not sick.

LIGARIUS. I am not sick if Brutus have in hand
Any exploit worthy the name of honour.

BRUTUS. Such an exploit have I in hand, Ligarius,
Had you a healthful ear to hear of it.

LIGARIUS. By all the gods that Romans bow before
I here discard my sickness. Soul of Rome!
Brave son, deriv'd from honourable loins!
Thou, like an exorcist, hast conjur'd up
My mortified spirit. Now bid me run,
And I will strive with things impossible;
Yea, get the better of them. What 's to do?

BRUTUS. A piece of work that will make sick men whole.

LIGARIUS. But are not some whole that we must make sick?

BRUTUS. That must we also. What it is, my Caius,
I shall unfold to thee as we are going
To whom it must be done.

LIGARIUS.　　　　　　　　Set on your foot,
And with a heart new-fir'd I follow you,
To do I know not what; but it sufficeth
That Brutus leads me on.

BRUTUS.　　　　　　　Follow me then.　　*Exeunt*

SCENE TWO

Cæsar's House.

Thunder and lightning. Enter Cæsar, in his night-gown

CÆSAR. Nor heaven nor earth have been at peace to-night:
  Thrice hath Calphurnia in her sleep cried out,
  'Help, ho! They murder Cæsar!' Who's within?

Enter a Servant

SERVANT. My lord!

CÆSAR. Go bid the priests do present sacrifice,
  And bring me their opinions of success.

SERVANT. I will, my lord.   *Exit*

Enter Calphurnia

CALPHURNIA. What mean you, Cæsar? Think you to walk
    forth?
  You shall not stir out of your house to-day.

CÆSAR. Cæsar shall forth: the things that threaten'd me
  Ne'er look'd but on my back; when they shall see
  The face of Cæsar, they are vanished.

CALPHURNIA. Cæsar, I never stood on ceremonies,
  Yet now they fright me. There is one within,
  Besides the things that we have heard and seen,
  Recounts most horrid sights seen by the watch.
  A lioness hath whelped in the streets;
  And graves have yawn'd, and yielded up their dead;
  Fierce fiery warriors fought upon the clouds,
  In ranks and squadrons and right form of war,
  Which drizzled blood upon the Capitol;
  The noise of battle hurtled in the air,
  Horses did neigh, and dying men did groan,
  And ghosts did shriek and squeal about the streets.
  O Cæsar! these things are beyond all use,
  And I do fear them.

CÆSAR.   What can be avoided
  Whose end is purpos'd by the mighty gods?
  Yet Cæsar shall go forth; for these predictions
  Are to the world in general as to Cæsar.

CALPHURNIA. When beggars die there are no comets seen;
  The heavens themselves blaze forth the death of princes.

CÆSAR. Cowards die many times before their deaths:

The valiant never taste of death but once.
Of all the wonders that I yet have heard,
It seems to me most strange that men should fear;
Seeing that death, a necessary end,
Will come when it will come.

Re-enter Servant

                    What say the augurers?

SERVANT. They would not have you to stir forth to-day.
Plucking the entrails of an offering forth,
They could not find a heart within the beast.

CÆSAR. The gods do this in shame of cowardice:
Cæsar should be a beast without a heart
If he should stay at home to-day for fear.
No, Cæsar shall not; danger knows full well
That Cæsar is more dangerous than he:
We are two lions litter'd in one day,
And I the elder and more terrible:
And Cæsar shall go forth.

CALPHURNIA.   Alas! my lord,
Your wisdom is consum'd in confidence.
Do not go forth to-day: call it my fear
That keeps you in the house, and not your own.
We 'll send Mark Antony to the senate-house,
And he shall say you are not well to-day:
Let me, upon my knee, prevail in this.

CÆSAR. Mark Antony shall say I am not well;
And, for thy humour, I will stay at home.

Enter Decius

Here 's Decius Brutus, he shall tell them so.

DECIUS. Cæsar, all hail! Good-morrow, worthy Cæsar:
I come to fetch you to the senate-house.

CÆSAR. And you are come in very happy time
To bear my greeting to the senators,
And tell them that I will not come to-day:
Cannot, is false, and that I dare not, falser;
I will not come to-day: tell them so, Decius.

CALPHURNIA. Say he is sick.

CÆSAR.   Shall Cæsar send a lie?
Have I in conquest stretch'd mine arm so far
To be afeard to tell greybeards the truth?
Decius, go tell them Cæsar will not come.

DECIUS. Most mighty Cæsar, let me know some cause,
  Lest I be laugh'd at when I tell them so.
CÆSAR. The cause is in my will: I will not come;
  That is enough to satisfy the senate:
  But for your private satisfaction,
  Because I love you, I will let you know:
  Calphurnia here, my wife, stays me at home:
  She dreamt to-night she saw my statua,
  Which, like a fountain with a hundred spouts,
  Did run pure blood; and many lusty Romans
  Came smiling, and did bathe their hands in it:
  And these does she apply for warnings and portents,
  And evils imminent; and on her knee
  Hath begg'd that I will stay at home to-day.
DECIUS. This dream is all amiss interpreted;
  It was a vision fair and fortunate:
  Your statue spouting blood in many pipes,
  In which so many smiling Romans bath'd,
  Signifies that from you great Rome shall suck
  Reviving blood, and that great men shall press
  For tinctures, stains, relics, and cognizance.
  This by Calphurnia's dream is signified.
CÆSAR. And this way have you well expounded it.
DECIUS. I have, when you have heard what I can say:
  And know it now: the senate have concluded
  To give this day a crown to mighty Cæsar.
  If you shall send them word you will not come,
  Their minds may change. Besides, it were a mock
  Apt to be render'd, for some one to say
  'Break up the senate till another time,
  When Cæsar's wife shall meet with better dreams.'
  If Cæsar hide himself, shall they not whisper
  'Lo! Cæsar is afraid'?
  Pardon me, Cæsar; for my dear dear love
  To your proceeding bids me tell you this,
  And reason to my love is liable.
CÆSAR. How foolish do your fears seem now, Calphurnia!
  I am ashamed I did yield to them.
  Give me my robe, for I will go:
    Enter Publius, Brutus, Ligarius, Metellus, Casca,
        Trebonius, and Cinna

And look where Publius is come to fetch me.

PUBLIUS. Good-morrow, Cæsar.

CÆSAR.   Welcome, Publius.
What! Brutus, are you stirr'd so early too?
Good-morrow, Casca. Caius Ligarius,
Cæsar was ne'er so much your enemy
As that same ague which hath made you lean.
What is 't o'clock?

BRUTUS.   Cæsar, 'tis strucken eight.

CÆSAR. I thank you for your pains and courtesy.

Enter Antony

See! Antony, that revels long o' nights,
Is notwithstanding up. Good-morrow, Antony.

ANTONY. So to most noble Cæsar.

CÆSAR.   Bid them prepare within:
I am to blame to be thus waited for.
Now, Cinna; now, Metellus; what, Trebonius!
I have an hour's talk in store for you;
Remember that you call on me to-day:
Be near me, that I may remember you.

TREBONIUS. Cæsar, I will:—(*Aside*) and so near will I be,
That your best friends shall wish I had been farther.

CÆSAR. Good friends, go in, and taste some wine with me;
And we, like friends, will straightway go together.

BRUTUS. (*Aside*) That every like is not the same, O Cæsar,
The heart of Brutus yearns to think upon.   *Exeunt*

SCENE THREE

A Street near the Capitol.

Enter Artemidorus, reading a paper

ARTEMIDORUS. 'Cæsar, beware of Brutus; take heed of Cassius; come not near Casca; have an eye to Cinna; trust not Trebonius; mark well Metellus Cimber; Decius Brutus loves thee not; thou hast wronged Caius Ligarius. There is but one mind in all these men, and it is bent against Cæsar. If thou be'st not immortal, look about you: security gives way to conspiracy. The mighty gods defend thee! Thy lover,
                    'Artemidorus.'

Here will I stand till Cæsar pass along,
And as a suitor will I give him this.
My heart laments that virtue cannot live
Out of the teeth of emulation.
If thou read this, O Cæsar! thou mayst live;
If not, the Fates with traitors do contrive.   *Exit*

SCENE FOUR

Another Part of the same Street, before the House of Brutus.

Enter Portia and Lucius

PORTIA. I prithee, boy, run to the senate-house;
Stay not to answer me, but get thee gone.
Why dost thou stay?
LUCIUS.   To know my errand, madam.
PORTIA. I would have had thee there, and here again,
Ere I can tell thee what thou shouldst do there.
O constancy! be strong upon my side;
Set a huge mountain 'tween my heart and tongue;
I have a man's mind, but a woman's might.
How hard it is for women to keep counsel!
Art thou here yet?
LUCIUS.   Madam, what shall I do?
Run to the Capitol, and nothing else?
And so return to you, and nothing else?
PORTIA. Yes, bring me word, boy, if thy lord look well,
For he went sickly forth; and take good note
What Cæsar doth, what suitors press to him.
Hark, boy! what noise is that?
LUCIUS. I hear none, madam.
PORTIA.   Prithee, listen well:
I heard a bustling rumour, like a fray,
And the wind brings it from the Capitol.
LUCIUS. Sooth, madam, I hear nothing.
                Enter the Soothsayer
PORTIA. Come hither, fellow: which way hast thou been?
SOOTHSAYER. At mine own house, good lady.
PORTIA. What is 't o'clock?
SOOTHSAYER.   About the ninth hour, lady.
PORTIA. Is Cæsar yet gone to the Capitol?

SOOTHSAYER. Madam, not yet: I go to take my stand,
　To see him pass on to the Capitol.
PORTIA. Thou hast some suit to Cæsar, hast thou not?
SOOTHSAYER. That I have, lady: if it will please Cæsar
　To be so good to Cæsar as to hear me,
　I shall beseech him to befriend himself.
PORTIA. Why, know'st thou any harm 's intended towards
　him?
SOOTHSAYER. None that I know will be, much that I fear
　may chance.
　Good-morrow to you. Here the street is narrow:
　The throng that follows Cæsar at the heels,
　Of senators, of prætors, common suitors,
　Will crowd a feeble man almost to death:
　I 'll get me to a place more void, and there
　Speak to great Cæsar as he comes along.　　　　*Exit*
PORTIA. I must go in. Ay me! how weak a thing
　The heart of woman is. O Brutus!
　The heavens speed thee in thine enterprise.
　Sure, the boy heard me: Brutus hath a suit
　That Cæsar will not grant. O! I grow faint.
　Run, Lucius, and commend me to my lord;
　Say I am merry: come to me again,
　And bring me word what he doth say to thee.
　　　　　　　　　　　　　　　　Exeunt, severally

ACT THREE

SCENE ONE

Rome. Before the Capitol; the Senate sitting above.

*A Crowd of People; among them Artemidorus and the
Soothsayer. Flourish. Enter Cæsar, Brutus, Cassius, Casca,
Decius, Metellus, Trebonius, Cinna, Antony,
Lepidus, Popilius, Publius, and Others*

CÆSAR. (*To the Soothsayer*) The ides of March are come.
SOOTHSAYER. Ay, Cæsar, but not gone.
ARTEMIDORUS. Hail, Cæsar! Read this schedule.
DECIUS. Trebonius doth desire you to o'er-read,
  At your best leisure, this his humble suit.
ARTEMIDORUS. O Cæsar! read mine first; for mine 's a suit
  That touches Cæsar nearer. Read it, great Cæsar.
CÆSAR. What touches us ourself shall be last serv'd.
ARTEMIDORUS. Delay not, Cæsar; read it instantly.
CÆSAR. What! is the fellow mad?
PUBLIUS.   Sirrah, give place.
CÆSAR. What! urge you your petitions in the street?
  Come to the Capitol.

               *Cæsar goes up to the Senate-
               House, the rest following. All the Senators rise*
POPILIUS. I wish your enterprise to-day may thrive.
CASSIUS. What enterprise, Popilius?
POPILIUS.   Fare you well.
                    Advances to Cæsar
BRUTUS. What said Popilius Lena?
CASSIUS. He wish'd to-day our enterprise might thrive.
  I fear our purpose is discovered.
BRUTUS. Look, how he makes to Cæsar: mark him.
CASSIUS. Casca, be sudden, for we fear prevention.
  Brutus, what shall be done? If this be known,
  Cassius or Cæsar never shall turn back,

For I will slay myself.

BRUTUS. Cassius, be constant:
Popilius Lena speaks not of our purposes;
For, look, he smiles, and Cæsar doth not change.

CASSIUS. Trebonius knows his time; for, look you, Brutus,
He draws Mark Antony out of the way.

> *Exeunt Antony and Trebonius.*
> *Cæsar and the Senators take their seats*

DECIUS. Where is Metellus Cimber? Let him go,
And presently prefer his suit to Cæsar.

BRUTUS. He is address'd; press near and second him.

CINNA. Casca, you are the first that rears your hand.

CASCA. Are we all ready? What is now amiss,
That Cæsar and his senate must redress?

METELLUS. Most high, most mighty, and most puissant
Cæsar,
Metellus Cimber throws before thy seat
A humble heart,— *Kneeling*

CÆSAR. I must prevent thee, Cimber.
These couchings and these lowly courtesies,
Might fire the blood of ordinary men,
And turn pre-ordinance and first decree
Into the law of children. Be not fond,
To think that Cæsar bears such rebel blood
That will be thaw'd from the true quality
With that which melteth fools; I mean sweet words,
Low-crooked curtsies, and base spaniel fawning.
Thy brother by decree is banished:
If thou dost bend and pray and fawn for him,
I spurn thee like a cur out of my way.
Know, Cæsar doth not wrong, nor without cause
Will he be satisfied.

METELLUS. Is there no voice more worthy than my own,
To sound more sweetly in great Cæsar's ear
For the repealing of my banish'd brother?

BRUTUS. I kiss thy hand, but not in flattery, Cæsar;
Desiring thee, that Publius Cimber may
Have an immediate freedom of repeal.

CÆSAR. What, Brutus!

CASSIUS. Pardon, Cæsar; Cæsar, pardon:
As low as to thy foot doth Cassius fall,
To beg enfranchisement for Publius Cimber.

CÆSAR. I could be well mov'd if I were as you;
  If I could pray to move, prayers would move me;
  But I am constant as the northern star,
  Of whose true fix'd and resting quality
  There is no fellow in the firmament.
  The skies are painted with unnumber'd sparks,
  They are all fire and every one doth shine,
  But there 's but one in all doth hold his place:
  So, in the world; 'tis furnish'd well with men,
  And men are flesh and blood, and apprehensive;
  Yet in the number I do know but one
  That unassailable holds on his rank,
  Unshak'd of motion: and that I am he,
  Let me a little show it, even in this,
  That I was constant Cimber should be banished,
  And constant do remain to keep him so.

CINNA. O Cæsar,—

CÆSAR. Hence! Wilt thou lift up Olympus!

DECIUS. Great Cæsar,—

CÆSAR.   Doth not Brutus bootless kneel?

CASCA. Speak, hands, for me!   *They stab Cæsar*

CÆSAR. Et tu, Brute? Then fall, Cæsar!   *Dies*

CINNA. Liberty! Freedom! Tyranny is dead!
  Run hence, proclaim, cry it about the streets.

CASSIUS. Some to the common pulpits, and cry out,
  'Liberty, freedom, and enfranchisement!'

BRUTUS. People and senators, be not affrighted;
  Fly not; stand still; ambition's debt is paid.

CASCA. Go to the pulpit, Brutus.

DECIUS.   And Cassius too.

BRUTUS. Where 's Publius?

CINNA. Here, quite confounded with this mutiny.

METELLUS. Stand fast together, lest some friend of Cæsar's
  Should chance—

BRUTUS. Talk not of standing. Publius, good cheer;
  There is no harm intended to your person,
  Nor to no Roman else; so tell them, Publius.

CASSIUS. And leave us, Publius; lest that the people,
  Rushing on us, should do your age some mischief.

BRUTUS. Do so; and let no man abide this deed
  But we the doers.

Re-enter Trebonius

CASSIUS. Where 's Antony?

TREBONIUS.   Fled to his house amaz'd.
Men, wives and children stare, cry out and run
As it were doomsday.

BRUTUS.   Fates, we will know your pleasures.
That we shall die, we know; 'tis but the time
And drawing days out, that men stand upon.

CASCA. Why, he that cuts off twenty years of life
Cuts off so many years of fearing death.

BRUTUS. Grant that, and then is death a benefit:
So are we Cæsar's friends, that have abridg'd
His time of fearing death. Stoop, Romans, stoop,
And let us bathe our hands in Cæsar's blood
Up to the elbows, and besmear our swords:
Then walk we forth, even to the market-place;
And waving our red weapons o'er our heads,
Let 's all cry, 'Peace, freedom, and liberty!'

CASSIUS. Stoop, then, and wash. How many ages hence
Shall this our lofty scene be acted o'er,
In states unborn and accents yet unknown!

BRUTUS. How many times shall Cæsar bleed in sport,
That now on Pompey's basis lies along
No worthier than the dust!

CASSIUS.   So oft as that shall be
So often shall the knot of us be call'd
The men that gave their country liberty.

DECIUS. What! shall we forth?

CASSIUS.   Ay, every man away:
Brutus shall lead; and we will grace his heels
With the most boldest and best hearts of Rome.

Enter a Servant

BRUTUS. Soft! who comes here? A friend of Antony's.

SERVANT. Thus, Brutus, did my master bid me kneel;
Thus did Mark Antony bid me fall down;
And, being prostrate, thus he made me say:
Brutus is noble, wise, valiant, and honest;
Cæsar was mighty, bold, royal, and loving:
Say I love Brutus, and I honour him;
Say I fear'd Cæsar, honour'd him, and lov'd him.
If Brutus will vouchsafe that Antony
May safely come to him, and be resolv'd
How Cæsar hath deserv'd to lie in death,

Mark Antony shall not love Cæsar dead
So well as Brutus living; but will follow
The fortunes and affairs of noble Brutus
Thorough the hazards of this untrod state
With all true faith. So says my master Antony.

BRUTUS. Thy master is a wise and valiant Roman;
I never thought him worse.
Tell him, so please him come unto this place,
He shall be satisfied; and, by my honour,
Depart untouch'd.

SERVANT.   I 'll fetch him presently.   *Exit*

BRUTUS. I know that we shall have him well to friend.

CASSIUS. I wish we may: but yet have I a mind
That fears him much; and my misgiving still
Falls shrewdly to the purpose.

Re-enter Antony

BRUTUS. But here comes Antony. Welcome, Mark Antony.

ANTONY. O mighty Cæsar! dost thou lie so low?
Are all thy conquests, glories, triumphs, spoils,
Shrunk to this little measure? Fare thee well.
I know not, gentlemen, what you intend,
Who else must be let blood, who else is rank:
If I myself, there is no hour so fit
As Cæsar's death's hour, nor no instrument
Of half that worth as those your swords, made rich
With the most noble blood of all this world.
I do beseech ye, if ye bear me hard,
Now, whilst your purpled hands do reek and smoke,
Fulfil your pleasure. Live a thousand years,
I shall not find myself so apt to die:
No place will please me so, no mean of death,
As here by Cæsar, and by you cut off,
The choice and master spirits of this age.

BRUTUS. O Antony, beg not your death of us.
Though now we must appear bloody and cruel,
As, by our hands and this our present act,
You see we do, yet see you but our hands
And this the bleeding business they have done.
Our hearts you see not; they are pitiful;
And pity to the general wrong of Rome—
As fire drives out fire, so pity pity—
Hath done this deed on Cæsar. For your part,

To you our swords have leaden points, Mark Antony.
Our arms, in strength of malice, and our hearts
Of brothers' temper, do receive you in
With all kind love, good thoughts, and reverence.

CASSIUS. Your voice shall be as strong as any man's
In the disposing of new dignities.

BRUTUS. Only be patient till we have appeas'd
The multitude, beside themselves with fear,
And then we will deliver you the cause
Why I, that did love Cæsar when I struck him,
Have thus proceeded.

ANTONY.   I doubt not of your wisdom.
Let each man render me his bloody hand:
First, Marcus Brutus, will I shake with you;
Next, Caius Cassius, do I take your hand;
Now, Decius Brutus, yours; now yours, Metellus;
Yours, Cinna; and, my valiant Casca, yours;
Though last, not least in love, yours, good Trebonius.
Gentlemen all,—alas! what shall I say?
My credit now stands on such slippery ground,
That one of two bad ways you must conceit me,
Either a coward or a flatterer.
That I did love thee, Cæsar, O! 'tis true:
If then thy spirit look upon us now,
Shall it not grieve thee dearer than thy death,
To see thy Antony making his peace,
Shaking the bloody fingers of thy foes,
Most noble! in the presence of thy corse?
Had I as many eyes as thou hast wounds,
Weeping as fast as they stream forth thy blood,
It would become me better than to close
In terms of friendship with thine enemies.
Pardon me, Julius! Here wast thou bay'd, brave hart;
Here didst thou fall; and here thy hunters stand,
Sign'd in thy spoil, and crimson'd in thy lethe.
O world! thou wast the forest to this hart;
And this, indeed, O world! the heart of thee.
How like a deer, strucken by many princes,
Dost thou here lie!

CASSIUS. Mark Antony,—

ANTONY.   Pardon me, Caius Cassius:
The enemies of Cæsar shall say this;

Then, in a friend, it is cold modesty.

CASSIUS. I blame you not for praising Cæsar so;
But what compact mean you to have with us?
Will you be prick'd in number of our friends,
Or shall we on, and not depend on you?

ANTONY. Therefore I took your hands, but was indeed
Sway'd from the point by looking down on Cæsar.
Friends am I with you all, and love you all,
Upon this hope, that you shall give me reasons
Why and wherein Cæsar was dangerous.

BRUTUS. Or else were this a savage spectacle.
Our reasons are so full of good regard
That were you, Antony, the son of Cæsar,
You should be satisfied.

ANTONY.   That 's all I seek:
And am moreover suitor that I may
Produce his body to the market-place;
And in the pulpit, as becomes a friend,
Speak in the order of his funeral.

BRUTUS. You shall, Mark Antony.

CASSIUS.   Brutus, a word with you.
(*Aside to Brutus*) You know not what you do; do not
    consent
That Antony speak in his funeral:
Know you how much the people may be mov'd
By that which he will utter?

BRUTUS.   By your pardon;
I will myself into the pulpit first,
And show the reason of our Cæsar's death:
What Antony shall speak, I will protest
He speaks by leave and by permission,
And that we are contented Cæsar shall
Have all true rites and lawful ceremonies.
It shall advantage more than do us wrong.

CASSIUS. I know not what may fall; I like it not.

BRUTUS. Mark Antony, here, take you Cæsar's body.
You shall not in your funeral speech blame us,
But speak all good you can devise of Cæsar,
And say you do 't by our permission;
Else shall you not have any hand at all
About his funeral; and you shall speak
In the same pulpit whereto I am going,

After my speech is ended.

ANTONY.   Be it so;
I do desire no more.

BRUTUS. Prepare the body then, and follow us.

Exeunt all but Antony

ANTONY. O! pardon me, thou bleeding piece of earth,
That I am meek and gentle with these butchers;
Thou art the ruins of the noblest man
That ever lived in the tide of times.
Woe to the hand that shed this costly blood!
Over thy wounds now do I prophesy,
Which like dumb mouths do ope their ruby lips
To beg the voice and utterance of my tongue,
A curse shall light upon the limbs of men;
Domestic fury and fierce civil strife
Shall cumber all the parts of Italy;
Blood and destruction shall be so in use,
And dreadful objects so familiar,
That mothers shall but smile when they behold
Their infants quarter'd with the hands of war;
All pity chok'd with custom of fell deeds:
And Cæsar's spirit, ranging for revenge,
With Ate by his side.come hot from hell,
Shall in these confines with a monarch's voice
Cry 'Havoc!' and let slip the dogs of war;
That this foul deed shall smell above the earth
With carrion men, groaning for burial.

Enter a Servant

You serve Octavius Cæsar, do you not?

SERVANT. I do, Mark Antony.

ANTONY. Cæsar did write for him to come to Rome.

SERVANT. He did receive his letters, and is coming;
And bid me say to you by word of mouth—

Seeing the body

O Cæsar!—

ANTONY. Thy heart is big, get thee apart and weep.
Passion, I see, is catching; for mine eyes,
Seeing those beads of sorrow stand in thine,
Began to water. Is thy master coming?

SERVANT. He lies to-night within seven leagues of Rome.

ANTONY. Post back with speed, and tell him what hath
chanc'd:

Here is a mourning Rome, a dangerous Rome,
No Rome of safety for Octavius yet;
Hie hence and tell him so. Yet, stay awhile;
Thou shalt not back till I have borne this corpse
Into the market-place; there shall I try,
In my oration, how the people take
The cruel issue of these bloody men;
According to the which thou shalt discourse
To young Octavius of the state of things.
Lend me your hand.   *Exeunt, with Cæsar's body*

SCENE TWO

The Forum.

Enter Brutus and Cassius, and a throng of Citizens

CITIZENS. We will be satisfied: let us be satisfied.
BRUTUS. Then follow me, and give me audience, friends.
    Cassius, go you into the other street,
    And part the numbers.
    Those that will hear me speak, let 'em stay here;
    Those that will follow Cassius, go with him;
    And the public reasons shall be rendered
    Of Cæsar's death.
FIRST CITIZEN. I will hear Brutus speak.
SECOND CITIZEN. I will hear Cassius; and compare their reasons,
    When severally we hear them rendered.
                            Exit Cassius, with some
                of the Citizens; Brutus goes into the pulpit
THIRD CITIZEN. The noble Brutus is ascended: silence!
BRUTUS. Be patient till the last.
    Romans, countrymen, and lovers! hear me for my cause;
    and be silent, that you may hear: believe me for mine
    honour, and have respect to mine honour, that you may
    believe: censure me in your wisdom, and awake your
    senses, that you may the better judge. If there be any in
    this assembly, any dear friend of Cæsar's, to him I say,
    that Brutus' love to Cæsar was no less that his. If then
    that friend demand why Brutus rose against Cæsar, this
    is my answer: Not that I loved Cæsar less, but that I

loved Rome more. Had you rather Cæsar were living,
and die all slaves, than that Cæsar were dead, to live all
free men? As Cæsar loved me, I weep for him; as he was
fortunate, I rejoice at it; as he was valiant, I honour him;
but, as he was ambitious, I slew him. There is tears for
his love; joy for his fortune; honour for his valour; and
death for his ambition. Who is here so base that would
be a bondman? If any, speak; for him have I offended.
Who is here so rude that would not be a Roman? If any,
speak; for him have I offended. Who is here so vile that
will not love his country? If any, speak; for him have I
offended. I pause for a reply.

CITIZENS. None, Brutus, none.

BRUTUS. Then none have I offended. I have done no more
to Cæsar, than you shall do to Brutus. The question of
his death is enrolled in the Capitol; his glory not exten-
uated, wherein he was worthy, nor his offences enforced,
for which he suffered death.

Enter Antony and Others, with Cæsar's body

Here comes his body, mourned by Mark Antony: who,
though he had no hand in his death, shall receive the
benefit of his dying, a place in the commonwealth; as
which of you shall not? With this I depart: that, as I
slew my best lover for the good of Rome, I have the
same dagger for myself, when it shall please my country
to need my death.

CITIZENS. Live, Brutus! live! live!

FIRST CITIZEN. Bring him with triumph home unto his
house.

SECOND CITIZEN. Give him a statue with his ancestors.

THIRD CITIZEN. Let him be Cæsar.

FOURTH CITIZEN.   Cæsar's better parts
Shall be crown'd in Brutus.

FIRST CITIZEN. We 'll bring him to his house with shouts
and clamours.

BRUTUS. My countrymen,—

SECOND CITIZEN. Peace! silence! Brutus speaks.

FIRST CITIZEN. Peace, ho!

BRUTUS. Good countrymen, let me depart alone,
And, for my sake, stay here with Antony.
Do grace to Cæsar's corpse, and grace his speech
Tending to Cæsar's glories, which Mark Antony,

By our permission, is allow'd to make.
I do entreat you, not a man depart,
Save I alone, till Antony have spoke.   *Exit*

FIRST CITIZEN. Stay, ho! and let us hear Mark Antony.

THIRD CITIZEN. Let him go up into the public chair;
We 'll hear him. Noble Antony, go up.

ANTONY. For Brutus' sake, I am beholding to you.   *Goes up*

FOURTH CITIZEN. What does he say of Brutus?

THIRD CITIZEN.   He says, for Brutus' sake,
He finds himself beholding to us all.

FOURTH CITIZEN. 'Twere best he speak no harm of Brutus
    here.

FIRST CITIZEN. This Cæsar was a tyrant.

THIRD CITIZEN.   Nay, that 's certain:
We are bless'd that Rome is rid of him.

SECOND CITIZEN. Peace! let us hear what Antony can say.

ANTONY. You gentle Romans,—

CITIZENS.   Peace, ho! let us hear him.

ANTONY. Friends, Romans, countrymen, lend me your ears;
I come to bury Cæsar, not to praise him.
The evil that men do lives after them,
The good is oft interred with their bones;
So let it be with Cæsar. The noble Brutus
Hath told you Cæsar was ambitious;
If it were so, it was a grievous fault,
And grievously hath Cæsar answer'd it.
Here, under leave of Brutus and the rest,—
For Brutus is an honourable man;
So are they all, all honourable men,—
Come I to speak in Cæsar's funeral.
He was my friend, faithful and just to me:
But Brutus says he was ambitious;
And Brutus is an honourable man.
He hath brought many captives home to Rome
Whose ransoms did the general coffers fill:
Did this in Cæsar seem ambitious?
When that the poor have cried, Cæsar hath wept;
Ambition should be made of sterner stuff:
Yet Brutus says he was ambitious;
And Brutus is an honourable man.
You all did see that on the Lupercal
I thrice presented him a kingly crown,

Which he did thrice refuse: was this ambition?
Yet Brutus says he was ambitious;
And, sure, he is an honourable man.
I speak not to disprove what Brutus spoke,
But here I am to speak what I do know.
You all did love him once, not without cause:
What cause withholds you then to mourn for him?
O judgment! thou art fled to brutish beasts,
And men have lost their reason. Bear with me.
My heart is in the coffin there with Cæsar,
And I must pause till it come back to me.

FIRST CITIZEN. Methinks there is much reason in his sayings.

SECOND CITIZEN. If thou consider rightly of the matter, Cæsar has had great wrong.

THIRD CITIZEN.　　　　　　　Has he, masters?
I fear there will a worse come in his place.

FOURTH CITIZEN. Mark'd ye his words? He would not take the crown;
Therefore 'tis certain he was not ambitious.

FIRST CITIZEN. If it be found so, some will dear abide it.

SECOND CITIZEN. Poor soul! his eyes are red as fire with weeping.

THIRD CITIZEN. There 's not a nobler man in Rome than Antony.

FOURTH CITIZEN. Now mark him; he begins again to speak.

ANTONY. But yesterday the word of Cæsar might
Have stood against the world; now lies he there,
And none so poor to do him reverence.
O masters! if I were dispos'd to stir
Your hearts and minds to mutiny and rage,
I should do Brutus wrong, and Cassius wrong,
Who, you all know, are honourable men.
I will not do them wrong; I rather choose
To wrong the dead, to wrong myself, and you,
Than I will wrong such honourable men.
But here 's a parchment with the seal of Cæsar;
I found it in his closet, 'tis his will.
Let but the commons hear this testament—
Which, pardon me, I do not mean to read—
And they would go and kiss dead Cæsar's wounds,
And dip their napkins in his sacred blood,

ANTONY.   I fear I wrong the honourable men
       Whose daggers have stabb'd Cæsar; I do fear it.

Yea, beg a hair of him for memory.
And, dying, mention it within their wills,
Bequeathing it as a rich legacy
Unto their issue.

FOURTH CITIZEN. We 'll hear the will: read it, Mark Antony.

CITIZENS. The will, the will! we will hear Cæsar's will.

ANTONY. Have patience, gentle friends; I must not read it:
It is not meet you know how Cæsar lov'd you.
You are not wood, you are not stones, but men;
And, being men, hearing the will of Cæsar,
It will inflame you, it will make you mad.
'Tis good you know not that you are his heirs;
For if you should, O! what would come of it.

FOURTH CITIZEN. Read the will! we 'll hear it, Antony;
You shall read us the will, Cæsar's will.

ANTONY. Will you be patient? Will you stay awhile?
I have o'ershot myself to tell you of it.
I fear I wrong the honourable men
Whose daggers have stabb'd Cæsar; I do fear it.

FOURTH CITIZEN. They were traitors: honourable men!

CITIZENS. The will! the testament!

SECOND CITIZEN. They were villains, murderers. The will!
read the will.

ANTONY. You will compel me then to read the will?
Then make a ring about the corpse of Cæsar,
And let me show you him that made the will.
Shall I descend? and will you give me leave?

CITIZENS. Come down.

SECOND CITIZEN. Descend.   *Antony comes down*

THIRD CITIZEN. You shall have leave.

FOURTH CITIZEN. A ring; stand round.

FIRST CITIZEN. Stand from the hearse; stand from the body.

SECOND CITIZEN. Room for Antony; most noble Antony.

ANTONY. Nay, press not so upon me; stand far off.

CITIZENS. Stand back! room! bear back!

ANTONY. If you have tears, prepare to shed them now.
You all do know this mantle: I remember
The first time ever Cæsar put it on;
'Twas on a summer's evening, in his tent,
That day he overcame the Nervii.
Look! in this place ran Cassius' dagger through:
See what a rent the envious Casca made:

Through this the well-beloved Brutus stabb'd;
And, as he pluck'd his cursed steel away,
Mark how the blood of Cæsar follow'd it,
As rushing out of doors, to be resolv'd
If Brutus so unkindly knock'd or no;
For Brutus, as you know, was Cæsar's angel:
Judge, O you gods! how dearly Cæsar lov'd him.
This was the most unkindest cut of all;
For when the noble Cæsar saw him stab,
Ingratitude, more strong than traitors' arms,
Quite vanquish'd him: then burst his mighty heart;
And, in his mantle muffling up his face,
Even at the base of Pompey's statua,
Which all the while ran blood, great Cæsar fell.
O! what a fall was there, my countrymen;
Then I, and you, and all of us fell down,
Whilst bloody treason flourish'd over us.
O! now you weep, and I perceive you feel
The dint of pity; these are gracious drops.
Kind souls, what! weep you when you but behold
Our Cæsar's vesture wounded? Look you here,
Here is himself, marr'd, as you see, with traitors.

FIRST CITIZEN. O piteous spectacle!

SECOND CITIZEN. O noble Cæsar!

THIRD CITIZEN. O woeful day!

FOURTH CITIZEN. O traitors! villains!

FIRST CITIZEN. O most bloody sight!

SECOND CITIZEN. We will be revenged.

CITIZENS. Revenge!—About!—Seek!—Burn!
Fire!—Kill!—Slay! Let not a traitor live.

ANTONY. Stay, countrymen!

FIRST CITIZEN. Peace there! Hear the noble Antony.

SECOND CITIZEN. We 'll hear him, we 'll follow him, we 'll die
for him.

ANTONY. Good friends, sweet friends, let me not stir you up
To such a sudden flood of mutiny.
They that have done this deed are honourable:
What private griefs they have, alas! I know not,
That made them do it; they are wise and honourable,
And will, no doubt, with reasons answer you.
I come not, friends, to steal away your hearts:
I am no orator, as Brutus is;

But, as you know me all, a plain blunt man,
That love my friend; and that they know full well
That gave me public leave to speak of him.
For I have neither wit, nor words, nor worth,
Action, nor utterance, nor the power of speech,
To stir men's blood: I only speak right on;
I tell you that which you yourselves do know,
Show you sweet Cæsar's wounds, poor poor dumb
  mouths,
And bid them speak for me: but were I Brutus,
And Brutus Antony, there were an Antony
Would ruffle up your spirits, and put a tongue
In every wound of Cæsar, that should move
The stones of Rome to rise and mutiny.

CITIZENS. We 'll mutiny.

FIRST CITIZEN. We 'll burn the house of Brutus.

THIRD CITIZEN. Away, then! come, seek the conspirators.

ANTONY. Yet hear me, countrymen; yet hear me speak.

CITIZENS. Peace, ho!—Hear Antony,—most noble Antony.

ANTONY. Why, friends, you go to do you know not what.
Wherein hath Cæsar thus deserv'd your loves?
Alas! you know not: I must tell you then.
You have forgot the will I told you of.

CITIZENS. Most true. The will! let 's stay and hear the will.

ANTONY. Here is the will, and under Cæsar's seal.
To every Roman citizen he gives,
To every several man, seventy-five drachmas.

SECOND CITIZEN. Most noble Cæsar! we 'll revenge his death.

THIRD CITIZEN. O royal Cæsar!

ANTONY. Hear me with patience.

CITIZENS. Peace, ho!

ANTONY. Moreover, he hath left you all his walks,
His private arbours, and new-planted orchards,
On this side Tiber; he hath left them you,
And to your heirs for ever; common pleasures,
To walk abroad, and recreate yourselves.
Here was a Cæsar! when comes such another?

FIRST CITIZEN. Never, never! Come, away, away!
We 'll burn his body in the holy place,
And with the brands fire the traitors' houses.
Take up the body.

SECOND CITIZEN. Go fetch fire.

THIRD CITIZEN. Pluck down benches.

FOURTH CITIZEN. Pluck down forms, windows, any thing.

Exeunt Citizens, with the body

ANTONY. Now let it work: mischief, thou art afoot,
Take thou what course thou wilt!

Enter a Servant

How now, fellow!

SERVANT. Sir, Octavius is already come to Rome.

ANTONY. Where is he?

SERVANT. He and Lepidus are at Cæsar's house.

ANTONY. And thither will I straight to visit him.
He comes upon a wish. Fortune is merry,
And in this mood will give us any thing.

SERVANT. I heard him say Brutus and Cassius
Are rid like madmen through the gates of Rome.

ANTONY. Belike they had some notice of the people,
How I had mov'd them. Bring me to Octavius.

Exeunt

SCENE THREE

A Street.

Enter Cinna, the Poet

CINNA. I dreamt to-night that I did feast with Cæsar.
And things unlucky charge my fantasy:
I have no will to wander forth of doors,
Yet something leads me forth.

Enter Citizens

FIRST CITIZEN. What is your name?

SECOND CITIZEN. Whither are you going?

THIRD CITIZEN. Where do you dwell?

FOURTH CITIZEN. Are you a married man, or a bachelor?

SECOND CITIZEN. Answer every man directly.

FIRST CITIZEN. Ay, and briefly.

FOURTH CITIZEN. Ay, and wisely.

THIRD CITIZEN. Ay, and truly, you were best.

CINNA. What is my name? Whither am I going? Where do
I dwell? Am I a married man, or a bachelor? Then, to answer every man directly and briefly, wisely and truly:
wisely I say, I am a bachelor.

SECOND CITIZEN. That 's as much as to say, they are fools
   that marry; you 'll bear me a bang for that, I fear. Proceed; directly.

CINNA. Directly, I am going to Cæsar's funeral.

FIRST CITIZEN. As a friend or an enemy?

CINNA. As a friend.

SECOND CITIZEN. That matter is answered directly.

FOURTH CITIZEN. For your dwelling, briefly.

CINNA. Briefly, I dwell by the Capitol.

THIRD CITIZEN. Your name, sir, truly.

CINNA. Truly, my name is Cinna.

SECOND CITIZEN. Tear him to pieces; he 's a conspirator.

CINNA. I am Cinna the poet, I am Cinna the poet.

FOURTH CITIZEN. Tear him for his bad verses, tear him for
   his bad verses.

CINNA: I am not Cinna the conspirator.

SECOND CITIZEN. It is no matter, his name 's Cinna; pluck
   but his name out of his heart, and turn him going.

THIRD CITIZEN. Tear him, tear him! Come, brands, ho! fire-
   brands! To Brutus', to Cassius'; burn all. Some to Decius'
   house, and some to Casca's; some to Ligarius'. Away! go!
                                                  Exeunt

ACT FOUR

SCENE ONE

Rome. A Room in Antony's House.

Antony, Octavius, and Lepidus, seated at a table

ANTONY.   These many then shall die; their names are prick'd.
OCTAVIUS.   Your brother too must die; consent you, Lepidus?
LEPIDUS.   I do consent.
OCTAVIUS.   Prick him down, Antony.
LEPIDUS.   Upon condition Publius shall not live,
  Who is your sister's son, Mark Antony.
ANTONY.   He shall not live; look, with a spot I damn him.
  But, Lepidus, go you to Cæsar's house;
  Fetch the will hither, and we shall determine
  How to cut off some charge in legacies.
LEPIDUS.   What! shall I find you here?
OCTAVIUS.   Or here or at the Capitol.   *Exit Lepidus*
ANTONY.   This is a slight unmeritable man,
  Meet to be sent on errands: is it fit,
  The three-fold world divided, he should stand
  One of the three to share it?
OCTAVIUS.   So you thought him;
  And took his voice who should be prick'd to die,
  In our black sentence and proscription.
ANTONY.   Octavius, I have seen more days than you:
  And though we lay these honours on this man,
  To ease ourselves of divers slanderous loads,
  He shall but bear them as the ass bears gold,
  To groan and sweat under the business,
  Either led or driven, as we point the way;
  And having brought our treasure where we will,
  Then take we down his load, and turn him off,
  Like to the empty ass, to shake his ears,
  And graze in commons.

OCTAVIUS.   You may do your will:
    But he 's a tried and valiant soldier.
ANTONY. So is my horse, Octavius; and for that
    I do appoint him store of provender.
    It is a creature that I teach to fight,
    To wind, to stop, to run directly on,
    His corporal motion govern'd by my spirit.
    And, in some taste, is Lepidus but so:
    He must be taught, and train'd, and bid go forth;
    A barren-spirited fellow; one that feeds
    On abject orts, and imitations,
    Which, out of use and stal'd by other men,
    Begin his fashion: do not talk of him
    But as a property. And now, Octavius,
    Listen great things: Brutus and Cassius
    Are levying powers; we must straight make head;
    Therefore let our alliance be combin'd,
    Our best friends made, and our best means stretch'd out;
    And let us presently go sit in council,
    How covert matters may be best disclos'd,
    And open perils surest answered.
OCTAVIUS. Let us do so: for we are at the stake,
    And bay'd about with many enemies;
    And some that smile have in their hearts, I fear,
    Millions of mischiefs.   *Exeunt*

SCENE TWO

Camp near Sardis. Before Brutus' Tent.

*Drum. Enter Brutus, Lucilius, Lucius, and Soldiers;
    Titinius and Pindarus meet them*

BRUTUS. Stand, ho!
LUCILIUS. Give the word, ho! and stand.
BRUTUS. What now, Lucilius! is Cassius near?
LUCILIUS. He is at hand; and Pindarus is come
    To do you salutation from his master.
                    Pindarus gives a letter to Brutus
BRUTUS. He greets me well. Your master, Pindarus,
    In his own change, or by ill officers,
    Hath given me some worthy cause to wish

Things done, undone; but, if he be at hand,
I shall be satisfied.

PINDARUS.   I do not doubt
But that my noble master will appear
Such as he is, full of regard and honour.

BRUTUS. He is not doubted. A word, Lucilius;
How he receiv'd you, let me be resolv'd.

LUCILIUS. With courtesy and with respect enough;
But not with such familiar instances,
Nor with such free and friendly conference,
As he hath us'd of old.

BRUTUS.   Thou hast describ'd
A hot friend cooling. Ever note, Lucilius,
When love begins to sicken and decay,
It useth an enforced ceremony.
There are no tricks in plain and simple faith;
But hollow men, like horses hot at hand,
Make gallant show and promise of their mettle;
But when they should endure the bloody spur,
They fall their crests, and, like deceitful jades,
Sink in the trial. Comes his army on?

LUCILIUS. They mean this night in Sardis to be quarter'd;
The greater part, the horse in general,
Are come with Cassius.

BRUTUS.   Hark! he is arriv'd.

                                        Low march within

March gently on to meet him.
                Enter Cassius and Soldiers

CASSIUS. Stand, ho!

BRUTUS. Stand, ho! Speak the word along.

FIRST SOLDIER. Stand!

SECOND SOLDIER. Stand!

THIRD SOLDIER. Stand!

CASSIUS. Most noble brother, you have done me wrong.

BRUTUS. Judge me, you gods! Wrong I mine enemies?
And, if not so, how should I wrong a brother?

CASSIUS. Brutus, this sober form of yours hides wrongs;
And when you do them—

BRUTUS.   Cassius, be content;
Speak your griefs softly: I do know you well.
Before the eyes of both our armies here,
Which should perceive nothing but love from us,

Let us not wrangle: bid them move away;
Then in my tent, Cassius, enlarge your griefs,
And I will give you audience.

CASSIUS.   Pindarus,
Bid our commanders lead their charges off
A little from this ground.

BRUTUS. Lucilius, do you the like; and let no man
Come to our tent till we have done our conference.
Let Lucius and Titinius guard our door.   *Exeunt*

SCENE THREE

Within the Tent of Brutus.

Enter Brutus and Cassius

CASSIUS. That you have wrong'd me doth appear in this:
You have condemn'd and noted Lucius Pella
For taking bribes here of the Sardians;
Wherein my letters, praying on his side,
Because I knew the man, were slighted off.

BRUTUS. You wrong'd yourself to write in such a case.

CASSIUS. In such a time as this it is not meet
That every nice offence should bear his comment.

BRUTUS. Let me tell you, Cassius, you yourself
Are much condemn'd to have an itching palm;
To sell and mart your offices for gold
To undeservers.

CASSIUS.   I an itching palm!
You know that you are Brutus that speak this,
Or, by the gods, this speech were else your last.

BRUTUS. The name of Cassius honours this corruption,
And chastisement doth therefore hide his head.

CASSIUS. Chastisement!

BRUTUS. Remember March, the ides of March remember:
Did not great Julius bleed for justice' sake?
What villain touch'd his body, that did stab,
And not for justice? What! shall one of us,
That struck the foremost man of all this world
But for supporting robbers, shall we now
Contaminate our fingers with base bribes,

And sell the mighty space of our large honours
For so much trash as may be grasped thus?
I had rather be a dog, and bay the moon,
Than such a Roman.

CASSIUS.   Brutus, bay not me;
I 'll not endure it: you forget yourself,
To hedge me in. I am a soldier, I,
Older in practice, abler than yourself
To make conditions.

BRUTUS.   Go to; you are not, Cassius.

CASSIUS. I am.

BRUTUS. I say you are not.

CASSIUS. Urge me no more, I shall forget myself;
Have mind upon your health; tempt me no further.

BRUTUS. Away, slight man!

CASSIUS. It 's possible?

BRUTUS.   Hear me, for I will speak.
Must I give way and room to your rash choler?
Shall I be frighted when a madman stares?

CASSIUS. O ye gods! ye gods! Must I endure all this?

BRUTUS. All this! ay, more: fret till your proud heart break;
Go show your slaves how choleric you are,
And make your bondmen tremble. Must I budge?
Must I observe you? Must I stand and crouch
Under your testy humour? By the gods,
You shall digest the venom of your spleen,
Though it do split you; for, from this day forth,
I 'll use you for my mirth, yea, for my laughter,
When you are waspish.

CASSIUS.   Is it come to this?

BRUTUS. You say you are a better soldier:
Let it appear so; make your vaunting true,
And it shall please me well. For mine own part,
I shall be glad to learn of noble men.

CASSIUS. You wrong me every way; you wrong me, Brutus;
I said an elder soldier, not a better:
Did I say 'better'?

BRUTUS.   If you did, I care not.

CASSIUS. When Cæsar liv'd, he durst not thus have mov'd
me.

BRUTUS. Peace, peace! you durst not so have tempted him.

CASSIUS. I durst not!

BRUTUS. No.

CASSIUS. What! durst not tempt him!

BRUTUS.   For your life you durst not

CASSIUS. Do not presume too much upon my love;
   I may do that I shall be sorry for.

BRUTUS. You have done that you should be sorry for.
   There is no terror, Cassius, in your threats;
   For I am arm'd so strong in honesty
   That they pass by me as the idle wind,
   Which I respect not. I did send to you
   For certain sums of gold, which you denied me;
   For I can raise no money by vile means:
   By heaven, I had rather coin my heart,
   And drop my blood for drachmas, than to wring
   From the hard hands of peasants their vile trash
   By any direction. I did send
   To you for gold to pay my legions,
   Which you denied me: was that done like Cassius?
   Should I have answer'd Caius Cassius so?
   When Marcus Brutus grows so covetous,
   To lock such rascal counters from his friends,
   Be ready, gods, with all your thunderbolts;
   Dash him to pieces!

CASSIUS.   I denied you not.

BRUTUS. You did.

CASSIUS.   I did not: he was but a fool
   That brought my answer back. Brutus hath riv'd my
      heart.
   A friend should bear his friend's infirmities,
   But Brutus makes mine greater than they are.

BRUTUS. I do not, till you practise them on me.

CASSIUS. You love me not.

BRUTUS.   I do not like your faults.

CASSIUS. A friendly eye could never see such faults.

BRUTUS. A flatterer's would not, though they do appear
   As huge as high Olympus.

CASSIUS. Come, Antony, and young Octavius, come,
   Revenge yourselves alone on Cassius,
   For Cassius is aweary of the world;
   Hated by one he loves; brav'd by his brother;
   Check'd like a bondman; all his faults observ'd,
   Set in a note-book, learn'd, and conn'd by rote,

To cast into my teeth. O! I could weep
My spirit from mine eyes. There is my dagger,
And here my naked breast; within, a heart
Dearer than Plutus' mine, richer than gold:
If that thou be'st a Roman, take it forth;
I, that denied thee gold, will give my heart:
Strike, as thou didst at Cæsar; for, I know,
When thou didst hate him worst, thou lov'dst him better
Than ever thou lov'dst Cassius.

BRUTUS.   Sheathe your dagger:
Be angry when you will, it shall have scope;
Do what you will, dishonour shall be humour.
O Cassius! you are yoked with a lamb
That carries anger as the flint bears fire,
Who, much enforced, shows a hasty spark,
And straight is cold again.

CASSIUS.   Hath Cassius liv'd
To be but mirth and laughter to his Brutus,
When grief and blood ill-temper'd vexeth him?

BRUTUS. When I spoke that I was ill-temper'd too.

CASSIUS. Do you confess so much? Give me your hand.

BRUTUS. And my heart too.

CASSIUS.   O Brutus!

BRUTUS.   What's the matter?

CASSIUS. Have not you love enough to bear with me,
When that rash humour which my mother gave me
Makes me forgetful?

BRUTUS.   Yes, Cassius; and from henceforth
When you are over-earnest with your Brutus,
He 'll think your mother chides, and leave you so.

                                        Noise within

POET. (*Within*) Let me go in to see the generals;
There is some grudge between 'em, 'tis not meet
They be alone.

LUCILIUS. (*Within*) You shall not come to them.

POET. (*Within*) Nothing but death shall stay me.

    Enter Poet, followed by Lucilius, Titinius, and Lucius

CASSIUS. How now! What's the matter?

POET. For shame, you generals! What do you mean?
Love, and be friends, as two such men should be;
For I have seen more years, I 'm sure, than ye.

CASSIUS. Ha, ha! how vilely doth this cynic rime!

BRUTUS. Get you hence, sirrah; saucy fellow, hence!

CASSIUS. Bear with him, Brutus; 'tis his fashion.

BRUTUS. I 'll know his humour, when he knows his time:
   What should the wars do with these jigging fools?
   Companion, hence!

CASSIUS.   Away, away! be gone.   *Exit Poet*

BRUTUS. Lucilius and Titinius, bid the commanders
   Prepare to lodge their companies to-night.

CASSIUS. And come yourselves, and bring Messala with you,
   Immediately to us.   *Exeunt Lucilius and Titinius*

BRUTUS.   Lucius, a bowl of wine!   *Exit Lucius*

CASSIUS. I did not think you could have been so angry.

BRUTUS. O Cassius! I am sick of many griefs.

CASSIUS. Of your philosophy you make no use
   If you give place to accidental evils.

BRUTUS. No man bears sorrow better: Portia is dead.

CASSIUS. Ha! Portia!

BRUTUS. She is dead.

CASSIUS. How 'scap'd I killing when I cross'd you so?
   O insupportable and touching loss!
   Upon what sickness?

BRUTUS.   Impatient of my absence,
   And grief that young Octavius with Mark Antony
   Have made themselves so strong;—for with her death
   That tidings came:—with this she fell distract,
   And, her attendants absent, swallow'd fire.

CASSIUS. And died so?

BRUTUS.   Even so.

CASSIUS.   O ye immortal gods!
            Re-enter Lucius, with wine and tapers

BRUTUS. Speak no more of her. Give me a bowl of wine.
   In this I bury all unkindness, Cassius.   *Drinks*

CASSIUS. My heart is thirsty for that noble pledge.
   Fill, Lucius, till the wine o'erswell the cup;
   I cannot drink too much of Brutus' love.   *Drinks*

BRUTUS. Come in, Titinius.   *Exit Lucius*
            Re-enter Titinius, with Messala
                        Welcome, good Messala.
   Now sit we close about this taper here,
   And call in question our necessities.

CASSIUS. Portia, art thou gone?

BRUTUS.   No more, I pray you.

Messala, I have here received letters,
That young Octavius and Mark Antony
Come down upon us with a mighty power,
Bending their expedition towards Philippi.

MESSALA. Myself have letters of the selfsame tenour.

BRUTUS. With what addition?

MESSALA. That by proscription and bills of outlawry,
Octavius, Antony, and Lepidus
Have put to death an hundred senators.

BRUTUS. Therein our letters do not well agree;
Mine speak of seventy senators that died
By their proscriptions, Cicero being one.

CASSIUS. Cicero one!

MESSALA.   Cicero is dead,
And by that order of proscription.
Had you your letters from your wife, my lord?

BRUTUS. No, Messala.

MESSALA. Nor nothing in your letters writ of her?

BRUTUS. Nothing, Messala.

MESSALA.   That, methinks, is strange.

BRUTUS. Why ask you? Hear you aught of her in yours?

MESSALA. No, my lord.

BRUTUS. Now, as you are a Roman, tell me true.

MESSALA. Then like a Roman bear the truth I tell:
For certain she is dead, and by strange manner.

BRUTUS. Why, farewell, Portia. We must die, Messala:
With meditating that she must die once,
I have the patience to endure it now.

MESSALA. Even so great men great losses should endure.

CASSIUS. I have as much of this in art as you,
But yet my nature could not bear it so.

BRUTUS. Well, to our work alive. What do you think
Of marching to Philippi presently?

CASSIUS. I do not think it good.

BRUTUS.   Your reason?

CASSIUS.   That is it:
'Tis better that the enemy seek us:
So shall he waste his means, weary his soldiers,
Doing himself offence; whilst we, lying still,
Are full of rest, defence, and nimbleness.

BRUTUS. Good reasons must, of force, give place to better.
The people 'twixt Philippi and this ground

Do stand but in a forc'd affection;
For they have grudg'd us contribution:
The enemy, marching along by them,
By them shall make a fuller number up,
Come on refresh'd, new-added, and encourag'd;
From which advantage shall we cut him off,
If at Philippi we do face him there,
These people at our back.

CASSIUS. Hear me, good brother.

BRUTUS. Under your pardon. You must note beside
That we have tried the utmost of our friends,
Our legions are brim-full, our cause is ripe:
The enemy increaseth every day;
We, at the height, are ready to decline.
There is a tide in the affairs of men,
Which, taken at the flood, leads on to fortune;
Omitted, all the voyage of their life
Is bound in shallows and in miseries.
On such a full sea are we now afloat;
And we must take the current when it serves,
Or lose our ventures.

CASSIUS.   Then, with your will, go on;
We 'll along ourselves, and meet them at Philippi.

BRUTUS. The deep of night is crept upon our talk,
And nature must obey necessity,
Which we will niggard with a little rest.
There is no more to say?

CASSIUS.   No more. Good-night:
Early to-morrow we will rise, and hence.

BRUTUS. Lucius!

Re-enter Lucius

          My gown.   *Exit Lucius*
                    Farewell, good Messala:
Good-night, Titinius. Noble, noble Cassius,
Good-night, and good repose.

CASSIUS.   O my dear brother!
This was an ill beginning of the night:
Never come such division 'tween our souls!
Let it not, Brutus.

BRUTUS.   Every thing is well.

CASSIUS. Good-night, my lord.

BRUTUS.   Good-night, good brother.

TITINIUS. ⎫ Good-night, Lord Brutus.
MESSALA. ⎭

BRUTUS.   Farewell, every one.

Exeunt Cassius, Titinius, and Messala
Re-enter Lucius, with the gown

Give me the gown. Where is thy instrument?

LUCIUS. Here in the tent.

BRUTUS.   What! thou speak'st drowsily?
Poor knave, I blame thee not: thou art o'er-watch'd.
Call Claudius and some other of my men;
I 'll have them sleep on cushions in my tent.

LUCIUS. Varro! and Claudius!

Enter Varro and Claudius

VARRO. Calls my lord?

BRUTUS. I pray you, sirs, lie in my tent and sleep:
It may be I shall raise you by and by
On business to my brother Cassius.

VARRO. So please you, we will stand and watch your
    pleasure.

BRUTUS. I will not have it so; lie down, good sirs;
It may be I shall otherwise bethink me.
Look, Lucius, here 's the book I sought for so;
I put it in the pocket of my gown.

Varro and Claudius lie down

LUCIUS. I was sure your lordship did not give it me.

BRUTUS. Bear with me, good boy, I am much forgetful.
Canst thou hold up thy heavy eyes awhile,
And touch thy instrument a strain or two?

LUCIUS. Ay, my lord, an 't please you.

BRUTUS.   It does, my boy:
I trouble thee too much, but thou art willing.

LUCIUS. It is my duty, sir.

BRUTUS. I should not urge thy duty past thy might;
I know young blood looks for a time of rest.

LUCIUS. I have slept, my lord, already.

BRUTUS. It was well done, and thou shalt sleep again;
I will not hold thee long: if I do live,
I will be good to thee.   *Music, and a song*
This is a sleepy tune: O murderous slumber!
Lay'st thou thy leaden mace upon my boy,
That plays thee music? Gentle knave, good-night;
I will not do thee so much wrong to wake thee.

If thou dost nod, thou break'st thy instrument;
I 'll take it from thee; and, good boy, good-night.
Let me see, let me see; is not the leaf turn'd down
Where I left reading? Here it is, I think.

Enter the Ghost of Cæsar

How ill this taper burns! Ha! who comes here?
I think it is the weakness of mine eyes
That shapes this monstrous apparition.
It comes upon me. Art thou any thing?
Art thou some god, some angel, or some devil,
That mak'st my blood cold and my hair to stare?
Speak to me what thou art.

GHOST. Thy evil spirit, Brutus.

BRUTUS.   Why com'st thou?

GHOST. To tell thee thou shalt see me at Philippi.

BRUTUS. Well; then I shall see thee again?

GHOST.   Ay, at Philippi.

BRUTUS. Why, I will see thee at Philippi then.

Ghost vanishes

Now I have taken heart thou vanishest:
Ill spirit, I would hold more talk with thee.
Boy, Lucius! Varro! Claudius! Sirs, awake!
Claudius!

LUCIUS. The strings, my lord, are false.

BRUTUS. He thinks he still is at his instrument.
Lucius, awake!

LUCIUS. My lord!

BRUTUS. Didst thou dream, Lucius, that thou so criedst out?

LUCIUS. My lord, I do not know that I did cry.

BRUTUS. Yes, that thou didst. Didst thou see any thing?

LUCIUS. Nothing, my lord.

BRUTUS. Sleep again, Lucius. Sirrah, Claudius! (*To Varro*)
Fellow thou! awake!

VARRO. My lord!

CLAUDIUS. My lord!

BRUTUS. Why did you so cry out, sirs, in your sleep?

VARRO.
CLAUDIUS. } Did we, my lord?

BRUTUS.   Ay: saw you any thing?

VARRO. No, my lord, I saw nothing.

CLAUDIUS.   Nor I, my lord.

BRUTUS. Go, and commend me to my brother Cassius.
Bid him set on his powers betimes before,
And we will follow.

VARRO.
CLAUDIUS. } It shall be done, my lord.

Exeunt

ACT FIVE

SCENE ONE

The Plains of Philippi.

Enter Octavius, Antony, and their Army

OCTAVIUS. Now, Antony, our hopes are answered:
  You said the enemy would not come down,
  But keep the hills and upper regions;
  It proves not so; their battles are at hand;
  They mean to warn us at Philippi here,
  Answering before we do demand of them.
ANTONY. Tut! I am in their bosoms, and I know
  Wherefore they do it: they could be content
  To visit other places; and come down
  With fearful bravery, thinking by his face
  To fasten in our thoughts that they have courage;
  But 'tis not so.

Enter a Messenger

MESSENGER.   Prepare you, generals:
  The enemy comes on in gallant show;
  The bloody sign of battle is hung out,
  And something to be done immediately.
ANTONY. Octavius, lead your battle softly on,
  Upon the left hand of the even field.
OCTAVIUS. Upon the right hand I; keep thou the left.
ANTONY. Why do you cross me in this exigent?
OCTAVIUS. I do not cross you; but I will do so.   *March*
  *Drum. Enter Brutus, Cassius, and their Army; Lucilius,
  Titinius, Messala, and Others*
BRUTUS. They stand, and would have parley.
CASSIUS. Stand fast, Titinius: we must out and talk.
OCTAVIUS. Mark Antony, shall we give sign of battle?
ANTONY. No, Cæsar, we will answer on their charge.
  Make forth; the generals would have some words.

OCTAVIUS. Stir not until the signal.

BRUTUS. Words before blows: is it so, countrymen?

OCTAVIUS. Not that we love words better, as you do.

BRUTUS. Good words are better than bad strokes, Octavius.

ANTONY. In your bad strokes, Brutus, you give good words:
  Witness the hole you made in Cæsar's heart,
  Crying, 'Long live! hail, Cæsar!'

CASSIUS.   Antony,
  The posture of your blows are yet unknown;
  But for your words, they rob the Hybla bees,
  And leave them honeyless.

ANTONY.   Not stingless too.

BRUTUS. O! yes, and soundless too;
  For you have stol'n their buzzing, Antony,
  And very wisely threat before you sting.

ANTONY. Villains! you did not so when your vile daggers
  Hack'd one another in the sides of Cæsar:
  You show'd your teeth like apes, and fawn'd like hounds,
  And bow'd like bondmen, kissing Cæsar's feet;
  Whilst damned Casca, like a cur, behind
  Struck Cæsar on the neck. O you flatterers!

CASSIUS. Flatterers! Now, Brutus, thank yourself:
  This tongue had not offended so to-day,
  If Cassius might have rul'd.

OCTAVIUS. Come, come, the cause: if arguing make us
    sweat,
  The proof of it will turn to redder drops.
  Look;
  I draw a sword against conspirators;
  When think you that the sword goes up again?
  Never, till Cæsar's three-and-thirty wounds
  Be well aveng'd; or till another Cæsar
  Have added slaughter to the sword of traitors.

BRUTUS. Cæsar, thou canst not die by traitors' hands,
  Unless thou bring'st them with thee.

OCTAVIUS.   So I hope;
  I was not born to die on Brutus' sword.

BRUTUS. O! if thou wert the noblest of thy strain,
  Young man, thou couldst not die more honourable.

CASSIUS. A peevish schoolboy, worthless of such honour,
  Join'd with a masker and a reveller.

ANTONY. Old Cassius still!

OCTAVIUS.   Come, Antony; away!
  Defiance, traitor, hurl we in your teeth.
  If you dare fight to-day, come to the field;
  If not, when you have stomachs.

                    Exeunt Octavius, Antony, and their Army

CASSIUS. Why now, blow wind, swell billow, and swim
      bark!
  The storm is up, and all is on the hazard.
BRUTUS. Ho!
  Lucilius! hark, a word with you.
LUCILIUS.   My lord?

                    Brutus and Lucilius talk apart

CASSIUS. Messala!
MESSALA.   What says my general?
CASSIUS.   Messala,
  This is my birth-day; as this very day
  Was Cassius born. Give me thy hand, Messala:
  Be thou my witness that against my will,
  As Pompey was, am I compell'd to set
  Upon one battle all our liberties.
  You know that I held Epicurus strong,
  And his opinion; now I change my mind,
  And partly credit things that do presage.
  Coming from Sardis, on our former ensign
  Two mighty eagles fell, and there they perch'd,
  Gorging and feeding from our soldiers' hands;
  Who to Philippi here consorted us:
  This morning are they fled away and gone,
  And in their stead do ravens, crows, and kites
  Fly o'er our heads, and downward look on us,
  As we were sickly prey: their shadows seem
  A canopy most fatal, under which
  Our army lies, ready to give up the ghost.
MESSALA. Believe not so.
CASSIUS.   I but believe it partly,
  For I am fresh of spirit and resolv'd
  To meet all perils very constantly.
BRUTUS. Even so, Lucilius.
CASSIUS.   Now, most noble Brutus,
  The gods to-day stand friendly, that we may,
  Lovers in peace, lead on our days to age!
  But since the affairs of men rest still incertain,

Let 's reason with the worst that may befall.
If we do lose this battle, then is this
The very last time we shall speak together:
What are you then determined to do?

BRUTUS. Even by the rule of that philosophy
By which I did blame Cato for the death
Which he did give himself; I know not how,
But I do find it cowardly and vile,
For fear of what might fall, so to prevent
The time of life: arming myself with patience,
To stay the providence of some high powers
That govern us below.

CASSIUS. Then, if we lose this battle,
You are contented to be led in triumph
Through the streets of Rome?

BRUTUS. No, Cassius, no: think not, thou noble Roman,
That ever Brutus will go bound to Rome;
He bears too great a mind: but this same day
Must end that work the ides of March begun;
And whether we shall meet again I know not.
Therefore our everlasting farewell take:
For ever, and for ever, farewell, Cassius!
If we do meet again, why, we shall smile!
If not, why then, this parting was well made.

CASSIUS. For ever, and for ever, farewell, Brutus!
If we do meet again, we 'll smile indeed;
If not, 'tis true this parting was well made.

BRUTUS. Why, then, lead on. O! that a man might know
The end of this day's business ere it come;
But it sufficeth that the day will end,
And then the end is known. Come, ho! away!   *Exeunt*

SCENE TWO

The Field of Battle.

Alarum. Enter Brutus and Messala

BRUTUS. Ride, ride, Messala, ride, and give these bills
Unto the legions on the other side.   *Loud alarum*
Let them set on at once, for I perceive
But cold demeanour in Octavius' wing,

And sudden push gives them the overthrow.
Ride, ride, Messala: let them all come down.   *Exeunt*

SCENE THREE

Another Part of the Field.

Alarum. Enter Cassius and Titinius

CASSIUS. O! look, Titinius, look, the villains fly:
Myself have to mine own turn'd enemy;
This ensign here of mine was turning back;
I slew the coward, and did take it from him.
TITINIUS. O Cassius! Brutus gave the word too early;
Who, having some advantage on Octavius,
Took it too eagerly: his soldiers fell to spoil,
Whilst we by Antony are all enclos'd.
                    Enter Pindarus
PINDARUS. Fly further off, my lord, fly further off;
Mark Antony is in your tents, my lord:
Fly, therefore, noble Cassius, fly far off.
CASSIUS. This hill is far enough. Look, look, Titinius;
Are those my tents where I perceive the fire?
TITINIUS. They are, my lord.
CASSIUS.   Titinius, if thou lov'st me,
Mount thou my horse, and hide thy spurs in him,
Till he have brought thee up to yonder troops
And here again; that I may rest assur'd
Whether yond troops are friend or enemy.
TITINIUS. I will be here again, even with a thought.   *Exit*
CASSIUS. Go, Pindarus, get higher on that hill;
My sight was ever thick; regard Titinius,
And tell me what thou not'st about the field.
                    Pindarus ascends the hill
This day I breathed first; time is come round,
And where I did begin, there shall I end;
My life is run his compass. Sirrah, what news?
PINDARUS. (*Above*) O my lord!
CASSIUS. What news?
PINDARUS. Titinius is enclosed round about
With horsemen, that make to him on the spur;
Yet he spurs on: now they are almost on him;

Now, Titinius! now some light; O! he lights too:
He 's ta'en; (*Shout*) and, hark! they shout for joy.
CASSIUS. Come down; behold no more.

O, coward that I am, to live so long,
To see my best friend ta'en before my face!

Pindarus descends

Come hither, sirrah;
In Parthia did I take thee prisoner;
And then I swore thee, saving of thy life,
That whatsoever I did bid thee do,
Thou shouldst attempt it. Come now, keep thine oath;
Now be a freeman; and with this good sword,
That ran through Cæsar's bowels, search this bosom.
Stand not to answer; here, take thou the hilts;
And, when my face is cover'd, as 'tis now,
Guide thou the sword. (*Pindarus stabs him*) Cæsar, thou
    art reveng'd,
Even with the sword that kill'd thee.   *Dies*

PINDARUS. So, I am free; yet would not so have been,
Durst I have done my will. O Cassius,
Far from this country Pindarus shall run,
Where never Roman shall take note of him.   *Exit*

Re-enter Titinius with Messala

MESSALA. It is but change, Titinius; for Octavius
Is overthrown by noble Brutus' power,
As Cassius' legions are by Antony.
TITINIUS. These tidings will well comfort Cassius.
MESSALA. Where did you leave him?
TITINIUS.   .   All disconsolate,
With Pindarus his bondman, on this hill.
MESSALA. Is not that he that lies upon the ground?
TITINIUS. He lies not like the living. O my heart!
MESSALA. Is not that he?
TITINIUS.   No, this was he, Messala,
But Cassius is no more. O setting sun!
As in thy red rays thou dost sink to-night,
So in his red blood Cassius' day is set;
The sun of Rome is set. Our day is gone;
Clouds, dews, and dangers come; our deeds are done.
Mistrust of my success hath done this deed.
MESSALA. Mistrust of good success hath done this deed.
O hateful error, melancholy's child!

Why dost thou show to the apt thoughts of men
The things that are not? O error! soon conceiv'd,
Thou never com'st unto a happy birth,
But kill'st the mother that engender'd thee.

TITINIUS. What, Pindarus! Where art thou, Pindarus?

MESSALA. Seek him, Titinius, whilst I go to meet
The noble Brutus, thrusting this report
Into his ears; I may say, thrusting it;
For piercing steel and darts envenomed
Shall be as welcome to the ears of Brutus
As tidings of this sight.

TITINIUS.   Hie you, Messala,
And I will seek for Pindarus the while.   *Exit Messala*
Why didst thou send me forth, brave Cassius?
Did I not meet thy friends? and did not they
Put on my brows this wreath of victory,
And bid me give it thee? Didst thou not hear their
    shouts?
Alas! thou hast misconstru'd every thing.
But, hold thee, take this garland on thy brow;
Thy Brutus bid me give it thee, and I
Will do his bidding. Brutus, come apace,
And see how I regarded Caius Cassius.
By your leave, gods: this is a Roman's part:
Come, Cassius' sword, and find Titinius' heart.
                                   Kills himself

Alarum. Re-enter Messala, with Brutus, Young Cato,
    Strato, Volumnius, and Lucilius

BRUTUS. Where, where, Messala, doth his body lie?

MESSALA. Lo, yonder: and Titinius mourning it.

BRUTUS. Titinius' face is upward.

CATO.   He is slain.

BRUTUS. O Julius Cæsar! thou art mighty yet!
Thy spirit walks abroad, and turns our swords
In our own proper entrails.   *Low alarums*

CATO.   Brave Titinius!
Look whe'r he have not crown'd dead Cassius!

BRUTUS. Are yet two Romans living such as these?
The last of all the Romans, fare thee well!
It is impossible that ever Rome
Should breed thy fellow. Friends, I owe more tears
To this dead man than you shall see me pay.—

I shall find time, Cassius, I shall find time.—
Come therefore, and to Thassos send his body:
His funerals shall not be in our camp,
Lest it discomfort us. Lucilius, come;
And come, young Cato;—let us to the field.
Labeo and Flavius, set our battles on:—
'Tis three o'clock; and, Romans, yet ere night
We shall try fortune in a second fight.   *Exeunt*

SCENE FOUR

Another Part of the Field.

*Alarum. Enter fighting, Soldiers of both armies; then
Brutus, Young Cato, Lucilius, and Others*

BRUTUS. Yet, countrymen, O! yet hold up your heads!
CATO. What bastard doth not? Who will go with me?
I will proclaim my name about the field:
I am the son of Marcus Cato, ho!
A foe to tyrants, and my country's friend;
I am the son of Marcus Cato, ho!
BRUTUS. And I am Brutus, Marcus Brutus, I;
Brutus, my country's friend; know me for Brutus!
                    Exit, charging the enemy.
                    Cato is overpowered, and falls
LUCILIUS. O young and noble Cato, art thou down?
Why, now thou diest as bravely as Titinius,
And mayst he honour'd, being Cato's son.
FIRST SOLDIER. Yield, or thou diest.
LUCILIUS. Only I yield to die:
There is so much that thou wilt kill me straight.
                    Offering money
Kill Brutus, and be honour'd in his death.
FIRST SOLDIER. We must not. A noble prisoner!
SECOND SOLDIER. Room, ho! Tell Antony, Brutus is ta'en.
FIRST SOLDIER. I'll tell the news: here comes the general.
                    Enter Antony
Brutus is ta'en, my lord.
ANTONY. Where is he?
LUCILIUS. Safe, Antony; Brutus is safe enough:
I dare assure thee that no enemy

Shall ever take alive the noble Brutus:
The gods defend him from so great a shame!
When you do find him, or alive or dead,
He will be found like Brutus, like himself.
ANTONY. This is not Brutus, friend; but, I assure you,
A prize no less in worth. Keep this man safe,
Give him all kindness: I had rather have
Such men my friends than enemies. Go on,
And see whe'r Brutus be alive or dead;
And bring us word unto Octavius' tent
How everything is chanc'd.   *Exeunt*

SCENE FIVE

Another Part of the Field.

Enter Brutus, Dardanius, Clitus, Strato, and Volumnius

BRUTUS. Come, poor remains of friends, rest on this rock.
CLITUS. Statilius show'd the torch-light; but, my lord,
He came not back: he is or ta'en or slain.
BRUTUS. Sit thee down, Clitus: slaying is the word;
It is a deed in fashion. Hark thee, Clitus.   *Whispers*
CLITUS. What, I, my lord? No, not for all the world.
BRUTUS. Peace, then! no words.
CLITUS.   I 'll rather kill myself.
BRUTUS. Hark thee, Dardanius.   *Whispers*
DARDANIUS.   Shall I do such a deed?
CLITUS. O, Dardanius!
DARDANIUS. O, Clitus!
CLITUS. What ill request did Brutus make to thee?
DARDANIUS. To kill him, Clitus. Look, he meditates.
CLITUS. Now is that noble vessel full of grief,
That it runs over even at his eyes.
BRUTUS. Come hither, good Volumnius: list a word.
VOLUMNIUS. What says my lord?
BRUTUS.   Why this, Volumnius:
The ghost of Cæsar hath appear'd to me
Two several times by night; at Sardis once,
And this last night here in Philippi fields.
I know my hour is come.
VOLUMNIUS.   Not so, my lord.

BRUTUS. Nay, I am sure it is, Volumnius.
  Thou seest the world, Volumnius, how it goes;
  Our enemies have beat us to the pit.   *Low alarums*
  It is more worthy to leap in ourselves,
  Than tarry till they push us. Good Volumnius,
  Thou know'st that we two went to school together;
  Even for that our love of old, I prithee,
  Hold thou my sword-hilts, whilst I run on it.
VOLUMNIUS. That 's not an office for a friend, my lord.
                                        Alarum still
CLITUS. Fly, fly, my lord! there is no tarrying here.
BRUTUS. Farewell to you; and you; and you, Volumnius.
  Strato, thou hast been all this while asleep;
  Farewell to thee too, Strato. Countrymen,
  My heart doth joy that yet, in all my life,
  I found no man but he was true to me.
  I shall have glory by this losing day,
  More than Octavius and Mark Antony
  By this vile conquest shall attain unto.
  So fare you well at once; for Brutus' tongue
  Hath almost ended his life's history:
  Night hangs upon mine eyes; my bones would rest,
  That have but labour'd to attain this hour.
                Alarum. Cry within, 'Fly, fly, fly!'
CLITUS. Fly, my lord, fly.
BRUTUS.   Hence! I will follow.
                Exeunt Clitus, Dardanius, and Volumnius
  I prithee, Strato, stay thou by thy lord:
  Thou art a fellow of good respect;
  Thy life hath had some smatch of honour in it:
  Hold then my sword, and turn away thy face,
  While I do run upon it. Wilt thou, Strato?
STRATO. Give me your hand first: fare you well, my lord.
BRUTUS. Farewell, good Strato.—(*He runs on his sword*)
                          Cæsar, now be still;
  I kill'd not thee with half so good a will.   *Dies*
      Alarum. Retreat. Enter Octavius, Antony, Messala,
                  Lucilius, and Army.
OCTAVIUS. What man is that?
MESSALA. My master's man. Strato, where is thy master?
STRATO. Free from the bondage you are in, Messala;
  The conquerors can but make a fire of him;

BRUTUS.   Cæsar, now be still;
I kill'd not thee with half so good a will.

CASSIUS.   Cæsar, now be still:
I killed not thee with half so good a will.

For Brutus only overcame himself,
And no man else hath honour by his death.

LUCILIUS. So Brutus should be found. I thank thee, Brutus,
That thou hast prov'd Lucilius' saying true.

OCTAVIUS. All that serv'd Brutus, I will entertain them.
Fellow, wilt thou bestow thy time with me?

STRATO. Ay, if Messala will prefer me to you.

OCTAVIUS. Do so, good Messala.

MESSALA. How died my master, Strato?

STRATO. I held the sword, and he did run on it.

MESSALA. Octavius, then take him to follow thee,
That did the latest service to my master.

ANTONY. This was the noblest Roman of them all;
All the conspirators save only he
Did that they did in envy of great Cæsar;
He only, in a general honest thought
And common good to all, made one of them.
His life was gentle, and the elements
So mix'd in him that Nature might stand up
And say to all the world, 'This was a man!'

OCTAVIUS. According to his virtue let us use him,
With all respect and rites of burial.
Within my tent his bones to-night shall lie,
Most like a soldier, order'd honourably.
So, call the field to rest; and let 's away,
To part the glories of this happy day.   *Exeunt.*

MACBETH

CAST OF CHARACTERS

DUNCAN, *King of Scotland*

MALCOLM
DONALBAIN } *his Sons*

MACBETH
BANQUO } *Generals of the King's Army*

MACDUFF
LENNOX
ROSS
MENTEITH
ANGUS
CAITHNESS
} *Noblemen of Scotland*

FLEANCE, *Son to Banquo*
SIWARD, *Earl of Northumberland, General of the English Forces*
YOUNG SIWARD, *his Son*
SEYTON, *an Officer attending on Macbeth*

Boy, *Son to Macduff*
An English Doctor
A Scotch Doctor
A Sergeant
A Porter
An Old Man

LADY MACBETH
LADY MACDUFF
Gentlewoman attending on Lady Macbeth

HECATE and three Witches

Lords, Gentlemen, Officers, Soldiers, Murderers, Attendants, and Messengers. The Ghost of Banquo, and other Apparitions

SCENE

Scotland; England

MACBETH

ACT ONE

SCENE ONE

Scotland. A desert Heath.

Thunder and lightning. Enter three Witches.

FIRST WITCH. When shall we three meet again
In thunder, lightning, or in rain?
SECOND WITCH. When the hurlyburly 's done,
When the battle 's lost and won.
THIRD WITCH. That will be ere the set of sun.
FIRST WITCH. Where the place?
SECOND WITCH.   Upon the heath.
THIRD WITCH. There to meet with Macbeth.
FIRST WITCH. I come, Graymalkin!
SECOND WITCH. Paddock calls.
THIRD WITCH. Anon.
ALL. Fair is foul, and foul is fair:
Hover through the fog and filthy air.   *Exeunt*

SCENE TWO

A Camp near Forres.

*Alarum within. Enter King Duncan, Malcolm, Donalbain,
Lennox, with Attendants, meeting a bleeding Sergeant*

DUNCAN. What bloody man is that? He can report,
As seemeth by his plight, of the revolt
The newest state.
MALCOLM.   This is the sergeant
Who, like a good and hardy soldier fought
'Gainst my captivity. Hail, brave friend!
Say to the king the knowledge of the broil
As thou didst leave it.

SERGEANT.   Doubtful it stood;
As two spent swimmers, that do cling together
And choke their art. The merciless Macdonwald—
Worthy to be a rebel, for to that
The multiplying villanies of nature
Do swarm upon him—from the western isles
Of kerns and gallowglasses is supplied;
And fortune, on his damned quarrel smiling,
Show'd like a rebel's whore: but all 's too weak;
For brave Macbeth,—well he deserves that name,—
Disdaining fortune, with his brandish'd steel,
Which smok'd with bloody execution,
Like valour's minion carv'd out his passage
Till he fac'd the slave;
Which ne'er shook hands, nor bade farewell to him,
Till he unseam'd him from the nave to the chaps,
And fix'd his head upon our battlements.

DUNCAN. O valiant cousin! worthy gentleman!

SERGEANT. As whence the sun 'gins his reflection
Shipwracking storms and direful thunders break,
So from that spring whence comfort seem'd to come
Discomfort swells. Mark, King of Scotland, mark:
No sooner justice had with valour arm'd
Compell'd these skipping kerns to trust their heels,
But the Norweyan lord surveying vantage,
With furbish'd arms and new supplies of men
Began a fresh assault.

DUNCAN.   Dismay'd not this
Our captains, Macbeth and Banquo?

SERGEANT.   Yes;
As sparrows eagles, or the hare the lion.
If I say sooth, I must report they were
As cannons overcharg'd with double cracks;
So they
Doubly redoubled strokes upon the foe:
Except they meant to bathe in reeking wounds,
Or memorize another Golgotha,
I cannot tell—
But I am faint, my gashes cry for help.

DUNCAN. So well thy words become thee as thy wounds;
They smack of honour both. Go, get him surgeons.
Exit Sergeant, attended

Enter Ross

Who comes here?

MALCOLM.   The worthy Thane of Ross.

LENNOX. What a haste looks through his eyes! So should he
  look

That seems to speak things strange.

ROSS.   God save the king!

DUNCAN. Whence cam'st thou, worthy thane?

ROSS.   From Fife, great king;

Where the Norweyan banners flout the sky
And fan our people cold. Norway himself,
With terrible numbers,
Assisted by that most disloyal traitor,
The Thane of Cawdor, began a dismal conflict;
Till that Bellona's bridegroom, lapp'd in proof,
Confronted him with self-comparisons,
Point against point, rebellious arm 'gainst arm,
Curbing his lavish spirit: and, to conclude,
The victory fell on us.—

DUNCAN.   Great happiness!

ROSS. That now

Sweno, the Norways' king, craves composition;
Nor would we deign him burial of his men
Till he disbursed, at Saint Colme's Inch,
Ten thousand dollars to our general use.

DUNCAN. No more that Thane of Cawdor shall deceive
Our bosom interest. Go pronounce his present death,
And with his former title greet Macbeth.

ROSS. I 'll see it done.

DUNCAN. What he hath lost noble Macbeth hath won.

                                   Exeunt

SCENE THREE

A Heath.

Thunder. Enter the three Witches

FIRST WITCH. Where hast thou been, sister?

SECOND WITCH. Killing swine.

THIRD WITCH. Sister, where thou?

FIRST WITCH. A sailor's wife had chestnuts in her lap,

And munch'd, and munch'd, and munch'd: 'Give me,'
   quoth I:
'Aroint thee, witch!' the rump-fed ronyon cries.
Her husband 's to Aleppo gone, master o' the Tiger:
But in a sieve I 'll thither sail,
And, like a rat without a tail,
I 'll do, I 'll do, and I 'll do.
SECOND WITCH. I 'll give thee a wind.
FIRST WITCH. Thou 'rt kind.
THIRD WITCH. And I another.
FIRST WITCH. I myself have all the other;
And the very ports they blow,
All the quarters that they know
I' the shipman's card.
I 'll drain him dry as hay:
Sleep shall neither night nor day
Hang upon his pent-house lid;
He shall live a man forbid.
Weary se'nnights nine times nine
Shall he dwindle, peak and pine:
Though his bark cannot be lost,
Yet it shall be tempest-tost.
Look what I have.
SECOND WITCH. Show me, show me.
FIRST WITCH. Here I have a pilot's thumb,
Wrack'd as homeward he did come.   *Drum within*
THIRD WITCH. A drum! a drum!
Macbeth doth come.
ALL. The weird sisters, hand in hand,
Posters of the sea and land,
Thus do go about, about:
Thrice to thine, and thrice to mine,
And thrice again, to make up nine.
Peace! the charm 's wound up.
       Enter Macbeth and Banquo
MACBETH. So foul and fair a day I have not seen.
BANQUO. How far is 't call'd to Forres? What are these,
So wither'd and so wild in their attire,
That look not like th' inhabitants o' the earth,
And yet are on 't? Live you? or are you aught
That man may question? You seem to understand me,

By each at once her choppy finger laying
Upon her skinny lips: you should be women,
And yet your beards forbid me to interpret
That you are so.

MACBETH.   Speak, if you can: what are you?

FIRST WITCH. All hail, Macbeth! hail to thee, Thane of
Glamis!

SECOND WITCH. All hail, Macbeth! hail to thee, Thane of
Cawdor!

THIRD WITCH. All hail, Macbeth; that shalt be king hereafter.

BANQUO. Good sir, why do you start, and seem to fear
Things that do sound so fair? I' the name of truth,
Are ye fantastical, or that indeed
Which outwardly ye show? My noble partner
You greet with present grace and great prediction
Of noble having and of royal hope,
That he seems rapt withal: to me you speak not.
If you can look into the seeds of time,
And say which grain will grow and which will not,
Speak then to me, who neither beg nor fear
Your favours nor your hate.

FIRST WITCH. Hail!

SECOND WITCH. Hail!

THIRD WITCH. Hail!

FIRST WITCH. Lesser than Macbeth, and greater.

SECOND WITCH. Not so happy, yet much happier.

THIRD WITCH. Thou shalt get kings, though thou be none:
So, all hail, Macbeth and Banquo!

FIRST WITCH. Banquo and Macbeth, all hail!

MACBETH. Stay, you imperfect speakers, tell me more:
By Sinel's death I know I am Thane of Glamis;
But how of Cawdor? the Thane of Cawdor lives,
A prosperous gentleman; and to be king
Stands not within the prospect of belief
No more than to be Cawdor. Say, from whence
You owe this strange intelligence? or why
Upon this blasted heath you stop our way
With such prophetic greeting? Speak, I charge you.

Witches vanish

BANQUO. The earth hath bubbles, as the water has,

And these are of them. Whither are they vanish'd?

MACBETH. Into the air, and what seem'd corporal melted
  As breath into the wind. Would they had stay'd!

BANQUO. Were such things here as we do speak about?
  Or have we eaten on the insane root
  That takes the reason prisoner?

MACBETH. Your children shall be kings.

BANQUO.   You shall be king.

MACBETH. And Thane of Cawdor too; went it not so?

BANQUO. To the selfsame tune and words. Who 's here?

Enter Ross and Angus

ROSS. The king hath happily receiv'd, Macbeth,
  The news of thy success; and when he reads
  Thy personal venture in the rebels' fight,
  His wonders and his praises do contend
  Which should be thine or his. Silenc'd with that,
  In viewing o'er the rest o' the selfsame day,
  He finds thee in the stout Norweyan ranks,
  Nothing afeard of what thyself didst make,
  Strange images of death. As thick as hail
  Came post with post, and every one did bear
  Thy praises in his kingdom's great defence,
  And pour'd them down before him.

ANGUS.   We are sent
  To give thee from our royal master thanks;
  Only to herald thee into his sight,
  Not pay thee.

ROSS. And, for an earnest of a greater honour,
  He bade me, from him, call thee Thane of Cawdor:
  In which addition, hail, most worthy thane!
  For it is thine.

BANQUO.   What! can the devil speak true?

MACBETH. The Thane of Cawdor lives: why do you dress
  me
  In borrow'd robes?

ANGUS.   Who was the thane lives yet;
  But under heavy judgment bears that life
  Which he deserves to lose. Whether he was combin'd
  With those of Norway, or did line the rebel
  With hidden help or vantage, or that with both
  He labour'd in his country's wrack, I know not;
  But treasons capital, confess'd and prov'd,

THIRD WITCH.　All hail, Macbeth; that shalt be king

Have overthrown him.

MACBETH. (*Aside*) Glamis, and Thane of Cawdor:
The greatest is behind. (*To Ross and Angus*) Thanks for
  your pains.
(*To Banquo*) Do you not hope your children shall be
  kings,
When those that gave the Thane of Cawdor to me
Promis'd no less to them?

BANQUO.   That, trusted home,
Might yet enkindle you unto the crown,
Besides the Thane of Cawdor. But 'tis strange:
And oftentimes, to win us to our harm,
The instruments of darkness tell us truths,
Win us with honest trifles, to betray 's
In deepest consequence.
Cousins, a word, I pray you.

MACBETH. (*Aside*)   Two truths are told,
As happy prologues to the swelling act
Of the imperial theme.—I thank you, gentlemen.
(*Aside*) This supernatural soliciting
Cannot be ill, cannot be good; if ill,
Why hath it given me earnest of success,
Commencing in a truth? I am Thane of Cawdor:
If good, why do I yield to that suggestion
Whose horrid image doth unfix my hair
And make my seated heart knock at my ribs,
Against the use of nature? Present fears
Are less than horrible imaginings;
My thought, whose murder yet is but fantastical,
Shakes so my single state of man that function
Is smother'd in surmise, and nothing is
But what is not.

BANQUO.   Look, how our partner 's rapt.

MACBETH. (*Aside*) If chance will have me king, why, chance
    may crown me,
Without my stir.

BANQUO.   New honours come upon him,
Like our strange garments, cleave not to their mould
But with the aid of use.

MACBETH. (*Aside*)   Come what come may,
Time and the hour runs through the roughest day.

BANQUO. Worthy Macbeth, we stay upon your leisure.

MACBETH. Give me your favour: my dull brain was wrought
With things forgotten. Kind gentlemen, your pains
Are register'd where every day I turn
The leaf to read them. Let us toward the king.
(*To Banquo*) Think upon what hath chanc'd; and, at
more time,
The interim having weigh'd it, let us speak
Our free hearts each to other.

BANQUO. Very gladly.

MACBETH. Till then, enough. Come, friends. *Exeunt*

SCENE FOUR

Forres. A Room in the Palace.

*Flourish. Enter Duncan, Malcolm, Donalbain,
Lennox, and Attendants*

DUNCAN. Is execution done on Cawdor? Are not
Those in commission yet return'd?

MALCOLM. My liege,
They are not yet come back; but I have spoke
With one that saw him die; who did report
That very frankly he confess'd his treasons,
Implor'd your Highness' pardon and set forth
A deep repentance. Nothing in his life
Became him like the leaving it; he died
As one that had been studied in his death
To throw away the dearest thing he ow'd,
As 'twere a careless trifle.

DUNCAN. There 's no art
To find the mind's construction in the face:
He was a gentleman on whom I built
An absolute trust.

Enter Macbeth, Banquo, Ross, and Angus
O worthiest cousin!
The sin of my ingratitude even now
Was heavy on me. Thou art so far before
That swiftest wing of recompense is slow
To overtake thee; would thou hadst less deserv'd,
That the proportion both of thanks and payment
Might have been mine! only I have left to say,
More is thy due than more than all can pay.

MACBETH. The service and the loyalty I owe,
In doing it, pays itself. Your Highness' part
Is to receive our duties; and our duties
Are to your throne and state, children and servants;
Which do but what they should, by doing everything
Safe toward your love and honour.

DUNCAN.   Welcome hither:
I have begun to plant thee, and will labour
To make thee full of growing. Noble Banquo,
That hast no less deserv'd, nor must be known
No less to have done so, let me infold thee
And hold thee to my heart.

BANQUO.   There if I grow,
The harvest is your own.

DUNCAN.   My plenteous joys,
Wanton in fulness, seek to hide themselves
In drops of sorrow. Sons, kinsmen, thanes,
And you whose places are the nearest, know
We will establish our estate upon
Our eldest, Malcolm, whom we name hereafter
The Prince of Cumberland; which honour must
Not unaccompanied invest him only,
But signs of nobleness, like stars, shall shine
On all deservers. From hence to Inverness,
And bind us further to you.

MACBETH. The rest is labour, which is not us'd for you:
I 'll be myself the harbinger, and make joyful
The hearing of my wife with your approach;
So, humbly take my leave.

DUNCAN.   My worthy Cawdor!

MACBETH. (*Aside*) The Prince of Cumberland! that is a
     step
On which I must fall down, or else o'erleap,
For in my way it lies. Stars, hide your fires!
Let not light see my black and deep desires;
The eye wink at the hand; yet let that be
Which the eye fears, when it is done, to see.   *Exit*

DUNCAN. True, worthy Banquo; he is full so valiant,
And in his commendations I am fed;
It is a banquet to me. Let 's after him,
Whose care is gone before to bid us welcome:
It is a peerless kinsman.   *Flourish. Exeunt*

SCENE FIVE

Inverness. Macbeth's Castle.

Enter Lady Macbeth, reading a letter

'They met me in the day of success; and I have learned by
the perfectest report, they have more in them than
mortal knowledge. When I burned in desire to question
them further, they made themselves air, into which they
vanished. Whiles I stood rapt in the wonder of it, came
missives from the king, who all-hailed me "Thane of
Cawdor"; by which title, before, these weird sisters sa-
luted me, and referred me to the coming on of time, with
"Hail, king that shalt be!" This have I thought good to
deliver thee, my dearest partner of greatness, that thou
mightest not lose the dues of rejoicing, by being ignorant
of what greatness is promised thee. Lay it to thy heart,
and farewell.'

Glamis thou art, and Cawdor; and shalt be
What thou art promis'd. Yet do I fear thy nature;
It is too full o' the milk of human kindness
To catch the nearest way; thou wouldst be great,
Art not without ambition, but without
The illness should attend it; what thou wouldst highly,
That thou wouldst holily; wouldst not play false,
And yet wouldst wrongly win; thou 'dst have, great
    Glamis,
That which cries 'Thus thou must do, if thou have it';
And that which rather thou dost fear to do
Than wishest should be undone. Hie thee hither,
That I may pour my spirits in thine ear,
And chastise with the valour of my tongue
All that impedes thee from the golden round,
Which fate and metaphysical aid both seem
To have thee crown'd withal.

Enter a Messenger

                    What is your tidings?
MESSENGER. The king comes here to-night.
LADY MACBETH.   Thou 'rt mad to say it!
Is not thy master with him? who, were 't so,
Would have inform'd for preparation.

MESSENGER. So please you, it is true: our thane is coming;
 One of my fellows had the speed of him,
 Who, almost dead for breath, had scarcely more
 Than would make up his message.

LADY MACBETH.   Give him tending;
 He brings great news.—(*Exit Messenger*) The raven him-
  self is hoarse
 That croaks the fatal entrance of Duncan
 Under my battlements. Come, you spirits
 That tend on mortal thoughts! unsex me here,
 And fill me from the crown to the toe top-full
 Of direst cruelty; make thick my blood,
 Stop up the access and passage to remorse,
 That no compunctious visitings of nature
 Shake my fell purpose, nor keep peace between
 The effect and it! Come to my woman's breasts,
 And take my milk for gall, you murdering ministers,
 Wherever in your sightless substances
 You wait on nature's mischief! Come, thick night,
 And pall thee in the dunnest smoke of hell,
 That my keen knife see not the wound it makes,
 Nor heaven peep through the blanket of the dark,
 To cry 'Hold, hold!'

       Enter Macbeth
       Great Glamis! worthy Cawdor!
Greater than both, by the all-hail hereafter!
 Thy letters have transported me beyond
 This ignorant present, and I feel now
 The future in the instant.

MACBETH.   My dearest love,
 Duncan comes here to-night.

LADY MACBETH.   And when goes hence?

MACBETH. To-morrow, as he purposes.

LADY MACBETH.   O! never
 Shall sun that morrow see.
 Your face, my thane, is as a book where men
 May read strange matters. To beguile the time,
 Look like the time; bear welcome in your eye,
 Your hand, your tongue: look like the innocent flower,
 But be the serpent under 't. He that 's coming
 Must be provided for; and you shall put
 This night's great business into my dispatch;

Which shall to all our nights and days to come
Give solely sovereign sway and masterdom.
MACBETH. We will speak further.
LADY MACBETH.   Only look up clear;
To alter favour ever is to fear.
Leave all the rest to me.   *Exeunt*

SCENE SIX

Inverness. Before the Castle.

*Hautboys and torches. Enter Duncan, Malcolm, Donalbain,
Banquo, Lennox, Macduff, Ross, Angus, and Attendants*

DUNCAN. This castle hath a pleasant seat; the air
Nimbly and sweetly recommends itself
Unto our gentle senses.
BANQUO.   This guest of summer,
The temple-haunting martlet, does approve
By his lov'd mansionry that the heaven's breath
Smells wooingly here: no jutty, frieze,
Buttress, nor coign of vantage, but this bird
Hath made his pendent bed and procreant cradle:
Where they most breed and haunt, I have observ'd
The air is delicate.
                    Enter Lady Macbeth
DUNCAN.   See, see, our honour'd hostess!
The love that follows us sometime is our trouble,
Which still we thank as love. Herein I teach you
How you shall bid God 'eyld us for your pains,
And thank us for your trouble.
LADY MACBETH.   All our service,
In every point twice done, and then done double,
Were poor and single business, to contend
Against those honours deep and broad wherewith
Your Majesty loads our house: for those of old,
And the late dignities heap'd up to them,
We rest your hermits.
DUNCAN.   Where 's the Thane of Cawdor?
We cours'd him at the heels, and had a purpose
To be his purveyor; but he rides well,
And his great love, sharp as his spur, hath holp him

To his home before us. Fair and noble hostess,
We are your guest to-night.
LADY MACBETH.   Your servants ever
Have theirs, themselves, and what is theirs, in compt,
To make their audit at your Highness' pleasure,
Still to return your own.
DUNCAN.   Give me your hand;
Conduct me to mine host: we love him highly,
And shall continue our graces towards him.
By your leave, hostess.   *Exeunt*

SCENE SEVEN

Inverness. A Room in the Castle.

*Hautboys and torches. Enter, and pass over the stage,
a Sewer, and divers Servants with dishes
and service. Then enter Macbeth*

MACBETH. If it were done when 'tis done, then 'twere well
It were done quickly; if the assassination
Could trammel up the consequence, and catch
With his surcease success; that but this blow
Might be the be-all and the end-all here,
But here, upon this bank and shoal of time,
We 'd jump the life to come. But in these cases
We still have judgment here; that we but teach
Bloody instructions, which, being taught, return
To plague the inventor; this even-handed justice
Commends the ingredients of our poison'd chalice
To our own lips. He 's here in double trust:
First, as I am his kinsman and his subject,
Strong both against the deed; then, as his host,
Who should against his murderer shut the door,
Not bear the knife myself. Besides, this Duncan
Hath borne his faculties so meek, hath been
So clear in his great office, that his virtues
Will plead like angels trumpet-tongu'd against
The deep damnation of his taking-off;
And pity, like a naked new-born babe,
Striding the blast, or heaven's cherubin, hors'd
Upon the sightless couriers of the air,

Shall blow the horrid deed in every eye,
That tears shall drown the wind. I have no spur
To prick the sides of my intent, but only
Vaulting ambition, which o'erleaps itself
And falls on the other.—

Enter Lady Macbeth

How now! what news?

LADY MACBETH. He has almost supp'd: why have you left
the chamber?

MACBETH. Hath he ask'd for me?

LADY MACBETH.   Know you not he has?

MACBETH. We will proceed no further in this business:
He hath honour'd me of late; and I have bought
Golden opinions from all sorts of people,
Which would be worn now in their newest gloss,
Not cast aside so soon.

LADY MACBETH.   Was the hope drunk
Wherein you dress'd yourself? hath it slept since,
And wakes it now, to look so green and pale
At what it did so freely? From this time
Such I account thy love. Art thou afeard
To be the same in thine own act and valour
As thou art in desire? Wouldst thou have that
Which thou esteem'st the ornament of life,
And live a coward in thine own esteem,
Letting 'I dare not' wait upon 'I would,'
Like the poor cat i' the adage?

MACBETH.   Prithee, peace.
I dare do all that may become a man;
Who dares do more is none.

LADY MACBETH.   What beast was 't, then,
That made you break this enterprise to me?
When you durst do it then you were a man;
And, to be more than what you were, you would
Be so much more the man. Nor time nor place
Did then adhere, and yet you would make both:
They have made themselves, and that their fitness now
Does unmake you. I have given suck, and know
How tender 'tis to love the babe that milks me:
I would, while it was smiling in my face,
Have pluck'd my nipple from his boneless gums,
And dash'd the brains out, had I so sworn as you

Have done to this.

MACBETH.   If we should fail,—

LADY MACBETH.   We fail!

But screw your courage to the sticking-place,
And we 'll not fail. When Duncan is asleep,
Whereto the rather shall his day's hard journey
Soundly invite him, his two chamberlains
Will I with wine and wassail so convince
That memory, the warder of the brain,
Shall be a fume, and the receipt of reason
A limbeck only; when in swinish sleep
Their drenched natures lie, as in a death,
What cannot you and I perform upon
The unguarded Duncan? what not put upon
His spongy officers, who shall bear the guilt
Of our great quell?

MACBETH.   Bring forth men-children only;

For thy undaunted mettle should compose
Nothing but males. Will it not be receiv'd,
When we have mark'd with blood those sleepy two
Of his own chamber, and us'd their very daggers,
That they have done 't?

LADY MACBETH.   Who dares receive it other,

As we shall make our griefs and clamour roar
Upon his death?

MACBETH.   I am settled, and bend up

Each corporal agent to this terrible feat.
Away, and mock the time with fairest show:
False face must hide what the false heart doth know.

                                        Exeunt

ACT TWO

SCENE ONE

Inverness. Court within the Castle.

*Enter Banquo and Fleance, with a Servant bearing
a torch before him*

BANQUO. How goes the night, boy?

FLEANCE. The moon is down; I have not heard the clock.

BANQUO. And she goes down at twelve.

FLEANCE.   I take 't, 'tis later, sir.

BANQUO. Hold, take my sword. There 's husbandry in
    heaven;
    Their candles are all out. Take thee that too.
    A heavy summons lies like lead upon me,
    And yet I would not sleep: merciful powers!
    Restrain in me the cursed thoughts that nature
    Gives way to in repose.
        Enter Macbeth, and a Servant with a torch
                Give me my sword.
    Who 's there?

MACBETH. A friend.

BANQUO. What, sir! not yet at rest? The king 's a-bed:
    He hath been in unusual pleasure, and
    Sent forth great largess to your offices.
    This diamond he greets your wife withal,
    By the name of most kind hostess; and shut up
    In measureless content.

MACBETH.   Being unprepar'd,
    Our will became the servant to defect,
    Which else should free have wrought.

BANQUO.   All 's well.
    I dreamt last night of the three weird sisters:
    To you they have show'd some truth.

MACBETH.   I think not of them:

Yet, when we can entreat an hour to serve,
We would spend it in some words upon that business,
If you would grant the time.
BANQUO.   At your kind'st leisure.
MACBETH. If you shall cleave to my consent, when 'tis,
It shall make honour for you.
BANQUO.   So I lose none
In seeking to augment it, but still keep
My bosom franchis'd and allegiance clear,
I shall be counsell'd.
MACBETH.   Good repose the while!
BANQUO. Thanks, sir: the like to you.
                    Exeunt Banquo and Fleance
MACBETH. Go bid thy mistress, when my drink is ready
She strike upon the bell. Get thee to bed.   *Exit Servant*
Is this a dagger which I see before me,
The handle toward my hand? Come, let me clutch thee:
I have thee not, and yet I see thee still.
Art thou not, fatal vision, sensible
To feeling as to sight? or art thou but
A dagger of the mind, a false creation,
Proceeding from the heat-oppressed brain?
I see thee yet, in form as palpable
As this which now I draw.
Thou marshall'st me the way that I was going;
And such an instrument I was to use.
Mine eyes are made the fools o' the other senses,
Or else worth all the rest: I see thee still;
And on thy blade and dudgeon gouts of blood,
Which was not so before. There 's no such thing:
It is the bloody business which informs
Thus to mine eyes. Now o'er the one half world
Nature seems dead, and wicked dreams abuse
The curtain'd sleep; witchcraft celebrates
Pale Hecate's offerings; and wither'd murder,
Alarum'd by his sentinel, the wolf,
Whose howl 's his watch, thus with his stealthy pace,
With Tarquin's ravishing strides, toward his design
Moves like a ghost. Thou sure and firm-set earth,
Hear not my steps, which way they walk, for fear
Thy very stones prate of my whereabout,
And take the present horror from the time,

Which now suits with it. Whiles I threat he lives:
Words to the heat of deeds too cold breath gives.

                                                A bell rings

I go, and it is done; the bell invites me.
Hear it not, Duncan; for it is a knell
That summons thee to heaven or to hell.   *Exit*

SCENE TWO

Inverness. Court within the Castle.

Enter Lady Macbeth

LADY MACBETH. That which hath made them drunk hath
      made me bold,
      What hath quench'd them hath given me fire. Hark!
      Peace!
      It was the owl that shriek'd, the fatal bellman,
      Which gives the stern'st good-night. He is about it:
      The doors are open, and the surfeited grooms
      Do mock their charge with snores: I have drugg'd their
          possets,
      That death and nature do contend about them,
      Whether they live or die.

MACBETH. (*Within*) Who's there? what, ho!

LADY MACBETH. Alack! I am afraid they have awak'd,
      And 'tis not done; the attempt and not the deed
      Confounds us. Hark! I laid their daggers ready;
      He could not miss them. Had he not resembled
      My father as he slept I had done 't. My husband!

Enter Macbeth

MACBETH. I have done the deed. Didst thou not hear a
      noise?

LADY MACBETH. I heard the owl scream and the crickets
      cry.
      Did not you speak?

MACBETH.   When?

LADY MACBETH.   Now.

MACBETH.   As I descended?

LADY MACBETH. Ay.

MACBETH. Hark!
      Who lies i' the second chamber?

LADY MACBETH.   Donalbain.

MACBETH. (*Looking on his hands*) This is a sorry sight.

LADY MACBETH. A foolish thought to say a sorry sight.

MACBETH. There's one did laugh in's sleep, and one cried
   'Murder!'
  That they did wake each other: I stood and heard them;
  But they did say their prayers, and address'd them
  Again to sleep.

LADY MACBETH. There are two lodg'd together.

MACBETH. One cried 'God bless us!' and 'Amen' the other:
  As they had seen me with these hangman's hands.
  Listening their fear, I could not say 'Amen,'
  When they did say 'God bless us!'

LADY MACBETH.   Consider it not so deeply.

MACBETH. But wherefore could not I pronounce 'Amen'?
  I had most need of blessing, and 'Amen'
  Stuck in my throat.

LADY MACBETH.   These deeds must not be thought
  After these ways; so, it will make us mad.

MACBETH. Methought I heard a voice cry 'Sleep no more!
  Macbeth does murder sleep,' the innocent sleep,
  Sleep that knits up the ravell'd sleave of care,
  The death of each day's life, sore labour's bath,
  Balm of hurt minds, great nature's second course,
  Chief nourisher in life's feast,—

LADY MACBETH.   What do you mean?

MACBETH. Still it cried 'Sleep no more!' to all the house:
  'Glamis hath murder'd sleep, and therefore Cawdor
  Shall sleep no more, Macbeth shall sleep no more!'

LADY MACBETH. Who was it that thus cried? Why, worthy
   thane,
  You do unbend your noble strength to think
  So brainsickly of things. Go get some water,
  And wash this filthy witness from your hand.
  Why did you bring these daggers from the place?
  They must lie there: go carry them, and smear
  The sleepy grooms with blood.

MACBETH.   I'll go no more:
  I am afraid to think what I have done;
  Look on't again I dare not.

LADY MACBETH.   Infirm of purpose!
  Give me the daggers. The sleeping and the dead

Are but as pictures; 'tis the eye of childhood
That fears a painted devil. If he do bleed,
I 'll gild the faces of the grooms withal;
For it must seem their guilt.   *Exit. Knocking within*
MACBETH.   Whence is that knocking?
How is 't with me, when every noise appals me?
What hands are here! Ha! they pluck out mine eyes.
Will all great Neptune's ocean wash this blood
Clean from my hand? No, this my hand will rather
The multitudinous seas incarnadine,
Making the green one red.

Re-enter Lady Macbeth

LADY MACBETH. My hands are of your color, but I shame
To wear a heart so white.—(*Knocking within*) I hear a
knocking
At the south entry; retire we to our chamber;
A little water clears us of this deed;
How easy is it, then! Your constancy
Hath left you unattended. (*Knocking within*) Hark! more
knocking.
Get on your nightgown, lest occasion call us,
And show us to be watchers. Be not lost
So poorly in your thoughts.
MACBETH. To know my deed, 'twere best not know myself.
Knocking within
Wake Duncan with thy knocking! I would thou couldst!
Exeunt

SCENE THREE

The Same.

Knocking within. Enter a Porter

PORTER. Here 's a knocking, indeed! If a man were porter
of hell-gate he should have old turning the key. (*Knocking within*) Knock, knock, knock! Who 's there, i' the
name of Beelzebub? Here 's a farmer that hanged himself on the expectation of plenty: come in time; have
napkins enough about you; here you 'll sweat for 't.
(*Knocking within*) Knock, knock! Who 's there, i' the
other devil's name! Faith, here 's an equivocator, that

could swear in both the scales against either scale; who
committed treason enough for God's sake, yet could not
equivocate to heaven: O! come in, equivocator. (*Knocking within*) Knock, knock, knock! Who 's there? Faith,
here 's an English tailor come hither for stealing out of a
French hose: come in, tailor; here you may roast your
goose. (*Knocking within*) Knock, knock; never at quiet!
What are you? But this place is too cold for hell. I'll
devil-porter it no further: I had thought to have let in
some of all professions, that go the primrose way to the
everlasting bonfire. (*Knocking within*) Anon, anon! I pray
you, remember the porter.   *Opens the gate*

Enter Macduff and Lennox

MACDUFF. Was it so late, friend, ere you went to bed,
That you do lie so late?

PORTER. Faith, sir, we were carousing till the second cock;
and drink, sir, is a great provoker of three things.

MACDUFF. What three things does drink especially provoke?

PORTER. Marry sir, nose-painting, sleep, and urine. Lechery, sir, it provokes, and unprovokes; it provokes the desire, but it takes away the performance. Therefore much
drink may be said to be an equivocator with lechery; it
makes him, and it mars him; it sets him on, and it takes
him off; it persuades him, and disheartens him; makes
him stand to, and not stand to, in conclusion, equivocates
him in a sleep, and, giving him the lie, leaves him.

MACDUFF. I believe drink gave thee the lie last night.

PORTER. That it did, sir, i' the very throat o' me: but I requited him for his lie; and, I think, being too strong for
him, though he took up my legs sometime, yet I made a
shift to cast him.

MACDUFF. Is thy master stirring?

Enter Macbeth

Our knocking has awak'd him; here he comes.

LENNOX. Good-morrow, noble sir.

MACBETH.   Good-morrow, both.

MACDUFF. Is the king stirring, worthy thane?

MACBETH.   Not yet.

MACDUFF. He did command me to call timely on him:
I have almost slipp'd the hour.

MACBETH.   I 'll bring you to him.

MACDUFF. I know this is a joyful trouble to you;
    But yet 'tis one.
MACBETH. The labour we delight in physics pain.
    This is the door.
MACDUFF.   I 'll make so bold to call,
    For 'tis my limited service.   *Exit*
LENNOX. Goes the king hence to-day?
MACBETH.   He does: he did appoint so.
LENNOX. The night has been unruly: where we lay,
    Our chimneys were blown down; and, as they say,
    Lamentings heard i' the air; strange screams of death,
    And prophesying with accents terrible
    Of dire combustion and confus'd events
    New hatch'd to the woeful time. The obscure bird
    Clamour'd the livelong night: some say the earth
    Was feverous and did shake.
MACBETH.   'Twas a rough night.
LENNOX. My young remembrance cannot parallel
    A fellow to it.

Re-enter Macduff

MACDUFF. O horror! horror! horror! Tongue nor heart
    Cannot conceive nor name thee!
MACBETH. ⎰
LENNOX. ⎱   What 's the matter?
MACDUFF. Confusion now hath made his masterpiece!
    Most sacrilegious murder hath broke ope
    The Lord's anointed temple, and stole thence
    The life o' the building!
MACBETH. What is 't you say? the life?
LENNOX. Mean you his majesty?
MACDUFF. Approach the chamber, and destroy your sight
    With a new Gorgon: do not bid me speak;
    See, and then speak yourselves.
                    Exeunt Macbeth and Lennox
                    Awake! awake!
    Ring the alarum-bell. Murder and treason!
    Banquo and Donalbain! Malcolm! awake!
    Shake off this downy sleep, death's counterfeit,
    And look on death itself! up, up, and see
    The great doom's image! Malcolm! Banquo!
    As from your graves rise up, and walk like sprites,
    To countenance this horror! Ring the bell.   *Bell rings*

Enter Lady Macbeth

LADY MACBETH. What 's the business,
  That such a hideous trumpet calls to parley
  The sleepers of the house? speak, speak!
MACDUFF.   O gentle lady!
  'Tis not for you to hear what I can speak;
  The repetition in a woman's ear
  Would murder as it fell.

Enter Banquo

                        O Banquo! Banquo!
  Our royal master 's murder'd!
LADY MACBETH.   Woe, alas!
  What! in our house?
BANQUO.   Too cruel any where.
  Dear Duff, I prithee, contradict thyself,
  And say it is not so.

Re-enter Macbeth and Lennox

MACBETH. Had I but died an hour before this chance
  I had liv'd a blessed time; for, from this instant,
  There 's nothing serious in mortality.
  All is but toys; renown and grace is dead,
  The wine of life is drawn, and the mere lees
  Is left this vault to brag of.

Enter Malcolm and Donalbain

DONALBAIN. What is amiss?
MACBETH.   You are, and do not know 't:
  The spring, the head, the fountain of your blood
  Is stopp'd; the very source of it is stopp'd.
MACDUFF. Your royal father 's murder'd.
MALCOLM.   O! by whom?
LENNOX. Those of his chamber, as it seem'd, had done 't:
  Their hands and faces were all badg'd with blood;
  So were their daggers, which unwip'd we found
  Upon their pillows: they star'd, and were distracted; no
    man's life
  Was to be trusted with them.
MACBETH. O! yet I do repent me of my fury,
  That I did kill them.
MACDUFF.   Wherefore did you so?
MACBETH. Who can be wise, amaz'd, temperate and furi-
    ous,
  Loyal and neutral, in a moment? No man:

The expedition of my violent love
Outran the pauser, reason. Here lay Duncan,
His silver skin lac'd with his golden blood;
And his gash'd stabs look'd like a breach in nature
For ruin's wasteful entrance: there, the murderers,
Steep'd in the colours of their trade, their daggers
Unmannerly breech'd with gore: who could refrain,
That had a heart to love, and in that heart
Courage to make 's love known?

LADY MACBETH.   Help me hence, ho!
MACDUFF. Look to the lady.
MALCOLM. (*Aside to Donalbain*) Why do we hold our
    tongues,
That most may claim this argument for ours?
DONALBAIN. (*Aside to Malcolm*) What should be spoken
Here where our fate, hid in an auger-hole,
May rush and seize us? Let 's away: our tears
Are not yet brew'd.
MALCOLM. (*Aside to Donalbain*) Nor our strong sorrow
Upon the foot of motion.
BANQUO.   Look to the lady:
                    Lady Macbeth is carried out
And when we have our naked frailties hid,
That suffer in exposure, let us meet,
And question this most bloody piece of work,
To know it further. Fears and scruples shake us:
In the great hand of God I stand, and thence
Against the undivulg'd pretence I fight
Of treasonous malice.
MACDUFF.   And so do I.
ALL.   So all.
MACBETH. Let 's briefly put on manly readiness,
And meet i' the hall together.
ALL.   Well contented.
                    Exeunt all but Malcolm and Donalbain
MALCOLM. What will you do? Let 's not consort with them:
To show an unfelt sorrow is an office
Which the false man does easy. I 'll to England.
DONALBAIN. To Ireland, I; our separated fortune
Shall keep us both the safer: where we are,
There 's daggers in men's smiles: the near in blood,
The nearer bloody.

MALCOLM.   This murderous shaft that 's shot
Hath not yet lighted, and our safest way
Is to avoid the aim: therefore, to horse;
And let us not be dainty of leave-taking,
But shift away: there 's warrant in that theft
Which steals itself when there 's no mercy left.   *Exeunt*

SCENE FOUR

The Same. Without the Castle.

Enter Ross and an Old Man

OLD MAN. Threescore and ten I can remember well;
Within the volume of which time I have seen
Hours dreadful and things strange, but this sore night
Hath trifled former knowings.
ROSS.   Ah! good father,
Thou seest, the heavens, as troubled with man's act,
Threaten his bloody stage: by the clock 'tis day,
And yet dark night strangles the travelling lamp.
Is 't night's predominance, or the day's shame,
That darkness does the face of earth entomb,
When living light should kiss it?
OLD MAN.   'Tis unnatural,
Even like the deed that 's done. On Tuesday last,
A falcon, towering in her pride of place,
Was by a mousing owl hawk'd at and kill'd.
ROSS. And Duncan's horses,—a thing most strange and cer-
    tain,—
Beauteous and swift, the minions of their race,
Turn'd wild in nature, broke their stalls, flung out,
Contending 'gainst obedience, as they would
Make war with mankind.
OLD MAN.   'Tis said they eat each other.
ROSS. They did so; to the amazement of mine eyes,
That look'd upon 't. Here comes the good Macduff.
                Enter Macduff
How goes the world, sir, now?
MACDUFF.   Why, see you not?
ROSS. Is 't known who did this more than bloody deed?
MACDUFF. Those that Macbeth hath slain.

ROSS.   Alas, the day!
What good could they pretend?
MACDUFF.   They were suborn'd.
Malcolm and Donalbain, the king's two sons,
Are stol'n away and fled, which puts upon them
Suspicion of the deed.
ROSS.   'Gainst nature still!
Thriftless ambition, that wilt ravin up
Thine own life's means! Then 'tis most like
The sovereignty will fall upon Macbeth.
MACDUFF. He is already nam'd, and gone to Scone
To be invested.
ROSS.   Where is Duncan's body?
MACDUFF. Carried to Colmekill;
The sacred storehouse of his predecessors
And guardian of their bones.
ROSS.   Will you to Scone?
MACDUFF. No, cousin, I 'll to Fife.
ROSS.   Well, I will thither.
MACDUFF. Well, may you see things well done there: adieu!
Lest our old robes sit easier than our new!
ROSS. Farewell, father.
OLD MAN. God's benison go with you; and with those
That would make good of bad, and friends of foes!
                                                Exeunt

ACT THREE

SCENE ONE

Forres. A Room in the Palace.

Enter Banquo

BANQUO. Thou hast it now: King, Cawdor, Glamis, all,
As the weird women promis'd; and, I fear,
Thou play'dst most foully for 't; yet it was said
It should not stand in thy posterity,
But that myself should be the root and father
Of many kings. If there come truth from them,--
As upon thee, Macbeth, their speeches shine,--
Why, by the verities on thee made good,
May they not be my oracles as well,
And set me up in hope? But, hush! no more.

*Sennet sounded. Enter Macbeth, as king; Lady Macbeth, as
    queen; Lennox, Ross, Lords, Ladies, and Attendants*

MACBETH. Here's our chief guest.

LADY MACBETH.   If he had been forgotten,
It had been as a gap in our great feast,
And all-thing unbecoming.

MACBETH. To-night we hold a solemn supper, sir,
And I 'll request your presence.

BANQUO.   Let your Highness
Command upon me; to the which my duties
Are with a most indissoluble tie
For ever knit.

MACBETH. Ride you this afternoon?

BANQUO. Ay, my good lord.

MACBETH. We should have else desir'd your good advice--
Which still hath been both grave and prosperous--
In this day's council; but we 'll take to-morrow.
Is 't far you ride?

BANQUO. As far, my lord, as will fill up the time

'Twixt this and supper; go not my horse the better,
I must become a borrower of the night
For a dark hour or twain.

MACBETH.   Fail not our feast.

BANQUO. My lord, I will not.

MACBETH. We hear our bloody cousins are bestow'd
In England and in Ireland, not confessing
Their cruel parricide, filling their hearers
With strange invention; but of that to-morrow,
When therewithal we shall have cause of state
Craving us jointly. Hie you to horse; adieu
Till you return at night. Goes Fleance with you?

BANQUO. Ay, my good lord: our time does call upon 's.

MACBETH. I wish your horses swift and sure of foot;
And so I do commend you to their backs.
Farewell.   *Exit Banquo*
Let every man be master of his time
Till seven at night; to make society
The sweeter welcome, we will keep ourself
Till supper-time alone; while then, God be with you!
                    Exeunt all but Macbeth and an Attendant
Sirrah, a word with you. Attend those men
Our pleasure?

ATTENDANT. They are, my lord, without the palace gate.

MACBETH. Bring them before us. (*Exit Attendant*) To be
thus is nothing;
But to be safely thus. Our fears in Banquo
Stick deep, and in his royalty of nature
Reigns that which would be fear'd: 'tis much he dares,
And, to that dauntless temper of his mind,
He hath a wisdom that doth guide his valour
To act in safety. There is none but he
Whose being I do fear; and under him
My genius is rebuk'd, as it is said
Mark Antony's was by Cæsar. He chid the sisters
When first they put the name of king upon me,
And bade them speak to him; then, prophet-like,
They hail'd him father to a line of kings.
Upon my head they plac'd a fruitless crown,
And put a barren sceptre in my gripe,
Thence to be wrench'd with an unlineal hand,
No son of mine succeeding. If 't be so,

For Banquo's issue have I fil'd my mind;
For them the gracious Duncan have I murder'd;
Put rancours in the vessel of my peace
Only for them; and mine eternal jewel
Given to the common enemy of man,
To make them kings, the seed of Banquo kings!
Rather than so, come fate into the list,
And champion me to the utterance! who 's there?
      Re-enter Attendant, with two Murderers
Now go to the door, and stay there till we call.
                                          Exit Attendant
Was it not yesterday we spoke together?
FIRST MURDERER. It was, so please your Highness.
MACBETH.   Well then, now
Have you consider'd of my speeches? Know
That it was he in the times past which held you
So under fortune, which you thought had been
Our innocent self. This I made good to you
In our last conference, pass'd in probation with you,
How you were borne in hand, how cross'd, the instru-
      ments,
Who wrought with them, and all things else that might
To half a soul and to a notion craz'd
Say 'Thus did Banquo.'
FIRST MURDERER. You made it known to us.
MACBETH. I did so; and went further, which is now
Our point of second meeting. Do you find
Your patience so predominant in your nature
That you can let this go? Are you so gospell'd
To pray for this good man and for his issue,
Whose heavy hand hath bow'd you to the grave
And beggar'd yours for ever?
FIRST MURDERER.   We are men, my liege.
MACBETH. Ay, in the catalogue ye go for men;
As hounds and greyhounds, mongrels, spaniels, curs,
Shoughs, water-rugs, and demi-wolves, are clept
All by the name of dogs: the valu'd file
Distinguishes the swift, the slow, the subtle,
The housekeeper, the hunter, every one
According to the gift which bounteous nature
Hath in him clos'd; whereby he does receive
Particular addition, from the bill

That writes them all alike: and so of men.
Now, if you have a station in the file,
Not i' the worst rank of manhood, say it;
And I will put that business in your bosoms,
Whose execution takes your enemy off,
Grapples you to the heart and love of us,
Who wear our health but sickly in his life,
Which in his death were perfect.

SECOND MURDERER.   I am one, my liege,
Whom the vile blows and buffets of the world
Have so incens'd that I am reckless what
I do to spite the world.

FIRST MURDERER.   And I another
So weary with disasters, tugg'd with fortune,
That I would set my life on any chance,
To mend it or be rid on 't.

MACBETH.   Both of you
Know Banquo was your enemy.

SECOND MURDERER.   True, my lord.

MACBETH. So is he mine; and in such bloody distance
That every minute of his being thrusts
Against my near'st of life: and though I could
With bare-fac'd power sweep him from my sight
And bid my will avouch it, yet I must not,
For certain friends that are both his and mine,
Whose loves I may not drop, but wail his fall
Whom I myself struck down; and thence it is
That I to your assistance do make love,
Masking the business from the common eye
For sundry weighty reasons.

SECOND MURDERER.   We shall, my lord,
Perform what you command us.

FIRST MURDERER.   Though our lives—

MACBETH. Your spirits shine through you. Within this hour
          at most
I will advise you where to plant yourselves,
Acquaint you with the perfect spy o' the time,
The moment on 't; for 't must be done to-night,
And something from the palace; always thought
That I require a clearness: and with him—
To leave no rubs nor botches in the work—
Fleance his son, that keeps him company,

Whose absence is no less material to me
Than is his father's, must embrace the fate
Of that dark hour. Resolve yourselves apart;
I 'll come to you anon.

SECOND MURDERER.   We are resolv'd, my lord.

MACBETH. I 'll call upon you straight: abide within.

Exeunt Murderers

It is concluded: Banquo, thy soul's flight,
If it find heaven, must find it out to-night.   *Exit*

SCENE TWO

Forres. Another Room in the Palace.

Enter Lady Macbeth and a Servant

LADY MACBETH. Is Banquo gone from court?

SERVANT. Ay, madam, but returns again to-night.

LADY MACBETH. Say to the king, I would attend his leisure
For a few words.

SERVANT.   Madam, I will.   *Exit*

LADY MACBETH.   Nought 's had, all 's spent,
Where our desire is got without content:
'Tis safer to be that which we destroy
Than by destruction dwell in doubtful joy.

Enter Macbeth

How now, my lord! why do you keep alone,
Of sorriest fancies your companions making,
Using those thoughts which should indeed have died
With them they think on? Things without all remedy
Should be without regard: what 's done is done.

MACBETH. We have scotch'd the snake, not kill'd it:
She 'll close and be herself, whilst our poor malice
Remains in danger of her former tooth.
But let the frame of things disjoint, both the worlds suf-
     fer,
Ere we will eat our meal in fear, and sleep
In the affliction of these terrible dreams
That shake us nightly. Better be with the dead,
Whom we, to gain our peace, have sent to peace,
Than on the torture of the mind to lie
In restless ecstasy. Duncan is in his grave;

After life's fitful fever he sleeps well;
Treason has done his worst: nor steel, nor poison,
Malice domestic, foreign levy, nothing
Can touch him further.

LADY MACBETH.   Come on;
Gentle my lord, sleek o'er your rugged looks;
Be bright and jovial among your guests to-night.

MACBETH. So shall I, love; and so, I pray, be you.
Let your remembrance apply to Banquo;
Present him eminence, both with eye and tongue:
Unsafe the while, that we
Must lave our honours in these flattering streams,
And make our faces vizards to our hearts,
Disguising what they are.

LADY MACBETH.   You must leave this.

MACBETH. O! full of scorpions is my mind, dear wife;
Thou know'st that Banquo, and his Fleance, lives.

LADY MACBETH. But in them nature's copy 's not eterne.

MACBETH. There 's comfort yet; they are assailable;
Then be thou jocund. Ere the bat hath flown
His cloister'd flight, ere, to black Hecate's summons
The shard-borne beetle with his drowsy hums
Hath rung night's yawning peal, there shall be done
A deed of dreadful note.

LADY MACBETH.   What 's to be done?

MACBETH. Be innocent of the knowledge, dearest chuck,
Till thou applaud the deed. Come, seeling night,
Scarf up the tender eye of pitiful day,
And with thy bloody and invisible hand
Cancel and tear to pieces that great bond
Which keeps me pale! Light thickens, and the crow
Makes wing to the rooky wood;
Good things of day begin to droop and drowse,
Whiles night's black agents to their preys do rouse.
Thou marvell'st at my words: but hold thee still;
Things bad begun make strong themselves by ill:
So, prithee, go with me.   *Exeunt*

SCENE THREE

Forres. A Park, with a Road leading to the Palace.

Enter three Murderers

FIRST MURDERER. But who did bid thee join with us?
THIRD MURDERER.   Macbeth.
SECOND MURDERER. He needs not our mistrust, since he de-
    livers
  Our offices and what we have to do
  To the direction just.
FIRST MURDERER.   Then stand with us.
  The west yet glimmers with some streaks of day:
  Now spurs the lated traveller apace
  To gain the timely inn; and near approaches
  The subject of our watch.
THIRD MURDERER.   Hark! I hear horses.
BANQUO. (*Within*) Give us a light there, ho!
SECOND MURDERER.   Then 'tis he: the rest
  That are within the note of expectation
  Already are i' the court.
FIRST MURDERER.   His horses go about.
THIRD MURDERER. Almost a mile; but he does usually,
  So all men do, from hence to the palace gate
  Make it their walk.
SECOND MURDERER.   A light, a light!
THIRD MURDERER.   'Tis he.
FIRST MURDERER. Stand to 't.
    Enter Banquo, and Fleance with a torch
BANQUO. It will be rain to-night.
FIRST MURDERER.   Let it come down.
               They set upon Banquo
BANQUO. O treachery! Fly, good Fleance, fly, fly, fly!
  Thou mayst revenge. O slave!   *Dies. Fleance escapes*
THIRD MURDERER. Who did strike out the light?
FIRST MURDERER.   Was 't not the way?
THIRD MURDERER. There 's but one down; the son is fled.
SECOND MURDERER.   We have lost
  Best half of our affair.
FIRST MURDERER. Well, let 's away, and say how much is
  done.

SCENE FOUR

Forres. A Room of State in the Palace.

A Banquet prepared. Enter Macbeth, Lady Macbeth, Ross,
Lennox, Lords, and Attendants

MACBETH. You know your own degrees; sit down: at first
　　and last,
　　The hearty welcome.

LORDS.　　　　　　　　Thanks to your Majesty.

MACBETH. Ourself will mingle with society
　　And play the humble host.
　　Our hostess keeps her state, but in best time
　　We will require her welcome.

LADY MACBETH. Pronounce it for me, sir, to all our friends;
　　For my heart speaks they are welcome.

　　　　　　Enter First Murderer to the door

MACBETH. See, they encounter thee with their hearts'
　　thanks;
　　Both sides are even: here I 'll sit i' the midst:
　　Be large in mirth; anon, we 'll drink a measure
　　The table round. (*Approaching the door*) There 's blood
　　upon thy face.

MURDERER. 'Tis Banquo's, then.

MACBETH. 'Tis better thee without than he within.
　　Is he dispatch'd?

MURDERER. My lord, his throat is cut; that I did for him.

MACBETH. Thou art the best o' the cut-throats; yet he 's
　　good
　　That did the like for Fleance: if thou didst it,
　　Thou art the nonpareil.

MURDERER.　　　　　　　　Most royal sir,
　　Fleance is 'scap'd.

MACBETH. Then comes my fit again: I had else been per-
　　fect;
　　Whole as the marble, founded as the rock,
　　As broad and general as the casing air:
　　But now I am cabin'd, cribb'd, confin'd, bound in
　　To saucy doubts and fears. But Banquo 's safe?

MURDERER. Ay, my good lord; safe in a ditch he bides,
　　With twenty trenched gashes on his head;

The least a death to nature.

MACBETH.   Thanks for that.
    There the grown serpent lies: the worm that 's fled
    Hath nature that in time will venom breed,
    No teeth for the present. Get thee gone; to-morrow
    We 'll hear ourselves again.   *Exit Murderer*

LADY MACBETH.   My royal lord,
    You do not give the cheer: the feast is sold
    That is not often vouch'd, while 'tis a-making,
    'Tis given with welcome: to feed were best at home;
    From thence, the sauce to meat is ceremony;
    Meeting were bare without it.

MACBETH.   Sweet remembrancer!
    Now good digestion wait on appetite,
    And health on both!

LENNOX.   May it please your Highness sit?
    The Ghost of Banquo enters, and sits in Macbeth's place

MACBETH. Here had we now our country's honour roof'd,
    Were the grac'd person of our Banquo present;
    Who may I rather challenge for unkindness
    Than pity for mischance!

ROSS.   His absence, sir,
    Lays blame upon his promise. Please 't your Highness
    To grace us with your royal company.

MACBETH. The table 's full.

LENNOX.   Here is a place reserv'd, sir.

MACBETH. Where?

LENNOX. Here, my good lord. What is 't that moves your
        Highness?

MACBETH. Which of you hath done this?

LORDS.   What, my good lord?

MACBETH. Thou canst not say I did it: never shake
    Thy gory locks at me.

ROSS. Gentlemen, rise; his Highness is not well.

LADY MACBETH. Sit, worthy friends: my lord is often thus,
    And hath been from his youth: pray you, keep seat;
    The fit is momentary; upon a thought
    He will again be well. If much you note him
    You shall offend him and extend his passion:
    Feed and regard him not. Are you a man?

MACBETH. Ay, and a bold one, that dare look on that
    Which might appal the devil.

LADY MACBETH.   O proper stuff!
This is the very painting of your fear;
This is the air-drawn dagger which, you said,
Led you to Duncan. O! these flaws and starts—
Impostors to true fear—would well become
A woman's story at a winter's fire,
Authoriz'd by her grandam. Shame itself!
Why do you make such faces? When all 's done
You look but on a stool.

MACBETH. Prithee, see there! behold! look! lo! how say you?
Why, what care I? If thou canst nod, speak too.
If charnel-houses and our graves must send
Those that we bury back, our monuments
Shall be the maws of kites.   *Ghost disappears*

LADY MACBETH.   What! quite unmann'd in folly?

MACBETH. If I stand here, I saw him.

LADY MACBETH.   Fie, for shame!

MACBETH. Blood hath been shed ere now, i' the olden time,
Ere human statute purg'd the gentle weal;
Ay, and since too, murders have been perform'd
Too terrible for the ear: the times have been,
That, when the brains were out, the man would die,
And there an end; but now they rise again,
With twenty mortal murders on their crowns,
And push us from our stools: this is more strange
Than such a murder is.

LADY MACBETH.   My worthy lord,
Your noble friends do lack you.

MACBETH.   I do forget.
Do not muse at me, my most worthy friends;
I have a strange infirmity, which is nothing
To those that know me. Come, love and health to all;
Then I 'll sit down. Give me some wine; fill full.
I drink to the general joy of the whole table,
And to our dear friend Banquo, whom we miss;
Would he were here! to all, and him, we thirst,
And all to all.

LORDS.   Our duties, and the pledge.

Re-enter Ghost

MACBETH. Avaunt! and quit my sight! Let the earth hide
thee!
Thy bones are marrowless, thy blood is cold;

Thou hast no speculation in those eyes
Which thou dost glare with.

LADY MACBETH.   Think of this, good peers,
But as a thing of custom: 'tis no other;
Only it spoils the pleasure of the time.

MACBETH. What man dare, I dare:
Approach thou like the rugged Russian bear,
The arm'd rhinoceros, or the Hyrcan tiger;
Take any shape but that, and my firm nerves
Shall never tremble: or be alive again,
And dare me to the desert with thy sword;
If trembling I inhabit then, protest me
The baby of a girl. Hence, horrible shadow!
Unreal mockery, hence!   *Ghost vanishes*
                    Why, so; being gone,
I am a man again. Pray you, sit still.

LADY MACBETH. You have displac'd the mirth, broke the
    good meeting,
With most admir'd disorder.

MACBETH.   Can such things be,
And overcome us like a summer's cloud,
Without our special wonder? You make me strange
Even to the disposition that I owe,
When now I think you can behold such sights,
And keep the natural ruby of your cheeks,
When mine are blanch'd with fear

ROSS.   What sights, my lord?

LADY MACBETH. I pray you, speak not; he grows worse and
    worse;
Question enrages him. At once, good-night:
Stand not upon the order of your going,
But go at once.

LENNOX.   Good-night; and better health
Attend his Majesty!

LADY MACBETH.   A kind good-night to all!
                    Exeunt Lords and Attendants

MACBETH. It will have blood, they say; blood will have
    blood:
Stones have been known to move and trees to speak;
Augurs and understood relations have
By maggot-pies and choughs and rooks brought forth
The secret'st man of blood. What is the night?

LADY MACBETH. Almost at odds with morning, which is
   which.

MACBETH. How sayst thou, that Macduff denies his person
   At our great bidding?

LADY MACBETH.   Did you send to him, sir?

MACBETH. I hear it by the way; but I will send.
   There 's not a one of them but in his house
   I keep a servant fee'd. I will to-morrow—
   And betimes I will—to the weird sisters:
   More shall they speak; for now I am bent to know,
   By the worst means, the worst. For mine own good
   All causes shall give way: I am in blood
   Stepp'd in so far, that, should I wade no more,
   Returning were as tedious as go o'er.
   Strange things I have in head that will to hand,
   Which must be acted ere they may be scann'd.

LADY MACBETH. You lack the season of all natures, sleep.

MACBETH. Come, we 'll to sleep. My strange and self-abuse
   Is the initiate fear that wants hard use:
   We are yet but young in deed.   *Exeunt*

SCENE FIVE

A Heath.

Thunder. Enter the three Witches, meeting Hecate

FIRST WITCH. Why, how now, Hecate! you look angerly.

HECATE. Have I not reason, beldams as you are,
   Saucy and overbold? How did you dare
   To trade and traffic with Macbeth
   In riddles and affairs of death;
   And I, the mistress of your charms,
   The close contriver of all harms,
   Was never call'd to bear my part,
   Or show the glory of our art?
   And, which is worse, all you have done
   Hath been but for a wayward son,
   Spiteful and wrathful; who, as others do,
   Loves for his own ends, not for you.
   But make amends now: get you gone,
   And at the pit of Acheron

MACBETH.   Thou canst not say I did it: never shake
    Thy gory locks at me.

Meet me i' the morning: thither he
Will come to know his destiny:
Your vessels and your spells provide,
Your charms and every thing beside.
I am for the air; this night I 'll spend
Unto a dismal and a fatal end:
Great business must be wrought ere noon:
Upon the corner of the moon
There hangs a vaporous drop profound;
I 'll catch it ere it come to ground:
And that distill'd by magic sleights
Shall raise such artificial sprites
As by the strength of their illusion
Shall draw him on to his confusion:
He shall spurn fate, scorn death, and bear
His hopes 'bove wisdom, grace, and fear;
And you all know security
Is mortals' chiefest enemy.

       Song within, 'Come away, come away,' &c.

Hark! I am call'd; my little spirit, see,
Sits in a foggy cloud, and stays for me.   *Exit*

FIRST WITCH. Come, let 's make haste; she 'll soon be back
   again.   *Exeunt*

SCENE SIX

Forres. A Room in the Palace.

Enter Lennox and another Lord

LENNOX. My former speeches have but hit your thoughts,
  Which can interpret further: only, I say,
  Things have been strangely borne. The gracious Duncan
  Was pitied of Macbeth: marry, he was dead:
  And the right-valiant Banquo walk'd too late;
  Whom, you may say, if 't please you, Fleance kill'd,
  For Fleance fled: men must not walk too late.
  Who cannot want the thought how monstrous
  It was for Malcolm and for Donalbain
  To kill their gracious father? damnèd fact!
  How it did grieve Macbeth! did he not straight
  In pious rage the two delinquents tear,

That were the slaves of drink and thralls of sleep?
Was not that nobly done? Ay, and wisely too;
For 'twould have anger'd any heart alive
To hear the men deny 't. So that, I say,
He has borne all things well; and I do think
That, had he Duncan's sons under his key,—
As, an 't please heaven, he shall not,—they should find
What 'twere to kill a father; so should Fleance.
But, peace! for from broad words, and 'cause he fail'd
His presence at the tyrant's feast, I hear,
Macduff lives in disgrace. Sir, can you tell
Where he bestows himself?

LORD.　　　　　　　　　　The son of Duncan,
From whom this tyrant holds the due of birth,
Lives in the English court, and is receiv'd
Of the most pious Edward with such grace
That the malevolence of fortune nothing
Takes from his high respect. Thither Macduff
Is gone to pray the holy king, upon his aid
To wake Northumberland and warlike Siward:
That, by the help of these—with him above
To ratify the work—we may again
Give to our tables meat, sleep to our nights,
Free from our feasts and banquets bloody knives,
Do faithful homage and receive free honours;
All which we pine for now. And this report
Hath so exasperate the king that he
Prepares for some attempt at war.

LENNOX.　　　　　　　　　Sent he to Macduff?

LORD. He did: and with an absolute, 'Sir, not I,'
The cloudy messenger turns me his back,
And hums, as who should say, 'You 'll rue the time
That clogs me with this answer.'

LENNOX.　　　　　　　　And that well might
Advise him to a caution to hold what distance
His wisdom can provide. Some holy angel
Fly to the court of England and unfold
His message ere he come, that a swift blessing
May soon return to this our suffering country
Under a hand accurs'd!

LORD.　　　　　　　I 'll send my prayers with him!

Exeunt

ACT FOUR

SCENE ONE

A Cavern. In the middle, a boiling Cauldron.

Thunder. Enter the three Witches

FIRST WITCH. Thrice the brinded cat hath mew'd.
SECOND WITCH. Thrice and once the hedge-pig whin'd.
THIRD WITCH. Harper cries: 'Tis time, 'tis time.
FIRST WITCH. Round about the cauldron go;
   In the poison'd entrails throw.
   Toad, that under cold stone
   Days and nights hast thirty-one
   Swelter'd venom sleeping got,
   Boil thou first i' the charmed pot.
ALL. Double, double toil and trouble;
   Fire burn and cauldron bubble.
SECOND WITCH. Fillet of a fenny snake,
   In the cauldron boil and bake;
   Eye of newt, and toe of frog,
   Wool of bat, and tongue of dog,
   Adder's fork, and blind-worm's sting,
   Lizard's leg, and howlet's wing,
   For a charm of powerful trouble,
   Like a hell-broth boil and bubble.
ALL. Double, double toil and trouble;
   Fire burn and cauldron bubble.
THIRD WITCH. Scale of dragon, tooth of wolf,
   Witches' mummy, maw and gulf
   Of the ravin'd salt-sea shark,
   Root of hemlock digg'd i' the dark,
   Liver of blaspheming Jew,
   Gall of goat, and slips of yew
   Sliver'd in the moon's eclipse,
   Nose of Turk, and Tartar's lips,

Finger of birth-strangled babe
Ditch-deliver'd by a drab,
Make the gruel thick and slab:
Add thereto a tiger's chaudron,
For the ingredients of our cauldron.

ALL. Double, double toil and trouble;
Fire burn and cauldron bubble.

SECOND WITCH. Cool it with a baboon's blood,
Then the charm is firm and good.

Enter Hecate

HECATE. O! well done! I commend your pains,
And every one shall share i' the gains.
And now about the cauldron sing,
Like elves and fairies in a ring,
Enchanting all that you put in. ·

Music and a song, 'Black Spirits,' &c.

SECOND WITCH. By the pricking of my thumbs,
Something wicked this way comes.
Open, locks,
Whoever knocks.

Enter Macbeth

MACBETH. How now, you secret, black, and midnight hags!
What is 't you do?

ALL. A deed without a name.

MACBETH. I conjure you, by that which you profess,—
Howe'er you come to know it,—answer me:
Though you untie the winds and let them fight
Against the churches; though the yesty waves
Confound and swallow navigation up;
Though bladed corn be lodg'd and trees blown down;
Though castles topple on their warders' heads;
Though palaces and pyramids do slope
Their heads to their foundations; though the treasure
Of Nature's germens tumble all together,
Even till destruction sicken; answer me
To what I ask you.

FIRST WITCH. Speak.

SECOND WITCH. Demand.

THIRD WITCH. We 'll answer.

FIRST WITCH. Say if thou 'dst rather hear it from our mouths,
Or from our master's?

MACBETH. Call 'em: let me see 'em.

FIRST WITCH. Pour in sow's blood, that hath eaten
  Her nine farrow; grease, that's sweaten
  From the murderer's gibbet throw
  Into the flame.
ALL.   Come, high or low;
  Thyself and office deftly show.
        Thunder. First Apparition of an armed Head
MACBETH. Tell me, thou unknown power,—
FIRST WITCH.   He knows thy thought:
  Hear his speech, but say thou nought.
FIRST APPARITION. Macbeth! Macbeth! Macbeth! beware
    Macduff;
  Beware the Thane of Fife. Dismiss me. Enough.
                                            Descends
MACBETH. Whate'er thou art, for thy good caution thanks;
  Thou hast harp'd my fear aright. But one word more,—
FIRST WITCH. He will not be commanded: here's another,
  More potent than the first.
        Thunder. Second Apparition, a bloody Child
SECOND APPARITION. Macbeth! Macbeth! Macbeth!—
MACBETH. Had I three ears, I'd hear thee.
SECOND APPARITION. Be bloody, bold, and resolute; laugh
    to scorn
  The power of man, for none of woman born
  Shall harm Macbeth.   *Descends*
MACBETH. Then live, Macduff; what need I fear of thee?
  But yet I'll make assurance double sure,
  And take a bond of fate: thou shalt not live;
  That I may tell pale-hearted fear it lies,
  And sleep in spite of thunder.
Thunder. Third Apparition, a Child crowned, with a tree in
                    his hand
                              What is this,
  That rises like the issue of a king,
  And wears upon his baby brow the round
  And top of sovereignty?
ALL.   Listen, but speak not to't.
THIRD APPARITION. Be lion-mettled, proud, and take no
    care
  Who chafes, who frets, or where conspirers are:
  Macbeth shall never vanquish'd be until
  Great Birnam wood to high Dunsinane hill

    Shall come against him.   *Descends*
MACBETH.   That will never be:
    Who can impress the forest, bid the tree
    Unfix his earth-bound root? Sweet bodements! good!
    Rebellion's head, rise never till the wood
    Of Birnam rise, and our high-plac'd Macbeth
    Shall live the lease of nature, pay his breath
    To time and mortal custom. Yet my heart
    Throbs to know one thing: tell me—if your art
    Can tell so much,—shall Banquo's issue ever
    Reign in this kingdom?
ALL.   Seek to know no more.
MACBETH. I will be satisfied: deny me this,
    And an eternal curse fall on you! Let me know.
    Why sinks that cauldron? and what noise is this?
                            Hautboys

FIRST WITCH. Show!
SECOND WITCH. Show!
THIRD WITCH. Show!
ALL. Show his eyes, and grieve his heart;
    Come like shadows, so depart.
A show of Eight Kings; the last with a glass in his hand:
        Banquo's Ghost following
MACBETH. Thou art too like the spirit of Banquo; down!
    Thy crown does sear mine eyeballs: and thy hair,
    Thou other gold-bound brow, is like the first:
    A third is like the former. Filthy hags!
    Why do you show me this? A fourth! Start, eyes!
    What! will the line stretch out to the crack of doom?
    Another yet? A seventh! I 'll see no more:
    And yet the eighth appears, who bears a glass
    Which shows me many more; and some I see
    That two-fold balls and treble sceptres carry.
    Horrible sight! Now I see 'tis true;
    For the blood-bolter'd Banquo smiles upon me,
    And points at them for his.   *Apparitions vanish*
               What! is this so?
FIRST WITCH. Ay, sir, all this is so: but why
    Stands Macbeth thus amazedly?
    Come, sisters, cheer we up his sprites,
    And show the best of our delights.
    I 'll charm the air to give a sound,

While you perform your antick round,
That this great king may kindly say,
Our duties did his welcome pay.

Music. The Witches dance,
and then vanish with Hecate

MACBETH. Where are they? Gone? Let this pernicious hour
Stand aye accursed in the calendar!
Come in, without there!

Enter Lennox

LENNOX.   What 's your Grace's will?
MACBETH. Saw you the weird sisters?
LENNOX.   No, my lord.
. MACBETH. Came they not by you?
LENNOX.   No indeed, my lord.
MACBETH. Infected be the air whereon they ride,
And damn'd all those that trust them! I did hear
The galloping of horse: who was 't came by?
LENNOX. 'Tis two or three, my lord, that bring you word
Macduff is fled to England.
MACBETH.   Fled to England!
LENNOX. Ay, my good lord.
MACBETH. (*Aside*) Time, thou anticipat'st my dread
    exploits;
The flighty purpose never is o'ertook
Unless the deed go with it; from this moment
The very firstlings of my heart shall be
The firstlings of my hand. And even now,
To crown my thoughts with acts, be it thought and done:
The castle of Macduff I will surprise;
Seize upon Fife; give to the edge of the sword
His wife, his babes, and all unfortunate souls
That trace him in his line. No boasting like a fool;
This deed I 'll do, before this purpose cool:
But no more sights! Where are these gentlemen?
Come, bring me where they are.   *Exeunt*

SCENE TWO

Fife. Macduff's Castle.

Enter Lady Macduff, her Son, and Ross

LADY MACDUFF. What had he done to make him fly the
    land?

ROSS. You must have patience, madam.

LADY MACDUFF.   He had none:
   His flight was madness: when our actions do not,
   Our fears do make us traitors.

ROSS.   You know not
   Whether it was his wisdom or his fear.

LADY MACDUFF. Wisdom! to leave his wife, to leave his
    babes,
   His mansion and his titles in a place
   From whence himself does fly? He loves us not;
   He wants the natural touch; for the poor wren,
   The most diminutive of birds, will fight—
   Her young ones in her nest—against the owl.
   All is the fear and nothing is the love;
   As little is the wisdom, where the flight
   So runs against all reason.

ROSS.   My dearest coz,
   I pray you, school yourself: but, for your husband,
   He is noble, wise, judicious, and best knows
   The fits o' the season. I dare not speak much further:
   But cruel are the times, when we are traitors
   And do not know ourselves, when we hold rumour
   From what we fear, yet know not what we fear,
   But float upon a wild and violent sea
   Each way and move. I take my leave of you:
   Shall not be long but I 'll be here again.
   Things at the worst will cease, or else climb upward
   To what they were before. My pretty cousin,
   Blessing upon you!

LADY MACDUFF. Father'd he is, and yet he 's fatherless.

ROSS. I am so much a fool, should I stay longer,
   It would be my disgrace, and your discomfort:
   I take my leave at once.   *Exit*

LADY MACDUFF.   Sirrah, your father 's dead:

And what will you do now? How will you live?

SON. As birds do, mother.

LADY MACDUFF.   What! with worms and flies?

SON. With what I get, I mean; and so do they.

LADY MACDUFF. Poor bird! thou 'dst never fear the net nor lime,

The pitfall nor the gin.

SON. Why should I, mother? Poor birds they are not set for.
My father is not dead, for all your saying.

LADY MACDUFF. Yes, he is dead: how wilt thou do for a father?

SON. Nay, how will you do for a husband?

LADY MACDUFF. Why, I can buy me twenty at any market.

SON. Then you 'll buy 'em to sell again.

LADY MACDUFF. Thou speak'st with all thy wit; and yet, i' faith,
With wit enough for thee.

SON. Was my father a traitor, mother?

LADY MACDUFF. Ay, that he was.

SON. What is a traitor?

LADY MACDUFF. Why, one that swears and lies.

SON. And be all traitors that do so?

LADY MACDUFF. Every one that does so is a traitor, and must be hanged.

SON. And must they all be hanged that swear and lie?

LADY MACDUFF. Every one,

SON. Who must hang them?

LADY MACDUFF. Why, the honest men.

SON. Then the liars and swearers are fools, for there are liars and swearers enow to beat the honest men, and hang up them.

LADY MACDUFF. Now God help thee, poor monkey!
But how wilt thou do for a father?

SON. If he were dead, you 'd weep for him: if you would not, it were a good sign that I should quickly have a new father.

LADY MACDUFF. Poor prattler, how thou talk'st!

Enter a Messenger

MESSENGER. Bless you, fair dame! I am not to you known,
Though in your state of honour I am perfect.
I doubt some danger does approach you nearly:
If you will take a homely man's advice,

Be not found here; hence, with your little ones.
To fright you thus, methinks, I am too savage;
To do worse to you were fell cruelty,
Which is too nigh your person. Heaven preserve you!
I dare abide no longer.   *Exit*

LADY MACDUFF.   Whither should I fly?
I have done no harm. But I remember now
I am in this earthly world, where, to do harm
Is often laudable, to do good sometime
Accounted dangerous folly; why then, alas!
Do I put up that womanly defence,
To say I have done no harm?

Enter Murderers

                                   What are these faces?
MURDERER. Where is your husband?
LADY MACDUFF. I hope in no place so unsanctified
    Where such as thou mayst find him.
MURDERER.   He 's a traitor.
SON. Thou liest, thou shag-hair'd villain.
MURDERER.   What! you egg.
    Young fry of treachery!   *Stabbing him*
SON.   He has killed me, mother:
    Run away, I pray you!   *Dies*
                            Exit Lady Macduff,
            crying 'Murder!' and pursued by the Murderers

SCENE THREE

England. Before the King's Palace.

Enter Malcolm and Macduff

MALCOLM. Let us seek out some desolate shade, and there
    Weep our sad bosoms empty.
MACDUFF.   Let us rather
    Hold fast the mortal sword, and like good men
    Bestride our down-fall'n birthdom; each new morn
    New widows howl, new orphans cry, new sorrows
    Strike heaven on the face, that it resounds
    As if it felt with Scotland and yell'd out
    Like syllable of dolour.
MALCOLM.   What I believe I 'll wail,

What know believe, and what I can redress,
As I shall find the time to friend, I will.
What you have spoke, it may be so perchance.
This tyrant, whose sole name blisters our tongues,
Was once thought honest: you have lov'd him well;
He hath not touch'd you yet. I am young; but something
You may deserve of him through me, and wisdom
To offer up a weak, poor, innocent lamb
To appease an angry god.

MACDUFF. I am not treacherous.

MALCOLM.   But Macbeth is.
A good and virtuous nature may recoil
In an imperial charge. But I shall crave your pardon;
That which you are my thoughts cannot transpose;
Angels are bright still, though the brightest fell;
Though all things foul would wear the brows of grace,
Yet grace must still look so.

MACDUFF.   I have lost my hopes.

MALCOLM. Perchance even there where I did find my
    doubts.
Why in that rawness left you wife and child—
Those precious motives, those strong knots of love—
Without leave-taking? I pray you,
Let not my jealousies be your dishonours,
But mine own safeties: you may be rightly just,
Whatever I shall think.

MACDUFF.   Bleed, bleed, poor country!
Great tyranny, lay thou thy basis sure,
For goodness dares not check thee! wear thou thy
    wrongs;
The title is affeer'd! Fare thee well, lord:
I would not be the villain that thou think'st
For the whole space that 's in the tyrant's grasp,
And the rich East to boot.

MALCOLM.   Be not offended:
I speak not as in absolute fear of you.
I think our country sinks beneath the yoke;
It weeps, it bleeds, and each new day a gash
Is added to her wounds: I think withal
There would be hands uplifted in my right;
And here from gracious England have I offer
Of goodly thousands: but, for all this,

When I shall tread upon the tyrant's head,
Or wear it on my sword, yet my poor country
Shall have more vices than it had before,
More suffer, and more sundry ways than ever,
By him that shall succeed.
MACDUFF.   What should he be?
MALCOLM. It is myself I mean; in whom I know
All the particulars of vice so grafted,
That, when they shall be open'd, black Macbeth
Will seem as pure as snow, and the poor state
Esteem him as a lamb, being compar'd
With my confineless harms.
MACDUFF.   .   Not in the legions
Of horrid hell can come a devil more damn'd
In evils to top Macbeth.
MALCOLM.   I grant him bloody,
Luxurious, avaricious, false, deceitful,
Sudden, malicious, smacking of every sin
That has a name; but there 's no bottom, none,
In my voluptuousness: your wives, your daughters,
Your matrons, and your maids, could not fill up
The cistern of my lust; and my desire
All continent impediments would o'erbear
That did oppose my will; better Macbeth
Than such an one to reign.
MACDUFF.   Boundless intemperance
In nature is a tyranny; it hath been
Th' untimely emptying of the happy throne,
And fall of many kings. But fear not yet
To take upon you what is yours; you may
Convey your pleasures in a spacious plenty,
And yet seem cold, the time you may so hoodwink.
We have willing dames enough; there cannot be
That vulture in you, to devour so many
As will to greatness dedicate themselves,
Finding it so inclin'd.
MALCOLM.   With this there grows
In my most ill-compos'd affection such
A stanchless avarice that, were I king,
I should cut off the nobles for their lands,
Desire his jewels and this other's house;
And my more-having would be as a sauce

To make me hunger more, that I should forge
Quarrels unjust against the good and loyal,
Destroying them for wealth.

MACDUFF.   This avarice
Sticks deeper, grows with more pernicious root
Than summer-seeming lust, and it hath been
The sword of our slain kings: yet do not fear;
Scotland hath foisons to fill up your will,
Of your mere own; all these are portable,
With other graces weigh'd.

MALCOLM. But I have none: the king-becoming graces,
As justice, verity, temperance, stableness,
Bounty, perseverance, mercy, lowliness,
Devotion, patience, courage, fortitude,
I have no relish of them, but abound
In the division of each several crime,
Acting it many ways. Nay, had I power, I should
Pour the sweet milk of concord into hell,
Uproar the universal peace, confound
All unity on earth.

MACDUFF.   O Scotland, Scotland!

MALCOLM. If such a one be fit to govern, speak:
I am as I have spoken.

MACDUFF.   Fit to govern!
No, not to live. O nation miserable,
With an untitled tyrant bloody-sceptr'd,
When shalt thou see thy wholesome days again,
Since that the truest issue of thy throne
By his own interdiction stands accurs'd,
And does blaspheme his breed? Thy royal father
Was a most sainted king; the queen that bore thee,
Oftener upon her knees than on her feet,
Died every day she liv'd. Fare thee well!
These evils thou repeat'st upon thyself
Have banish'd me from Scotland. O my breast,
Thy hope ends here!

MALCOLM.   Macduff, this noble passion,
Child of integrity, hath from my soul
Wip'd the black scruples, reconcil'd my thoughts
To thy good truth and honour. Devilish Macbeth
By many of these trains hath sought to win me
Into his power, and modest wisdom plucks me

From over-credulous haste; but God above
Deal between thee and me! for even now
I put myself to thy direction, and
Unspeak mine own detraction, here abjure
The taints and blames I laid upon myself,
For strangers to my nature. I am yet
Unknown to woman, never was forsworn,
Scarcely have coveted what was mine own,
At no time broke my faith, would not betray
The devil to his fellow, and delight
No less in truth than life; my first false speaking
Was this upon myself. What I am truly,
Is thine and my poor country's to command;
Whither indeed, before thy here-approach,
Old Siward, with ten thousand warlike men,
Already at a point, was setting forth.
Now we 'll together, and the chance of goodness
Be like our warranted quarrel. Why are you silent?

MACDUFF. Such welcome and unwelcome things at once
'Tis hard to reconcile.

Enter a Doctor

MALCOLM. Well; more anon. Comes the king forth, I pray
you?

DOCTOR. Ay, sir; there are a crew of wretched souls
That stay his cure; their malady convinces
The great assay of art; but, at his touch,
Such sanctity hath heaven given his hand,
They presently amend.

MALCOLM.   I thank you, doctor.

Exit Doctor

MACDUFF. What 's the disease he means?
MALCOLM.   'Tis call'd the evil:
A most miraculous work in this good king,
Which often, since my here-remain in England,
I have seen him do. How he solicits heaven,
Himself best knows; but strangely-visited people,
All swoln and ulcerous, pitiful to the eye,
The mere despair of surgery, he cures;
Hanging a golden stamp about their necks,
Put on with holy prayers; and 'tis spoken
To the succeeding royalty he leaves
The healing benediction. With this strange virtue,

He hath a heavenly gift of prophecy,
And sundry blessings hang about his throne
That speak him full of grace.

MACDUFF.   See, who comes here?

MALCOLM. My countryman; but yet I know him not.

Enter Ross

MACDUFF. My ever-gentle cousin, welcome hither.

MALCOLM. I know him now. Good God, betimes remove
The means that makes us strangers!

ROSS.   Sir, amen.

MACDUFF. Stands Scotland where it did?

ROSS.   Alas! poor country:
Almost afraid to know itself. It cannot
Be call'd our mother, but our grave; where nothing,
But who knows nothing, is once seen to smile;
Where sighs and groans and shrieks that rent the air
Are made, not mark'd; where violent sorrow seems
A modern ecstasy; the dead man's knell
Is there scarce ask'd for who; and good men's lives
Expire before the flowers in their caps,
Dying or ere they sicken.

MACDUFF.   O! relation
Too nice, and yet too true!

MALCOLM.   What 's the newest grief?

ROSS. That of an hour's age doth hiss the speaker;
Each minute teems a new one.

MACDUFF.   How does my wife?

ROSS. Why, well.

MACDUFF.   And all my children?

ROSS.   Well too.

MACDUFF. The tyrant has not batter'd at their peace?

ROSS. No; they were well at peace when I did leave 'em.

MACDUFF. Be not a niggard of your speech: how goes 't?

ROSS. When I came hither to transport the tidings,
Which I have heavily borne, there ran a rumour
Of many worthy fellows that were out;
Which was to my belief witness'd the rather
For that I saw the tyrant's power a-foot.
Now is the time of help; your eye in Scotland
Would create soldiers, make our women fight,
To doff their dire distresses.

MALCOLM.   Be 't their comfort

We are coming thither. Gracious England hath
Lent us good Siward and ten thousand men;
An older and a better soldier none
That Christendom gives out.

ROSS.   Would I could answer
This comfort with the like! But I have words
That would be howl'd out in the desert air,
Where hearing should not latch them.

MACDUFF.   What concern they?
The general cause? or is it a fee-grief
Due to some single breast?

ROSS.   No mind that 's honest
But in it shares some woe, though the main part
Pertains to you alone.

MACDUFF.   If it be mine
Keep it not from me; quickly let me have it.

ROSS. Let not your ears despise my tongue for ever,
Which shall possess them with the heaviest sound
That ever yet they heard.

MACDUFF.   Hum! I guess at it.

ROSS. Your castle is surpris'd; your wife and babes
Savagely slaughter'd; to relate the manner,
Were, on the quarry of these murder'd deer,
To add the death of you.

MALCOLM.   Merciful heaven!
What! man; ne'er pull your hat upon your brows;
Give sorrow words; the grief that does not speak
Whispers the o'er-fraught heart and bids it break.

MACDUFF. My children too?

ROSS.   Wife, children, servants, all
That could be found.

MACDUFF.   And I must be from thence!
My wife kill'd too?

ROSS.   I have said.

MALCOLM.   Be comforted:
Let 's make us medicine of our great revenge,
To cure this deadly grief.

MACDUFF. He has no children. All my pretty ones?
Did you say all? O hell-kite! All?
What! all my pretty chickens and their dam
At one fell swoop?

MALCOLM.   Dispute it like a man.

MACDUFF.   I shall do so;
  But I must also feel it as a man:
  I cannot but remember such things were,
  That were most precious to me. Did heaven look on,
  And would not take their part? Sinful Macduff!
  They were all struck for thee. Naught that I am,
  Not for their own demerits, but for mine,
  Fell slaughter on their souls. Heaven rest them now!
MALCOLM. Be this the whetstone of your sword: let grief
  Convert to anger; blunt not the heart, enrage it.
MACDUFF. O! I could play the woman with mine eyes,
  And braggart with my tongue. But, gentle heavens,
  Cut short all intermission; front to front
  Bring thou this fiend of Scotland and myself;
  Within my sword's length set him; if he 'scape,
  Heaven forgive him too!
MALCOLM.   This tune goes manly.
  Come, go we to the king; our power is ready;
  Our lack is nothing but our leave. Macbeth
  Is ripe for shaking, and the powers above
  Put on their instruments. Receive what cheer you may;
  The night is long that never finds the day.   *Exeunt*

ACT FIVE

SCENE ONE

Dunsinane. A Room in the Castle.

Enter a Doctor of Physic and a Waiting-Gentlewoman

DOCTOR. I have two nights watched with you, but can perceive no truth in your report. When was it she last walked?

GENTLEWOMAN. Since his majesty went into the field, I have seen her rise from her bed, throw her nightgown upon her, unlock her closet, take forth paper, fold it, write upon 't, read it, afterwards seal it, and again return to bed; yet all this while in a most fast sleep.

DOCTOR. A great perturbation in nature, to receive at once the benefit of sleep and do the effects of watching! In this slumbery agitation, besides her walking and other actual performances, what, at any time, have you heard her say?

GENTLEWOMAN. That, sir, which I will not report after her.

DOCTOR. You may to me, and 'tis most meet you should.

GENTLEWOMAN. Neither to you nor any one, having no witness to confirm my speech.

Enter Lady Macbeth, with a taper

Lo you! here she comes. This is her very guise; and, upon my life, fast asleep. Observe her; stand close.

DOCTOR. How came she by that light?

GENTLEWOMAN. Why, it stood by her: she has light by her continually; 'tis her command.

DOCTOR. You see, her eyes are open.

GENTLEWOMAN. Ay, but their sense is shut.

DOCTOR. What is it she does now? Look, how she rubs her hands.

GENTLEWOMAN. It is an accustomed action with her, to seem thus washing her hands. I have known her to continue in this a quarter of an hour.

LADY MACBETH. Yet here 's a spot.

DOCTOR. Hark! she speaks. I will set down what comes from her, to satisfy my remembrance the more strongly.

LADY MACBETH. Out, damned spot! out, I say! One; two: why, then, 'tis time to do 't. Hell is murky! Fie, my lord, fie! a soldier, and afeard? What need we fear who knows it, when none can call our power to account? Yet who would have thought the old man to have had so much blood in him?

DOCTOR. Do you mark that?

LADY MACBETH. The Thane of Fife had a wife: where is she now? What! will these hands ne'er be clean? No more o' that, my lord, no more o' that: you mar all with this starting.

DOCTOR. Go to, go to; you have known what you should not.

GENTLEWOMAN. She has spoke what she should not, I am sure of that: Heaven knows what she has known.

LADY MACBETH. Here 's the smell of the blood still: all the perfumes of Arabia will not sweeten this little hand. Oh! oh! oh!

DOCTOR. What a sigh is there! The heart is sorely charged.

GENTLEWOMAN. I would not have such a heart in my bosom for the dignity of the whole body.

DOCTOR. Well, well, well.

GENTLEWOMAN. Pray God it be, sir.

DOCTOR. This disease is beyond my practice: yet I have known those which have walked in their sleep who have died holily in their beds.

LADY MACBETH. Wash your hands, put on your nightgown; look not so pale. I tell you yet again, Banquo 's buried; he cannot come out on 's grave.

DOCTOR. Even so?

LADY MACBETH. To bed, to bed: there 's knocking at the gate. Come, come, come, come, give me your hand. What 's done cannot be undone. To bed, to bed, to bed.   *Exit*

DOCTOR. Will she go now to bed?

GENTLEWOMAN. Directly.

DOCTOR. Foul whisperings are abroad. Unnatural deeds
Do breed unnatural troubles; infected minds
To their deaf pillows will discharge their secrets;
More needs she the divine than the physician.

God, God forgive us all! Look after her;
Remove from her the means of all annoyance,
And still keep eyes upon her. So, good-night:
My mind she has mated, and amaz'd my sight.
I think, but dare not speak.

GENTLEWOMAN. Good-night, good doctor.

Exeunt

SCENE TWO

The Country near Dunsinane.

*Enter, with drum and colours, Menteith, Caithness,
Angus, Lennox, and Soldiers*

MENTEITH. The English power is near, led on by Malcolm,
His uncle Siward, and the good Macduff.
Revenges burn in them; for their dear causes
Would to the bleeding and the grim alarm
Excite the mortified man.

ANGUS. Near Birnam wood
Shall we well meet them; that way are they coming.

CAITHNESS. Who knows if Donalbain be with his brother?

LENNOX. For certain, sir, he is not: I have a file
Of all the gentry: there is Siward's son,
And many unrough youths that even now
Protest their first of manhood.

MENTEITH. What does the tyrant?

CAITHNESS. Great Dunsinane he strongly fortifies.
Some say he 's mad; others that lesser hate him
Do call it valiant fury; but, for certain,
He cannot buckle his distemper'd cause
Within the belt of rule.

ANGUS. Now does he feel
His secret murders sticking on his hands;
Now minutely revolts upbraid his faith-breach;
Those he commands move only in command,
Nothing in love; now does he feel his title
Hang loose about him, like a giant's robe
Upon a dwarfish thief.

MENTEITH. Who then shall blame
His pester'd senses to recoil and start,

LADY MACBETH.   Yet who would have thought the old man
to have had so much blood in him?

When all that is within him does condemn
Itself for being there?
CAITHNESS.   Well, march we on,
To give obedience where 'tis truly ow'd;
Meet we the medicine of the sickly weal,
And with him pour we in our country's purge
Each drop of us.
LENNOX.   Or so much as it needs
To dew the sovereign flower and drown the weeds.
Make we our march towards Birnam.   *Exeunt, marching*

SCENE THREE

Dunsinane. A Room in the Castle.

Enter Macbeth, Doctor, and Attendants

MACBETH. Bring me no more reports; let them fly all:
Till Birnam wood remove to Dunsinane
I cannot taint with fear. What 's the boy Malcolm?
Was he not born of woman? The spirits that know
All mortal consequences have pronounc'd me thus:
'Fear not, Macbeth; no man that 's born of woman
Shall e'er have power upon thee.' Then fly, false thanes,
And mingle with the English epicures:
The mind I sway by and the heart I bear
Shall never sag with doubt nor shake with fear.
Enter a Servant
The devil damn thee black, thou cream-fac'd loon!
Where gott'st thou that goose look?
SERVANT. There is ten thousand—
MACBETH.   Geese, villain?
SERVANT.   Soldiers, sir.
MACBETH. Go, prick thy face, and over-red thy fear,
Thou lily-liver'd boy. What soldiers, patch?
Death of thy soul! those linen cheeks of thine
Are counsellors to fear. What soldiers, whey-face?
SERVANT. The English force, so please you.
MACBETH. Take thy face hence. (*Exit Servant*) Seyton!—
I am sick at heart
When I behold—Seyton, I say!—This push
Will cheer me ever or disseat me now.

I have liv'd long enough: my way of life
Is fall'n into the sear, the yellow leaf;
And that which should accompany old age,
As honour, love, obedience, troops of friends,
I must not look to have; but, in their stead,
Curses, not loud but deep, mouth-honour, breath,
Which the poor heart would fain deny, and dare not.
Seyton!

Enter Seyton

SEYTON. What is your gracious pleasure?
MACBETH.   What news more?
SEYTON. All is confirm'd, my lord, which was reported.
MACBETH. I'll fight till from my bones my flesh be hack'd.
Give me my armour.
SEYTON.   'Tis not needed yet.
MACBETH. I'll put it on.
Send out more horses, skirr the country round;
Hang those that talk of fear. Give me mine armour.
How does your patient, doctor?
DOCTOR.   Not so sick, my lord,
As she is troubled with thick-coming fancies,
That keep her from her rest.
MACBETH.   Cure her of that:
Canst thou not minister to a mind diseas'd,
Pluck from the memory a rooted sorrow,
Raze out the written troubles of the brain,
And with some sweet oblivious antidote
Cleanse the stuff'd bosom of that perilous stuff
Which weighs upon the heart?
DOCTOR.   Therein the patient
Must minister to himself.
MACBETH. Throw physic to the dogs; I'll none of it.
Come, put mine armour on; give me my staff.
Seyton, send out.—Doctor, the thanes fly from me.—
Come, sir, dispatch.—If thou couldst, doctor, cast
The water of my land, find her disease,
And purge it to a sound and pristine health,
I would applaud thee to the very echo,
That should applaud again.—Pull 't off, I say.—
What rhubarb, senna, or what purgative drug
Would scour these English hence? Hear'st thou of them?
DOCTOR. Ay, my good lord; your royal preparation

Makes us hear something.

MACBETH.   Bring it after me.
I will not be afraid of death and bane
Till Birnam forest come to Dunsinane.

DOCTOR. (*Aside*) Were I from Dunsinane away and clear,
Profit again should hardly draw me here.   *Exeunt*

SCENE FOUR

Country near Birnam Wood.

Enter, with drum and colours, Malcolm, Old Siward and his Son, Macduff, Menteith, Caithness, Angus, Lennox, Ross, and Soldiers, marching

MALCOLM. Cousins, I hope the days are near at hand
That chambers will be safe.

MENTEITH.   We doubt it nothing.

SIWARD. What wood is this before us?

MENTEITH. The wood of Birnam.

MALCOLM. Let every soldier hew him down a bough
And bear 't before him: thereby shall we shadow
The numbers of our host, and make discovery
Err in report of us.

SOLDIERS.   It shall be done.

SIWARD. We learn no other but the confident tyrant
Keeps still in Dunsinane, and will endure
Our setting down before 't.

MALCOLM.   'Tis his main hope;
For where there is advantage to be given,
Both more and less have given him the revolt,
And none serve with him but constrained things
Whose hearts are absent too.

MACDUFF.   Let our just censures
Attend the true event, and put we on
Industrious soldiership.

SIWARD.   The time approaches
That will with due decision make us know
What we shall say we have and what we owe.
Thoughts speculative their unsure hopes relate,
But certain issue strokes must arbitrate,
Towards which advance the war.   *Exeunt, marching*

SCENE FIVE

Dunsinane. Within the Castle.

Enter, with drum and colours, Macbeth, Seyton,
and Soldiers

MACBETH. Hang out our banners on the outward walls;
　The cry is still, 'They come'; our castle's strength
　Will laugh a siege to scorn; here let them lie
　Till famine and the ague eat them up;
　Were they not forc'd with those that should be ours,
　We might have met them dareful, beard to beard,
　And beat them backward home.　*A cry of women within*
　　　　　　　　　　What is that noise?
SEYTON. It is the cry of women, my good lord.　*Exit*
MACBETH. I have almost forgot the taste of fears.
　The time has been my senses would have cool'd
　To hear a night-shriek, and my fell of hair
　Would at a dismal treatise rouse and stir
　As life were in 't. I have supp'd full with horrors;
　Direness, familiar to my slaughterous thoughts,
　Cannot once start me.
　　　　　　　　Re-enter Seyton
　　　　　　　Wherefore was that cry?
SEYTON. The queen, my lord, is dead.
MACBETH. She should have died hereafter;
　There would have been a time for such a word.
　To-morrow, and to-morrow, and to-morrow,
　Creeps in this petty pace from day to day,
　To the last syllable of recorded time;
　And all our yesterdays have lighted fools
　The way to dusty death. Out, out, brief candle!
　Life 's but a walking shadow, a poor player
　That struts and frets his hour upon the stage,
　And then is heard no more; it is a tale
　Told by an idiot, full of sound and fury,
　Signifying nothing.　　　　　*Enter a Messenger*
　Thou com'st to use thy tongue; thy story quickly.
MESSENGER. Gracious my lord,
　I should report that which I say I saw,
　But know not how to do it.
MACBETH　　　　　　　Well, say, sir,

MESSENGER. As I did stand my watch upon the hill,
  I look'd towards Birnam, and anon, methought,
  The wood began to move.
MACBETH.   Liar and slave!
MESSENGER. Let me endure your wrath if 't be not so:
  Within this three mile may you see it coming;
  I say, a moving grove.
MACBETH.   If thou speak'st false,
  Upon the next tree shalt thou hang alive,
  Till famine cling thee; if thy speech be sooth,
  I care not if thou dost for me as much.
  I pull in resolution and begin
  To doubt the equivocation of the fiend
  That lies like truth; 'Fear not, till Birnam wood
  Do come to Dunsinane'; and now a wood
  Comes toward Dunsinane. Arm, arm, and out!
  If this which he avouches does appear,
  There is nor flying hence, nor tarrying here.
  I 'gin to be aweary of the sun,
  And wish the estate o' the world were now undone.
  Ring the alarum-bell! Blow, wind! come, wrack!
  At least we 'll die with harness on our back.   *Exeunt*

SCENE SIX

Dunsinane. A Plain before the Castle.

*Enter, with drum and colours, Malcolm, Old Siward,
  Macduff, &c., and their Army, with boughs*

MALCOLM. Now near enough; your leavy screens throw
    down,
  And show like those you are. You, worthy uncle,
  Shall, with my cousin, your right-noble son,
  Lead our first battle; worthy Macduff and we
  Shall take upon 's what else remains to do,
  According to our order.
SIWARD.   Fare you well.
  Do we but find the tyrant's power to-night,
  Let us be beaten, if we cannot fight.
MACDUFF. Make all our trumpets speak; give them all
    breath,
  Those clamorous harbingers of blood and death.   *Exeunt*

SCENE SEVEN

Another Part of the Plain.

Alarums. Enter Macbeth

MACBETH. They have tied me to a stake; I cannot fly,
But bear-like I must fight the course. What 's he
That was not born of woman? Such a one
Am I to fear, or none.

Enter Young Siward

YOUNG SIWARD. What is thy name?
MACBETH.   Thou 'lt be afraid to hear it.
YOUNG SIWARD. No; though thou call'st thyself a hotter name
Than any is in hell.
MACBETH.   My name 's Macbeth.
YOUNG SIWARD. The devil himself could not pronounce a title
More hateful to mine ear.
MACBETH.   No, nor more fearful.
YOUNG SIWARD. Thou liest, abhorred tyrant; with my sword
I 'll prove the lie thou speak'st.

      They fight, and Young Siward is slain

MACBETH.   Thou wast born of woman:
But swords I smile at, weapons laugh to scorn,
Brandish'd by man that 's of a woman born. *Exit*

Alarums. Enter Macduff

MACDUFF. That way the noise is. Tyrant, show thy face:
If thou be'st slain and with no stroke of mine,
My wife and children's ghosts will haunt me still.
I cannot strike at wretched kerns, whose arms
Are hir'd to bear their staves: either thou, Macbeth,
Or else my sword with an unbatter'd edge
I sheathe again undeeded. There thou shouldst be;
By this great clatter, one of greatest note
Seems bruited. Let me find him, fortune!
And more I beg not.   *Exit. Alarums*

Enter Malcolm and Old Siward

SIWARD. This way, my lord; the castle 's gently render'd:
The tyrant's people on both sides do fight;
The noble thanes do bravely in the war;

The day almost itself professes yours,
And little is to do.

MALCOLM.   We have met with foes
That strike beside us.

SIWARD.   Enter, sir, the castle.

Exeunt. Alarums

Re-enter Macbeth

MACBETH. Why should I play the Roman fool, and die
On mine own sword? whilst I see lives, the gashes
Do better upon them.

Re-enter Macduff

MACDUFF.   Turn, hell-hound, turn!

MACBETH. Of all men else I have avoided thee:
But get thee back, my soul is too much charg'd
With blood of thine already.

MACDUFF.   I have no words;
My voice is in my sword, thou bloodier villain
Than terms can give thee out!   *They fight*

MACBETH.   Thou losest labour:
As easy mayst thou the intrenchant air
With thy keen sword impress as make me bleed:
Let fall thy blade on vulnerable crests;
I bear a charmed life, which must not yield
To one of woman born.

MACDUFF.   Despair thy charm;
And let the angel whom thou still hast serv'd
Tell thee, Macduff was from his mother's womb
Untimely ripp'd.

MACBETH. Accursed be that tongue that tells me so,
For it hath cow'd my better part of man:
And be these juggling fiends no more believ'd,
That palter with us in a double sense;
That keep the word of promise to our ear,
And break it to our hope. I 'll not fight with thee.

MACDUFF. Then yield thee, coward,
And live to be the show and gaze o' the time:
We 'll have thee, as our rarer monsters are,
Painted upon a pole, and underwrit,
'Here may you see the tyrant.'

MACBETH.   I will not yield,
To kiss the ground before young Malcolm's feet,
And to be baited with the rabble's curse.

Though Birnam wood be come to Dunsinane,
And thou oppos'd, being of no woman born,
Yet I will try the last: before my body
I throw my warlike shield. Lay on, Macduff,
And damn'd be him that first cries, 'Hold, enough!'

Exeunt fighting

Retreat. Flourish. Re-enter, with drum and colours,
Malcolm, Old Siward, Ross, Thanes, and Soldiers

MALCOLM. I would the friends we miss were safe arriv'd.
SIWARD. Some must go off; and yet, by these I see,
So great a day as this is cheaply bought.
MALCOLM. Macduff is missing, and your noble son.
ROSS. Your son, my lord, has paid a soldier's debt:
He only liv'd but till he was a man;
The which no sooner had his prowess confirm'd
In the unshrinking station where he fought,
But like a man he died.
SIWARD.   Then he is dead?
ROSS. Ay, and brought off the field. Your cause of sorrow
Must not be measur'd by his worth, for then
It hath no end.
SIWARD.   Had he his hurts before?
ROSS. Ay, on the front.
SIWARD.   Why then, God's soldier be he!
Had I as many sons as I have hairs,
I would not wish them to a fairer death:
And so, his knell is knoll'd.
MALCOLM.   He's worth more sorrow,
And that I'll spend for him.
SIWARD.   He's worth no more;
They say, he parted well, and paid his score:
And so, God be with him! Here comes newer comfort.

Re-enter Macduff, with Macbeth's head

MACDUFF. Hail, king! for so thou art. Behold, where stands
The usurper's cursed head: the time is free:
I see thee compass'd with thy kingdom's pearl,
That speak my salutation in their minds;
Whose voices I desire aloud with mine;
Hail, King of Scotland!
ALL.   Hail, King of Scotland!

Flourish

MALCOLM. We shall not spend a large expense of time
  Before we reckon with your several loves,
  And make us even with you. My thanes and kinsmen,
  Henceforth be earls, the first that ever Scotland
  In such an honour nam'd. What 's more to do,
  Which would be planted newly with the time,
  As calling home our exil'd friends abroad
  That fled the snares of watchful tyranny;
  Producing forth the cruel ministers
  Of this dead butcher and his fiend-like queen,
  Who, as 'tis thought, by self and violent hands
  Took off her life; this, and what needful else
  That calls upon us, by the grace of Grace
  We will perform in measure, time, and place:
  So, thanks to all at once and to each one,
  Whom we invite to see us crown'd at Scone.

                              Flourish. Exeunt